Business Skills

ALL-IN-ONE

by John A. Tracy, Mary Ann Anderson,
Dr. Edward G. Anderson, Jr., Dr. Geoffrey
Parker, Dawna Jones, Stan Portny,
Joel Elad, Natalie Canavor,
Ryan Deiss, Russ Henneberry

for
dummies®

A Wiley Brand

Business Skills All-in-One For Dummies®

Published by: **John Wiley & Sons, Inc.,** 111 River Street, Hoboken, NJ 07030-5774, www.wiley.com

Copyright © 2018 by John Wiley & Sons, Inc., Hoboken, New Jersey

Published simultaneously in Canada

For general information on our other products and services, please contact our Customer Care Department within the U.S. at 877-762-2974, outside the U.S. at 317-572-3993, or fax 317-572-4002. For technical support, please visit https://hub.wiley.com/community/support/dummies.

Wiley publishes in a variety of print and electronic formats and by print-on-demand. Some material included with standard print versions of this book may not be included in e-books or in print-on-demand. If this book refers to media such as a CD or DVD that is not included in the version you purchased, you may download this material at http://booksupport.wiley.com. For more information about Wiley products, visit www.wiley.com.

Library of Congress Control Number: 2018933542

ISBN 978-1-119-47397-8 (pbk); ISBN 978-1-119-47400-5 (ebk); ISBN 978-1-119-47398-5 (ebk)

Manufactured in the United States of America

10 9 8 7 6 5 4 3 2 1

Table of Contents

Introduction

When was the last time you received an email and cringed at the muddled organization and horrible grammar? Or you felt so overwhelmed that your productivity plummeted? Or how about the last time you were so unsure about making a big decision that you came across as unprepared or worse — unprofessional?

Unfortunately, business professionals in all stages of their careers encounter these situations at one point or another. Although these instances may seem benign on the surface, they harm your professional reputation, which is hard to reverse. Would you want to do business with someone who is so unorganized that he constantly misses project deadlines or turns in shoddy work because he's rushed? Of course not! Project management and having a solid organizational system are just a couple of the secrets to success that we discuss in this book.

About This Book

This book provides you with detailed information on topics that will help you gain the confidence needed to grow and advance in your business life. You'll read about the ins and outs of the income statement, balance sheet, and statement of cash flows, how to craft the perfect written document that gets results, how to plan a project like a pro, and more.

Foolish Assumptions

There's a time and a place for just about everything and assumptions are no different. First, we assume that you are a business professional and you're ready, willing, and able to devote some time and energy into honing your business skills.

We also assume that you have at least a general knowledge of the major software packages that businesses use and are interested in utilizing them to advance in your professional activities. If that's the case, this is the book for you!

Icons Used in This Book

Throughout this book, you'll find special icons to call attention to important information. Here's what to expect.

TIP

"If you see people falling asleep during your presentations, bang a book against the table to wake them up." Kidding!

This icon is used for helpful suggestions and things you may find useful at some point. No worries, though: No one will be falling asleep during your presentations if you take to heart the tip written here!

REMEMBER

This icon is used when something is essential and bears repeating. Again, this icon is used when something is essential and bears repeating. (See what we did there?)

TECHNICAL
STUFF

The little Dummies Man is information to share with the people who handle the technical aspect of things. You can skip technical-oriented information without derailing any of the hard work you're putting toward achieving your best professional self.

WARNING

Pay attention to these warnings to avoid potential pitfalls. Nothing suggested will get you fired or arrested (unless you do something like practice mindfulness *so well* that you start to nod off while driving or during meetings with the CEO — we can't help you there). If you see this icon, slow down and proceed with caution.

Beyond the Book

Although this book is a one-stop shop for your professional development, we can cover only so much in a set number of pages! If you find yourself at the end of this book thinking, "This was an amazing book! Where can I learn more about how to advance my career by working on my business skills?" head over to www.dummies.com for more resources.

For details about significant updates or changes that occur between editions of this book, go to www.dummies.com, search for *Business Skills All-in-One For Dummies*, and open the Downloads tab on this book's dedicated page.

In addition, check out the cheat sheet for this book for tips on making informed decisions, avoiding common project management pitfalls, building your LinkedIn network, and more. To get to the cheat sheet, go to www.dummies.com, and then type *Business Skills All-in-One For Dummies* in the Search box.

Where to Go from Here

The minibooks and chapters are written to stand on their own, so you can start reading anywhere and skip around as you see fit.

If you don't know where to start, check out Book 1, Chapter 1. However, if you see a particular topic that piques your interest, feel free to jump right into its chapter.

1

Accounting

Contents at a Glance

Chapter 1

Introducing Financial Statements

I n this chapter, you get interesting tidbits about the three primary business financial statements, or *financials,* as they're sometimes called: the income statement, the balance sheet, and the statement of cash flows.

For each financial statement, we introduce its basic information components. The purpose of financial statements is to communicate information that is useful to the readers of the financial statements, to those who are entitled to the information. Financial statement readers include the managers of the business and its lenders and investors. These constitute the primary audience for financial statements. (Beyond this primary audience, others are also interested in a business's financial statements, such as its labor union or someone considering buying the business.) Think of yourself as a shareholder in a business. What sort of information would you want to know about the business? The answer to this question should be the touchstone for the accountant in preparing the financial statements.

The financial statements explained in this chapter are for businesses. Business financial statements serve as a useful template for not-for-profit (NFP) entities and other organizations (social clubs, homeowners' associations, retirement communities, and so on). In short, business financial statements are a good reference point for the financial statements of non-business entities. There are differences but not as many as you may think. As you go along in this and the following chapters, we point out the differences between business and non-business financial statements.

Toward the end of this chapter, we briefly discuss accounting standards and financial reporting standards. Notice here that we distinguish accounting from financial reporting. *Accounting standards* deal primarily with how to record transactions for measuring profit and for putting values on assets, liabilities, and owners' equity. *Financial reporting standards* focus on additional aspects such as the structure and presentation of financial statements, disclosure in the financial statements and elsewhere in the report, and other matters. We use the term *financial accounting* to include both types of standards.

TIP

The philosophy behind the need for standards is that all businesses should follow uniform methods for measuring and reporting profit performance and reporting financial condition. Consistency in financial accounting across all businesses is the name of the game. We won't bore you with a lengthy historical discourse on the development of accounting and financial reporting standards in the United States. The general consensus (backed by law) is that businesses should use consistent accounting methods and terminology. General Motors and Microsoft should use the same accounting methods; so should Wells Fargo and Apple. Of course, businesses in different industries have different types of transactions, but the same types of transactions should be accounted for in the same way. That is the goal.

Setting the Stage for Financial Statements

This chapter focuses on the basic *information components* of each financial statement reported by a business.

Offering a few preliminary comments about financial statements

Realistic examples are needed to illustrate and explain financial statements, which presents a slight problem. The information content of a business's financial statements depends on whether it sells products or services, invests in other businesses, and so on. For example, the financial statements of a movie theater chain are different from those of a bank, which are different from those of an airline, which are different from an automobile manufacturer's, which are different from — well, you name it.

The classic example used to illustrate financial statements involves a business that sells products and sells on credit to its customers. Therefore, the assets in the example include *receivables* from the business's sales on credit and *inventory* of products it has purchased or manufactured that are awaiting future sale. Keep in mind, however, that many businesses that sell products do not sell on credit to their customers. Many retail businesses sell only for cash (or accept credit or debit cards that are near cash). Such businesses do not have a receivables asset.

REMEMBER

The financial statements of a business do not present a history of the business. Financial statements are, to a large extent, limited to the recent profit performance and financial condition of the business. A business may add some historical discussion and charts that aren't strictly required by financial reporting standards. (Public corporations that have their ownership shares and debt traded in open markets are subject to various disclosure requirements under federal law, including certain historical information.)

The illustrative financial statements that follow do not include a historical narrative of the business. Nevertheless, whenever you see financial statements, we encourage you to think about the history of the business. To help you out in this regard, here are some particulars about the business example in this chapter:

>> It sells products to other businesses (not on the retail level).

>> It sells on credit, and its customers take a month or so before they pay.

>> It holds a fairly large stock of products awaiting sale.

>> It owns a wide variety of long-term operating assets that have useful lives from 3 to 30 years or longer (building, machines, tools, computers, office furniture, and so on).

>> It has been in business for many years and has made a profit most years.

>> It borrows money for part of the total assets it needs.

>> It's organized as a corporation and pays federal and state income taxes on its annual taxable income.

>> It has never been in bankruptcy and is not facing any immediate financial difficulties.

The following sections present the company's annual income statement for the year just ended, its balance sheet at the end of the year, and its statement of cash flows for the year.

Looking at other aspects of reporting financial statements

TIP

Dollar amounts in financial statements are typically rounded off, either by not presenting the last three digits (when rounded to the nearest thousand) or by not presenting the last six digits (when rounded to the nearest million by large corporations). We strike a compromise on this issue and show the last three digits for each item as 000, which means that we rounded off the amount but still show all digits. Many smaller businesses report their financial statement dollar amounts to the last dollar or even the last penny, for that matter. Keep in mind that having too many digits in a dollar amount makes it hard to comprehend.

Actual financial statements use only one- or two-word account titles on the assumption that you know what all these labels mean. What you see in this chapter, on the other hand, are the basic information components of each financial statement. We provide descriptions for each financial statement element rather than the terse and technical account titles you find in actual financial statements. Also, we strip out subtotals that you see in actual financial statements because they aren't necessary at this point. So, with all these caveats in mind, let's get going.

REMEMBER

Oops! We forgot to mention a few things about financial reports. Financial reports are rather stiff and formal. No slang or street language is allowed, and we've never seen a swear word in one. Financial statements would get a G in the movies rating system. Seldom do you see any graphics or artwork in a financial statement itself, although you do see a fair amount of photos and graphics on other pages in the financial reports of public companies. And there's virtually no humor in financial reports. However, Warren Buffet, in his annual letter to the stockholders of Berkshire Hathaway, includes some wonderful humor to make his points.

Income Statement

First on the minds of financial report readers is the profit performance of the business. The *income statement* is the all-important financial statement that summarizes the profit-making activities of a business over a period of time. Figure 1-1 shows the basic information content of an external income statement for our company example. *External* means that the financial statement is released outside the business to those entitled to receive it — primarily its shareowners and lenders. Internal financial statements stay within the business and are used mainly by its managers; they aren't circulated outside the business because they contain competitive and confidential information.

Company's Name Income Statement For Most Recent Year	
Total amount of revenue from sales of products to customers during year, excluding returns.	$10,400,000
Total cost of goods sold that are included in sales revenue, which is based on purchase or manufacturing costs of the products. Might also include cost of products written off as unsalable.	($6,240,000)
Selling, general, and administrative expenses, which is the total amount of operating expenses of the business for the year. Excludes other expenses listed in the income statement, of course.	($3,235,000)
Total interest charged to the business on the amount of its interest-bearing debt during the year. May include other financing costs as well.	($125,000)
Total amount paid or payable to federal and state income tax authorities based on taxable income for year.	($280,000)
Net income, which may be called net earnings, or just earnings, but seldom profit.	$520,000

FIGURE 1-1:
Income
statement
information
components for
a business that
sells products.

Presenting the components of the income statement

Figure 1-1 presents the major ingredients, or information packets, in the income statement for a company that sells products. As you may expect, the income statement starts with *sales revenue* on the top line. There's no argument about this, although in the past, certain companies didn't want to disclose their annual sales revenue (to hide the large percent of profit they were earning on sales revenue).

Sales revenue is the total amount that has been or will be received from the company's customers for the sales of products to them. Simple enough, right? Well, not really. The accounting profession is currently reexamining the technical accounting standards for recording sales revenue, and this has proven to be a challenging task. Our business example, like most businesses, has adopted a certain set of procedures for the timeline of recording its sales revenue.

Recording expenses involves much more troublesome accounting problems than revenue problems for most businesses. Also, there's the fundamental question regarding which information to disclose about expenses and which information to bury in larger expense categories in the external income statement. Direct your attention to the four kinds of expenses in Figure 1-1. Expenses are deducted from sales revenue to determine the final profit for the period, which is referred to as the *bottom line.* The preferred label is *net income,* as you see in the figure.

TIP

The four expense categories you see in Figure 1-1 should almost always be disclosed in external income statements. These constitute the minimum for adequate disclosure of expenses. The *cost of goods sold expense* is just what it says: the cost of the products sold to customers. The cost of the products should be matched against the revenue from the sales, of course.

Only one conglomerate operating expense has to be disclosed. In Figure 1-1, it's called *selling, general, and administrative expenses,* which is a popular title in income statements. This all-inclusive expense total mixes together many kinds of expenses, including labor costs, utility costs, depreciation of assets, and so on. But it doesn't include interest expenses or income tax expense; these two expenses are always reported separately in an income statement.

The cost of goods sold expense and the selling, general, and administrative expenses take the biggest bites out of sales revenue. The other two expenses (interest and income tax) are relatively small as a percent of annual sales revenue but are important enough in their own right to be reported separately. And though you may not need this reminder, *bottom-line profit* (net income) is the amount of sales revenue in excess of the business's total expenses. If either sales revenue or any of the expense amounts are wrong, profit is wrong

REMEMBER

A service business does not sell products; therefore, it doesn't have the cost of goods sold expense. In place of cost of goods sold, it has other types of expenses. Most service businesses are labor extensive; they have relatively large labor costs as a percent of sales revenue. Service companies differ in how they report their operating expenses. For example, United Airlines breaks out the cost of aircraft fuel and landing fees. The largest expense of the insurance company State Farm is payments on claims. The movie chain AMC reports film exhibition costs separate from its other operating expenses. We offer these examples to remind you that accounting should always be adapted to the way the business operates and makes profit. In other words, accounting should follow the business model.

Income statement pointers

TIP

Most businesses break out one or more expenses instead of disclosing just one very broad category for all selling, general, and administrative expenses. For example, Apple, in its condensed income statement, discloses research and development expenses separate from its selling, general, and administrative expenses. A business could disclose expenses for advertising and sales promotion, salaries and wages, research and development (as does Apple), and delivery and shipping — though reporting these expenses varies quite a bit from business to business. Businesses do not disclose the compensation of top management in their external financial reports, although this information can be found in the proxy statements of public companies that are filed with the Securities and Exchange Commission (SEC). In summary, the extent of details disclosed about operating expenses in externally reported financial reports varies quite a bit from business to business. Financial reporting standards are rather permissive on this point.

Inside most businesses, a profit statement is called a *P&L (profit and loss) report.* These internal profit performance reports to the managers of a business include more detailed information about expenses and about sales revenue — a good deal more! Reporting just four expenses to managers (as shown in Figure 1-1) would not do.

Sales revenue refers to sales of products or services to customers. In some income statements, you also see the term *income,* which generally refers to amounts earned by a business from sources other than sales. For example, a real estate rental business receives rental income from its tenants. (In the example in this chapter, the business has only sales revenue.)

The income statement gets the most attention from business managers, lenders, and investors (not that they ignore the other two financial statements). The much-abbreviated versions of income statements that you see in the financial press, such as in *The Wall Street Journal,* report the top line (sales revenue and income) and the bottom line (net income) and not much more. Refer to Chapter 2 in this minibook for more information on income statements.

Balance Sheet

A more accurate name for a balance sheet is *statement of financial condition* or *statement of financial position,* but the term *balance sheet* has caught on, and most people use this term. Keep in mind that the most important thing is not the balance but rather the information reported in this financial statement.

In brief, a balance sheet summarizes on the one hand the assets of the business and on the other hand the sources of the assets. However, looking at assets is only half the picture. The other half consists of the liabilities and owner equity of the business. Cash is listed first, and other assets are listed in the order of their nearness to cash. Liabilities are listed in order of their due dates (the earliest first, and so on). Liabilities are listed ahead of owners' equity. We discuss the ordering of the components in a balance sheet in Chapter 3 in this minibook.

Presenting the components of the balance sheet

Figure 1-2 shows the building blocks of a typical balance sheet for a business that sells products on credit. As mentioned, one reason the balance sheet is called by this name is that its two sides balance, or are equal in total amounts. In this example, the $5.2 million total assets equals the $5.2 million total liabilities and owners' equity. The balance or equality of total assets on the one side of the scale and the sum of liabilities plus owners' equity on the other side of the scale is expressed in the *accounting equation*. *Note:* The balance sheet in Figure 1-2 shows the essential elements in this financial statement. In a financial report, the balance sheet includes additional features and frills, which we explain in Chapter 3 of this minibook.

Company's Name Balance Sheet At End of Most Recent Year	
Assets	
Cash and cash equivalents.	$1,000,000
Receivables from sales made on credit at amount expected to be collected.	$800,000
Inventory of unsold products, at purchase cost or manufacturing cost.	$1,560,000
Long-term operating assets, at original costs less cumulative amount recorded to expense over the years.	$1,840,000
Total assets	$5,200,000
Liabilities and Owners' Equity	
Non-interest bearing liabilities from purchases on credit and for unpaid expenses.	$650,000
Interest-bearing debt owed by the business — both short-term and long-term.	$2,080,000
Owners' equity capital invested in business plus profit earned and retained in business.	$2,470,000
Total liabilities and owners' equity	$5,200,000

FIGURE 1-2: Balance sheet information components for a business that sells products and makes sales on credit.

Take a quick walk through the balance sheet. For a company that sells products on credit, assets are reported in the following order: First is cash, then receivables, then cost of products held for sale, and finally the long-term operating assets of the business. Moving to the other side of the balance sheet, the liabilities section starts with the trade liabilities (from buying on credit) and liabilities for unpaid expenses. Following these operating liabilities is the interest-bearing debt of the business. Owners' equity sources are then reported below liabilities. So a balance sheet is a composite of assets on one hand and a composite of liabilities and owners' equity sources on the other hand.

REMEMBER

A balance sheet is a reflection of the fundamental two-sided nature of a business (expressed in the *accounting equation*). In the most basic terms, assets are what the business owns, and liabilities plus owners' equity are the sources of the assets. The sources have claims against the assets. Liabilities and interest-bearing debt have to be paid, of course, and if the business were to go out of business and liquidate all its assets, the residual after paying all its liabilities would go to the owners.

A company that sells services doesn't has an inventory of products being held for sale. A service company may or may not sell on credit. Airlines don't sell on credit, for example. If a service business doesn't sell on credit, it won't have two of the sizable assets you see in Figure 1-2: receivables from credit sales and inventory of products held for sale. Generally, this means that a service-based business doesn't need as much total assets compared with a products-based business with the same size sales revenue.

The smaller amount of total assets of a service business means that the other side of its balance sheet is correspondingly smaller. In plain terms, this means that a service company doesn't need to borrow as much money or raise as much capital from its equity owners.

As you may suspect, the particular assets reported in the balance sheet depend on which assets the business owns. We include just four basic types of assets in Figure 1-2. These are the hardcore assets that a business selling products on credit would have. It's possible that such a business could lease (or rent) virtually all its long-term operating assets instead of owning them, in which case the business would report no such assets. In this example, the business owns these so-called *fixed assets*. They're *fixed* because they are held for use in the operations of the business and are not for sale, and their usefulness lasts several years or longer.

Balance sheet pointers

So, where does a business get the money to buy its assets? Most businesses borrow money on the basis of interest-bearing notes or other credit instruments for part of the total capital they need for their assets. Also, businesses buy many things on credit and, at the balance sheet date, owe money to their suppliers, which will be paid in the future.

These operating liabilities are never grouped with interest-bearing debt in the balance sheet. The accountant would be tied to the stake for doing such a thing. Liabilities are not intermingled with assets — this is a definite no-no in financial reporting. You can't subtract certain liabilities from certain assets and report only the net balance.

Introducing Financial Statements

Could a business's total liabilities be greater than its total assets? Well, not likely — unless the business has been losing money hand over fist. In the vast majority of cases, a business has more total assets than total liabilities. Why? For two reasons:

>> Its owners have invested money in the business.

>> The business has earned profit over the years, and some (or all) of the profit has been retained in the business. Making profit increases assets; if not all the profit is distributed to owners, the company's assets rise by the amount of profit retained.

WARNING

In the product company example (see Figure 1-2), owners' equity is about $2.5 million, or $2.47 million to be more exact. Sometimes this amount is referred to as *net worth* because it equals total assets minus total liabilities. However, net worth can be misleading because it implies that the business is worth the amount recorded in its owners' equity accounts. The market value of a business, when it needs to be known, depends on many factors. The amount of owners' equity reported in a balance sheet, which is called the business's *book value*, is not irrelevant in setting a market value on the business, but it usually isn't the dominant factor. The amount of owners' equity in a balance sheet is based on the history of capital invested in the business by its owners and the history of its profit performance and distributions from profit.

TIP

A balance sheet could be whipped up anytime you want — say, at the end of every day. In fact, some businesses (such as banks and other financial institutions) need daily balance sheets, but few businesses prepare balance sheets that often. Typically, preparing a balance sheet at the end of each month is adequate for general management purposes — although a manager may need to take a look at the business's balance sheet in the middle of the month. In external financial reports (those released outside the business to its lenders and investors), a balance sheet is required at the close of business on the last day of the income statement period. If its annual or quarterly income statement ends, say, September 30, then the business reports its balance sheet at the close of business on September 30.

The profit *for the most recent period* is found in the income statement; periodic profit is not reported in the balance sheet. The profit reported in the income statement is before any distributions from profit to owners. The cumulative amount of profit over the years that hasn't been distributed to the business's owners is reported in the owners' equity section of the company's balance sheet.

By the way, note that the balance sheet in Figure 1-2 is presented in a top-and-bottom format instead of a left-and-right format. Either the vertical (portrait) or horizontal (landscape) mode of display is acceptable. You see both layouts in financial reports. Of course, the two sides of the balance sheet should be kept together, either on one page or on facing pages in the financial report. You can't put assets up front and hide the other side of the balance sheet in the rear of the financial report.

Statement of Cash Flows

To survive and thrive, business managers confront three financial imperatives:

>> **Make an adequate profit (or at least break even, for a not-for-profit entity).** The income statement reports whether the business made a profit or suffered a loss for the period.

>> **Keep the financial condition in good shape.** The balance sheet reports the financial condition of the business at the end of the period.

>> **Control cash flows.** Management's control over cash flows is reported in the *statement of cash flows,* which presents a summary of the business's sources and uses of cash during the same period as the income statement.

This section introduces you to the statement of cash flows. Financial reporting standards require that the statement of cash flows be reported when a business reports an income statement.

Presenting the components of the statement of cash flows

Successful business managers tell you that they have to manage both profit and cash flow; you can't do one and ignore the other. Business managers have to deal with a two-headed dragon in this respect. Ignoring cash flow can pull the rug out from under a successful profit formula.

REMEMBER

Figure 1-3 shows the basic information components of the statement of cash flows for the business example we use in the chapter. The cash activity of the business during the period is grouped into three sections:

>> The first reconciles net income for the period with the cash flow from the business's profit-making activities, or *operating activities*.

>> The second summarizes the company's *investing* transactions during the period.

>> The third reports the company's *financing* transactions.

FIGURE 1-3:
Information
components of
the statement of
cash flows.

Company's Name Statement of Cash Flows For Most Recent Year	
Cash increase or decrease during period from profit-making operating activities (collecting cash from sales and paying cash for expenses)	$400,000
Cash increase or decrease during period from making investments in and disposals of long-term operating assets	($450,000)
Cash increase or decrease during period from transactions with lenders and owners, including increases and decreases in debt and ownership shares and cash dividends from profit paid to owners	$200,000
Cash increase during period	$150,000
Cash balance at start of period	$850,000
Cash balance at end of period	$1,000,000

The net increase or decrease in cash from the three types of cash activities during the period is added to or subtracted from the beginning cash balance to get the cash balance at the end of the year.

The business earned $520,000 profit (net income) during the year (refer to Figure 1-1). The cash result of its operating activities was to increase its cash by $400,000, which you see in the first part of the statement of cash flows (see Figure 1-3). This still leaves $120,000 of profit to explain. This doesn't mean that the profit number is wrong. The actual cash inflows from revenues and outflows for expenses run on a different timetable from when the sales revenue and expenses are recorded for determining profit. For a more comprehensive explanation of the differences between cash flows and sales revenue and expenses, see Book 1, Chapter 4.

The second part of the statement of cash flows sums up the long-term investments the business made during the year, such as constructing a new production plant or replacing machinery and equipment. If the business sold any of its long-term assets, it reports the cash inflows from these divestments in this section of the statement of cash flows. The cash flows of other investment activities (if any) are reported in this part of the statement as well. As you can see in Figure 1-3, the business invested $450,000 in new long-term operating assets (trucks, equipment, tools, and computers).

The third part of the statement sums up the dealings between the business and its sources of capital during the period — borrowing money from lenders and raising capital from its owners. Cash outflows to pay debt are reported in this section, as are cash distributions from profit paid to the owners of the business. The third part of the example statement shows that the result of these transactions was to increase cash by $200,000. (By the way, in this example, the business didn't make cash distributions from profit to its owners. It probably could have, but it didn't — which is an important point that we discuss later in "Why no cash distribution from profit?")

As you see in Figure 1-3, the net result of the three types of cash activities was a $150,000 increase during the year. The increase is added to the cash balance at the start of the year to get the cash balance at the end of the year, which is $1.0 million. We should make one point clear: The $150,000 cash increase during the year (in this example) is never referred to as a cash flow *bottom line* or any such thing.

REMEMBER

The term *bottom line* is reserved for the final line of the income statement, which reports net income — the final amount of profit after all expenses are deducted.

Statement of cash flows pointers

In 1987, the American rulemaking body for financial accounting standards (the Financial Accounting Standards Board) made the cash flow statement a required statement. Relatively speaking, this financial statement hasn't been around that long. How has it gone? Well, in our humble opinion, this financial statement is a disaster for financial report readers.

Statements of cash flows of most businesses are frustratingly difficult to read and far too technical. The average financial report reader understands the income statement and balance sheet. Certain items may be hard to fathom, but overall, the reader can make sense of the information in the two financial statements. In contrast, trying to follow the information in a statement of cash flows — especially the first section of the statement — can be a challenge even for a CPA. (More about this issue in Chapter 4 of this minibook.)

TIP

Imagine you have a highlighter and the three basic financial statements of a business in front of you. What are the most important numbers to mark? *Bottom-line profit* (net income) in the income statement is one number you'd mark. Another key number is *cash flow from operating activities* in the statement of cash flows. You don't have to understand the technical steps of how the accountant gets this cash flow number, but pay attention to how it compares with the profit number for the period. (We explain this point in detail in Chapter 5 of this minibook.)

WARNING

Cash flow is almost always different from net income. The sales revenue reported in the income statement does not equal cash collections from customers during the year, and expenses do not equal cash payments during the year. Cash collections from sales minus cash payments for expenses gives cash flow from a company's profit-making activities; sales revenue minus expenses gives the net income earned for the year. Sorry, mate, but that's how the cookie crumbles.

A Note about the Statement of Changes in Shareowners' Equity

Many business financial reports include a *fourth* financial statement — or at least it's called a "statement." It's really a summary of the changes in the constituent elements of owners' equity (stockholders' equity of a corporation). The corporation is one basic type of legal structure that businesses use. We don't show a statement of changes in owners' equity here.

When a business has a complex owners' equity structure, a separate summary of changes in the components of owners' equity during the period is useful for the owners, the board of directors, and the top-level managers. On the other hand, in some cases, the only changes in owners' equity during the period were earning profit and distributing part of the cash flow from profit to owners. In this situation, there isn't much need for a summary of changes in owners' equity. The financial statement reader can easily find profit in the income statement and cash distributions from profit (if any) in the statement of cash flows. For details, see the later section "Why no cash distribution from profit?"

Gleaning Important Information from Financial Statements

The whole point of reporting financial statements is to provide important information to people who have a financial interest in the business — mainly its investors and lenders. From that information, investors and lenders are able to answer key questions about the financial performance and condition of the business. We discuss a few of these key questions in this section.

How's profit performance?

Investors use two important measures to judge a company's annual profit performance. Here, we use the data from Figures 1-1 and 1-2 for the product company. You can do the same ratio calculations for a service business. For convenience, the dollar amounts are expressed in thousands:

>> **Return on sales = profit as a percent of annual sales revenue:**

$$\frac{\$520 \text{ bottom} - \text{line annual profit (net income)}}{\$10,400 \text{ annual sales revenue}} = 5.0\%$$

» Return on equity = profit as a percent of owners' equity:

$$\frac{\$520 \text{ bottom} - \text{line annual profit (net income)}}{\$2,470 \text{ owners' equity}} = 21.1\%$$

Profit looks pretty thin compared with annual sales revenue. The company earns only 5 percent return on sales. In other words, 95 cents out of every sales dollar goes for expenses, and the company keeps only 5 cents for profit. (Many businesses earn 10 percent or higher return on sales.) However, when profit is compared with owners' equity, things look a lot better. The business earns more than 21 percent profit on its owners' equity. We'd bet you don't have many investments earning 21 percent per year.

Is there enough cash?

Cash is the lubricant of business activity. Realistically, a business can't operate with a zero cash balance. It can't wait to open the morning mail to see how much cash it will have for the day's needs (although some businesses try to operate on a shoestring cash balance). A business should keep enough cash on hand to keep things running smoothly even when there are interruptions in the normal inflows of cash. A business has to meet its payroll on time, for example. Keeping an adequate balance in the checking account serves as a buffer against unforeseen disruptions in normal cash inflows.

At the end of the year, the company in our example has $1 million cash on hand (refer to Figure 1-2). This cash balance is available for general business purposes. (If there are restrictions on how the business can use its cash balance, the business is obligated to disclose the restrictions.) Is $1 million enough? Interestingly, businesses do not have to comment on their cash balance. We've never seen such a comment in a financial report.

The business has $650,000 in operating liabilities that will come due for payment over the next month or so (refer to Figure 1-2). Therefore, it has enough cash to pay these liabilities. But it doesn't have enough cash on hand to pay its operating liabilities and its $2.08 million interest-bearing debt. Lenders don't expect a business to keep a cash balance more than the amount of debt; this condition would defeat the very purpose of lending money to the business, which is to have the business put the money to good use and be able to pay interest on the debt.

Lenders are more interested in the ability of the business to control its cash flows so that when the time comes to pay off loans, it will be able to do so. They know that the other, non-cash assets of the business will be converted into cash flow. Receivables will be collected, and products held in inventory will be sold, and the sales will generate cash flow. So you shouldn't focus just on cash; you should look at the other assets as well.

Taking this broader approach, the business has $1 million cash, $800,000 receivables, and $1.56 million inventory, which adds up to $3.36 million in cash and cash potential. Relative to its $2.73 million total liabilities ($650,000 operating liabilities plus $2.08 million debt), the business looks like it's in pretty good shape. On the other hand, if it turns out that the business isn't able to collect its receivables and isn't able to sell its products, the business would end up in deep doo-doo.

TIP

One other way to look at a business's cash balance is to express its cash balance in terms of how many days of sales the amount represents. In the example, the business has an ending cash balance equal to 35 days of sales, calculated as follows:

$$\frac{\$10,400,000 \text{ annual sales revenue}}{365 \text{ days}} = \$28,493 \text{ sales per day}$$

$$\frac{\$1,000,000 \text{ cash balance}}{\$28,493 \text{ sales per day}} = 35 \text{ days}$$

The business's cash balance equals a little more than one month of sales activity, which most lenders and investors would consider adequate.

Can you trust financial statement numbers?

Whether the financial statements are correct depends on the answers to two basic questions:

>> Does the business have a reliable accounting system in place and employ competent accountants?

>> Have its managers manipulated the business's accounting methods or deliberately falsified the numbers?

WARNING

We'd love to tell you that the answer to the first question is always yes and that the answer to the second question is always no. But you know better, don't you? A recent survey of 400 chief financial officers and financial executives revealed that they think that about 20 percent of corporations distort their earnings reports (income statements) — even though the companies stay within the boundaries of accepted accounting standards. We would estimate that for most businesses, you should take their financial statements with a grain of salt and keep in mind that the numbers could be manipulated in the range of 10 to 20 percent higher or lower. Even though most people think accounting is an exact science, it isn't. There's a fair amount of play in the numbers.

Furthermore, there are a lot of crooks and dishonest persons in the business world who think nothing of manipulating the accounting numbers and cooking the books. Also, organized crime is involved in many businesses. And we have to tell you that in our experience, many businesses don't put much effort into keeping their accounting systems up to speed, and they skimp on hiring competent accountants. In short, there's a risk that the financial statements of a business could be incorrect and seriously misleading.

To increase the credibility of their financial statements, many businesses hire independent CPA auditors to examine their accounting systems and records and to express opinions on whether the financial statements conform to established standards. In fact, some business lenders insist on an annual audit by an independent CPA firm as a condition of making a loan. The outside, non-management investors in a privately owned business could vote to have annual CPA audits of the financial statements. Public companies have no choice; under federal securities laws, a public company is required to have annual audits by an independent CPA firm.

WARNING

Two points: CPA audits are not cheap, and these audits aren't always effective in rooting out financial reporting fraud by managers. Unfortunately, there have been many cases of CPA auditors not detecting serious financial fraud that had been going on for years, right under their auditing noses. Cleverly concealed fraud is difficult to uncover, unless you stumble over it by accident. CPAs are supposed to apply *professional skepticism* in doing their audits, but this doesn't always lead to discovery of fraud.

IS MAKING PROFIT ETHICAL?

Many people have the view that making profit is unethical; they think profit is a form of theft — from employees who aren't paid enough, from customers who are charged too much, from the government (by finding loopholes in the tax laws), and so on. (Profit critics usually don't say anything about the ethical aspects regarding who should absorb the effects of a loss.) We must admit that profit critics are sometimes proved right because some businesses make profit by using illegal or unethical means, such as using false advertising, selling unsafe products, paying employees lower wages than they're legally entitled to, or deliberately underfunding retirement plans for employees. Of course, in making profit, a business should comply with all applicable laws, conduct itself in an ethical manner, and play fair with everyone it deals with.

In our experience, most businesses strive to behave according to high ethical standards, although they will cut corners and take the low road in certain areas when under pressure. Keep in mind that businesses provide jobs, pay several kinds of taxes, and are essential cogs in the economic system. Even though they aren't perfect angels, where would we be without them?

Why no cash distribution from profit?

Distributions from profit by a business corporation are called *dividends* (because the total amount distributed is divided up among the stockholders). Cash distributions from profit to owners are included in the third section of the statement of cash flows (refer to Figure 1-3). But in our example, the business didn't make any cash distributions from profit — even though it earned $520,000 net income (refer to Figure 1-1). Why not?

The business realized $400,000 cash flow from its profit-making (operating) activities (refer to Figure 1-3). In most cases, this would be the upper limit on how much cash a business would distribute from profit to its owners. Should the business have distributed, say, at least half of its cash flow from profit, or $200,000, to its owners? If you owned 20 percent of the ownership shares of the business, you would have received 20 percent, or $40,000, of the distribution. But you got no cash return on your investment in the business. Your shares should be worth more because the profit for the year increased the company's owners' equity, but you didn't see any of this increase in your wallet.

REMEMBER

Deciding whether to make cash distributions from profit to shareowners is in the hands of the directors of a business corporation. Its shareowners elect the directors, and in theory the directors act in the best interests of the shareowners. So, evidently, the directors thought the business had better use for the $400,000 cash flow from profit than distributing some of it to shareowners. Generally, the main reason for not making cash distributions from profit is to finance the growth of the business — to use all the cash flow from profit for expanding the assets needed by the business at the higher sales level. Ideally, the directors of the business would explain their decision not to distribute any money from profit to the shareowners. But generally, no such comments are made in financial reports.

Keeping in Compliance with Accounting and Financial Reporting Standards

When an independent CPA audits the financial report of a business, there's no doubt regarding which accounting and financial reporting standards the business uses to prepare its financial statements and other disclosures. The CPA explicitly states which standards are being used in the auditor's report. What about unaudited financial reports? Well, the business could clarify which accounting and financial reporting standards it uses, but you don't see such disclosure in all cases.

When the financial report of a business is not audited and does not make clear which standards are being used to prepare its financial report, the reader is entitled to assume that appropriate standards are being used. However, a business may be way out in left field (or out of the ballpark) in the guideposts it uses for recording profit and in the preparation of its financial statements. A business may make up its own rules for measuring profit and preparing financial statements. In this minibook, we concentrate on authoritative standards, of course.

Imagine the confusion that would result if every business were permitted to invent its own accounting methods for measuring profit and for putting values on assets and liabilities. What if every business adopted its own individual accounting terminology and followed its own style for presenting financial statements? Such a state of affairs would be a Tower of Babel.

The goal is to establish broad-scale uniformity in accounting methods for all businesses. The idea is to make sure that all accountants are singing the same tune from the same hymnal. The authoritative bodies write the tunes that accountants have to sing.

Looking at who makes the standards

Who are the authoritative bodies that set the standards for financial accounting and reporting? In the United States, the highest-ranking authority in the private (nongovernment) sector for making pronouncements on accounting and financial reporting standards — and for keeping these standards up-to-date — is the Financial Accounting Standards Board (FASB). This rulemaking body has developed a *codification* of all its pronouncements. This is where accountants look to first.

Outside the United States, the main authoritative accounting-standards setter is the International Accounting Standards Board (IASB), which is based in London. The IASB was founded in 2001. More than 7,000 public companies have their securities listed on the several stock exchanges in the European Union (EU) countries. In many regards, the IASB operates in a manner similar to the Financial Accounting Standards Board (FASB) in the United States, and the two have very similar missions. The IASB has already issued many standards, which are called International Financial Reporting Standards. Without going into details, FASB and IASB are not in perfect harmony (even though congruence of their standards was the original goal of the two organizations).

Also, in the United States, the federal Securities and Exchange Commission (SEC) has broad powers over accounting and financial reporting standards for companies whose securities (stocks and bonds) are publicly traded. Actually, because it derives its authority from federal securities laws that govern the public issuance and trading in securities, the SEC outranks the FASB. The SEC has on occasion overridden the FASB, but not very often.

Consider taking the time to Google the acronyms of these three authoritative sources of financial accounting standards. You'll find which particular financial accounting standards and problem areas are under active review and development. In late 2015, for instance, lease accounting and revenue accounting were under active review and transition to new standards, to say nothing about a host of other financial accounting problems.

Knowing about GAAP

The authoritative standards and rules that govern financial accounting and reporting by businesses in the United States are called *generally accepted accounting principles (GAAP)*. The financial statements of an American business should be in full compliance with GAAP regarding reporting its cash flows, profit-making activities, and financial condition — *unless* the business makes very clear that it has prepared its financial statements using some other basis of accounting or has deviated from GAAP in one or more significant respects.

If GAAP are not the basis for preparing a business's financial statements, the business should make very clear which other basis of accounting it's using and avoid using titles for its financial statements that are associated with GAAP. For example, if a business uses a simple cash receipts and cash disbursements basis of accounting — which falls way short of GAAP — it should not use the terms *income statement* and *balance sheet*. These terms are part and parcel of GAAP, and their use as titles for financial statements implies that the business is using GAAP.

There are upwards of 10,000 public companies in the United States and easily more than a million privately owned businesses. Now, are we telling you that all these businesses should use the same accounting methods, terminology, and presentation styles for their financial statements? Putting it in such a stark manner makes us suck in our breath a little. The ideal answer is that all businesses *should* use the same rulebook of GAAP. However, the rulebook permits alternative accounting methods for some transactions. Furthermore, accountants have to interpret the rules as they apply GAAP in actual situations. The devil is in the detail.

In the United States, GAAP constitute the gold standard for preparing financial statements of business entities. The presumption is that any deviations from GAAP would cause misleading financial statements. If a business honestly thinks it should deviate from GAAP — to better reflect the economic reality of its transactions or situation — it should make very clear that it has not complied with GAAP in one or more respects. If deviations from GAAP are not disclosed, the business may have legal exposure to those who relied on the information in its financial report and suffered a loss attributable to the misleading nature of the information.

FINANCIAL ACCOUNTING AND REPORTING BY GOVERNMENT AND NOT-FOR-PROFIT ENTITIES

In the grand scheme of things, the world of financial accounting and reporting can be divided into two hemispheres: for-profit business entities and not-for-profit (NFP) entities. GAAP have been hammered out over the years to govern accounting methods and financial reporting of business entities in the United States. Accounting and financial reporting standards have also evolved and been established for government entities.

The rulemaking body for government entities is the Governmental Accounting Standards Board (GASB). Financial reporting by government entities is a broad and diverse territory, which is beyond the scope of this minibook.

People generally don't demand financial reports from government and not-for-profit organizations. Federal, state, and local government entities issue financial reports that are in the public domain, although few taxpayers are interested in reading them. When you donate money to a charity, school, or church, you don't always get financial reports in return. On the other hand, many private, not-for-profit organizations issue financial reports to their members — credit unions, homeowners' associations, country clubs, mutual insurance companies (owned by their policyholders), pension plans, labor unions, healthcare providers, and so on. The members or participants may have an equity interest or ownership share in the organization, and thus they need financial reports to apprise them of their financial status with the entity.

GAAP also include requirements for *disclosure*, which refers to the following:

>> The types of information that have to be included with the financial statements

>> How information is classified and presented in financial statements (mainly in the form of footnotes)

The SEC makes the disclosure rules for public companies. Disclosure rules for private companies are controlled by GAAP.

Divorcing public and private companies

Traditionally, GAAP and financial reporting standards were viewed as equally applicable to public companies (generally large corporations) and private companies (generally smaller). For some time, private companies have argued that some of the standards issued by the FASB are too complex and burdensome for private companies to apply. Although most accountants don't like to admit it, there's always been a de facto divergence in actual financial reporting practices by private companies compared with the more rigorously enforced standards for public companies. For example, a surprising number of private companies still do not include a statement of cash flows in their financial reports, even though this has been a GAAP requirement for 30 years.

REMEMBER

Although it's hard to prove one way or the other, our view is that the financial reports of private businesses generally measure up to GAAP standards in all significant respects. At the same time, however, there's little doubt that the financial reports of some private companies fall short. In fact, in the invitation to comment on the proposal to establish an advisory committee for private company accounting standards, the FASB said, "Compliance with GAAP standards for many for-profit private companies is a choice rather than a requirement because private companies can often control who receives their financial information." Recently, a *Private Company Council (PCC)* was established; it's separate from the FASB but subject to oversight by the FASB.

Private companies do not have many of the accounting problems of large, public companies. For example, many public companies deal in complex derivative instruments, issue stock options to managers, provide highly developed defined-benefit retirement and health benefit plans for their employees, enter into complicated intercompany investment and joint venture operations, have complex organizational structures, and so on. Most private companies don't have to deal with these issues.

Finally, we should mention in passing that the AICPA, the national association of CPAs, has started a project to develop an *Other Comprehensive Basis of Accounting* for privately held small and medium-sized entities. Oh my! What a time we live in regarding accounting standards. The upshot seems to be that we're drifting toward separate accounting standards for larger public companies versus smaller private companies — and maybe even a third branch of standards for small and medium-sized companies.

Following the rules and bending the rules

An often-repeated story concerns three persons interviewing for an important accounting position. They're asked one key question: "What's 2 plus 2?" The first candidate answers, "It's 4," and is told, "Don't call us. We'll call you." The second candidate answers, "Well, most of the time the answer is 4, but sometimes it's 3, and sometimes it's 5." The third candidate answers, "What do you want the answer to be?" Guess who gets the job. This story exaggerates, of course, but it does have an element of truth.

DEPENDING ON ESTIMATES AND ASSUMPTIONS

The importance of estimates and assumptions in financial accounting is illustrated in a footnote like the following, which you see in many annual financial reports:

"The preparation of financial statements in conformity with generally accepted accounting principles requires management to make estimates and assumptions that affect reported amounts. Examples of the more significant estimates include: accruals and reserves for warranty and product liability losses, post-employment benefits, environmental costs, income taxes, and plant closing costs."

Accounting estimates should be based on the best available information, of course, but most estimates are subjective and arbitrary to some extent. The accountant can choose either pessimistic or optimistic estimates and thereby record either conservative profit numbers or more aggressive profit numbers.

One key prediction made in preparing financial statements is called the *going-concern assumption.* The accountant assumes that the business is not facing imminent shutdown of its operations and the forced liquidation of its assets and assumes that it will continue as usual for the foreseeable future. If a business is in the middle of bankruptcy proceedings, the accountant changes focus to the liquidation values of its assets.

The point is that interpreting GAAP is not cut-and-dried. Many accounting standards leave a lot of wiggle room for interpretation. *Guidelines* would be a better word to describe many accounting rules. Deciding how to account for certain transactions and situations requires seasoned judgment and careful analysis of the rules. Furthermore, many estimates have to be made. (See the sidebar "Depending on estimates and assumptions.") Deciding on accounting methods requires, above all else, *good faith.*

WARNING

A business may resort to so-called creative accounting to make profit for the period look better or to make its year-to-year profit less erratic than it really is (which is called *income smoothing*). Like lawyers who know where to find loopholes, accountants can come up with inventive interpretations that stay within the boundaries of GAAP. We warn you about these creative accounting techniques — also called *massaging the numbers* — at various points in this minibook. Massaging the numbers can get out of hand and become accounting fraud, also called *cooking the books.* Massaging the numbers has some basis in honest differences for interpreting the facts. Cooking the books goes way beyond interpreting facts; this fraud consists of *inventing* facts and good old-fashioned chicanery.

IN THIS CHAPTER

» Looking at typical income statements

» Being an active reader of income statements

» Asking about the substance of profit

» Handling out-of-the-ordinary gains and losses in an income statement

» Correcting misconceptions about profit

Chapter **2**

Reporting Profit or Loss in the Income Statement

I n this chapter, we lift up the hood and explain how the profit engine runs. Making a profit is the main financial goal of a business. (Not-for-profit organizations and government entities don't aim to make profit, but they should break even and avoid a deficit.) Accountants are the profit scorekeepers in the business world and are tasked with measuring the most important financial number of a business. We warn you right here that measuring profit is a challenge in most situations. Determining the correct amounts for revenue and expenses (and for special gains and losses, if any) to record is no walk in the park.

Managers have the demanding tasks of making sales and controlling expenses, and accountants have the tough job of measuring revenue and expenses and preparing financial reports that summarize the profit-making activities. Also, accountants help business managers analyze profit for decision-making as well as prepare profit budgets for managers.

This chapter explains how profit-making activities are reported in a business's external financial reports to its owners and lenders. Revenue and expenses change the financial condition of the business, a fact often overlooked when reading a profit report. Keep in mind that recording revenue and expenses (and gains and losses) and then reporting these profit-making activities in external financial reports are governed by authoritative accounting standards, which we discuss in Chapter 1 of this minibook.

Presenting Typical Income Statements

At the risk of oversimplification, we would say that businesses make profit in three basic ways:

>> **Selling products** (with allied services) and controlling the cost of the products sold and other operating costs

>> **Selling services** and controlling the cost of providing the services and other operating costs

>> **Investing** in assets that generate investment income and market value gains and controlling operating costs

Obviously, this list isn't exhaustive, but it captures a large swath of business activity. In this chapter, we show you typical externally reported income statements for the three types of businesses. Products range from automobiles to computers to food to clothes to jewelry. The customers of a company that sells products may be final consumers in the economic chain, or a business may sell to other businesses. Services range from transportation to entertainment to consulting. Investment businesses range from mutual funds to credit unions to banks to real estate development companies.

Looking at businesses that sell products

Figure 2-1 presents a classic profit report for a *product-oriented* business; this report, called the *income statement,* would be sent to its outside, or external, owners and lenders. (The report could just as easily be called the *net income statement* because the bottom-line profit term preferred by accountants is *net income,* but the word *net* is dropped from the title, and it's most often called the income statement.) Alternative titles for the external profit report include *earnings statement, operating statement, statement of operating results,* and *statement of earnings.* *Note:* Profit reports prepared for managers that stay inside a business are usually called *P&L* (profit and loss) statements, but this moniker isn't used much in external financial reporting.

The heading of an income statement identifies the business (which in this example is incorporated — thus the "Inc." following the name), the financial statement title ("Income Statement"), and the time period summarized by the statement ("Year Ended December 31, 2017").

Typical Product Business, Inc. Income Statement For Year Ended December 31, 2017	
Sales Revenue	$26,000,000
Cost of Goods Sold Expense	14,300,000
Gross Margin	$11,700,000
Selling, General, and Administrative Expenses	8,700,000
Operating Earnings	$3,000,000
Interest Expense	400,000
Earnings Before Income Tax	$2,600,000
Income Tax Expense	910,000
Net Income	$1,690,000
Earnings Per Share	$3.38

FIGURE 2-1:
Typical income
statement for
a business that
sells products.

You may be tempted to start reading an income statement at the bottom line. But this financial report is designed for you to read from the top line (sales revenue) and proceed down to the last — the bottom line (net income). Each step down the ladder in an income statement involves the deduction of an expense. In Figure 2-1, four expenses are deducted from the sales revenue amount, and four profit lines are given: gross margin, operating earnings, earnings before income tax, and net income:

>> **Gross margin (also called gross profit)** = sales revenue minus the cost of goods (products) sold expense but before operating and other expenses are considered

>> **Operating earnings (or loss)** = profit (or loss) before interest and income tax expenses are deducted from gross margin

>> **Earnings (or loss) before income tax** = profit (or loss) after deducting interest expense from operating earnings but before income tax expense

>> **Net income** = final profit for period after deducting all expenses from sales revenue, which is commonly called the *bottom line*

Although you see income statements with fewer than four profit lines, you seldom see an income statement with more.

Terminology in income statements varies somewhat from business to business, but you can usually determine the meaning of a term from its context and placement in the income statement.

Note in Figure 2-1 that below the net income line, the *earnings per share* (EPS) amount is reported. This important number equals net income divided by the number of ownership shares the business corporation has issued and that are being held by its shareholders. All public corporations whose stock shares are traded in stock markets must report this key metric. EPS is compared to the current market price of the stock to help judge whether the stock is over- or under-priced. Private companies aren't required to report EPS, but they may decide to do so. If a private business decides to report its EPS, it should follow the accounting standard for calculating this number.

The standard practice for almost all businesses is to report two-year comparative financial statements in side-by-side columns — for the period just ended and for the same period one year ago. Indeed, some companies present three-year comparative financial statements. Two-year or three-year financial statements may be legally required, such as for public companies whose debt and ownership shares are traded in a public market. We have to confess that the income statement in Figure 2-1 is incomplete in this regard. It should have a companion column for the year ended December 31, 2016. To ease up on the amount of numbers, however, we show only the most recent year.

Looking at businesses that sell services

Figure 2-2 presents a typical income statement for a *service-oriented* business. We keep the sales revenue and operating earnings the same amount for both the product and the service businesses so you can more easily compare the two.

Typical Service Business, Inc. Income Statement For Year Ended December 31, 2017	
Sales Revenue	$26,000,000
Marketing and Selling Expenses	4,325,000
Operating and Administrative Expenses	8,700,000
Employee Compensation Expense	9,975,000
Operating Earnings	$3,000,000
Interest Expense	200,000
Earnings Before Income Tax	$2,800,000
Income Tax Expense	980,000
Net Income	$1,820,000
Earnings Per Share	$3.64

FIGURE 2-2: Typical income statement for a business that sells services.

If a business sells services and doesn't sell products, it doesn't have a cost of goods sold expense; therefore, the company doesn't show a gross margin line. Some service businesses report a *cost of sales* expense line, but this isn't uniform at all. Even if they do, the business might not deduct this expense line from sales revenue to show a gross margin line equivalent to the one product companies report.

In Figure 2-2, the first profit line is *operating earnings,* which is profit before interest and income tax. The service business example in Figure 2-2 discloses three broad types of expenses. In passing, you may notice that the interest expense for the service business is lower than for the product business (compare with Figure 2-1). Therefore, it has higher earnings before income tax and higher net income.

TIP

The premise of financial reporting is that of *adequate disclosure,* but you find many variations in the reporting of expenses. A business — whether a product or service company or an investment company — has fairly wide latitude regarding the number of expense lines to disclose in its external income statement. A CPA auditor (assuming the company's financial report is audited) may not be satisfied that just three expenses provide enough detail about the operating activities of the business. Accounting standards do not dictate that particular expenses must be disclosed (other than cost of goods sold expense).

Public companies must disclose certain expenses in their publicly available fillings with the federal Securities and Exchange Commission (SEC). Filing reports to the SEC is one thing; in their reports to shareholders, most businesses are relatively stingy regarding how many expenses are revealed in their income statements.

Looking at investment businesses

Figure 2-3 presents an income statement for an investment business. Notice that this income statement discloses three types of revenue: interest and dividends that were earned, gains from sales of investments during the year, and unrealized gains of the market value of its investment portfolio. Instead of gains, the business could've had realized and unrealized losses during a down year, of course. Generally, investment businesses are either required or are under a good deal of pressure to report their three types of investment return. Investment companies might not borrow money and thus have no interest expense. Or they might. We show interest expense in Figure 2-3 for the investment business example.

REMEMBER

We should mention in passing that public investment companies, such as mutual funds and exchange traded securities (ETS), are heavily regulated by the SEC as well as other types of investment entities that raise capital in public offerings. Our purpose in showing the income statement for an investment business (Figure 2-3) is simply for comparison with businesses that sell products and those that sell services (see Figures 2-1 and 2-2).

Typical Investment Business, Inc. Income Statement For Year Ended December 31, 2017	
Interest and Dividends	$14,000,000
Realized Gain (Loss) from Investments	3,000,000
Unrealized Gain (Loss) on Investments	9,000,000
Total Return on Investments	$26,000,000
Marketing and Selling Expenses	4,325,000
Operating and Administrative Expenses	8,700,000
Employee Compensation Expense	9,975,000
Operating Earnings	$3,000,000
Interest Expense	200,000
Earnings Before Income Tax	$2,800,000
Income Tax Expense	980,000
Net Income	$1,820,000
Earnings Per Share	$3.38

FIGURE 2-3: Typical income statement for an investment business.

Taking Care of Housekeeping Details

REMEMBER

We want to point out a few things about income statements that accountants assume everyone knows but, in fact, are not obvious to many people. (Accountants do this a lot: They assume that the people using financial statements know a good deal about the customs and conventions of financial reporting, so they don't make things as clear as they could.) For an accountant, the following facts are second nature, but you may not be aware of them:

>> **Minus signs are missing.** Expenses are deductions from sales revenue, but hardly ever do you see minus signs in front of expense amounts to indicate that they're deductions. Forget about minus signs in income statements and in other financial statements as well. Sometimes parentheses are put around a deduction to signal that it's a negative number, but that's the most you can expect to see.

>> **Your eye is drawn to the bottom line.** Putting a double underline under the final (bottom-line) profit number for emphasis is common practice but not universal. Instead, net income may be shown in bold type. You generally don't see anything as garish as a fat arrow pointing to the profit number or a big smiley encircling the profit number — but again, tastes vary.

>> **Profit isn't usually called *profit*.** As you see in Figures 2-1, 2-2, and 2-3, bottom-line profit is called *net income.* Businesses use other terms as well, such as *net earnings* or just *earnings.* (Can't accountants agree on anything?) In this minibook, we use the terms *net income* and *profit* interchangeably, but when showing a formal income statement, we stick to *net income.*

>> **You don't get details about sales revenue.** The sales revenue amount in an income statements of a product or a service company is the combined total of all sales during the year; you can't tell how many different sales were made, how many different customers the company sold products or services to, or how the sales were distributed over the 12 months of the year. (Public companies are required to release quarterly income statements during the year, and they include a special summary of quarter-by-quarter results in their annual financial reports; private businesses may or may not release quarterly sales data.) Sales revenue does not include sales and excise taxes that the business collects from its customers and remits to the government.

Note: In addition to sales revenue from selling products and/or services, a business may have income from other sources. For instance, a business may have earnings from investments in marketable securities. In its income statement, investment income goes on a separate line and is not commingled with sales revenue. (The businesses featured In Figures 2-1 and 2-2 do not have investment income.)

>> **Gross margin matters.** The *cost of goods sold* expense of a business that sells products is the cost of products sold to customers, the sales revenue of which is reported on the *sales revenue* line. The idea is to match up the sales revenue of goods sold with the cost of goods sold and show the *gross margin* (also called *gross profit*), which is the profit before other expenses are deducted. The other expenses could in total be more than gross margin, in which case the business would have a net loss for the period. (By the way, a bottom-line loss usually has parentheses around it to emphasize that it's a negative number.)

Note: Companies that sell services rather than products (such as airlines, movie theaters, and CPA firms) do *not* have a cost of goods sold expense line in their income statements, as you see in Figure 2-2. Nevertheless, some service companies report a cost of sales expense, and these businesses may also report a corresponding gross margin line of sorts. This is one more example of the variation in financial reporting from business to business that you have to live with if you read financial reports.

>> **Operating costs are lumped together.** The broad category *selling, general, and administrative expenses* (refer to Figure 2-1) consists of a wide variety of costs of operating the business and making sales. Some examples are

- Labor costs (employee wages and salaries, plus retirement benefits, health insurance, and payroll taxes paid by the business)

- Insurance premiums

- Property taxes on buildings and land

- Cost of gas and electric utilities

- Travel and entertainment costs

- Telephone and Internet charges

- Depreciation of operating assets that are used more than one year (including buildings, land improvements, cars and trucks, computers, office furniture, tools and machinery, and shelving)

- Advertising and sales promotion expenditures

- Legal and audit costs

As with sales revenue, you don't get much detail about operating expenses in a typical income statement as it's presented to the company's debtholders and shareholders. A business may disclose more information than you see in its income statement — mainly in the footnotes that are included with its financial statements. Public companies have to include more detail about the expenses in their filings with the SEC, which are available to anyone who looks up the information (probably over the Internet).

Being an Active Reader

The worst thing you can do when presented with an income statement is to be a passive reader. You should be inquisitive. An income statement is not fulfilling its purpose unless you grab it by its numbers and start asking questions.

For example, you should be curious regarding the size of the business (see the nearby sidebar "How big is a big business, and how small is a small business?"). Another question to ask is "How does profit compare with sales revenue for the year?" Profit (net income) equals what's left over from sales revenue after you deduct all expenses. The business featured in Figure 2-1 squeezed $1.69 million profit from its $26 million sales revenue for the year, which equals 6.5 percent. (The service business did a little better; see Figure 2-2.) This ratio of profit to sales revenue means expenses absorbed 93.5 percent of sales revenue. Although it may seem rather thin, a 6.5 percent profit margin on sales is quite acceptable for many businesses. (Some businesses consistently make a bottom-line profit of 10 to 20 percent of sales, and others are satisfied with a 1 or 2 percent profit on sales revenue.) Profit ratios on sales vary widely from industry to industry.

HOW BIG IS A BIG BUSINESS, AND HOW SMALL IS A SMALL BUSINESS?

One key measure of the size of a business is the number of employees it has on its payroll. Could the business shown in Figure 2-1 have 500 employees? Probably not. This would mean that the annual sales revenue per employee would be only $52,000 ($26 million annual sales revenue divided by 500 employees). But the annual wage per employee in many industries today is over $35,000 and much higher in some industries. Much more likely, the number of full-time employees in this business is closer to 100. This number of employees yields $260,000 sales revenue per employee, which means that the business could probably afford an average annual wage of $40,000 per employee or higher. Do the math to check this out.

Public companies generally disclose their numbers of employees in their annual financial reports, but private businesses generally don't. United States accounting standards do not require that the total number and total compensation of employees be reported in the external financial statements of a business or in the footnotes to the financial statements.

The definition of a small business isn't uniform. Generally, the term refers to a business with fewer than 100 full-time employees, but in some situations, it refers to businesses with fewer than 20 employees or even fewer than 10 full-time employees. Say a business has 20 full-time employees on its payroll who earn an average of $40,000 in annual wages (a relatively low amount). This costs $800,000 for its annual payroll before figuring in employee benefits (such as Social Security taxes, 401(k) matching retirement plans, health insurance, and so on). Product businesses need to earn annual gross margin equal to two or three times their basic payroll expense.

REMEMBER

Accounting standards are relatively silent regarding which expenses have to be disclosed on the face of an income statement or elsewhere in a financial report. For example, the amount a business spends on advertising doesn't have to be disclosed. (In contrast, the rules for filing financial reports with the SEC require disclosure of certain expenses, such as repairs and maintenance expenses. Keep in mind that the SEC rules apply only to public businesses.)

In the product business example in Figure 2-1, expenses such as labor costs and advertising expenditures are buried in the all-inclusive *selling, general, and administrative expenses* line. (If the business manufactures the products it sells instead of buying them from another business, a good part of its annual labor cost is included in its *cost of goods sold* expense.) Some companies disclose specific expenses such as advertising and marketing costs, research and development costs, and other significant expenses. In short, income statement expense-disclosure practices vary considerably from business to business.

TALKING ABOUT PROFIT: THE *P* WORD

We're sure you won't be surprised to hear that the financial objective of every business is to earn an adequate profit on a sustainable basis. In the pursuit of profit, a business should behave ethically, stay within the law, care for its employees, and be friendly to the environment. We don't mean to preach here. But the blunt truth of the matter is that *profit* is a dirty word to many people, and the profit motive is a favorite target of many critics who blame the push for profit for unsafe working conditions, outsourcing, wages that are below the poverty line, and other ills of the economic system. The profit motive is an easy target for criticism.

You hear a lot about the profit motive of business, but you don't see the *p* word in many external financial reports. The financial press uses the term *profit* but also alternative terms — in particular, *earnings*. For example, *The Wall Street Journal* and *The New York Times* use the term *earnings reports.* If you look in financial statements, the term *net income* is used most often for the bottom-line profit that a business earns. Accountants prefer *net income,* although they also use other names, like *net earnings* and *net operating earnings.*

In short, *profit* is more of a street name; in polite company, you generally say *net income.* However, we must point out one exception. We've followed the financial reports of Caterpillar, Inc., for many years. Caterpillar uses the term *profit* for the bottom line of its income statement; it's one of the few companies that call a spade a spade.

Another set of questions you should ask in reading an income statement concerns the *profit performance* of the business. Refer again to the product company's profit performance report (Figure 2-1). Profitwise, how did the business do? Underneath this question is the implicit question, "Relative to *what?*" Generally speaking, three sorts of benchmarks are used for evaluating profit performance:

>> Broad, industrywide performance averages

>> Immediate competitors' performances

>> The business's own performance in recent years

Deconstructing Profit

Now that you've had the opportunity to read an income statement (see Figures 2-1, 2-2, and 2-3), let us ask you a question: What *is* profit? Our guess is that you'll answer that profit is revenue less expenses. In our class, you'd get only a C grade for this answer. Your answer is correct, as far as it goes, but it doesn't go far enough. This answer doesn't strike at the core of profit. The answer doesn't tell us what profit consists of or the substance of profit.

In this section, we explain the anatomy of profit. Having read the product company's income statement, you now know that the business earned net income for the year ending December 31, 2017 (see Figure 2-1). Where's the profit? If you had to put your finger on the profit, where would you touch?

Recording profit works like a pair of scissors: You have the positive revenue blade and the negative expenses blade. Revenue and expenses have opposite effects. This leads to two questions: What is a revenue? And what is an expense?

Figure 2-4 summarizes the financial natures of revenue and expenses in terms of impacts on assets and liabilities. Notice the symmetrical framework of revenue and expenses. It's beautiful in its own way, don't you think? In any case, this summary framework is helpful for understanding the financial effects of revenue and expenses.

FIGURE 2-4: Fundamental natures of revenue and expenses.

	Asset	Liability
Revenue	+	−
Expense	−	+

Revenue and expense effects on assets and liabilities

Here's the gist of the two-by-two matrix shown in Figure 2-4. In recording a sale, the bookkeeper increases a revenue account. The revenue account accumulates sale after sale during the period. So at the end of the period, the total sales revenue for the period is the balance in the account. This amount is the cumulative end-of-period total of all sales during the period. All sales revenue accounts are combined for the period, and one grand total is reported in the income statement on the top line. As each sale (or other type of revenue event) is recorded, either an asset account is increased or a liability account is decreased.

TIP

We're reasonably sure you follow that revenue increases an asset. For example, if all sales are made for cash, the company's cash account increases accordingly. On the other hand, you may have trouble understanding that certain revenue transactions are recorded with a decrease in a liability. Here's why: Customers may pay in advance for a product or service to be delivered later (examples are prepaying for theater or airline tickets and making a down payment for future delivery of products). In recording such advance payments from customers, the business increases cash, of course, and increases a liability account usually called *deferred revenue*. The term *deferred* simply means postponed. When the product or service is delivered to the customer — and not before then — the bookkeeper records the amount of revenue that has now been earned *and* decreases the deferred revenue liability by the same amount.

Recording expenses is rather straightforward. When an expense is recorded, a specific expense account is increased, and either an asset account is decreased or a liability account is increased the same amount. For example, to record the cost of goods sold, the expense with this name is increased, say, $35,000, and in the same entry, the inventory asset account is decreased $35,000. Alternatively, an expense entry may involve a liability account instead of an asset account. For example, suppose the business receives a $10,000 bill from its CPA auditor that it will pay later. In recording the bill from the CPA, the audit expense account is increased $10,000, and a liability account called *accounts payable* is increased $10,000.

The summary framework of Figure 2-4 has no exceptions. Recording revenue and expenses (as well as gains and losses) always follow these rules. So where does this leave you for understanding profit? Profit itself doesn't show up in Figure 2-4, does it? Profit depends on amounts recorded for revenue and expenses, of course, as we show in the next section.

Comparing three scenarios of profit

Figure 2-5 presents three scenarios of profit in terms of changes in the assets and liabilities of a business. In all three cases, the business makes the same amount of profit: $10, as you see in the abbreviated income statements on the right side. (We keep the numbers small, but you can think of $10 million instead of $10 if you prefer.)

To find the amount of profit, first determine the amount of revenue and expenses for each case. In all three cases, total expenses are $90, but the changes in assets and liabilities differ:

>> In Case A, revenue consists of $100 asset increase; no liability was involved in recording revenue.

>> In Case B, revenue was from $100 decrease in a liability.

>> In Case C, you see both asset increases and liability decreases for revenue.

Case A

	Asset	Liability	Income Statement	
Revenue	+ $100		Revenue	$100
Expense	- $60	+ $30	Expenses	$90
			Profit	$10

Case B

	Asset	Liability	Income Statement	
Revenue		- $100	Revenue	$100
Expense	- $60	+ $30	Expenses	$90
			Profit	$10

Case C

	Asset	Liability	Income Statement	
Revenue	+ $50	- $50	Revenue	$100
Expense	- $45	+ $45	Expenses	$90
			Profit	$10

FIGURE 2-5:
Comparing asset and liability changes for three profit scenarios.

REMEMBER

Revenue and expenses are originally recorded as increases or decreases in different asset and liability accounts. Cash is just one asset. We explain the other assets and the liabilities in the later section "Pinpointing the Assets and Liabilities Used to Record Revenue and Expenses."

Some businesses make sales for cash; cash is received at the time of the sale. In recording these sales, a revenue account is increased and the cash account is increased. Some expenses are recorded at the time of cutting a check to pay the expense. In recording these expenses, an appropriate expense account is increased and the cash asset account is decreased. However, for most businesses, the majority of their revenue and expense transactions do not simultaneously affect cash.

For most businesses, cash comes into play before or after revenue and expenses are recorded. For example, a business buys products from its supplier that it will sell sometime later to its customers. The purchase is paid for before the goods are sold. No expense is recorded until products are sold. Here's another example: A business makes sales on credit to its customers. In recording credit sales, a sales revenue account is increased and an asset account called *accounts receivable* is increased. Sometime later, the receivables are collected in cash. The amount of cash actually collected through the end of the period may be less than the amount of sales revenue recorded.

Cash inflow from revenue is almost always different from revenue for the period. Furthermore, cash outflow for expenses is almost always different from expenses for the period. The lesson is this: Do not equate revenue with cash inflow, and do not equate expenses with cash outflows. The net cash flow from profit for the period — revenue inflow minus expense outflow — is bound to be higher or lower than the accounting-based measure of profit for the period. The income statement does not report cash flows!

This chapter lays the foundation for Chapter 4 of this minibook, where we explain cash flow from profit. Cash flow is an enormously important topic in every business. We're sure even Apple, with its huge treasure of marketable investments, worries about its cash flow.

Folding profit into retained earnings

After profit is determined for the period, which means that all revenue and expenses have been recorded for the period, the profit amount is entered as an increase in *retained earnings*. Doing this keeps the accounting equation in balance. For Case A in Figure 2-5, for example, the changes in the accounting equation for the period are as follows:

$$+\$40 \text{ Assets} = +\$30 \text{ Liabilities} + \$10 \text{ Retained Earnings}$$

The $40 increase on the asset side is balanced by the $30 increase in liabilities and the $10 increase in retained earnings on the opposite side of the accounting equation. The books are in balance.

In most situations, not all annual profit is distributed to owners; some is retained in the business. Unfortunately, the retained earnings account sounds like an asset in the minds of many people. It isn't! It's a source-of-assets account, not an asset account. It's on the right-hand side of the accounting equation; assets are on the left side. For more information, see the sidebar "So why is it called retained earnings?"

The product business in Figure 2-1 earned $1.69 million profit for the year. Therefore, during the year, its retained earnings increased this amount because net income is recorded in this owners' equity account. You know this for sure, but what you can't tell from the income statement is how the assets and liabilities of the business were affected by its sale and expense activities during the period. The product company's $1.69 million net income resulted in some mixture of changes in its assets and liabilities, such that its owners' equity increased $1.69 million. It could be that its assets increased $1.0 million and its liabilities increased $0.69 million, but you can't tell this from the income statement.

SO WHY IS IT CALLED RETAINED EARNINGS?

The ending balance reported in the retained earnings account is the amount after recording increases and decreases in the account during the period, starting with the opening balance at the start of the period, of course. The retained earnings account increases when the business makes a profit and decreases when the business distributes some of the profit to its owners. That is, the total amount of profit paid out to the owners is recorded as a decrease in the retained earnings account.

Bonus question: Why doesn't a business pay out all its annual profit to owners? One reason is that the business may not have converted all its profit into cash by the end of the year and may not have enough cash to distribute. Or the business may have had the cash but needed it for other purposes, such as growing the company by buying new buildings and equipment or spending the money on research and development of new products. Reinvesting the profit in the business in this way is often referred to as *plowing back* earnings. A business should always make good use of its cash flow instead of letting the cash pile up in the cash account. See Chapter 4 in this minibook for more on cash flow from profit.

The financial gyrations in assets and operating liabilities from profit-making activities are especially important for business managers to understand and pay attention to because they have to manage and control the changes. It would be dangerous to assume that making a profit has only beneficial effects on assets and liabilities. One of the main purposes of the statement of cash flows, which we discuss in Chapter 4 in this minibook, is to summarize the financial changes caused by the profit activities of the business during the year.

Pinpointing the Assets and Liabilities Used to Record Revenue and Expenses

The sales and expense activities of a business involve cash inflows and outflows, as we're sure you know. What you may not know, however, is that the profit-making activities of a business that sells products on credit involves four other basic assets and three basic types of liabilities. Cash is the pivotal asset. You may have heard the old saying that "all roads lead to Rome." In like manner, revenue and expenses, sooner or later, lead to cash. But in the meantime, other asset and liability accounts are used to record the flow of profit activity. This section explains the main assets and liabilities used in recording revenue and expenses.

Making sales: Accounts receivable and deferred revenue

TIP

Many businesses allow their customers to buy their products or services on credit, or "on the cuff," as they said in the old days. The customer buys now and pays later. To record credit sales, a business uses an asset account called *accounts receivable.* Recording a credit sale increases sales revenue and increases accounts receivable. The business records now and collects later. The immediate recording of credit sales is one aspect of the *accrual basis of accounting.* When the customer pays the business, cash is increased and accounts receivable is decreased. In most cases, a business doesn't collect all of its credit sales by the end of the year, so it reports a balance for its accounts receivable in its end-of-period balance sheet (see Chapter 3 in this minibook).

In contrast to making sales on credit, some businesses collect cash before they deliver their products or services to customers. For example, you might pay *The New York Times* for a one-year subscription at the start of the year. During the year, the newspaper delivers the product one day at a time. Another example is when you buy and pay for an airline ticket days or weeks ahead of your flight. There are many examples of advance payments by customers. When a business receives advance payments from customers, it increases cash (of course) and increases a liability account called *deferred revenue.* Sales revenue isn't recorded until the product or service is delivered to the customer. When delivered sales revenue is increased, the liability account is decreased, which reflects that part of the liability has been paid down by delivery of the product or service.

REMEMBER

Increases or decreases in the asset *accounts receivable* and the liability account *deferred revenue* affect cash flow during the year from the profit-making activities of the business. We explain cash flow in Chapter 4 in this minibook. Until then, keep in mind that the balance of accounts receivable is money waiting in the wings to be collected in the near future, and the balance in deferred revenue is the amount of money collected in advance from customers. These two accounts appear in the balance sheet, which we discuss in Chapter 3 in this minibook.

Selling products: Inventory

The *cost of goods sold* is one of the primary expenses of businesses that sell products. (In Figure 2-1, notice that this expense equals more than half the sales revenue for the year.) This expense is just what its name implies: the cost that a business pays for the products it sells to customers. A business makes profit by setting its sales prices high enough to cover the costs of products sold, the costs of operating the business, interest on borrowed money, and income taxes (assuming that the business pays income tax), with something left over for profit.

When the business acquires products (by purchase or manufacture), the cost of the products goes into an *inventory* asset account (and, of course, the cost is either deducted from the cash account or added to a liability account, depending on whether the business pays cash or buys on credit). When a customer buys that product, the business transfers the cost of the products sold from the inventory asset account to the *cost of goods sold* expense account because the products are no longer in the business's inventory; the products have been delivered to the customer.

In the first layer in the income statement of a product company, the cost of goods sold expense is deducted from the sales revenue for the goods sold. Almost all businesses that sell products report the cost of goods sold as a separate expense in their income statements, as you see in Figure 2-1. Most report this expense as shown in Figure 2-1 so that *gross margin* is reported. But some product companies simply report cost of goods sold as one expense among many and do not call attention to gross margin. Actually, you see many variations on the theme of reporting gross margin. Some businesses use the broader term *cost of sales*, which includes cost of goods sold as well as other costs.

REMEMBER

A business that sells products needs to have a stock of those products on hand for ready sale to its customers. When you drive by an auto dealer and see all the cars, SUVs, and pickup trucks waiting to be sold, remember that these products are inventory. The cost of unsold products (goods held in inventory) is not yet an expense; only after the products are actually sold does the cost get recorded as an expense. In this way, the cost of goods sold expense is correctly matched against the sales revenue from the goods sold. Correctly matching expenses against sales revenue is the essential starting point of accounting for profit.

Prepaying operating costs: Prepaid expenses

Prepaid expenses are the opposite of unpaid expenses. For example, a business buys fire insurance and general liability insurance (in case a customer who slips on a wet floor or is insulted by a careless salesperson sues the business). Insurance premiums must be paid ahead of time, before coverage starts. The premium cost is allocated to expense in the actual periods benefited. At the end of the year, the business may be only halfway through the insurance coverage period, so it should allocate only half the premium cost as an expense. (For a six-month policy, you charge one-sixth of the premium cost to each of the six months covered.) At the time the premium is paid, the entire amount is recorded as an increase in the prepaid expenses asset account. For each period of coverage, the appropriate fraction of the cost is recorded as a decrease in the asset account and as an increase in the insurance expense account.

In another example, a business pays cash to stock up on office supplies that it may not use up for several months. The cost is recorded in the prepaid expenses asset account at the time of purchase; when the supplies are used, the appropriate amount is subtracted from the prepaid expenses asset account and recorded in the office supplies expense account.

Using the prepaid expenses asset account is not so much for the purpose of reporting all the assets of a business, because the balance in the account compared with other assets and total assets is typically small. Rather, using this account is an example of allocating costs to expenses in the period benefited by the costs, which isn't always the same period in which the business pays those costs. The prepayment of these expenses lays the groundwork for continuing operations seamlessly into the next year.

Fixed assets: Depreciation expense

Long-term operating assets that are not held for sale in the ordinary course of business are called generically *fixed assets*; these include buildings, machinery, office equipment, vehicles, computers and data-processing equipment, shelving and cabinets, and so on. The term *fixed assets* is informal, or accounting slang. The more formal term used in financial reports is *property, plant, and equipment.* It's easier to say *fixed assets,* which we do in this section.

Depreciation refers to spreading out the cost of a fixed asset over the years of its useful life to a business, instead of charging the entire cost to expense in the year of purchase. That way, each year of use bears a share of the total cost. For example, autos and light trucks are typically depreciated over five years; the idea is to charge a fraction of the total cost to depreciation expense during each of the five years. (The actual fraction each year depends on the method of depreciation used.)

Depreciation applies only to fixed assets that a business owns, not those it rents or leases. If a company leases or rents fixed assets, which is quite common, the rent it pays each month is charged to *rent expense.* Depreciation is a real expense but not a cash outlay expense in the year it's recorded. The cash outlay occurred when the fixed asset was acquired. See the sidebar "The special character of depreciation" for more information.

Suppose a business records $100,000 depreciation for the period. You'd think that the depreciation expense account would be increased $100,000 and one or more fixed asset accounts would be decreased $100,000. Well, not so fast. Instead of directly decreasing the fixed asset account, the bookkeeper increases a contra asset account called *accumulated depreciation.* The balance in this negative account is deducted from the balance of the fixed asset account. In this manner, the original acquisition cost of the fixed asset is preserved, and the historical cost is reported in the balance sheet. We discuss this practice in Book 1, Chapter 3.

THE SPECIAL CHARACTER OF DEPRECIATION

To start with, let's agree that fixed assets wear out and lose their economic usefulness over time. Some fixed assets, such as office furniture and buildings, last many years. Other fixed assets, such as delivery trucks and computers, last just a few. Accountants argue, quite logically, that the cost of a fixed asset should be spread out or allocated over its predicted useful life to the business. Depreciation methods are rather arbitrary, but any reasonable method is much better than the alternative of charging off the entire cost of a fixed asset in the year it's acquired.

A business has to pass the cost of its fixed assets through to its customers and recover the cost of its fixed assets through sales revenue. For example, consider a taxicab driver who owns his cab. He sets his fares high enough to pay for his time; to pay for the insurance, license, gas, and oil; and to recover the cost of the cab. Included in each fare is a tiny fraction of the cost of the cab, which over the course of the year adds up to the depreciation expense that he passed on to his passengers and collected in fares. At the end of the year, he has collected a certain amount of money that pays him back for part of the cost of the cab.

In summary, fixed assets are gradually sold off and turned back into cash each year. Part of sales revenue recovers some of the cost of fixed assets, which is why the decrease in the fixed assets account to record depreciation expense has the effect of increasing cash (assuming your sales revenue is collected in cash during the year). What the company does with this cash recovery is another matter. Sooner or later, you need to replace fixed assets to continue in business.

TIP

Take a look back at the product company income statement example in Figure 2-1. From the information supplied in this income statement, you don't know the amount of depreciation expense the business recorded in 2017. However, the footnotes to the business's financial statements and its statement of cash flows reveal this amount. In 2017, the business recorded $775,000 depreciation expense. Basically, this expense decreases the book value (the recorded value) of its depreciable assets. *Book value* equals original cost minus the accumulated depreciation recorded so far. Book value may be different — indeed, quite a bit different — compared with the current replacement value of fixed assets.

Unpaid expenses: Accounts payable, accrued expenses payable, and income tax payable

A typical business pays many expenses *after* the period in which the expenses are recorded. Following are common examples:

>> A business hires a law firm that does a lot of legal work during the year, but the company doesn't pay the bill until the following year.

>> A business matches retirement contributions made by its employees but doesn't pay its share of the latest payroll until the following year.

>> A business has unpaid bills for telephone service, gas, electricity, and water that it used during the year.

Accountants use three types of liability accounts to record a business's unpaid expenses:

>> **Accounts payable:** This account is used for items that the business buys on credit and for which it receives an invoice (a bill) either in hard copy or over the Internet. For example, your business receives an invoice from its lawyers for legal work done. As soon as you receive the invoice, you record in the accounts payable liability account the amount that you owe. Later, when you pay the invoice, you subtract that amount from the accounts payable account, and your cash goes down by the same amount.

>> **Accrued expenses payable:** A business has to make estimates for several unpaid costs at the end of the year because it hasn't received invoices or other types of bills for them. Examples of accrued expenses include the following:

- Unused vacation and sick days that employees carry over to the following year, which the business has to pay for in the coming year

- Unpaid bonuses to salespeople

- The cost of future repairs and part replacements on products that customers have bought and haven't yet returned for repair

- The daily accumulation of interest on borrowed money that won't be paid until the end of the loan period

Without invoices to reference, you have to examine your business operations carefully to determine which liabilities of this sort to record.

>> **Income tax payable:** This account is used for income taxes that a business still owes to the IRS at the end of the year. The income tax expense for the year is the total amount based on the taxable income for the entire year. Your

business may not pay 100 percent of its income tax expense during the year; it may owe a small fraction to the IRS at year's end. You record the unpaid amount in the income tax payable account.

Note: A business may be organized legally as a *pass-through tax entity* for income tax purposes, which means that it doesn't pay income tax itself but instead passes its taxable income on to its owners. The business we refer to here is an ordinary corporation that pays income tax.

Reporting Unusual Gains and Losses

We have a small confession to make: The income statement examples in Figures 2-1, 2-2, and 2-3 are sanitized versions when compared with actual income statements in external financial reports. Suppose you took the trouble to read 100 income statements. You'd be surprised at the wide range of things you'd find in these statements. But we do know one thing for certain you'd discover.

Many businesses report *unusual gains and losses* in addition to their usual revenue and expenses. Remember that recording a gain increases an asset or decreases a liability. And recording a loss decreases an asset or increases a liability. The road to profit is anything but smooth and straight. Every business experiences an occasional gain or loss that's off the beaten path — a serious disruption that comes out of the blue, doesn't happen regularly, and impacts the bottom-line profit. Such unusual gains and losses are perturbations in the continuity of the business's regular flow of profit-making activities.

Here are some examples of unusual gains and losses:

>> **Downsizing and restructuring the business:** Layoffs require severance pay or trigger early retirement costs. Major segments of the business may be disposed of, causing large losses.

>> **Abandoning product lines:** When you decide to discontinue selling a line of products, you lose at least some of the money that you paid for obtaining or manufacturing the products, either because you sell the products for less than you paid or because you just dump the products you can't sell.

>> **Settling lawsuits and other legal actions:** Damages and fines that you pay — as well as awards that you *receive* in a favorable ruling — are obviously nonrecurring losses or gains (unless you're in the habit of being taken to court every year).

>> **Writing down (also called *writing off*) damaged and impaired assets:** If products become damaged and unsellable or if fixed assets need to be replaced unexpectedly, you need to remove these items from the assets accounts. Even when certain assets are in good physical condition, if they lose their ability to generate future sales or other benefits to the business, accounting rules say that the assets have to be taken off the books or at least written down to lower book values.

>> **Changing accounting methods:** A business may decide to use a different method for recording revenue and expenses than it did in the past, in some cases because the accounting rules (set by the authoritative accounting governing bodies — see Book 1, Chapter 1) have changed. Often, the new method requires a business to record a one-time cumulative effect caused by the switch in accounting method. These special items can be huge.

>> **Correcting errors from previous financial reports:** If you or your accountant discovers that a past financial report had a serious accounting error, you make a catch-up correction entry, which means that you record a loss or gain that has nothing to do with your performance this year.

The basic tests for an unusual gain or loss are that it is unusual in nature or infrequently occurring. Deciding what qualifies as an unusual gain or loss is not a cut-and-dried process. Different accountants may have different interpretations of what fits the concept of an unusual gain or loss.

According to financial reporting standards, a business should disclose unusual gains and losses on a separate line in the income statement or, alternatively, explain them in a footnote to its financial statements. There seems to be a general preference to put an unusual gain or loss on a separate line in the income statement. Therefore, in addition to the usual lines for revenue and expenses, the income statement would disclose separate lines for these out-of-the-ordinary happenings.

WARNING

Every company that stays in business for more than a couple of years experiences an unusual gain or loss of one sort or another. But beware of a business that takes advantage of these discontinuities in the following ways:

>> **Discontinuities become continuities:** This business makes an extraordinary loss or gain a regular feature on its income statement. Every year or so, the business loses a major lawsuit, abandons product lines, or restructures itself. It reports certain nonrecurring gains or losses on a recurring basis.

>> **A discontinuity is used as an opportunity to record all sorts of write-downs and losses:** When recording an unusual loss (such as settling a lawsuit), the business opts to record other losses at the same time, and everything but the kitchen sink (and sometimes that, too) gets written off. This so-called *big-bath* strategy says that you may as well take a big bath now in order to avoid taking little showers in the future.

A business may just have bad (or good) luck regarding unusual events that its managers couldn't have predicted. If a business is facing a major, unavoidable expense this year, cleaning out all its expenses in the same year so it can start off fresh next year can be a clever, legitimate accounting tactic. But where do you draw the line between these accounting manipulations and fraud? All we can advise you to do is stay alert to these potential problems.

Watching for Misconceptions and Misleading Reports

One broad misconception about profit is that the numbers reported in the income statement are precise and accurate and can be relied on down to the last dollar. Call this the *exactitude* misconception. Virtually every dollar amount you see in an income statement probably would have been different if a different accountant had been in charge. We don't mean that some accountants are dishonest and deceitful. It's just that business transactions can get very complex and require forecasts and estimates. Different accountants would arrive at different interpretations of the so-called facts and therefore record different amounts of revenue and expenses. Hopefully, the accountant is consistent over time so that year-to-year comparisons are valid.

Another serious misconception is that if profit is good, the financial condition of the business is good. As we write this sentence, the profit of Apple is very good. But we didn't automatically assume that its financial condition was equally good. We looked in Apple's balance sheet and found that its financial condition is very good indeed. (It has more cash and marketable investments on hand than the economy of many countries.) Our point is that its bottom line doesn't tell you anything about the financial condition of the business. You find this in the balance sheet, which we explain in Chapter 3 of this minibook.

The income statement occupies center stage; the bright spotlight is on this financial statement because it reports profit or loss for the period. But remember that a business reports *three* primary financial statements — the other two being the balance sheet and the statement of cash flows, which we discuss in the next two chapters. The three statements are like a three-ring circus. The income statement may draw the most attention, but you have to watch what's going on in all three places. As important as profit is to the financial success of a business, the income statement is not an island unto itself.

Keep in mind that financial statements are supplemented with footnotes and contain other commentary from the business's executives. If the financial statements have been audited, the CPA firm includes a short report stating whether the financial statements have been prepared in conformity with the appropriate accounting standards.

We don't like closing this chapter on a sour note, but we must point out that an income statement you read and rely on — as a business manager, an investor, or a lender — may not be true and accurate. In most cases (we'll even say in the large majority of cases), businesses prepare their financial statements in good faith, and their profit accounting is honest. They may bend the rules a little, but basically their accounting methods are within the boundaries of GAAP even though the business puts a favorable spin on its profit number.

But some businesses resort to accounting fraud and deliberately distort their profit numbers. In this case, an income statement reports false and misleading sales revenue and/or expenses in order to make the bottom-line profit appear to be better than the facts would support. If the fraud is discovered at a later time, the business puts out revised financial statements. Basically, the business in this situation rewrites its profit history.

We wish we could say that financial reporting fraud doesn't happen very often, but the number of high-profile accounting fraud cases over the recent two decades (and longer in fact) has been truly alarming. The CPA auditors of these companies didn't catch the accounting fraud, even though this is one purpose of an audit. Investors who relied on the fraudulent income statements ended up suffering large losses.

Anytime we read a financial report, we keep in mind the risk that the financial statements may be stage managed to some extent — to make year-to-year reported profit look a little smoother and less erratic and to make the financial condition of the business appear a little better. Regrettably, financial statements don't always tell it as it is. Rather, the chief executive and chief accountant of the business fiddle with the financial statements to some extent.

IN THIS CHAPTER

» Reading the balance sheet

» Categorizing business transactions

» Connecting revenue and expenses with their assets and liabilities

» Examining where businesses go for capital

» Understanding values in balance sheets

Chapter **3**

Reporting Financial Condition in the Balance Sheet

This chapter explores one of the three primary financial statements reported by business and not-for-profit entities: the *balance sheet*, which is also called the *statement of financial condition* and the *statement of financial position*. This financial statement summarizes the assets of a business and its liabilities and owners' equity sources at a point in time. The balance sheet is a two-sided financial statement.

The balance sheet may seem to stand alone because it's presented on a separate page in a financial report, but keep in mind that the assets and liabilities reported in a balance sheet are the results of the activities, or transactions, of the business. *Transactions* are economic exchanges between the business and the parties it deals with: customers, employees, vendors, government agencies, and sources of capital. The other two financial statements — the income statement and the statement of cash flows (see Book 1, Chapter 4) — report transactions, whereas the balance sheet reports values at an instant in time. The balance sheet is prepared at the end of the income statement period.

Unlike the income statement, the balance sheet doesn't have a natural bottom line, or one key figure that's the focus of attention. The balance sheet reports various assets, liabilities, and sources of owners' equity. Cash is the most important asset, but other assets are important as well. Short-term liabilities are compared to cash and assets that can be converted into cash quickly. The balance sheet, as we explain in this chapter, has to be read as a whole — you can't focus only on one or two items in this financial summary of the business. You shouldn't put on blinders in reading a balance sheet by looking only at two or three items. You might miss important information by not perusing the whole balance sheet.

Expanding the Accounting Equation

The *accounting equation* is a condensed version of a balance sheet. In its most concise form, the accounting equation is as follows:

$$\text{Assets} = \text{Liabilities} + \text{Owners' Equity}$$

Figure 3-1 expands the accounting equation to identify the basic accounts reported in a balance sheet.

Assets	=	Liabilities	+	Owners' Equity
Cash		Accounts Payable		Invested Capital Account
Accounts Receivable		Accrued Expenses Payable		Retained Earnings
Inventory		Income Tax Payable		
Prepaid Expenses		Short-term Debt		
Fixed Assets		Long-term Debt		

FIGURE 3-1: Expanded accounting equation.

Many of the balance sheet accounts you see in Figure 3-1 are introduced in Book 1, Chapter 2, which explains the income statement and the profit-making activities of a business. In fact, most balance sheet accounts are driven by profit-making transactions.

TIP

Certain balance sheet accounts are not involved in recording the profit-making transactions of a business. Short- and long-term debt accounts aren't used in recording revenue and expenses, and neither is the invested capital account, which records the investment of capital from the owners of the business. Transactions involving debt and owners' invested capital accounts have to do with *financing* the business — that is, securing the capital needed to run the business.

Presenting a Proper Balance Sheet

Figure 3-2 presents a two-year comparative balance sheet for the business example introduced in Chapter 2 of this minibook. This business sells products and makes sales on credit to its customers. The balance sheet is at the close of business, December 31, 2016 and 2017. In most cases, financial statements are not completed and released until a few weeks after the balance sheet date. Therefore, by the time you read this financial statement, it's already somewhat out of date, because the business has continued to engage in transactions since December 31, 2017. When significant changes have occurred in the interim between the closing date of the balance sheet and the date of releasing its financial report, a business should disclose these subsequent developments in the footnotes to the financial statements.

The balance sheet in Figure 3-2 is in the vertical (portrait) layout, with assets on top and liabilities and owners' equity on the bottom. Alternatively, a balance sheet may be in the horizontal (landscape) mode, with liabilities and owners' equity on the right side and assets on the left.

TIP

The financial statement in Figure 3-2 is called a *classified* balance sheet because certain accounts are grouped into classes (groups). Although the accounts in the class are different, they have common characteristics. Two such classes are *current assets* and *current liabilities*. Notice that subtotals are provided for each class. We discuss the reasons for reporting these classes of accounts later in the chapter (see "Current assets and liabilities"). The total amount of assets and the total amount of liabilities plus owners' equity are given at the bottom of the columns for each year. We probably don't have to remind you that these two amounts should be equal; otherwise, the company's books aren't in balance.

WARNING

If a business doesn't release its annual financial report within a few weeks after the close of its fiscal year, you should be alarmed. The reasons for such a delay are all bad. One reason might be that the business's accounting system isn't functioning well and the controller (chief accounting officer) has to do a lot of work at year-end to get the accounts up to date and accurate for preparing its financial statements. Another reason is that the business is facing serious problems and can't decide on how to account for the problems. Perhaps a business is delaying the reporting of bad news. Or the business may have a serious dispute with its independent CPA auditor that hasn't been resolved.

Typical Product Business, Inc. Statement of Financial Condition at December 31, 2016 and 2017 (Dollar amounts in thousands)			
Assets	**2016**	**2017**	**Change**
Cash	$2,275	$2,165	($110)
Accounts Receivable	$2,150	$2,600	$450
Inventory	$2,725	$3,450	$725
Prepaid Expenses	$525	$600	$75
Current Assets	$7,675	$8,815	
Property, Plant, and Equipment	$11,175	$12,450	$1,275
Accumulated Depreciation	($5,640)	($6,415)	($775)
Net of Depreciation	$5,535	$6,035	
Total Assets	$13,210	$14,850	$1,640
Liabilities and Owners' Equity	**2016**	**2017**	**Change**
Accounts Payable	$640	$765	$125
Accrued Expenses Payable	$750	$900	$150
Income Tax Payable	$90	$115	$25
Short-term Notes Payable	$2,150	$2,250	$100
Current Liabilities	$3,630	$4,030	
Long-term Notes Payable	$3,850	$4,000	$150
Owners' Equity:			
Capital Stock	$3,100	$3,250	$150
Retained Earnings	$2,630	$3,570	$940
Total Owners' Equity	$5,730	$6,820	
Total Liabilities and Owners' Equity	$13,210	$14,850	$1,640

FIGURE 3-2: Illustrative two-year comparative balance sheet for a product business.

The balance sheet in Figure 3-2 includes a column for *changes* in the assets, liabilities, and owners' equity over the year (from year end 2016 through year end 2017). Including these changes is not required by financial reporting standards, and in fact most businesses do not include the changes. It's certainly acceptable to report balance sheet changes, but it's not mandated, and most companies don't. We include the changes for ease of reference in this chapter. Transactions generate changes in assets, liabilities, and owners' equity, which we summarize later in the chapter (see the section "Understanding That Transactions Drive the Balance Sheet").

Doing an initial reading of the balance sheet

Now suppose you own the business whose balance sheet is in Figure 3-2. (Most likely, you wouldn't own 100 percent of the ownership shares of the business; you'd own the majority of shares, giving you working control of the business.) You've already digested your most recent annual income statement (refer to Book 1, Chapter 2's Figure 2-1), which reports that you earned $1,690,000 net income on annual sales of $26,000,000. What more do you need to know? Well, you need to check your financial condition, which is reported in the balance sheet.

Is your financial condition viable and sustainable to continue your profit-making endeavor? The balance sheet helps answer this critical question. Perhaps you're on the edge of going bankrupt, even though you're making a profit. Your balance sheet is where to look for telltale information about possible financial troubles.

In reading through a balance sheet, you may notice that it doesn't have a punchline like the income statement does. The income statement's punchline is the net income line, which is rarely humorous to the business itself but can cause some snickers among analysts. (Earnings per share is also important for public corporations.) You can't look at just one item on the balance sheet, murmur an appreciative "ah-ha," and rush home to watch the game. You have to read the whole thing (sigh) and make comparisons among the items. Book 1, Chapter 5 offers information on interpreting financial statements.

At first glance, you might be somewhat alarmed that your cash balance decreased $110,000 during the year (refer to Figure 3-2). Didn't you make a tidy profit? Why would your cash balance go down? Well, think about it. Many other transactions affect your cash balance. For example, did you invest in new long-term operating assets (called *property, plant, and equipment* in the balance sheet)? Yes you did, as a matter of fact. These fixed assets increased $1,275,000 during the year.

Overall, your total assets increased $1,640,000. All assets except cash increased during the year. One big reason is the $940,000 increase in your retained earnings owners' equity. We explain in Book 1, Chapter 2 that earning profit increases retained earnings. Profit was $1,690,000 for the year, but retained earnings increased only $940,000. Therefore, part of profit was distributed to the owners, decreasing retained earnings. We discuss these things and other balance sheet interpretations as you move through the chapter. For now, the preliminary read of the balance sheet doesn't indicate any earth-shattering financial problems facing your business.

The balance sheet of a service business looks pretty much the same as a product business (see Figure 3-2) — except a service business doesn't report an inventory of products held for sale. If it sells on credit, a service business has an accounts receivable asset, just like a product company that sells on credit. The size of its total assets relative to annual sales revenue for a service business varies greatly from industry to industry, depending on whether the service industry is *capital intensive* or not. Some service businesses, such as airlines, for-profit hospitals, and hotel chains, need to make heavy investments in long-term operating assets. Other service businesses do not.

REMEMBER

The balance sheet is unlike the income and cash flow statements, which report flows over a period of time (such as sales revenue that is the cumulative amount of all sales during the period). The balance sheet presents the *balances* (amounts) of a company's assets, liabilities, and owners' equity at an instant in time. Notice the two quite different meanings of the term *balance*. As used in *balance sheet,* the term refers to the equality of the two opposing sides of a business — total assets on the one side and total liabilities and owners' equity on the other side, like a scale. In contrast, the *balance* of an account (asset, liability, owners' equity, revenue, and expense) refers to the amount in the account after recording increases and decreases in the account — the net amount after all additions and subtractions have been entered. Usually, the meaning of the term is clear in context.

TIP

An accountant can prepare a balance sheet at any time that a manager wants to know how things stand financially. Some businesses — particularly financial institutions such as banks, mutual funds, and securities brokers — need balance sheets at the end of each day in order to track their day-to-day financial situation. For most businesses, however, balance sheets are prepared only at the end of each month, quarter, or year. A balance sheet is always prepared at the close of business on the last day of the profit period. In other words, the balance sheet should be in sync with the income statement.

Kicking balance sheets out into the real world

The statement of financial condition, or balance sheet, in Figure 3-2 is about as lean and mean as you'll ever read. In the real world, many businesses are fat and complex. Also, we should make clear that Figure 3-2 shows the content and format for an *external* balance sheet, which means a balance sheet that's included in a financial report released outside a business to its owners and creditors. Balance sheets that stay within a business can be quite different.

Internal balance sheets

REMEMBER

For internal reporting of financial condition to managers, balance sheets include much more detail, either in the body of the financial statement itself or, more likely, in supporting schedules. For example, just one cash account is shown in Figure 3-2, but the chief financial officer of a business needs to know the balances on deposit in each of the business's checking accounts.

As another example, the balance sheet in Figure 3-2 includes just one total amount for accounts receivable, but managers need details on which customers owe money and whether any major amounts are past due. Greater detail allows for better control, analysis, and decision-making. Internal balance sheets and their supporting schedules should provide all the detail that managers need to make good business decisions.

External balance sheets

Balance sheets presented in external financial reports (which go out to investors and lenders) don't include a whole lot more detail than the balance sheet in Figure 3-2. However, as mentioned, external balance sheets must *classify* (or group together) short-term assets and liabilities. These are called *current assets* and *current liabilities*, as you see in Figure 3-2. Internal balance sheets for management use only don't have to be classified if the managers don't want the information.

Let us make clear that the NSA (National Security Agency) doesn't vet balance sheets to prevent the disclosure of secrets that would harm national security. The term *classified*, when applied to a balance sheet, means that assets and liabilities are sorted into basic classes, or groups, for external reporting. Classifying certain assets and liabilities into *current* categories is done mainly to help readers of a balance sheet compare current assets with current liabilities for the purpose of judging the short-term solvency of a business.

Judging Liquidity and Solvency

REMEMBER

Solvency refers to the ability of a business to pay its liabilities on time. Delays in paying liabilities on time can cause serious problems for a business. In extreme cases, a business can be thrown into *involuntary bankruptcy*. Even the threat of bankruptcy can cause serious disruptions in the normal operations of a business, and profit performance is bound to suffer. The *liquidity* of a business isn't a well-defined term; it can take on different meanings. However, generally it refers to the ability of a business to keep its cash balance and its cash flows at adequate levels so that operations aren't disrupted by cash shortfalls.

If current liabilities become too high relative to current assets — which constitute the first line of defense for paying current liabilities — managers should move quickly to resolve the problem. A perceived shortage of current assets relative to current liabilities could ring alarm bells in the minds of the company's creditors and owners.

Therefore, notice the following points in Figure 3-2 (dollar amounts refer to year-end 2017):

>> **Current assets:** The first four asset accounts (cash, accounts receivable, inventory, and prepaid expenses) are added to give the $8,815,000 subtotal for *current assets.*

>> **Current liabilities:** The first four liability accounts (accounts payable, accrued expenses payable, income tax payable, and short-term notes payable) are added to give the $4.03 million subtotal for *current liabilities.*

>> **Notes payable:** The total interest-bearing debt of the business is divided between $2.25 million in *short-term* notes payable (those due in one year or sooner) and $4 million in *long-term* notes payable (those due after one year).

Read on for details on current assets and liabilities and on the current and quick ratios.

Current assets and liabilities

Short-term, or *current*, assets include the following:

>> Cash

>> Marketable securities that can be immediately converted into cash

>> Assets converted into cash within one operating cycle, the main components being accounts receivable and inventory

The *operating cycle* refers to the repetitive process of putting cash into inventory, holding products in inventory until they're sold, selling products on credit (which generates accounts receivable), and collecting the receivables in cash. In other words, the operating cycle is the "from cash, through inventory and accounts receivable, back to cash" sequence. The operating cycles of businesses vary from a few weeks to several months, depending on how long inventory is held before being sold and how long it takes to collect cash from sales made on credit.

PREPARING MULTIYEAR STATEMENTS

The three primary financial statements of a business, including the balance sheet, are generally reported in a two- or three-year comparative format. To give you a sense of comparative financial statements, we present a two-year comparative format for the balance sheet example in Figure 3-2. Two- or three-year comparative financial statements are *de rigueur* in filings with the Securities and Exchange Commission (SEC). Public companies have no choice, but private businesses aren't under the SEC's jurisdiction. Accounting standards favor presenting comparative financial statements for two or more years, but we've seen financial reports of private businesses that don't present information for prior years.

The main reason for presenting two- or three-year comparative financial statements is for *trend analysis.* The business's managers, as well as its outside investors and creditors, are extremely interested in the general trend of sales, profit margins, ratio of debt to equity, and many other vital signs of the business. Slippage in the ratio of gross margin to sales from year to year, for example, is a serious matter.

Short-term, or *current*, liabilities include non-interest-bearing liabilities that arise from the operating (sales and expense) activities of the business. A typical business keeps many accounts for these liabilities — a separate account for each vendor, for example. In an external balance sheet, you usually find only three or four operating liabilities, and they aren't labeled as non-interest-bearing. We assume that you know that these operating liabilities don't bear interest (unless the liability is seriously overdue and the creditor has started charging interest because of the delay in paying the liability).

The balance sheet example in Figure 3-2 discloses three operating liabilities: accounts payable, accrued expenses payable, and income tax payable. Be warned that the terminology for these short-term operating liabilities varies from business to business.

In addition to operating liabilities, interest-bearing notes payable that have maturity dates one year or less from the balance sheet date are included in the current liabilities section. The current liabilities section may also include certain other liabilities that must be paid in the short run (which are too varied and technical to discuss here).

Current and quick ratios

The sources of cash for paying current liabilities are the company's current assets. That is, current assets are the first source of money to pay current liabilities when these liabilities come due. Remember that current assets consist of cash and assets that will be converted into cash in the short run.

TIP

The *current ratio* lets you size up current assets against total current liabilities. Using information from the balance sheet (refer to Figure 3-2), you compute the company's year-end 2017 current ratio as follows:

$$\frac{\$8,815,000 \text{ current assets}}{\$4,030,000 \text{ current liabilities}} = 2.2 \text{ current ratio}$$

Generally, businesses do not provide their current ratio on the face of their balance sheets or in the footnotes to their financial statements — they leave it to the reader to calculate this number. On the other hand, many businesses present a financial highlights section in their financial report, which often includes the current ratio.

The *quick ratio* is more restrictive. Only cash and assets that can be immediately converted into cash are included, which excludes accounts receivable, inventory, and prepaid expenses. The business in this example doesn't have any short-term marketable investments that could be sold on a moment's notice, so only cash is included for the ratio. You compute the quick ratio as follows (see Figure 3-2):

$$\frac{\$2,165,000 \text{ quick assets}}{\$4,030,000 \text{ current liabilities}} = 0.54 \text{ quick ratio}$$

Folklore has it that a company's current ratio should be at least 2.0, and its quick ratio, 1.0. However, business managers know that acceptable ratios depend a great deal on general practices in the industry for short-term borrowing. Some businesses do well with current ratios less than 2.0 and quick ratios less than 1.0, so take these benchmarks with a grain of salt. Lower ratios don't necessarily mean that the business won't be able to pay its short-term (current) liabilities on time. Chapter 5 of this minibook explains solvency in more detail.

Understanding That Transactions Drive the Balance Sheet

REMEMBER

A balance sheet is a snapshot of the financial condition of a business at an instant in time — the most important moment in time being at the end of the last day of the income statement period. The *fiscal*, or accounting, year of our business example ends on December 31. So its balance sheet is prepared at the close of business at midnight December 31. (A company should end its fiscal year at the close of its natural business year or at the close of a calendar quarter — September 30, for example.)

This freeze-frame nature of a balance sheet may make it appear that a balance sheet is static. Nothing is further from the truth. A business doesn't shut down to prepare its balance sheet. The financial condition of a business is in constant motion because the activities of the business go on nonstop.

Transactions change the makeup of a company's balance sheet — that is, its assets, liabilities, and owners' equity. The transactions of a business fall into three fundamental types:

>> **Operating activities, which also can be called profit-making activities:** This category refers to making sales and incurring expenses, and it also includes accompanying transactions that lead or follow the recording of sales and expenses. For example, a business records sales revenue when sales are made on credit and then, later, records cash collections from customers. The transaction of collecting cash is the indispensable follow-up to making the sale on credit.

For another example, a business purchases products that are placed in its inventory (its stock of products awaiting sale), at which time it records an entry for the purchase. The expense (the cost of goods sold) is not recorded until the products are actually sold to customers. Keep in mind that the term *operating activities* includes the associated transactions that precede or are subsequent to the recording of sales and expense transactions.

>> **Investing activities:** This term refers to making investments in assets and (eventually) disposing of the assets when the business no longer needs them. The primary examples of investing activities for businesses that sell products and services are *capital expenditures,* which are the amounts spent to modernize, expand, and replace the long-term operating assets of a business. A business may also invest in *financial assets,* such as bonds and stocks or other types of debt and equity instruments. Purchases and sales of financial assets are also included in this category of transactions.

>> **Financing activities:** These activities include securing money from debt and equity sources of capital, returning capital to these sources, and making distributions from profit to owners. Note that distributing profit to owners is treated as a financing transaction. For example, when a business corporation pays cash dividends to its stockholders, the distribution is treated as a financing transaction. The decision of whether to distribute some of its profit depends on whether the business needs more capital from its owners to grow the business or to strengthen its solvency. Retaining part or all of the profit for the year is one way of increasing the owners' equity in the business. We discuss this topic later in "Financing a Business: Sources of Cash and Capital."

Figure 3-3 presents a summary of changes in assets, liabilities, and owners' equity during the year for the business example introduced in Book 1, Chapter 2 and continued in this chapter. Notice the middle three columns, which show each of the three basic types of transactions of a business. One column is for changes caused by its revenue and expenses and their connected transactions during the year, which collectively are called *operating activities* (although we prefer to call them *profit-making* activities). The second column is for changes caused by its *investing activities* during the year. The third column is for the changes caused by its *financing activities*.

Typical Product Business, Inc. Summary of Changes in Assets, Liabilities, and Owners' Equity For Year Ended December 31, 2017 (Dollar amounts in thousands)					
Assets	Beginning Balances	Operating Activities	Investing Activities	Financing Activities	Change
Cash	$2,275	$1,515	($1,275)	($350)	($110)
Accounts Receivable	$2,150	$450			$450
Inventory	$2,725	$725			$725
Prepaid Expenses	$525	$75			$75
Property, Plant, and Equipment	$11,175		$1,275		$1,275
Accumulated Depreciation	($5,640)	($775)			($775)
Totals	$13,210	$1,990	$0	($350)	$1,640
Liabilities and Owners' Equity					
Accounts Payable	$640	$125			$125
Accrued Expenses Payable	$750	$150			$150
Income Tax Payable	$90	$25			$25
Short-term Notes Payable	$2,150			$100	$100
Long-term Notes Payable	$3,850			$150	$150
Owners' Equity — Capital Stock	$3,100			$150	$150
Owners' Equity — Retained Earnings	$2,630	$1,690		($750)	$940
Totals	$13,210	$1,990		($350)	$1,640

Note: Figure 3-3 doesn't include subtotals for current assets and liabilities; the formal balance sheet for this business is in Figure 3-2. Businesses don't report a summary of changes in their assets, liabilities, and owners' equity (though we think such a summary would be helpful to users of financial reports). The purpose of Figure 3-3 is to demonstrate how the three major types of transactions during the year change the assets, liabilities, and owners' equity accounts of the business during the year.

The 2017 income statement of the business is shown in Book 1, Chapter 2's Figure 2-1. You may want to flip back to this financial statement. On sales revenue of $26 million, the business earned $1.69 million bottom-line profit (net income) for the year. The sales and expense transactions of the business during the year plus the associated transactions connected with sales and expenses cause the changes shown in the operating-activities column in Figure 3-3. You can see that the $1.69 million net income has increased the business's owners' equity–retained earnings by the same amount. (The business paid $750,000 distributions from profit to its owners during the year, which decreases the balance in retained earnings.)

The operating-activities column in Figure 3-3 is worth lingering over because it shows the financial outcomes of making profit. In our experience, most people see a profit number, such as the $1.69 million in this example, and stop thinking any further about the financial outcomes of making the profit. This is like going to a movie because you like its title, without knowing anything about the plot and characters. You probably noticed that the $1,515,000 increase in cash in this operating-activities column differs from the $1,690,000 net income figure for the year. The cash effect of making profit (which includes the associated transactions connected with sales and expenses) is almost always different from the net income amount for the year. Book 1, Chapter 4 explains this difference.

The summary of changes in Figure 3-3 gives you a sense of the balance sheet in motion, or how the business got from the start of the year to the end of the year. Having a good sense of how transactions propel the balance sheet is important. This kind of summary of balance sheet changes can be helpful to business managers who plan and control changes in the assets and liabilities of the business. Managers need a solid understanding of how the three basic types of transactions change assets and liabilities. Figure 3-3 also provides a useful platform for the statement of cash flow in Book 1, Chapter 4.

TURNING OVER ASSETS

Assets should be *turned over*, or put to use, by making sales. The higher the turnover — the more times the assets are used and then replaced — the better, because every sale is a profit-making opportunity. The *asset turnover ratio* compares annual sales revenue with total assets. In our example, the company's asset turnover ratio is computed as follows for the year 2017:

$$\frac{\$26,000,000 \text{ annual sales revenue}}{\$14,850,000 \text{ total assets}} = 1.75 \text{ asset turnover ratio}$$

Some industries are capital-intensive, which means that they have low asset turnover ratios; they need a lot of assets to support their sales. For example, gas and electric utilities are capital-intensive. Many retailers, on the other hand, don't need a lot of assets to make sales. Their asset turnover ratios are relatively high; their annual sales are three, four, or five times their assets. The example business, with a 1.75 asset turnover ratio, falls in the broad middle range of businesses that sell products.

Sizing Up Assets and Liabilities

TIP

When you first read the balance sheet in Figure 3-2, did you wonder about the size of the company's assets, liabilities, and owners' equities? Did you ask, "Are the balance sheet accounts about the right size?" The balances in a company's balance sheet accounts should be compared with the sales revenue size of the business. The amounts of assets that are needed to carry on the profit-making transactions of a business depend mainly on the size of its annual revenue. And the sizes of its assets, in turn, largely determine the sizes of its liabilities — which, in turn, determines the size of its owners' equity accounts (although the ratio of liabilities and owners' equity depends on other factors as well).

Although the business example we use in this chapter is hypothetical, we didn't make up the numbers at random. We use a modest-sized business that has $26 million in annual sales revenue. The other numbers in its income statement and balance sheet are realistic relative to each other. We assume that the business earns 45 percent gross margin ($11.7 million gross margin ÷ $26 million sales revenue = 45 percent), which means its cost of goods sold expense is 55 percent of sales revenue. The sizes of particular assets and liabilities compared with their relevant income statement numbers vary from industry to industry and even from business to business in the same industry.

Based on the business's history and operating policies, the managers of a business can estimate what the size of each asset and liability should be; these estimates provide useful *control benchmarks* to which the actual balances of the assets and liabilities are compared. Assets (and liabilities, too) can be too high or too low relative to the sales revenue and expenses that drive them, and these deviations can cause problems that managers should try to remedy.

For example, based on the credit terms extended to its customers and the company's actual policies regarding how aggressively it acts in collecting past-due receivables, a manager determines the range for the proper, or within-the-boundaries, balance of accounts receivable. This figure is the control benchmark. If the actual balance is reasonably close to this control benchmark, accounts receivable is under control. If not, the manager should investigate why accounts receivable is smaller or larger than it should be.

This section discusses the relative sizes of the assets and liabilities in the balance sheet that result from sales and expenses (for the fiscal year 2017). The sales and expenses are the *drivers*, or causes, of the assets and liabilities. If a business earned profit simply by investing in stocks and bonds, it wouldn't need all the various assets and liabilities explained in this chapter. Such a business — a mutual fund, for example — would have just one income-producing asset: investments in securities. This chapter focuses on businesses that sell products on credit.

Sales revenue and accounts receivable

Annual sales revenue for the year 2017 is $26 million in our example (see Book 1, Chapter 2's Figure 2-1). The year-end accounts receivable is one-tenth of this, or $2.6 million (see Figure 3-2). So the average customer's credit period is roughly 36 days: 365 days in the year times the 10 percent ratio of ending accounts receivable balance to annual sales revenue. Of course, some customers' balances are past 36 days, and some are quite new; you want to focus on the average. The key question is whether a customer credit period averaging 36 days is reasonable.

Suppose that the business offers all customers a 30-day credit period, which is common in business-to-business selling (although not for a retailer selling to individual consumers). The relatively small deviation of about 6 days (36 days average credit period versus 30 days normal credit terms) probably isn't a significant cause for concern. But suppose that, at the end of the period, the accounts receivable had been $3.9 million, which is 15 percent of annual sales, or about a 55-day average credit period. Such an abnormally high balance should raise a red flag; the responsible manager should look into the reasons for the abnormally high accounts receivable balance. Perhaps several customers are seriously late in paying and shouldn't be extended new credit until they pay up.

Cost of goods sold expense and inventory

In the example, the cost of goods sold expense for the year 2017 is $14.3 million. The year-end inventory is $3.45 million, or about 24 percent. In rough terms, the average product's inventory holding period is 88 days   365 days in the year times the 24 percent ratio of ending inventory to annual cost of goods sold. Of course, some products may remain in inventory longer than the 88-day average, and some products may sell in a much shorter period than 88 days. You need to focus on the overall average. Is an 88-day average inventory holding period reasonable?

REMEMBER

The "correct" average inventory holding period varies from industry to industry. In some industries, especially heavy equipment manufacturing, the inventory holding period is long — three months or more. The opposite is true for high-volume retailers, such as retail supermarkets, that depend on getting products off the shelves as quickly as possible. The 88-day average holding period in the example is reasonable for many businesses but would be too high for others.

The managers should know what the company's average inventory holding period should be — they should know what the control benchmark is for the inventory holding period. If inventory is much above this control benchmark, managers should take prompt action to get inventory back in line (which is easier said than done, of course). If inventory is at abnormally low levels, this should be investigated as well. Perhaps some products are out of stock and should be restocked to avoid lost sales.

Fixed assets and depreciation expense

Depreciation is like other expenses in that all expenses are deducted from sales revenue to determine profit. Other than this, however, depreciation is different from most other expenses. (Amortization expense, which we get to later, is a kissing cousin of depreciation.) When a business buys or builds a long-term operating asset, the cost of the asset is recorded in a specific fixed asset account. *Fixed* is an overstatement; although the assets may last a long time, eventually they're retired from service. The main point is that the cost of a long-term operating or fixed asset is spread out, or allocated, over its expected useful life to the business. Each year of use bears some portion of the cost of the fixed asset.

The depreciation expense recorded in the period doesn't require any cash outlay during the period. (The cash outlay occurred when the fixed asset was acquired, or perhaps later when a loan was secured for part of the total cost.) Rather, *depreciation expense* for the period is that quota of the total cost of a business's fixed assets that is allocated to the period to record the cost of using the assets during the period. Depreciation depends on which method is used to allocate the cost of fixed assets over their estimated useful lives.

The higher the total cost of a business's fixed assets (called *property, plant, and equipment* in a formal balance sheet), the higher its depreciation expense. However, there's no standard ratio of depreciation expense to the cost of fixed assets. The annual total depreciation expense of a business seldom is more than 10 to 15 percent of the original cost of its fixed assets. Either the depreciation expense for the year is reported as a separate expense in the income statement, or the amount is disclosed in a footnote.

REMEMBER

Because depreciation is based on the gradual charging off or writing-down of the cost of a fixed asset, the balance sheet reports not one but two numbers: the original (historical) cost of its fixed assets and the *accumulated depreciation* amount (the total amount of depreciation that has been charged to expense from the time of acquiring the fixed assets to the current balance sheet date). The purpose isn't to confuse you by giving you even more numbers to deal with. Seeing both numbers gives you an idea of how old the fixed assets are and also tells you how much these fixed assets originally cost.

In the example in this chapter, the business has, over several years, invested $12,450,000 in its fixed assets (that it still owns and uses), and it has recorded total depreciation of $6,415,000 through the end of the most recent fiscal year, December 31, 2017. The business recorded $775,000 depreciation expense in its most recent year.

You can tell that the company's collection of fixed assets includes some old assets because the company has recorded $6,415,000 total depreciation since assets were bought — a fairly sizable percent of original cost (more than half). But many businesses use accelerated depreciation methods that pile up a lot of the depreciation expense in the early years and less in the back years, so it's hard to estimate the average age of the company's assets. A business could discuss the actual ages of its fixed assets in the footnotes to its financial statements, but hardly any businesses disclose this information — although they do identify which depreciation methods they're using.

Operating expenses and their balance sheet accounts

The sales, general, and administrative (SG&A) expenses of a business connect with three balance sheet accounts: the prepaid expenses asset account, the accounts payable liability account, and the accrued expenses payable liability account (see Figure 3-2). The broad SG&A expense category includes many types of expenses in making sales and operating the business. (Separate detailed expense accounts are maintained for specific expenses; depending on the size of the business and the needs of its various managers, hundreds or thousands of specific expense accounts are established.)

Many expenses are recorded when paid. For example, wage and salary expenses are recorded on payday. However, this record-as-you-pay method doesn't work for many expenses. For example, insurance and office supplies costs are prepaid and then released to expense gradually over time. The cost is initially put in the *prepaid expenses* asset account. (Yes, we know that *prepaid expenses* doesn't sound like an asset account, but it is.) Other expenses aren't paid until weeks after the expenses are recorded. The amounts owed for these unpaid expenses are recorded in an *accounts payable* or in an *accrued expenses payable* liability account.

For details regarding the use of these accounts in recording expenses, see Book 1, Chapter 2. Remember that the accounting objective is to match expenses with sales revenue for the year, and only in this way can the amount of profit be measured for the year. So expenses recorded for the year should be the correct amounts, regardless of when they're paid.

Intangible assets and amortization expense

Although our business example doesn't include tangible assets, many businesses invest in them. *Intangible* means without physical existence, in contrast to tangible assets like buildings, vehicles, and computers. Here are some examples of intangible assets:

>> A business may purchase the customer list of another company that's going out of business.

» A business may buy patent rights from the inventor of a new product or process.

» A business may buy another business lock, stock, and barrel and may pay more than the individual assets of the company being bought are worth — even after adjusting the particular assets to their current values. The extra amount is for *goodwill*, which may consist of a trained and efficient workforce, an established product with a reputation for high quality, or a valuable location.

REMEMBER

Only intangible assets that are purchased are recorded by a business. A business must expend cash, or take on debt, or issue owners' equity shares for an intangible asset in order to record the asset on its books. Building up a good reputation with customers or establishing a well-known brand is not recorded as an intangible asset. You can imagine the value of Coca-Cola's brand name, but this asset isn't recorded on the company's books. However, Coca-Cola protects its brand name with all the legal means at its disposal.

KEEPING A CASH BALANCE

A business's cash account consists of the money it has in its checking accounts plus the money that it keeps on hand. Cash is the essential lubricant of business activity. Sooner or later, virtually all business transactions pass through the cash account. Every business needs to maintain a working cash balance as a buffer against fluctuations in day-to-day cash receipts and payments. You can't really get by with a zero cash balance, hoping that enough customers will provide enough cash to cover all the cash payments that you need to make that day.

At year-end 2017, the cash balance of the business whose balance sheet is presented in Figure 3-2 is $2,165,000, which equals a little more than four weeks of annual sales revenue. How large of a cash balance should a business maintain? There's no simple answer. A business needs to determine how large of a cash safety reserve it's comfortable with to meet unexpected demands on cash while keeping the following points in mind:

• Excess cash balances are unproductive and don't earn any profit for the business.

• Insufficient cash balances can cause the business to miss taking advantage of opportunities that require quick action, such as snatching up a prized piece of real estate that just came on the market or buying out a competitor.

The cost of an intangible asset is recorded in an appropriate asset account, just like the cost of a tangible asset is recorded in a fixed asset account. Whether or when to allocate the cost of an intangible asset to expense has proven to be a difficult issue in practice, not easily amenable to accounting rules. At one time, the cost of most intangible assets were charged off according to some systematic method. The fraction of the total cost charged off in one period is called *amortization expense*.

Currently, however, the cost of an intangible asset isn't charged to expense unless its value has been impaired. A study of 8,700 public companies found that they collectively recorded $26 billion of write-downs for goodwill impairment in 2014. Testing for impairment is a messy process. The practical difficulties of determining whether impairment has occurred and the amount of the loss in value of an intangible asset have proven to be a real challenge to accountants. For the latest developments, search for *impairment of intangible assets* on the Internet, which will lead you to several sources. We don't go into the technical details here; because our business example doesn't include any intangible assets, there's no amortization expense.

Debt and interest expense

Look back at the balance sheet shown in Figure 3-2. Notice that the sum of this business's short-term (current) and long-term notes payable at year-end 2017 is $6.25 million. From the income statement in Book 1, Chapter 2's Figure 2-1, you see that the business's interest expense for the year is $400,000. Based on the year-end amount of debt, the annual interest rate is about 6.4 percent. (The business may have had more or less borrowed at certain times during the year, of course, and the actual interest rate depends on the debt levels from month to month.)

For most businesses, a small part of their total annual interest is unpaid at year-end; the unpaid part is recorded to bring interest expense up to the correct total amount for the year. In Figure 3-2, the accrued amount of interest is included in the *accrued expenses payable* liability account. In most balance sheets, you don't find accrued interest payable on a separate line; rather, it's included in the accrued expenses payable liability account. However, if unpaid interest at year-end happens to be a rather large amount, or if the business is seriously behind in paying interest on its debt, it should report the accrued interest payable as a separate liability.

Income tax expense and income tax payable

In its 2017 income statement, the business reports $2.6 million earnings before income tax — after deducting interest and all other expenses from sales revenue. The actual taxable income of the business for the year probably is different from this amount because of the many complexities in the income tax law. In the example, we use a realistic 35 percent tax rate, so the income tax expense is $910,000 of the pretax income of $2.6 million.

A large part of the federal and state income tax amounts for the year must be paid before the end of the year. But a small part is usually still owed at the end of the year. The unpaid part is recorded in the *income tax payable* liability account, as you see in Figure 3-2. In the example, the unpaid part is $115,000 of the total $910,000 income tax for the year, but we don't mean to suggest that this ratio is typical. Generally, the unpaid income tax at the end of the year is fairly small, but just how small depends on several technical factors.

Net income and cash dividends (if any)

The business in our example earned $1.69 million net income for the year (see Book 1, Chapter 2's Figure 2-1). Earning profit increases the owners' equity account *retained earnings* by the same amount. Either the $1.69 million profit (here we go again using *profit* instead of *net income*) stays in the business, or some of it is paid out and divided among the owners of the business.

During the year, the business paid out $750,000 total cash distributions from its annual profit. This is included in Figure 3-3's summary of transactions — look in the financing-activities column on the retained earnings line. If you own 10 percent of the shares, you'd receive one-tenth, or $75,000 cash, as your share of the total distributions. Distributions from profit to owners (shareholders) are not expenses. In other words, bottom-line net income is before any distributions to owners. Despite the importance of distributions from profit, you can't tell from the income statement or the balance sheet the amount of cash dividends. You have to look in the statement of cash flows for this information (which we explain in Book 1, Chapter 4). You can also find distributions from profit (if any) in the *statement of changes in stockholders' equity.*

Financing a Business: Sources of Cash and Capital

REMEMBER

To run a business, you need financial backing, otherwise known as *capital*. In overview, a business raises capital needed for its assets by buying things on credit, waiting to pay some expenses, borrowing money, getting owners to invest money in the business, and making profit that is retained in the business. Borrowed money is known as *debt*; capital invested in the business by its owners and retained profits are the two sources of *owners' equity.*

How did the business whose balance sheet is shown in Figure 3-2 finance its assets? Its total assets are $14,850,000 at fiscal year-end 2017. The company's profit-making activities generated three liabilities — accounts payable, accrued expenses payable, and income tax payable — and in total these three liabilities provided $1,780,000 of the total assets of the business. Debt provided $6,250,000, and the two sources of owners' equity provided the other $6,820,000. All three sources add up to $14,850,000, which equals total assets, of course. Otherwise, its books would be out of balance, which is a definite no-no.

Accounts payable, accrued expenses payable, and income tax payable are short-term, non-interest-bearing liabilities that are sometimes called *spontaneous liabilities* because they arise directly from a business's expense activities — they aren't the result of borrowing money but rather are the result of buying things on credit or delaying payment of certain expenses.

It's hard to avoid these three liabilities in running a business; they're generated naturally in the process of carrying on operations. In contrast, the mix of debt (interest-bearing liabilities) and equity (invested owners' capital and retained earnings) requires careful thought and high-level decisions by a business. There's no natural or automatic answer to the debt-versus-equity question. The business in the example has a large amount of debt relative to its owners' equity, which would make many business owners uncomfortable.

Debt is both good and bad, and in extreme situations, it can get very ugly. The advantages of debt are as follows:

>> Most businesses can't raise all the capital they need from owners' equity sources, and debt offers another source of capital (though, of course, many lenders are willing to provide only part of the capital that a business needs).

>> Interest rates charged by lenders are lower than rates of return expected by owners. Owners expect a higher rate of return because they're taking a greater risk with their money — the business isn't required to pay them back the same way that it's required to pay back a lender. For example, a business may pay 6 percent annual interest on its debt and be expected to earn a 12 percent annual rate of return on its owners' equity. (See Book 1, Chapter 5 for more on earning profit for owners.)

Here are the disadvantages of debt:

>> A business must pay the fixed rate of interest for the period even if it suffers a loss for the period or earns a lower rate of return on its assets.

>> A business must be ready to pay back the debt on the specified due date, which can cause some pressure on the business to come up with the money on time. (Of course, a business may be able to *roll over* or renew its debt, meaning that it replaces its old debt with an equivalent amount of new debt, but the lender has the right to demand that the old debt be paid and not rolled over.)

WARNING

If a business defaults on its debt contract — it doesn't pay the interest on time or doesn't pay back the debt on the due date — it faces some major unpleasantness. In extreme cases, a lender can force it to shut down and liquidate its assets (that is, sell off everything it owns for cash) to pay off the debt and unpaid interest. Just as you can lose your home if you don't pay your home mortgage, a business can be forced into involuntary bankruptcy if it doesn't pay its debts. A lender may allow the business to try to work out its financial crisis through bankruptcy procedures, but bankruptcy is a nasty affair that invariably causes many problems and can really cripple a business.

FINANCIAL LEVERAGE: TAKING A CHANCE ON DEBT

The large majority of businesses borrow money to provide part of the total capital needed for their assets. The main reason for debt is to close the gap between how much capital the owners can come up with and the amount the business needs. Lenders are willing to provide the capital because they have a senior claim on the assets of the business. Debt has to be paid back before the owners can get their money out of the business. A business's owners' equity provides a relatively permanent base of capital and gives its lenders a cushion of protection.

The owners use their capital invested in the business as the basis for borrowing. For example, for every two bucks the owners have in the business, lenders may be willing to add another dollar (or even more). Using owners' equity as the basis for borrowing is referred to as *financial leverage,* because the equity base of the business can be viewed as the fulcrum, and borrowing is the lever for lifting the total capital of the business.

A business can realize a financial leverage gain by making more EBIT (earnings before interest and income tax) on the amount borrowed than the interest on the debt. On the flip side, using debt may yield not a financial leverage gain but rather a financial leverage *loss.* Suppose EBIT equals zero for the year. Nevertheless, the business must pay the interest on its debt, so the business would have a bottom-line loss for the year.

Recognizing the Hodgepodge of Values Reported in a Balance Sheet

In our experience, the values reported for assets in a balance sheet can be a source of confusion for business managers and investors, who tend to put all dollar amounts on the same value basis. In their minds, a dollar is a dollar, whether it's in accounts receivable; inventory; property, plant, and equipment; accounts payable; or retained earnings. But some dollars are much older than other dollars.

The dollar amounts reported in a balance sheet are the result of the transactions recorded in the assets, liabilities, and owners' equity accounts. (Hmm, where have you heard this before?) Some transactions from years ago may still have life in the present balances of certain assets. For example, the land owned by the business that is reported in the balance sheet goes back to the transaction for the purchase of the land, which could be 20 or 30 years ago. The balance in the land asset is standing in the same asset column, for example, as the balance in the accounts receivable asset, which likely is only 1 or 2 months old.

REMEMBER

Book values are the amounts recorded in the accounting process and reported in financial statements. Don't assume that the book values reported in a balance sheet equal the current *market values.* Generally speaking, the amounts reported for cash, accounts receivable, and liabilities are equal to or are very close to their current market or settlement values. For example, accounts receivable will be turned into cash for the amount recorded on the balance sheet, and liabilities will be paid off at the amounts reported in the balance sheet. It's the book values of fixed assets, as well as any other assets in which the business invested some time ago, that are likely lower than their current replacement values.

Also, keep in mind that a business may have unrecorded assets. These off-balance-sheet assets include such things as a well-known reputation for quality products and excellent service, secret formulas (think Coca-Cola here), patents that are the result of its research and development over the years, and a better-trained workforce than its competitors. These are intangible assets that the business did not purchase from outside sources but, rather, accumulated over the years through its own efforts. These assets, though not reported in the balance sheet, should show up in better-than-average profit performance in the business's income statement.

WARNING

The current replacement values of a company's fixed assets may be quite a bit higher than the recorded costs of these assets, in particular for buildings, land, heavy machinery, and equipment. For example, the aircraft fleet of United Airlines, as reported in its balance sheet, is hundreds of millions of dollars less than the current cost it would have to pay to replace the planes. Complicating matters is the fact that many of its older planes aren't being produced anymore, and United would replace the older planes with newer models.

Businesses are not permitted to write up the book values of their assets to current market or replacement values. (Well, investments in marketable securities held for sale or available for sale have to be written up, or down, but this is an exception to the general rule.) Although recording current market values may have intuitive appeal, a market-to-market valuation model isn't practical or appropriate for businesses that sell products and services. These businesses do not stand ready to sell their assets (other than inventory); they need their assets for operating the business into the future. At the end of their useful lives, assets are sold for their disposable values (or traded in for new assets).

Don't think that the market value of a business is simply equal to its owners' equity reported in its most recent balance sheet. Putting a value on a business depends on several factors in addition to the latest balance sheet of the business.

IN THIS CHAPTER

» Clarifying why the statement of cash flows is reported

» Presenting the statement of cash flows in two flavors

» Earning profit versus generating cash flow from profit

» Reading lines and between the lines in the statement of cash flows

» Offering advice and observations on cash flow

Chapter **4**

Reporting Cash Sources and Uses in the Statement of Cash Flows

You could argue that the income statement (see Book 1, Chapter 2) and balance sheet (see Book 1, Chapter 3) are enough. These two financial statements answer the most important questions about the financial affairs of a business. The income statement discloses revenue and how much profit the business squeezed from its revenue, and the balance sheet discloses the amounts of assets used to make sales and profit, as well as its capital sources. What more do you need to know? Well, it's also helpful to know about the cash flows of the business.

This chapter explains the third primary financial statement reported by businesses: the *statement of cash flows.* This financial statement has two purposes: It explains why cash flow from profit differs from bottom-line profit, and it summarizes the investing and financing activities of the business during the period. This may seem an odd mix to put into one financial statement, but it makes sense.

Earning profit (net income) generates net cash inflow (at least, it should). Making profit is a primary source of cash to a business. The investing and financing transactions of a business hinge on its cash flow from profit. All sources and uses of cash hang together and should be managed in an integrated manner.

Meeting the Statement of Cash Flows

The income statement has a natural structure:

Revenue − Expenses = Profit (Net Income)

So does the balance sheet:

Assets = Liabilites + Owners' Equity

The statement of cash flows doesn't have an obvious natural structure, so the accounting rule-making body had to decide on the basic format for the statement. They settled on the following structure:

± Cash Flow from Operating Activities

± Cash Flow from Investing Activities

± Cash Flow from Financing Activities

= Cash Increase or Decrease during Period

+ Beginning Cash Balance

= Ending Cash Balance

The ± signs mean that the cash flow could be positive or negative. Generally, the cash flow from investing activities of product businesses is negative, which means that the business spent more on new investments in long-term assets than cash received from disposals of previous investments. And generally, the cash flow from operating activities (profit-making activities) should be positive, unless the business suffered a big loss for the period that drained cash out of the business.

REMEMBER

The threefold classification of activities (transactions) reported in the statement of cash flows — operating, investing, and financing — are the same ones we introduce in Book 1, Chapter 3, in which we explain the balance sheet. In that chapter, Figure 3-3 summarizes these transactions for the product company example that we continue with in this chapter.

In the example, the business's cash balance decreases $110,000 during the year. You see this decrease in the company's balance sheets for the years ended December 31, 2016 and 2017 (refer to Book 1, Chapter 3, Figure 3-2). The business started the year with $2,275,000 cash and ended the year with $2,165,000. What does the balance sheet, by itself, tell you about the reasons for the cash decrease? The two-year comparative balance sheet provides some clues about the reasons for the cash decrease. However, answering such a question isn't the purpose of a balance sheet.

Presenting the direct method

REMEMBER

The statement of cash flows begins with the cash from making profit, or *cash flow from operating activities,* as accountants call it. *Operating activities* is the term accountants adopted for sales and expenses, which are the operations that a business carries out to earn profit. Furthermore, the term *operating activities* also includes the transactions that are coupled with sales and expenses. For example, making a sale on credit is an operating activity, and so is collecting the cash from the customer at a later time. Recording sales and expenses can be thought of as primary operating activities because they affect profit. Their associated transactions are secondary operating activities because they don't affect profit. However, they do affect cash flow, which we explain in this chapter.

Figure 4-1 presents the statement of cash flows for the product business example we introduce in Chapters 2 and 3 in this minibook. What you see in the first section of the statement of cash flows is called the *direct method* for reporting cash flow from operating activities. The dollar amounts are the cash flows connected with sales and expenses. For example, the business collected $25,550,000 from customers during the year, which is the direct result of making sales. The company paid $15,025,000 for the products it sells, some of which went toward increasing the inventory of products awaiting sale next period.

Note: Because we use the same business example in this chapter that we use in Chapters 2 and 3 in this minibook, you may want to take a moment to review the 2017 income statement in Figure 2-1. And you may want to review Figure 3-3, which summarizes how the three types of activities changed the business's assets, liabilities, and owners' equity accounts during the year 2017. (Go ahead, we'll wait.)

TIP

The basic idea of the direct method is to present the sales revenue and expenses of the business on a cash basis, in contrast to the amounts reported in the income statement, which are on the accrual basis for recording revenue and expenses. *Accrual basis* accounting is real-time accounting that records transactions when economic events happen: Accountants record sales on credit when the sales take place, even though cash isn't collected from customers until sometime later. Cash payments for expenses occur before or after the expenses are recorded. *Cash basis* accounting is just what it says: Transactions aren't recorded until there's actual cash flow (in or out).

Typical Product Business, Inc. Statement of Cash Flows for Year Ended December 31, 2017 (Dollar amounts in thousands)		
Cash Flow From Operating Activities		
Collections from sales		$25,550
Payments for products	($15,025)	
Payments for selling, general, and administrative costs	($7,750)	
Payments for interest on debt	($375)	
Payments on income tax	($885)	($24,035)
Cash Flow From Operating Activities		$1,515
Cash Flows From Investing Activities		
Expenditures on Property, Plant & Equipment		($1,275)
Cash Flows From Financing Activities		
Short-term Debt Increase	$100	
Long-term Debt Increase	$150	
Capital Stock Issue	$150	
Dividends Paid Stockholders	($750)	($350)
Decrease In Cash During Year		($110)
Beginning Cash Balance		$2,275
Ending Cash Balance		$2,165

FIGURE 4-1: The statement of cash flows, illustrating the direct method for cash flow from operating activities.

The revenue and expense cash flows you see in Figure 4-1 differ from the amounts you see in the accrual accounting basis income statement (see Book 1, Chapter 2's Figure 2-1). Herein lies a problem with the direct method. If you, a conscientious reader of the financial statements of a business, compare the revenues and expenses reported in the income statement with the cash flow amounts reported in the statement of cash flows, you may get confused. Which set of numbers is the correct one? Well, both are. The numbers in the income statement are the true numbers for measuring profit for the period. The numbers in the statement of cash flows are additional information for you to ponder.

Notice in Figure 4-1 that cash flow from operating activities for the year is $1,515,000, which is less than the company's $1,690,000 net income for the year (refer to Book 1, Chapter 2's Figure 2-1). The accounting rule–making board thought that financial report readers would want an explanation for the difference between these two important financial numbers. Therefore, the board decreed that a statement of cash flows that uses the direct method of reporting cash flow from operating liabilities should include a reconciliation schedule that explains the difference between cash flow from operating activities and net income.

Opting for the indirect method

Having to read both the operating activities section of the cash flow statement and a supplemental schedule gets to be rather demanding for financial statement readers. Accordingly, the accounting rule–making body decided to permit an alternative method for reporting cash flow from operating activities. The alternative method starts with net income and then makes adjustments in order to reconcile cash flow from operating activities with net income. This alternative method is called the *indirect method*, which we show in Figure 4-2. The rest of the cash flow statement is the same, no matter which option is selected for reporting cash flow from operating activities. Compare the investing and financing activities in Figures 4-1 and 4-2; they're the same.

Typical Product Business, Inc. Statement of Cash Flows for Year Ended December 31, 2017 (Dollar amounts in thousands)		
Cash Flows From Operating Activities		
Net Income		$1,690
Adjustments to Net Income For Determining Cash Flow:		
Accounts Receivable Increase	($450)	
Inventory Increase	($725)	
Prepaid Expenses Increase	($75)	
Depreciation Expense	$775	
Accounts Payable Increase	$125	
Accrued Expenses Increase	$150	
Income Tax Payable Increase	$25	($175)
Cash Flow From Operating Activities		$1,515
Cash Flows From Investing Activities		
Expenditures on Property, Plant & Equipment		($1,275)
Cash Flows From Financing Activities		
Short-term Debt Increase	$100	
Long-term Debt Increase	$150	
Capital Stock Issue	$150	
Dividends Paid Stockholders	($750)	($350)
Decrease In Cash During Year		($110)
Beginning Cash Balance		$2,275
Ending Cash Balance		$2,165

FIGURE 4-2: The statement of cash flows, illustrating the indirect method for presenting cash flow from operating activities.

TIP

By the way, the adjustments to net income in the indirect method for reporting cash flow from operating activities (see Figure 4-2) constitute the supplemental schedule of changes in assets and liabilities that has to be included under the direct method. So the indirect method kills two birds with one stone: Net income is adjusted to the cash flow basis, and the changes in assets and liabilities affecting cash flow are included in the statement. It's no surprise that the vast majority of businesses use the indirect method.

The indirect method for reporting cash flow from operating activities focuses on the *changes* during the year in the assets and liabilities that are directly associated with sales and expenses. We explain these connections between revenue and expenses and their corresponding assets and liabilities in Book 1, Chapter 2. (You can trace the amounts of these changes back to Book 1, Chapter 3's Figure 3-2.)

REMEMBER

Both the direct method and the indirect method report the same cash flow from operating activities for the period. Almost always, this important financial metric for a business differs from the amount of its bottom-line profit, or net income, for the same period. Why? Read on.

Explaining the Variance between Cash Flow and Net Income

The amount of cash flow from profit, in the large majority of cases, is a different amount from profit. Both revenue and expenses are to blame. Cash collected from customers during the period is usually higher or lower than the sales revenue booked for the period. And cash actually paid out for operating costs is usually higher or lower than the amounts of expenses booked for the period. You can see this by comparing cash flows from operating activities in Figure 4-1 with sales revenue and expenses in the company's income statement (see Book 1, Chapter 2's Figure 2-1). The accrual-based amounts (Figure 2-1) are different from the cash-based amounts (Figure 4-1).

Now, how to report the divergence of cash flow and profit? A business could, we suppose, present only one line for cash flow from operating activities (which in our example is $1,515,000). Next, the financial report reader would move on to the investing and financing sections of the cash flow statement. But this approach won't do, according to financial reporting standards.

REMEMBER

The premise of financial reporting is that financial statement readers want more information than just a one-line disclosure of cash flow from operating activities. The standard practice is to disclose the major factors that cause cash flow to be higher or lower than net income. Smaller factors are often collapsed on one line called "other factors" or something like that. The business example we use in Chapters 2, 3, and 4 of this minibook is tractable. You can trace all the specific reasons that cause the variance between cash flow and net income.

The business in our example experienced a strong growth year. Its accounts receivable and inventory increased by relatively large amounts. In fact, all its assets and liabilities intimately connected with sales and expenses increased; the ending balances are larger than the beginning balances (which are the amounts carried forward from the end of the preceding year). Of course, this may not always be the case in a growth situation; one or more assets and liabilities could decrease during the year. For flat, no-growth situations, it's likely that there will be a mix of modest-sized increases and decreases.

In this section, we explain how asset and liability changes affect cash flow from operating activities. As a business manager, you should keep a close watch on the changes in each of your assets and liabilities and understand the cash flow effects of these changes. Investors and lenders should focus on the business's ability to generate a healthy cash flow from operating activities, so they should be equally concerned about these changes. In some situations, these changes indicate serious problems!

We realize that you may not be too interested in the details of these changes, so at the start of each section, we present the synopsis. If you want, you can just read the short explanation and move on (though the details are fascinating — well, at least to accountants).

Note: Instead of using the full phrase *cash flow from operating activities* every time, we use the shorter term *cash flow.* All data for assets and liabilities are found in the two-year comparative balance sheet of the business (see Book 1, Chapter 3's Figure 3-2).

Accounts receivable change

Synopsis: An increase in accounts receivable hurts cash flow; a decrease helps cash flow.

REMEMBER

The accounts receivable asset shows how much money customers who bought products on credit still owe the business; this asset is a promise of cash that the business will receive. Basically, accounts receivable is the amount of uncollected sales revenue at the end of the period. Cash doesn't increase until the business collects money from its customers.

The business started the year with $2.15 million and ended the year with $2.6 million in accounts receivable. The beginning balance was collected during the year, but the ending balance hadn't been collected at the end of the year. Thus, the *net* effect is a shortfall in cash inflow of $450,000. The key point is that you need to keep an eye on the increase or decrease in accounts receivable from the beginning of the period to the end of the period. Here's what to look for:

>> **Increase in accounts receivable:** If the amount of credit sales you made during the period is greater than what you collected from customers during the period, your accounts receivable increased over the period, and you need to *subtract* from net income that difference between start-of-period accounts receivable and end-of-period accounts receivable. In short, an increase in accounts receivable hurts cash flow by the amount of the increase.

>> **Decrease in accounts receivable:** If the amount you collected from customers during the period is greater than the credit sales you made during the period, your accounts receivable decreased over the period, and you need to *add* to net income that difference between start-of-period accounts receivable and end-of-period accounts receivable. In short, a decrease in accounts receivable helps cash flow by the amount of the decrease.

In our business example, accounts receivable increased $450,000. Cash collections from sales were $450,000 less than sales revenue. Ouch! The business increased its sales substantially over the last period, so its accounts receivable increased. When credit sales increase, a company's accounts receivable generally increases about the same percent, as it did in this example. (If the business takes longer to collect its credit sales, its accounts receivable would increase even more than can be attributed to the sales increase.) In this example, the higher sales revenue was good for profit but bad for cash flow.

REMEMBER

The lagging behind effect of cash flow is the price of growth — business managers, lenders, and investors need to understand this point. Increasing sales without increasing accounts receivable is a happy situation for cash flow, but in the real world, you usually can't have one increase without the other.

Inventory change

Synopsis: An increase in inventory hurts cash flow; a decrease helps cash flow.

Inventory is usually the largest short-term, or *current*, asset of businesses that sell products. If the inventory account is greater at the end of the period than at the start of the period — because unit costs increased or because the quantity of products increased — the amount the business actually paid out in cash for inventory purchases (or for manufacturing products) is more than what the business recorded in the cost of goods sold expense for the period. To refresh your memory here: The cost of inventory is not charged to cost of goods sold expense until products are sold and sales revenue is recorded.

In our business example, inventory increased $725,000 from start-of-year to end-of-year. In other words, to support its higher sales levels in 2017, this business replaced the products that it sold during the year *and* increased its inventory by $725,000. The business had to come up with the cash to pay for this inventory increase. Basically, the business wrote checks amounting to $725,000 more than its cost of goods sold expense for the period. This step-up in its inventory level was necessary to support the higher sales level, which increased profit even though cash flow took a hit.

Prepaid expenses change

Synopsis: An increase in prepaid expenses (an asset account) hurts cash flow; a decrease helps cash flow.

A change in the prepaid expenses asset account works the same way as a change in inventory and accounts receivable, although changes in prepaid expenses are usually much smaller than changes in the other two asset accounts.

The beginning balance of prepaid expenses is charged to expense this year, but the cash of this amount was actually paid out last year. This period (the year 2017 in our example), the business paid cash for next period's prepaid expenses, which affects this period's cash flow but doesn't affect net income until next period. In short, the $75,000 increase in prepaid expenses in this business example has a negative effect on cash flow.

REMEMBER

As a business grows, it needs to increase its prepaid expenses for such things as fire insurance (premiums have to be paid in advance of the insurance coverage) and its stocks of office and data processing supplies. Increases in accounts receivable, inventory, and prepaid expenses are the cash-flow price a business has to pay for growth. Rarely do you find a business that can increase its sales revenue without increasing these assets.

Depreciation: Real but noncash expense

Synopsis: No cash outlay is made in recording depreciation. In recording depreciation, a business simply decreases the book (recorded) value of the asset being depreciated. Cash isn't affected by the recording of depreciation (keeping in mind that depreciation is deductible for income tax).

Recording depreciation expense decreases the value of long-term, fixed operating assets that are reported in the balance sheet. The original costs of fixed assets are recorded in a *property, plant, and equipment* type account. Depreciation is recorded in an *accumulated depreciation* account, which is a so-called *contra* account because its balance is deducted from the balance in the fixed asset account (see Book 1, Chapter 3's Figure 3-2). Recording depreciation increases the accumulated depreciation account, which decreases the book value of the fixed asset.

TIP

There's no cash outlay when recording depreciation expense. Sales prices should be set high enough so that the cash inflow from revenue reimburses the business for the use of its long-term operating assets as they gradually wear out over time. The amount of depreciation expense recorded in the period is a portion of the original cost of the business's fixed assets, most of which were bought and paid for years ago. (Chapters 2 and 3 in this minibook explain more about depreciation.) Because the depreciation expense isn't a cash outlay this period, the amount is added to net income to determine cash flow from operating activities (see Figure 4-2). Depreciation is just one adjustment factor to get from net income reported in the income statement to cash flow from operating activities reported in the statement of cash flows.

For measuring profit, depreciation is definitely an expense — no doubt about it. Buildings, machinery, equipment, tools, vehicles, computers, and office furniture are all on an irreversible journey to the junk heap (although buildings usually take a long time to get there). Fixed assets (except for land) have a finite life of usefulness to a business; depreciation is the accounting method that allocates the total cost of fixed assets to each year of their use in helping the business generate sales revenue. In our example, the business recorded $775,000 depreciation expense for the year.

TIP

Instead of looking at depreciation only as an expense, consider the investment-recovery cycle of fixed assets. A business invests money in fixed assets that are then used for several or many years. Over the life of a fixed asset, a business has to recover through sales revenue the cost invested in the fixed asset (ignoring any salvage value at the end of its useful life). In a real sense, a business sells some of its fixed assets each period to its customers — it factors the cost of fixed assets into the sales prices that it charges its customers.

For example, when you go to a supermarket, a very small slice of the price you pay for that quart of milk goes toward the cost of the building, the shelves, the refrigeration equipment, and so on. (No wonder they charge so much!) Each period, a business recoups part of the cost invested in its fixed assets. In the example, $775,000 of sales revenue went toward reimbursing the business for the use of its fixed assets during the year.

COMPARING DEPRECIATION AND AMORTIZATION

The business in our example doesn't own any intangible assets and thus doesn't record any amortization expense. (See Book 1, Chapter 3 for an explanation of intangible assets and amortization.) If a business does own intangible assets, the amortization expense on these assets for the year is treated the same as depreciation is treated in the statement of cash flows. In other words, the recording of amortization expense doesn't require cash outlay in the year being charged with the expense. The cash outlay occurred in prior periods when the business invested in intangible assets. But in contrast to tangible depreciable assets, amortization expense is recorded as a decrease in the intangible asset account; the accountant doesn't use a contra account. There's no accumulated amortization account. That's just one of the quirks of accounting.

Changes in operating liabilities

Synopsis: An increase in a short-term operating liability helps cash flow; a decrease hurts cash flow.

The business in our example, like almost all businesses, has three basic liabilities inextricably intertwined with its expenses:

>> Accounts payable

>> Accrued expenses payable

>> Income tax payable

When the beginning balance of one of these liability accounts is the same as its ending balance (not too likely, of course), the business breaks even on cash flow for that liability. When the end-of-period balance is higher than the start-of-period balance, the business didn't pay out as much money as was recorded as an expense in the year. You want to refer to the company's comparative balance sheet of the business to compare the beginning and ending balances of these three liability accounts (see Book 1, Chapter 3's Figure 3-2).

In our business example, the business disbursed $640,000 to pay off last year's accounts payable balance. (This $640,000 was the accounts payable balance at December 31, 2016, the end of the previous fiscal year.) Its cash this year decreased $640,000 because of these payments. But this year's ending balance sheet (at December 31, 2017) shows accounts payable of $765,000 that the business won't pay until the following year. This $765,000 amount was recorded to expense in the year 2017. So the amount of expense was $125,000 more than the cash outlay for the year, or, in reverse, the cash outlay was $125,000 less than the expense. An increase in accounts payable benefits cash flow for the year. In other words, an increase in accounts payable has a positive cash flow effect (until the liability is paid). An increase in accrued expenses payable or income tax payable works the same way.

REMEMBER

In short, liability increases are favorable to cash flow — in a sense, the business ran up more on credit than it paid off. Such an increase means that the business delayed paying cash for certain things until next year. So you need to add the increases in the three liabilities to net income to determine cash flow, as you see in the statement of cash flows (refer to Figure 4-2). The business avoided cash outlays to the extent of the increases in these three liabilities. In some cases, of course, the ending balance of an operating liability may be lower than its beginning balance, which means that the business paid out more cash than the corresponding expenses for the period. In that case, the decrease is a negative cash flow factor.

Putting the cash flow pieces together

TIP

Taking into account all the adjustments to net income, the company's cash balance increased $1,515,000 from its operating activities during the course of the year. The operating activities section in the statement of cash flows (refer to Figure 4-2) shows the stepping-stones from net income to the amount of cash flow from operating activities.

Recall that the business experienced sales growth during this period. The downside of sales growth is that assets and liabilities also grow — the business needs more inventory at the higher sales level and also has higher accounts receivable. The business's prepaid expenses and liabilities also increased, although not nearly as much as accounts receivable and inventory. Still, the business had $1,515,000 cash at its disposal. What did the business do with this $1,515,000 in available cash? You have to look to the remainder of the cash flow statement to answer this very important question.

Sailing through the Rest of the Statement of Cash Flows

After you get past the first section of the statement of cash flows, the remainder is a breeze. Well, to be fair, you *could* encounter some rough seas in the remaining two sections. But generally speaking, the information in these sections isn't too difficult to understand. The last two sections of the statement report on the other sources of cash to the business and the uses the business made of its cash during the year.

Understanding investing activities

The second section of the statement of cash flows (see Figure 4-1 or 4-2) reports the investment actions that a business's managers took during the year. Investments are like tea leaves indicating what the future may hold for the company. Major new investments are sure signs of expanding or modernizing the production and distribution facilities and capacity of the business. Major disposals of long-term assets and shedding off a major part of the business could be good news or bad news for the business, depending on many factors. Different investors may interpret this information differently, but all would agree that the information in this section of the cash flow statement is very important.

Certain long-lived operating assets are required for doing business. For example, Federal Express and UPS wouldn't be terribly successful if they didn't have airplanes and trucks for delivering packages and computers for tracking deliveries. When these assets wear out, the business needs to replace them. Also, to remain competitive, a business may need to upgrade its equipment to take advantage of the latest technology or to provide for growth. These investments in long-lived, tangible, productive assets, which are called *fixed assets,* are critical to the future of the business. In fact, these cash outlays are called *capital expenditures* to stress that capital is being invested for the long haul.

One of the first claims on the $1,515,000 cash flow from operating activities is for capital expenditures. Notice that the business spent $1,275,000 on fixed assets, which are referred to more formally as *property, plant,* and *equipment* in the cash flow statement (to keep the terminology consistent with account titles used in the balance sheet; the term *fixed assets* is rather informal).

A typical statement of cash flows doesn't go into much detail regarding what specific types of fixed assets the business purchased (or constructed): how many additional square feet of space the business acquired, how many new drill presses it bought, and so on. Some businesses do leave a clearer trail of their investments, though. For example, in the footnotes or elsewhere in their financial reports, airlines generally describe how many new aircraft of each kind were purchased to replace old equipment or to expand their fleets.

TIP

Usually, a business disposes of some of its fixed assets every year because they reached the end of their useful lives and will no longer be used. These fixed assets are sent to the junkyard, traded in on new fixed assets, or sold for relatively small amounts of money. The value of a fixed asset at the end of its useful life is called its *salvage value.* The disposal proceeds from selling fixed assets are reported as a source of cash in the investing activities section of the statement of cash flows. Usually, these amounts are fairly small. Also, a business may sell off fixed assets because it's downsizing or abandoning a major segment of its business; these cash proceeds can be fairly large.

Looking at financing activities

Note that in the annual statement of cash flows for the business example, cash flow from operating activities is a positive $1,515,000, and the negative cash flow from investing activities is $1,275,000 (refer to Figure 4-1 or 4-2). The result to this point, therefore, is a net cash increase of $240,000, which would have increased the company's cash balance this much if the business had no financing activities during the year. However, the business increased its short-term and long-term debt during the year, its owners invested additional money in the business, and it distributed some of its profit to stockholders. The third section of the cash flow statement summarizes these *financing activities* of the business over the period.

The managers didn't have to go outside the business for the $1,515,000 cash increase generated from its operating activities for the year. Cash flow from operating activities is an *internal* source of money generated by the business itself, in contrast to *external* money that the business raises from lenders and owners. A business doesn't have to go hat in hand for external money when its internal cash flow is sufficient to provide for its growth. Making profit is the cash flow spigot that should always be turned on.

TIP

A business that earns a profit could, nevertheless, have a *negative* cash flow from operating activities — meaning that despite posting a net income for the period, the changes in the company's assets and liabilities cause its cash balance to decrease. In contrast, a business could report a bottom-line *loss* for the year yet have a *positive* cash flow from its operating activities. The cash recovery from depreciation plus the cash benefits from decreases in accounts receivable and inventory could be more than the amount of loss. However, a loss usually leads to negative cash flow or very little positive cash flow.

The term *financing* refers to a business raising capital from debt and equity sources — by borrowing money from banks and other sources willing to loan money to the business and by its owners putting additional money in the business. The term also includes the flip side — that is, making payments on debt and returning capital to owners. The term *financing* also includes cash distributions by the business from profit to its owners. (Keep in mind that interest on debt is an expense reported in the income statement.)

Most businesses borrow money for the short term (generally defined as less than one year) as well as for longer terms (generally defined as more than one year). In other words, a typical business has both short-term and long-term debt. (Book 1, Chapter 3 explains that short-term debt is presented in the current liabilities section of the balance sheet.)

The business in our example has both short-term and long-term debt. Although this isn't a hard-and-fast rule, most cash flow statements report just the *net* increase or decrease in short-term debt, not the total amounts borrowed and total payments on short-term debt during the period. In contrast, both the total amounts of borrowing from and repayments on long-term debt during the year are generally reported in the statement of cash flows — the numbers are reported gross, instead of net.

In our example, no long-term debt was paid down during the year, but short-term debt was paid off during the year and replaced with new short-term notes payable. However, only the $100,000 net increase is reported in the cash flow statement. The business also increased its long-term debt by $150,000 (refer to Figure 4-1 or 4-2).

The financing section of the cash flow statement also reports the flow of cash between the business and its owners (stockholders of a corporation). Owners can be both a *source* of a business's cash (capital invested by owners) and a *use* of a business's cash (profit distributed to owners). The financing activities section of the cash flow statement reports additional capital raised from its owners, if any, as well as any capital returned to the owners. In the cash flow statement, note that the business issued additional stock shares for $150,000 during the year, and it paid a total of $750,000 cash dividends from profit to its owners.

Reading actively

As a business lender or investor, your job is to ask questions (at least in your own mind) when reading an external financial statement. You should be an active reader, not a ho-hum passive reader, when reading the statement of cash flows. You should mull over certain questions to get full value out of the financial statement.

The statement of cash flows reveals what financial decisions the business's managers made during the period. Of course, management decisions are always subject to second-guessing and criticism, and passing judgment based on reading a financial statement isn't totally fair because it doesn't capture the pressures the managers faced during the period. Maybe they made the best possible decisions in the circumstances. Then again, maybe not.

TIP

One issue comes to the forefront when reading the company's statement of cash flows. The business in our example (see Figure 4-1 or 4-2) distributed $750,000 cash from profit to its owners — a 44 percent *payout ratio* (which equals the $750,000 distribution divided by its $1,690,000 net income). In analyzing whether the payout ratio is too high, too low, or just about right, you need to look at the broader context of the business's sources of and needs for cash.

The company's $1,515,000 cash flow from operating activities is enough to cover the business's $1,275,000 capital expenditures during the year and still leave $240,000 available. The business increased its total debt $250,000. Combined, these two cash sources provided $490,000 to the business. The owners also kicked in another $150,000 during the year, for a grand total of $640,000. Its cash balance didn't increase by this amount because the business paid out $750,000 in dividends from profit to its stockholders. Therefore, its cash balance dropped $110,000.

If we were on the board of directors of this business, we certainly would ask the chief executive why cash dividends to shareowners weren't limited to $240,000 to avoid the increase in debt and to avoid having shareowners invest additional money in the business. We'd probably ask the chief executive to justify the amount of capital expenditures as well.

WARNING

Some small and privately owned businesses don't report a statement of cash flows — though according to current financial reporting standards that apply to all businesses, they should. We've seen several small, privately owned businesses that don't go to the trouble of preparing this financial statement. Perhaps someday accounting standards for private and smaller businesses will waive the requirement for the cash flow statement. (We discuss developments of accounting standards for larger public versus smaller private companies in Book 1, Chapter 1.) Without a cash flow statement, the reader of the financial report could add back depreciation to net income to get a starting point. From there on, it gets more challenging to determine cash flow from profit. Adding depreciation to net income is no more than a first step in determining cash flow from profit — but we have to admit it's better than nothing.

Pinning Down Free Cash Flow

WARNING

The term *free cash flow* has emerged in the lexicon of finance and investing. This piece of language is not — we repeat, *not* — officially defined by the rule-making body of any authoritative accounting or financial institution. Furthermore, the term does not appear in cash flow statements reported by businesses.

Rather, *free cash flow* is street language, and the term appears in *The Wall Street Journal* and *The New York Times*. Securities brokers and investment analysts use the term freely (pun intended). Unfortunately, the term *free cash flow* hasn't settled down into one universal meaning, although most usages have something to do with cash flow from operating activities.

TIP

The term *free cash flow* can refer to the following:

>> Net income plus depreciation expense, plus any other expense recorded during the period that doesn't involve the outlay of cash — such as amortization of costs of the intangible assets of a business and other asset write-downs that don't require cash outlay

>> Cash flow from operating activities as reported in the statement of cash flows, although the very use of a different term *(free cash flow)* suggests that a different meaning is intended

>> Cash flow from operating activities minus the amount spent on capital expenditures during the year (purchases or construction of property, plant, and equipment)

>> Earnings before interest, tax, depreciation, and amortization (EBITDA) — although this definition ignores the cash flow effects of changes in the short-term assets and liabilities directly involved in sales and expenses, and it obviously ignores that interest and income tax expenses in large part are paid in cash during the period

In the strongest possible terms, we advise you to be very clear on which definition of *free cash flow* a speaker or writer is using. Unfortunately, you can't always determine what the term means even in context. Be careful out there.

One definition of free cash flow is quite useful: cash flow from operating activities minus capital expenditures for the year. The idea is that a business needs to make capital expenditures in order to stay in business and thrive. And to make capital expenditures, the business needs cash. Only after providing for its capital expenditures does a business have free cash flow that it can use as it likes. For the example in this chapter, the free cash flow according to us is

$1,515,000 cash flow from operating activities

$1,275,000 capital expenditures = $240,000 free cash flow

In many cases, cash flow from operating activities falls short of the money needed for capital expenditures. To close the gap, a business has to borrow more money, persuade its owners to invest more money in the business, or dip into its cash reserve. Should a business in this situation distribute any of its profit to owners? After all, it has a cash *deficit* after paying for capital expenditures. But, in fact, many businesses make cash distributions from profit to their owners even when they don't have any free cash flow (as we just defined it).

Limitations of the Statement of Cash Flows

We remember the days before the cash flow statement was required in the externally reported financial statements of businesses. In 1987, the cash flow statement was made mandatory. Most financial report users thought that this new financial statement would be quite useful and should open the door for deeper insights into the business. However, over the years, we've seen serious problems develop in the actual reporting of cash flows.

Focusing on cash flows is understandable. If a business runs out of money, it will likely come to an abrupt halt and may not be able to start up again. Even running low on cash (as opposed to running out of cash) makes a business vulnerable to all sorts of risks that could be avoided if it had enough sustainable cash flow. Managing cash flow is as important as making sales and controlling expenses. You'd think that the statement of cash flows would be carefully designed to make it as useful as possible and reasonably easy to read so that the financial report reader could get to the heart of the matter.

Would you like to hazard a guess on the average number of lines in the cash flow statements of publicly owned corporations? Typically, their cash flow statements have 30 to 40 or more lines of information. So it takes quite a while to read the cash flow statement — more time than the average reader probably has available. Each line in a financial statement should be a truly useful piece of information. Too many lines baffle the reader rather than clarify the overall cash flows of the business. We have to question why companies overload this financial statement with so much technical information. One could even suspect that many businesses deliberately obscure their statements of cash flows.

The main problem in understanding the statement of cash flows is the first section for cash flow from operating activities. What a terrible way to start the statement of cash flows! As it is now, the financial report reader has to work down numerous adjustments that are added or deducted from net income to determine the amount of cash flow from operating activities (see Figure 4-2). You could read quickly through the whole balance sheet or income statement in the time it takes to do this. In short, the first section of the cash flow statement isn't designed for an easy read. Something needs to be done to improve this opening section of the cash flow statement.

We don't hear a lot of feedback on the cash flow statement from principal external users of financial reports, such as business lenders and investors. We wonder how financial report users would react if the cash flow statement were accidently omitted from a company's annual financial report. How many would notice the missing financial statement and complain? The SEC and other regulators would take action, of course. But few readers would even notice the omission. In contrast, if a business failed to include an income statement or balance sheet, the business would hear from its lenders and owners, that's for sure.

Instead of the statement of cash flows, we favor presenting a summary of operating, investing, and financial transactions such as Book 1, Chapter 3's Figure 3-3. You might compare this summary with the statement of cash flows shown in Figure 4-2. Which is better for the average financial report reader? You be the judge.

IN THIS CHAPTER

» Looking after your investments

» Using ratios to interpret profit performance

» Using ratios to interpret financial condition

» Scanning footnotes and sorting out important ones

» Checking out the auditor's report

Chapter 5

Reading a Financial Report

This chapter focuses on the *external* financial report that a business sends to its lenders and shareowners. Many of the topics and ratios explained in the chapter apply to not-for-profit (NFP) entities as well. But the main focus is reading the financial reports of profit-motivated business entities. External financial reports are designed for the *non-manager* stakeholders in the business. The business's managers should definitely understand how to read and analyze its external financial statements, and managers should do additional financial analysis. This additional financial analysis by managers uses confidential accounting information that is not circulated outside the business.

You could argue that this chapter goes beyond the domain of accounting. Yes, this chapter ventures into the field of financial statement analysis. Some argue that this is in the realm of finance and investments, not accounting. Well, our answer is this: We assume one of your reasons for reading this book is to understand and learn how to read financial statements. From this perspective, this chapter definitely should be included, whether or not the topics fit into a strict definition of accounting.

Some years ago, a private business needed additional capital to continue its growth. Its stockholders could not come up with all the additional capital the business needed. So they decided to solicit several people to invest money in the company.

After studying the financial report, several people concluded that the profit prospects of this business looked promising and that they probably would receive reasonable cash dividends on their investment. They also thought the business might be bought out by a bigger business someday, and they would make a capital gain. That proved to be correct: The business was bought out a few years later, and they doubled their money (and earned dividends along the way).

Not all investment stories have a happy ending, of course. As you know, stock share market prices go up *and* down. A business may go bankrupt, causing its lenders and shareowners large losses. This chapter isn't about guiding you toward or away from making specific types of investments. Our purpose is to explain basic ratios and other tools lenders and investors use for getting the most information value out of a business's financial reports — to help you become a more intelligent lender and investor.

Knowing the Rules of the Game

When you invest money in a business venture or lend money to a business, you receive regular financial reports from the business. The primary premise of financial reporting is *accountability* — to inform the sources of a business's ownership and debt capital about the financial performance and condition of the business. Abbreviated financial reports are sent to owners and lenders every three months. A full and comprehensive financial report is sent annually. The ratios and techniques of analysis we explain in the chapter are useful for both quarterly and annual financial reports.

There are written rules for financial reports, and there are unwritten rules. The written rules in the United States are called *generally accepted accounting principles* (GAAP). The movement toward adopting international accounting standards isn't dead, but it is on life support, so in this chapter, we assume that U.S. GAAP are used to prepare the financial statements.

The unwritten rules don't have a name. For example, there's no explicit rule prohibiting the use of swear words and vulgar expressions in financial reports. Yet, quite clearly, there is a strict unwritten rule against improper language in financial reports. There's one unwritten rule in particular that you should understand:

A financial report isn't a confessional. A business doesn't have to lay bare all its problems in its financial reports. A business doesn't comment on all its difficulties in reporting its financial affairs to the outside world.

Making Investment Choices

An investment opportunity in a private business won't show up on your doorstep every day. However, if you make it known that you have money to invest as an equity shareholder, you may be surprised at how many offers come your way. Alternatively, you can invest in publicly traded *securities,* those stocks and bonds traded every day in major securities markets. Your stockbroker would be delighted to execute a buy order for 100 shares of, say, Caterpillar for you. Keep in mind that your money doesn't go to Caterpillar; the company isn't raising additional money. Your money goes to the seller of the 100 shares. You're investing in the *secondary capital market* — the trading in stocks by buyers and sellers after the shares were originally issued some time ago.

In contrast, you can invest in the *primary capital market,* which means that your money goes directly to the business. These days, a growing tactic of raising money is *crowdfunding,* which is done over the Internet. On a website, a new or early-stage business invites anyone with money to join in the venture and become a stockholder. Usually, you can invest a relatively small amount of money in a crowdfunding appeal. The business seeking the money is counting on a large number of people to invest money in the venture.

You may choose not to manage your securities investments yourself. Instead, you can put your money in any of the thousands of mutual funds available today, or in an exchange-traded fund (ETF), or in closed-end investment companies, or in unit investment trusts, and so on. You'll have to read other books to gain an understanding of the choices you have for investing your money and managing your investments. Be very careful about books that promise spectacular investment results with no risk and little effort. One book that is practical, well written, and levelheaded is *Investing For Dummies,* by Eric Tyson (Wiley).

TIP

Investors in a private business have just one main pipeline of financial information about the business they've put their hard-earned money in: its financial reports. Of course, investors should carefully read these reports. By *carefully,* we mean they should look for the vital signs of progress and problems. The financial statement ratios that we explain in this chapter point the way — like signposts on the financial information highway.

LOOKING BEYOND FINANCIAL REPORTS

Investors don't rely solely on financial reports when making investment decisions. Analyzing a business's financial reports is just one part of the process. You should consider these additional factors, depending on the business you're thinking about investing in:

- Industry trends and problems

- National economic and political developments

- Threatened action by regulatory agencies against the business

- Possible mergers, friendly acquisitions, and hostile takeovers

- Turnover of key executives

- Labor problems

- International markets and currency exchange ratios

- Supply shortages

- Product surpluses

Whew! This kind of stuff goes way beyond accounting, obviously, and is just as significant as financial statement analysis when you're picking stocks and managing investment portfolios.

Investors in securities of public businesses have many sources of information at their disposal. Of course, they can read the financial reports of the businesses they have invested in and those they're thinking of investing in. Instead of thoroughly reading these financial reports, they may rely on stockbrokers, the financial press, and other sources of information. Many individual investors turn to their stockbrokers for investment advice. Brokerage firms put out all sorts of analyses and publications, and they participate in the placement of new stock and bond securities issued by public businesses. A broker will be glad to provide you with information from companies' latest financial reports. So why should you bother reading this chapter if you can rely on other sources of investment information?

REMEMBER

The more you know about interpreting a financial report, the better prepared you are to evaluate the commentary and advice of stock analysts and other investment experts. If you can at least nod intelligently while your stockbroker talks about a business's P/E and EPS, you'll look like a savvy investor — and you may get more favorable treatment. (P/E and EPS, by the way, are two of the key ratios explained later in the chapter.) You may regularly watch financial news on television or listen to one of today's popular radio financial talk shows. The ratios explained in this chapter are frequently mentioned in the media. As a matter of fact, a business may include one or more of the ratios in its financial report (public companies have to disclose earnings per share, or EPS).

This chapter covers financial statement ratios that you should understand as well as signs to look for in audit reports. We also suggest how to sort through the footnotes that are an integral part of every financial report to identify those that have the most importance to you.

Contrasting Reading Financial Reports of Private versus Public Businesses

REMEMBER

Public companies make their financial reports available to the public at large; they don't limit distribution only to their present shareowners and lenders. We don't happen to own any stock shares of Caterpillar. So how did we get its annual financial report? We simply went to Cat's website. In contrast, private companies generally keep their financial reports private — they distribute their financial reports only to their shareowners and lenders. Even if you were a close friend of the president of a private business, we doubt that the president would let you see a copy of its latest financial report. You may as well ask to see the president's latest individual income tax return. (You're not going to see it, either.)

WARNING

Although accountants are loath to talk about it, the blunt fact is that many private companies simply ignore some authoritative standards in preparing their financial reports. This doesn't mean that their financial reports are misleading — perhaps substandard, but not seriously misleading. In any case, a private business's annual financial report is generally bare bones. It includes the three primary financial statements (balance sheet, income statement, and statement of cash flows) plus some footnotes — and that's about it. We've seen private company financial reports that don't even have a letter from the president. In fact, we've seen financial reports of private businesses (mostly very small companies) that don't include a statement of cash flows, even though this financial statement is required according to U.S. GAAP.

Public businesses are saddled with the additional layer of requirements issued by the Securities and Exchange Commission. (This federal agency has no jurisdiction over private businesses.) The financial reports and other forms filed with the SEC are available to the public at www.sec.gov. The anchor of these forms is the annual 10-K, which includes the business's financial statements in prescribed formats, with many supporting schedules and detailed disclosures that the SEC requires.

TIP

Most publicly owned businesses present very different annual financial reports to their stockholders compared with their filings with the SEC. A large number of public companies include only *condensed* financial information in their annual stockholder reports (not their full-blown and complete financial statements). They refer the reader to their more detailed SEC financial report for specifics. The financial information in the two documents can't differ in any material way. In essence, a stock investor can choose from two levels of information — one quite condensed and the other very technical.

A typical annual financial report by a public company to its stockholders is a glossy booklet with excellent art and graphic design, including high-quality photographs. The company's products are promoted, and its people are featured in glowing terms that describe teamwork, creativity, and innovation — we're sure you get the picture. In contrast, the reports to the SEC look like legal briefs — there's nothing fancy in these filings. The SEC filings contain information about certain expenses and require disclosure about the history of the business, its main markets and competitors, its principal officers, any major changes on the horizon, the major risks facing the business, and so on. Professional investors and investment managers definitely should read the SEC filings. By the way, if you want information on the compensation of the top-level officers of the business, you have to go to its *proxy statement* (see the sidebar "Studying the proxy statement").

Using Ratios to Digest Financial Statements

Financial statements have lots of numbers in them. (Duh!) All these numbers can seem overwhelming when you're trying to see the big picture and make general conclusions about the financial performance and condition of the business. Instead of actually reading your way through the financial statements — that is, carefully reading every line reported in all the financial statements — one alternative is to compute certain ratios to extract the main messages from the financial statements. Many financial report readers go directly to ratios and don't bother reading everything in the financial statements. In fact, five to ten ratios can tell you a lot about a business.

TIP

Financial statement ratios enable you to compare a business's current performance with its past performance or with another business's performance, regardless of whether sales revenue or net income was bigger or smaller for the other years or the other business. In other words, using ratios cancels out size differences. (We bet you knew that, didn't you?)

As a rule, you don't find too many ratios in financial reports. Publicly owned businesses are required to report just one ratio (earnings per share, or EPS), and privately owned businesses generally don't report any ratios. GAAP don't demand that any ratios be reported (except EPS for publicly owned companies). However, you still see and hear about ratios all the time, especially from stockbrokers and other financial professionals, so you should know what the ratios mean, even if you never go to the trouble of computing them yourself.

REMEMBER

Ratios do not provide final answers — they're helpful indicators, and that's it. For example, if you're in the market for a house, you may consider cost per square foot (the total cost divided by total square feet) as a way of comparing the prices of the houses you're looking at. But you have to put that ratio in context: Maybe one neighborhood is closer to public transportation than another, and maybe one house needs more repairs than another. In short, the ratio isn't the only factor in your decision.

Figures 5-1 and 5-2 present an income statement and balance sheet for a business that serves as the example for the rest of the chapter. We don't include a statement of cash flows because no ratios are calculated from data in this financial statement. Well, we should say that no cash flow ratios have yet become household names. We don't present the footnotes to the company's financial statements, but we discuss reading footnotes in the upcoming section "Frolicking through the Footnotes." In short, the following discussion focuses on ratios from the income statement and balance sheet. Later, we return to the topic of cash flow ratios and why cash flow ratios haven't become widespread benchmarks among financial statement analysts.

Income Statement For Year	
(Dollar amounts in thousands, except per share amounts)	
Sales Revenue	$ 457,000
Cost of Goods Sold Expense	298,750
Gross Margin	$ 158,250
Sales, Administration, and General Expenses	102,680
Earnings Before Interest and Income Tax	$ 55,570
Interest Expense	6,250
Earnings Before Income Tax	$ 49,320
Income Tax Expense	16,850
Net Income	$ 32,470
Basic Earnings Per Share	$3.82
Diluted Earnings Per Share	$3.61

FIGURE 5-1: Income statement example.

Balance Sheet at End of Year		
(Dollar amounts in thousands)		
Assets		
Cash	$ 14,850	
Accounts Receivable	42,500	
Inventory	75,200	
Prepaid Expenses	4,100	
Current Assets		$136,650
Fixed Assets	$ 246,750	
Accumulated Depreciation	(46,825)	199,925
Total Assets		$336,575
Liabilities		
Accounts Payable	$ 8,145	
Accrued Expenses Payable	9,765	
Income Tax Payable	945	
Short-term Notes Payable	40,000	
Current Liabilities		$ 58,855
Long-term Notes Payable		60,000
Owners' Equity		
Capital Stock (8,500,000 shares)	$ 85,000	
Retained Earnings	132,720	217,720
Total Liabilities and Owners' Equity		$336,575

FIGURE 5-2: Balance sheet example.

Gross margin ratio

Making bottom-line profit begins with making sales and earning sufficient gross margin from those sales. By *sufficient*, we mean that your gross margin must cover the expenses of making sales and operating the business, as well as paying interest and income tax expenses, so that there's still an adequate amount left over for profit. You calculate the *gross margin ratio* as follows:

$$\frac{\text{Gross margin}}{\text{Sales revenue}} = \text{Gross margin ratio}$$

So a business with a $158.25 million gross margin and $457 million in sales revenue (refer to Figure 5-1) earns a 34.6 percent gross margin ratio. Now, suppose the business had been able to reduce its cost of goods sold expense and had earned a 35.6 percent gross margin. That one additional point (one point equals 1 percent) would have increased gross margin $4.57 million (1 percent × $457 million sales revenue) — which would have trickled down to earnings before income tax, assuming other expenses below the gross margin line had been the same (except income tax). Earnings before income tax would have been 9.3 percent higher:

$$\frac{\$4,570,000 \text{ bump in gross margin}}{\$49,320,000 \text{ earnings before income tax}} = 9.3\% \text{ increase}$$

Never underestimate the impact of even a small improvement in the gross margin ratio!

Investors can track the gross margin ratios for the two or three years whose income statements are included in the annual financial report, but they really can't get behind gross margin numbers for the inside story. In their financial reports, public companies include a *management discussion and analysis* (MD&A) section that should comment on any significant change in the gross margin ratio. But corporate managers have wide latitude in deciding what exactly to discuss and how much detail to go into. You definitely should read the MD&A section, but it may not provide all the answers you're looking for. You have to search further in stockbroker releases, in articles in the financial press, or at the next professional business meeting you attend.

Business managers pay close attention to margin per unit and total margin in making and improving profit. *Margin* does not mean *gross margin*; rather, it refers to sales revenue minus product cost and all other variable operating expenses of a business. In other words, *margin* is profit before the company's total fixed operating expenses (and before interest and income tax). Margin is an extremely important factor in the profit performance of a business. Profit hinges directly on margin.

REMEMBER

In an external financial report, the income statement discloses gross margin and operating profit, or earnings before interest and income tax expenses (see Figure 5-1). However, the expenses between these two profit lines in the income statement are not classified into *variable* and *fixed*. Therefore, businesses do not disclose margin information in their external financial reports — they wouldn't even think of doing so. This information is considered to be proprietary in nature; it's kept confidential and out of the hands of competitors. In short, investors don't have access to information about a business's margin or its fixed expenses. Neither GAAP nor the SEC requires that such information be disclosed — and it isn't!

Profit ratio

Business is motivated by profit, so the profit ratio is important, to say the least. The bottom line is called *the bottom line* with good reason. The *profit ratio* indicates how much net income was earned on each $100 of sales revenue:

$$\frac{\text{Net income}}{\text{Sales revenue}} = \text{Profit ratio}$$

The business in Figure 5-1 earned $32.47 million net income from its $457 million sales revenue, so its profit ratio equals 7.1 percent, meaning that the business earned $7.10 net income for each $100 of sales revenue. (Thus, its expenses were $92.90 per $100 of sales revenue.) Profit ratios vary widely from industry to industry. A 5- to 10-percent profit ratio is common in many industries, although some high-volume retailers, such as supermarkets, are satisfied with profit ratios around 1 or 2 percent.

TECHNICAL
STUFF

You can turn any ratio upside down and come up with a new way of looking at the same information. If you flip the profit ratio over to be sales revenue divided by net income, the result is the amount of sales revenue needed to make $1 profit. Using the same example, $457 million sales revenue ÷ $32.47 million net income = 14.08, which means that the business needs $14.08 in sales to make $1.00 profit. So you can say that net income is 7.1 percent of sales revenue, or you can say that sales revenue is 14.08 times net income.

Earnings per share (EPS), basic and diluted

Publicly owned businesses, according to GAAP, must report earnings per share (EPS) below the net income line in their income statements — giving EPS a certain distinction among ratios. Why is EPS considered so important? Because it gives investors a means of determining the amount the business earned on their stock share investments: EPS tells you how much net income the business earned for each stock share you own. The essential equation for *EPS* is as follows:

$$\frac{\text{Net income}}{\text{Total number of capital stock shares}} = \text{EPS}$$

For the example in Figures 5-1 and 5-2, the company's $32.47 million net income is divided by the 8.5 million shares of stock the business has issued to compute its $3.82 EPS.

Note: EPS is extraordinarily important to the stockholders of businesses whose stock shares are publicly traded. These stockholders pay close attention to market price per share. They want the net income of the business to be communicated to them on a per-share basis so they can easily compare it with the market price of their stock shares. The stock shares of privately owned corporations aren't actively traded, so there's no readily available market value for the stock shares. Private businesses don't have to report EPS. The thinking behind this exemption is that their stockholders don't focus on per-share values and are more interested in the business's total net income.

The business in the example could be listed on the New York Stock Exchange (NYSE) or another securities exchange. Suppose that its capital stock is being traded at $70 per share. With 8.5 million shares trading at $70 per share, the company's market cap is $595 million, which equals the current market price of its stock shares multiplied by the number of shares in the hands of stockholders. The word *cap* means *capitalization,* which in turn means the total amount of capital invested, as it were, in the business. (The actual, historical amount of capital invested in the business is found in the balance sheet, in particular in its capital stock and retained earnings accounts.) *Market cap* simply refers to the total market value of the business. Stock investors pay much more attention to EPS than market cap. As just explained, EPS expresses the net income (earnings) of the business on a per-share basis.

At the end of the year, this corporation has 8.5 million stock shares *outstanding,* which refers to the number of shares that have been issued and are owned by its stockholders. But here's a complication: The business is committed to issuing additional capital stock shares in the future for stock options that the company has granted to its executives, and it has borrowed money on the basis of debt instruments that give the lenders the right to convert the debt into its capital stock. Under terms of its management stock options and its convertible debt, the business may have to issue 500,000 additional capital stock shares in the future. Dividing net income by the number of shares outstanding plus the number of shares that could be issued in the future gives the following computation of EPS:

$$\frac{\$32,470,000 \text{ net income}}{9,000,000 \text{ capital stock shares issued and potentially issuable}} = \$3.61 \text{ EPS}$$

This second computation, based on the higher number of stock shares, is called the *diluted* earnings per share. (*Diluted* means thinned out or spread over a larger number of shares.) The first computation, based on the number of stock shares actually issued and outstanding, is called *basic* earnings per share. Both are reported at the bottom of the income statement — see Figure 5-1.

WARNING

Publicly owned businesses report two EPS figures — unless they have a *simple capital structure* that doesn't require the business to issue additional stock shares in the future. Generally, publicly owned corporations have *complex capital structures* and have to report two EPS figures, as you see in Figure 5-1. Sometimes it's not clear which of the two EPS figures is being used in press releases and in articles in the financial press. You have to be careful to determine which EPS ratio is being used — and which is being used in the calculation of the P/E ratio (explained in the next section). The more conservative approach is to use diluted EPS, although this calculation includes a hypothetical number of shares that may or may not actually be issued in the future.

TECHNICAL STUFF

Calculating basic and diluted EPS isn't always as simple as the example may suggest. Here are just two examples of complicating factors that require the accountant to adjust the EPS formula. During the year, a company may do the following:

>> **Issue additional stock shares and buy back some of its stock shares:** (Shares of its stock owned by the business itself that aren't formally cancelled are called *treasury stock*.) The weighted average number of outstanding stock shares is used in these situations.

>> **Issue more than one class of stock, causing net income to be divided into two or more pools — one pool for each class of stock:** EPS refers to the *common* stock, or the most junior of the classes of stock issued by a business. (Let's not get into *tracking stocks* here, in which a business divides itself into two or more sub-businesses and you have an EPS for each sub-part of the business; few public companies do this.)

Price/earnings (P/E) ratio

The price/earnings (P/E) ratio is another ratio that's of particular interest to investors in public businesses. The P/E ratio gives you an idea of how much you're paying in the current price for stock shares for each dollar of earnings (the net income being earned by the business). Remember that earnings prop up the market value of stock shares.

TIP

The P/E ratio is, in one sense, a reality check on just how high the current market price is in relation to the underlying profit that the business is earning. Extraordinarily high P/E ratios are justified when investors think that the company's EPS has a lot of upside potential in the future.

The P/E ratio is calculated as follows:

$$\frac{\text{Current market price of stock}}{\text{Most recent trailing 12 months diluted EPS}^{*}} = \text{P/E ratio}$$

* If the business has a simple capital structure and doesn't report a diluted EPS, its basic EPS is used for calculating its P/E ratio (see the preceding section).

The capital stock shares of the business in our example are trading at $70, and its diluted EPS for the latest year is $3.61. *Note:* For the remainder of this section, we use the term EPS; we assume you understand that it refers to diluted EPS for businesses with complex capital structures or to basic EPS for businesses with simple capital structures.

Stock share prices of public companies bounce around day to day and are subject to big changes on short notice. To illustrate the P/E ratio, we use the $70 price, which is the closing price on the latest trading day in the stock market. This market price means that investors trading in the stock think that the shares are worth about 19 times EPS ($70 market price ÷ $3.61 EPS = 19). This P/E ratio should be compared with the average stock market P/E to gauge whether the business is selling above or below the market average.

Over the last century, average P/E ratios have fluctuated more than you may think. We remember when the average P/E ratio was less than 10 and a time when it was more than 20. Also, P/E ratios vary from business to business, industry to industry, and year to year. One dollar of EPS may command only a $12 market value for a mature business in a no-growth industry, whereas a dollar of EPS for dynamic businesses in high-growth industries may be rewarded with a $35 market value per dollar of earnings (net income).

Dividend yield

The *dividend yield ratio* tells investors how much cash income they're receiving on their stock investment in a business:

$$\frac{\text{Annual cash dividend per share}}{\text{Current market price of stock}} = \text{Dividend yield}$$

Suppose that our example business paid $1.50 in cash dividends per share over the last year, which is less than half of its EPS. (We should mention that the ratio of annual dividends per share divided by annual EPS is called the *payout ratio.*) You calculate the dividend yield ratio for this business as follows:

$$\frac{\$1.50 \text{ annual cash dividend per share}}{\$70 \text{ current market price of stock}} = 2.1\% \text{ dividend yield}$$

You can compare the dividend yields of different companies. However, the company that pays the highest dividend yield isn't necessarily the best investment. The best investment depends on many factors, including forecasts of earnings and EPS in particular.

Traditionally, the interest rates on high-grade debt securities (U.S. Treasury bonds and Treasury notes being the safest) were higher than the average dividend yield on public corporations. In theory, market price appreciation of the stock shares made up for this gap. Of course, stockholders take the risk that the market value won't increase enough to make their total return on investment rate higher than a benchmark interest rate. Recently, however, the yields on U.S. debt securities have fallen below the dividend yields on many corporate stocks.

Market value, book value, and book value per share

The amount reported in a business's balance sheet for owners' equity is called its *book value*. In the Figure 5-2 example, the book value of owners' equity is $217.72 million at the end of the year. This amount is the sum of the accounts that are kept for owners' equity, which fall into two basic types: *capital accounts* (for money invested by owners minus money returned to them) and *retained earnings* (profit earned and not distributed to the owners). Just like accounts for assets and liabilities, the entries in owners' equity accounts are for the actual, historical transactions of the business.

Book value is *not* market value. The book value of owners' equity isn't directly tied to the market value of a business. You could say that a disconnect exists between book value and market value, although this might go a little too far. Book value may be considered heavily in putting a market value on a business and its ownership shares, or it may play only a minor role. Other factors come into play in setting the market value of a business and its ownership shares. Market value may be quite a bit more or considerably less than book value. In any case, market value is *not* reported in the balance sheet of a business. For example, you don't see the market value of Apple reported in its latest balance sheet (although public companies include the market price ranges of their capital stock shares for each quarter of the year).

Public companies have one advantage: You can easily determine the current market value of their ownership shares and the market cap for the business as a whole (equal to the number of shares times the market value per share.) The market values of capital stock shares of public companies are easy to find. Stock market prices of the largest public companies are reported every trading day in many newspapers and are available on the Internet.

Private companies have one disadvantage: There's no active trading in their ownership shares to provide market value information. The shareowners of a private business probably have some idea of the price per share that they would be willing to sell their shares for, but until an actual buyer for their shares or for the business as a whole comes down the pike, market value isn't known. Even so, in some situations, someone has to put a market value on the business and/or its ownership shares. For example, when a shareholder dies or gets a divorce, there's need for a current market value estimate of the owner's shares for estate tax or divorce settlement purposes. When making an offer to buy a private business, the buyer puts a value on the business, of course. The valuation of a private business is beyond the scope of this book.

In addition to or in place of market value per share, you can calculate book value per share. Generally, the actual number of capital stock shares issued is used for this ratio, not the higher number of shares used in calculating diluted EPS (see the earlier section "Earnings per share [EPS], basic and diluted"). The formula for *book value per share* is

$$\frac{\text{Owners' equity}}{\text{Actual number of stock shares outstanding}} = \text{Book value per share}$$

The business shown in Figure 5-2 has issued 8.5 million capital stock shares, which are outstanding (in the hands of stockholders). The book value of its $217.72 million owners' equity divided by this number of stock shares gives a book value per share of $25.61. If the business sold off its assets exactly for their book values and paid all its liabilities, it would end up with $217.72 million left for the stock-holders, and it could therefore distribute $25.61 per share to them. But, of course, the company doesn't plan to go out of business, liquidate its assets, and pay off its liabilities anytime soon.

REMEMBER

Is book value the major determinant of market value? No, generally speaking, book value is not the dominant factor that drives the market price of stock shares — not for a public company whose stock shares are traded every day, nor for a private business when a value is being put on the business. EPS is much more important than book value per share for public companies. However, let's not throw out the baby with the bath water — book value per share isn't entirely irrelevant. Book value per share is the measure of the recorded value of the company's assets less its liabilities — the net assets backing up the business's stock shares.

Book value per share is important for *value investors*, who pay as much attention to the balance sheet factors of a business as to its income statement factors. They search out companies with stock market prices that aren't much higher, or are even lower, than book value per share. Part of their theory is that such a business has more assets to back up the current market price of its stock shares, compared with businesses that have relatively high market prices relative to their book value per share. In the example, the business's stock is selling for about 2.8 times its book value per share ($70 market price per share ÷ $25.61 book value per share = 2.8 times). This may be too high for some investors and would certainly give value investors pause before deciding to buy stock shares of the business.

Book value per share can be calculated for a private business, of course. But its capital stock shares aren't publicly traded, so there's no market price to compare the book value per share with. Suppose someone owns 1,000 shares of stock of a private business, and offers to sell 100 of those shares to you. The book value per share might play some role in your negotiations. However, a more critical factor would be the amount of dividends per share the business will pay in the future, which depends on its earnings prospects. Your main income would be dividends, at least until you had an opportunity to liquidate the shares (which is uncertain for a private business).

Return on equity (ROE) ratio

The *return on equity (ROE) ratio* tells you how much profit a business earned in comparison to the book value of its owners' equity. This ratio is especially useful for privately owned businesses, which have no easy way of determining the market value of owners' equity. ROE is also calculated for public corporations, but just like book value per share, it generally plays a secondary role and isn't the dominant factor driving market prices. Here's how you calculate this ratio:

$$\frac{\text{Net income}}{\text{Owners' equity}} = \text{ROE}$$

The business whose income statement and balance sheet are shown in Figures 5-1 and 5-2 earned $32.47 million net income for the year just ended and has $217.72 million owners' equity at the end of the year. Therefore, its ROE is 14.9 percent:

$$\frac{\$32,470,000 \text{ net income}}{\$217,720,000 \text{ owners' equity}} = 14.9\% \text{ ROE}$$

Net income increases owners' equity, so it makes sense to express net income as the percentage of improvement in the owners' equity. In fact, this is exactly how Warren Buffett does it in his annual letter to the stockholders of Berkshire Hathaway. Over the 50 years ending in 2014, Berkshire Hathaway's average annual ROE was 19.4 percent, which is truly extraordinary. See the sidebar "If you had invested $1,000 in Berkshire Hathaway in 1965."

Current ratio

The current ratio is a test of a business's *short-term solvency* — its capability to pay its liabilities that come due in the near future (up to one year). The ratio is a rough indicator of whether cash on hand plus the cash to be collected from accounts receivable and from selling inventory will be enough to pay off the liabilities that will come due in the next period.

IF YOU HAD INVESTED $1,000 IN BERKSHIRE HATHAWAY IN 1965

You've probably heard about Berkshire Hathaway and its CEO, Warren Buffett, who's usually among the top few in *Forbes* magazine's annual listing of the 400 richest people in America. Suppose you had invested $1,000 in Berkshire Hathaway in 1965 and held onto your shares for 51 years, to the end of 2015. At that time, the book value of your shares would be over $8 million. The market value of Berkshire Hathaway shares was usually higher than their book value over this time period.

This Berkshire Hathaway investment example demonstrates the power of compounding at a high earnings rate over a long stretch of time. Under Mr. Buffett's time as CEO starting in 1965 through the end of 2015, the company earned an average 19.2 percent annual ROE. The actual annual ROE rates for Berkshire Hathaway fluctuated over the 51 years. In fact, ROE was lower than this average in 28 of the 51 years, and ROE was actually negative in 2 of the 51 years. (Data is from Warren Buffett's 2015 annual letter to Berkshire Hathaway's stockholders, which is part of its 2015 annual financial report.)

As you can imagine, lenders are particularly keen on punching in the numbers to calculate the current ratio. Here's how they do it:

$$\frac{\text{Current assets}}{\text{Current liabilities}} = \text{Current ratio}$$

Note: Unlike most other financial ratios, you don't multiply the result of this equation by 100 and represent it as a percentage.

Businesses are generally expected to maintain a minimum 2-to-1 current ratio, which means a business's current assets should be twice its current liabilities. In fact, a business may be legally required to stay above a minimum current ratio as stipulated in its contracts with lenders. The business in Figure 5-2 has $136,650,000 in current assets and $58,855,000 in current liabilities, so its current ratio is 2.3. The business shouldn't have to worry about lenders coming by in the middle of the night to break its legs. Book 1, Chapter 3 discusses current assets and current liabilities and how they're reported in the balance sheet.

Acid-test (quick) ratio

Most serious investors and lenders don't stop with the current ratio for testing the business's short-term solvency (its capability to pay the liabilities that will come due in the short term). Investors, and especially lenders, calculate the *acid-test ratio* — also known as the *quick ratio* or less frequently as the *pounce ratio* — which is a more severe test of a business's solvency than the current ratio. The acid-test ratio excludes inventory and prepaid expenses, which the current ratio includes, and it limits assets to cash and items that the business can quickly convert to cash. This limited category of assets is known as *quick* or *liquid* assets.

You calculate the acid-test ratio as follows:

$$\frac{\text{Liquid assets}}{\text{Current liabilities}} = \text{Acid-test ratio}$$

Note: Like the current ratio, you don't multiply the result of this equation by 100 and represent it as a percentage.

The business example in Figure 5-2 has two quick assets: $14.85 million cash and $42.5 million accounts receivable, for a total of $57.35 million. (If it had any short-term marketable securities, this asset would be included in its total quick assets.) Total quick assets are divided by current liabilities to determine the company's acid-test ratio, as follows:

$$\frac{\$57,350,000 \text{ quick assets}}{\$58,855,000 \text{ current liabilities}} = 0.97 \text{ acid-test ratio}$$

The 0.97 to 1.00 acid-test ratio means that the business would be just about able to pay off its short-term liabilities from its cash on hand plus collection of its accounts receivable. The general rule is that the acid-test ratio should be at least 1.0, which means that liquid (quick) assets should equal current liabilities. Of course, falling below 1.0 doesn't mean that the business is on the verge of bankruptcy, but if the ratio falls as low as 0.5, that may be cause for alarm.

REMEMBER

This ratio is also called the *pounce ratio* to emphasize that you're calculating for a worst-case scenario, where a pack of wolves (known as *creditors*) could pounce on the business and demand quick payment of the business's liabilities. But don't panic. Short-term creditors don't have the right to demand immediate payment, except under unusual circumstances. This ratio is a conservative way to look at a business's capability to pay its short-term liabilities — too conservative in most cases.

Return on assets (ROA) ratio and financial leverage gain

As we discuss in Book 1, Chapter 3, one factor affecting the bottom-line profit of a business is whether it uses debt to its advantage. For the year, a business may realize a *financial leverage gain*, meaning it earns more profit on the money it has borrowed than the interest paid for the use of that borrowed money. A good part of a business's net income for the year could be due to financial leverage.

The first step in determining financial leverage gain is to calculate a business's *return on assets (ROA) ratio,* which is the ratio of EBIT (earnings before interest and income tax) to the total capital invested in operating assets. Here's how to calculate ROA:

$$\frac{\text{EBIT}}{\text{Net operating assets}} = \text{ROA}$$

Note: This equation uses *net operating assets,* which equals total assets less the non-interest-bearing operating liabilities of the business. Actually, many stock analysts and investors use the total assets figure because deducting all the non-interest-bearing operating liabilities from total assets to determine net operating assets is, quite frankly, a nuisance. But we strongly recommend using net operating assets because that's the total amount of capital raised from debt and equity.

Compare ROA with the interest rate: If a business's ROA is, say, 14 percent and the interest rate on its debt is, say, 6 percent, the business's net gain on its debt capital is 8 percent more than what it's paying in interest. There's a favorable spread of 8 points (1 point = 1 percent), which can be multiplied times the total debt of the business to determine how much of its earnings before income tax is traceable to financial leverage gain.

In Figure 5-2, notice that the business has $100 million total interest-bearing debt: $40 million short-term plus $60 million long-term. Its total owners' equity is $217.72 million. So its net operating assets total is $317.72 million (which excludes the three short-term non-interest-bearing operating liabilities). The company's ROA, therefore, is

$$\frac{\$55,570,000 \text{ EBIT}}{\$317,720,000 \text{ net operating assets}} = 17.5\% \text{ ROA}$$

The business earned $17.5 million (rounded) on its total debt — 17.5 percent ROA times $100 million total debt. The business paid only $6.25 million interest on its debt. So the business had $11.25 million financial leverage gain before income tax ($17.5 million less $6.25 million).

TIP

ROA is a useful ratio for interpreting profit performance, aside from determining financial gain (or loss). ROA is a *capital utilization* test — how much profit before interest and income tax was earned on the total capital employed by the business. The basic idea is that it takes money (assets) to make money (profit); the final test is how much profit was made on the assets. If, for example, a business earns $1 million EBIT on $25 million assets, its ROA is only 4 percent. Such a low ROA signals that the business is making poor use of its assets and will have to improve its ROA or face serious problems in the future.

Cash flow ratios — not

No cash flow ratios serve as important benchmarks among financial statement analysts. You can find websites that feature cash flow ratios, but frankly, these ratios don't have much clout. The statement of cash flows has been around for 30 years, but you'd be hard-pressed to point to even one cash flow ratio that has achieved the status and widespread use as the financial statement ratios we discuss earlier.

Cash flow ratios are in the minor leagues — for good reason. Ratios compare one number against another. Take, for example, the current ratio. Current assets are divided by current liabilities to get the current ratio. This result is a good indicator of the short-run solvency of the business — that is, its ability to pay its short-term liabilities on time from its cash balance plus the cash flow to be generated by its short-term liquid assets. A low ratio signals trouble ahead. What cash flow ratio could you use instead? You might try using cash flow from operating activities instead of current assets and dividing by current liabilities, but there's not a natural pairing off of the two components of the ratio like there is in pitting current assets against current liabilities.

The proponents of cash flow ratios will have to come up with ratios that do a better job of providing insights into the financial affairs of a business. Given the relatively easy access to financial statement information databases, perhaps cash flow ratios will become more prominent in the future, but we doubt it.

More ratios?

The previous list of ratios is bare bones; it covers the hardcore, everyday tools for interpreting financial statements. You could certainly calculate many more ratios from the financial statements, such as the inventory turnover ratio and the debt-to-equity ratio. How many ratios to calculate is a matter of judgment and is limited by the time you have for reading a financial report.

Computer-based databases are at our disposal, and it's relatively easy to find many other financial statement ratios. Which of these additional ratios provide valuable insight?

TIP

Be careful about wasting time on ratios that don't really add anything to the picture you get from the basic ratios explained in this chapter. Almost any financial statement ratio is interesting, we suppose. For instance, you could calculate the ratio of inventory divided by retained earnings to see what percent of retained earnings is tied up in the inventory asset. (This ratio isn't generally computed in financial statement analysis.) But we'd advise you to limit your attention to the handful of ratios that play a central role in looking after your investments.

Frolicking through the Footnotes

Reading the footnotes in annual financial reports is no walk in the park. The investment pros read them because in providing service and consultation to their clients, they're required to comply with due diligence standards — or because of their legal duties and responsibilities of managing other peoples' money. But beyond the group of people who get paid to read financial reports, does anyone read footnotes?

For a company you've invested in (or are considering investing in), we suggest that you do a quick read-through of the footnotes and identify the ones that seem to have the most significance. Generally, the most important footnotes are those dealing with the following:

>> **Stock options awarded by the business to its executives:** The additional stock shares issued under stock options dilute (thin out) the earnings per share of the business, which in turn puts downside pressure on the market value of its stock shares, assuming everything else remains the same.

>> **Pending lawsuits, litigation, and investigations by government agencies:** These intrusions into the normal affairs of the business can have enormous consequences.

>> **Employee retirement and other post-retirement benefit plans:** Your concerns here should be whether these future obligations of the business are seriously underfunded. We have to warn you that this particular footnote is one of the most complex pieces of communication you'll ever encounter. Good luck.

>> **Debt problems:** It's not unusual for companies to get into problems with their debt. Debt contracts with lenders can be very complex and are financial straitjackets in some ways. A business may fall behind in making interest and principal payments on one or more of its debts, which triggers provisions in the debt contracts that give its lenders various options to protect their rights. Some debt problems are normal, but in certain cases, lenders can threaten drastic action against a business, which should be discussed in its footnotes.

>> **Segment information for the business:** Public businesses have to report information for the major segments of the organization — sales and operating profit by territories or product lines. This gives a better glimpse of the parts making up the whole business. (Segment information may be reported elsewhere in an annual financial report than in the footnotes, or you may have to go to the SEC filings of the business to find this information.)

TIP

Stay alert for other critical matters that a business may disclose in its footnotes. We suggest scanning each and every footnote for potentially important information. Finding a footnote that discusses a major lawsuit against the business, for example, may make the stock too risky for your stock portfolio.

Checking Out the Auditor's Report

TIP

There are two types of businesses: those that have audits of their financial reports by independent CPAs and those that don't. All public companies are required by federal securities laws to have annual audits. Private companies aren't covered by these laws and generally don't have regular audits. For one thing, audits by CPAs are expensive, and smaller businesses simply can't afford them. On the other hand, many privately owned businesses have audits done because they know that an audit report adds credibility to their financial report, even though the audit is expensive.

If a private business's financial report doesn't include an audit report, you have to trust that the business has prepared accurate financial statements according to applicable accounting and financial reporting standards and that the footnotes to the financial statements cover all important points and issues. One thing you could do is to find out the qualifications of the company's chief accountant. Is the accountant a CPA? Does the accountant have a college degree with a major in accounting? Does the financial report omit a statement of cash flows or have any other obvious deficiencies?

Why audits?

The top managers, along with their finance and accounting officers, oversee the preparation of the company's financial statements and footnotes. These executives have a vested interest in the profit performance and financial condition of the business; their yearly bonuses usually depend on recorded profit, for example. This situation is somewhat like the batter in a baseball game calling the strikes and balls. Where's the umpire? Independent CPA auditors are like umpires in the financial reporting game. The CPA comes in, does an audit of the business's accounting system and methods, critically examines the financial statements, and gives a report that's attached to the company's financial statements.

We hope we're not the first to point this out to you, but the business world is not like Sunday school. Not everything is honest and straight. A financial report can be wrong and misleading because of innocent, unintentional *errors* or because of deliberate, cold-blooded *fraud*. Errors can happen because of incompetence and carelessness. Audits are one means of keeping misleading financial reporting to a minimum. The CPA auditor should definitely catch all major errors. The auditor's responsibility for discovering fraud isn't as clear-cut. You may think catching fraud is the purpose of an audit, but we're sorry to tell you it's not as simple as that.

WARNING

Sometimes the auditor fails to discover major accounting fraud. Furthermore, the implementation of accounting methods is fairly flexible, leaving room for interpretation and creativity that's just short of *cooking the books* (deliberately defrauding and misleading readers of the financial report). Some massaging of the numbers is tolerated by auditors, which may mean that what you see on the financial report isn't exactly an untarnished picture of the business.

What's in an auditor's report?

The large majority of financial statement audit reports give the business a clean bill of health, or what's called a *clean opinion*. (The technical term for this opinion is an *unmodified opinion*, which means that the auditor doesn't qualify or restrict his opinion regarding any significant matter.) At the other end of the spectrum, the auditor may state that the financial statements are misleading and shouldn't be relied upon. This negative, disapproving audit report is called an *adverse opinion*. That's the big stick that auditors carry: They have the power to give a company's financial statements a thumbs-down opinion, and no business wants that.

The threat of an adverse opinion almost always motivates a business to give way to the auditor and change its accounting or disclosure in order to avoid getting the kiss of death of an adverse opinion. An adverse audit opinion says that the financial statements of the business are misleading. The SEC doesn't tolerate adverse opinions by auditors of public businesses; it would suspend trading in a company's securities if the company received an adverse opinion from its CPA auditor.

If the auditor finds no serious problems, the CPA firm gives the business's financial report an *unmodified* or *clean* opinion. The key phrase auditors love to use is that the financial statements *present fairly* the financial position and performance of the business. However, we should warn you that the standard audit report has enough defensive, legalistic language to make even a seasoned accountant blush. If you have any doubts, go to the website of any public corporation and look at its most recent financial statements, particularly the auditor's report.

The following summary cuts through the jargon and explains what the clean audit report really says:

Audit Report (Unmodified or Clean Opinion)

1st paragraph	We did an audit of the financial report of the business at the date and for the periods covered by the financial statements (which are specifically named).
2nd paragraph	Here's a description of management's primary responsibility for the financial statements, including enforcing internal controls for the preparation of the financial statements.
3rd paragraph	We carried out audit procedures that provide us a reasonable basis for expressing our opinion, but we didn't necessarily catch everything.
4th paragraph	The company's financial statements conform to accounting and financial reporting standards and are not misleading in any significant respect.

Unfortunately, auditors' reports have become increasingly difficult to read. Even seasoned stock analysts have trouble figuring out the nuances of wording in an audit opinion. Much of this creeping obfuscation of audit report language has been caused by the legal responsibilities imposed on CPA auditors. In any case, be prepared to struggle through the language in reading an audit report. Sorry, but that's how it is in our litigation-prone society.

An audit report that does *not* give a clean opinion may look similar to a clean-opinion audit report to the untrained eye. Some investors see the name of a CPA firm next to the financial statements and assume that everything is okay — after all, if the auditor had seen a problem, the Feds would have pounced on the business and put everyone in jail, right? Well, not exactly. For example, the auditor's report may point out a flaw in the company's financial statements but not a fatal flaw that would require an adverse opinion. In this situation, the CPA issues a *modified opinion.* The auditor includes a short explanation of the reasons for the modification. You don't see this type of audit opinion that often, but you should read the auditor's report to be sure.

One type of an auditor's report is very serious — when the CPA expresses substantial doubts about the capability of the business to continue as a going concern. A *going concern* is a business that has sufficient financial wherewithal and momentum to continue its normal operations into the foreseeable future and that would be able to absorb a bad turn of events without having to default on its liabilities. A business could be under some financial distress but overall still be judged a going concern. Unless there is evidence to the contrary, the CPA auditor assumes that the business is a going concern.

Discovering fraud, or not

Auditors have trouble discovering fraud for several reasons. The most important reason is that managers who are willing to commit fraud understand that they must do a good job of concealing it. Managers bent on fraud are clever in devising schemes that look legitimate, and they're good at generating false evidence to hide the fraud. These managers think nothing of lying to their auditors. Also, they're aware of the standard audit procedures used by CPAs and design their fraud schemes to avoid audit scrutiny as much as possible.

Over the years, the auditing profession has taken somewhat of a wishy-washy position on the issue of whether auditors are responsible for discovering accounting and financial reporting fraud. The general public is confused because CPAs seem to want to have it both ways. CPAs don't mind giving the impression to the general public that they catch fraud, or at least catch fraud in most situations. However, when a CPA firm is sued because it didn't catch fraud, the CPA pleads that an audit conducted according to generally accepted auditing standards doesn't necessarily discover fraud in all cases.

In the court of public opinion, it's clear that people think that auditors should discover material accounting fraud — and, for that matter, auditors should discover any other fraud against the business by its managers, employees, vendors, or customers. CPAs refer to the difference between their responsibility for fraud detection (as they define it) and the responsibility of auditors perceived by the general public as the *expectations gap*. CPAs want to close the gap — not by taking on more responsibility for fraud detection but by lowering the expectations of the public regarding their responsibility.

You'd have to be a lawyer to understand in detail the case law on auditors' legal liability for fraud detection. But quite clearly, CPAs are liable for gross negligence in the conduct of an audit. If the judge or jury concludes that gross negligence was the reason the CPA failed to discover fraud, the CPA is held liable. (CPA firms have paid millions and millions of dollars in malpractice lawsuit damages.)

REMEMBER

In a nutshell, standard audit procedures don't always uncover fraud, except when the perpetrators of the fraud are particularly inept at covering their tracks. Using tough-minded forensic audit procedures would put auditors in adversarial relationships with their clients, and CPA auditors want to maintain working relationships with clients that are cooperative and friendly. A friendly auditor, some would argue, is an oxymoron. Also, there's the cost factor. Audits are already expensive. The CPA audit team spends many hours carrying out many audit procedures.

An audit would cost a lot more if extensive fraud detection procedures were used in addition to normal audit procedures. To minimize their audit costs, businesses assume the risk of not discovering fraud. They adopt internal controls designed to minimize the incidence of fraud. But they know that clever fraudsters can circumvent the controls. They view fraud as a cost of doing business (as long as it doesn't get out of hand).

One last point: In many accounting fraud cases that have been reported in the financial press, the auditor knew about the accounting methods of the client but didn't object to the misleading accounting — you may call this an *audit judgment failure.* In these cases, the auditor was overly tolerant of questionable accounting methods used by the client. Perhaps the auditor had serious objections to the accounting methods, but the client persuaded the CPA to go along with the methods.

In many respects, the failure to object to bad accounting is more serious than the failure to discover accounting fraud, because it strikes at the integrity and backbone of the auditor. CPA ethical standards demand that a CPA resign from an audit if the CPA judges that the accounting or financial reporting by the client is seriously misleading. The CPA may have a tough time collecting a fee from the client for the hours worked up to the point of resigning.

2

Operations Management

Contents at a Glance

Chapter **1**

Designing Processes to Meet Goals

B efore you can begin designing smart processes, you need to know what you want to accomplish. We're talking about establishing goals. Defining meaningful goals for a process requires knowing what really matters to your customers and having a clear sense of the anticipated demand for the process outcome. With these prerequisites in the bag, you can design a process to meet your goals and expectations.

In this chapter, we show you how to design a process that reduces flow time and maximizes capacity. We also point out how to use line balancing and flexible resources to improve process performance. The key to improving a process is to follow a structured process improvement plan instead of trying to wing it. Without this structured plan, you'll find yourself lost, wasting valuable time and resources. Keep your eye on the ball; the intent here is continuous improvement. Always look for ways to improve your processes because there is always room for improvement.

Getting Started with Process Improvement

Companies spend a lot of time and resources on process improvement projects that fail to produce the desired results. A primary reason that many projects fall short of expectations is because they fail to follow a structured approach. Documenting where a process has been and where it needs to go provides a road map — with directions — that can save an enormous amount of time and resources that may otherwise be wasted on dead·ends and cul-de-sacs. How novel, right?

Follow these steps when undertaking an improvement project:

1. **Map your process.**

2. **Determine your current process metrics.**

3. **Determine whether you have enough capacity to meet your demand requirements.**

4. **Decide what process metrics you need to improve and set goals for each.**

5. **Use the process improvement techniques presented in this chapter to design changes that will accomplish your desired goals.**

6. **Draw the new process map, implement the design changes, and observe the new process.**

7. **Reassess your process metrics and goals.**

8. **Repeat Steps 1 through 7 for continuous improvement.**

TIP

Start by creating a "what we do now" process flow. Many companies skip this step because it's time-consuming, but having a visual of the current system can reveal valuable information. For instance, a visual of the status quo highlights cross-departmental interaction points, which can give you insights into matters involving delay and waste. A baseline process map can also facilitate buy-in for the improvement effort throughout the organization.

Planning Operations

You can design a process in countless ways. What constitutes a good or bad design depends on your objectives. Some general rules can help you maximize your process design and achieve your goals.

In this section, we look at the effects of the placement of activities in the process. Serial processes have operations that must occur one after the other; parallel processes can occur simultaneously.

Considering a serial process

In a system with a serial process design, activities occur one after the other; no activities occur simultaneously. Figure 1-1 shows a typical serial process in which activities take place one at a time in a defined sequence. A resource performs an operation and places the output in a waiting area until the next operation is ready to receive it as an input. We refer to the part or customer in this section as the *flow unit*.

FIGURE 1-1:
Example of a
serial process.

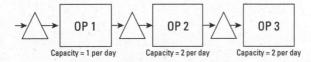

In this serial process, the resource performing OP1 has the smallest capacity and is the bottleneck with a capacity of one flow unit per day. The time it takes one flow unit to get through the system is two days (one day for OP1 and a half day each for OP2 and OP3). Because this calculation does not include any wait times, it's really a rush order flow time and not the actual flow time. But for simplicity, we call this variable the flow time.

A major problem with a serial process is that the flow time can be very long; after all, the flow unit must go through the system one step at a time. It may be possible to reduce flow time if you can identify where in the process operations can happen simultaneously. An example of this opportunity is in a medical clinic where a customer can see the doctor at the same time that office staff processes paperwork for insurance. Operations that happen at the same time are said to be in *parallel*.

Placing operations in parallel

Placing two or more operations *in parallel*, a term that indicates operations perform their functions at the same time, can either reduce flow time or increase capacity, depending on whether the parallel operations perform different functions (*unlike operations*) or perform the same function on different parts (*like operations*).

Placing unlike operations in parallel reduces the flow time but doesn't affect capacity. Placing like operations in parallel increases the operation's capacity — and the system capacity if the operation is the bottleneck — but doesn't affect the flow time.

Unlike operations

Multiple operations that perform different processes on the same flow unit at the same time are referred to as *unlike operations*. For example, a cashier at a fast-food restaurant can take your money at the same time the fry cook is preparing your order.

Figure 1-2 shows the serial process in Figure 1-1 transformed by placing OP1 and OP2 in parallel.

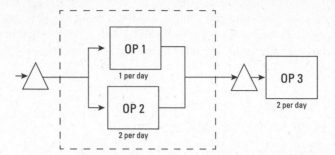

FIGURE 1-2:
Unlike operations
in parallel.

In Figure 1-2, OP1 and OP2 are completed at the same time, but both operations must be completed before the flow unit can proceed to OP3. The capacity of the bottleneck stays the same, so the system capacity remains one per day, but the flow time is reduced.

When unlike operations are parallel and both must be completed before the flow unit can proceed, the flow time for the pair is the greater of the two. In other words, the slowest one is the pacesetter. The flow time in Figure 1-2 decreases by the 0.5 days of OP2 because this operation begins and ends inside the time it takes to complete OP1; total flow time for the process is now 1.5 days.

REMEMBER

You can place unlike operations in parallel for the same flow unit only if they can work on the flow unit at the same time. For example, operations that attach each of four different doors and the hood of a car in assembly can be placed in parallel. But you can't attach a door to a car in assembly at the same time the flow unit (the car) is going through the paint booth unless you also desire to paint the equipment and operators.

Like operations

When *like operations* are in parallel, more than one of the same type of resource is performing the identical operation but on different flow units. In a restaurant, for example, several servers take orders from different customers. In this case, the servers are functioning in parallel.

Adding like operations in parallel to a system usually requires adding equipment or an employee to the process. Because the bottleneck determines system capacity, if your goal is to increase capacity, you want to add resources only to the bottleneck operation; adding them to another operation won't change capacity.

Figure 1-3 shows what a process looks like when another resource is added at OP1. A flow unit is now positioned at each of the OP1 stations. Because OP1 was the bottleneck, the system capacity is increased. You now have two resources, each producing one per day, making the new capacity two per day.

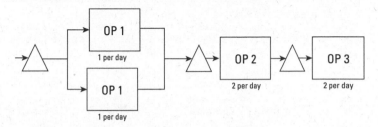

FIGURE 1-3:
Like operations in parallel.

OP1 now has the same capacity as OP2 and OP3. You've effectively balanced the production line! (More on this later.) Now, all operations can be considered a bottleneck; to improve capacity any further, you need to take action on all three of the bottlenecks.

Although you increased the system capacity, the flow time — the time needed to get one unit through the entire process — holds steady. Even though you have two resources performing OP1, they're doing so on different flow units, and each flow unit still takes one day at OP1. Therefore, the flow time remains the same at two days.

Improving Processes According to a Goal

Any given business has a variety of objectives that are related to different parts of the business. Designing your processes to operate effectively can help you meet those objectives. In this section, we examine how one process can be arranged in many configurations to produce a different outcome. Starting with a simple serial configuration, we then look at ways to improve the process based on an objective to reduce the flow time. We make different adjustments to increase capacity, and show you one more variation to improve both flow time and capacity. We also look at the effect of each version of the process on its utilization of the workers.

Figure 1-4 illustrates the simple service process of obtaining a passport at a post office. We use this example to show the required steps to either reduce the flow time, increase capacity, or accomplish both goals. In the analysis that follows, we make the following assumptions:

>> A waiting period (WIP) exists between each operation.

>> Customers arrive at the post office and enter the process at the speed of the process bottleneck.

>> No variability exists in customer arrival rates and operation cycle times.

FIGURE 1-4:
Passport application process.

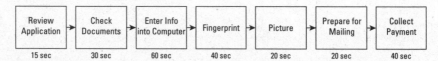

Review Application	Check Documents	Enter Info into Computer	Fingerprint	Picture	Prepare for Mailing	Collect Payment
15 sec	30 sec	60 sec	40 sec	20 sec	20 sec	40 sec

In this example process, a customer enters the post office and is greeted by a clerk who reviews the individual's application. Another clerk checks all of the customer's documents for completeness and hands the documents to another who enters the information into the computer.

The customer then proceeds to an employee who takes his fingerprints (not part of a real passport process but included here to emphasize the process structure issues) and then to another who takes his picture. Next, the application is prepared for mailing, and the customer pays a clerk before leaving.

This system has a capacity of 60 passports per hour, and the bottleneck in this process is the clerk who enters customer information into the computer. The rush order flow time for any customer without wait times is 225 seconds (sum of all of the cycle times).

If you're thinking that this kind of efficiency at your local post office is but a pipe dream, you're probably not alone. But if you're the operations manager of this post office, you may be concerned with the utilization of your resources. Assuming that you're lucky enough to have unlimited demand and smart enough to only let customers in the door at the rate your bottleneck can process them, you avoid the temptation to push too many customers into your process (find more on this in the "Managing Bottlenecks" section, later in this chapter).

In our example, customers arrive at the speed of the bottleneck, which is one every 60 seconds. Here's the utilization for the resource at each operation:

Review application	15/60 = 25%
Check documents	30/60 = 50%
Enter info	60/60 = 100%
Fingerprint	40/60 = 66.7%
Take picture	20/60 = 33.3%
Prepare for mailing	20/60 = 33.3%
Collect payment	40/60 = 66.7%

Another metric that may be important to you is *average labor utilization*. As the name states, this metric is the sum of all worker utilizations divided by the number of workers. The post office example includes seven employees (one worker assigned to each station), so the average labor utilization is 225/420 or 53.6%.

Many different process configurations exist for even this simple system. How you design your process depends on what you want to accomplish.

Reducing customer flow time

If your goal is to reduce customer rush order flow time in the process, you need to start by removing any non-value-added time from each of the operations. Every second removed from any operation reduces the flow time. After that is accomplished, you can further reduce flow time by placing unlike operations in parallel, as described in the "Placing operations in parallel" section, earlier in this chapter.

Figure 1-5 shows the process in Figure 1-4 when the "Enter info" operation is placed in parallel with the "Fingerprint" and Take picture" operations. This can only be done because the customer is not needed to interact with the clerk who enters the information. In this case, the customer goes one direction, and the paperwork goes another. The customer then meets back up with his paperwork before proceeding to the clerk who prepares all of the documents for mailing.

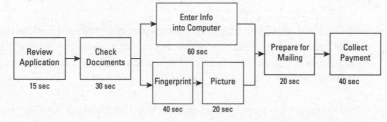

FIGURE 1-5: Reducing customer flow time.

In this new configuration, the bottleneck (entering the information into the computer) still needs to be addressed; that's why process capacity remains the same. However, flow time has been reduced by 60 seconds because the time the customer spent waiting for the clerk to enter information into the computer is eliminated now that it happens at the same time a different clerk takes fingerprints and a picture. The new flow time is 165 seconds.

Flow time is an important metric for a customer, so if improving customer service is on your wish list, you may seriously consider this design. The improvement involves no additional expense because the number of resources stays the same, so you can improve customer service for free!

By the way, the utilizations for each resource also remain the same because customers still enter the system at the rate of one per minute.

Increasing system capacity

To increase the process's capacity, you must address the speed of the bottleneck. The first step is to analyze all actions related to the bottleneck and removing all non-value added operations. (See the "Managing Bottlenecks" section, later in this chapter, for more ideas.) Then you want to break down the bottleneck's task into specific actions and assign some of the actions to other resources, if possible, to improve the bottleneck's pace.

TIP

To further increase the bottleneck's capacity, you need to add another resource to the bottleneck operation, placing it in parallel with the original.

Figure 1-6 shows the new process. Note that you added another employee, which brings the staff head count to eight. What is the new system capacity?

FIGURE 1-6:
Increasing capacity by adding a resource to the bottleneck.

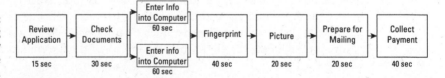

To find out, first calculate the new capacity of the original bottleneck. You now have two workers with each processing one customer every minute; that's 60 customers per hour per worker. The new capacity at this operation is 120 customers per hour.

But this isn't the new system capacity. You now have a new bottleneck — actually, two bottlenecks. The resources at fingerprint and collect payment are the new bottlenecks in this system because they both have a cycle time of 40 seconds per customer, making the new system capacity

$$\text{System Capacity} = \frac{1 \text{ Customer}}{40 \text{ Seconds}} \times \frac{3,600 \text{ Seconds}}{1 \text{ Hour}} = 90 \text{ Customers per Hour}$$

Although this version of the process significantly increases capacity, flow time remains the same at 225 seconds. Despite having two workers entering information, each flow unit still takes 60 seconds at this operation.

Assuming that you have demand of 90 customers per hour (1 customer arrives every 40 seconds), here are the new utilizations:

Review application	15/40 = 37.5%
Check documents	30/40 = 75%
Enter info (clerk 1)	60/80 = 75%
Enter info (clerk 1)	60/80 = 75%
Fingerprint	40/40 = 100%
Take picture	20/40 = 50%
Prepare for mailing	20/40 = 50%
Collect payment	40/40 = 100%

You may be wondering how the utilization of the clerks entering information was calculated. There are two ways to look at this:

>> **Clerks as separate units:** Customers come into the process at the rate of one every 40 seconds. They proceed through the process and arrive in the WIP in front of the clerks entering the information. The first available clerk processes the customer. Theoretically, each clerk processes every other customer, so from an individual clerk's perspective, the arrival rate is one every 80 seconds, making the utilization of each clerk 75%.

>> **Clerks as a single unit:** If you calculate utilization by looking at the clerks as one unit and it takes 60 seconds to process a customer and one arrives every 40 seconds, total congestion is 60/40 or 150%. Because you have two workers, the utilization of each is 150/2 or 75%.

The average labor utilization in this configuration with eight employees is 225/320 or 70.3%. This reveals that this configuration, to some extent, better balances the worker utilizations.

Adding capacity usually means adding costs — possibly in the form of hiring additional employees, purchasing additional equipment, and even acquiring additional space. In the post office example in this section, implementing this configuration increases expenses by one employee as well as an additional computer, and you may need to change the facility layout to accommodate the new flow.

Balancing the line

Moving assembly lines require a balanced line because an assembly line can only move at the speed of the bottleneck. If it moves any faster, the bottleneck cannot complete its operation. To avoid idle time at the other stations, the process design must ensure that the processing time for all of the operations comes as close as possible to the bottleneck's cycle time.

Balancing the line also has many advantages in service operations — namely, it allows you to spread work across resources so that every employee has approximately the same volume of work. Dividing the work such as by breaking a long operation into smaller tasks can lead to reduced cycle times thus increasing your system capacity. Line balancing also prevents some employees from doing all the work while others are idle. This can have a remarkable effect on worker morale.

In the post office example, adding an additional resource at the original bottleneck creates two new bottlenecks. If demand remains greater than capacity, you must find a way to increase capacity at both bottleneck operations. One way to do this is to look for ways to equalize work content across your resources through *line balancing.*

If you combine the fingerprint operation with the picture-taking function and also combine the mailing prep operation with payment collection, the processing time becomes 60 seconds for each combination, the same as the original bottleneck.

If you combine these operations, you have two clerks that you can place in parallel to perform the combined operations. Figure 1-7 shows this process with two clerks performing each of the three new operations.

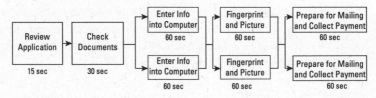

FIGURE 1-7: Balancing the process.

The process now has three operations that take 60 seconds to complete. With two employees assigned to each, the new capacity is two customers per minute, and the new process cycle time is 30 seconds.

These adjustments balance the line, except the review application operation. The new process capacity is 120 customers per hour, but it does not change the time it takes for a customer to get through the system. It still takes 225 seconds.

If demand is 120 customers per hour, here are the worker utilizations:

Review application	15/30 = 50%
Check documents	30/30 = 100%
Enter info (clerk 1)	60/60 = 100%
Enter info (clerk 1)	60/60 = 100%
Fingerprint/picture	60/60 = 100%
Fingerprint/picture	60/60 = 100%
Mailing/payment	60/60 = 100%
Mailing/payment	60/60 = 100%

The average labor utilization with eight employees is 750/8 = 93.75%.

Implementing this configuration will most likely require that you alter your facility layout. You not only have two computers in this configuration, but this version also requires an additional camera as well as equipment to take fingerprints. The additional expense of the eighth employee is also a factor.

Utilizing flexible resources

Another possible configuration for a process is to cross train workers to perform more than one task in a process. Figure 1-8 shows the case where all of the workers in the post office example can perform every operation in the process.

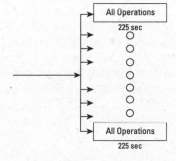

FIGURE 1-8: Flexible resources.

With eight workers, the process capacity is 128 customers per hour (8 customers every 225 seconds). The flow time remains 225 seconds and the utilization for every worker is 100% if the demand exists.

This process requires additional equipment and space because every station needs a computer, a camera, and fingerprinting supplies. That eighth employee also needs to be paid. In addition, all employees need to be trained to perform each function. Depending on the complexity of the different functions, this option may be cost prohibitive for some systems.

Table 1-1 summarizes the effect that each process configuration has on system performance. The right process configuration for a specific situation depends wholly on the objectives you want to achieve and any constraints you have on resources.

TABLE 1-1 ## Comparison of Process Configurations

Process	Action	Flow Time	System Capacity	Average Labor Utilization
Base case		225 seconds	60 per hour	53.6%
Reducing customer flow time	Place unlike activities in parallel	165 seconds	60 per hour	53.6%
Increasing system capacity	Add another resource to the bottleneck	225 seconds	90 per hour (bottleneck as moved)	70.3%
Balancing the line	Make each operation have about the same cycle time	225 seconds	120 per hour	93.8%
Utilizing flexible resources	All employees perform all the operations on the same flow unit	225 seconds	128 per hour	100%

Improving a process that has excess capacity

Although every businessperson's dream is to have unlimited demand for his or her product or service, many businesses have more than enough capacity; customer demand is the actual bottleneck. In this case, an internal bottleneck no longer exists. Until you can increase the demand, there are some concrete things you can do to reduce your process expenses. These savings can then be used on activities to increase demand.

Line balancing can reduce resource requirements. By combining operations until each new resulting station has a processing time as close to the bottleneck as possible, the process can be staffed with fewer employees or completed with less equipment. Figure 1-9 shows the example process with combined operations.

FIGURE 1-9:
Balancing the process to meet demand.

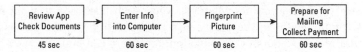

With one employee assigned to each operation, the system capacity is 60 customers per hour; the new process requires only four employees. The flow time for any customer remains 225 seconds, and our average utilization is 93.75% if demand is equal to the capacity.

Implementing a flexible process with four employees enables you to increase system capacity to 64 customers per hour (4 customers every 225 seconds).

The key to minimizing expenses is to design process so that the maximum cycle time is as close to demand as possible. In this case, with just one full-time employee, the process capacity would be 16 customers per hours. As you add employees and maintain a flexible configuration, you increase capacity by 16 per hour with each employee. Of course you can always add part-time employees if you know your demand patterns over the course of the day so you can schedule the resources to work when needed.

Keep in mind that variability in the real world — variability in processing time, customer arrival rates, equipment breakdowns, and other types of unpredictable fluctuations in a given process — affects the clean calculations of this example and the different configurations we describe. This chapter is intended to simply point out the theoretical results of different adjustments you can make to a process design to meet specific business objectives.

Managing Bottlenecks

If you're lucky enough to be in a situation where demand for your product or service exceeds your ability to make the products or deliver the service, you want to find ways to increase your production so you can sell more. Effective management of your *bottleneck*, or constraint — resources that limit a process's output — is a key to productivity and profitability.

In this section, we point out how overproduction can conceal the true process bottleneck and provide tips on how to get the most out of an existing bottleneck.

Getting tripped up by overproduction

Overproduction occurs when you allow each operation to work as fast as it can without regard to the ability of other operations in the process to keep up. If you're in a state of overproduction, inventory can build up anywhere in the process before the bottleneck where successive operations have different cycle times. Figure 1-10 represents such a situation.

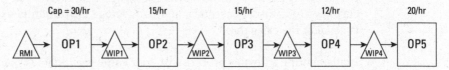

FIGURE 1-10: Hidden bottleneck.

For example, assume that you're releasing material into the process at the rate of the first operation. OP1 processes a part every 2 minutes and places it in WIP1, where it waits for OP2. However, OP2 requires 4 minutes to process each part. Because OP2 has a capacity of only 15 parts per hour and OP1 is processing 30 per hour, WIP1 grows by 15 parts per hour (30 – 15). Imagine the scene after an 8-hour shift.

WARNING

If you think you can easily spot the bottleneck by finding the operation with the most inventory in front of it, you may be making a big mistake. Here's why: OP2 feeds parts to OP3 at the rate of 15 units per minute, and OP3 processes them at the same rate. With no variability in the cycle times of these operations, inventory shouldn't accumulate in WIP2. The output of OP3 waits in WIP3 for the true bottleneck — the resource(s) at OP4. Because OP4 can process only 12 of the 15 parts it receives per hour, 3 parts per hour accumulate in WIP3 — significantly fewer than the 15 parts per hour that accumulate in WIP1.

This situation applies to services as well. Instead of parts waiting for an operation, customers would be waiting in line.

REMEMBER

Overproduction at OP1 can lead a less experienced operations manager to mistakenly conclude that the resource at OP2 is the bottleneck because it appears to be the operation that's holding up production. In reality, the bottleneck is at OP4 because it's the slowest operation.

A firm might allow a process to overproduce for many reasons. For example, look to a common accounting practice that leads companies to make this mistake. When costing products, accountants often calculate the cost per piece at each operation by dividing the total expense for the operation by the number of units it produces. By producing more units, the operation can seem to be improving and cost less per item.

If the line manager's performance is only evaluated by the artificial cost per piece or utilization of the resources, overproduction becomes a desired situation. But if a combination of different, more bottom-line friendly metrics are used to measure the performance of the process and its manager, such as the cost to actually produce a piece compared to the cost of producing it with a perfectly efficient process, a different outcome is likely. Other factors may also cause a firm to overproduce, such as inaccurate forecasts of demand or the desire to build inventory in anticipation of future demand.

TIP

Employees tend to perform to the metric on which you evaluate them, so be sure to consider the priorities and outcomes you may facilitate when setting up an evaluation system.

Increasing process capacity

Increasing capacity of an overall process relies on increasing the capacity of the bottleneck. The system's capacity can't exceed the capacity of the bottleneck, so increasing the capacity of OP4 in Figure 1-10 is the priority. If improvement resources are limited, focus on OP4 first.

REMEMBER

As you improve any bottleneck resource, you may move the bottleneck to another resource. It is vital that you continually monitor the effects of your process changes to identify when the bottleneck does indeed change. After it does, you want to change your focus to the new bottleneck.

Here are some ways for you to increase capacity at the bottleneck:

>> **Add resources at the bottleneck operation.** You can increase the number of resources that are performing the operation without adding head count if you can assign an employee from another operation to help perform the bottleneck operation during unutilized time.

>> **Always have a part for the bottleneck to process.** Be sure to monitor the WIP in front of the bottleneck and that it always has a part to process. This involves managing the resources feeding the bottleneck to ensure that nothing is slowing them down, such as equipment failures. If scheduling overtime, you must also make sure that the bottleneck has enough parts to process during the overtime period. Overtime can be expensive, especially if the bottleneck resource is idle during this time because it runs out of material.

- **» Assure that the bottleneck works only on quality parts.** Don't waste the bottleneck's time on bad parts. If you need quality checks in the process, place them before the bottleneck operation. This increases the throughput of the process.

- **» Examine your production schedule.** If a process is used to make several different products that use varying amounts of the bottleneck's time, an analysis of the production schedule can create a product mix that minimizes overall demand on the bottleneck.

- **» Increase the time the operation is working.** Keep the bottleneck resource working. Always have someone assigned to the operation, including during scheduled breaks and lunch periods, and use overtime if necessary. Although doing so won't technically reduce the cycle time, it will allow the bottleneck to produce when other operations are idle. The more time the bottleneck works, the more parts the system produces.

- **» Minimize downtime.** Avoid scheduled and unscheduled downtime. If the bottleneck equipment suffers a breakdown during scheduled operations, dispatch repair personnel immediately to get the bottleneck up and running as quickly as possible. This may involve keeping replacement parts on hand and easily accessible. Perform preventive maintenance on equipment during non-operating hours when possible. In addition, do what you can to reduce changeover times from one product to the next, because this time takes away from actual production time.

- **» Perform process improvement on the bottleneck resource.** A good place to start is to document everything the resource does. Then eliminate all non-value-added activities and look for ways to reduce the time it takes to do value-added activities by getting rid of all the waste in the operation. This results in a shorter cycle time. Process improvement is almost always focused on eliminating waste.

- **» Reassign some of the bottleneck's work.** If possible, break the operation down into smaller activities and reassign some to other resources. Doing so results in a shorter cycle time and increased capacity.

Chapter **2**

Planning for Successful Operations

B en Franklin said, "If you fail to plan, you are planning to fail." This saying is particularly true of operations management because of the interdependencies of all the various components, including resources, materials, and processes. Trying to manage complex business operations with a seat-of-your-pants approach, hoping that the process will somehow evolve into something efficient without planning, is a losing proposition. To win at the game of operations, you need to plan.

In this chapter, we show you how to plan operations with a hierarchical approach. We describe tools you can use to plan operations at both the corporate and facility levels and point out how to apply your plans to process scheduling. Near the end of this chapter, we also cover software systems that are particular popular in the operations management set.

Planning from the Top Down

The planning and control of operations usually occurs in a hierarchical manner. Figure 2-1 illustrates the typical organization for operations planning. Strategies and goals are determined at the corporate level; detailed plans for meeting the firm's objectives are developed at the facility level; and operations are executed at the plant-floor (or, for services, front-line) level. In this section, we examine these three levels of planning and look at the decisions made in each.

Hierarchy of Planning

Corporate Level
Strategic Planning

Facility Level
Aggregate Planning

Plant-floor Level
Detailed Control

FIGURE 2-1: The hierarchy of operations planning.

Determining corporate strategy

At the top of the pyramid is the corporate strategy, which ideally establishes the organization's direction and the basis upon which the business will compete. Michael Porter, a leading expert on corporate strategy and competitiveness, proposed basic strategies for competitive advantage. They include a focus on being the low-cost provider (Walmart), a focus on being the leader in innovation (Apple) or product quality (Toyota), or a focus on the differentiated needs of the customer (American Express). Each of these strategies requires a different approach to operations management.

The key to executing the corporate strategy is the *business plan,* which answers the core questions of running the business, such as what products or services the firm wants to provide and where and how it will produce, market, and distribute them. The business plan also describes market dynamics and competition.

The business plan has a long-term effect on the health of the company and its shareholders. It covers many aspects of running the business, including these:

>> **Goals:** What financial and performance goals will the company set?

>> **Markets:** What markets and which customers will the firm pursue?

>> **Product portfolio:** What products will the business offer, and how quickly will the company introduce and update the products?

The business plan also covers the key strategic operations management decisions within the scope of this chapter on operations, including these considerations and others:

>> **Facility location:** Will the company have multiple facilities, and if so, where will they be located?

>> **Long-term capacity:** What is the forecast for expected demand, and how much capacity will the firm need to meet the demand?

>> **Outsourcing strategy:** What will the company produce or provide itself and what will it outsource?

>> **Production allocation:** What facilities will make which products, and will a product be produced at multiple facilities or will a facility make multiple products?

>> **Production policy:** How will the firm face the market? Will the company make its product to order or make it to stock?

These high-level decisions have long-term implications and must be considered over a long time horizon. Given the long-term nature of corporate strategy decisions, company leaders must look into the future and create a shared vision of what the company will be before making those decisions.

Preparing for success

After a firm determines its corporate strategy and establishes its long-term capacity needs and production policies, focus shifts to intermediate planning, which is often referred to as *aggregate planning*. Aggregate planning usually presents a detailed plan for sales and operations that covers a period of 2 to 12 months. A company's aggregate plan typically addresses the following three specific operational considerations:

>> **Employment levels:** How much manpower is needed to meet the set production rates?

>> **Inventory levels:** How much inventory (both raw material and finished goods) does the company need?

>> **Production or output rates:** How much will the company produce in the designated time period?

Develop an aggregate plan by following these steps:

1. **Determine demand for each time period covered in the plan.**

2. **Determine the available capacities for each time period.**

   Be sure to calculate capacities for all resources, including labor and machine capacities.

3. **Identify corporate policies and external constraints such as regulation and market forces that may influence the plan.**

   These policies include limitations on workers over time, inventory targets, and outsourcing policies.

4. **Determine product cost, based on direct labor and material costs as well as indirect or overhead (fixed) manufacturing expenses.**

5. **Develop contingency plans to account for surges and downturns in the market.**

   For example, each plan may utilize different levels of overtime, outsourcing, and inventory to meet the demand requirements, thus resulting in a different product cost and availability.

6. **Select the plan that best meets the corporate objectives.**

   Compare your various plans and determine how well each one meets your business objectives. Some plans may present tradeoffs in different performance metrics such as utilization versus inventory levels.

7. **Test the plan for robustness (its ability to perform well under varying conditions).**

   This step may involve changing the demand requirements or the unit costs for things such as overtime to simulate different scenarios. If the outcome of the plan varies greatly from your ideal scenario, revisit one of the alternative plans available in Step 5.

REMEMBER

Aggregate planning is an ongoing process. A plan usually provides details at the monthly level over the course of a year, and you should update it as conditions change. For example, you need to account for changes in expected demand as well as unexpected events such as material shortages and production disruptions.

WARNING

Avoid the temptation to change your aggregate plan too often. The purpose of the plan is to provide an intermediate path into the future. Reacting too quickly to perceived changes in demand or variability in production output could create unnecessary disruptions in your overall plan, such as layoffs, unnecessary hiring, or changes in supply purchasing contracts. Until you recognize an undisputable, reoccurring change in demand or production output, allow your short-term planning to accommodate the blips in demand that are only temporary because of such things as weather events or short-term shifts in customer preference.

Executing the plan

Armed with the aggregate plan, plant personnel or those who schedule and control actual production develop the short-term detailed plans for implementation. This level of planning generally includes the weekly and daily schedules for specific tasks:

>> **Inventory levels:** How much raw material, work-in-process, and finished goods should be in the operation?

>> **Machine loading:** What items will be processed by what resources and when?

>> **Production lot sizes:** How large should batch sizes be, and how should changeovers be scheduled?

>> **Work schedules:** What are the staffing needs, including overtime?

REMEMBER

A critical aspect of successful operations is managing bottleneck operations. Because the bottleneck is the resource that limits the processes output, start your detailed planning with a focus on the bottleneck. This increases the likelihood that the facility will use its resources in the best way possible.

The detailed plan needs to be responsive to sudden changes in conditions such as a rush order for a product, a disruption in material supply, or an unexpected equipment failure. The operations manager can schedule overtime or reassign workers to different tasks to adjust for many of these issues.

Exploring the Components of an Aggregate Plan

An aggregate plan provides the road map for business operations; it translates corporate strategy into a plan that can be implemented on the plant floor or on the front-line of service. For companies that sell physical products, this map details the production process. For service-based companies, the aggregate map identifies staffing levels and other resources needed to accommodate customer demand. In this section, find out how the aggregate plan evolves from the corporate strategy and how it becomes a detailed plan for production.

Putting together a plan

The operations planning process starts at the corporate level with a strategic plan for the company. The overarching corporate strategy guides the aggregate operations plan; this relationship is shown in Figure 2-2.

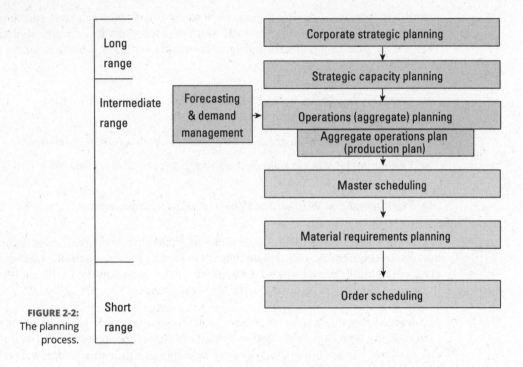

FIGURE 2-2: The planning process.

The purpose of the aggregate plan is to match the firm's capacity with anticipated customer demand to ensure that the company is utilizing its available capacity to best meet anticipated demand. An aggregate plan requires two sets of information:

>> **Strategic capacity plan:** A *capacity plan* emerges from the corporate strategic plan and provides aggregate planners with details on current and future capacity levels.

>> **Forecast of anticipated demand:** The demand forecast provides an overview on how much product the facility needs to manufacture in the coming months to satisfy anticipated customer demand.

REMEMBER

In their general form, aggregate plans deal with the total demand. They typically don't focus on individual models or items. For example, when allocating space in a grocery store, the aggregate plan would indicate a certain amount of space to be used for breakfast cereals, but the plan wouldn't address how much shelf space each type or brand of cereal gets. In some cases, the plan may allocate a specific amount of space to a particular manufacturer, such as Kellogg's, but this is usually as specific as it gets.

The end product of aggregate planning is the production plan, which guides the development of a master schedule (MS), which informs detailed schedules for operations. These relationships are illustrated in Figure 2-2.

Creating the master schedule

Based on the production plan, facility personnel (such as a retail store manager) create a detailed schedule to give specific direction on what to do when to employees who are actually doing the work or providing the service. The master schedule shows the quantity and timing for a specific product to be delivered to customers over a specific period of time, but it doesn't show how many products actually need to be produced because the demanded products can be provided using inventory in some cases.

The master schedule and inventory levels provide information for the master production schedule, which communicates how many units need to be produced at a given time.

For example, a computer manufacturer's production plan may show that the company forecasts sales of 1,200 portable computers in September, 1,500 in October, and 1,700 in November. But it doesn't give any information about what quantity of each model is needed. The master schedule shows how many of each model is needed and when it needs to be produced.

Figure 2-3 shows the aggregate plan and the master schedule for a company that manufactures three different models of a product.

Getting to the specifics of the master schedule can be difficult. Breaking a production plan into the number of specific models to produce isn't always easy. Because disaggregate forecasts are less accurate than aggregate forecasts, it's often difficult to predict what actual models the customer will desire. You must take care when developing the forecast. Because short-term forecasts are typically more accurate than long-term forecasts, the longer you can delay making the line item (model) forecast, the better off everyone will be. When creating a master schedule, follow a structured method (such as the one described earlier in this chapter in the "Preparing for success" section).

Disaggregating the Plan

Aggregate Plan	Month	September	October	November
	Planned Output	1,200	1,500	1,700
Master Schedule	Month	September	October	November
	Planned Output			
	Model 360	500	700	800
	Model 183	450	500	575
	Model 71	250	300	325

FIGURE 2-3:
Disaggregating the plan.

Considering Materials

A company's master schedule focuses on creating the product or delivering the service that a company is in business to sell. This commodity often requires materials and processes, and the collection of parts and activity can become complicated very quickly. In this section, we present the basics of material requirements planning (or MRP).

Gathering information for the system

Material requirements planning (MRP) is a computerized information system designed to help manage the ordering and scheduling of the components, parts, and raw material that make up a company's end product. Demand for these components is often referred to as *dependent demand* because the quantity demanded depends on the consumer demand for the end product.

An MRP system requires these major inputs:

>> **Master production schedule:** This input is described in the "Creating the master schedule" section, earlier in this chapter.

>> **Product structure:** This diagram shows all inputs needed to produce the product. It may also show assembly order. Figure 2-4 shows an abbreviated product structure for an automobile. The automobile consists of two axle assemblies, one body, and one engine assembly. Each axle assembly consists of two wheels and one axle subassembly.

>> **Bill of materials (BOM):** This input is a listing of all the items needed to produce an end product. It's much like the list of ingredients in a recipe.

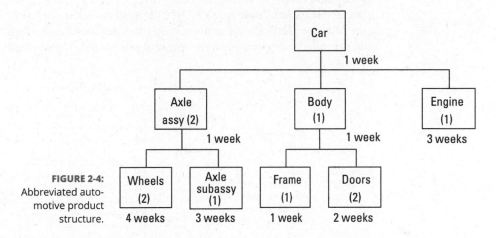

Product Structure for an Automobile

FIGURE 2-4:
Abbreviated automotive product structure.

>> **Inventory record:** Tallies of all the raw material, parts, subassemblies (partial assemblies), and assemblies for each time period are included in this input. Here are the primary data points contained in this file:

- *Gross requirements:* Total demand for the item during the time period

- *Scheduled receipts:* Orders placed but not yet received, often referred to as *open orders*

- *Expected on-hand inventory:* Estimate of the inventory on hand

- *Net requirements:* Actual amount needed

- *Planned receipts:* Quantity expected to be received

- *Planned releases:* Quantity expected to be ordered

For MRP, you must also know the expected *lead time*, the time between the ordering of parts and their delivery.

Getting system results

The MRP system takes the master production schedule, product structure, BOM, inventory record, and lead time information and creates a material requirement plan for each item. The process starts with the number of end products desired in any given period. The software uses the product structure and the BOM to determine how many of each assembly and subassembly are needed — and when — to make the end product. Using current inventory levels, the system provides the manufacturing staff with a work release, which points out how many items they need to actually produce. This process repeats down to the raw material level.

To visualize this process, consider the BOM in Figure 2-4. If you need 100 automobiles in week 7 and 120 in week 8, the MRP system breaks out the master schedule into separate plans for the automobile, the axle assemblies, the subassemblies, and the wheels. Figure 2-5 shows a traditional output from an MRP system.

MRP Output

		1	2	3	4	5	6	7	8
	Week Number	1	2	3	4	5	6	7	8
	Quantity							100	120
Automobile LT 1 week	Gross requirements							100	120
	Scheduled receipts								
	Expected on hand								
	Planned receipts							100	120
	Planned releases						100	120	
Axle Assembly (2 required) LT 1 week	Gross requirements						200	240	
	Scheduled receipts								
	Expected on hand								
	Planned receipts						200	240	
	Planned releases					200	240		
Axle Subassembly (1 required) LT 3 weeks	Gross requirements						200	240	
	Scheduled receipts								
	Expected on hand								
	Planned receipts						200	240	
	Planned releases		200	240					
Wheels (2 required) LT 4 weeks	Gross requirements					400	480		
	Scheduled receipts								
	Expected on hand								
	Planned receipts					400	480		
	Planned releases	400	480						

FIGURE 2-5: MRP output.

Figure 2-5 shows that the company needs 100 automobiles in week 7. Because the company has a one-week lead time, it needs to release the required materials into the plant during week 6, which means that 200 axle assemblies must be ready at this time. (Each automobile needs two axle assemblies.) Given the one-week lead time to produce an axle assembly, the company must release the material needed to produce the assemblies at week 5. Note that producing a subassembly takes 3 weeks, so the company must release materials for 200 axle subassemblies at week 2. For the same reasons, it needs to release materials for 400 wheels at week 1 (two wheels per axle assembly; four-week lead time). These calculations are repeated for the 120 automobiles needed at week 8, although, because of the 20 percent increase in demand, all the quantities grow by 20 percent.

MRP reporting makes it quick and easy for an operations manager to see the required timing for future operations. For example, if you're managing the axle subassembly operations, you know that at week 2 you need to begin production for the 200 subassemblies required for a week-5 delivery to the axle assembly area.

Taking MRP data to the factory floor

MRP releases raw material onto the factory floor as needed but doesn't schedule the individual resources (machines and people) needed to produce the product. Scheduling jobs can be problematic when specific resources are required for multiple products or jobs. Which jobs do you schedule first?

Several methods to prioritize jobs are available. Here are some of the most common options:

>> **First-come, first-served (FCFS):** Process jobs in the order that they arrive. Also known as *first-in, first-out* (FIFO).

>> **Shortest operating time (SOT):** Start with the job that has the shortest processing time.

>> **Earliest due date (EDD) first:** Begin with the job that has the earliest required date.

>> **Critical ratio (CR) method:** Calculate the time remaining until the due date and divide it by the total processing time remaining. Start with the job with the smallest ratio.

The metrics you use to evaluate the advantages of each scheduling method include the flow time and the job lateness. *Flow time* (covered in Book 2, Chapter 1) is the length of time a job spends in the facility. It includes not only processing time but also the time the job waits to be processed. Measure lateness against the promised due date to the customer; that is, calculate job lateness as the difference between the actual completion date and the due date.

Unfortunately, no one method is better than the others in all circumstances. Evaluate all the methods for each series of jobs to find the best approach for a given situation.

Here are some general trends:

>> FCFS is the worst performer in most situations because long jobs often delay other jobs behind them in the process. However, FCFS is often used in service operations because it's the simplest method to implement and perceived to be the fairest to customers.

>> SOT always results in the lowest flow time for a group of jobs. This typically results in lower work-in-progress inventory because jobs move through the process quickly. The major drawback is that long-processing-time jobs often spend much more time waiting than with FCFS or EDD.

>> EDD usually minimizes the number of jobs missing their delivery date, but it also can increase the flow time of jobs through the system because they aren't processed until the last possible moment.

Planning for Services

Aggregate planning is rooted in the manufacturing sector, but many of its concepts apply to service industries, too. In this section, we point out how operations planning typically happens in service-based companies. We highlight the factors that make planning for service unique and describe how to develop a plan for serve operations.

Seeing the difference in services

All sorts of businesses sell services, and some service products — such as those provided by restaurants and retail stores — contain many of the same operational elements as manufacturing-based organizations. For starters, these particular service industries require a business to maintain inventory. In fact, much of the activity in the banking industry (think processing deposits and withdraws) can be automated in a way that's quite similar to what you may see on a production line. However, other kinds of service-based businesses, including healthcare, are significantly different from a manufacturing operation because patients cannot be inventoried and their care cannot be automated.

Most service industries share a handful of characteristics that don't apply to most manufacturing operations:

>> **High level of customization:** No two customers are alike in most service environments, and each requires at least some level of customization, if not complete customization.

>> **No inventory:** Customers cannot be inventoried for services, and the service process cannot be initiated until a customer expresses demand for the service. For example, a bank cannot approve a mortgage loan until an applicant finds a house he wants to purchase and submits the loan application. Similarly, a doctor cannot perform most medical procedures until a patient is present.

>> **Variable arrival rates:** In manufacturing, the operations manager has a fairly high level of control over the arrival rates of material. This isn't the case for services, where the arrival of customers is often difficult to control. Even with the use of appointments and reservations, customer arrival rates are difficult to predict and control. If a manufacturing company produces using a make-to-order system (only producing when an order is received), its arrival rate variability will be more like that of a service operation.

>> **Variable service times:** In services, the *cycle time* (time to complete the task) can vary significantly, much more than in a typical manufacturing operation. Service time variability makes capacity planning more difficult in service industries.

WARNING

Because inventory isn't present in most service-based operations, capacity becomes the prime leverage point when managing product availability, and the variability in arrival rates and service times makes capacity management difficult, resulting in potentially significant waiting time for customers, which often impacts customer satisfaction.

Establishing the service plan

Service planning is usually completed in a hierarchical manner. At the corporate level, company leaders decide what types of services to provide and set goals and metrics. These parameters are communicated to the facility level where detailed plans are made. As in manufacturing, these plans are then carried out on the service floor, or front line.

In services the primary focus is on capacity, and service capacity is usually of the human variety, so the goal of planning is to determine how many people are needed for certain periods of time and when individual employees should work. In aggregate planning terms, customer demand is specified for each time period and employees are assigned to meet this demand. For example, when staffing a restaurant, additional kitchen and waitstaff are scheduled during lunch and dinner hours to meet the increased demand.

Although an MRP system isn't too useful in services, many services utilize a scheduling optimization software program that can help managers best utilize resources and provide better customer service.

Consider a popular retail chain. At the corporate level, the strategic plans for the company are established. Corporate leaders determine what customer market to target and what products to sell. Each facility takes these strategic plans and determines how to implement them at its local branch. In the clothing industry, for example, a store in southern Texas has limited need for winter parkas, so the store's managers may decide to carry a larger stock of lightweight jackets instead.

Although general management employment levels are established at the strategic level, it is typically up to the facility management to determine how many employees are needed on the store floor to service customers. These employees are usually assigned to departments based on projected demand. For example, the days before Mother's Day, more employees may be assigned to the women's apparel and jewelry departments to service the anticipated increase in demand in these areas.

Applying Information to the Entire Organization

MRP led to the development of *enterprise resource planning* (ERP). As the name implies, ERP integrates an entire company into one information system that operates on real-time data it receives from throughout the organization. The shared database ensures that every location and department can access the most reliable and up-to-date information (see Figure 2-6).

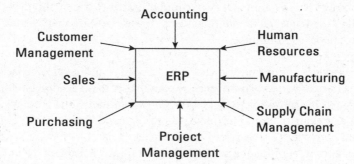

FIGURE 2-6: Spanning the organization.

An ERP system incorporates many of the topics, including process design and management, aggregate planning, capacity and inventory management, scheduling, quality control, and project management.

WARNING

An ERP system has many advantages, but beware of the silver bullet perception. ERP systems require significant investments, including purchasing the system and then implementing and maintaining it. Many companies under-estimate the amount of time and money involved with implementing and maintaining an ERP system.

We recommend the following steps for implementing a successful ERP system:

1. Assess your needs.

Do you really need such a sophisticated system? The system itself won't fix all the problems of an organization. Often, some process reengineering and communication across the organization can do the trick, and you can handle data management in a much simpler and inexpensive way. Many world-class manufacturing and service operations use relatively simple, unsophisticated systems to manage their ERP needs.

2. Fix your processes.

Implementing an ERP system won't fix broken, inefficient processes. Before investing in an ERP system, evaluate and, if needed, redesign your processes.

3. Acquire and verify consistent data.

When you begin populating an ERP system with data, remember that the outputs are only as good as the data going in. If different departments are operating on different sets of data — say, sales data in one department is different from sales data in another —the software system isn't going to produce accurate data for the company.

4. Customize your software.

ERP vendors offer highly standardized software, typically with optimized modules for particular industries. One of the major concerns companies have about implementing an ERP system is that it locks the company into standard-ized processes. This inhibits process innovation within a company because deviating from the ERP's process ends up requiring many software work-arounds. When setting up an ERP, make sure the system can accommodate process improvements from Step 2 and not force you into the standard processes that have been built into its software.

WARNING

When customizing software to accommodate an improved process, be sure your competitors don't get ahold of the same programs and eliminate any competitive advantage you've gained.

5. Train your employees.

Employees must understand the purpose of the system and how to input data and interpret the reports that the system generates.

6. Continuously improve your processes.

Continuous improvement is the heartbeat of all successful companies, and changing processes almost certainly involves modifications to ERP software. Many companies find themselves locked into their current processes to avoid the time and money needed to update their software. Avoid stagnation by developing a good relationship with your software provider.

Chapter **3**

Creating a Quality Organization

A quality mind-set must be part of the corporate culture for a company to produce true quality products. Planning for quality must begin in the executive suite, and the entire organization must embrace quality to create it and deliver it to customers.

Not long ago, quality improvement efforts were the sole responsibility of a few selected individuals in an organization. Most manufacturing plants had a quality control department, and many times those departments were located far from the factory floor. Unfortunately, those responsible for quality acted alone and at times were considered a nuisance to the personnel responsible for doing the work.

By now, most companies realize that the quality mentality must be part of what happens in every department — not just manufacturing. In this chapter, we examine the evolution of a company becoming a quality organization. We introduce the tools necessary for building such an organization and highlight the obstacles that firms face on their journey toward quality central.

Reaching Beyond Traditional Improvement Programs

Quality improvement programs aren't a new concept or late-breaking fad in business. Companies have been using methods such as *total quality management* (TQM) and *statistical process control* (SPC) for decades. In this section, we examine how these traditional quality improvement initiatives have turned into what's become known as *Six Sigma* quality.

Multiplying failures

Most companies typically operate their process at a 3 sigma quality level. This means that the process mean is 3 standard deviations away from the nearest *specification limit*, which defines the boundaries of a good part.

Figure 3-1 shows a process operating at 2.6, 3, and 6 sigma. The figure reveals that 1 percent of the output of a 2.6 sigma process will be defective, assuming a normal distribution. By increasing the quality level to 3 sigma, you can reduce the defective rate to 0.3 percent. Even at this level, a company can lose a significant amount of profits, because 3 of every 1,000 products it makes have a defect.

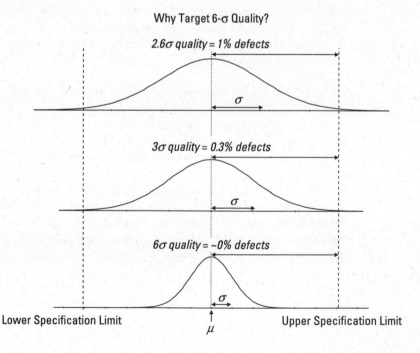

Why Target 6-σ Quality?

2.6σ quality = 1% defects

σ

3σ quality = 0.3% defects

σ

6σ quality = ~0% defects

σ

FIGURE 3-1: Six Sigma quality.

Lower Specification Limit μ Upper Specification Limit

Realizing that 3 sigma just wasn't good enough, the Motorola Corporation embarked on a quality journey starting in 1985, which led to the birth of what's now called *Six Sigma.* Other companies picked up on the concept, and a quality revolution was launched in the world of business operations.

So you may be asking, if 6 sigma quality is so good, wouldn't 7, 8, or even 9 sigma be even better? Not necessarily. You start bumping into the point of diminishing returns. In other words, Figure 3-1 reveals that after you reach 6 sigma, the defect rate is very close to zero. Going beyond 6 sigma can get very expensive because you eliminate all the easy problems to get to this point; any gains you receive from further improvement are small — perhaps not worth the effort and cost required to achieve them.

TECHNICAL
STUFF

For various obscure reasons, Motorola assumed that the mean could drift up to 1.5 standard deviations off center toward one side of the customer specifications or the other. So you may hear that a 6 sigma capability translates into a defect rate of 3.4 parts per million. In this minibook, we don't follow this assumption but instead assume that 6 sigma means the process mean (average parameter value) is 6 standard deviations away from the nearest specification limit.

Because most products are assembled from multiple components, the quality level of each component is critical; each one has a compounding influence on the quality of the end product. Therefore, the expected quality of the end product diminishes as the number of components increases. You can calculate the expected quality of a product using this equation:

$$\% \text{ Defective products} = 1 - \left[1 - \left(\% \text{ Defective} / 100\right)\right]^{Number\ of\ components}$$

For example, operating at 3 sigma quality for each of 10 components that make up a final product may sound like a reasonable quality level because only approximately 0.3 percent of each component will be defective. But the expected end quality of the final product when the 10 components are assembled is only 97 percent; 3 percent of the final products are defective. This only gets worse as the number of components increases, as shown in Table 3-1. Here, each component is at a 3 sigma quality level.

TABLE 3-1

Final Product Quality

Number of Components	Defective Rate of Final Product
200-part DVR	45%
500-part laptop computer	78%
3,000-part automobile	Approximately 100%

Raising the bar

Six Sigma emphasizes the following set of values:

>> Achieving quality improvement requires participation across the organization.

>> The process characteristics must be measured, analyzed, improved, and controlled.

>> To achieve high quality, a company must focus on continuous improvement.

Here are the fundamentals that separate Six Sigma from its predecessors and living relatives:

>> Efforts to improve quality are prioritized by return on investment. Projects are selected based on a cost-benefit analysis.

>> Decisions are made on concrete, verifiable data. Great attempts are made to remove qualitative assertions.

>> Experts of different degrees with formalized training (covered in the next section) handle implementation.

>> An increased emphasis is placed on benchmarking competitive performance.

The Six Sigma concept applies an increased focus on concrete results that can be measured. Improvement projects are chosen based on the potential financial results the organization can achieve. All improvement is measured and documented. The firm's attention is squarely trained on actions that produce tangible results when Six Sigma is in action.

Varying skill levels

Perhaps one of the greatest differences that separates Six Sigma from other quality improvement programs is its emphasis on differentiated skill levels among employee training. Following the structure of martial arts training, Six Sigma uses a belt color system to designate the level of training the employee has received in the methods of Six Sigma:

>> **Black belts:** At the top of the skill chain are the black belts. These employees are highly trained experts and are responsible for leading Six Sigma projects. In many organizations, their full-time position involves implementing projects and training others.

>> **Green belts:** Next in line are the green belts. Although not experts, they're proficient in Six Sigma methodologies and are part-time participants in the implementation effort.

>> **Yellow belts:** Yellow belts make up the majority of a Six Sigma project team. Often, these people perform in the process being improved. The success of any project rests on the shoulders of these people because they not only work to improve the process but also maintain the gains after the others move on to their next project in the continuous improvement cycle.

Implementation of a Six Sigma initiative starts in the executive suite. Upper management must be fully committed to the program. Champions of the cause in upper management are usually tasked to oversee implementation of chosen projects. Although upper management may not be black belts, they do require some understanding of the dedication required to successfully implement Six Sigma in their organization.

Adding to the Tool Box

At the foundation of Six Sigma quality lies a powerful tool box of techniques and methods that employees use throughout all phases of a successful project. In this section, we introduce you to the must-have tools and explain how to best use them.

At the heart of any project is what has become known as DMAIC (define-measure-analyze-improve-control). DMAIC, pronounced "dah-*may*-ik," is a standardized process in which employees follow a series of well-defined steps throughout the project and repeat the process repeatedly for continuous improvement.

Figure 3-2 shows the five phases of the DMAIC process:

>> **Define:** Choose the project, determine what you'll accomplish in concrete terms, select the project team, and devise a plan for executing the next phases of the project.

>> **Measure:** Document the current state of the process that you're targeting for improvement. After all, you need to know where you started to determine whether the process achieved improvements and met the objectives you established in the define phase.

>> **Analyze:** Examine the current process to find out how it works. Identify the main process drivers and the causes of problems. In the "Analyzing the problem" section, later in the chapter, we describe many of the tools you use during this phase.

>> **Improve:** Implement solutions to the problems you've identified. Be sure to measure and validate any improvements to find out whether your improvement efforts actually produced measurable results.

>> **Control:** Establish a plan to monitor the ongoing performance of the changes. You can use statistical process controls to monitor and control the new process.

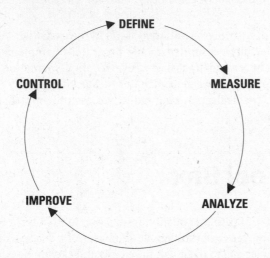

FIGURE 3-2: The DMAIC process.

In addition to DMAIC, Six Sigma utilizes DMADV (define, measure, analyze, design, and verify), particularly on new processes or when a process requires a radical change. The DMADV process mirrors DMAIC except the improve step is replaced with a design step.

Defining the problem

All DMAIC projects start with a well-defined problem statement that states what the issue is and what needs to be improved. After you define the problem, you write an *objective statement,* which outlines the project's scope, defines its concrete and measurable goals, and provides a timeline for project completion. During the define phase of the project, you also identify all stakeholders and assemble the project team.

You can use *benchmarking* — comparing your performance to others — to set targets for your improvement goals. Find out who's best in class, study what those companies do, and determine whether you can duplicate their attributes and habits in your organization.

When benchmarking, don't limit yourself to companies in your industry. Looking outside your immediate realm can offer new insights into the problems you're facing and possibly help you leapfrog the performance of your competition.

Measuring the process

After defining the project and establishing objectives, you must measure the current state of the process. Although many undisciplined firms want to skip this step and consider it a waste of time, documenting the status quo is critical for successful improvement projects. You must know where you started to claim improvement victory.

Start by creating an as-is process flow diagram and include metrics such as cycle time, flow time, process capacity, and current quality levels.

Analyzing the problem

The output of any process is determined by the inputs into the process and the transformation activities that occur. Simply put, the output y is a function of the input x:

$$y = f(x)$$

In the analyze phase, find out which inputs influence the outcome and how they do it. Be vigilant about finding the root cause of your undesirable output. Several tools can help you do this; we describe them in the following sections.

Brainstorming

Brainstorming sessions can help extract possible causes of offending outcomes. By gathering a cross-functional array of employees, including management and line workers, you can get a wide assortment of ideas and often find the reasoning behind certain ideas.

Conduct a meeting in which you encourage everyone to voice his opinion about the problem's root causes. Place ideas on sticky notes and display them on a board. (Sticky notes allow for later rearranging.)

TIP

Companies often use *affinity diagrams* to organize possible causes into clusters. An affinity diagram is a tool that helps group ideas and concepts into similar sets. Affinity diagrams are useful because they make it easy to see how identified causes fit into a small number of categories, making the potential causes easier to analyze.

Brainstorming and the resulting affinity diagrams tend to open the door to meaningful discussions on the key issues influencing performance. In practice, a brainstorming session may begin with a high-level question, such as, "Why are our sales down?" Comments from employees might include "We don't have enough salespeople to service potential customers"; "Production can't deliver the products within the time the customer wants"; and "Our products have a bad quality reputation." You can probably imagine how discussions may proceed from there.

Determining cause and effect

Brainstorming usually results in several potential answers to the brainstorming question. From this information you can choose an area on which to focus your effort. Because this is a chapter on quality, we focus on the quality comments, which you'd probably group together on your affinity diagram.

The next step is to get to the root cause of the problem. Poor quality may be due to many problems. To to help quantify the important reasons, you can use the following tools.

CHARTING THE CAUSES

The *Pareto chart* is named after the Italian economist Vilfredo Pareto. In the early 1900s he observed that 80 percent of the land in Italy was held by 20 percent of the people. Further studies showed that this principle was true for many things, and it became known as the 80-20 rule or the law of the vital few. The principle states that 80 percent of the effects (problems, complaints, sales, and so on) come from 20 percent of the causes.

The Pareto chart is a bar graph in which the independent variables or events are on the horizontal axis, and the vertical axis is the number of occurrences. The values are plotted in decreasing order of frequency. For example, you can analyze customer product-return data and graph the reasons why customers return a product and the frequency that the product is returned for that reason. Figure 3-3 illustrates a Pareto chart.

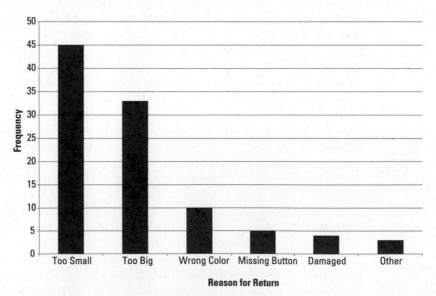

FIGURE 3-3:
A Pareto chart.

Using the Pareto chart, you can quickly identify the vital few events that are causing most of your problems. You can then determine where you should focus improvement efforts.

BONING THE FISH

After you identify an event or events to address, use a cause-and-effect diagram to get to the root cause of an issue. One such tool is the *fishbone* or *Ishikawa* diagram. As the name implies, the diagram resembles the skeleton of a fish (see Figure 3-4).

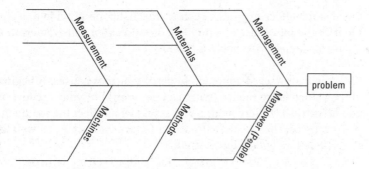

FIGURE 3-4:
A fishbone diagram.

At the head of the diagram is a statement of the problem. If, for example, you discover from a Pareto chart that a top reason for customer returns is that parts are missing from the package, "Missing parts" would become the problem statement in the fishbone diagram.

Running along the central spine is a list of what could cause parts to be missing from the package. These causes are grouped into categories that make up sections, and each section can contain one or more specific causes.

Although the categories can vary, many companies use the six Ms to separate the causes:

>> **Machines:** The state or characteristics of the equipment required to perform the operations

>> **Management:** The policies and procedures that govern the company

>> **Manpower:** The people performing the operation, and the training or ability of the workers

>> **Materials:** The raw materials that go into the process and the tools or materials required to complete the operation

>> **Measurement:** The ways and accuracy of measuring the process

>> **Methods:** The how's of the process or the process steps necessary to complete the task

REMEMBER

When building a diagram, remember that these categories are flexible. However, make sure that you cover everything. A good fishbone diagram contains many sections from the spine, and each section should contain its own cluster of bones projecting from it.

ANALYZING FAILURE MODES

Cause-and-effect diagrams such as the fishbone provide a useful visual tool to identify the root cause of a problem. Another root cause determination tool is the *failure mode and effects analysis* (FMEA).

REMEMBER

FMEA is a structured approach to getting at root causes. It begins by identifying all possible failure modes (what can go wrong) of your product or process. After you identify the failure modes, you assess what effect the failure mode would have if it occurred, the likelihood that the failure will occur, as well as the likelihood that the failure will be undetected.

Rank each failure mode on three dimensions and give each dimension a value of 1 to 10. Here are the dimensions and the rating systems:

>> **Severity (SEV):** How significantly does the failure affect the customer? A ranking of 1 indicates that the customer probably won't notice the effect or considers it insignificant; a ranking of 10 indicates a catastrophic event such as a customer injury.

>> **Occurrence (OCC):** How likely is the cause of this failure to occur? A ranking of 1 indicates that it isn't likely; a ranking of 10 means that failures nearly always occur.

>> **Detectability (DET):** What are the odds that the failure will be discovered? A ranking of 1 means that the defect will most certainly be detected before reaching the customer; a ranking of 10 indicates that the failure will most likely go out undetected.

After you determine the rankings, calculate a risk priority number (RPN), which is simply the product of the three rankings:

$$RPN = SEV \cdot OCC \cdot DET$$

The higher the RPN, the more critical the failure mode and the greater need for taking action. As a final step, after implementing corrective action, be sure to reevaluate the failure mode.

WARNING

FMEA is a powerful tool for analyzing possible failure modes of products and processes. But take care when using the FMEA methodology. This ranking system is very subjective because it relies on the opinions of the employees taking part in the activity and results may be biased.

Correlating the variables

It's a safe bet to assume that every outcome will be the result of two or more factors. Therefore, you can't study variables in isolation. Analyzing the correlation among variables is a significant component of Six Sigma projects.

Correlation is the degree to which two or more attributes show a tendency to vary together. A positive correlation means that the attributes move in the same direction — up or down. A negative correlation means that the attributes move in opposite directions; one goes up and the other goes down.

CHARTING CORRELATION

The simplest tool for looking at correlation between variables is the *correlation chart,* which plots two factors together and shows the visual relationship. Figure 3-5 shows a correlation chart with a positive correlation.

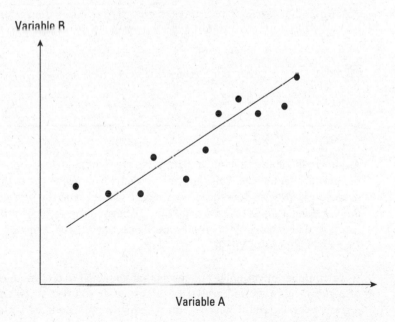

Variable B

Variable A

FIGURE 3-5:
A correlation
chart.

DESIGNING EXPERIMENTS

Correlation charts are useful when looking at two variables, but a more powerful tool is necessary when multiple variables can interact. *Design of experiments* (DOE) is a methodology in which you change the levels of one or more factors according to a predesigned plan and then record the outcome of each experiment.

You can use a properly conducted DOE to identify the effect of the variables independently or the effect of the variables' interaction. In a typical DOE, you assign several levels of each variable and conduct experiments by changing the levels of each variable. Table 3-2 shows a DOE with three variables (X, Y, and Z) and two levels for each variable (H and L). When conducting the experiments, you want to randomize the order in which you test.

TABLE 3-2

Design of Experiments

Experiment Number	X	Y	Z
4	H	H	H
6	H	H	L
1	H	L	H
8	H	L	L
5	L	H	H
3	L	H	L
7	L	L	H
2	L	L	L

As shown in Table 3-2, eight experiments are required to capture all combinations of variables and levels. You can then statistically analyze the data using a variety of methods to determine the effects of each variable and the interactions that exist among them. Details on how to do this are beyond the scope of this book. If you're interested in exploring this topic, check out *Statistics For Dummies,* 2nd Edition, by Deborah J. Rumsey (Wiley).

As the number of variables and levels that you want to test increases, the number of experiments required grows. For example, if you test three variables at three different levels, you'd have to run 27 experiments; four variables at two levels would require 16 experiments.

In general, the number of experiments in a full factorial design is equal to

$$\text{Number of experiments} = \text{Number of levels}^{\text{number of variables}}$$

Fractional factorial methods can help reduce the number of experiments without sacrificing statistical results. However, you must choose how you conduct these experiments carefully because they all carry some risk in accuracy; they do not account for all interactions of the variables.

Implementing a solution

After you identify the root cause of the problem, you need to select and implement a solution. Chances are the problem has many solutions. So a decision matrix can help you decide which solution to pursue.

REMEMBER

A *decision matrix*, often called a *Pugh matrix*, evaluates alternative solutions by comparing each along a series of objectives. Often, the current method serves as a baseline.

Say your team comes up with three solutions (A, B, and C) to a problem. Follow these steps to construct a decision matrix (see example in Table 3-3):

1. **Select the solutions you want to evaluate**

   Find out what improvement you can expect from each solution. The solutions are listed in the top row of the matrix in Table 3-3.

2. **Decide what the criteria for evaluation are.**

   Choose the most important criteria that relate to the issues that made you decide to focus your efforts on the project. The criteria are listed in the first column of the matrix in Table 3-3.

3. **Score each solution against each of the criteria.**

   Always give the baseline a score of 0. Typically, a 3-point scale is great for this, but if more differentiation among the solutions is desirable, you can use a 5-point scale (as shown in Table 3-3). In a 5-point scale, use the following numbers:

+2	Much better than baseline
+1	Better than baseline
0	Equal to baseline
−1	Worse than baseline
−2	Much worse than baseline

4. **Rate the importance of the criteria if necessary.**

   If one or more of the decision criteria are considered more critical than the others, you can assign a weight to each. Then multiply the score from Step 3 by the criteria ranking, giving it a final score. The matrix in Table 3-3 omits this step.

5. **Sum the assigned scores.**

   Add the scores for each solution along the criteria to get a net score.

6. **Choose your solution.**

   In most cases, you want to choose the solution with the highest score. (In Table 3-3, for example, solution B is best.) If all alternatives score less than zero, the baseline (current) process is considered the best option. You may want to consider other solutions if the current batch doesn't offer improvements worth the cost of implementation.

Keep in mind that rating the criteria, as described in Step 4, may have a great effect on your solution decision. For example, if you rate the importance of criteria 1 in Table 3-3 higher than the others, solution C may well end up being the preferred solution.

TABLE 3-3   ## Decision Matrix

Criteria	Baseline	A	B	C
1	0	+2	+1	+2
2	0	0	+1	+2
3	0	+1	+2	−1
4	0	−1	0	0
Total	0	+2	+4	+3

Maintaining the gain

After you analyze the situation, identify root causes, and implement the new process, you must continue to monitor the new process to assure that you maintain the improvements you've achieved. One statistical method you can use to do this is the *process control chart*.

Two other tools, the run chart and the histogram, are also used to monitor the process. These tools are easy to set up and maintain and don't require the statistical calculations found in a control chart.

The *run chart* plots an individual metric over time and makes it easy to spot trends and patterns over time. Figure 3-6 shows a sample run chart.

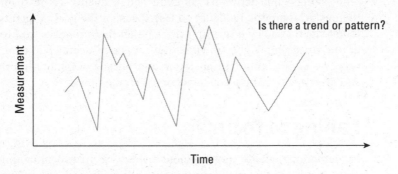

FIGURE 3-6:
A sample
run chart.

Here are some things to look for in a run chart that may indicate an unstable or problem process:

>> **Cluster:** Several observations surrounding a certain value

>> **Mean shift:** Several observations above or below the process average

>> **Oscillations:** Observations that go up and down with recognizable frequency

>> **Trends:** Several observations in a row that all go up or down

A *histogram* displays the frequency of different measurements. As shown in Figure 3-7, the histogram shows the distribution of the measurements and highlights measurements that are considered outliers from the rest. Histograms are useful to identify special cause variation.

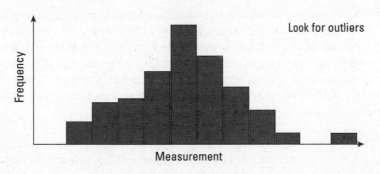

FIGURE 3-7:
A sample
histogram.

Overcoming Obstacles

Many things stand between a company and its quality-centered end game. Among the obstacles are the tendency to lose focus on the goal of quality improvement, to get sidetracked by a seeming silver bullet that promises to solve all the quality issues, or to simply give up when the gains don't come fast enough. In this section, we explore common obstacles and pitfalls of quality improvement efforts and offer advice to help you avoid or overcome them.

Failing to focus

Implementing quality improvement requires a great deal of time and commitment. A mistake that many organizations make is to jump headfirst into too many projects. At the start of the journey, everyone is excited about the potential that quality improvement promises, and the firm may embark on several projects at a time. This reduces the focus on any one project and often stretches resources too thin.

Instead, we advise that you start by choosing a project that involves a process that employees have a lot of knowledge about and understand well. This helps ensure that the results are successful and encourages others to get behind future projects.

When adding projects, choose carefully. Tools such as the Pareto chart (see the "Charting the causes" section, earlier in the chapter) can help you select the most important issues to address.

Prioritizing into paralysis

Some companies fall into the trap of spending so much time on prioritizing potential projects that they never get down to the real work. When selecting projects, companies typically rank them based on anticipated benefit, which is often the expected *return on investment* (ROI). This often leads to disagreement across the organization as to which project is the most important and should get first priority. And as you may know, benefits data — especially expected ROI — is easy to manipulate.

TIP

Don't get caught in this trap. If you must choose between two or more improvement projects that have roughly the same value, just choose one and get started. Completing any project that provides benefit to the business is much better than waiting to find the perfect project.

You may want to start with the project that's easiest and quickest to implement. A quick victory at the beginning of a quality improvement initiative can provide momentum to the organization on future projects.

Falling for the lure of magical solutions

Falling victim to the silver bullet quality program happens to the best of'em. Magical, fix-it-all, pain-free programs are usually touted as the program that is going to save the company, but easy, catch-all solutions often involve a consulting agency coming into the company with grand ideas and beautiful presentations that are likely to fail because they don't follow the proven methods (outlined in this chapter). After a few months with few results, firms that embrace such programs often end up moving on to the next program that promises quick and easy results.

This approach may ultimately sabotage your quality improvement efforts. Employees become tired and complacent about these programs, and they dismiss future programs as a waste of time; after all, none of the past programs ever panned out very well.

Lacking employee involvement

For quality improvement projects to be successful, all levels of an organization must commit to the effort. This means all employees must understand the importance of the quality projects and contribute to their success.

Employees sometimes view improvement efforts as a threat to their job security or as an examination into whether they can do the job. Therefore, when identifying and implementing any process changes, be sure to consult with and educate the people involved with performing the process targeted for improvement. Often, just knowing why the change is being made is enough to earn buy-in from the employees.

Not knowing what to do

One of the biggest obstacles to quality success is not knowing what to do if a process is discovered to be *out of control,* or unstable. Setting up and monitoring the control charts require significant time and resources. Employees must take samples, perform the necessary observations and measurements, and record the results on the chart. That's the easy part.

WARNING

What happens when a sample indicates that the process has changed and is now out of control? That's the hard part. A company must establish procedures and train employees to enact them to deal with an out-of-control situation. Failure to act or acting inappropriately won't lead to improved quality and may even make the situation worse.

Not learning from the experience

Few firms make the effort to learn from past quality projects. After completing a project, companies often just move on to the next effort and lose what they learned from the last one. Projects should have a formal documentation process (often called *after-action* or *after-project review*) to record what happened, what the results were, and why.

Companies should also conduct after-project reviews to share project lessons. But don't limit these reviews to the project team; include personnel who may be working on other projects so they can duplicate successes and learn from mistakes.

Calling it a program

A *program* implies something that has a defined beginning and end. Quality improvement shouldn't be a program; it should occur naturally as part of the everyday job. Quality must become institutionalized and become an underlying foundation for the company. Without this shift in culture, true quality success is only a passing dream.

Giving up

Achieving improvement and implementing change is a slow, continuous process. It doesn't happen overnight. Expecting instant improvements is a recipe for disaster, and giving up too quickly because your first efforts don't produce the desired results only leads to failure. But with continual focus and a commitment to the methods and tools presented in this book, you *will* see improvement. Stick with it!

3

Decision-Making

Contents at a Glance

Chapter **1**

The Key Ingredients for Effective Decisions

D ecision-making is rarely logical, despite assertions that it's based on rational thinking. Different ideas don't have a chance when they fail to fit into what decision-makers believe will or won't work. Just ask anyone who has ever put together a perfectly good proposal on how to increase profitability only to have the proposal shot down. Nor can innovation take place when decision-makers are unaware of how thinking influences perspective or risk perception.

Knowing what is going on under the surface drives results and gives you a chance to improve and adjust. In this chapter, we introduce you to decision-making styles and discuss what the rational mind can't see when it comes to risk perception. We also show you the three key elements that make decisions effective: a common language, the workplace culture, and your self-knowledge.

Distinguishing the Different Kinds of Decisions

The kinds of decisions you face fall anywhere on a spectrum from strategic to operational or frontline. If you're a small business owner — until you add staff and distribute responsibility, that is — you make decisions across the full spectrum. If you're in a medium-sized to large company, the kinds of decisions you face depend on how your organization distributes decision-making authority and responsibility: centralized at the top or decentralized through all levels, for example. In addition, the type of decisions you're responsible for depends on your role in the company. In this section, we describe the different kinds of business decisions. Each kind of decision calls for a different kind of thinking and decision-making style.

REMEMBER

Traditionally, big companies are organized hierarchically, with authority allocated at each level of management down to the front line. In theory, direction comes from the top and moves down through the company for implementation. The speed and complexity of the business environment challenges this way of assigning decision-making power because it is slow. Still, this is the prevalent organizational style; even medium-sized companies lean toward using the combination of hierarchy and authority. For that reason, in this section, we lay out ways that decisions are typically thought or talked about. Different organizational structures and sources may use different terminology.

Strategic decisions

Strategic decisions are executive-level decisions. Strategic decisions are made in every area, from IT (information technology), HR (human resources), finance, and CRM (customer relations), for example. Strategic decisions look ahead to the longer term and direct the company to its destiny. They tend to be high risk and high stakes. They are complex and rely on intuition supported by information based on analysis and experience. When you face a strategic decision, you may have time to consider options reinforced by the gathered information, or you may have moments to decide.

To make good strategic-level decisions, you need to be comfortable working with a lot of information and have the ability to see the interrelationships among the company and its employees, clients, suppliers, and the communities it reaches. You need to be collaborative, in touch with what is going on, open-minded, and flexible without being wishy-washy. You can read more about what you rely on as a decision-maker in Chapter 3 of this minibook.

Tactical decisions

Tactical decisions translate strategic decisions into action. Tactical decisions are more straightforward and less complex than strategic-level decisions. When they are in alignment with your company's core values or its overall mission, tactical decisions add even more value to the outcomes of the implementation. Conversely, if tactical decisions become detached from the company's direction, you and your employees end up expending a lot of effort on tasks that don't help the company achieve its goals or vision.

Tactical decisions fall in the scope of middle management. Middle managers are the proverbial meat in the sandwich; they make things happen. In vertically organized hierarchies, middle managers translate top-level decisions into goals that can be operationalized.

Operational and frontline decisions

Operational and frontline decisions are made daily. Many operational decisions are guided by company procedures and processes, which help new employees get up to speed and serve as a backdrop for more experienced employees, who, having mastered the current procedures and processes, can detect and rapidly collate additional information, such as cues, patterns, and sensory data, that aren't covered by the procedures. For example, master mechanics are able to apply procedures and specifications to fix a problem, and their accumulated experiences (and intuition) strengthen their troubleshooting abilities. Detecting subtleties is an intuitive intelligence. The effect is faster and more accurate diagnosis or assessment of a particular situation.

WARNING

Because conditions are more concrete and predictable, operational and frontline decisions as a rule hold less risk strategically and tend to follow a more routine pattern. But therein lies the danger: They can hold more risk for health and safety for the simple reason that complacency sets in, and people become less alert.

Identifying the Different Decision-Making Styles

What kind of decision-maker are you? To help you find out, we explain the different styles of decision-making. These styles are conveniently labeled, but how you apply them depends on each situation you're in and the people you're with. The following is a list of decision-making styles, which we've drawn from the work of Kenneth Brousseau, CEO of Decision Dynamics:

>> **Decisive:** With decisive decision-makers, time is of the essence. Their mantra is "Get things done quickly and consistently, and stick to the plan." This decision-making style applies one course of action, using relatively little information. Being decisive comes in handy in emergency situations or when you have to clearly communicate operational-level health and safety decisions.

- » **Flexible:** Flexible decision-makers are focused on speed and adaptability. They acquire just enough data to decide what to do next and are willing to change course if needed. This decision-making style works with several options that can change or be replaced as new information becomes available. Being flexible comes in handy when you have to make decisions in dynamic, uncertain situations. Flexible decision-making is relevant to all levels of decision-making.

- » **Hierarchic:** Hierarchic decision-makers analyze a lot of information and seek input from others. They like to challenge differing views or approaches and value making decisions that will withstand scrutiny. After their minds are made up, their decisions are final. This decision-making style incorporates lots of information to produce one option. This characteristic can be handy, depending on the application; financial forecasting and capital procurement decisions come to mind.

- » **Integrative:** Integrative decision-makers take into account multiple elements and work with lots of input. They cultivate a wider perspective of the situation and invite a wide range of views (even ones with which they don't agree). They flex as changes arise until time is up and a decision must be made. This decision-making style uses lots of information and produces lots of options. It's handy for executive-level or managerial decision-making in fast-moving, dynamic conditions where the decision has a big impact on people or resources.

If you don't feel like you fit into any one of the decision-making characteristics we list here, rest assured. First, you bring more than what is described here to the business decision-making process. Second, these styles are not exclusive: You may use characteristics of more than one style, or you may use different styles in different situations.

REMEMBER

Your approach to decision-making must change as you move into different levels of responsibility and into new decision-making territory. What works at the operational level, for example, is a disaster at the strategic level. To change your mindset as a decision-maker, you must be willing to increase your flexibility and flex your brain muscles. You must let go of what you're comfortable with to enter different decision-making territory, which will expand your decision-making skill.

Recognizing the Workplace Environment and Culture as a Force

Workplace health and effective decision-making are linked. We'll spare you the details (are you relieved?). Suffice it to say that the workplace environment directly guides your decisions. This was a key point in Malcolm Gladwell's book *Blink: The Power of Thinking without Thinking* (Back Bay Books), in which he explains what he calls the *power of context.* In a nutshell, the simple question "Am I safe or unsafe?" can trigger growth (when you feel safe) or protection and risk aversion (when you feel unsafe).

One of the biggest mistakes companies make is not paying attention to how workplace environment and cultural assumptions and beliefs influence decision-making. Fortunately, more and more are becoming aware that healthy cultures and environments that are both emotionally and physically safe produce better decisions. In this section, we show you how growth impacts decision-making and workplace health and explain how the design of the organization affects how decisions get made.

Mapping your company on the innovation curve

A company's culture is revealed in the quality of the workplace relationships and how well the company treats change or handles the unexpected. One way to find out whether your company embraces or fears change is to determine where it falls on the innovation curve. In this section, we tell you what the innovation curve is and what it can reveal about you and your company.

Introducing the innovation curve

A company's position on the innovation curve indicates how it thinks about, embraces, or adapts to change. On one end of the innovation curve are Innovators; on the other end are Laggards:

REMEMBER

>> **Innovators:** A small percentage (2.5 percent) of companies and decision makers fall into this category. They break the rules because, as far as they're concerned, there are no rules. They instigate *disruptive technologies,* technologies that change how people live and see the world. Innovators brought us downloadable music, Google Maps, and social networking. Innovators are incubators for start-up companies that thrive on the edge of uncertainty and boldly lead where no other company has gone before.

Question for you: How long did it take you to experiment with social media in your business? When did your business get its Facebook page or start monitoring customer feedback on Yelp.com? The longer you took to explore the effects of new technology on your business, the further behind you become, exposing your company to greater uncertainty.

- » **Early adopters:** Early adopters are people and companies who are quick to grasp a good idea when they see one. They prefer to lead, not follow, and they aren't afraid to invent or adopt different ways of doing things if doing so gives them an edge. About 13.5 percent of people and businesses fall into this category. They are risk takers.

- » **Early majority:** People and companies in this category are open to change as long as it doesn't rock the boat too much. They operate in the zone between the early adopters and the late majority folks, veering back and forth between the two. They want innovation, but only after the bugs have been ironed out. Their business culture can be in transformation for several reasons, one of which is that they are moving from a command-and-control structure to a more adaptive and flexible culture.

- » **Late majority:** People in this group, which constitutes 34 percent of people and companies, prefer to wait until they feel absolutely certain about what is going on. Results have to be consistent before they feel comfortable introducing new ideas into their culture. When it's no longer practical to resist, they'll transplant an idea from elsewhere but will do so without adapting it to fit. If this quick fix fails, which is highly probable, they blame the idea rather than examine how the implementation process may have sabotaged their success. Late majority companies prefer to avoid risk and prevent mistakes, value perfectionism and predictability, and don't like surprises. They have a low level of trust in their employees' abilities and insert tons of controls to ensure that no one colors outside the lines. (Note that some of these characteristics also apply to early majority companies that still have one foot stuck in old habits.)

- » **Laggards:** The laggards are the real old-timers who prefer to use a rotary phone, still fax messages, and don't know how to turn on a computer. Get the picture? About 16 percent of people and companies fall into this category.

Companies that don't manage their cultures can unintentionally punish or block the creativity and innovation they expect employees to deliver. In the next section, we tell you how to avoid creating this issue.

Building a culture that values innovation

Over-controlling cultures block innovation, which is a product of flexible thinking and a company's mind-set, as well as the ability to spot insights.

An unexpected event or a disruption to the routine can be an opportunity to take a serious look at processes that stymie progress, to reinvent how things get done, and to open the door to creative solutions. Answering the following questions can shed light on how tightly you control situations and data rather than allow intuition or insight to prevail:

>> **Do you have excessive procedures and processes in place to control how things get done?** If you or your company put too many controls in place, you foster an environment that isn't conducive to innovation.

>> **Do you listen to or ignore information that doesn't fit the norm or red flags that an employee may raise?** If you ignore information that doesn't fit your or your company's beliefs or business culture, you are missing the moment to adapt, check for ethical issues, or discover a totally different approach to routine situations.

>> **To what extent do you trust your employees to do what is required to achieve a goal?** Put simply, in low-trust workplace cultures, employees become conditioned to not take initiative or innovate. Conversely, high-trust workplaces foster employee initiative; they trust their employees to get the job done.

>> **Do you punish mistakes or use failures to learn?** Trust and the ability to learn from failure are part of an Innovator's tool kit; they are also key indicators of whether your organization has the capacity for flexibility.

WARNING

Perfectionism can undermine your company's ability to adapt. Companies that seek perfection squelch creativity and insight. To avoid this trap, try to cultivate a culture that instills higher levels of trust in individuals. This, combined with the organization's collective talent, can counterbalance fear of mistakes.

REMEMBER

When you move closer to the Innovator category, you shift perspective. Instead of seeing a mistake as a failure, you treat it as another step in the experimentation process. Had 3M been locked into perfection, the Post-it Note wouldn't exist. Post-it Notes came about when a glue that was being formulated wasn't sticky enough — a happy accident born out of a production mistake. Similarly, Thomas Edison, who was told he was too stupid to learn anything, viewed his 1,000 attempts to invent the light bulb as 1,000 steps rather than failures. When you become an Innovator, you adopt the spirit of patience and perseverance by staying focused on the goal.

Accounting for company organizational structures

The number of employees impacts a company's organizational structure. When companies are small, working relationships and roles are more transparent to everyone. Making decisions is a matter of agreeing on what tool will be used in relation to the importance of the decision. As the number of employees increases, decision-makers recognize a need to organize how work gets done, yet unless an intentional decision is made to choose how to organize, companies tend to fall back on a hierarchical decision-making structure that distributes decision-making to different levels of authority. The problem with command-and-control structures is that, as a company continues to grow, such structures are too slow to make or implement decisions in fast-changing situations.

At the point where a company feels the need to organize working relationships, it can choose a different structure, one in which everyone is responsible and accountable for achieving the mission of the company. This option is one that many companies are exploring.

Organizational challenges and company size

For effective and participatory decision-making, relationships must be stable and people must know whom to go to — and this is where size comes into play. In theory, at a certain point, an organization just becomes too large to accommodate those kinds of relationships. So what's the tipping point? According to Robin Dunbar, a British anthropologist, it's about 150. In fact, there seem to be two points at which companies alter how work gets done: when they grow beyond 50 employees and when they grow beyond 150 employees. In the following list, we outline the organizational challenges businesses of different sizes face:

>> **From 1 to 50 employees:** Companies of this size can take two approaches to organization: They can implement an organizational structure right at the beginning by agreeing on how decisions will be made and what kind of organization would work effectively, and by selecting the clientele profile they want to work with. Or they can wait until things get so dysfunctional that the business is at risk of failure and they're forced to put systems in place.

>> **From 50 to 150 employees:** If you haven't made clear decisions on how you'll decide or whom you'll engage in different kinds of decisions, you must do so now. Consider this your company's awkward teenage stage. By putting in place systems and processes, you help your company graduate from winging it to being more organized. Gaining employee engagement in gathering or relaying market intelligence keeps a company current with new developments. Similarly, supplier relations become an integral part of reputation-building, so making sure your employees have shared commitment to quality and customers reduces risk as your company continues to grow.

>> **More than 150 employees:** At this stage in a company's growth, whatever decisions a company has made about how it gets things done stabilize and settle. Dunbar's rule, noted earlier, states that in groups with more than 150 members, relationships destabilize. One solution, used by W. L. Gore, a sportswear manufacturing company with 10,000 employees, is to work in units of 150. This structure enables the company to gain flexibility without sacrificing growth.

REMEMBER

Not all companies run into the 150 rule. Companies that use a self-management model organize around how work gets done. They set up clearly defined roles and accountabilities long before they reach the 150 employee stage. Self-managing companies, such as the world's largest tomato processing company, Morning Star (400 employees), has strong processes and agreements in place that allow them to grow while maintaining clear guidelines for internal relationships and decision-making.

Reviewing organizational options for small and medium-sized companies

Basically, you can organize people by their relationship and expertise to a specific function, or you can organize how work gets done. The distinction separates a traditional structure, which aims to manage people, from one that organizes how each person contributes to the achievement of the overall mission of the company. Autonomy and self-managing are built in to a governance approach that centers on individual and collective achievement of a mission.

Organizations are made of relationships, so you have options around how to arrange the relationships in your company so that decision-making is participatory and effective. If you run a company that has fewer than 150 employees, you have several organizational options; which of these options will work best for your company depends on what you hope to achieve for employees and customers:

TIP

» **Establish a self-management structure.** This self-managed approach brings in more structure, not around who has power but around how each person contributes to the mission.

Follow the lead of Morning Star, which has worked out the agreements and accountabilities necessary to operate with 400 employees. You'll find sample contracts on http://www.self-managementinstitute.org.

» **Create job titles to designate areas of responsibility, and then decentralize the decision-making, using clearly defined participatory decision-making processes.** The functional lead accepts accountability but works as a peer with his or her team to bring value to the company and customer. Remaining open to hearing feedback from employees and customers keeps your decision-making in stride with emerging requirements.

» **Designate job titles, areas of responsibility, and accountability, and then delegate specific levels of decision-making authority to each level of management.** This is the organizational structure that most businesses are accustomed to. It centers on an organization in which a manager exercises control over people to get work done.

At the very least, give some thought to your decision-making structure. If you don't make the decision intentionally, the traditional hierarchical business structure (the one where decision-making resides at top echelons and is handed down from on high) becomes the default decision-making structure. In this situation, areas of responsibility, such as marketing or human resources, are often assigned to a lead. Competitive silos and groups of power can form, distracting attention away from performance goals.

Choosing a structure conducive to fast growth

The traditional approach in pyramid-style company organizations is to assign decision-making authority to each level of command and to mandate that each lower level must ferry the decision up to the next before approval is granted. This structure is too slow to be effective when change is occurring quickly.

To combat this, some growing companies purposely select a decision-making process that fits their values: They either decentralize or use participatory decision-making processes in which the final decision rests with the lead person. These approaches, which promote making decisions as a community, give a company greater flexibility and match company growth with company values. This kind of structure works well for small companies and, if done well, it can also work well in medium-sized companies that prefer the flexibility that comes with self-organizing and the autonomy that comes with personal responsibility.

Morning Star is a pioneer of the flat organizational approach. (You can read more about the flat organizational approach at http://www.self-managementinstitute. org.) Another innovative company is gaming company Valve, which employs a self-organizing structure based on the *wisdom of crowds,* the idea that the many are collectively smarter than the few. Valve has turned this concept into a uniquely creative approach to customer and employee relationships and decision-making. To read more about this theory, check out James Surowiecki's book *The Wisdom of Crowds* (Anchor).

The strongest innovators are found in the technology sector and come from young entrepreneurs who haven't gotten locked into a conventional way of thinking. If you're looking for new ways of thinking that also seem to scale nicely, explore what companies such as Cocoon Projects in Italy are doing, for instance. For more information visit http://cocoonprojects.com/en/ or http://LiquidOrganization.info.

Putting together your decision-making structure

The best organizational structure is one that offers clarity, flexibility, solid processes, and agreements about how decisions are made; clear communication regarding goals; and ways to monitor and provide feedback. Such structures create the stable framework upon which working relationships can function effectively.

The methods you put in place must be clear, thoughtful, and intentional, and you must be willing to adjust as your company's relationships evolve. To agree on the decision-making process you want to work with internally, follow these steps:

1. **List all the decisions you typically make in a day, week, month, or quarter.**

2. **Identify who is best positioned to make the decisions you list in Step 1, based on speed, access to information, or other key criteria.**

3. **For each type of decision, create guidelines for which people to include, which process to use, and which shared company values apply to the decision-making process.**

   Include the following kinds of information in your guidelines:

   - **The decision-making tools to be used:** Select and apply your own principles to fit your business. If a decision-making tool such as dot voting will work, use it. If you need something more sophisticated, select a tool that fits the importance of the decision and the need for employee input. Cocoon Projects, for example, applies the principle of using the smallest tool possible to get the job done.

REMEMBER

   By matching the decision-making tool to the kind of decision, you replace random decision-making with a process that ideally ensures employee contribution, resolves issues quickly, and is relevant to the situation. In short, you gain speed and accuracy.

   - **The amount of time allocated for each level of decision:** This timeline marks the time available from input through to the final decision. Some decisions, depending on their magnitude, may take no more than a few minutes; others may take weeks or months.

   - **Guidelines regarding employee involvement:** These guidelines would cover how long and in what capacity employees participate in the decision-making process.

TIP

As you create your process, keep these suggestions in mind:

>> Decentralize decision-making so that the people with real-time information are the ones making the decisions.

>> Use technology to ensure that internal information flows openly.

>> Let go of decisions that are better made elsewhere. Doing so frees your desk of decisions that frontline employees are better qualified to make. If you find it difficult to give away control, read the upcoming section "Developing the Decision-Maker: To Grow or Not."

Assessing the health of the workplace

A company is a community of people, each having unlimited potential, who agree to work with others. The quality of the interactions and relationships within the workplace dictates what gets done and how well. So when the workplace isn't healthy, neither is the company.

An unhealthy company is not an environment conducive to sound decision-making. Therefore, it's important to monitor the health of your company. Here are a few key indicators:

>> **Stress-related illness:** Frequent incidences of stress-related illness suggest that a company's workplace is unhealthy. This doesn't mean that a small business should panic if someone calls in sick. But if the employee repeatedly calls in sick, take the time to look more deeply.

>> **Ethical versus unethical decision-making:** The business culture can reinforce ethical behavior or encourage unethical behavior. The following conditions influence the likelihood of ethical decision-making:

- **A person's well-being and sense of security:** Do employees feel valued? Are they part of an important endeavor? Companies that demonstrate care and compassion for employees emphasize well-being and sustain an environment for ethical decisions.

- **Workplace conditions:** How well do your employees relate to one another? The healthier the workplace, the higher the probability of ethical decisions. Companies that don't pay attention to the workplace environment set themselves up for poor decisions at every level but more likely at the top.

- **How power is used:** How much influence do employees have on the company's direction and relationships?

Developing the Decision-Maker: To Grow or Not?

Today, the lines between private and public life and between work and personal time are blurred, and it's easy to lose touch with what is important to you and to what you want from life. Beliefs you're unaware of also get in the way of your changing course, even when you want to. They can also prevent you from recognizing changes that are going on around you, putting you and your company in a vulnerable position.

To counter these forces so that you can become the manager and leader you want to be and effectively manage in diverse environments, decision-making today demands that you expand your self-awareness and become more flexible in your thinking.

Knowing thyself

All the tools and techniques in the world don't make you a better decision-maker or communicator. To become a better decision-maker, you must know yourself. Consider that you play the most important role in effective decision-making for these simple reasons:

>> You take yourself with you wherever you go. In other words, whether you make a decision through a knee-jerk reaction (who hasn't?) or take a more deliberate approach, the information you receive is interpreted through filters that you use to make sense of reality. You must know what those filters are because you can't get away from yourself when you're making decisions. This is why knowing yourself — being aware of your triggers, your beliefs (both conscious and unconscious), your assumptions, your preferences, and so on — is so important to *your* being able to make effective decisions.

>> Your communication skills and style dictate how effective you are in your interaction and relationships with your colleagues and subordinates.

Avoiding temptations that obstruct sound decisions

Company performance and achievement of goals get traded off when key decision-makers — often in executive, management, or supervisory roles — give into one or more temptations, such as the following:

>> **Putting career aspirations ahead of the company's success:** When you succumb to this temptation, your priority is to protect your career status or reputation. Examples include taking credit for someone else's idea or failing to recognize another's contribution. Although people who engage in this behavior say that this is just how business gets done, it's unethical, and the consequence is that lousy decisions get made. Turf wars result, and any attempts to improve the situation result in defensiveness. The opportunity you have is to help others succeed, which helps you succeed as well. If the company culture doesn't reward achievement of goals, a leadership and cultural overhaul may be in order.

» **Insisting on absolutely correct decisions to achieve certainty:** When management yields to this temptation, there is no tolerance for error, especially human error. The result? Employees feel set up for failure. There is never enough information to finally decide (100 percent certainty is an unattainable goal), and confusing directions to employees combined with the desire to make the right decision can result in procrastination and delay. Ultimately, companies that succumb to this temptation lose out to more agile and flexible companies. The cure for this temptation is to trust in yourself and your team to creatively achieve results, which involves learning from mistakes.

» **Letting the desire for peace and harmony in the workplace result in avoiding conflict and being uncomfortable with delivering unexpected news:** The problems? First, the harmony you're so intent on preserving is fake. Relationships seem friendly on the surface, but people will release their frustrations in nonproductive ways, such as backstabbing around the water cooler. Second, this environment is conducive to poor decision-making simply because good decisions need diverse views and perspectives to be out in the open for discussion. When no one wants to talk about the big issues, decision-making is severely compromised.

To cure this temptation, flip the perspective on conflict. Don't see it as bad; see it simply as a way to look at things from a different perspective. Allow your decision-making conversations to air diverse perspectives on the issue, and have a zero-tolerance policy for personal attacks or the belittling of others' ideas — behaviors that are distracting and destructive when you want to gain value from the different thinking in the room. In Chapter 2 of this minibook, we explain how to use different perspectives to generate options for consideration.

TIP

Courage is needed to grow as a decision-maker. To read a fable on how these temptations show up in business environments, see *The Five Temptations of a CEO: A Leadership Fable,* by Patrick Lencioni (Jossey-Bass).

IN THIS CHAPTER

» **Identifying why a decision needs to be made**

» **Amassing and analyzing data**

» **Generating viable options and making the final decision**

» **Communicating and implementing the decision**

» **Understanding intuitive decision-making**

Chapter **2**

Walking through the Decision-Making Process

As a decision-maker, you face all kinds of situations in your business, and each situation calls for a different decision-making approach. Some approaches are rational and analytical; some are more intuitive. Despite their differences, both rational thought and intuitive thought gather and make sense of information in an attempt to arrive at the best course of action.

Whatever approach you use, you can benefit from understanding the basic steps to making sound decisions. In fact, for every decision you make, you'll touch on — accidentally or intentionally — the steps we outline in this chapter. We also show how your intuition enables you to make rapid-fire decisions in quickly changing, high-risk situations.

Clarifying the Purpose of the Decision

Being clear on why you're taking action guides implementation. Establishing purpose (the *why*) is a must-do, front-end task because you reduce the risk of mistakes and misunderstandings when circumstances change. Purpose provides the focus for thinking, action, and all the micro-decisions that lead to the result.

Identifying the reason for the decision

Decisions are made for several reasons. In business, the two most common reasons for making a decision and taking action are to address a problem or to seize an opportunity:

>> **Addressing a problem:** Operationally, when equipment isn't working, products aren't delivered on time, or customers don't receive what they ordered when you promised it, it's a problem. When problems occur, you need to take action to find out why the problem exists. In a flower shop, for example, having the fridge that supposed to store today's shipment break down and not having a backup is a problem. The question is, is this simply a mechanical glitch or is the situation far more serious?

>> **Seizing an opportunity:** Opportunities take many forms: a serendipitous encounter with someone who has the potential to become your biggest buyer, for example, or a change in zoning laws in an area where you want to expand. Other opportunities come dressed as problems: Employee disengagement, for example, is an opportunity to create a better workplace. Recognizing opportunities means seeing situations like these not as problems to be solved, but as a chance to do things differently.

When the reason for making the decision is clarified, being super clear about what you're hoping to achieve (the outcome or result) provides the focus for getting there. Make sure you can articulate the following:

>> Why you're taking action now and not later

>> What will be in place when the action plan is complete

>> What conditions you want the solution to meet

REMEMBER

Providing a compelling picture of the desired outcome mobilizes the minds and hearts of employees and other affected parties.

Taking a tactical or strategic approach

Actions can be propelled by urgency (you need to do something fast) or inspired by vision and opportunity in the longer term. Articulating what you want the decision to achieve gives you a good idea about whether you need to take a tactical or strategic approach.

To understand the difference between strategic and tactical actions, consider this situation: The workload at your company has become intolerable, and your employees are stressed and requesting overtime pay. In addressing the problem, you can take a tactical approach or a strategic approach:

>> **Tactical:** You look at options that solve the immediate problem, such as outsourcing some of the work or hiring someone to alleviate the burden on your employees.

>> **Strategic:** You step back to observe how work is being delegated and communicated, how existing resources are being used, and so on, so that you can discover and address what is creating the pressure in the first place. With this knowledge, you can institute changes that in the long run will reduce employees' stress and workload.

WARNING

It's easy to make the pain go away by taking action quickly before you truly understand the situation. Doing so can result in having to revisit the problem when the solution proves to be ineffective. Companies, for example, sometimes fix undesirable employee behavior by sending them off to training rather than exploring what is creating the situation in the system (culture) itself.

Eliciting All Relevant Info

Many decisions that fail do so because they were made using narrow thinking. You don't know what you don't know. Narrow thinking can torpedo your business decisions. Consider the business owner who, when her decisions were questioned, always answered, "I know what I'm doing." She carried on . . . right into bankruptcy. To avoid the dangers of limited thinking, try to gather relevant information from as many different perspectives as possible, especially the ones you disagree with.

In this section, we outline sources of information and tell you how to vet the info you find.

Doing your research

Depending on the issue you're confronting or the reason you're taking action, you may have to conduct extensive research, consult with colleagues who have already successfully faced a similar question, and consult with employees and customers. When doing so, your intention must be to learn rather than to confirm that your own ideas are right. A genuine inquiry builds trust and uncovers key factors critical to decision-making.

The primary goal at this stage of the decision-making process is to look at the situation from as many different angles as you possibly can. Sometimes this task can be difficult, especially when you don't agree with the ideas you hear, but it is well worth doing nonetheless. Doing a thorough job of gathering information gives you a wide variety of viewpoints to consider, uncovers potential pitfalls, and reveals unstated needs that must be addressed if your decision is to be effective.

Following are some ways you can gain the varied insight and information you seek:

>> Monitor and participate in LinkedIn discussions relevant to your business.

>> Subscribe to online newsfeeds such as the *Huffington Post* or other international, national, and regional news outlets.

>> Participate in professional associations where you find your clients and customers.

>> Ask employees, customers, and clients for input and information by using focus groups or surveys.

>> Host information sessions to find out how constituent groups see the situation.

>> Consult with colleagues to find out their views on the project or initiative.

>> Give employees an opportunity to ask questions of people in leadership and management positions in an open and honest fashion.

REMEMBER

The information-gathering stage is typically fluid and fast rather than overly structured.

Gaining distance to stay objective

You can see a situation more clearly when you haven't got your nose in it. For that reason, when you gather information, you want to maintain some distance. Doing so helps you objectively assess the information you receive. You'll be better able to see which questions you need to ask and to recognize who needs to be involved.

Gaining distance is easier said than done, for two reasons:

>> **You have to remember to pull back and reflect.** If you don't build time to reflect into your decision-making process, it won't happen.

>> **You have a blind side — unknown biases or, worse, prejudices — that work against your decision-making.** Chances are you're unaware of these biases in yourself but can spot them easily in others. To avoid being blind-sided by what you can't see in yourself, ask someone you trust to point out when you're overlooking the obvious.

TIP

Your beliefs guide which cues you pay attention to and how you interpret them. Yet your views and perceptions are limited — limited by how much information you've had access to and the experiences you've acquired in your lifetime. Keeping an open mind is a way to maintain a check and balance on your perceptions. It opens your eyes to what others see that you can't. It also helps you be more effective. To ensure that you aren't restricting information to only what you're familiar with, follow these suggestions:

>> **Remain curious.** Approaching each situation with an inquisitive mind expands perception.

>> **Notice when you're being defensive or feel compelled to prove that you're right.** Take these emotional reactions as signals that you're thinking rigidly or feel threatened. They're good indicators that you're overlooking important information that can change how you lead.

Paying attention to different perspectives

Gathering accurate information in a highly interconnected communication environment is challenging, especially because each person can see only a part of the overall picture. What people see depends on their unique perspectives, and what they understand is determined by what they know about their part of the picture. For this reason, you need to pay attention to as many different perspectives as possible. When gathering intelligence, try to do the following:

>> **Use as many different sources as you can.** Take into account personal experience, factual data, and the social and emotional factors that will affect both the decision-making environment and the implementation situation.

>> **Pay attention to conflicting information.** Conflicting info points to holes in the picture and is a signal that you need to keep seeking information from different people. Try asking the kinds of questions a person completely unfamiliar with the topic would ask. This strategy can shine a light on how the different views converge to form the big picture.

> » **Incorporate diverse perspectives, especially ones you may not agree with, into your thinking.** Such perspectives highlight the things you need to consider when making the decision. They also provide insight into the factors that should be addressed when putting together the action and implementation plans.

Separating fact from speculation

Facts — such as the amount of money allocated for a project and the amount spent, the number of employees who work for the company, and the employee turnover rate — can be verified and proven. At some point, however, facts can get mixed up with opinions (based on perceptions) and ideas. The key is being able to discern between them, and the challenge is being able to do so in the midst of change.

When people are in the midst of change and the future is unknown or uncertain, they start guessing about what will happen to feel more certain about what lies ahead. Before long, speculation is running amok because people don't know what to expect or lose confidence in where and how they fit into the changing world.

REMEMBER

When people start filling in the blanks themselves because they don't know how they fit into the company's bigger picture, you know that the company has failed to communicate its intent and the direction of its decisions sufficiently. When you hear speculation, you know that more open communication is necessary and that the decision must take into account the shaky confidence among the company's employees. Whatever you do, don't confuse speculation with information for decision-making.

You can address speculation in two ways:

> » **Find out what people are saying.** Do they see the consequences of the initiative in a positive or negative light? Discover important concerns related to the decision's outcome so that you can address them, if necessary.

> » **Communicate.** Outline what is known and not known. Explain the direction. Doing so helps reduce worry.

Including feelings as information

The idea that humans are logical beings is nice, but it's not realistic. Although facts appeal to the rational mind, feelings guide what people do. Therefore, when you're gathering information, you want to include the emotional environment. Doing so can provide valuable data.

WARNING

When one of your decisions isn't being implemented or, worse, it backfires, chances are you've failed to consider what matters to people. Unless you consider both the emotional needs and the social needs of the people affected by the decision, you risk being out of sync with customer needs or overlooking small things that can make a big difference to employee well-being and performance or to customer loyalty.

You don't find this kind of information in reports or data charts. You find it by making connections with people, being genuinely curious, and listening actively, with your mind — not your mouth — wide open.

Whether you use surveys combined with in-person relationships, engage in joint projects, or facilitate open lines of communication with employees and customers, you can follow these simple strategies to discover what matters to your employees and customers:

>> **Ask questions about what works and what doesn't.** If you're testing a new product, the best way to elicit useful information is to give staff or potential customers the product and find out how it works for them both practically ("Did your clothes come out clean?") and in terms of meeting values or specific preferences ("How did you feel about using the product?"). The responses offer insight into what works and what doesn't for the market you're reaching.

>> **Build trust with your employees so they don't fear reprisal or punishment when they tell you things you'd rather not hear.** Not every business owner is prepared to hear that he or she sounds like Attila the Hun. But you must be able to receive difficult-to-hear information without breaking down into a pool of tears or going into a fit of rage. Neither approach builds confidence or credibility.

>> **Engage with the community by building partnerships with local nonprofits and other local businesses.** Such partnerships provide a steady stream of information on what matters. For example, in the Sustainable Food Lab (https://sustainablefoodlab.org/), companies partner with nonprofits to insert sustainable practices into the food supply chain. This large collaboration, in which the partners bring totally different mind-sets, develops internal leadership skills while simultaneously tackling a bigger issue.

Knowing when you have enough

Gathering information isn't about feeling absolutely certain or waiting until everything is perfect before you act. It is about feeling 80 percent satisfied that you've looked at the situation from as many directions as possible and that you have enough information to make a good decision. Then you're ready to move on. When determining how much information is enough, consider the following factors:

>> **The amount of time you have available:** Stay open to new information until the full-stop deadline for making the final choice arrives.

>> **Whether you're satisfied that you've asked enough questions and have enough information:** You'll know by answering the question, "Do we have enough information to analyze the merits of each option or scenario under consideration?" If your answer is yes, you're good to go.

REMEMBER

Knowing when enough information is enough is never a precise calculation. Only after you reflect on the decision to gain knowledge from the process do you learn, one decision at a time, how to determine how much info you need. Intuitively, you'll most likely feel a sense of calm centered in your gut or heart.

Sifting and Sorting Data: Analysis

After you gather information, the next step is to make sense of it. In short, it's time to analyze the data. Factors that determine how you'll proceed include how much time is available and whether you need to justify your decision to investors, customers, employees, or shareholders.

Conducting your analysis

Follow these steps to sort and analyze the information you've gathered:

1. **Identify the facts, data, and raw numbers relevant to the decision and determine how you'll crunch the numbers so they can inform the decision or selection of options.**

TIP

Big data is the term given to the proliferation and abundance of data decision-makers must consider. Computer programs available for analyzing complex data include spatial, visual, and cloud-based presentations. For an example, see www.spatialdatamining.org/software. You can find a list of the top free data analysis software at www.predictiveanalyticstoday.com/top-data-analysis-software/.

2. **Sort the social and emotional information into themes.**

The themes can be *trends* (the direction for societal preferences), *dynamics* (the interrelationships that exist), and needs or preferences (which point to the underlying values that inform decisions), for example. These things tell you about what lies ahead so that you can predict what the response will be to your decision. Use them as a lens to identify what you need to consider in choosing options, or to ensure that you meet social and emotional needs during the implementation process.

3. **Identify the considerations you see as relevant to either making the decision or implementing it.**

   To synthesize what's important to consider in your decision-making, explore the facts (the rational-logical portion) and what is going on in the situation (feelings/emotions or relationships/social). Pull out the main ideas to use in subsequent steps. You can either use a mind map (a method to visually map related ideas) or you can tuck related ideas under the key points so you can see the relationships between the information you've gathered.

   For example, if you were launching into a new market, as Target did into Canada, you'd want to ask Canadian customers what Target products they prefer. Customer preferences would be a theme; the product, price point, and customer expectations for service would form a part of the background decision-making.

4. **Map out consequences — how the decision will affect staff, customers, employees, and suppliers, for example.**

   Knowing the consequences helps you make adjustments and informs what and how you'll communicate any changes to your listeners, based on what they currently expect or are familiar with.

5. **If you're using a rational decision-making process, select criteria you'll use to consider options before making a final selection.**

   You need to identify the criteria you'll use to assess the options under consideration. Refer to the later section "Establishing and weighing criteria" for details.

By now, you'll know which information is most relevant, whether you're relying exclusively on analysis of the data or combining it with your intuitive know-how. If you're making your decision purely intuitively, you'll use what you perceive to be important and will rely on how the data is presented to pull out key points.

TIP

Throughout your analysis, keep communicating with your team. Doing so not only helps everyone know what is going on, but it also encourages dissenting views and alternative perspectives to come forward.

Critically evaluating your data

Mistakes get made when critical thinking isn't applied. When you think critically, you become your own devil's advocate, so to speak. You examine and reflect on your own thinking and question assumptions or conclusions. If you find critical thinking hard to do solo, enlist a colleague's help or engage the entire team by doing some individual reflection first and then coming together to exchange observations.

To critically evaluate your data, ask these questions:

>> What aren't we saying? What are we overlooking?

>> Where are we making assumptions, or what assumptions are we making?

>> Where are we superimposing our own values and views on top of the information we are looking at?

>> What could possibly go wrong?

WARNING

Critical thinking and skepticism aren't the same, although they can both bring value. Whereas critical thinking is an intellectual exercise that challenges the validity of an idea to test its worthiness, skepticism is a whole different kettle of fish. When skepticism rears its head, you hear comments such as, "We've tried that before" and "This will never work!" The skeptic offers criticism without offering insight. If you fall into this trap, you run the risk of dismissing an idea without truly evaluating whether it has merit, and if you dismiss a skeptic simply because his or her comments aren't helpful, you're missing an opportunity to learn something valuable. If you have a skeptic on the team (or you begin to hear your own inner skeptic), find out what can be learned from the skeptic's past experience that may help the current situation.

Making assumptions intentionally . . . or not

Decisions get made all the time based on assumptions. Assumptions can be calculated guesses you make when you're missing essential information, or they can be ideas you accept as true without proof and without thought. Depending on what kind of assumption you're making — the educated-guess kind or the I-believe-it-just-because kind — assumptions can help or hinder your decision-making.

REMEMBER

Making assumptions allows you to convert uncertainties into something you can work with, at least temporarily. Assumptions also give you a way to move forward until new information clarifies any uncertainty and presents an opportunity to think through your priorities so that, if something unexpected happens, you can quickly change direction. (For more on priorities, head to the later section "Implementing the Decision.")

Using assumptions works under these conditions:

>> **You know you're making them.** When essential information is missing, you intentionally convert the unknowns into assumptions. Suppose, for example, that your office is planning to move to a larger location. You don't have data regarding your company's growth rate or the number of telecommuters it employs — information you need when determining which of the new sites has enough room to accommodate your work force. Therefore, you make the assumption that, over the next five years, the staff count will double and that telecommuters will be physically in the office one day each week. These assumptions let you fill in the blanks and move on.

>> **You adjust your assumptions as new data becomes available.** As conditions change, you review your assumptions and adjust them to fit the emerging reality. If the information you needed in the first place becomes available, you can eliminate the assumption altogether.

WARNING

Assumptions don't work when you're not aware that you're making them or when they are left unchecked and then prove to be inaccurate. If you aren't aware of your assumptions, or you don't test the assumptions you've knowingly made against the reality of the situation you're in, you may be operating under a dangerous illusion.

TIP

Check your assumptions before making a decision to see what unnoticed thoughts are sneaking into your deliberations. To uncover underlying beliefs, openly ask what assumptions you and your team are making. Without declaring the assumptions, you risk making a poor decision that seems sound initially but undermines your efforts later.

Establishing and weighing criteria

In a rational decision-making process, you use the information you gather to establish criteria that specify what each of the alternatives under consideration must meet to accomplish your goal. You can create the criteria on your own (for personal decisions) or collectively, as you do when you work in a team or in a collaborative venture.

Establishing a list of criteria by which to judge the options in front of you offers benefits such as the following:

>> Helps you think the decision through

>> Brings the most practical alternatives to the surface

>> Provides a clear structure that guides the evaluation process

>> Helps the decision-making team agree on what it is looking for

>> Makes the thinking behind your final choice visible, clear, and precise — which is especially important when you make decisions that are subject to open scrutiny

Criteria specify the conditions that must be met for an option to be considered. We explain how to establish and weigh criteria in this section.

Listing and sorting your criteria

Start by making a short yet complete list of the conditions that must be met. If you're hiring, for example, list the criteria any viable candidate must have. You don't want to be the company who hired a VP only to find out he is afraid of flying!

Sort the list items into one of the following two categories:

>> **Must Haves category:** Think of the Must Haves category as the go or no go category. The option being considered (or the candidate in the case of a hiring decision) either meets the criteria or doesn't. If it meets the criteria, it moves on in the review process. If it doesn't meet the criteria, it's out.

TIP

Be sure to test the items on the Must Haves list to make sure list they're essential. For example, imagine that you're hiring a new sales manager, and you think a degree is essential. To test this criterion, ask, "If a candidate comes along who brings experience worth far more than a degree or who lacks a degree but has a proven track record, do we still reject that candidate because of his or her lack of degree?" If you say that you would still consider this candidate, even without the degree, the criterion of having a degree is comparative, not essential.

>> **Comparative category:** The Comparative category holds the measures you'll apply to options that pass through the first screen (the Must Haves). You assign each criterion a rating (weight) based on how important you or your team think it is. We explain how to assign and use ratings in the next section.

Weighing your criteria

Comparative criteria are usually assigned a weighting from 1 to 10, with 1 indicating not important and 10 indicating very important. (Anything below 6 probably isn't important enough to be a criterion.) In this section, we give you two tools to help you apply criteria in your decision-making.

SCORING YOUR OPTIONS WITH A LITTLE MATH

When you're considering several comparative criteria, each with a different relative importance, follow these steps to see how the different options stack up:

1. **Create a table in which you list each comparative criterion and assign each a numeric value out of a total possible 10 points.**

   Importance, or relative value, is determined relative to the other criterion.

2. **For each option being considered, assign a score assessing how well the option meets that criteria.**

   Measure each option against the criteria, scoring each by using the relative weighting you've assigned. If the comparative criteria has a high possible score of 8, for example, and the option under consideration fully meets the criteria, give it an 8. If it doesn't meet the criteria, give it a lower score.

3. **After you score each of the options, multiply the option's score by the criterion's relative value and — voila! — you have a final tally.**

   For example, if the relative value of a criterion is 8, and the option was scored a 6, the final tally is 48. Table 2-1 illustrates how to use criteria's' relative values to evaluate the options. Place the option at the top of the table and evaluate each alternative, using the scoring sheet. When you're finished, you'll have a score that tells you how well the option did against the criteria you set.

4. **Add the scores for each option to get a total for each alternative.**

   Taking this extra step lets you compare, at a glance, the total scores to see which of all your options has the highest score.

TABLE 2-1   ## Scoring Option A — an Example

Criteria	Relative Value	Option #1 Score	Final Tally for Option #1
User-friendly for the customer	10	8	80
Easy to repeat	8	5	40
Fits into an airplane storage space	8	6	48

REMEMBER

Using such a scoring sheet enables everyone to see the collective thinking. You can either have team members fill out the scores together (assuming you're all on-site), or have them fill it out online. The scores are then compiled to show how the decision-making team ranked the options.

APPLYING THINKING TOOLS: THE PUGH MATRIX

The Pugh Matrix, designed by Professor Stuart Pugh, answers the question, "Which option will most improve what is in place now?" by including a baseline in the calculations used to weigh comparative criteria. The use of the baseline indicates whether the option will positively improve or negatively subtract from what is currently in place.

To use the Pugh Matrix, follow these steps:

1. **Make a list of five or fewer of your most important criteria or conditions.**

   More than five and the list gets cumbersome. Ten is way too many.

2. **As you consider each criterion and each option, ask, "Will the result be better or worse than the current system?"**

   If the option is better than the current system, assign it a +1. If it is worse, assign it a –1. Table 2-2 shows an example of the Pugh Matrix in action.

3. **Tally the pluses and minuses to see which is the best option.**

   In this example, Option 3 dominates with three pluses and one minus, making it the logical choice.

TABLE 2-2   **Assessing Options by Using the Pugh Matrix**

Criteria	Baseline (What We Have Now)	Option 1	Option 2	Option 3
1	0	+1	–1	+1
2	0	+1	+1	–1
3	0	–1	–1	+1
4	0	–1	–1	+1

Avoiding analysis paralysis

An organization that delays making a decision for too long is most likely stuck in the analysis stage. If you were to ask why a decision hadn't been made, you'd hear reasons such as, "There isn't enough information," or "Conditions are changing too quickly," or "We have too many options to choose from." The result? No decision is made or no option chosen.

Companies and people find themselves in this predicament for a few reasons:

>> They overthink and overanalyze the information, the options, or the implications of the decision.

>> They operate from an underlying fear of making a mistake.

>> They are totally overwhelmed by uncertainty or internal chaos from too much change.

>> They see either no clear option or far too many options to choose from.

WARNING

Not making a decision that needs to be made increases the pressure that employees feel, which in turn leads to consequences such as stress-related illness, frustration, low morale, and poor performance. Not good. In this situation, employees have lost trust in the company's intuitive intelligence.

How do you shift out of analysis paralysis? What can you do to restore employee morale? Start by recognizing that conditions are changing constantly. To regain control and pave a path that enables you to make concrete decisions and action plans, follow these suggestions:

>> **Identify decisions that are easy and ready to go, and take action.** A bit of success will build momentum, and these low-stakes, low-risk decisions are not hard to implement. So take action on them.

>> **Make one decision at a time.** Limiting yourself to one decision at a time allows for the smoke of confusion and frustration to clear. Solve one problem and then move on to the next.

>> **Get a fresh new perspective on the decisions under consideration.** Ask someone from outside the unit what he or she would do. Or change your environment to see the decision from a different context.

REMEMBER

Research shows that more information doesn't necessarily mean better decisions. Hesitating to make the decision because you don't have the absolute best information is a trap. It means that you need to be perfect or right. Avoid it.

>> **Trust in yourself and your colleagues.** Working from a base of trust is much easier than working from a base of fear. Sure, it may require a leap of faith, but let go of hesitation and move forward. Although a bit unsettling initially, if you take gradual steps, you can help build momentum and restore confidence, and soon things will get rolling again.

REMEMBER

Analysis isn't bad or good. It is just one way of thinking. Other ways of thinking offer different benefits. Analysis reduces. In analytical thinking, you take the picture apart. Yet in a business environment where complexity and diversity dominate, big-picture thinking is necessary. For that reason, analytical thinking may not be the best option. Flexibility is necessary.

Generating Options

In decision-making, the term *options* refers to the different alternatives or solutions under consideration. Whether you're buying a computer, upgrading office space, or hiring an accountant, for example, you must decide which alternative offers the best solution. Some decisions, such as purchasing equipment, must result in the selection of only one out of several alternatives. Other decisions may benefit from working with more than one option simultaneously.

In this section, we explain how to come up with options, how to work with the risk of uncertainty, and what to do when you have too few or too many options to choose from.

Avoiding the one-option-only trap

When you're making a decision, having only one option to consider isn't really an option. When you focus on only one idea to address your dilemma, you face two risks: that your (or your team's) tunnel vision has bypassed potentially better solutions and that any decision you make will keep you safely, and potentially stagnantly, in the status quo.

People think that they have only one choice for the following reasons:

>> **Narrow thinking:** You consider only what has been done before, regardless of whether it's worked. You disregard creative or unproven ideas.

>> **Fearful thinking:** The decision is being triggered by fear, or the decision-making environment is characterized by fear or being afraid to take a risk.

WARNING

The rationale underlying narrow or fearful thinking when making a decision is that, if nothing changes, nothing will change. It's a way to stay on familiar ground and stick to the status quo. And it brings on employee disengagement, the inability to retain talent, stress, and, ultimately, poor decisions.

Tapping into others' creativity

The solution to overcoming narrow or fearful thinking is to reawaken and apply creativity. Seek ideas and additional options by involving employees, customers, suppliers, and other involved parties (and don't forget to give credit where credit is due!). Tapping into additional sources' creative ideas helps you avoid missing an optimal solution no one has thought of yet.

TIP

Think of options as opportunities. You can generate options by taking creative steps to reach out and look for ideas that would otherwise escape notice.

Brainstorming has long been used to come up with ideas, but in brainstorming, strong-willed people too often end up pressuring others to conform to one view — theirs! Because creative work is best accomplished privately — many brilliant ideas come up in the shower or when you're gardening — we recommend that you take a different approach. Follow these steps:

1. **Ask team members to identify one or more solutions on their own.**

Independently coming up with ideas enables creative ideas to come forward that might otherwise not be heard in a group setting.

2. **Collate potential solutions so that you have access to a wider range of possibilities.**

Bringing the ideas together allows the team, whether working remotely or in the same location, to see which alternatives fit.

3. **Discuss the merits of top ideas.**

Bring the top ideas forward to work with. Solicit team members' perspectives on which alternative appeals and why it has merit. Include any risks associated with the option, as well as its pros and cons.

REMEMBER

Always consider dissenting views because they hold valued insights. Collaborating may result in creating a new solution or, at minimum, identifying the most viable alternatives.

4. **After discussion, short-list the alternatives — have participants select their top three choices, for example — and then gain consensus from the team.**

An easy and reliable way to short list is to use dot voting, in which you give participants dots (you can buy these little dots from stationary stores) that they then use to identify the alternative(s) they find most appealing.

TIP

Dot voting is a great way to rank ideas or to see where the preferences lie. It's not used to make the final decision. Dot voting has several rules, such as how many dots you hand out (this number is based on how many people you're working with and how many choices are under consideration) and whether you can let participants load up their dots on one idea (it's generally a no-no!). For detailed instructions on dot voting, go to http://dotmocracy.org/dot-voting/.

At this point, you should have a short list of viable options that you keep open as you move forward.

Vetting your top options

If you're using a criteria-based decision-making process, you can now match your options against the criteria you set earlier on. Refer to the earlier section "Establishing and weighing criteria" for details. Otherwise, you can select one or several to move forward on simultaneously. Keep reading for the details.

And the winner is! Selecting one option

Looking for one option or solution works best when you need only one solution, such as when you buy a software package, select a new location for your office, and so on. In these cases, you need to select the single, best option that meets your needs.

A super-rational decision-making process works well in predictable environments where the information isn't moving at breakneck speed and you can take the time to deliberate. The process we outline in the earlier section "Establishing and weighting criteria" — especially in regards to using a scoring sheet or the Pugh Matrix to discover the best option in front of you — can help you do that.

Using scenario forecasting

In the case of project implementation or, at a higher level, determining strategic direction, new information pops up all the time. The situation is unpredictable and quite fluid. Selecting a single option to adhere to is like trying to put a foot down while the train is still moving. Instead, view your options as scenarios. Doing so helps in situations where there are multiple possibilities in fast-changing circumstances.

REMEMBER

In uncertain decision-making environments or when you're forecasting into the future, keeping your options open is a better approach because fixing on one solution too early can create stress (you're forcing a solution that doesn't quite work) or result in a missed opportunity (you overlooked a solution that would work better). When the decision-making environment is complex and rapidly changing, you can't afford to be inflexible in your approach.

Scenario forecasting, an approach to risk management, is a way to keep options open by exploring scenarios and changing how you allocate resources. In scenario forecasting, you prepare for a world with multiple possible futures by creating a concrete plan for dealing with an abstract but probable future event.

When you use scenarios to prepare for future events, you're truly thinking big and mitigating risk exposure. Fortune favors the prepared. Consider FedEx, for example, which relies on petroleum as its energy source. If the global forecast predicts a world shortage of petroleum, rising gas prices will increase FedEx's risk of relying solely on one fuel source. By working through this kind of scenario — imagining a world in which petroleum is in short supply or imagining options that address the problems caused by a shortage of petroleum — FedEx can identify various ways to mitigate its risk. It may look at strategies that reduce energy use, identify reliable sources of alternative energy such as biofuels, or investigate other options that alleviate reliance on petroleum.

Assessing Immediate and Future Risk

Working with risk is risky. Although your mind can assess risk logically, psychologically, you handle risk in a totally different way. In this section, we explain how to calculate risk in your mind, look at how human psychology works when facing risk, and, finally, show you how to avoid underestimating risk.

Identifying risks

Calculating risk rationally engages your mind in a way that identifies the risk and assigns a value to how serious that risk is. Follow these steps:

1. **Start by asking the question, "What can possibly go wrong?"**

   The answer identifies potential risks arising from different sources. These are unique to the situation. For instance, in bridge building, one way you'd use this lens is to uncover potential engineering flaws. In marketing, you'd use it to identify assumptions being made about the market.

2. **Ask yourself, "What is the probability of this event happening?"**

   Assign the probability a high, medium, or low rating. This step separates the big risks from the tiny ones and helps you identify the likelihood that you'll face the risk in reality.

   TIP

   If you detect a risk that is lying on the periphery of what everyone is paying attention to, name it.

3. **Identify the seriousness of the event's effect on your business, using the high, medium, or low rating.**

   This step isolates the risks that may have a low probability of happening but very serious consequences if they do — a reactor failure in a nuclear power plant, for example. On the other hand, a number of risks may surface that have both high probability and high seriousness.

   By looking at probability and seriousness together, you identify risks that you need to address in the decision-making process, either by making a contingency plan or by addressing the risk early on in the process to prevent it entirely or mitigate its effects.

4. **Develop and incorporate ways to prevent, mitigate, or eliminate the risk into your decision-making process.**

   If you can't prevent it, plan to have a backup plan. For instance, in the case of electrical outage, most buildings have a backup generator. How far you take efforts to mitigate risk depends on the seriousness of the consequences.

Considering people's response to risk

When a risk is real, specific, concrete, or immediate, it is much easier to relate to. For instance, when you jaywalk across the street in a high traffic zone, the risk of being hit by a car is pretty real. Conversely, a risk that is possible but not tangible — such as the chance of needing trip interruption insurance — is treated differently. Why? Human psychology. Consider the following points:

>> **People naturally tend to focus on the tangible and discount the theoretical.** In other words, you're more likely to pay attention to a specific risk you're facing in the moment than to anticipate a risk that may happen in the future. This tendency explains why attention goes to what actresses wear to the Oscars rather than rising sea levels, or why a contractor substitutes inferior, low-cost materials to meet budget rather than focus on probable future risk (the stability of the building and the possibility that the inferior product may fail).

>> **Especially when making complex decisions, few people see *unintended consequences,* the unanticipated, wider effects that result from an action.** Think of a spider web. If you jiggle one strand, the whole system is affected. The decisions you make can have similar effects. If you limit your attention to only one strand — that is, you make a decision looking only at one part of the whole picture — you won't see how the strands are interconnected. Such tunnel vision causes decision-making errors.

TIP

When you see the big picture, you can more accurately identify the direct consequences of a decision and action plans, and you can predict the indirect effects. Doing so reduces the chance that you'll be blindsided or make a decision that takes a nosedive. Use a mind-mapping process to see how a decision may play out and to see who will be affected directly and indirectly.

>> **People perceive the future as distant, unknown, and not concrete.** Traditionally, the majority of companies have operated on the assumption that climate change wasn't relevant to business sustainability over the longer term. The probability of climate change, given the way risk is assessed psychologically, has not traditionally been factored into decisions about how resources are used or the carbon footprint of business activity. Consequently, actions that could have reduced carbon outputs were not taken. Now, according to the Carbon Disclosure Project's survey, S&P 500 companies estimate that 45 percent of the risk will surface in the next one to five years, with some costs of production already being felt. The effect of the psychological tendency to see potential futures as a slide show is that action is delayed, resulting in a higher cost later on.

In the traditional sequence of think-plan-do, risk isn't real until you reach the doing stage. As long as you're thinking or planning, things that go bump in the night — the consequences of your actions — aren't real. But when you take action, people react, and consequences show up. To assess risk, you must be able to conceive the reality of things going wrong. You can reduce the risk of making errors in risk planning by imagining the possible scenarios and describing in real terms what would happen as a result of the options you're considering. This exercise gives you a better sense of whether a particular path improves the situation, makes it worse, or has no effect. Looking at each option through this lens better prepares you for implementation.

TIP

A fresh mind sees things a tired mind can't. If you're confused, hold off your decision until you have regained clarity, which may take only minutes or a day or two. Sometimes the best way to gain clarity is to relax and not think about the decision or situation at all. Take a break and remove yourself from the environment: Take a walk in the woods, see a show, go to the gym, spend time with family. We explain the value of a relaxed emotional state in the later section "Making the Decision."

REMEMBER

In situations where uncertainty reigns, the human tendency is to decide now — even if it means being wrong — just to restore certainty. Those who are uncomfortable with the unfamiliar or who feel unsure may commit to an option far too soon.

Mapping the Consequences: Knowing Who Is Affected and How

Most decisions that backfire do so for two reasons:

>> The people who must implement them aren't involved in the decision-making.

>> The decision fails to take into account the emotional needs and values of the customer (or anyone else affected by the implementation). These needs and values aren't limited solely to the effect that the decision has on people. The effect of the decision on the environment and on the community the business resides in is also an important consideration.

A popular tool for mapping out whom or what the decision affects is a mind map (the brainchild of Tony Buzan, expert on the brain, memory, creativity, and innovation). Mind maps are incredibly useful because they help participants tap into both creative thinking and linear-logical thinking. Mind maps graphically represent the various aspects of a topic. In the case of decision-making, they can bring the pieces of the puzzle or process into one visible picture.

TIP

To create a mind map of internal relationships, start by mapping out which staff or internal business units are involved (ask questions such as "Which departments are required for implementation?" and "Who needs to handle sensitive issues?"). Then add maps to include the implications on those directly or indirectly affected by the decision. Be sure to include social, emotional, and environmental effects such as employment opportunities, a decrease in property values, the destruction of wildlife habitat, and so on. Such a map helps you see the relationships between different parts of the situation so that you can better prepare and build in ways to either reduce the risk of negative effect or devise a strategy for addressing it.

Making the Decision

An effective decision has these characteristics:

REMEMBER

>> **Reflects a positive attitude:** Negativity is like glue. It slows everything down, saps energy, and undermines momentum. If your attitude is negative during the decision-making process, or if the decision-making environment is highly stressful, you'll make a poor choice. Period.

Negative attitudes and critical thinking are not the same thing. Critical thinking improves a decision. Head to the earlier section "Critically evaluating your data" for an explanation of the difference.

>> **Aligns what you think and how you feel about the final choice:** Pushing forward because you feel obligated is draining. When your heart just isn't in it, even if you think the idea is a good one, nothing happens, or if it does, it takes a lot of effort and can feel quite depleting.

>> **Balances your intuition with your rational, analytical work:** Ideally, you want your gut and your mind working together, each providing a check and balance to the other. One entrepreneur told us, for example, that he'd been to an investor's meeting where the pitch sounded good and the numbers looked sound, but he didn't opt in because he had a bad feeling about the deal.

>> **Includes time to contemplate and reflect:** Time can be your ally when you're deciding on a course of action. Often the best ideas occur when you're relaxed and doing something other than concentrating on the decision.

TIP

Bias, prejudice, and doubt influence decisions whether you realize it or not. Here are some suggestions to help you overcome the three:

>> **Doubt:** Doubt simply signals that a hidden fear is getting in your way. Ask yourself, "What's the worry?" When you put the fear out in the open, you often find that the doubts and worry lose their power over you.

>> **Bias and prejudice:** Prejudice and bias create a blind side, and you need help from others who can point out what you can't see. To minimize the chances that unseen bias and prejudice are influencing your choices, notice when you're leaning toward one solution or perspective over another.

Communicating the Decision Effectively

Transparency of information creates trust, which is important in business environments and vital when change is being made. Decisions made behind closed doors are always suspect. Therefore, after the decision is made, you need to communicate it. *How* you communicate the decision is everything. Basically, you want your message to summarize the decision you've made, why you've made it, and what it means for the audience you're addressing. When you communicate your decision, include the following:

>> **The reason the decision was necessary:** Include a brief summary of the opportunity or issue the decision and action plan address. Explain the "why."

>> **The final decision:** Pretty straightforward.

>> **The implications:** What the decision means to both your internal network and your customers or clientele. Address how the solutions will help and speak directly to the changes that these groups would be likely to see as losses.

REMEMBER

Few things are worse than hearing that tired old phrase "Out with the old, in with the new." People fear loss and change more than they value gain. Meeting emotional needs when you're both making and communicating a decision is frequently overlooked but of vital importance. People are less interested in the decision itself and more interested in what that decision means to them.

>> **What will happen next and what you need them to do to support the decision:** Feedback and feed-forward information allows for adjusting to change.

TIP

To avoid a backlash, make sure you address the key concerns that were raised during the information-gathering process; refer to the earlier section "Paying attention to different perspectives."

REMEMBER

Credibility comes from speaking from the heart, genuinely and honestly. Tell your team and all parties involved what you know and what you don't know. Don't feel you have to cover the nitty-gritty details. What they need to know is just what is expected and what the resulting decision means to them personally and professionally.

Implementing the Decision

Finally — it's time for action (as if you've been sitting around all this time)! Getting things done is where rational and logical thinking really delivers. So what do you do? You create an action plan. This section has the details.

Putting together your action plan

An action plan guides the implementation of the decision and helps monitor progress. The more complex the task, the more people involved and the more key activities and sub-activities are needed. In an action plan, you list the tasks that need to get done, identify the parties responsible for each task, set timelines for completion, and indicate what successful completion of a task looks like.

To put together your action plan, follow these steps:

1. Individually or collectively list all the steps that need to be accomplished to get the job done.

Involve the team and any other units that will be involved in the implementation of the decision. Doing so ensures that no task gets inadvertently left out.

TIP

If you're doing this task in person, put one action step on a sticky note or 3-x-5-inch index card. Then you can rearrange them easily to get the timing and order worked out.

2. Set priorities.

Some actions are immediate and some can wait. To establish which decisions or parts of an action plan are more critical, set priorities. For additional information on priorities, refer to the next section.

3. Pull out higher-level action items and then rearrange the sub-activities so that each appears below the higher-level action with which it is associated.

The higher-level actions are like parents to the rest; taking care of them resolves other issues down the line. (The term *parent-child* refers to actions that are related to one another. By taking action on the parent, you look after the child. Noticing such relationships allows you to leverage your efforts.)

For instance, if you're starting a company, the higher-level action may be to get the company legally registered. Sub-activities could include deciding what legal registration fits, generating and submitting names for the company so that your company's name isn't already taken, and so on.

This step lets you see how each sub-activity contributes toward your overall goal; it also helps you identify the tasks associated with each action step.

4. **For each task, indicate who is responsible for the task.**

5. **Set time frames for completion or, at minimum, checkpoints for review.**

   Avoid the label "ongoing," which may lead people to assume that things are moving along on this action item when, in fact, it may be stalled or overlooked.

6. **Define what the task will accomplish so that the endpoint is clear.**

   Agree on what successful completion will fulfill. Everyone involved in implementation needs to be on the same page, holding the same picture of what the result must accomplish so that everyone can adapt during implementation as conditions change.

REMEMBER

Action plans change all the time as new information alters the course. Be prepared to adjust. Use this kind of framework to jump-start the launch. After that, communication with your team will keep track of what is happening.

TIP

For large, multiparty projects, sophisticated project management software is necessary. Here are some helpful links:

>> For a list of top ten free (open source) project management software programs, go to www.cyberciti.biz/tips/open-source-project-management-software.html.

>> For programs for remote teams, visit www.hongkiat.com/blog/project-management-software/.

>> For general project management programs, go to https://www.software advice.com/project-management/.

In addition, social collaboration tools help facilitate information exchange. A range of solutions is available, and new software products pop up all the time. Companies such as http://www.Nooq.co.uk facilitate rapid information exchange in small to medium-sized companies. IBM social platforms or Microsoft's products, such as SharePoint, offer large-scale content management solutions. Go to http://mashable.com/2012/09/07/social-collaboration-tools/ for details.

Deciding what is important: Metrics

You've probably heard the business maxim, "What gets measured, gets managed." In short, metrics matter. Establishing the measures you'll use to track performance ensures you pay attention to what matters and to whom — the customer or internal operations. Choose the right metrics, and you get information that helps you make good decisions; choose the wrong metrics, and you may inadvertently create issues that you then have to deal with. In this section, we offer two examples of how your choice of metric can support or undermine your business goals.

Example 1: Customer service

Getting the metric right can take awhile, but knowing what you want to achieve is the place to start. Suppose, for example, that you work for a telecommunications company, and your company wants to improve customer retention. To achieve that goal, it targets the customer service function and decides to use length of call time as its metric, assuming that shortened call time will result in greater customer satisfaction and retention. Sounds reasonable, right? After all, no one likes being on a customer service line for what seems like an eternity.

Now put yourself in the customers' shoes. Imagine being on a call with your mobile provider where your problem *never got solved* but they had you off the line in less than five minutes. Do you, as the customer, consider the call a success? Not a chance. If customer service performance is measured by the length of call time rather than whether the customer's problem was successfully resolved, you have not improved customer satisfaction or retention, although you may have improved call time. The customer will be a long way from feeling delighted. In fact, you may have annoyed the customer so much that he looks for another provider.

Now suppose that the metric you use is whether the customer's problem was solved to his or her satisfaction. Chances are your company would have happier customers who are more likely to continue to use your service.

Example 2: Employee retention

Suppose that you want to reduce turnover rate because you know that replacing people is costly. The metrics you use to measure the actual costs of losing an employee direct the focus of your efforts to retain people:

>> **Viewing the situation from a mathematical perspective:** When an employee resigns, you can calculate the costs in a relatively simple mathematical equation:

cost of one lost employee = that employee's salary + replacement cost + training time

With this calculation, you may discover, for example, that having to replace an employee costs you 2.5 times the lost employee's salary.

>> **Taking a holistic view of the costs:** Note that the preceding equation misses the hidden costs. How much, for example, does it cost to replace the knowledge and experience that walked out the door? The lost clients? The customer loyalty to staff? The damage to your company's reputation? These factors can't be measured and yet are important for weighing how well things are working.

Setting priorities

To ensure that you do the tasks in the correct order and to allocate resources, which tend to be in chronically short supply in most businesses, you must set priorities. By setting priorities, you know what to pay attention to first and where to direction your attention so that you don't try to do everything at once.

In establishing priorities, think in terms of these three categories:

>> **Essential (1):** These action items must be started immediately after the decision and action plan are finalized. Indicate essential action items by using the number 1.

>> **Important (2):** These action items are not essential but are still important to the overall success of the plan. Indicate these by using the number 2.

>> **Nice (3):** Think of these action items as frosting on the cake. They're not essential but would be nice to implement. Assign them a 3.

Learning from the implementation process

As the implementation of the decision unfolds, you'll find yourself making adjustments to your plan due to practical and emerging realities as unintended consequences and changing conditions unfold.

Adapting to changing realities

As you implement your changes, monitor the consequences of the decision and adjust the implementation plan to reflect what is happening. Here are some suggestions:

>> **Pay attention to whether too many negative results show up and you find your red flags working overtime.** So that you can adapt quickly to the emerging realities, try these tactics:

- *Agree with the team ahead of time that any team member can call a review meeting in the event that a concern or opportunity to improve the action plan arises.* During this meeting, the team can collectively decide how to respond to the changing conditions.

- *Have a contingency plan ready.* This is one way you can use the scenarios developed during your planning phase. You can also develop contingency plans out of your risk assessment. See the earlier section "Using scenario forecasting" for details.

>> **Treat unexpected occurrences as a potential opportunity to creatively improve the work you're doing.** Some unexpected events might be negative consequences, but a creative approach can convert a potential problem into a creative opportunity.

Reflecting on what happened

Unless you and your company are devoted to learning, you'll fall into a pattern of recycling the same decisions over and over again. You can use self- and organizational awareness to avoid this fate. Companies that develop this awareness have a clear edge. One way to increase self- and organizational awareness is to take time for reflection. Following are two approaches:

>> **For bigger decisions that went badly sideways, collectively reflect on each part of the decision-making process.** Ask probing questions, such as

- What kind of thinking was applied (analytical, big picture, causal, and so on)?

- What assumptions were made?

- What questions weren't asked?

- What flags were ignored?

Applying a critical and constructive review allows the organization to learn from the decision-making process.

>> **Schedule a time weekly or monthly to engage in reflection within the business unit.** As a group, ask questions such as, "What do we need to stop (or start) doing?" and "What do we need to improve?" Then incorporate results back into your day-to-day work. This systematic method lets you stay on top of what's going on and gives you an opportunity to identify actions that are habitual but useless as conditions change.

REMEMBER

When a decision turns out to be a failure or doesn't play out according to plan, reflection gives you the tools to recognize what went wrong, learn how to avoid repeating the errors, and improve your future decision-making endeavors.

Decision-Making on Auto-Pilot

Most decisions happen instantly (the whole decision-making process may be over in milliseconds) and are made entirely without your conscious knowledge. When you don't have time to consciously work through the decision-making process, what do you do — take a wild guess? No, you use your intuition.

Intuition is the ability to know or identify a solution without conscious thought. And where does this ability come from? One source is from experience you gain by making decisions, something called *implicit knowledge*. With implicit knowledge, the most recognized form of intuition, the more experience you have making decisions in diverse, complex, unstructured situations, the faster and more accurate your decisions are. In this section, we provide more details into how intuition works in both stable and highly volatile situations.

Grasping intuitive decision-making

When you're under pressure, you may not have time to mentally generate different options, evaluate their practicality, and then choose one. You need to act quickly! Intuition equips you to make fast, accurate, and workable decisions in complex, dynamically changing, and unfamiliar conditions. Higher-level strategic decisions rely heavily on intuitive intelligence, for instance. Here is how your supercomputer, your intuition, operates:

1. Processes incoming information at high speeds.

2. Selects pertinent factual and situational information from a ton of data.

3. Scans for cues and patterns you've come across before.

4. Decides whether this situation is typical or unfamiliar.

5. Runs scenarios from your inventory of what has worked before to see how the solution will play out in the current situation and then adjusts the solution to fit the situation.

6. Chooses one and — shazaam! — the decision is made.

And it does all of this in milliseconds!

Examining intuition in different situations

As the preceding steps indicate, part of the intuitive decision-making process is an assessment of whether the situation is typical or atypical. If the situation is typical, your supercomputer retrieves options that have worked before, rapidly tests them, scans them for weaknesses, and modifies them if necessary before selecting one. This process, described by Gary Klein in several of his books, most notably *Streetlights and Shadows: Searching for the Keys to Adaptive Decision Making* (Bradford), is illustrated in Figure 2-1.

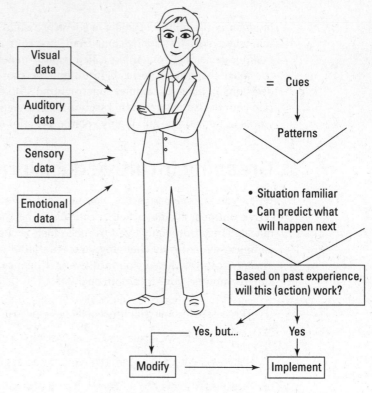

Situation:
- Low levels of uncertainty
- Stable, fairly predictable conditions

Visual data

Auditory data

Sensory data

Emotional data

= Cues

Patterns

- Situation familiar
- Can predict what will happen next

Based on past experience, will this (action) work?

Yes, but...   Yes

Modify → Implement

Time elapsed: Milliseconds

FIGURE 2-1:
Intuitive decision-making in stable, fairly predictable conditions.

If the situation isn't typical, your supercomputer goes into overdrive. This is where experience matters. Your internal supercomputer looks for more information until it senses that enough has been gathered, and then it runs through some scenarios to see which one will work, makes any necessary adjustments, and then the decision is made. Figure 2-2 shows this process.

Quite frankly, neuroscientists still aren't sure how the brain selects the right information from so many signals. One thing is for sure: Intuition is efficient, and it works, especially when there isn't any structure to lean on, when you aren't really sure what will happen next, when conditions are volatile or ambiguous, and when there is an immediate reaction to events.

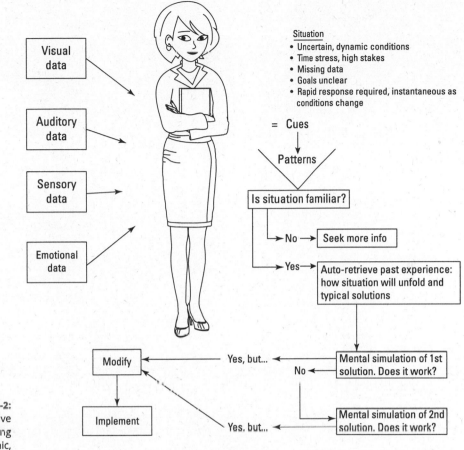

Visual data

Auditory data

Sensory data

Emotional data

Situation
- Uncertain, dynamic conditions
- Time stress, high stakes
- Missing data
- Goals unclear
- Rapid response required, instantaneous as conditions change

= Cues

Patterns

Is situation familiar?

No → Seek more info

Yes → Auto-retrieve past experience: how situation will unfold and typical solutions

Modify ← Yes, but... ← No ← Mental simulation of 1st solution. Does it work?

Implement

Yes, but... ← Mental simulation of 2nd solution. Does it work?

Time elapsed: Milliseconds

FIGURE 2-2:
Intuitive decision-making in highly dynamic, uncertain conditions.

Chapter **3**

Becoming a More Effective Decision-Maker

Big advances in your skills and leadership don't happen when things are going swimmingly. Your character and your strengths grow when you face tough judgment calls, deal with inner or interpersonal conflicts, or face unfamiliar territory, such as a new career. Making tough decisions is only one half of being a successful businessperson. The other half is unearthing who you become as a result of the decisions you make. Such character-defining decisions — ones that determine the quality of your key personal and professional relationships from that point on — affect what happens next in your business and in your life.

In this chapter, we show you how to use challenging moments to develop your influence as a decision-maker and how to adapt your thinking by taking increased responsibility for your company's direction. We also explain how to handle yourself when things go wrong or when you find yourself confronting bad behavior. No matter what the crucible, you can grow leadership capacity and build character and your relationships in the process.

Upping Your Game: Transitioning from Area-Specific to Strategic Decisions

When small companies grow big fast, CEOs who want to stay CEOs pretty much have to grow to keep pace with the expansion. And, according to one Harvard study, 79 percent of top-performing CEOs are hired from within. This means that if you're aiming for an executive position, your thinking and approach to decision-making have to evolve to meet your career aspirations. Accepting higher levels of responsibility changes your decision-making game.

As your responsibilities grow, no matter how that growth unfolds or how large your business, you'll be challenged in two ways:

>> You'll move from making straightforward decisions to strategic and more ambiguous decisions. Ambiguous decisions don't lend themselves to a "right" answer or a step-by-step approach.

>> Whereas in the past, you could specialize in — and remain comfortable with — one area of expertise, you now must embrace and understand the bigger picture.

TIP

The business environment is both complex and interconnected. For that reason, relying on only one area of expertise limits your view as a decision-maker, and you'll make mistakes as a result. To combat this tendency, try tackling decisions where more is at stake. Doing so gives you the chance to push the boundaries of your comfort zone. The idea is to give yourself a chance to stretch, not to the snapping point, but to the point where you can discover that you're capable of more than you think. The rewards? By accepting higher levels of personal responsibility, you gain freedom to make decisions for yourself instead of following directives without question.

REMEMBER

Any company, regardless of size, can benefit from working with a longer-term view. In fact, if you want to do more than survive as a company, you need to blend strategy (the thinking part) with creativity (the innovation element) so that you can continue to adapt.

Highlighting strategic decisions

Whether you make strategic decisions or not, your decisions benefit from strategic thinking. When you think strategically, you look ahead to the direction you're heading, and you weigh risk, consequence, and other aspects of the decision-making process. In short, strategic thinking allows you to work with the uncertainty of the future and use the details you pay attention to day by day to set a direction for your company. When you think strategically, you take the big-picture view as you move from your current position to the desired possibilities.

In this section, we focus on strategic thinking because, without it, the chances that your company will fail increase.

Balancing short-term actions with long-term direction

Many companies fail to think past the end of next month or next quarter, and most equate being constantly busy with making progress. The problem with this mind-set is that, if you don't know where you're going, you could end up going in circles and never make progress, or you can wind up someplace you'd rather not be. Strategic thinking puts the compass in your hands, enabling you to balance short-term, immediate actions (which everyone loves) with the longer-term direction that makes a company resilient and valued.

Taking a bird's-eye view

Strategic thinking entails thinking conceptually to see patterns and relationships among seemingly unrelated pieces of information and then adding a dose of imagination (without getting too carried away) to find opportunity. The best way to see new opportunities is to view circumstances from a higher vantage point. When you think conceptually, you can separate what's important from what's not important, or you can take a solution that works in one place and apply it successfully to a totally different situation somewhere else.

British explorer Mark Wood approached Skype, a computer-based video and audio chat software company, to install a cybercafe in Nepal, where tourists would pay a nominal fee to use Skype to call home. The fee gave the local Nepalese children connection to the rest of the world.

WARNING

If you're like many, you may prefer to avoid thinking conceptually because concepts don't tell you what to do differently on Monday morning when you show up at work. After all, the security of routinely knowing exactly what to do Monday morning is comforting . . . and a trap:

>> If you don't visualize or articulate where you want to go, you're left without direction or purpose.

>> Routines can blind you to what can be achieved if you were to look beyond the end of the month, the end of the project, and so on.

>> Feeling certain can lull you into thinking that nothing is changing, but it is — and at rapid rates.

REMEMBER

As a decision-maker, you'll make fewer strategic decisions than tactical ones (head to the next section to find out the difference), but these decisions can make or break your company's fortunes and future.

Developing your strategic thinking capabilities

As a small business owner or someone who works at the operational or managerial level, you make a lot of decisions. The practice you gain in those positions gives you the experience you need to steer through fairly predictable situations, operationally and tactically. However, with increased responsibility, your decisions change from tactical ones, which take care of current needs and projects, to strategic ones, which attempt to answer the question, "What do we want to accomplish?" The mind-set shifts from managing or controlling the process (tactical) to looking for the results (strategic).

You can develop your strategic thinking by doing the following:

>> **Step back and shift perspective.** Try to observe your business and its position in the community or market from as many angles as possible. Doing so is crucial because it gives you time to reflect so that you can see the big picture.

TIP

Don't hesitate to explore how a totally different kind of company is tackling the same kinds of issues. The idea isn't to transplant their ideas into your company but to gain inspiration from their thinking and come up with something that fits your situation.

>> **Dedicate time each month to reflect on your position in the market, in the community, and in the world.** Reflect alone first and then reflect with your team. This enables you and your team to refresh your thinking with enough perspective to make creative decisions and plan for the future.

>> **Use the insights you gain from your observations and reflection to modify or affirm your direction.** Beware the trap of thinking that once you develop a strategy you're done and have only to periodically update it. Defining and setting out your strategy doesn't mean you suddenly have the ability to control the future, and in the rapidly changing conditions of the modern business environment, things are going to change. Monitoring changes in the market conditions and then incorporating new information into your thinking allows you to stay on top of change or even totally change direction.

Avoiding the perils of micromanaging

Anywhere along the path to increased responsibility, you may be tempted to hang on to control, thinking that it's part of being "in charge." Actually, letting go of control is the basic skill needed. If you don't learn to let go, you run the risk of micromanaging. As a micromanager, you direct every action and must verify the accuracy of every decision because you don't trust that your employees are competent.

WARNING

Micromanaging is a really good way to demoralize staff. It shows that you don't trust your staff or that your need for perfection compels you to retain control over everything. Can you say, "Control freak"? To solve the problem, you have to first recognize that you're micromanaging and then shift your approach to a more strategic style. You do so either by identifying the tendency on your own or by asking staff.

Overcoming your micromanaging tendencies offers many benefits:

>> You reduce your stress levels and gain engagement with your staff.

>> Delegating lets you see the big picture, which gives you the perspective you need to think strategically.

>> You can accomplish more when you work together with your team than you can by doing everything by yourself.

>> Realizing that you're human and need the support of staff to get the job done makes you a more compassionate and better leader.

Are you a micromanager?

Although you likely won't admit to being a micromanager, it is a guarantee that your staff knows. Here is a set of characteristics that indicate you're probably a micromanager:

>> **You frequently feel overwhelmed by work while others wait for you to tell them what to do.** This indicates that you're bearing the brunt of the workload and not delegating.

>> **You dictate the end result rather than work with staff to clarify expectations.** Dictating the end results indicates that you need to be in complete control and you're not using the assets and brain trust at your disposal.

>> **You may delegate a task, but if it isn't being done the way you want it done, you retract the assignment and put it back on your desk.** This behavior indicates that you believe you're the only person who can do the job right.

>> **You hear these words running through your mind or coming out of your mouth:**

  - **"If you want something done right, do it yourself."** If you think along these lines, you believe that you're the only one who can do the job right.

  - **"Nothing can move forward until it is approved by me."** This is another way of saying that you need to be happy with the details. It also suggests that you have expectations you either haven't told staff about or haven't articulated clearly enough; otherwise, your staff would know how to accurately interpret your meaning and produce what you want on their own.

REMEMBER

See yourself? If so, you need to overcome this tendency. Micromanaging sends the message that you don't trust that your staff will perform. Lack of trust causes confidence to deteriorate. It's also baggage that you have to shed if you want to progress to higher levels of decision-making. No single person is perfect, and one person alone, even one with a superhero cape, simply can't be a company.

Letting go of micromanaging

If you've confessed that you're a micromanager, how do you let go? Follow these steps:

1. **Name, boldly and honestly, what you're attached to and why.**

   For example, perhaps you have a hard time letting go because of a fear of failure or a fear you won't get the result you want.

Control stems from fear, so knowing what you're afraid of losing and why helps you decide whether it's a real concern and opens up the space to trust in what comes to you rather than force results.

2. **Decide whether you're ready to let go of control.**

   Keep in mind that there will never be a perfect time. Knowing that the timing is right is an intuitive instinct that fear blocks access to. Ask yourself whether letting go of intervening in team decisions, for example, would give you more freedom. If the answer is yes, then it's time. Remember, the goal is to recognize that, by opening up to new results, you'll be able to handle what happens next.

3. **Accept what happens next and trust all will be well, without your intervention.**

   There is always an empty space between what you've always done and what's next. To avoid reverting back to control, simply be patient with yourself, visualize the better approach, and trust that you'll be all right. To navigate personally, consider working with a mindfulness coach who can help you stay calm. At work, letting go of micromanaging might mean you give up making decisions team members are better equipped to make. They'll be expecting you to step in when they hesitate. Don't bite on that invite! Keep asking them what they'd do and then wait.

Often, when people hear they need to let go, panic results because they think it means letting go of responsibility or quality. But in actuality, you're simply replacing the need to be in control with trust in yourself, your management capabilities, and others on your staff. At the end of the day, the only one you can control is yourself.

If you don't want to let go, not because you need to be in control but because your staff isn't ready to independently assume the necessary responsibilities, then release slowly. Make sure you give inexperienced staff the mentoring and support to bring them up to speed. Also, encourage them to ask questions when they aren't sure. Doing so helps them grow in their careers.

Taking even more steps to improve your leadership style

As you recover from your experimental stint as a micromanager, you can continue to expand your leadership skills, and the easiest way to do so is to take time to listen to what each person on your team brings — or wants to bring — to the table. By listening deeply to your staff, you'll be able to discover breakthroughs and unique solutions. Leadership, as we explain in more detail later in this chapter, isn't about having all the right answers; it's about asking the right questions.

To strengthen your leadership style, ask these questions:

>> **Do you expect staff to get the job done the way you would do it, or do you simply want it successfully accomplished?** The difference is a focus on the process (how it's accomplished) or the end point (success!). Micromanagers focus on every single aspect of how things get done by others. You want to focus on achieving results, using a process that respects and engages your team.

>> **What do your staff members see as each other's strengths and what responsibilities does each want to grow into?** The information you glean from this question guides you as you decide how to allocate staff members' current skills while helping them develop new skills. It also helps staff see where their growth aspirations lie.

Based on the responses to these questions, return decision-making power to the appropriate level and people. When you give decision-making power back, the result is that decision-making has sustainability; that is, the team can perform well past the assumed targets. U.S. naval commanders who develop ship personnel as decision-makers find that they can leave and performance doesn't plummet, even if the next commander brings a less enlightened approach. In short, the crew can lead itself.

TIP

Support the team as team members come up with ways to have fun, work together, and support one another. Doing so shows that you trust your team members to solve problems on their own.

Moving from specializing in one area to working across functions

Several forces are pushing decision-makers to hold an expanded view not only of their businesses, but of their roles as well. Here are the highlights:

>> **The shift away from the old notion that you're either a specialist or a generalist:** You may specialize in a function, but you'll always need to know where you fit in terms of the company's success and how the company dovetails into the rest of the world. Understanding what the higher purpose of a company is helps employees stay engaged while achieving that purpose.

>> **The trend toward combining complementary functions into one role so that all can function more cooperatively:** Internal functions, such as sales versus marketing, for example, used to compete with each other. But businesses can no longer afford to waste productive energy on unproductive competition among staff members or company divisions. The idea behind combining complementary functions is to serve the employee community and the customer, not feed competitive conflict.

>> **The shift away from centralized decision-making, in which decisions are made by a few, to decentralized decision-making:** This structure fosters collaboration and timelier responses to change, and everyone contributes to the company's success.

As a decision-maker, how can you prepare for these changes? By taking the actions we outline here:

>> **Seek out opportunities to work in different areas of expertise.** Working with others whose expertise differs from yours makes you a well-rounded individual and gives you insight into other areas of the company. This exposure to multiple areas gives you a new, broader perspective that can inform your decisions and help you predict what impact your decisions will have.

>> **Participate in decision-making related to the best projects to move forward on.** Quality, not quantity, of projects aids success. You'll gain experience in seeing how projects bring together expertise from within and beyond your company's boundaries. Even if you're working on a joint venture, you'll gain insight into how very different values, criteria, and beliefs guide decision-making.

>> **Practice empathy.** Use every conflict or misunderstanding to see through someone else's eyes. Doing so lets you use your team's diverse outlooks to your advantage. Plus, this capability is an essential quality for anyone paying attention to the workplace culture and customer relationships. Your greatest ally is your ability to listen.

>> **Embrace the idea that you don't know everything there is to know.** Don't believe everything you think. There is more knowledge, excitement, and opportunity waiting, and the only thing required to tap into it is curiosity! Through social media and other resources, information can flow instantly around the world. This new reality expands what is available, and it opens new relationships from many different sources.

Displaying Character through Decision-Making

Character — essentially your moral fiber, ethics, and integrity all rolled into one — counts at every level. How you use power, whether it's personal power, which you earn by overcoming adversity, or delegated power, which you possess as you attain positions of authority, reveals your character. Character separates those who lead their lives with integrity from those who abuse authority or use force.

Mirror, mirror, on the wall: Taking a close look at yourself

TIP

How can you tell where you stand, character-wise? Use the Waiter Rule. Basically, this rule says that how you treat a waiter reveals who you are as a person. According to Bill Swanson, a now retired CEO of Raytheon, "If someone is friendly to you (someone higher in authority) but rude to the waiter, he or she isn't a nice person." In addition, saying things such as, "I know the owner and can get you fired" speaks volumes about how a person uses his or her personal power. Someone who throws the power of his position around doesn't respect his position or the power it holds and doesn't embody the traits of a good leader.

To discover how you view power, ask yourself these questions:

>> **Do I think I have all the answers, or can others offer a view that I can learn from?** Reflecting on this question reveals your approach to learning. If you think you have all the answers and need to be the resident expert, incorporating the wisdom of the team will be tough. Take this mind-set to the extreme, and you could qualify for dictator!

>> **Do I treat those who report to me with the same respect I treat those in higher positions?** If you treat everyone with the same respect, regardless of his or her position, you'll know you're comfortable with authority. If not, you'll know that you attach authority to power and so might not respect its use.

>> **Does my confidence shrink when I am confronted by an authority figure? Do I feel I need to manipulate to get what I want?** If your default, go-to strategy is to exert control over others or use manipulation to get your way, there's a good chance your self-esteem needs a boost. Low self-esteem leads to lousy decisions. Building confidence in yourself can help you increase trust.

>> **Do I feel more powerful when I am delivering orders or when I am collaborating to achieve a team goal?** In other words, what floats your boat: being in charge or working collaboratively toward a common goal? Perhaps you're comfortable doing both. If you need to be in charge, can you step back and let others take the helm without feeling you've lost control?

WARNING

Out of all the questions listed, the last one points to the ego. In this context, *ego* refers to your concept of self and your relationship with yourself. Most business folks still hang onto the old and generally inaccurate belief that an overblown ego is a prerequisite to achieving success. The younger generation, on the other hand, doesn't subscribe to this idea, and these "kids" are leading companies that are growing like crazy. Many people who have poor relationships with their egos protect the ego by trying to make themselves feel better by putting down or comparing themselves to others, but this is a career limiting mind-set, especially in environments where collaboration is critical. When your concept of self is low, your decisions suffer because making yourself feel better becomes more important than making a better decision.

Using defining moments to build character

In the same way that career-defining moments of a company's leader shape the company's future, personal defining moments build character. In these defining moments, you're typically presented with two equally held, highly important values that you must choose between.

Suppose, for example, that you discover you're booked to meet a potential new client at the same time you promised your daughter you'd attend her school play. What do you do in this situation? There is no going back and no right answer, and your response may uncover something you didn't know about yourself or another person involved. Do you do what you believe is more important or what you feel obligated to do? Cumulatively, tough decisions build character. They also change relationships.

How can you use character-revealing conflicts to transform character? There are two ways:

>> **Find out what is important to you and then identify the underlying values.** Look at a conflicting feeling not as gut wrenching, even though it may feel that way, but as tension between two equally acceptable values. To identify the conflict, ask yourself what is important to you about each demand. Then chose the higher, more difficult path that is aligned with what matters more to you.

>> **Take your mind off what is immediate and in your face to allow your creative side to go to work.** Step out of the workplace "noise" and do something you love to do: ski, hike, bike, knit, garden . . . whatever, but before you do so, ask yourself for insight. Then, when you're out doing the thing you enjoy, insights will pop up when you least expect. Notice when the light bulb goes on to reveal deeper values.

TIP

The idea is to free your mind, not numb it. So step away from the TV, remote control, and mini-bar.

Handling yourself when things go wrong

You may have heard the saying, "Conflict builds character, but crisis defines it." Sooner or later, something you're working on will not go as planned — perhaps with disastrous results — and you'll have to deal with it. How you handle yourself in such situations is a defining moment in the development of your leadership ability.

As a leader and decision-maker, you must be prepared to handle unexpected crises with honesty and integrity. Following are some actions you can take to prepare for, deal with, and learn from when the going gets rough:

>> **Plan ahead.** If you don't have a team plan for a crisis, put one together and make sure that all members are on the same page regarding the following:

- An explanation of what constitutes a crisis for your business

- How to address all legal issues

- How to address public perception of what happened and what it means

- The people responsible for putting the plan into action to ensure that, when bad things happen, the plan is brought forward to guide immediate action

>> **At the time of the crisis, take action.** Move immediately to address risks to public or employee safety and offer clear information about what is going on.

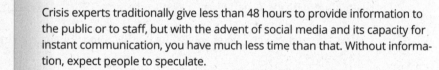

Crisis experts traditionally give less than 48 hours to provide information to the public or to staff, but with the advent of social media and its capacity for instant communication, you have much less time than that. Without information, expect people to speculate.

>> **Show true compassion for the people affected.** Due to the violence people are exposed to every day — violent TV shows and video games, ongoing military operations, and so on — the public psyche is often numbed to general tragedy. However, when loss is experienced at a personal level, it's very real. Therefore, when you take action during a crisis in which your business or product harms the public — whether that harm is physical or to the public trust — you must speak from your heart and put yourself in their shoes. Otherwise, your response comes across as insincere.

>> **After the dust has settled, find out what happened and then share that knowledge.** Your goal after the crisis is not to seek someone or something to blame, but to learn from the situation. Put together a team of employees from throughout the organization and give them the job of collectively reflecting, documenting, and then sharing what is learned. Remember, sound organizational judgment comes from learning and then sharing.

A crisis can be the catalyst for doing things differently for greater benefit. It breaks up patterns and gives you an opportunity to replace useless or ineffective habits. But you don't have to wait for a crisis before you decide to think creatively about your processes.

A STUDY IN CHARACTER: AKIO TOYODA

At the end of 2009 and into early 2010, Toyota recalled over 7.5 million cars due to unintentional acceleration (and subsequent deaths) traced back to the gas pedal made by one supplier. After recalling over 7 million vehicles, Toyota President Akio Toyoda accepted full responsibility, saying, "In the past few months, our customers have started to feel uncertain about the safety of Toyota's vehicles, and I take full responsibility for that." His next step was to learn what happened and to address it. He did not shy away from what he discovered:

> I would like to point out that Toyota's priority has traditionally been the following: First, safety; second, quality; third, volume. These priorities became confused, and we were not able to stop, think, and make improvements as much as we were able to before, and our basic stance to listen to customers' voices to make better products has weakened somewhat. We pursued growth over the speed at which we were able to develop our people and our organization, and we should be sincerely mindful of that."

Toyota has a learning culture, and, true to form, company leaders focused on learning why the errors leading to the recall occurred. The company's president accepted full responsibility and didn't pin the blame on a scapegoat further down in the ranks. Loyalty is inspired by care and honesty.

Improving Your Decision-Making by Becoming a Better Leader

Who do people turn to in times of uncertainty, when they need to take action but don't know what action to take, or when they have a problem they can't solve on their own? Leaders. In short, leaders are the people others look to when a decision must be made. But you already knew that. What you may not know is what a leader isn't: He or she is not the one with all the answers, and not necessarily the one with the authority. In this section, we tell you how you can become a better leader, which will, in turn, transform you into a better decision–maker.

Differentiating between leadership and authority

Despite their similarities, being a leader is not the same as having authority. Knowing the difference between being a leader and being in a position of authority is necessary for operating in a world where collaboration is essential. Here are some basic definitions:

>> *Authority* refers to officially possessing, often through a position, decision-making power.

>> *Leadership* refers to the quality that inspires others to move toward a common goal, to overcome hardship or difficulties, and to work together to achieve the objectives placed before them. Leadership combines vision with inspiration and telling the truth.

You can see the confusion anytime someone asks, "Who is the leader?" and everyone points to the person in charge. That isn't leadership. It's where authority resides. Now that same person may also be a leader, but it isn't a forgone conclusion.

Although authority specifies which decisions you have the power to make, authority does not necessarily make you a leader. Plenty of people in authority have been ineffective leaders, and plenty of important leaders have come from the ranks of those without official authority.

Using your power for good

Leaders inspire. They turn the mundane into the meaningful and motivate others to pursue this higher purpose. They don't have all the answers, but they ask the right questions. Leaders are decisive and visionary.

Anyone can be a leader. The notion that people fall into one of two groups — either leaders or followers — just isn't accurate and has been debunked in the last place you'd expect: marine naval vessels. Even in strong command-and-control structures such as the military, each person can demonstrate leadership because it doesn't have anything to do with authority. It has to do with responsibility. People are encouraged to take the initiative, come up with solutions, and act on them. This kind of trust in the capabilities of people up and down the chain of command is vital for success, not only in the military but in the civilian world, too. In fact, sustained high performance depends on it.

In environments where people are expected to take the initiative and act on the solutions they devise, the person in authority — you, as a business owner or manager — plays a completely different role: Your role is to facilitate the emergence of leadership. To foster leadership in your team, ask your employees what solutions they have to the issue at hand, and keep asking them for their ideas, even when they turn to you for direction. Then help them think through the solution (a mentoring role) and support implementation.

Some people in positions of authority wield power inappropriately just to boost their self-esteem, ego, and confidence. Doing so undermines staff morale and contribution. How you handle power and personnel when in a position of authority says everything about you.

Being a leader good enough to ask the tough questions

Groupthink — when people feel they need to conform to one view without question — is toxic for effective teamwork. It leads to important issues not being addressed and creative ideas not being offered. It preserves the status quo and leaves you and your company vulnerable.

WARNING

If you move forward without clearing out the hidden issues, your leadership and your company's growth get stuck in a holding pattern, and moving forward will feel like running waist-deep in glue. You'll miss breakthrough moments in personal, team, and organizational performance.

Fortunately, effective leadership can overcome groupthink. Leaders must have the courage to ask the tough questions of themselves and their teams. Doing so puts the "unmentionables" on the table. By asking tough questions, you ensure that routine thinking doesn't block achievement of your goal. The best time to ask a powerful question or two is when things are at a standstill or when agreement has come too easily. What is a powerful question? Here's one example: "Is there something we're missing here?"

TIP

To profit from powerful questions, do the following before finalizing the decision; this exercise is especially important when you're making big, strategic decisions, such as whether to accept an offer to sell your business:

1. **Take a time-out between discussions.**

   The purpose of this time-out is to give everyone a chance to ruminate on the issue at hand. Team members can take a walk together or alone. Don't give specific instructions (you don't want to lead them to a conclusion), but you can say, "Let's take some time to think about this."

2. **When you reconvene, ask for questions or offer one yourself.**

   Breakthroughs can often result when you open up the conversation to explore alternatives not usually on the table. If allowing space for reflection hasn't produced any questions, you can move to conclude the decision.

Creating Safe and Stable Workplaces

Trauma occurs when an individual is psychologically overwhelmed and unable to cope intellectually or emotionally. When the source of the trauma is a single, catastrophic event, such as a hurricane or an office shooting, or ongoing and pervasive danger (such as exists in war zones), it's easy to identify. But people can also experience trauma as a result of an accumulation of factors, such as unclear expectations, excessive workloads, repeated negative judgments, prejudicial behaviors and opinions, pathologically difficult people, or abusive treatment by superiors. Sound familiar? Unfortunately, one or more of these factors affects too many workplaces.

Trauma caused by the work environment has a negative effect on creativity, mental processing of information, productivity, and the ability to adjust to change. In other words, poor workplace environments cultivate poor performance and bad decisions. Conversely, when workplaces are safe, people contribute beyond what is expected, without fear of reprimand. They also make better decisions because they aren't stressed out.

A safe workplace is one in which employees feel emotionally safe, financially secure, recognized, and acknowledged. In this section, we explain how you can create a workplace that fosters well-being, creativity, and improved problem-solving and decision-making.

Adapting your management style

Management by fear works against sound decision-making and performance. It creates an emotionally charged workplace that is not conducive to rational or intuitive decision-making. Although productivity is possible in such a workplace, this type of environment is bad for a few key reasons:

THE TROUBLE WITH BOSSES

Research conducted by the Hay Group, a global management consulting firm, found that globally the majority of leaders, most likely in management roles, are blocking performance and instilling workplaces with unmotivated employees, which results in poor decision-making. These leaders give instructions and then focus on what was wrong over what was right. The subjects of the Hay Group study aren't alone. Many in leadership roles default to a command-and-control management style as a way to feel in power, particularly when things seem uncertain. The command-and-control style has its place, but for day-to-day performance, it's demoralizing. In an environment like this, decision-making can come to a standstill because people are afraid of making mistakes.

>> **It makes creatively adapting to changing conditions impossible.** People will follow the rules before achieving goals or taking risks.

>> **It compromises innovation.** Innovation requires creativity and risk-taking. In fear-based decision-making environments, people watch their backs and avoid taking risks.

>> **It impedes seeing ahead.** Vision for the future requires intuition and empathy, two things that are in very short supply in fear-based environments.

Relying on coercion isn't logical or rational, yet it's the prevailing leadership style around the world. If you work in a complex decision-making environment, you (and your managers) need to access leadership styles that are more appropriate to creating better decisions. Managers who follow management styles that free up employee creativity and open communication to difficult conversations share these characteristics:

>> They engage employees to creatively find solutions to issues.

>> They focus decisions on achieving business goals rather than personal career aspirations.

>> They engage in difficult conversations aimed at understanding the situation instead of seeking fault.

>> They care about employee well-being, do not judge, and approach issues with open minds and hearts, enabling open and honest communication that springs from a genuine place.

>> They inspire trust in the working relationships.

REMEMBER

Workplaces that don't work for the employees don't work for the company's sustainability. A healthy, trusting work environment lets you go beyond your current productivity goals and quotas to achieve much higher performance. It really is that simple.

Taking steps to improve the quality of the working environment

One way to address negative aspects in the workplace and ensure that employees can work well together as a team is to pay attention to working relationships. The world may be unpredictable, but the quality of working relationships provides stability. In workplaces where trust, a sense of belonging, and genuine care for each other are cultivated, employees can focus on giving the company or the project their absolute best.

When the environment doesn't support high-quality working relationships, your employees spend more time dealing with office politics or covering their backs to reduce personal risk. If your goal is to create high-quality working relationships among employees, supervisors, and upper management, give the items we discuss in this section prime consideration.

Improving emotional safety

To improve emotional safety, identify barriers to trustworthy interpersonal relationships (punishing disclosure of safety risk, for example) and then work with managers and supervisors to establish accountability for better practices. Here are some suggestions:

>> **Sustain caring, respectful working relationships.** Rather than confirm the negative, relationships must support the positive. Solid emotional support helps people recover from stressful situations, whereas relationships that confirm negativity in the workplace affirm the trauma.

>> **Provide opportunities to talk about traumas and release emotion.** Trauma results from a painful, stressful, or shocking event that can be sudden or prolonged over time. Traumatic experiences include losing a coworker, an insensitively handled layoff, violence in the workplace, or a bullying boss. Be sure to acknowledge and look after your own feelings, as well.

>> **Plan casual events that support social interaction, in a comforting environment.** Doing so allows the workplace community to collectively process its experience.

WARNING

Often management sends the message that employees just need to get over it or that their feelings about the situation indicate weakness. This attitude only makes the trauma worse. Conversely, excessive focus can strengthen the trauma by reinforcing the sense of powerlessness. The difference lies between allowing the emotions to be processed versus repeatedly reliving the experience.

TIP

Anne Murray Allen, in her former role as Senior Director for Knowledge and Intranet Management for Hewlett-Packard, suggests saying something like this to get the conversation going: "We are missing a process here. If we had it, it would make everyone's life easier. How about we all get together to create this process so it works?"

Ensuring physical safety

To ensure physical safety, set standards and live by them. In industries such as construction and manufacturing, workplace safety requires watchfulness. Give experienced employees the assignment of identifying potential hazards or practices.

In companies where speed of production can undermine personal safety, employees will "take one for the team" if meeting quotas has a higher priority than workplace safety. In some workplace environments, such a priority can mean a limb lost — not something you want credit for.

Ensuring high-quality interactions

To ensure high-quality interactions between employees, supervisors, and upper management, create an atmosphere that affirms employee confidence by genuinely acknowledging effort. This suggestion doesn't mean you have to be Mr. or Ms. Nice 24/7. It means that recognition is a natural part of the interaction between you and all the employees you come in contact with.

Spontaneously praise employees for jobs well done. Include fun as part of the working day. When you have fun, don't do so at anyone's expense, but out of the pure pleasure of working with a great group of people. Your genuine enthusiasm and sincere appreciation for their efforts can make a big different, even when your employees aren't feeling so great about themselves or their work.

Being the leader you expect to see in others

When morale is low or the thinking small, small issues end up looking pretty big and people act out their frustration and lack of control. One cause of low morale is often unaddressed bad behavior — bullying, threats, and intimidation, for example — in the workplace. If you truly want your company or department to succeed, you need to address these issues.

Staff look to your actions to find out what the unwritten rules are. The *unwritten rules* are the de facto rules that govern behavior and expectations in the workplace, regardless of what the stated policy is. Often, the term refers to the difference between what is said — "We value respect in the workplace," for example — and what is done — managers overlook bullying behavior. Although no one may be running around the workplace waving a sign that declares, "Bad behavior is permissible!" not doing anything about bad behavior pretty much amounts to saying that it's acceptable.

Being a leader means you must firmly, yet professionally, confront tough interpersonal issues, including bad behavior in the workplace. Here's how:

>> **Challenge bad behavior, including bullying and overtly expressed prejudice.** Bullies tend to be people who feel that they lack power and use anger and aggressive behavior to reclaim it. Have no tolerance for inappropriate behavior or judgment of others, but offer professional coaching or

personal development opportunities so the individual can gain better interpersonal skills. In the workplace, holding people accountable for their behavior reinforces your commitment to higher standards.

Deal with prejudice differently because it is a hard-wired belief. To deal with prejudice, pair people up so that the successes resulting from the working relationship transforms the belief.

>> **Draw clear boundaries around what is acceptable and respectful and what is not.** When dealing with an interpersonal issue, take the individual aside, and, if the employee is receptive, provide a coach.

TIP

You can also try a game that builds empathy. One such game is Know Me, developed in the thick of apartheid reconciliation, as a means to respectfully disagree, learn, and forge better solutions. For details about this game and others, go to `http://knowmegame.com/johari_window.html`.

>> **Reject pervasive negativity.** In some workplaces, grumbling could qualify as an Olympic sport. Pessimism and crankiness can be momentarily useful, but if they become persistent habits, they bring everyone down.

REMEMBER

Negativity is not the same as critical thinking. Critical thinking is required as a check and balance; it doesn't have to be negative or punitive.

>> **Tackle difficult issues.** Many issues negatively affecting the workplace are left unresolved for fear that careers will be in jeopardy if the problem is reported. When you encounter a difficult issue, openly gather the facts, skip blame or judgment, and involve all parties to develop options and solutions. Be hard on the problem and soft on the people. When you face a difficult issue head-on and with integrity, you open up confidence and reinforce that all people matter, not just the ones considered to be of higher value.

REMEMBER

It takes courage and strength to deal with adversarial or difficult situations in the workplace, but when you do, you display — and inspire — integrity and are more likely to make ethical decisions and engage in the kind of risk-taking that saves companies.

>> **Establish clear expectations about what are and aren't acceptable behaviors for everyone in the workplace, including contract employees.** When the expectations you set aren't being followed, you must follow up and put your foot down. Trust is breached otherwise.

REMEMBER

Management guru Edwards Deming said, "Managers talk about getting rid of deadwood, but there are only two possible explanations of why the deadwood exists: You hired deadwood in the first place or, you hired live wood, and then you killed it." Nonperforming employees are often created when you don't pay attention to how workplace conditions affect performance. You can change the workplace conditions to make them better.

4
Project Management

Contents at a Glance

Chapter **1**

Achieving Results

Successful organizations create projects that produce desired results in established time frames with assigned resources. As a result, businesses are increasingly driven to find individuals who can excel in this project-oriented environment.

Because you're reading this minibook, chances are good that you've been asked to manage a project. So, hang on tight — you're going to need a new set of skills and techniques to steer that project to successful completion. But not to worry! This chapter gets you off to a smooth start by showing you what projects and project management really are and by helping you separate projects from non-project assignments. This chapter also offers the rationale for why projects succeed or fail and gets you into the project-management mind-set.

Determining What Makes a Project a Project

No matter what your job is, you handle a myriad of assignments every day. For example, you may prepare a memo, hold a meeting, design a sales campaign, or move to new offices. Or you may make the information systems more user-friendly, develop a research compound in the laboratory, or improve the organization's public image. Not all these assignments are projects. How can you tell which ones are and which ones aren't? This section is here to help.

Understanding the three main components that define a project

A *project* is a temporary undertaking performed to produce a unique product, service, or result. Large or small, a project always has the following three components:

>> **Specific scope:** Desired results or products

>> **Schedule:** Established dates when project work starts and ends

>> **Required resources:** Necessary number of people and funds and other resources

REMEMBER

As illustrated in Figure 1-1, each component affects the other two. For example: Expanding the type and characteristics of desired outcomes may require more time (a later end date) or more resources. Moving up the end date may necessitate paring down the results or increasing project expenditures (for instance, by paying overtime to project staff). Within this three-part project definition, you perform work to achieve your desired results.

```
                    Product
                   /       \
                  /         \
                 /           \
            Schedule <----> Resources
```

FIGURE 1-1:
The relationship between the three main components of a project.

Although many other considerations may affect a project's performance (see the later section "Defining Project Management" for details), these three components are the basis of a project's definition for the following three reasons:

>> The only reason a project exists is to produce the results specified in its scope.

>> The project's end date is an essential part of defining what constitutes successful performance; the desired result must be provided by a certain time to meet its intended need.

>> The availability of resources shapes the nature of the products the project can produce.

A Guide to the Project Management Body of Knowledge, PMBOK Guide 6th Edition (*PMBOK 6*), published by Project Management Institute, elaborates on these components by

>> Emphasizing that *product* includes both the basic nature of what is to be produced (for example, a new training program or a new prescription drug) and its required characteristics (for example, the topics that the training program must address), which are defined as the product's *quality*

>> Noting that *resources* refers to funds, as well as to other nonmonetary resources, such as people, equipment, raw materials, and facilities

PMBOK 6 also emphasizes that *risk* (the likelihood that not everything will go exactly according to plan) plays an important role in defining a project and that guiding a project to success involves continually managing tradeoffs among the three main project components — the products to be produced and their characteristics, the schedule, and the resources required to do the project work.

Recognizing the diversity of projects

Projects come in a wide assortment of shapes and sizes. For example, projects can

>> **Be large or small**

- Installing a new subway system, which may cost more than $1 billion and take 10 to 15 years to complete, is a project.

- Preparing an ad hoc report of monthly sales figures, which may take you one day to complete, is also a project.

>> **Involve many people or just you**

- Training all 10,000 of your organization's staff in a new affirmative-action policy is a project.

- Rearranging the furniture and equipment in your office is also a project.

>> **Be defined by a legal contract or by an informal agreement**

- A signed contract between you and a customer that requires you to build a house defines a project.

- An informal promise you make to install a new software package on your colleague's computer also defines a project.

>> **Be business-related or personal**

- Conducting your organization's annual blood drive is a project.

- Having a dinner party for 15 people is also a project.

A PROJECT BY ANY OTHER NAME JUST ISN'T A PROJECT

People often confuse the following two terms with *project*:

- **Process:** A *process* is a series of routine steps to perform a particular function, such as a procurement process or a budget process. A process isn't a one-time activity that achieves a specific result; instead, it defines *how* a particular function is to be done every time. Processes, like the activities that go into buying materials, are often parts of projects.

- **Program:** This term can describe two different situations. First, a *program* can be a set of goals that gives rise to specific projects. But, unlike a project, a program can never be completely accomplished. For example, a health-awareness program can never completely achieve its goal (the public will never be totally aware of all health issues as a result of a health-awareness program), but one or more projects may accomplish specific results related to the program's goal (such as a workshop on minimizing the risk of heart disease). Second, a *program* sometimes refers to a group of specified projects that achieve a common goal.

REMEMBER

Regardless of the individual characteristics of your project, you define it by the same three components described in the previous section: results (or scope), start and end dates, and resources. The information you need to plan and manage your project is the same for any project you manage, although the ease and the time to develop it may differ. The more thoroughly you plan and manage your projects, the more likely you are to succeed.

Describing the four stages of a project

Every project, whether large or small, passes through the following four stages:

- **Starting the project:** This stage involves generating, evaluating, and framing the business need for the project and the general approach to performing it and agreeing to prepare a detailed project plan. Outputs from this stage may include approval to proceed to the next stage, documentation of the need for the project and rough estimates of time and resources to perform it (often included in a project charter), and an initial list of people who may be interested in, involved with, or affected by the project.

- **Organizing and preparing:** This stage involves developing a plan that specifies the desired results; the work to do; the time, cost, and other resources required; and a plan for how to address key project risks. Outputs from this stage may include a project plan that documents the intended project results and the time, resources, and supporting processes needed to create them.

>> **Carrying out the work:** This stage involves establishing the project team and the project support systems, performing the planned work, and monitoring and controlling performance to ensure adherence to the current plan. Outputs from this stage may include project results, project progress reports, and other communications.

>> **Closing out the project:** This stage involves assessing the project results, obtaining customer approvals, transitioning project team members to new assignments, closing financial accounts, and conducting a post-project evaluation. Outputs from this stage may include final, accepted, and approved project results and recommendations and suggestions for applying lessons learned from this project to similar efforts in the future.

For small projects, this entire life cycle can take just a few days. For larger projects, it can take many years! In fact, to allow for greater focus on key aspects and to make it easier to monitor and control the work, project managers often subdivide larger projects into separate phases, each of which is treated as a miniproject and passes through these four life cycle stages. Regardless of the project's simplicity or complexity, however, these four stages are the same.

REMEMBER

In a perfect world, you complete one stage of your project before you move on to the next one; and after you complete a stage, you never return to it again. But the world isn't perfect, and project success often requires a flexible approach that responds to real situations that you may face, such as the following:

>> **You may have to work on two (or more) project stages at the same time to meet tight deadlines.** Working on the next stage before you complete the current one increases the risk that you may have to redo tasks, which may cause you to miss deadlines and spend more resources than you originally planned. If you choose this strategy, be sure people understand the potential risks and costs associated with it.

>> **Sometimes you learn by doing.** Despite doing your best to assess feasibility and develop detailed plans, you may realize you can't achieve what you thought you could. When this situation happens, you need to return to the earlier project stages and rethink them in light of the new information you've acquired.

>> **Sometimes things change unexpectedly.** Your initial feasibility and benefits assessments are sound and your plan is detailed and realistic. However, certain key project team members leave the organization without warning during the project. Or a new technology emerges, and it's more appropriate to use than the one in your original plans. Because ignoring these occurrences may seriously jeopardize your project's success, you need to return to the earlier project stages and rethink them in light of these new realities.

Achieving Results

Defining Project Management

Project management is the process of guiding a project from its beginning through its performance to its closure. Project management includes five sets of processes, which are described in more detail in the following sections:

>> **Initiating processes:** Clarifying the business need, defining high-level expectations and resource budgets, and beginning to identify audiences that may play a role in your project

>> **Planning processes:** Detailing the project scope, time frames, resources, and risks, as well as intended approaches to project communications, quality, and management of external purchases of goods and services

>> **Executing processes:** Establishing and managing the project team, communicating with and managing project audiences, and implementing the project plans

>> **Monitoring and controlling processes:** Tracking performance and taking actions necessary to help ensure that project plans are successfully implemented and the desired results are achieved

>> **Closing processes:** Ending all project activity

As illustrated in Figure 1-2, these five process groups help support the project through the four stages of its life cycle. Initiating processes support the work to be done when starting the project, and planning processes support the organizing-and-preparing stage. Executing processes guide the project tasks performed when carrying out the work, and closing processes are used to perform the tasks that bring the project to an end.

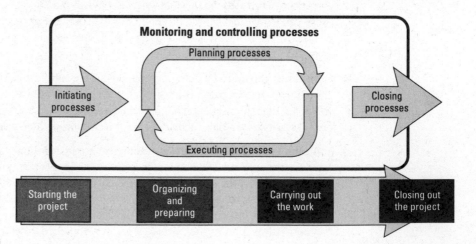

FIGURE 1-2:
The five project-management process groups that support the four project life cycle stages.

Figure 1-2 highlights how you may cycle back from executing processes to planning processes when you have to return to the organizing–and–preparing stage to modify existing plans to address problems you encounter or new information you acquire while carrying out the project work. Finally, you use monitoring and controlling processes in each of the four stages to help ensure that work is being performed according to plans.

Successfully performing these processes requires the following:

>> **Information:** Accurate, timely, and complete data for the planning, performance monitoring, and final assessment of the project

>> **Communication:** Clear, open, and timely sharing of information with appropriate individuals and groups throughout the project's duration

>> **Commitment:** Team members' personal promises to produce the agreed-upon results on time and within budget

Starting with the initiating processes

All projects begin with an idea. Perhaps your organization's client identifies a need; or maybe your boss thinks of a new market to explore; or maybe you think of a way to refine your organization's procurement process.

Sometimes the initiating process is informal. For a small project, it may consist of just a discussion and a verbal agreement. In other instances, especially for larger projects, a project requires a formal review and decision by your boss and other members of your organization's senior management team.

Decision-makers consider the following two questions when deciding whether to move ahead with a project:

>> *Should* **we do it?** Are the benefits we expect to achieve worth the costs we'll have to pay? Are there better ways to approach the issue?

>> *Can* **we do it?** Is the project technically feasible? Are the required resources available?

If the answer to both questions is "Yes," the project can proceed to the organizing-and-preparing stage (see the following section), during which a project plan is developed. If the answer to either question is a definite, ironclad "No," under no circumstances should the project go any further. If nothing can be done to make it desirable and feasible, the decision-makers should cancel the project immediately. Doing anything else guarantees wasted resources, lost opportunities, and a frustrated staff. (Check out the later sidebar "Performing a benefit-cost analysis" if you need extra help determining the answer to the first question.)

Suppose you're in charge of the publications department in your organization. You've just received a request to have a 20,000-page document printed in 10 minutes, which requires equipment that can reproduce at the rate of 2,000 pages per minute.

You check with your staff and confirm that your document-reproducing equipment has a top speed of 500 pages per minute. You check with your suppliers and find out that the fastest document-reproducing equipment available today has a top speed of 1,000 pages per minute. Do you agree to plan and perform this project when you know you can't possibly meet the request? Of course not.

Rather than promising something you know you can't achieve, consider asking your customer whether she can change the request. For example, can she accept the document in 20 minutes? Can you reproduce certain parts of the document in the first 10 minutes and the rest later?

During some projects, you may be convinced that you can't meet a particular request or that the benefits of the project aren't worth the costs involved. Be sure to check with the people who developed or approved the project. They may have information you don't, or you may have additional information that they weren't aware of when they approved the request.

WARNING

Beware of assumptions that you or other people make when assessing your project's potential value, cost, and feasibility. For example, just because your requests for overtime have been turned down in the past doesn't guarantee they'll be turned down this time.

Outlining the planning processes

When you know what you hope to accomplish and you believe it's possible, you need a detailed plan that describes how you and your team will make it happen. Include the following in your project-management plan:

>> An overview of the reasons for your project. (See Chapter 3 of this minibook.)

>> A detailed description of intended results. (Chapter 3 of this minibook explains how to describe desired results.)

>> A list of all constraints the project must address. (Chapter 3 of this minibook explores the different types of constraints a project may face.)

>> A list of all assumptions related to the project. (Chapter 3 of this minibook discusses how to frame assumptions.)

PERFORMING A BENEFIT-COST ANALYSIS

A *benefit-cost analysis* is a comparative assessment of all the benefits you anticipate from your project and all the costs required to introduce the project, perform it, and support the changes resulting from it. Benefit-cost analyses help you to

- Decide whether to undertake a project or decide which of several projects to undertake

- Frame appropriate project objectives

- Develop appropriate *before* and *after* measures of project success

- Prepare estimates of the resources required to perform the project work

You can express some anticipated benefits in monetary equivalents (such as reduced operating costs or increased revenue). For other benefits, numerical measures can approximate some, but not all, aspects. If your project is to improve staff morale, for example, you may consider associated benefits to include reduced turnover, increased productivity, fewer absences, and fewer formal grievances. Whenever possible, express benefits and costs in monetary terms to facilitate the assessment of a project's net value.

Consider costs for all phases of the project. Such costs may be nonrecurring (such as labor, capital investment, and certain operations and services) or recurring (such as changes in personnel, supplies, and materials or maintenance and repair). In addition, consider the following:

- Potential costs of not doing the project

- Potential costs if the project fails

- Opportunity costs (in other words, the potential benefits if you had spent your funds successfully performing a different project)

The farther into the future you look when performing your analysis, the more important it is to convert your estimates of benefits over costs into today's dollars. Unfortunately, the farther you look, the less confident you can be of your estimates. For example, you may expect to reap benefits for years from a new computer system, but changing technology may make your new system obsolete after only one year.

Thus, the following two key factors influence the results of a benefit-cost analysis:

- How far into the future you look to identify benefits

- On which assumptions you base your analysis

(continued)

Achieving Results

(continued)

Although you may not want to go out and design a benefit-cost analysis by yourself, you definitely want to see whether your project already has one and, if it does, what the specific results of that analysis were.

The excess of a project's expected benefits over its estimated costs in today's dollars is its *net present value (NPV)*. The net present value is based on the following two premises:

- **Inflation:** The purchasing power of a dollar will be less one year from now than it is today. If the rate of inflation is 3 percent for the next 12 months, $1 today will be worth $0.97 one year from today. In other words, 12 months from now, you'll pay $1 to buy what you paid $0.97 for today.

- **Lost return on investment:** If you spend money to perform the project being considered, you'll forego the future income you could earn by investing it conservatively today. For example, if you put $1 in a bank and receive simple interest at the rate of 3 percent compounded annually, 12 months from today you'll have $1.03 (assuming 0 percent inflation).

To address these considerations when determining the NPV, you specify the following numbers:

- **Discount rate:** The factor that reflects the future value of $1 in today's dollars, considering the effects of both inflation and lost return on investment

- **Allowable payback period:** The length of time for anticipated benefits and estimated costs

In addition to determining the NPV for different discount rates and payback periods, figure the project's *internal rate of return* (the value of the discount rate that would yield an NPV of 0) for each payback period.

>> A list of all required work. (Chapter 4 of this minibook discusses how to identify all required project work.)

>> A breakdown of the roles you and your team members will play.

>> A detailed project schedule.

>> Needs for personnel, funds, and non-personnel resources (such as equipment, facilities, and information).

>> A description of how you plan to manage any significant risks and uncertainties.

» Plans for project communications. (Chapter 5 of this minibook discusses how to keep everyone who's involved in your project up-to-date.)

» Plans for ensuring project quality.

TIP

Always put your project plans in writing; doing so helps you clarify details and reduces the chances that you'll forget something. Plans for large projects can take hundreds of pages, but a plan for a small project can take only a few lines on a piece of paper (or a tablecloth!).

The success of your project depends on the clarity and accuracy of your plan and on whether people believe they can achieve it. Considering past experience in your project plan makes your plan more realistic; involving people in the plan's development encourages their commitment to achieving it.

WARNING

Don't let the pressure to get fast results convince you to skip the planning and get right to the tasks. Although this strategy can create a lot of immediate activity, it also creates significant chances for waste and mistakes.

TIP

Be sure your project's drivers and supporters review and approve the plan in writing before you begin your project (see Chapter 2 of this minibook). For a small project, you may need only a brief email or someone's initials on the plans. For a larger project, though, you may need a formal review and signoff by one or more levels of your organization's management.

Examining the executing processes

After you've developed your project-management plan and set your appropriate project baselines, it's time to get to work and start executing your plan. This is often the phase when management gets more engaged and excited to see things being produced.

Preparing

Preparing to begin the project work involves the following tasks:

» **Assigning people to all project roles:** Confirm the individuals who'll perform the project work and negotiate agreements with them and their managers to make sure they'll be available to work on the project team.

» **Introducing team members to each other and to the project:** Help people begin developing interpersonal relationships with each other. Help them appreciate the overall purpose of the project and explain how the different parts will interact and support each other.

>> **Giving and explaining tasks to all team members:** Describe to all team members what work they're responsible for producing and how the team members will coordinate their efforts.

>> **Defining how the team will perform its essential functions:** Decide how the team will handle routine communications, make different project decisions, and resolve conflicts. Develop any procedures that may be required to guide performance of these functions.

>> **Setting up necessary tracking systems:** Decide which system(s) and accounts you'll use to track schedules, work effort, and expenditures and then set them up.

>> **Announcing the project to the organization:** Let the project audiences know that your project exists, what it will produce, and when it will begin and end.

REMEMBER

Suppose you don't join your project team until the actual work is getting underway. Your first task is to understand how people decided initially that the project was possible and desirable. If the people who participated in the start-of-the-project and the organizing-and-preparing stages overlooked important issues, you need to raise them now. When searching for the project's history, check minutes from meetings, memos, letters, emails, and technical reports. Then consult with all the people involved in the initial project decisions.

Performing

Finally, you get to perform the project work! The performing subgroup of the executing processes includes the following:

>> **Doing the tasks:** Perform the work that's in your plan.

>> **Assuring quality:** Continually confirm that work and results conform to requirements and applicable standards and guidelines.

>> **Managing the team:** Assign tasks, review results, and resolve problems.

>> **Developing the team:** Provide needed training and mentoring to improve team members' skills.

>> **Sharing information:** Distribute information to appropriate project audiences.

Surveying the monitoring and controlling processes

As the project progresses, you need to ensure that plans are being followed and desired results are being achieved. The monitoring and controlling processes include the following tasks:

>> **Comparing performance with plans:** Collect information on outcomes, schedule achievements, and resource expenditures; identify deviations from your plan; and develop corrective actions.

>> **Fixing problems that arise:** Change tasks, schedules, or resources to bring project performance back on track with the existing plan, or negotiate agreed-upon changes to the plan itself.

>> **Keeping everyone informed:** Tell project audiences about the team's achievements, project problems, and necessary revisions to the established plan.

Ending with the closing processes

Finishing your assigned tasks is only part of bringing your project to a close. In addition, you must do the following:

>> Get your clients' approvals of the final results.

>> Close all project accounts (if you've been charging time and money to special project accounts).

>> Help team members move on to their next assignments.

>> Hold a post-project evaluation with the project team to recognize project achievements and to discuss lessons you can apply to the next project. (At the very least, make informal notes about these lessons and your plans for using them in the future.)

Knowing the Project Manager's Role

The project manager's job is challenging. For instance, she often coordinates technically specialized professionals — who may have limited experience working together — to achieve a common goal. Although the project manager's own work experience is often technical in nature, her success requires a keen ability to identify and resolve sensitive organizational and interpersonal issues. This section describes the main tasks that a project manager handles and notes potential challenges she may encounter.

Looking at the project manager's tasks

Historically, the performance rules in traditional organizations were simple: Your boss made assignments; you carried them out. Questioning your assignments was a sign of insubordination or incompetence.

But these rules have changed. Today your boss may generate ideas, but you assess how to implement them. You confirm that a project meets your boss's (and your organization's) real need and then determine the work, schedules, and resources you require to implement it.

Handling a project any other way simply doesn't make sense. The project manager must be involved in developing the plans because she needs the opportunity to clarify expectations and proposed approaches and then to raise any questions she may have *before* the project work begins.

REMEMBER

The key to project success is being proactive. Instead of waiting for others to tell you what to do, you should

>> Seek out information because you know you need it.

>> Follow the plan because you believe it's the best way.

>> Involve people whom you know are important for the project.

>> Identify issues and risks, analyze them, and elicit support to address them.

>> Share information with the people you know need to have it.

>> Put all-important information in writing.

>> Ask questions and encourage other people to do the same.

>> Commit to your project's success.

Staving off excuses for not following a structured project-management approach

Be prepared for other people to fight your attempts to use proven project-management approaches. You need to be prepared for everything! The following list provides a few examples of excuses you may encounter as a project manager and the appropriate responses you can give:

>> **Excuse:** Our projects are all crises; we have no time to plan.

Response: Unfortunately for the excuse giver, this logic is illogical! In a crisis, you have limited time and resources to address critical issues, and you definitely can't afford to make mistakes. Because acting under pressure and emotion (the two characteristics of crises) practically guarantees that mistakes will occur, you can't afford not to plan.

>> **Excuse:** Structured project management is only for large projects.

Response: No matter what size the project is, the information you need to perform it is the same. What do you need to produce? What work has to be accomplished? Who's going to do that work? When will the work end? Have you met expectations?

Large projects may require many weeks or months to develop satisfactory answers to these questions. Small projects that last a few days or less may take only 15 minutes. Either way, you still have to answer the questions.

>> **Excuse:** These projects require creativity and new development. They can't be predicted with any certainty.

Response: Some projects are more predictable than others. However, people awaiting the outcomes of any project still have expectations for what they'll get and when. Therefore, a project with many uncertainties needs a manager to develop and share initial plans and then to assess and communicate the effects of unexpected occurrences.

Even if you don't encounter these specific excuses, you can adapt the response examples provided here to address your own situations.

Avoiding shortcuts

The short-term pressures of your job as a project manager may encourage you to act today in ways that cause you, your team, or your organization to pay a price tomorrow. Especially with smaller, less formal projects, you may feel no need for organized planning and control.

WARNING

Don't be seduced into the following, seemingly easier shortcuts:

>> **Jumping directly from starting the project to carrying out the work:** You have an idea and your project is on a short schedule. Why not just start doing the work? Sounds good, but you haven't defined the work to be done!

Other variations on this shortcut include the following:

- **"This project's been done many times before, so why do I have to plan it out again?"** Even though projects can be similar to past ones, some

Achieving Results

elements are always different. Perhaps you're working with some new people or using a new piece of equipment. Take a moment now to be sure your plan addresses the current situation.

- **"Our project's different than it was before, so what good is trying to plan?"** Taking this attitude is like saying you're traveling in an unknown area, so why try to lay out your route on a road map? Planning for a new project is important because no one's taken this particular path before. Although your initial plan may have to be revised during the project, you and your team need to have a clear statement of your intended plan from the outset.

>> **Failing to prepare in the carrying-out-the-work stage:** Time pressure is often the apparent justification for this shortcut. However, the real reason is that people don't appreciate the need to define procedures and relationships before jumping into the actual project work.

>> **Jumping right into the work when you join the project in the carrying-out-the-work stage:** The plan has already been developed, so why go back and revisit the starting-the-project and the organizing-and-preparing stages? Actually, you need to do so for two reasons:

- To identify any issues that the developers may have overlooked

- To understand the reasoning behind the plan and decide whether you feel the plan is achievable

>> **Only partially completing the closing stage:** At the end of one project, you often move right on to the next. Scarce resources and short deadlines encourage this rapid movement, and starting a new project is always more challenging than wrapping up an old one.

However, you never really know how successful your project is if you don't take the time to ensure that all tasks are complete and that you've satisfied your clients. If you don't take positive steps to apply the lessons this project has taught you, you're likely to make the same mistakes you made in this project again or fail to repeat this project's successful approaches.

Staying aware of other potential challenges

WARNING

Projects are temporary; they're created to achieve particular results. Ideally, when the results are achieved, the project ends. Unfortunately, the transitory nature of projects may create some project–management challenges, including the following:

>> **Additional assignments:** People may be asked to accept an assignment to a new project in addition to — not in lieu of — existing assignments. They may

not be asked how the new work might affect their existing projects. (Higher management may just assume the project manager can handle everything.) When conflicts arise over a person's time, the organization may not have adequate guidelines or procedures to resolve those conflicts.

>> **New people on new teams:** People who haven't worked together before and who may not even know each other may be assigned to the same project team. This lack of familiarity may slow down the project because team members may

- Have different operating and communicating styles
- Use different procedures for performing the same type of activity
- Not have time to develop mutual respect and trust

>> **No direct authority:** For most projects, the project manager and team members have no direct authority over each other. Therefore, the rewards that usually encourage top performance (such as salary increases, superior performance appraisals, and job promotions) aren't available. In addition, conflicts over time commitments or technical direction may require input from a number of sources. As a result, they can't be settled with one, unilateral decision.

Do You Have What It Takes to Be an Effective Project Manager?

You're reading this book because you want to be a better project manager, right? Well, before you jump in, we suggest you do a quick self-evaluation to determine your strengths and weaknesses. By answering the following ten questions, you can get an idea of what subjects you need to spend more time on so you can be as effective as possible. Good luck!

1. Are you more concerned about being everyone's friend or getting a job done right?

Answer: Although maintaining good working relations is important, the project manager often must make decisions that some people don't agree with for the good of the project.

2. Do you prefer to do technical work or manage other people doing technical work?

Answer: Most project managers achieve their positions because of their strong performance on technical tasks. But after you become a project manager, your job is to encourage other people to produce high-quality technical work rather than to do it all yourself.

3. Do you think the best way to get a tough task done is to do it yourself?

   Answer: Believing in yourself is important. However, the project manager's task is to help other people develop to the point where they can perform tasks with the highest quality.

4. Do you prefer your work to be predictable or constantly changing?

   Answer: The project manager tries to minimize unexpected problems and situations through responsive planning and timely control. When problems do occur, the project manager must deal with them promptly to minimize their impact on the project.

5. Do you prefer to spend your time developing ideas rather than explaining those ideas to other people?

   Answer: Although coming up with ideas can help your project, the project manager's main responsibility is to ensure that every team member correctly understands all ideas that are developed.

6. Do you handle crises well?

   Answer: The project manager's job is to provide a cool head to size up the situation, choose the best action, and encourage all members to do their parts in implementing the solution.

7. Do you prefer to work by yourself or with others?

   Answer: Self-reliance and self-motivation are important characteristics for a project manager. However, the key to any project manager's success is to facilitate interaction among a diverse group of technical specialists.

8. Do you think you shouldn't have to monitor people after they've promised to do a task for you?

   Answer: Although you may feel that honoring one's commitments is a fundamental element of professional behavior, the project manager needs both to ensure that people maintain their focus and to model how to work cooperatively with others.

9. Do you believe people should be self-motivated to perform their jobs?

   Answer: People should be self-motivated, but the project manager has to encourage them to remain motivated by their job assignments and related opportunities.

10. Are you comfortable dealing with people at all organizational levels?

    Answer: The project manager deals with people at all levels — from upper management to support staff — who perform project-related activities.

IN THIS CHAPTER

» **Compiling an audience list**

» **Identifying drivers, supporters, and observers**

» **Using an effective format**

» **Determining who has authority in your project**

» **Prioritizing your audiences**

Chapter **2**

Knowing Your Project's Audiences

O ften a project is like an iceberg: Nine-tenths of it lurks below the surface. You receive an assignment and think you know what it entails and who needs to be involved. Then, as the project unfolds, new people emerge who may affect your goals, approach, and chances for project success.

You risk compromising your project in the following two ways when you don't involve key people or groups in your project in a timely manner:

» You may miss important information that can affect the project's performance and ultimate success.

» You may insult people. And you can be sure that when people feel that you have slighted or insulted them, they will take steps to make sure you don't do it again!

As soon as you begin to think about a new project, start to identify people who may play a role. This chapter shows you how to identify these candidates; how to decide whether, when, and how to involve them; and how to determine who has the authority, power, and interest to make critical decisions.

Understanding Your Project's Audiences

A *project audience* is any person or group that supports, is affected by, or is interested in your project. Your project's audiences can be inside or outside your organization, and knowing who they are helps you

>> Plan whether, when, and how to involve them.

>> Determine whether the scope of the project is bigger or smaller than you originally anticipated.

You may hear other terms used in the business world to describe project audiences, but these terms address only some of the people from your complete project audience list. Here are some examples:

>> **A *stakeholder list* identifies people and groups who support or are affected by your project.** The stakeholder list doesn't usually include people who are merely interested in your project.

>> **A *distribution list* identifies people who receive project communications.** These lists are often out-of-date for a couple of reasons. Some people remain on the list simply because no one removes them; other people are on the list because no one wants to run the risk of insulting them by removing them. In either case, having their names on this list doesn't ensure that these people actually support, are affected by, or are interested in your project.

>> ***Team members* are people whom the project manager directs.** All team members are stakeholders and, as such, are part of the project audience, but the audience list includes more than just team members.

Developing an Audience List

As you identify the different audiences for your project, record them in an audience list. Check out the following sections for information on how to develop this list.

Starting your audience list

A project audience list is a living document. You need to start developing your list as soon as you begin thinking about your project. Write down any names that occur to you; when you discuss your project with other people, ask them who they think may be affected by or interested in your project. Then select a small group of the audiences you identify and conduct a formal brainstorming session. Continue to add and subtract names to your audience list until you can't think of anyone else.

In the following sections, you discover how to refine your audience list by dividing it into specific categories and recognizing important potential audiences. This section ends with a sample to show you how to put together your own list.

Using specific categories

To increase your chances of identifying all appropriate people, develop your audience list in categories. You're less likely to overlook people when you consider them department by department or group by group instead of trying to identify everyone from the organization individually at the same time.

REMEMBER

Start your audience list by developing a hierarchical grouping of categories that covers the universe of people who may be affected by, be needed to support, or be interested in your project. You might want to start with the following groups:

>> **Internal:** People and groups inside your organization

- **Upper management:** Executive-level management responsible for the general oversight of all organization operations

- **Requesters:** The person who came up with the idea for your project and all the people through whom the request passed before you received it

- **Project manager:** The person with overall responsibility for successfully completing the project

- **End users:** People who will use the goods or services the project will produce

- **Team members:** People assigned to the project whose work the project manager directs

- **Groups normally involved:** Groups typically involved in most projects in the organization, such as the human resources, finance, contracts, and legal departments

- **Groups needed just for this project:** Groups or people with special knowledge related to this project

>> **External:** People and groups outside your organization

- **Clients or customers:** People or groups that buy or use your organization's products or services

- **Collaborators:** Groups or organizations with which you may pursue joint ventures related to your project

- **Vendors, suppliers, and contractors:** Organizations that provide personnel, raw materials, equipment, or other resources required to perform your project's work

- **Regulators:** Government agencies that establish regulations and guidelines that govern some aspect of your project work

- **Professional societies:** Groups of professionals that may influence or be interested in your project

- **The public:** The local, national, and international community of people who may be affected by or interested in your project

TIP

Continue to subdivide these categories further until you arrive at job titles or position descriptions and the names of the people who occupy them. (The process of systematically separating a whole into its component parts is called *decomposition*, which you can read about in Chapter 4 in this minibook.)

THE TRUE PURPOSE OF THE AUDIENCE LIST

Suppose your boss had assigned you a project that you have to finish in two months. You immediately develop an audience list, following the steps in this chapter, but, much to her horror, the list included more than 150 names! How are you supposed to involve more than 150 people in a two-month project? You might conclude that the audience list is clearly of no help.

In fact, your audience list has served its purpose perfectly. Identifying the people at the outset who would affect the success of your project gives you three options:

- Plan how and when to involve each person during the project.

- Assess the potential consequences of not involving one or more of your audiences.

- Discuss extending the project deadline or reducing its scope with your boss if you realize that you can't ignore any of the audiences.

The audience list itself doesn't decide whom you should involve in your project. Instead, it specifies those people who may affect the success of your project so you can weigh the benefits and the costs of including or omitting them.

Considering often overlooked audiences

As you develop your audience list, be sure not to overlook the following potential audiences:

>> **Support groups:** These people don't tell you what you should do (or help you deal with the trauma of project management); instead, they help you accomplish the project's goals. If support groups know about your project early, they can fit you into their work schedules more readily. They can also tell you information about their capabilities and processes that may influence what your project can accomplish and by when you can do so. Such groups include

- Facilities
- Finance
- Human resources
- Information technology (IT)
- Legal services
- Procurement or contracting
- Project management office
- Quality
- Security

>> **End users of your project's products:** *End users* are people or groups who will use the goods and services your project produces. Involving end users at the beginning of and throughout your project helps ensure that the goods and services produced are as easy as possible to implement and use and are most responsive to their true needs. It also confirms that you appreciate the fact that the people who will use a product may have important insights into what it should look like and do, which increases the chances that they'll work to implement the products successfully.

In some cases, you may omit end users on your audience list because you don't know who they are. In other situations, you may think you have taken them into account through *liaisons* — people who represent the interests of the end users. (Check out the nearby sidebar "Discovering the real end users" for a costly example of what can happen when you depend solely on liaisons.)

>> **People who will maintain or support the final product:** People who will service your project's final products affect the continuing success of these products. Involving these people throughout your project gives them a chance to make your project's products easier to maintain and support. It also allows them to become familiar with the products and effectively build their maintenance into existing procedures.

CHAPTER 2 **Knowing Your Project's Audiences** 267

Examining the beginning of a sample audience list

Suppose you're asked to coordinate your organization's annual blood drive. Figure 2-1 illustrates some of the groups and people you might include in your project's audience list as you prepare for your new project.

Ensuring a complete and up-to-date audience list

Many different groups of people may influence the success of or have an interest in your project. Knowing who these people are allows you to plan to involve them at the appropriate times during your project. Therefore, identifying all project audiences as soon as possible and reflecting any changes in those audiences as soon as you find out about them are important steps to take as you manage your project.

REMEMBER

To ensure that your audience list is complete and up-to-date, consider the following guidelines:

>> **Eventually identify each audience by position description and name.** You may, for example, initially identify people from sales and marketing as an audience. Eventually, however, you want to specify the particular people from that group — such as *brand manager for XYZ product, Sharon Wilson* — and their contact information.

Category			
Level 1	**Level 2**	**Level 3**	**Level 4**
Internal	Upper management	Executive oversight committee	
		VP, Sales and Marketing	
		VP, Operations	
		VP, Administration	
	Requester	VP, Sales and Marketing	
		Manager, Community Relations	
	Project team	Project manager	
		Team members	Customer service rep
			Community relations rep
			Human resources rep
	Groups normally involved	Finance	
		Facilities	
		Legal	
		Human resources	
	Groups just for this project	Project manager and team members from last year's blood drive	
External	Clients/customers	Donors	Prior
			New
		Hospital and medical centers receiving blood from the drive	
	Vendors and contractors	Attending nurses, food-service provider, facility's landlord, local blood center	
	Regulatory agencies	Local board of health	
	Professional societies	American Medical Association	
		American Association of Blood Banks	
	Public	Local community	
		Local media	Local newspapers
			Local TV stations
			Local radio stations

FIGURE 2-1: The beginning of a sample audience list for an annual blood drive.

>> **Speak with a wide range of people.** Check with people in different organizational units, from different disciplines, and with different tenures in the organization. Ask every person whether he or she can think of anyone else you should speak with. The more people you speak with, the less likely you are to overlook someone important.

>> **Allow sufficient time to develop your audience list.** Start to develop your list as soon as you become project manager. The longer you think about your project, the more potential audiences you can identify. Throughout the project, continue to check with people to identify additional audiences.

>> **Include audiences who may play a role at any time during your project.** Your only job at this stage is to identify names so you don't forget them. At a later point, you can decide whether, when, and how to involve these people (see the later section "Considering the Drivers, Supporters, and Observers").

>> **Include team members' functional managers.** Include the people to whom the project manager and team members directly report. Even though functional managers usually don't perform project tasks themselves, they can help ensure that the project manager and team members devote the time they originally promised to the project and that they have the resources necessary to perform their project assignments.

>> **Include a person's name on the audience list for every role she plays.** Suppose your boss plans to provide expert technical advice to your project team. Include your boss's name twice — once as your direct supervisor and once as the technical expert. If your boss is promoted but continues to serve as a technical advisor to your project, the separate listings remind you that a new person now occupies your direct supervisor's slot.

>> **Continue to add and remove names from your audience list throughout your project.** Your audience list evolves as you understand more about your project and as your project changes. Plan to review your list at regular intervals throughout the project to identify names that should be added or deleted. Encourage people involved in your project to continually identify new audiences as they think of them.

>> **When in doubt, write down a person's name.** Your goal is to avoid overlooking someone who may play an important part in your project. Identifying a potential audience member doesn't mean you have to involve that person; it simply means you have to consider him or her. Eliminating the name of someone who won't be involved is a lot easier than trying to add the name of someone who should be.

Using an audience list template

An *audience list template* is a predesigned audience list that contains typical categories and audiences for a particular type of project. You may develop and maintain your own audience list templates for tasks you perform, functional groups may develop and maintain audience list templates for tasks they typically conduct, or your organization's project management office may develop and maintain templates for the entire organization.

Regardless of who maintains the template, it reflects people's cumulative experiences. As the organization continues to perform projects of this type, audiences who were overlooked in earlier efforts may be added and audiences who proved unnecessary removed. Using these templates can save you time and improve your accuracy.

Suppose you prepare the budget for your department each quarter. After doing a number of these budgets, you know most of the people who give you the necessary information, who draft and print the document, and who have to approve the final budget. Each time you finish another budget, you revise your audience list template to include new information from that project. The next time you prepare your quarterly budget, you begin your audience list with your template. You then add and subtract names as appropriate for that particular budget preparation.

REMEMBER

When using audience list templates, keep the following guidelines in mind:

>> **Develop templates for frequently performed tasks and for entire projects.** Audience list templates for kicking off the annual blood drive or submitting a newly developed drug to the Food and Drug Administration are valuable. But so are templates for individual tasks that are part of these projects, such as awarding a competitive contract or printing a document. Many times, projects that appear new contain some tasks that you've performed before. You can still reap the benefits of your experience by including the audience list templates for these tasks in your overall project audience list.

>> **Focus on position descriptions rather than the names of prior audiences.** Identify an audience as *accounts payable manager* rather than *Bill Miller*. People come and go, but functions endure. For each specific project, you can fill in the appropriate names.

>> **Develop and modify your audience list template from previous projects that worked, not from initial plans that looked good but lacked key information.** Often you develop a detailed audience list at the start of your project but don't revise the list during the project or add audiences that you overlooked in your initial planning. If you update your template with information from an initial list only, your template can't reflect the discoveries you made throughout the earlier project.

>> **Encourage your team members to brainstorm possible audiences before you show them an existing audience list template.** Encouraging people to identify audiences without guidance or restrictions increases the chances that they'll think of audiences that were overlooked on previous projects.

>> **Use templates as starting points, not ending points.** Make clear to your team that the template isn't the final list. Every project differs in some ways from similar ones. If you don't critically examine the template, you may miss people who weren't involved in previous projects but whom you need to consider for this one.

>> **Reflect your different project experiences in your audience list templates.** The post-project evaluation is an excellent time to review, critique, and modify your audience list for a particular project.

WARNING

Templates can save time and improve accuracy. However, starting with a template that's too polished can suggest you've already made up your mind about the contents of your final list, which may discourage people from freely sharing their thoughts about other potential audiences. In addition, their lack of involvement in the development of the project's audience list may lead to their lack of commitment to the project's success.

Considering the Drivers, Supporters, and Observers

After you identify everyone in your project audience, you need to determine which of the following groups those people fall into. Then you can decide whether to involve them and, if so, how and when.

>> **Drivers:** People who have some say in defining the results of your project. You're performing your project for these people.

>> **Supporters:** The people who help you perform your project. Supporters include individuals who authorize or provide the resources for your project as well as those who work on it.

>> **Observers:** People who are neither drivers nor supporters but who are interested in the activities and results of your project. Observers have no say in your project, and they're not actively involved in it. However, your project may affect them at some point.

Separating audiences into these three categories helps you decide what information to seek from and share with each audience, as well as to clarify the project decisions in which to involve them.

Suppose an IT group has the job of modifying the layout and content of a monthly sales report for all sales representatives. The vice president of sales requested the project, and the *chief information officer* (CIO — the boss of the head of the IT group) approved it. As the project manager for this project, consider categorizing your project's audiences as follows:

>> **Drivers:** The vice president of sales is a driver because he has specific reasons for revising the report. The CIO is a potential driver because she may hope to develop certain new capabilities for her group through this project. Individual sales representatives are all drivers for this project because they'll use the redesigned report to support their work.

>> **Supporters:** The systems analyst who designs the revised report, the training specialist who trains the users, and the vice president of finance who authorizes the funds for changing the manual are all supporters.

>> **Observers:** The head of the customer service department is a potential observer because he hopes your project will lead to an improved problem-tracking system this year.

WARNING

Beware of supporters who try to act like drivers. In the preceding example, the analyst who finalizes the content and format of the report may try to include certain items that she thinks are helpful. However, only the real drivers should determine the specific data that goes into the report. The analyst just determines whether including the desired data is possible and what doing so will cost.

INCLUDING A PROJECT CHAMPION

A *project champion* is a person in a high position in the organization who strongly supports your project; advocates for your project in disputes, planning meetings, and review sessions; and takes whatever actions are necessary to help ensure the successful completion of your project.

As soon as you start planning, find out whether your project has a champion. If it doesn't, try to recruit one. An effective project champion has the following characteristics:

• Sufficient power and authority to resolve conflicts over resources, schedules, and technical issues

• A keen interest in the results of your project

• A willingness to have his or her name cited as a strong supporter of your project

REMEMBER

Keep in mind that the same person can be both a driver and a supporter. For example, the vice president of sales is a driver for the project to develop a revised monthly sales report but also a supporter if he has to transfer funds from the sales department budget to pay for developing the report.

The following sections help you identify when you need to involve drivers, supporters, and observers, and how to keep them involved.

Deciding when to involve your audiences

Projects pass through the following four stages as they progress from an idea to completion (see Chapter 1 of this minibook for detailed explanations of these stages):

>> Starting the project

>> Organizing and preparing

>> Carrying out the work

>> Closing the project

Plan to involve drivers, supporters, and observers in each stage of your project's life cycle. The following sections tell you how you can do so.

Drivers

Keeping drivers involved in your project from start to finish is critical because they define what your project should produce, and they evaluate your project's success when it's finished. Their desires and your assessment of feasibility can influence whether you should pursue the project. Check out Table 2-1 to see how to involve drivers during the four stages of your project.

TABLE 2-1   **Involving Drivers in the Different Project Stages**

Stage	Involvement Level	How to Involve
Starting the project	Heavy	Identify and speak with as many drivers as possible. If you uncover additional drivers later, explore with them the issues that led to the project; ask them to identify and assess any special expectations they may have.
Organizing and preparing	Moderate to heavy	Consult with drivers to ensure that your project plan addresses their needs and expectations. Have them formally approve the plan before you start the project work.

Stage	Involvement Level	How to Involve
Carrying out the work	Moderate	As the project gets under way, introduce the drivers to the project team. Have the drivers talk about their needs and interests to reinforce the importance of the project and help team members form a more accurate picture of project goals. In addition, have the team members talk to the drivers to increase the drivers' confidence that the team members can successfully complete the project.
		While performing the project work, keep drivers apprised of project accomplishments and progress to sustain their ongoing interest and enthusiasm. Continually confirm that the results are meeting their needs.
Closing the project	Heavy	Have drivers assess the project's results and determine whether their needs and expectations were met. Identify their recommendations for improving performance on similar projects in the future.

Supporters

Involving supporters from start to finish is important because they perform and support the project work; supporters need to know about changing requirements so they can promptly identify and address problems. Keeping them actively involved also sustains their ongoing motivation and commitment to the project. Check out Table 2-2 to see how to involve supporters during your project's four stages.

TABLE 2-2 ## Involving Supporters in the Different Project Stages

Stage	Involvement Level	How to Involve
Starting the project	Moderate	Wherever possible, have key supporters assess the feasibility of meeting driver expectations. If you identify key supporters later in the project, have them confirm the feasibility of previously set expectations.
Organizing and preparing	Heavy	Supporters are the major contributors to the project plan. Because they facilitate or do all the work, have them determine necessary technical approaches, schedules, and resources. Also have them formally commit to all aspects of the plan.

(continued)

TABLE 2-2 *(continued)*

Stage	Involvement Level	How to Involve
Carrying out the work	Heavy	Familiarize all supporters with the planned work. Clarify how the supporters will work together to achieve the results. Have supporters decide how they'll communicate, resolve conflicts, and make decisions throughout the project. Throughout the project, keep supporters informed of project progress, encourage them to identify performance problems they encounter or anticipate, and work with them to develop and implement solutions to these problems.
Closing the project	Heavy	Have supporters conclude their different tasks. Inform them of project accomplishments and recognize their roles in project achievements. Elicit their suggestions for handling similar projects more effectively in the future.

Observers

After you choose the observers with whom you want to actively share project information, involve them minimally throughout the project because they neither tell you what should be done nor help you do it. Table 2-3 shows how you may keep observers involved.

TABLE 2-3 ## Involving Observers in the Different Project Stages

Stage	Involvement Level	How to Involve
Starting the project	Minimal	Inform observers of your project's existence and its main goals.
Organizing and preparing	Minimal	Inform observers about the project's planned outcomes and time frames.
Carrying out the work	Minimal	Tell observers that the project has started and confirm the dates for planned milestones. Inform observers of key project achievements.
Closing the project	Minimal	When the project is done, inform observers about the project's products and results.

TIP

Because observers don't directly influence or affect your project, be sure to carefully manage the time and effort you spend sharing information with them. When deciding whom to involve and how to share information with them, consider the following:

>> Their level of interest in your project

>> The likelihood that your project will affect them at some point in the future

>> The need to maintain a good working relationship with them

See the "Assessing Your Audience's Power and Interest" section, later in this chapter, for information on what to consider when deciding how to involve different audiences.

Using different methods to involve your audiences

Keeping drivers, supporters, and observers informed as you progress in your project is critical to the project's success. Choosing the right method for involving each audience group can stimulate that group's continued interest and encourage its members to actively support your work. Consider the following approaches for keeping your project audiences involved throughout your project:

>> **One-on-one meetings:** One-on-one meetings (formal or informal discussions with one or two other people about project issues) are particularly useful for interactively exploring and clarifying special issues of interest with a small number of people.

>> **Group meetings:** These meetings are planned sessions for some or all team members or audiences. Smaller meetings are useful to brainstorm project issues, reinforce team member roles, and develop mutual trust and respect among team members. Larger meetings are useful to present information of general interest.

>> **Informal written correspondence:** Informal written correspondence (notes, memos, letters, and emails) helps you document informal discussions and share important project information.

>> **More formal information-sharing vehicles:** Information resources such as project newsletters or sites on the organization's intranet may be useful for sharing nonconfidential and noncontroversial information with larger audiences.

>> **Written approvals:** Written approvals (such as a technical approach to project work or formal agreements about a product, schedule, or resource commitment) serve as records of project decisions and achievements.

Flip to Chapter 5 in this minibook for additional suggestions for sharing information about your project's ongoing performance.

Making the most of your audiences' involvement

To maximize your audiences' involvement and contributions, follow these guidelines throughout your project:

>> **Involve audiences early in the project planning if they have a role later.** Give your audiences the option to participate in planning even if they don't perform until later in the project. Sometimes they can share information that'll make their tasks easier. At the least, they can reserve time to provide their services when you need them.

>> **If you're concerned with the legality of involving a specific audience, check with your legal department or contracts office.** Suppose you're planning to award a competitive contract to buy certain equipment. You want to know whether prospective bidders typically have this equipment on hand and how long it will take to receive it after you award the contract. However, you're concerned that speaking to potential contractors in the planning stage may tip them off about the procurement and lead to charges of favoritism by unsuccessful bidders who didn't know about the procurement in advance.

>> Instead of ignoring this important audience, check with your contracts office or legal department to determine how you can get the information you want and still maintain the integrity of the bidding process.

>> **Develop a plan with all key audiences to meet their information needs and interests as well as yours.** Determine the information they want and the information you believe they need. Also decide when to provide that information and in what format. Finally, clarify what you want from them and how and when they can provide it.

>> **Always be sure you understand each audience's *what's in it for me* (WIIFM).** Clarify why seeing your project succeed is in each audience's interest. Throughout your project, keep reminding your audiences of the benefits they'll realize when your project is complete and the progress your project has made toward achieving those benefits.

Displaying Your Audience List

You're concerned with two issues when developing the format and content of your audience list:

>> Increasing your confidence that you identified all appropriate audiences

>> Helping others suggest people not on the list who should be included and people on the list who possibly should not

Figure 2-2 shows a sample audience list format you might want to use for your audience list. The format includes three major categories of information:

>> The hierarchical structure of the categories in which audiences are located

>> The specific identifiers of each audience (job title and name)

>> The audience's role with regard to the project (driver, supporter, or observer; see the earlier section "Considering the Drivers, Supporters, and Observers")

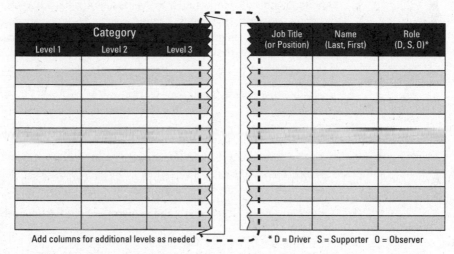

FIGURE 2-2: Sample audience list format.

Note: You can add additional columns on the right for optional information, such as email and phone.

Confirming Your Audience's Authority

In project terms, *authority* refers to the overall right to make project decisions that others must follow, including the right to apply project resources, expend funds, or give approvals. Having opinions about how an aspect should be addressed is different from having the authority to decide how it will be addressed. Mistaking a person's level of authority can lead to frustration as well as wasted time and money.

Confirm that the people you've identified as audiences have the authority to make the decisions they need to make to perform their tasks. If they don't have that authority, find out who does and how to bring those people into the process.

At the beginning of the carrying out the work stage in your projects, take the following steps to define each audience member's authority:

1. **Clarify each audience member's tasks and decisions.**

   Define with each person his tasks and his role in those tasks. For example, will he just work on the task, or will he also approve the schedules, resource expenditures, and work approaches?

2. **Ask each audience member what his authority is regarding each decision and task.**

   Ask about individual tasks rather than all issues in a particular area. For example, a person can be more confident about his authority to approve supply purchases up to $5,000 than about his authority to approve all equipment purchases, no matter the type or amount.

   Clarify decisions that the audience member can make himself. For decisions needing someone else's approval, find out whose approval he needs. (Ask, never assume!)

3. **Ask each audience member how he knows what authority he has.**

   Does a written policy, procedure, or guideline confirm the authority? Did the person's boss tell him in conversation? Is the person just assuming? If the person has no specific confirming information, encourage him to get it.

4. **Check out each audience member's history of exercising authority.**

   Have you or other people worked with this person in the past? Has he been overruled on decisions that he said he was authorized to make? If so, ask him why he believes he won't be similarly overruled this time.

5. **Verify whether anything has recently changed regarding each audience member's authority.**

   Do you have any reason to believe that this person's authority has changed? Is he new to his current group or position? Has he recently started working for a new boss? If any of these situations exists, encourage the person to find specific documentation to confirm his authority for his benefit as well as yours.

Reconfirm the information in these steps when a particular audience's decision-making assignments change. Suppose, for example, that you initially expect all individual purchases on your project to be at or under $2,500. Bill, the team representative from the finance group, assures you that he has the authority to approve such purchases for your project without checking with his boss. Midway through the project, you find that you have to purchase a piece of equipment for $5,000. Be sure to verify with Bill that he can personally authorize this larger expenditure. If he can't, find out whose approval you need and plan how to get it.

Assessing Your Audience's Power and Interest

An audience's potential effect on a project depends on the power he or she can exercise and the interest the person has in exercising that power. Assessing the relative levels of each helps you decide with whom you should spend your time and effort to realize the greatest benefits.

Power is a person's ability to influence the actions of others. This ability can derive either from the direct authority the person has to require people to respond to her requests *(ascribed power)* or the ability she has to induce others to do what she asks because of the respect they have for her professionally or personally *(achieved power)*. In either case, the more power a person has, the better able she is to marshal people and resources to support your project. Typically, drivers and supporters have higher levels of power over your project than observers do.

On the other hand, a person's *interest* in something is how much she cares about it, is curious about it, or pays attention to it. The more interested a person is in your project, the more likely she is to want to use her power to help the project succeed.

You can define an audience's relative levels of power and interest related to your project as being either *high* or *low.* You then have four possible combinations for each audience's relative levels of power and interest. The particular values of an audience's power and interest ratings suggest the chances that the audience may have a significant effect on your project and, therefore, the relative importance of keeping that audience interested and involved in your project.

TIP

Most often, you base the assessments of an audience's power over and interest in your project on the aggregated individual, subjective opinions of several parties: you, your team members, your project's other audiences, people who have worked with the audience on other projects, subject matter experts, the audience himself or herself, or a combination. If you assign a value of 1 to each individual rating of *high* and 0 to each individual rating of *low,* you'd rate an audience's power or interest as *high* if the average of the individual assessments were 0.5 or greater and *low* if the average were below 0.5.

Figure 2-3 depicts a *power-interest grid*, which represents these four possible power-interest combinations as distinct quadrants on a two-dimensional graph.

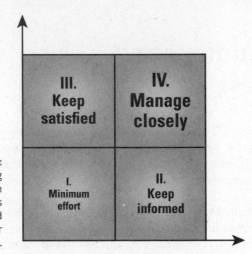

FIGURE 2-3:
Involving audiences with different levels of power and interest in your project.

As the project manager, you should spend a minimal amount of time and effort with audiences who have low levels of both power and interest (quadrant I). Spend increasingly greater amounts of time and effort with audiences that have a low level of power and a high level of interest (quadrant II) and a low level of interest and a high level of power (quadrant III), respectively. You should spend the most time and effort keeping audiences with high degrees of both power and interest (quadrant IV) informed and involved. (Check out Chapter 5 of this minibook for different ways to communicate with your project's audiences.)

Chapter **3**

Clarifying Your Project

All projects are created for a reason; someone identifies a need and devises a project to address that need. How well the project ultimately addresses that need defines the project's success or failure.

This chapter helps you develop a mutual agreement between your project's requesters and your project team about the project's goals and expectations. It also helps you establish the conditions necessary to perform the project work.

Defining Your Project with a Scope Statement

A *scope statement* is a written confirmation of the results your project will produce and the constraints and assumptions under which you will work. Both the people who requested the project and the project team should agree to all terms in the scope statement before project work begins.

A good scope statement includes the following information:

» **Justification:** A brief statement regarding the business need your project addresses

» **Product scope description:** The characteristics of the products, services, and/ or results that your project will produce

>> **Acceptance criteria:** The conditions that must be met before project deliverables are accepted

>> **Deliverables:** The products, services, and/or results that your project will produce (also referred to as *objectives*)

>> **Project exclusions:** Statements about what the project will not accomplish or produce

>> **Constraints:** Restrictions that limit what you can achieve, how and when you can achieve it, and how much achieving it can cost

>> **Assumptions:** Statements about how you will address uncertain information as you conceive, plan, and perform your project

REMEMBER

Think of your scope statement, when viewed with the other components of your project plan, as a binding agreement in which

>> You and your team commit to producing certain results. Your project's requesters commit that they'll consider your project 100 percent successful if you produce these results.

>> You and your team identify all restrictions regarding your approach to the work and the resources you need to support your work. Your project's requesters agree that there are no restrictions other than the ones you've identified and that they'll provide you the support you declare you need.

>> You and your team identify all assumptions you made when setting the terms of your scope statement. Your project's requesters agree that, if any of these assumptions prove to be invalid, you may have to modify some or all of your project plans.

A well-written scope statement is an important resource for helping to manage stakeholder expectations.

REMEMBER

Of course, predicting the future is impossible. In fact, the further into the future you try to look, the less certain your predictions can be. However, your scope statement represents your project commitments based on what you know today and expect to be true in the future. If and when situations change, you have to assess the effect of the changes on all aspects of your project and propose the necessary changes to your scope statement. Your project's requesters always have the option of either accepting your proposed changes (and allowing the project to continue) or canceling your project.

DOCUMENTS RELATED TO THE SCOPE STATEMENT

Your organization may use a number of other documents, such as the ones listed here, to address issues similar to those included in the scope statement. When you use these other documents as sources of information to prepare or describe your project plan, be careful to note how they differ from the scope statement:

- **Market requirements document:** A formal request to develop or modify a product. This document (typically prepared by a member of your organization's sales and marketing group) may lead to the creation of a project. However, in its original form, this document reflects only the *desires* of the person who wrote it. It doesn't reflect an assessment of whether meeting the request is possible or in the organization's best interest, nor is it a commitment to meet the request.

- **Business requirements document:** A description of the business needs that a requested product, service, or system must address.

- **Technical requirements, specifications document, or product requirements document:** A description of the characteristics that the products and services produced must have.

- **Project request:** A written request for a project by a group in the organization. The project request indicates a desire for a project rather than a mutual agreement and commitment to perform it.

- **Statement of work:** A narrative description of products, services, or results to be supplied by a project.

- **Project profile:** A document that highlights the key information about a project, sometimes also called a *project summary* or a *project abstract*.

- **Project charter:** A document issued by upper management that formally establishes a project and authorizes the project manager to use organizational resources to perform project activities.

- **Work order:** A written description of work that people or groups in your organization will perform in support of your project. The signed work order focuses on work performance rather than overall project outcomes.

- **Contract:** A legal agreement for providing specified goods or services.

Looking at the Big Picture: Explaining the Need for Your Project

Understanding the situation and thought processes that led to your project's creation helps ensure that you and your project successfully meet people's expectations. This section helps you clarify your project's justification and the desired deliverables.

Figuring out why you're doing the project

When you take on a project, *why* you're doing it may seem obvious — because your boss told you to. The real question, however, isn't why you chose to accept the assignment but why the project must be done (by you or anyone else) in the first place.

The following sections help you identify people who may benefit from your project so you can then determine how their expectations and needs help justify the project.

Identifying the initiator

Your first task in discovering your project's underlying justification is to determine who had the original idea that led to your project (this person is called the *project's initiator*). Project success requires that, at a minimum, you meet this person's needs and expectations.

MAKING A POSITIVE FIRST IMPRESSION: THE PROJECT TITLE

To accomplish a successful project, a group of focused and motivated people must effectively and efficiently work together to produce an agreed-upon set of desired results. From the beginning of the project, these people must have all the information they need to perform their assigned tasks, as well as the motivation and commitment to overcome any challenges they may encounter as they proceed with their project work. One of the first items you can use to develop these essential information-sharing and commitment-building processes is your project's title.

Although one important use of the project title is to serve as an identifier for project information and materials, the title, if written well, can also serve to

- Announce your project's existence.

- Reveal what the project is about.

- Stimulate curiosity and interest in the project.

- Evoke positive feelings about the project.

For the title to accomplish these goals, the following must happen:

- People must read the title.

- The title must include information about the project's intended results.

- People must be able to relate to the title.

- People must remember the title.

You can help ensure that your title meets all these requirements by adhering to the following guidelines when writing it:

- Know your audience — their interests, knowledge, and communication preferences.

- Keep the title to one sentence.

- Make it reader-friendly by printing it in a sufficiently large font in a color that contrasts effectively with its background.

- Make it a mini-abstract of your project by stating the main intended results.

- Include the most important words first.

- Triple-check that all information is accurate.

- Remove unnecessary words (like *a* and *the*) and any redundant information.

- Minimize your use of technical jargon and acronyms.

If you aren't feeling especially creative, consider asking the marketing or graphics department for some ideas or soliciting the assistance of team members and others you might know.

Whether or not you acknowledge it, your project title will affect people's knowledge and feelings about your project. You can choose to write a title that will influence people in ways that you want, or you can write it with no consideration for how it will affect your project's potential audience. Just know that not considering how it will affect others doesn't mean it won't affect them.

Identifying your project's initiator is easy when he's the person who directly assigns it to you. More likely, however, the person who gives you the project is passing along an assignment she received from someone else. If your project has passed through several people before it reaches you, you may have difficulty determining who really had the initial idea. Not to mention, the original intent may have become blurred if people in the chain purposely or inadvertently changed the assignment a little as they passed it on.

To determine who came up with the original idea for your project, take the following steps:

1. **Ask the person who assigns you the project whether he originated the idea.**

2. **If that person didn't initiate the idea, ask the following questions:**

   - Who gave her the assignment?
   - Who else, if anyone, was involved in passing the assignment to her?
   - Who had the original idea for the project?

3. **Check with all the people you identified in Step 2 and ask them the same questions.**

4. **Check the following written records that may confirm who originally had the idea:**

   - Minutes from division-, department-, and organization-wide planning and budget sessions
   - Correspondence and email referring to the project
   - Reports of planning or feasibility studies

   A *feasibility study* is a formal investigation to determine the likely success of performing certain work or achieving certain results.

   In addition to helping you identify the people who initiated your project, these written sources may shed light on what these people hope to get from it.

5. **Consult with people who may be affected by or are needed to support your project; they may know who originated the idea.**

Be as specific as possible when specifying your project initiator. In other words, don't write "The sales department requested promotional literature for product Alpha." Instead, write "Mary Smith, the sales representative for the northeast region, requested promotional literature for product Alpha."

Be sure to distinguish between drivers and supporters as you seek to find your project's initiator (see Chapter 2 in this minibook for more information about drivers and supporters):

>> *Drivers* have some say when defining the results of the project. They tell you what you *should* do.

>> *Supporters* help you perform your project. They tell you what you *can* do.

For example, the vice president of finance who requests a project to upgrade the organization's financial information systems is a project driver. The manager of the computer center who must provide staff and resources to upgrade the organization's information systems is a project supporter.

Sometimes supporters claim to be drivers. For example, when you ask the manager of the computer center, he may say he initiated the project. In reality, however, the manager authorized the people and funds to perform the project, but the vice president of finance initiated the project.

Recognizing other people who may benefit

Although they may not have initiated the idea, other people may benefit from your completed project. They may be people who work with, support, or are clients of your project's drivers, or they may have performed similar projects in the past. They may have expressed interests or needs in areas addressed by your project in meetings, correspondence, or informal conversations.

Identify these other people as soon as possible to determine what their particular needs and interests are and how you can appropriately address them. These additional audiences may include people who

>> Know the project exists and have expressed an interest in it

>> Know it exists but don't realize it can benefit them

>> Are unaware of your project

Identify these additional audiences by doing the following:

>> Review all written materials related to your project.

>> Consult with your project's drivers and supporters.

>> Encourage everyone you speak to about the project to identify others who may benefit from it.

As you identify people who can benefit from your project, also identify people who strongly oppose it. Figure out why they oppose your project and whether you can address their concerns. Take the time to determine whether they may be able to derive any benefits from your project, and, if they can, explain these benefits to them. If they continue to oppose your project, make a note in your risk-management plan about their opposition and how you plan to deal with it.

Distinguishing the project champion

A *project champion* is a person in a high position in the organization who strongly supports your project; advocates for your project in disputes, planning meetings, and review sessions; and takes necessary actions to help ensure that your project is successful.

Sometimes the best champion is one whose support you never have to use. Just knowing that this person supports your project helps other people appreciate its importance and encourages them to work diligently to ensure its success.

Check with your project's drivers and supporters to find out whether your project already has a champion. If it doesn't, work hard to recruit one by looking for people who can reap benefits from your project and who have sufficient power and influence to encourage serious, ongoing organizational commitment to your project. Explain to these people why the success of your project is in their best interest and how you may need their specific help as your project progresses. Assess how interested they are in your project and how much help they're willing to provide.

Considering those who will implement the project's results

Most projects create a product or service to achieve a desired result. Often, however, the person who asks you to create the product or service isn't the one who'll use it.

Suppose your organization's director of sales and marketing wants to increase annual sales by 10 percent in the next fiscal year. She decides that developing and introducing a new product, XYZ, will allow her to achieve this goal. However, she won't go to all your organization's customers and sell them XYZ; her sales staff will. Even though they didn't come up with the idea to develop XYZ, the sales staff may have strong opinions about the characteristics XYZ should have — and so will the customers who ultimately buy (or don't buy!) the product.

To identify the real users of project products and services, try to do the following early in your project planning:

>> Clarify the products and services that you anticipate producing.

>> Identify exactly who will use these products and services and how they'll use them.

After you identify these people, consult with them to determine any additional interests or needs they may have that your project should also address.

Determining your project drivers' expectations and needs

The needs that your project addresses may not always be obvious. Suppose, for example, that your organization decides to sponsor a blood drive. Is the real reason for your project to address the shortage of blood in the local hospital or to improve your organization's image in the local community?

The needs your project must satisfy to successfully achieve its purpose are termed your project's *requirements*.

When you clearly understand your project's requirements, you can

>> Choose project activities that enable you to accomplish the true desired results (see Chapter 4 in this minibook for information on identifying project activities).

>> Monitor performance during and at the end of the project to ensure that you're meeting the real needs.

>> Realize when the project isn't meeting the real needs so that you can suggest modifying or canceling it.

When you're initially assigned a project, you hope you're told the products you're supposed to produce and the needs you're supposed to address. However, often you're told what to produce (the outcomes), but you have to figure out the needs yourself.

REMEMBER

Consider the following questions as you work to define your project's requirements:

>> **What needs do people want your project to address?** Don't worry at this point whether your project can address these needs or whether it's the best way to address the needs. You're just trying to identify the hopes and expectations that led to this project in the first place.

>> **How do you know the needs you identify are the real hopes and expectations that people have for your project?** Determining people's real thoughts and feelings can be difficult. Sometimes they don't want to share them; sometimes they don't know how to clearly express them.

When speaking with people to determine the needs your project should address, try the following techniques:

>> Encourage them to speak at length about their needs and expectations.

>> Listen carefully for any contradictions.

>> Encourage them to clarify vague ideas.

>> Try to confirm your information from two or more independent sources.

>> Ask them to indicate the relative importance of addressing each of their needs.

The following scheme is useful for prioritizing a person's needs:

>> **Must have:** The project must address these needs, at the very least.

>> **Should have:** The project should address these needs, if at all possible.

>> **Nice to have:** It would be nice for the project to address these needs, if doing so doesn't negatively affect anything else.

See whether your organization performed a formal benefit-cost analysis for your project. A *benefit-cost analysis* is a formal identification and assessment of the following (see Chapter 1 in this minibook for details):

>> The benefits anticipated from your project

>> The costs of performing your project and using and supporting the products or services produced by your project

The benefit-cost analysis documents the results that people were counting on when they decided to proceed with your project. Therefore, the analysis is an important source for the real needs that your project should address.

Confirming that your project can address people's needs

Although needs may be thoroughly documented (see the preceding section), you may have difficulty determining whether your project can successfully address those needs. On occasion, companies fund formal feasibility studies to determine whether a project can successfully address a particular need.

Other times, however, your project may be the result of a brainstorming session or someone's creative vision. In this case, you may have less confidence that your project can accomplish its expected results. Don't automatically reject a project at this point, but do aggressively determine the chances for success and the actions you can take to increase these chances. If you can't find sufficient information to support your analysis, consider asking for a formal feasibility study.

REMEMBER

If you feel the risk of project failure is too great, share your concerns with the key decision makers and explain why you recommend not proceeding with your project.

Uncovering other activities that relate to your project

Your project doesn't exist in a vacuum. It may require results from other projects, it may generate products that other projects will use, and it may address needs that other projects also address. For these reasons, you need to identify projects related to yours as soon as possible so you can coordinate the use of shared personnel and resources and minimize unintended overlap in project activities and results.

Check the following sources to identify projects that may be related to yours:

>> Your project's audiences

>> Centrally maintained lists of projects planned or being performed by your organization

>> Organization-wide information-sharing vehicles, such as newsletters or your organization's intranet

>> The project management office (PMO)

>> Upper-management committees responsible for approving and overseeing your organization's projects

>> The finance department, which may have established labor or cost accounts for such projects

>> The procurement department, which may have purchased goods or services for such projects

>> The information technology department, which may be storing, analyzing, or preparing progress reports for such projects

>> Functional managers whose people may be working on such projects

Emphasizing your project's importance to your organization

How much importance your organization places on your project directly influences the chances for your project's success. When conflicting demands for scarce resources arise, resources usually go to those projects that can produce the greatest benefits for the organization.

Your project's perceived value depends on its intended benefits and people's awareness of those benefits. Take the following steps to help people understand how your project will support the organization's priorities:

>> **Look for existing statements or documents that confirm your project's support of your organization's priorities.** Consult the following sources to find out more about your organization's priorities:

- **Long-range plan:** A formal report that identifies your organization's overall direction, specific performance targets, and individual initiatives for the next one to five years

- **Annual budget:** The detailed list of categories and individual initiatives that your organization will financially support during the year

- **Capital appropriations plan:** The itemized list of all planned expenditures (over an established minimum amount) for facilities and equipment purchases, renovations, and repairs during the year

- **Your organization's key performance indicators (KPIs):** Performance measures that describe your organization's progress toward its goals

When you review these documents, note whether your project or its intended outcome is specifically mentioned.

In addition, determine whether your organization has made specific commitments to external customers or upper management related to your project's completion.

>> **Describe in your brief statement of justification how your project relates to the organization's priorities.** Mention existing discussions of your project from the information sources mentioned in the preceding point. If your project isn't specifically referenced in these sources, prepare a written explanation of how your project and its results will affect the organization's priorities.

Occasionally, you may have a hard time identifying specific results that people expect your project to generate. Perhaps the person who initiated the project has assumed different responsibilities and no longer has any interest in it, or maybe the original need the project was designed to address has changed. If people have trouble telling you how your project will help your organization, ask them what would happen if you didn't perform your project. If they conclude that it wouldn't make a difference, ask them how you can modify your project to benefit the organization. If they don't think your project can be changed to produce useful results, consider suggesting that the project be canceled.

REMEMBER

Organizations are consistently overworked and understaffed. Spending precious time and resources on a project that everyone agrees will make no difference is the last thing your organization needs or wants. More likely, people do realize that your project can have a positive effect on the organization. Your job, then, is to help these people consistently focus on the valuable results your project has to offer.

Being exhaustive in your search for information

TIP

In your quest to find out what your project is supposed to accomplish and how it fits into your organization's overall plans, you have to seek information that is sensitive, sometimes contradictory, and often unwritten. Getting this information isn't always easy, but following these tips can help make your search more productive:

>> **Try to find several sources for the same piece of information.** The more independent sources that contain the same information, the more likely the information is to be correct.

>> **Whenever possible, get information from primary sources.** A *primary source* contains the original information. A *secondary source* is someone else's report of the information from the primary source.

Suppose you need information from a recently completed study. You can get the information from the primary source (the actual report of the study written by the scientists who performed it), or you can get it from secondary sources (such as articles in magazines or scientific journals by authors who paraphrased and summarized the original report).

WARNING

The further your source is from the primary source, the more likely the secondary information differs from the real information.

>> **Look for written sources because they're the best.** Check relevant minutes from meetings, correspondence, email, reports from other projects, long-range plans, budgets, capital improvement plans, market requirement documents, and benefit-cost analyses.

>> **Speak with two or more people from the same area to confirm information.** Different people have different styles of communication as well as different perceptions of the same situation. Speak with more than one person, and compare their messages to determine any contradictions.

If you get different stories, speak with the people again to verify their initial information. Determine whether the people you consulted are primary or secondary sources (primary sources tend to be more accurate than secondary ones). Ask the people you consulted to explain or reconcile any remaining differences.

>> **When speaking with people about important information, arrange to have at least one other person present.** Doing so allows two different people to interpret what they hear from the same individual.

>> **Write down all information you obtain from personal meetings.** Share your written notes and summaries with other people who were present at the meeting to ensure that your interpretation is correct and to serve as a reminder of agreements made during the meeting.

>> **Plan to meet at least two times with your project's key audiences.** Your first meeting starts them thinking about issues. Allow some time for them to think over your initial discussions and to think of new ideas related to those issues. A second meeting gives you a chance to clarify any ambiguities or inconsistencies from the first session. (See Chapter 2 in this minibook for more information on project audiences.)

>> **Practice active listening skills in all your meetings and conversations.** See Chapter 5 in this minibook for information on how to practice active listening.

>> **Wherever possible, confirm what you heard in personal meetings with written sources.** When you talk with people, they share their perceptions and opinions. Compare those perceptions and opinions with written, factual data (from primary sources, if possible). Discuss any discrepancies with those same people.

Drawing the line: Where your project starts and stops

Sometimes your project stands alone, but more often it's only one of several related efforts to achieve a common result. You want to avoid duplicating the work of these other related projects, and, where appropriate, you want to coordinate your efforts with theirs.

Your description of your project's scope of work should specify clearly where your project starts and where it ends. Suppose your project is to develop a new product for your organization. You may frame your project's scope description as follows:

This project entails designing, developing, and testing a new product.

If you feel your statement is in any way ambiguous, you may clarify your scope further by stating what you will not do:

> This project won't include finalizing the market requirements or launching the new product.

To make sure your project's scope of work description is clear, do the following:

>> **Check for hidden inferences.** Suppose your boss has asked you to design and develop a new product. Check to be sure she doesn't assume you'll also perform the market research to determine the new product's characteristics.

>> **Use words that clearly describe intended activities.** Suppose your project entails *the implementation of a new information system.* Are you sure that everyone defines *implementation* in the same way? For instance, do people expect it to include installing the new software, training people to use it, evaluating its performance, fixing problems with it, or something else?

>> **Confirm your understanding of your project's scope with your project's drivers and supporters.**

> Suppose that you have an assignment to prepare for the competitive acquisition of certain equipment. You develop a plan to include the selection of the vendor, awarding of the contract, and production and delivery of the equipment. Your boss, however, is stunned with your project estimate of six months and $500,000. He thought it would take less than two months and cost less than $25,000.

> After a brief discussion with your boss, you realize that your job was to select the potential vendor, not place the order and have the equipment manufactured and delivered. Although you clarified your misunderstanding, you still wondered aloud, "But why would we select a vendor if we didn't want to buy the equipment?"

> You missed the point. The question wasn't whether the company planned to buy the equipment. (Certainly the intention to buy the equipment was the reason for the project.) The real question was whether the project or a different project in the future would purchase the equipment.

Stating your project's objectives

As mentioned previously in this chapter, *objectives* are outcomes your project will produce (they're also referred to as *deliverables*). Your project's outcomes may be products or services you develop or the results of using these products and services. The more clearly you define your project's objectives, the more likely you are to achieve them. Include the following elements in your objectives:

>> **Statement:** A brief narrative description of what you want to achieve

>> **Measures:** Indicators you'll use to assess your achievement

>> **Performance targets:** The value(s) of each measure that define success

Suppose you take on a project to reformat a report that summarizes monthly sales activity. You may frame your project's objective as follows:

Statement	Measures	Performance Targets
A revised report that summarizes monthly sales activity	Content	Report must include total number of items sold, total sales revenue, and total number of returns for each product line.
	Schedule	Report must be operational by August 31.
	Budget	Development expenditures are not to exceed $40,000.
	Approvals	New report format must be approved by the vice president of sales, regional sales manager, district sales manager, and sales representatives.

WARNING

Sometimes people try to avoid setting a specific target by establishing a range of values that defines successful performance. But setting a range is the same as avoiding the issue. Suppose you're a sales representative and your boss says you'll be successful if you achieve $20 million to $25 million in sales for the year. As far as you're concerned, you'll be 100 percent successful as soon as you reach $20 million. Most likely, however, your boss will consider you 100 percent successful only when you reach $25 million. Although you and your boss appeared to reach an agreement, you didn't.

The following sections explain how to create clear and specific objectives, identify all types of objectives, and respond to resistance to objectives.

Making your objectives clear and specific

REMEMBER

You need to be crystal clear when stating your project's objectives. The more specific your project objectives, the greater your chances of achieving them. Here are some tips for developing clear objectives:

» **Be brief when describing each objective.** If you take an entire page to describe a single objective, most people won't read it. Even if they do read it, your objective probably won't be clear and may have multiple interpretations.

» **Don't use technical jargon or acronyms.** Each industry (such as pharmaceuticals, telecommunications, finance, and insurance) has its own vocabulary, and so does each company within that industry. Within companies, different departments (such as accounting, legal, and information services) also have their own jargon. Because of this proliferation of specialized languages, the same three-letter acronym (TLA) can have two or more meanings in the same organization! To reduce the chances for misunderstandings, express your objectives in language that people of all backgrounds and experiences are familiar with.

» **Make your objectives SMART, as follows:**

- **Specific:** Define your objectives clearly, in detail, with no room for misinterpretation.

- **Measurable:** State the measures and performance specifications you'll use to determine whether you've met your objectives.

- **Aggressive:** Set challenging objectives that encourage people to stretch beyond their comfort zones.

- **Realistic:** Set objectives the project team believes it can achieve.

- **Time sensitive:** Include the date by which you'll achieve the objectives.

» **Make your objectives controllable.** Make sure that you and your team believe you can influence the success of each objective. If you don't believe you can, you may not commit 100 percent to achieving it (and most likely you won't even try). In that case, it becomes a wish, not an objective.

» **Identify all objectives.** Time and resources are always scarce, so if you don't specify an objective, you won't (and shouldn't) work to achieve it.

» **Be sure drivers and supporters agree on your project's objectives.** When drivers buy into your objectives, you feel confident that achieving the objectives constitutes true project success. When supporters buy into your objectives, you have the greatest chance that people will work their hardest to achieve them.

If drivers don't agree with your objectives, revise them until they do agree. After all, your drivers' needs are the whole reason for your project! If supporters don't buy into your objectives, work with them to identify their concerns and develop approaches they think can work.

Probing for all types of objectives

When you start a project, the person who makes the initial project request often tells you the major results she wants to achieve. However, she may want the project to address other items that she forgot to mention to you. And other (as yet unidentified) people may also want your project to accomplish certain results.

REMEMBER

You need to identify *all* project objectives as early as possible so you can plan for and devote the necessary time and resources to accomplishing each one. When you probe to identify all possible objectives, consider that projects may have objectives in the following three categories:

>> Physical products or services

>> The effects of these products or services

>> General organizational benefits that weren't the original reason for the project

Suppose that your information technology department is about to purchase and install a new software package for searching for and analyzing information in the company's parts-inventory database. The following are examples of objectives this project may have in each category:

>> **Physical product or service:** The completed installation and integration of the new software package with the parts-inventory database

>> **The effect of the product or service:** Reduced costs of inventory and storage due to timelier ordering facilitated by the new software

>> **A general organizational benefit:** Use of the new software with other company databases

REMEMBER

An objective is different from *serendipity* (a chance occurrence or coincidence). In the previous example of the new software package, consider that one project driver won't be completely satisfied unless the software for the parts-inventory database is also installed and integrated with the company's product-inventory database. In this case, installing the system on the company's product-inventory database must be an objective of your project so you must devote specific time and resources to accomplish it. On the other hand, if your audience will be happy whether you do or don't install the software on the second database, being able to use the software on that database is serendipity — meaning you shouldn't devote any time or resources specifically to accomplishing it.

Determining all project objectives requires you to identify all drivers who may have specific expectations for your project. See Chapter 2 in this minibook for a discussion of the different types of audiences and tips on how to identify each one.

Anticipating resistance to clearly defined objectives

Some people are uncomfortable committing to specific objectives because they're concerned they may not achieve them. Unfortunately, no matter what the reason, not having specific objectives makes knowing whether you're addressing (and meeting) your drivers' true expectations a lot more difficult. In other words, when your objectives aren't specific, you increase the chances that your project won't succeed.

Here are some excuses people give for not defining their objectives too specifically, along with suggestions for addressing those excuses:

>> **Excuse 1: Too much specificity stifles creativity.**

   Response: Creativity should be encouraged — the question is where and when. Your project's drivers should be clear and precise when stating their objectives; your project's supporters should be creative when figuring out ways to meet those objectives. You need to understand what people *do* expect from your project, not what they *may* expect. The more clearly you can describe your objectives, the more easily you can determine whether (and how) you can meet them.

>> **Excuse 2: Your project entails research and new development, and you can't tell today what you'll be able to accomplish.**

   Response: Objectives are targets, not guarantees. Certain projects have more risks than others. When you haven't performed a task before, you don't know whether it's possible. And if it is possible, you don't know how long it will take and how much it will cost. But you must state at the outset exactly what you want to achieve and what you think is possible, even though you may have to change your objectives as the project progresses.

>> **Excuse 3: What if interests or needs change?**

   Response: Objectives are targets based on what you know and expect today. If conditions change in the future, you may have to revisit one or more of your objectives to see whether they're still relevant and feasible or whether they, too, must change.

>> **Excuse 4: The project's requestor doesn't know what she specifically wants her project to achieve.**

   Response: Ask her to come back when she does. If you begin working on this project now, you have a greater chance of wasting time and resources to produce results that the requestor later decides she doesn't want.

> **» Excuse 5: Even though specific objectives help determine when you've succeeded, they also make it easier to determine when you haven't.**
>
> **Response: Yep. That's true.** However, because your project was framed to accomplish certain results, you need to know if your project achieved those results. If it didn't, you may have to perform additional work to accomplish them. In addition, you want to determine the benefits the organization is realizing from the money it's spending.

Marking Boundaries: Project Constraints

You'd like to operate in a world where everything is possible — that is, where you can do anything necessary to achieve your desired results. Your clients and your organization, on the other hand, would like to believe that you can achieve everything they want with minimal or no cost to them. Of course, neither situation is true.

Defining the constraints you must work within introduces reality into your plans and helps clarify expectations. As you plan and implement your project, think in terms of the following two types of constraints:

- **» Limitations:** Restrictions other people place on the results you have to achieve, the time frames you have to meet, the resources you can use, and the way you can approach your tasks.

- **» Needs:** Requirements you stipulate must be met so you can achieve project success.

This section helps you determine your project's limitations and needs.

Working within limitations

Project limitations may influence how you perform your project and may even determine whether or not you (and your project's drivers and supporters) decide to proceed with your project. Consult with your project's drivers and supporters to identify limitations as early as possible so you can design your plan to accommodate them.

Understanding the types of limitations

Project limitations typically fall into several categories. By recognizing these categories, you increase the chances that you'll discover all the limitations affecting your project. Your project's drivers and supporters may have preset expectations or requirements in one or more of the following categories:

>> **Results:** The products and effect of your project. For example, the new product must cost no more than $300 per item to manufacture, or the new book must be fewer than 384 pages in length.

>> **Time frames:** When you must produce certain results. For example, your project must be done by June 30. You don't know whether you can finish by June 30; you just know that someone expects the product to be produced by then.

>> **Resources:** The type, amount, and availability of resources to perform your project work. Resources can include people, funds, equipment, raw materials, facilities, information, and so on. For example, you have a budget of $100,000; you can have two people full time for three months; or you can't use the test laboratory during the first week in June.

>> **Activity performance:** The strategies for performing different tasks. For example, you're told that you must use your organization's printing department to reproduce the new users' manuals for the system you're developing. You don't know what the manual will look like, how many pages it'll be, how many copies you'll need, or when you'll need them. Therefore, you can't know whether your organization's printing department is up to the task. But at this point, you do know that someone expects you to have the printing department do the work.

WARNING

Be careful of vague limitations; they provide poor guidance for what you can or can't do, and they can demoralize people who have to deal with them. Here are some examples of vague limitations and how you can improve them:

>> **Time frame limitation:**

- **Vague:** "Finish this project as soon as possible." This statement tells you nothing. With this limitation, your audience may suddenly demand your project's final results — with no warning.

- **Specific:** "Finish this project by close of business June 30."

>> **Resource limitation:**

- **Vague:** "You can have Laura Webster on your project part time in May." How heavily can you count on her? From Laura's point of view, how can she juggle all her assignments in that period if she has no idea how long each one will take?

- **Specific:** "You can have Laura Webster on your project four hours per day for the first two weeks in May."

REMEMBER

When people aren't specific about their constraints, you can't be sure whether you can honor their requests. The longer people wait to be specific, the less likely you are to adhere to the limitation and successfully complete your project.

Looking for project limitations

Determining limitations is a fact–finding mission, so your job is to identify and examine all possible sources of information. You don't want to miss anything, and you want to clarify any conflicting information. After you know what people expect, you can determine how (or whether) you can meet those expectations. Try the following approaches:

>> **Consult your audiences.** Check with drivers about limitations regarding desired results; check with supporters about limitations concerning activity performance and resources.

>> **Review relevant written materials.** These materials may include long-range plans, annual budgets and capital appropriations plans, benefit-cost analyses, feasibility studies, reports of related projects, minutes of meetings, and individuals' performance objectives.

>> **When you identify a limitation, note its source.** Confirming a limitation from different sources increases your confidence in its accuracy. Resolve conflicting opinions about a limitation as soon as possible.

Addressing limitations in the scope statement

List all project limitations in your scope statement. If you have to explore ways to modify your project plan in the future, this list of limitations can help define alternatives that you can and can't consider.

You can reflect limitations in your project in two ways:

>> **Incorporate limitations directly into your plan.** For example, if a key driver says you have to finish your project by September 30, you may

choose to set September 30 as your project's completion date. Of course, because September 30 is the outside limit, you may choose to set a completion date of August 31. In this case, the limitation influences your target completion date but isn't equivalent to it.

>> **Identify any project risks that result from a limitation.** For example, if you feel the target completion date is unusually aggressive, the risk of missing that date may be significant. Your goal is to develop plans to minimize and manage that risk throughout your project.

Dealing with needs

As soon as possible, decide on the situations or conditions necessary for your project's success. Most of these needs relate to project resources. Here are a few examples of resource-related needs:

>> **Personnel:** "I need a technical editor for a total of 40 hours in August."

>> **Budget:** "I need a budget of $10,000 for computer peripherals."

>> **Other resources:** "I need access to the test laboratory during June."

TIP

Be as clear as possible when describing your project's needs. The more specific you are, the more likely other people are to understand and meet those needs.

Sometimes you can identify needs early in your project planning. More often, however, particular needs surface as you create a plan that addresses the drivers' expectations. As your list of needs grows, check with your project's supporters to decide how the new needs can be met and at what cost. Check with your project's drivers to confirm that the estimated additional cost is justified, and modify your project documentation to reflect any changes in planned results, activities, schedules, or resources.

Documenting Your Assumptions

As you proceed through your planning process, you can identify issues or questions that may affect your project's performance. Unfortunately, just identifying these issues or questions doesn't help you address them.

TIP

For every potential issue you identify, make assumptions regarding unknowns associated with it. Then use these assumptions as you plan your project. Consider the following examples:

>> **Issue:** You don't have a final, approved budget for your project.

Approach: *Assume* you'll get $50,000 for your project. *Plan* for your project to spend up to, but no more than, $50,000. Develop detailed information to demonstrate why your project budget must be $50,000, and share that information with key decision-makers.

>> **Issue:** You don't know when you'll get authorization to start work on your project.

Approach: *Assume* you'll receive authorization to start work on August 1. *Plan* your project work so that no activities start before August 1. Explain to key decision-makers why your project must start on August 1, and work with them to facilitate your project's approval by that date.

Note: Don't forget to consider all project assumptions when you develop your project's risk-management plan.

Presenting Your Scope Statement

Figure 3-1 presents an example of how you can display your scope statement in a table format. In this example, the information in the statement is grouped by major categories, starting with a brief statement of the justification for the project and its importance to the organization, moving through the specific results the project is intended to produce, and finishing with important constraints and assumptions that will define the environment in which the project is performed.

This table format is effective for the following reasons:

>> The category headings serve as reminders of the information you should include in the document.

>> The prepared format presents the information in the document in a logical order for the reader to digest.

>> The category headings make it easy for readers to find the particular information they are seeking.

>> The premeasured space for each category of information encourages you to choose your words carefully and keep the length of your entries to a minimum.

Project Title	Project Manager	Date: (mm/dd/yy)
		/ /

SCOPE STATEMENT

Justification	(To be written by the document's author)

Brief statement of the reason for the project
(to be summarized from the project charter)

Objectives/Deliverables (continue on additional pages as necessary)

Statement (continue on additional pages as necessary)

1.	(To be written by the document's author)

Product Scope Description/Product Acceptance Criteria

Measures	Performance Targets
1.1. (To be written by the document's author)	1.1.1. (To be written by the document's author)
1.2.	1.1.2.
Etc. (Continue on additional pages as necessary)	Etc. (Continue on additional pages as necessary)

Constraints

Limitations	
1.	
2.	(To be written by the document's author)
3.	
Etc.	(Continue on additional pages as necessary)
Needs	
1.	(To be written by the document's author)
2.	
3.	
Etc.	(Continue on additional pages as necessary)

Assumptions

1.	(To be written by the document's author)
2.	
3.	
Etc.	(Continue on additional pages as necessary)

Approvals

Project Manager	Client	Other
Date	Date	Date

FIGURE 3-1:
Sample scope
statement.

Clarifying Your Project

Chapter **4**

Developing a Game Plan

The keys to successful project planning and performance are completeness and continuity. You want to identify all important information in your project plan and address every aspect of your project while it's in progress.

Describing in detail all the tasks required to complete your project helps you accomplish them. Your description of project work provides the basis for scheduling, planning resources, defining roles and responsibilities, assigning work to team members, capturing key project performance data, and reporting on completed project work. This chapter helps you break down your project work into manageable pieces.

Breaking Your Project into Manageable Chunks

Two major concerns when starting a new project are remembering to plan for all important pieces of work and accurately estimating the time and resources required to perform that work. To address both issues, you should develop a logical framework to define all work that's necessary to complete the project.

Suppose you're asked to design and present a training program. You and a colleague work intensely for a couple of months developing the content and materials, arranging for the facilities, and inviting the participants. A week before the session, you ask your colleague whether he's made arrangements to print the training manuals. He says that he thought you were dealing with it, and you say that you thought he was dealing with it. Unfortunately, neither of you arranged to have the manuals printed because you each thought the other person was handling it. Now you have a training session in a week, and you don't have the time or money to print the needed training notebooks.

How can you avoid a situation like this one? By using a structured approach in the organizing and preparing stage of your project to identify all required project work. The following sections explain how to accomplish this task by subdividing your project's intermediate and final products into finer levels of detail and specifying the work required to produce them.

Thinking in detail

The most important guideline to remember when identifying and describing project work is this: Think in detail! People consistently underestimate the time and resources they need for their project work because they just don't recognize everything they have to do to complete it.

Suppose you have to prepare a report of your team's most recent meeting. Based on your past experience with preparing many similar reports, you quickly figure you'll need a few days to do this one. But how confident are you that this estimate is correct? Are you sure you've considered all the work that writing this particular report will entail? Will the differences between this report and others you've worked on mean more time and work for you? How can you tell?

The best way to determine how long and how much work a project will take to complete is to break down the required project work into its component deliverables, a process called *decomposition*. (A *deliverable* is an intermediate or final product, service, and/or result your project will produce. See Chapter 3 in this minibook for more information on project deliverables, or *objectives*, as they're often called.)

The greater the detail in which you decompose a project, the less likely you are to overlook anything significant. For example, creating the report in the preceding example actually entails producing three separate deliverables: a draft, reviews of the draft, and the final version. Completing the final version of the report, in turn, entails producing two deliverables: the initial version and the edited version. By decomposing the project into the deliverables necessary to generate the final report, you're more likely to identify all the work you need to do to complete the project.

TIP

Follow these two guidelines when decomposing your project:

>> **Allow no gaps.** Identify all components of the deliverable you're decomposing. In the example of creating a meeting report, if you have *allowed no gaps,* you'll have the desired final product in hand after you've produced the draft, the reviews of the draft, and the final version. However, if you feel that you'll have to do additional work to transform these three subproducts into a final product, you need to define the subproduct(s) that this additional work will produce.

>> **Allow no overlaps.** Don't include the same subproduct in your decomposition of two or more different deliverables. For example, don't include completed reviews of the draft by your boss and the vice president of your department as parts of the draft (the first deliverable) if you've already included them with all other reviews under reviews of the draft (the second deliverable).

Using these guidelines as you specify the parts and subparts of your project decreases the chance that you'll overlook something significant, which, in turn, helps you develop more accurate estimates of the time and resources needed to do the project.

Identifying necessary project work with a work breakdown structure

Thinking in detail is critical when you're planning your project, but you also need to consider the big picture. If you fail to identify a major part of your project's work, you won't have the chance to detail it! Thus, you must be both comprehensive and specific.

Figure 4-1 shows how you can depict necessary project work in a *work breakdown structure* (WBS), a deliverable-oriented decomposition of the work required to produce the necessary project products and achieve the project's objectives. The different levels in a WBS have had many different names. The top element is typically called a *project* and the lowest level of detail is typically called a *work package.* However, the levels in between have been called *phases, subprojects, work assignments, tasks, subtasks,* and *deliverables.* In this minibook, the top-level box (the Level 1 component) is a *project,* the lowest level of detail is a *work package,* and the elements in between are *Level 2 components, Level 3 components,* and so forth. A work package is comprised of activities that must be performed to produce the deliverable it represents.

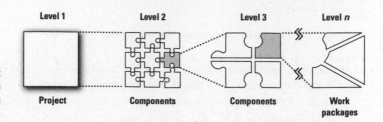

FIGURE 4-1:
Developing a
work breakdown
structure.

Level 1 — Project
Level 2 — Components
Level 3 — Components
Level n — Work packages

Specifically, Figure 4-1 shows that you can subdivide the entire project, represented as a Level 1 component, into Level 2 components and then subdivide some or all Level 2 components into Level 3 components. You can continue to subdivide all the components you create in the same manner until you reach a point at which you think the components you defined are sufficiently detailed for planning and management purposes. These Level *n* components, where *n* is the number of the lowest-level component in a particular WBS branch, are called *work packages.*

Suppose you're responsible for a project titled *Training Program Creation and Presentation* that entails creating and presenting a new training program for your organization. To get started, you develop a WBS for this project as follows:

1. **Determine the major deliverables or products to be produced.**

Ask yourself, "What major intermediate or final products or deliverables must be produced to achieve the project's objectives?"

You may identify the following items:

- Training program needs statement
- Training program design
- Participant notebooks
- Trained instructor
- Program testing
- Training program presentation

REMEMBER

Creating the WBS with deliverables rather than activities is important because

- It reinforces that in almost all instances, you achieve project success by producing desired outcomes, not by performing certain activities.
- It creates a link between the scope statement and the WBS, which helps ensure that you identify and perform all required work (and only work that is, in fact, required).

2. **Divide each major deliverable from Step 1 into its component deliverables.**

If you start with *Training program needs statement,* ask, "What intermediate deliverables must I have so I can create the needs statement?"

You may determine that you require the following:

- Interviews of potential participants

- A review of materials discussing the needs for the program

- A report summarizing the needs this program will address

3. **Divide each intermediate deliverable from Step 2 into its component parts.**

   If you start with *Interviews of potential participants,* ask, "What deliverables must I have to complete these interviews?"

   You may decide that you have to produce the following deliverables:

   - Selected interviewees

   - Interview questionnaire

   - Interview schedule

   - Completed interviews

   - Report of interview findings

   But why stop here? You can break each of these five items into its component parts and then break those pieces into even more parts. How far should you go? The following sections can help you answer that question.

Asking four key questions

Determining how much detail you need isn't a trivial task. You want to describe your work in sufficient detail to support accurate planning and meaningful tracking. But the benefits of this detail must justify the additional time you spend developing and maintaining your plans and reporting your progress.

REMEMBER

Asking the following four questions about each WBS component can help you decide whether you've defined it in enough detail:

>> Do you require two or more intermediate deliverables to produce this deliverable?

>> Can you estimate the resources you need to perform the work to produce this deliverable? (Resources include personnel, equipment, raw materials, money, facilities, and information.)

>> Can you accurately estimate how long producing this deliverable will take?

>> If you have to assign the work to produce this deliverable to someone else, are you confident that person will understand exactly what to do?

If you answer yes to the first question or no to any one of the other three, break down the deliverable into the components necessary to produce it.

Your answers to these questions depend on how familiar you are with the work, how critical the activity is to the success of your project, what happens if something goes wrong, whom you may assign to perform the activity, how well you know that person, and so on. In other words, the correct level of detail for your WBS depends on your judgment.

TIP

If you're a little uneasy about answering these four questions, try this even simpler test: Subdivide your WBS component into additional deliverables if you think either of the following situations applies:

>> The component will take much longer than two calendar weeks to complete.

>> The component will require much more than 80 person-hours to complete.

Remember that these estimates are just guidelines. For example, if you estimate that it will take two weeks and two days to prepare a report, you've probably provided sufficient detail. But if you think it will take two to three months to finalize requirements for your new product, you need to break the deliverable *finalized requirements* into more detail because

>> Experience has shown that there can be so many different interpretations of what is supposed to occur during these two to three months that you can't be sure your time and resource estimates are correct, and you can't confidently assign the task to someone to perform.

>> You don't want to wait two or three months to confirm that work is on schedule by verifying that a desired product has been produced on time.

Making assumptions to clarify planned work

Sometimes you want to break down a particular WBS component further, but certain unknowns stop you from doing so. How do you resolve this dilemma? You make assumptions regarding the unknowns. If, during the course of your project, you find that any of your assumptions are wrong, you can change your plan to reflect the correct information.

Regarding the *Training Program Creation and Presentation* project example presented previously in this section — suppose you decide that the *Completed interviews* deliverable from Step 3 needs more detail so you can estimate its required time and resources. However, you don't know how to break it down further because you don't know how many people you'll interview or how many separate sets of interviews you'll conduct. If you assume you'll interview five groups of seven people each, you can then develop specific plans for arranging and conducting each of these sessions. In most situations, it's best to consider a guess in the middle of the possible range. To determine how sensitive your results are to the different values, you may want to analyze for several different assumptions.

TIP

Be sure to write down your assumption so you remember to change your plan if you conduct more or less than five interview sessions. See the discussion in Chapter 3 of this minibook for more information about detailing assumptions.

Focusing on results when naming deliverables

Whenever possible, name a deliverable based on the result you need to achieve rather than the activity you need to perform to achieve that result. For example, you might title a deliverable that signifies completion of a needs assessment survey you have to conduct in one of two ways:

>> Survey completed

>> Needs assessment finished

Both options state that something has been finished. However, although the deliverable *Survey completed* indicates that a survey was performed, it doesn't explain what type of information the survey was supposed to obtain or whether it successfully obtained that information. On the other hand, *Needs assessment finished* confirms that the information from the completed survey successfully fulfilled the purpose for which it was intended.

Using action verbs to title activities

Use action verbs in the titles of activities that make up a work package to clarify the nature of the work the activities entail. Action verbs can improve your time and resource estimates, your work assignments to team members, and your tracking and reporting because they provide a clear picture of the work included in the activities and, thereby, the work packages of which they are a part.

Consider the assignment to prepare a report after a team meeting. Suppose you choose *Draft report* to be one of its work packages. If you don't break down *Draft report* further, you haven't indicated clearly whether it includes any or all of the following actions:

>> Collecting information for the draft

>> Determining length and format expectations and restrictions

>> Writing the draft

>> Reviewing the draft yourself before officially circulating it to others

But if you simply break down the work package into two activities that are titled "Design the draft report" and "Write the draft report," your scope of work is instantly clearer. A few well-chosen words at this level go a long way.

Developing a WBS for large and small projects

You need to develop a WBS for very large projects, very small projects, and everything in between. Building a skyscraper, designing a new airplane, researching and developing a new drug, and revamping your organization's information systems all need a WBS. So, too, do writing a report, scheduling and conducting a meeting, coordinating your organization's annual blood drive, and moving into your new office. The size of the WBS may vary immensely depending on the project, but the hierarchical scheme used to develop each one is the same.

REMEMBER

Occasionally, your detailed WBS may seem to make your project more complex than it really is. Seeing 100 tasks (not to mention 10,000) on paper can be a little unnerving! However, the WBS doesn't create a project's complexity; it just displays that complexity. In fact, by clearly portraying all aspects of your project work, the WBS simplifies your project.

Check out the sidebar "Conducting a survey using a WBS" for an illustration of how a work breakdown structure helps you develop a more accurate estimate of the time you need to complete your work.

CONDUCTING A SURVEY USING A WBS

Suppose your boss asks you to estimate how long it will take to survey people regarding the characteristics they would like to see in a new product your company may develop. Based on your experience doing similar types of assessments, you figure you'll need to contact people at the company headquarters, at two regional activity centers, and from a sampling of current clients. You tell your boss that the project will take you between one and six months to complete.

Have you ever noticed that bosses aren't happy when you respond to their question of "How long will it take?" with an answer of "Between one and six months"? You figure that finishing any time before six months meets your promise, but your boss expects you to be done in one month, given some (okay, a lot of) hard work. The truth is, though, you don't have a clue how long the survey will take because you have no idea how much work you have to do to complete it.

Developing a WBS encourages you to define exactly what you have to do and thereby improves your estimate of how long each step will take. In this example, you decide to conduct three different surveys: personal interviews with people at your headquarters, phone conference calls with people at the two regional activity centers, and a mail survey of a sample of your company's clients. Realizing you need to describe each survey in more detail, you begin by considering the mail survey and decide it includes five deliverables:

- **A sample of clients to survey:** You figure you need one week to select your sample of clients if the sales department has a current record of all company clients. You check with that department, and, thankfully, it does.

- **A survey questionnaire:** As far as this deliverable is concerned, you get lucky. A colleague tells you that she thinks the company conducted a similar survey of a different target population a year ago and that extra questionnaires from that effort may still be around. You find that a local warehouse has 1,000 of these questionnaires and — yes! — they're perfect for your survey. How much time do you need to allow for designing and printing the questionnaires? Zero!

- **Survey responses:** You determine that you need a response rate of at least 70 percent for the results to be valid. You consult with people who've conducted these types of surveys before and find out that you have to use the following three-phased approach to have an acceptable chance of achieving a minimum response rate of 70 percent:

  1. Initial mailing and receiving of questionnaires (estimated time is four weeks)

  2. Second mailing and receiving of questionnaires to non-respondents (estimated time is four weeks)

  3. Phone follow-ups with people who still haven't responded, encouraging them to complete and return their surveys (estimated time is two weeks)

- **Data analyses:** You figure you'll need about two weeks to enter and analyze the data you expect to receive.

- **A final report:** You estimate you'll need two weeks to prepare the final report.

Now, instead of one to six months, you can estimate the time you need to complete your mail survey to be 15 weeks. Because you've clarified the work you have to do and how you'll do it, you're more confident that you can reach your goal, and you've increased the chances that you will!

Note: To develop the most accurate estimates of your project's duration, in addition to the nature of the work you do, you need to consider the types and amounts of resources you require, together with their capacities and availabilities. However, this example illustrates that using just a WBS to refine the definition of your project's work components significantly improves your estimates.

Understanding a project's deliverable/activity hierarchy

Figure 4-2 shows a portion of the *deliverable/activity hierarchy* for the project of surveying people to determine the characteristics a new product your organization may develop should have (refer to the nearby sidebar "Conducting a survey using a WBS" for details on this example). As illustrated in the figure, a project's deliverable/activity hierarchy is comprised of three types of components:

>> **Deliverables:** Intermediate or final products created during the performance of the project (see Chapter 3 of this minibook)

>> **Work packages:** Deliverables at the lowest point in each branch of the hierarchy that can be further subdivided into activities

>> **Activities:** Work that's performed to produce a deliverable

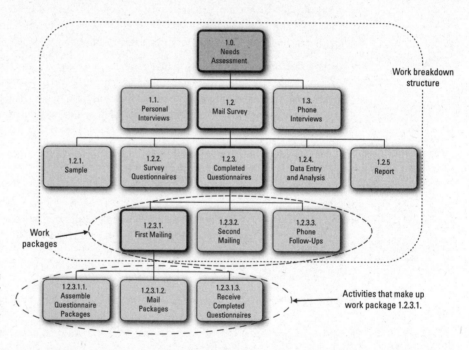

FIGURE 4-2:
The hierarchy of deliverables and activities for surveying people.

The WBS is the portion of the hierarchy that contains the deliverables (from the topmost level down to and including all work packages) that will be produced during the project. The activities that make up the work packages are recorded in a comprehensive activity list. While not considered to be part of the WBS, each activity is a component of a work package, so you need to identify it as such. (For convenience, you should include activities in the WBS dictionary under the work package to which they relate; see the later section "Documenting Your Planned Project Work" for details on the WBS dictionary.)

Dealing with special situations

With a little thought, you can break down most WBS elements into components. However, in some situations, like the ones described in the following sections, you have to get creative.

Representing conditionally repeating work

Suppose your project contains a deliverable (such as an approved report) that requires an unknown number of repetitive cycles (such as reviewing and revising the latest version of the draft report) to produce, each of which generates at least one intermediate deliverable. In reality, you write the report and submit it for review and approval. If the reviewers approve the report, you obtain your deliverable of an approved report and proceed to the next phase of your project (such as a distributed report). But if the reviewers don't approve the report, you have to revise it to incorporate their comments and then resubmit it for a second review and approval. If they approve the second draft, you obtain your deliverable of an approved report and proceed to the next phase of your project. But if they still don't approve your report, you have to repeat the process (or try to catch them in a better mood).

Revising the draft is *conditional work*; it will be completed only if a certain condition (in this case, not receiving the reviewers' approval) comes to pass. Unfortunately, a WBS doesn't include conditional work; you plan to perform every piece of work you detail in your WBS. However, you can indirectly represent conditional work in the following two ways:

>> **You can define a single deliverable as an *Approved report* and assign it a duration.** In effect, you're saying that you can create as many *Reviewed but not approved versions of the report* as necessary (each of which is an intermediate deliverable) to obtain the final reviewed and approved version within the established time period.

>> **You can assume that you'll need a certain number of revisions and include the intermediate deliverable created after each one (a different *Reviewed but not approved version of the report*) in your WBS.** This approach allows more meaningful tracking.

Whichever approach you choose, be sure to document it in your project plan.

Assuming that your project needs three reviews and two revisions doesn't guarantee that your draft will be good to go after only the third review. If your draft is approved after the first review, congratulations! You can move on to the next piece of work immediately — that is, you don't perform two revisions just because the plan assumed you would have to!

However, if you still haven't received approval after the third review, you continue to revise it and submit it for further review until you do get the seal of approval you need. Of course, then you have to reexamine your plan to determine the effect of the additional reviews and revisions on the schedule and budget of future project activities.

A plan isn't a guarantee of the future; it's your statement of what you will work to achieve. If you're unable to accomplish any part of your plan, you must revise it accordingly (and promptly).

Handling work with no obvious break points

Sometimes you can't see how to break a piece of work into two-week intervals. Other times that amount of detail just doesn't seem necessary. Even in these situations, however, you want to divide the work into smaller chunks to remind yourself to periodically verify that your current schedule and resource estimates are still valid.

KEEPING A CLOSE EYE ON YOUR PROJECT

A number of years ago, a young engineer was asked to design and build a piece of equipment for a client. He submitted a purchase request to his procurement department for the raw materials he needed and was told that, if they didn't arrive by the promised delivery date in six months, he should notify the procurement specialist he was working with so she could investigate the situation. He was uneasy about waiting six months without checking periodically to see whether everything was still on schedule, but being young, inexperienced, and new to the organization, he wasn't comfortable trying to fight this established procedure. So he waited six months.

When he didn't receive his raw materials by the promised delivery date, he notified the procurement specialist, who, in turn, checked with the vendor. Apparently, there had been a major fire in the vendor's facilities five months earlier, and production had just resumed the previous week. The vendor estimated his materials would be shipped in about five months!

He could have divided the waiting time into one-month intervals and called the vendor at the end of each month to see whether anything had occurred that changed the projected delivery date. Although checking periodically wouldn't have prevented the fire, the engineer would have known about it five months sooner and could have made other plans immediately.

In these instances, arbitrarily define intermediate milestones to occur every two weeks that are defined as "progress confirmed as being on schedule" or "expenditures confirmed as being on budget." Check out the sidebar "Keeping a close eye on your project" for an illustration of why it's important to have frequent milestones to support project tracking and how to deal with WBS components that have no obvious break points.

Planning a long-term project

A long-term project presents a different challenge. Often the work you perform a year or more in the future depends on the results of the work you do between now and then. Even if you can accurately predict the work you'll perform later, the further into the future you plan, the more likely it is that something will change and require you to modify your plans.

When developing a WBS for a long-term project, use a *rolling-wave approach,* in which you continually refine your plans throughout the life of your project as you discover more about the project and its environment. This approach acknowledges that uncertainties may limit your plan's initial detail and accuracy, and it encourages you to reflect more accurate information in your plans as soon as you discover it. Apply the rolling-wave approach to your long-term project by taking the following steps:

1. **Break down the first three months' work into components that take two weeks or less to complete.**

2. **Plan the remainder of the project in less detail, perhaps describing the work in packages you estimate to take between one and two months to complete.**

3. **Revise your initial plan at the end of the first three months to detail your work for the next three months in components that take two weeks or less to complete.**

4. **Modify any future work as necessary, based on the results of your first three months' work.**

5. **Continue revising your plan in this way throughout the project.**

REMEMBER

No matter how carefully you plan, something unanticipated can always occur. The sooner you find out about such an occurrence, the more time you have to minimize any negative effect on your project.

Issuing a contract for services you will receive

Generally speaking, you use a WBS that you include in a contract for services to be provided to you by another person or organization differently from the way you use one to guide project work that you or your organization performs itself. When you perform the project yourself, the WBS provides the basis for developing detailed project schedules, estimating personnel and other resource requirements, detailing the project roles and responsibilities of project team members, and assessing all aspects of the ongoing work. However, when you manage a contract with an external organization that's performing the project for you, you use the WBS to

>> Support responsive progress assessment to help ensure that the overall project is on track to finish on time and within budget.

>> Provide the contractor with a framework for tracking and reporting periodic assessments of project schedule achievement and resource expenditures.

>> Confirm that product, schedule, and resource performance is sufficient to justify the making of scheduled progress payments.

In addition, you don't want the WBS to unduly restrict the contractor's ability to use his experience, skills, and professional judgment to achieve the results detailed in the contract. Typically, developing the WBS to two or three levels of detail is sufficient to meet the preceding needs without creating unnecessary restrictions.

Creating and Displaying a WBS

You can use several schemes to develop and display your project's WBS; each one can be effective under different circumstances. This section looks at a few of the most common schemes and provides some examples and advice on how and when to apply them.

Considering different schemes

The following five schemes (and their examples) can help you subdivide project work into WBS components:

>> **Product components:** Floor plan, training manuals, or screen design

>> **Functions:** Design, launch, review, or test

>> **Project phases:** Initiation, design, or construction

>> **Geographical areas:** Region 1 or the northwest

>> **Organizational units:** Marketing, operations, or facilities

Project phases, product components, and functions are the most often used.

When you choose a scheme to organize the sub-elements of a WBS component, continue to use that same scheme for all the sub-elements under that component to prevent possible overlap in categories. For example, consider that you want to develop finer detail for the WBS component titled *Report.* You may choose to break out the detail according to function, such as *Draft report, Reviews of draft report,* and *Final report.* Or you may choose to break it out by product component, such as *Section 1, Section 2,* and *Section 3.*

Don't define a WBS component's sub-elements by using some items from two different schemes. For instance, for the component *Report,* don't use the sub-elements *Section 1, Section 2, Reviews of draft report,* and *Final report.* Combining schemes in this way increases the chances of either including work twice or overlooking it completely. For example, the work to prepare the final version of Section 2 could be included in either of two sub-elements: *Section 2* or *Final report.*

Consider the following questions when choosing a scheme:

>> **What higher-level milestones will be most meaningful when reporting progress?** For example, is it more helpful to report that *Section 1* is completed or that the entire *Draft report* is done?

>> **How will you assign responsibility?** For example, is one person responsible for the draft, reviews, and final report of Section 1, or is one person responsible for the drafts of Sections 1, 2, and 3?

>> **How will you and your team members actually do the work?** For example, is the drafting, reviewing, and finalizing of Section 1 separate from the same activities for Section 2, or are all chapters drafted together, reviewed together, and finalized together?

Developing your WBS

How you develop your WBS depends on how familiar you and your team are with your project, whether similar projects have been successfully performed in the past, and how many new methods and approaches you'll use. Choose one of the following two approaches for developing your WBS based on your project's characteristics:

>> **Top-down:** Start at the top level in the hierarchy and systematically break WBS elements into their component parts.

This approach is useful when you have a good idea of the project work involved before the actual work begins. The top-down approach ensures that you thoroughly consider each category at each level, and it reduces the chances that you overlook work in any of your categories.

>> **Brainstorming:** Generate all possible work and deliverables for this project and then group them into categories.

Brainstorming is helpful when you don't have a clear sense of a project's required work at the outset. This approach encourages you to generate any and all possible pieces of work that may have to be performed, without worrying about how to organize them in the final WBS. After you decide that a proposed piece of work is a necessary part of the project, you can identify any related work that is also required.

TIP

Whichever approach you decide to use, consider using stick-on notes to support your WBS development. As you identify pieces of work, write them on the notes and put them on the wall. Add, remove, and regroup the notes as you continue to think through your work. This approach encourages open sharing of ideas and helps all people appreciate — in detail — the nature of the work that needs to be done.

The top-down approach

Use the following top-down approach for projects that you or others are familiar with:

1. **Specify all Level 2 components for the entire project.**

2. **Determine all necessary Level 3 components for each Level 2 component.**

3. **Specify the Level 4 components for each Level 3 component as necessary.**

4. **Continue in this way until you've completely detailed all project intermediate and final deliverables.**

    The lowest-level components in each WBS chain are your project's work packages.

The brainstorming approach

Use the following brainstorming approach for projects involving untested methods or for projects you and your team members aren't familiar with:

1. **Identify all the intermediate and final deliverables that you think your project will produce.**

    Don't worry about overlap or level of detail.

    Don't discuss wording or other details of the work items.

    Don't make any judgments about the appropriateness of the work.

2. **Group these items into a few major categories with common characteristics and eliminate any deliverables that aren't required.**

These groups are your *Level 2* categories.

3. **Divide the deliverables under each Level 2 category into groups with common characteristics.**

These groups are your *Level 3* categories.

4. **Use the top-down method to identify any additional deliverables that you overlooked in the categories you created.**

5. **Continue in this manner until you've completely described all project deliverables and work components.**

The lowest-level components in each WBS chain are your project's work packages.

Categorizing your project's work

Although you eventually want to use only one WBS for your project, early in the development of your WBS, you can look at two or more different hierarchical schemes. Considering your project from two or more perspectives helps you identify work you may have overlooked.

Suppose a local community wants to open a halfway house for substance abusers. Figures 4-3 and 4-4 depict two different schemes to categorize the work for this community-based treatment facility. The first scheme classifies the work by product component, and the second classifies the work by function:

>> Figure 4-3 defines the following components as Level 2 categories: staff, facility, residents (people who'll be living at the facility and receiving services), and community training.

FIGURE 4-3: A product component scheme for a WBS.

>> Figure 4-4 defines the following functions as Level 2 categories: planning, recruiting, buying, and training.

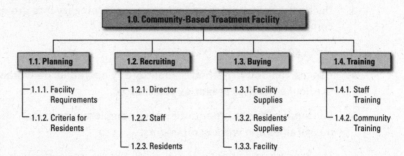

FIGURE 4-4: A functional scheme for a WBS.

Both WBSs contain the same lowest-level components or work packages.

When you think about your project in terms of major functions (rather than final product components), you realize that you forgot the following work:

>> Planning for staff recruiting

>> Buying staff supplies

>> Planning for your community training

After you identify the work components you overlooked, you can include them in either of the two WBSs.

WARNING

Be sure you choose only one WBS before you leave your project's planning phase. Nothing confuses people faster than trying to use two or more different WBSs to describe the same project.

Labeling your WBS entries

As the size of a project grows, its WBS becomes increasingly complex. Losing sight of how a particular piece of work relates to other parts of the project is easy to do. Unfortunately, this problem can lead to poor coordination between related work efforts and a lack of urgency on the part of people who must perform the work.

TIP

Figure 4-5 illustrates a scheme for labeling your WBS components so you can easily see their relationships with each other and their relative positions in the overall project WBS:

>> The first digit (1), the Level 1 identifier, indicates the project in which the item is located.

>> The second digit (5) indicates the Level 2 component of the project in which the item is located.

>> The third digit (7) refers to the Level 3 component under the Level 2 component *1.5.* in which the item is located.

>> The fourth and last digit (3) is a unique identifier assigned to distinguish this item from the other Level 4 components under the Level 3 component *1.5.7.* If *1.5.7.3. Materials Ordered* isn't subdivided further, it's a work package.

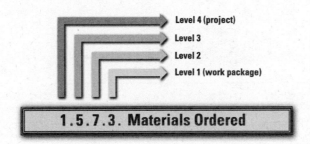

FIGURE 4-5:
Identifying your WBS components.

TIP

When you're ready to label the activities that fall under a given work package, use a combination of the WBS code of the work package and a unique code that specifically refers to each activity. For example, suppose an activity under the work package 1.5.7.3. is *Prepare list of items to order.* You may give this activity the identifier code depicted in Figure 4-6. In this instance, the first four digits of the activity code are the WBS code for the work package of which this activity is a part. The fifth digit distinguishes this activity from the others in work package 1.5.7.3.

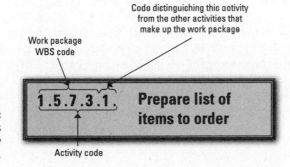

FIGURE 4-6:
The components of an activity code.

Developing a Game Plan

Displaying your WBS in different formats

You can display your WBS in several different formats. This section looks at three of the most common ones.

The organization-chart format

Figure 4-7 shows a WBS in the *organization-chart format* (also referred to as a *hierarchy diagram* or a *graphical view*). This format effectively portrays an overview of your project and the hierarchical relationships of different WBS components at the highest levels. However, because this format generally requires a lot of space, it's less effective for displaying large WBSs.

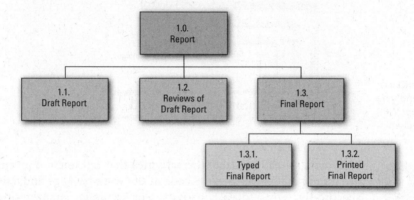

FIGURE 4-7:
Your WBS in the organization-chart format.

The indented-outline format

The *indented-outline format* in Figure 4-8 is another way to display your WBS. This format allows you to read and understand a complex WBS with many components. However, you can easily get lost in the details of a large project with this format and forget how the pieces all fit together.

TIP

Both the organization-chart format and the indented-outline format can be helpful for displaying the WBS for a small project. For a large project, however, consider using a combination of the organization-chart and the indented-outline formats to explain your WBS. You can display the Level 1 and Level 2 components in the organization-chart format and portray the detailed breakout for each Level 2 component in the indented-outline format.

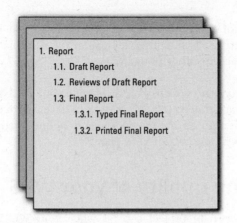

FIGURE 4-8:
Your WBS in the
indented-outline
format.

The bubble-chart format

The *bubble-chart format* in Figure 4-9 is particularly effective for displaying the results of the brainstorming approach to develop your WBS for both small and large projects (see the earlier section "The brainstorming approach"). You interpret the bubble-chart format as follows:

>> The bubble in the center represents your entire project (in this case, *Report*).

>> Lines from the center bubble lead to Level 2 breakouts (in this case, *Draft Report*, *Reviews of Draft*, and *Final Report*).

>> Lines from each Level 2 component lead to Level 3 components related to the Level 2 component. (In this case, the Level 2 component *Final Report* consists of the two Level 3 components *Typed Final Report* and *Printed Final Report*.)

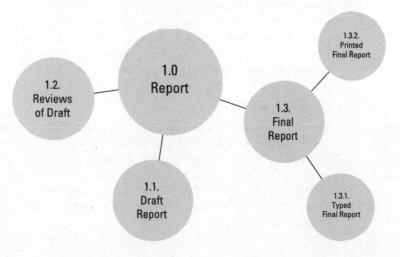

FIGURE 4-9:
Your WBS in the
bubble-chart
format.

The freeform nature of the bubble-chart format allows you to easily record thoughts generated during a brainstorming session. You can also easily rearrange components as you proceed with your analysis.

The bubble-chart format isn't effective for displaying your WBS to audiences who aren't familiar with your project. Use this format to develop your WBS with your team, but transpose it into an organization-chart or indented-outline format when you present it to people outside your team.

Improving the quality of your WBS

You increase the chances for project success when your WBS is accurate and complete *and* when people who will be performing the work understand and agree with it. The following guidelines suggest some ways to improve your WBS's accuracy and acceptance:

>> **Involve the people who'll be doing the work.** When possible, involve them during the initial development of the WBS. If they join the project after the initial planning, have them review and critique the WBS before they begin work.

>> **Review and include information from WBSs from similar projects.** Review plans and consult people who've worked on projects similar to yours that were successful. Incorporate your findings into your WBS.

>> **Keep your WBS current.** When you add, delete, or change WBS elements during your project, be sure to reflect these changes in your WBS. (See the "Documenting Your Planned Project Work" section, later in this chapter, for more about sharing the updated WBS with the team.)

>> **Make assumptions regarding uncertain activities.** If you're not sure whether you'll do a particular activity, make an assumption and prepare your WBS based on that assumption. Be sure to document that assumption. If your assumption proves to be wrong during the project, change your plan to reflect the true situation. (See the earlier sections "Making assumptions to clarify planned work" and "Representing conditionally repeating work" for more about assumptions.)

>> **Remember that your WBS identifies only your project's deliverables; it doesn't depict their chronological order.** Nothing is wrong with listing deliverables from left to right or top to bottom in the approximate order that you'll create them. In complex projects, however, you may have difficulty showing detailed interrelationships among intermediate and final deliverables in the WBS format. The purpose of the WBS is to ensure that you identify all project deliverables.

Using templates

A *WBS template* is an existing WBS that contains deliverables typical for a particular type of project. This template reflects people's cumulative experience from performing many similar projects. As people perform more projects, they add deliverables to the template that were overlooked and remove deliverables that weren't needed. Using templates can save you time and improve your accuracy.

Don't inhibit people's active involvement in the development of the WBS by using a template that's too polished. Lack of people's involvement can lead to missed activities and lack of commitment to project success.

This section looks at how you can develop a WBS template and improve its accuracy and completeness.

Drawing on previous experience

By drawing on previous experience, you can prepare your WBS in less time than it takes to develop a new WBS and be more confident that you've included all essential pieces of work.

Suppose you prepare your department's quarterly budget. After doing a number of these budgets, you know most of the work you have to perform. Each time you finish another budget, you revise your WBS template to include new information you gleaned from the recently completed project.

The next time you start to plan a quarterly budget, begin with the WBS template you've developed from your past projects. Then add and subtract elements as appropriate for this particular budget preparation.

Improving your WBS templates

The more accurate and complete your WBS templates are, the more time they can save on future projects. This section offers several suggestions for continually improving the quality of your WBS templates.

When using templates, keep in mind the following guidelines:

>> **Develop templates for frequently performed tasks as well as for entire projects.** Templates for the annual organization blood drive or the submission of a newly developed drug to the Food and Drug Administration are valuable. So are templates for individual tasks that are part of these projects, such as awarding a competitive contract or having a document printed. You can always incorporate templates for individual pieces of work into a larger WBS for an entire project.

» **Develop and modify your WBS template from previous projects that worked, not from initial plans that looked good.** Often you develop a detailed WBS at the start of your project, but you may forget to add intermediate or final deliverables that you overlooked in your initial planning. If you update your template from a WBS that you prepared at the *start* of your project, it won't reflect what you discovered *during* the performance of the project.

» **Use templates as starting points, not ending points.** Clarify to your team members and others involved in the project that the template is only the start for your WBS, not the final version. Every project differs in some ways from similar ones performed in the past. If you don't critically examine the template, you may miss work that wasn't done in previous projects but that needs to be done in this one.

» **Continually update your templates to reflect your experiences from different projects.** The post-project evaluation is a great opportunity to review and critique your original WBS. At the end of your project, take a moment to revise your WBS template to reflect what you found.

Identifying Risks While Detailing Your Work

In addition to helping you identify work you need to complete, a WBS helps you identify unknowns that may cause problems when you attempt to perform that work. As you think through the work you have to do to complete your project, you often identify considerations that may affect how or whether you can perform particular project activities. Sometimes you have the information you need to assess and address a consideration and sometimes you don't. Identifying and dealing effectively with information you need but don't have can dramatically increase your chances for project success.

Unknown information falls into one of two categories:

» **Known unknown:** Information you know you need that someone else has

» **Unknown unknown:** Information you know you need that neither you nor anyone else has because it doesn't exist yet

You deal with known unknowns by finding out who has the information you need and then getting it. You deal with unknown unknowns by using one or more of the following strategies:

>> Buying insurance to minimize damage that occurs if something doesn't turn out the way you expected

>> Developing contingency plans to follow if something doesn't turn out the way you expected

>> Trying to influence what the information eventually turns out to be

In the project *Conducting a survey* discussed in the "Conducting a survey using a WBS" sidebar, presented previously in this chapter, you figure you'll need a week to select a sample of clients to survey if the sales department has a current customer relationship manager (CRM) program listing all the company's clients. At this point, whether the listing exists is a *known unknown* — it's unknown to you, but if it exists, someone else knows about it. You deal with this unknown by calling people to find someone who knows whether such a listing does or doesn't exist.

You experience a different situation when you become aware that the person who managed the CRM program has left the job. As part of your *Conducting a survey* project, you need to have the new person work with the list and you're concerned that he doesn't know that it's part of his job.

Whether or not the operator knows it's his job is an unknown unknown when you prepare the WBS for your project plan. You can't determine beforehand that the first person would leave the company and the new one wouldn't be properly trained because it's an unintended, unplanned act (at least you hope so).

Because you can't find out for certain whether or not this occurrence will happen, you consider taking one or more of the following approaches to address this risk:

>> **Develop a contingency plan.** For example, in addition to developing a scheme for the computerized selection of names directly from the original database, have the statistician who guides the selection of the sample develop a scheme for selecting names randomly by hand from the database.

>> **Take steps to reduce the likelihood that only one person knows what is going on with the CRM.** For example, check with the department head to see whether another employees can be trained to run the CRM program.

Of course, if you feel the chance that only one operator will know how to run the program is sufficiently small, you can always choose to do nothing beforehand and just deal with the situation if and when it actually occurs.

Developing the WBS helps you identify a situation that may compromise your project's success. You then must decide how to deal with that situation.

Documenting Your Planned Project Work

After preparing your project WBS, take some time to gather essential information about all your work packages (lowest-level WBS components), and keep it in the *WBS dictionary* that's available to all project team members. You and your team will use this information to develop the remaining parts of your plan, as well as to support the tracking, controlling, and replanning of activities during the project. The project manager (or her designee) should approve all changes to information in this dictionary.

The WBS dictionary can contain but isn't limited to the following information for all WBS components:

>> **WBS component title and WBS identification code:** Descriptors that uniquely identify the WBS component

>> **Activities included:** List of all the activities that must be performed to create the deliverable identified in the work package

>> **Work detail:** Narrative description of work processes and procedures

>> **Schedule milestones:** Significant events in the component's schedule

>> **Quality requirements:** Desired characteristics of the deliverables produced in the WBS component

>> **Acceptance criteria:** Criteria that must be met before project deliverables are accepted

>> **Required resources:** People, funds, equipment, facilities, raw materials, information, and so on that these activities need

TIP

For larger projects, you maintain the entire WBS — including all its components from Level 1 down to and including the work packages — in the same hierarchical representation, and you keep all the activities that make up the work packages in an activity list or in the WBS dictionary or in both. Separating the WBS components in this way helps you more easily see and understand the important interrelationships and aspects of the project deliverables and work.

On smaller projects, however, you may combine the deliverable-oriented WBS components and the activities in each work package in the same hierarchical display.

IN THIS CHAPTER

» **Highlighting important elements of communication**

» **Deciding how to share news**

» **Writing your project-progress report**

» **Getting familiar with different meeting styles**

» **Creating a project communications plan**

Chapter **5**

Keeping Everyone Informed

Imagine standing at one end of a large room filled with assorted sofas, chairs, and tables. You've accepted a challenge to walk to the other end without bumping into any of the furniture. But as you set off on your excursion, the lights go off and you have to complete your trip in darkness, with only your memory of the room's layout to guide you.

Sounds like a pretty tough assignment, doesn't it? How much easier it would be if the lights went on every few seconds — you could see exactly where you were, where you had to go, and where the furniture got in the way. The walk would still be challenging, but it would be much more successful than in total darkness.

Surprisingly, many projects are just like that walk across the room. People plan how they'll perform the project — who will do what, by when, and for how much — and they share this information with the team members and other people who will support the project. But as soon as the project work begins, people receive no information about their progress, the work remaining, or any obstacles that may lie ahead.

Effective communication — sharing the right messages with the right people in a timely manner — is a key to successful projects. Informative communications support the following:

>> Continued buy-in and support from key audiences and team members

>> Prompt problem identification and decision-making

>> A clear project focus

>> Ongoing recognition of project achievements

>> Productive working relationships among team members

Planning your project communications enables you to choose the appropriate media for sharing different messages. This chapter can help you keep everyone in the loop so no one's left wondering about the status of your project.

Successful Communication Basics

Have you ever played the game of telephone with a group of people sitting around a table? The first person at the table has a written message, and the object of the game is for the group to transmit that message accurately to the last person at the table by having each person in turn whisper the contents of the message to the next person in line. The rules are simple: No one other than the first person can see the original written message, and each person must ensure that only the next in line hears the message she whispers. Invariably, the message received by the last person bears little, if any, resemblance to the original message because, even in this controlled setting, a myriad of factors influence how well people send and receive messages.

Sadly, sometimes this type of miscommunication can occur in a project-management environment. But don't worry! This section is here to help. It explores important parts of the communication process, distinguishes different types of communication, and offers suggestions to improve the chances that the message a receiver gets is the one the sender intended to give.

Breaking down the communication process

Communication is the transmitting of information from a sender to a receiver. Whenever you communicate, during the life of a project or at any other time, your goal is to ensure that the right person correctly receives your intended message in a timely manner.

REMEMBER

The process of transmitting information includes the following components:

>> **Message:** The thoughts or ideas being transmitted.

>> **Sender:** The person transmitting the message.

>> **Encoded message:** The message translated into a language understandable to others. (This language may consist of words, pictures, or actions.)

>> **Medium:** The method used to convey the message. (The different mediums are described in detail in the later section "Choosing the Appropriate Medium for Project Communication.")

>> **Noise:** Anything that hinders successfully transmitting the message. (Noise may include preconceived notions, biases, difficulty with the language used, personal feelings, nonverbal cues, and emotions.)

>> **Receiver:** The person getting the message.

>> **Decoded message:** The message translated back into thoughts or ideas.

Depending on the nature of a particular communication, any or all of these elements can affect the chances that the sender receives the message as intended.

Distinguishing one-way and two-way communication

Certain types of communication are more effective for transmitting particular types of information. The two main types are

>> **One-way communication:** Going from the sender to the receiver with no opportunity for clarification or confirmation that the receiver received and correctly understood the intended message. This type of communication can be effective for presenting facts, confirming actions, and sharing messages that have little chance of being misinterpreted.

One-way communications are either push or pull:

- *Push:* Proactively distributed to particular people; examples include memos, reports, letters, faxes, and emails.

- *Pull:* Available to people who must access the communications themselves; examples include Internet and intranet sites, knowledge repositories, and bulletin boards.

>> **Two-way communication:** Going from the sender to the receiver and from the receiver back to the sender to help ensure that the intended audience received and correctly interpreted the message. Examples include face-to-face discussions, phone calls, in-person group meetings, interactive teleconferences, and online instant messaging. Two-way communication is effective for ensuring that more complex content is correctly received and for conveying the sender's beliefs and feelings about the message.

Can you hear me? Listening actively

The one skill that most strongly influences the quality of your communications is your ability to listen actively. Although you can assume that the information contained in a message and the format in which it's presented affect how well that message is received, you can find out whether the recipient received the message as you intended by listening carefully to the recipient's reactions.

Active listening is exploring and discussing a message that's being sent to help ensure that the message is understood as intended. If you're sending a message, you should encourage your intended recipient to use active listening techniques to help ensure that she correctly understands your message. If you're receiving a message, you should use these techniques to verify to yourself that you have correctly received the intended message.

Because listening to and observing your recipient's response to a message you sent her involves information flowing first from you to the recipient and then from the recipient back to you, active listening is, by definition, a form of two-way communication.

Active listening techniques include the following:

>> **Visualizing:** Forming a mental picture of the content of a message. Forming this picture gives the receiver the opportunity to identify pieces of the message that may be missing or misunderstood, as well as to seek additional information that may improve the overall understanding of the original message.

Consider that you've been asked to redesign the layout of your group's offices to create a more open environment that will encourage people to feel more relaxed and to engage in more informal working group discussions. To help clarify what's expected, you may try to visualize how the office environment will look and how people will behave after the changes in the layout are made. In particular, you may think about the following:

- Whether you'll have to use the existing furnishings or you'll be able to buy new ones

- Where people might hold informal meetings

- How much soundproofing partitions of differing heights will provide

As you try to visualize these different parts of the new office layout, you realize that the following aspects aren't quite clear to you:

- Will window offices have couches or just chairs?

- How many people should be able to sit comfortably in an office?

- Should you install white noise machines?

As you talk with people to find answers to your questions, you get a better idea of what your boss does and doesn't want.

>> **Paraphrasing:** Explaining the message and its implications, as the receiver understands them, back to the sender in different words than the original message. To be most effective, the receiver should repeat the message in her own words to give the sender the best chance of identifying any misinterpretations.

Consider that your boss asks you to prepare a report of your company's recent sales activity by the end of the week. Many aspects of this request are unclear, such as the time period the report should cover, the specific time by when the report must be finished, the format in which you should prepare the report, and so forth. To clarify these items, you can paraphrase the request back to your boss as follows:

"I'd like to confirm that you're asking me to prepare for you a PowerPoint presentation on the company's total gross and net sales of products a, b, and c for the period from January 1 to March 31 of this year and that you'd like me to have it for you by this coming Friday at 5:00 p.m."

>> **Checking inferences:** Clarifying assumptions and interpretations that the receiver makes about the message received.

Consider the previous example in which your boss asks you to redesign the layout of your group's offices. As you start to calculate the numbers of desks and chairs you'll need in the new arrangement, you realize you're assuming that the group will have the same number of people now and after the move. Instead of making this assumption, you can check with your boss to find out how many people he would like you to plan for as you design the new layout.

REMEMBER

Active listening is particularly useful in situations that are emotionally charged, situations in which understanding is critical, situations in which consensus and clarity are desired in resolving conflict, and situations in which trust is sought.

Keeping Everyone Informed

Choosing the Appropriate Medium for Project Communication

When deciding how to communicate with your team and your project's audiences, choosing the right medium is as important as deciding what information to share (check out Chapter 2 of this minibook for a detailed discussion of project audiences). Your choice of medium helps ensure that people get the information they need when they need it.

Project communications come in two forms:

>> **Formal:** Formal communications are planned and conducted in a standard format in accordance with an established schedule. Examples include weekly team meetings and monthly progress reports.

>> **Informal:** Informal communications occur as people think of information they want to share. These communications occur continuously in the normal course of business. Examples include brief conversations by the water cooler and spur-of-the-moment emails you dash off during the day.

WARNING

Take care not to rely on informal communications to share important information about your project because these interchanges often involve only a small number of the people who should hear what you have to say. To minimize the chances for misunderstandings and hurt feelings among your project's team members and other audiences, follow these guidelines:

- Confirm in writing any important information you share in informal discussions.

- Avoid having an informal discussion with only some of the people who are involved in the topic.

Formal and informal communications can be either written or oral. The following sections suggest when to use each format and how to make it most effective.

Just the facts: Written reports

Unlike informal oral communication, written reports enable you to present factual data efficiently, choose your words carefully to minimize misunderstandings, provide a historical record of the information you share, and share the same message with a wide audience.

Although written reports have quite a few benefits, they also have some drawbacks that you need to consider:

>> They don't allow your audience to ask questions to clarify the content, meaning, or implication of your message.

>> With written reports, you can't verify that your audience received and interpreted your message as you intended.

>> They don't enable you to pick up nonverbal signals that suggest your audience's reactions to the message.

>> They don't support interactive discussion and brainstorming about your message.

>> You may never know whether your audience reads the report!

Keep the following pointers in mind to improve the chances that people read and understand your written reports (see the later section "Preparing a Written Project-Progress Report" for specifics on writing this special type of communication):

>> **Prepare regularly scheduled reports in a standard format.** This consistency helps your audience find specific types of information quickly.

>> **Stay focused.** Preparing several short reports to address different topics is better than combining several topics into one long report. People are more likely to pick up the important information about each topic.

>> **Minimize the use of technical jargon and acronyms.** If people are unfamiliar with the language in your report, they'll miss at least some of your messages.

>> **Use written reports to share facts, and be sure to identify a person or people to contact for clarification or further discussion of any information in the reports.** Written reports present hard data with a minimum of subjective interpretation, and they provide a useful, permanent reference. A contact person can address any questions a recipient has about the information or the reasons for sharing it.

>> **Clearly describe any actions you want people to take based on information in the report.** The more specifically you explain what you want people to do, the more likely they are to do it.

>> **Use different approaches to emphasize key information.** For example, print key sections in a different color or on colored paper, or mention particularly relevant or important sections in a cover memo. This additional effort increases the chances that your audience will see the report *and* read it.

>> **After you send your report, discuss one or two key points that you addressed in it with people who received it.** These follow-up conversations can quickly tell you whether your recipients have read your report.

When you come across people who clearly haven't read your report, in addition to following the other suggestions in this section, explain to them the specific parts of the document that are most important for them to review and why. Then tell them that you'd like to set up a follow-up meeting with them to discuss any questions or issues they may have regarding the information contained in those parts of the document.

>> **Keep your reports to one page, if possible.** If you can't fit your report on one page, include a short summary (one page or less) at the beginning of the report (check out the nearby sidebar "Keep it short — and that means you!").

Move it along: Meetings that work

Few words elicit the same reactions of anger and frustration that the word *meeting* can provoke. People consider meetings to be everything from the last vestige of interpersonal contact in an increasingly technical society to the biggest time waster in business today.

KEEP IT SHORT — AND THAT MEANS YOU!

Be careful of the "yes, but" syndrome, in which you think an idea sounds great for others, but your *special* situation requires a different approach. In a training program a number of years ago, the speaker suggested that project reports should be one page or less. Most people agreed that doing so made sense, but one participant rejected the notion. He proceeded to explain that his project was so important and so complex that he sent his boss monthly project reports that were a minimum of ten pages. "And," he added, "My boss reads every word."

A few weeks after the training session, the speaker had the opportunity to talk to this participant's boss about an unrelated matter. In the course of the conversation, he happened to mention his frustration with a person on his staff who felt his project was so important that he had to submit monthly progress reports no fewer than ten pages. He said that he usually read the first paragraph, but he rarely had time to review the reports thoroughly. He added that he hoped this person had listened carefully to the suggestion that reports fit on one page!

You've probably been in meetings where you wanted to bang your head against the wall. Ever been to a meeting that didn't start on time? How about a meeting that didn't have an agenda or didn't stick to the agenda it did have? Or how about a meeting at which people discussed issues you thought were resolved at a previous meeting?

REMEMBER

Meetings don't have to be painful experiences. If you plan and manage them well, meetings can be effective forms of communication. They can help you find out about other team members' backgrounds, experiences, and styles; stimulate brainstorming, problem analysis, and decision-making; and provide a forum to explore the reasons for and interpretations of a message.

You can improve your meetings by using the suggestions in the following sections. (In addition, check out the later section "Holding Key Project Meetings" for tips on planning different types of meetings.)

Planning for a successful meeting

TIP

To have a good meeting, you need to do some pre-meeting planning. Keep these pointers in mind as you plan:

>> **Clarify the purpose of the meeting.** This step helps you ensure that you invite the right people and allows attendees to prepare for the meeting.

>> **Decide who needs to attend and why.** If you need information, decide who has it, and make sure they attend the meeting. If you want to make decisions at the meeting, decide who has the necessary authority and who needs to be part of the decision-making, and make sure they attend.

>> **Give plenty of notice of the meeting.** This step increases the chances that the people you want to attend will be able to do so.

>> **Let the people who should attend the meeting know its purpose.** People are more likely to attend a meeting when they understand why their attendance is important.

>> **Prepare a written agenda that includes topics and their allotted discussion times.** This document helps people see why attending the meeting is worth their time. The agenda is also your guideline for running the meeting.

>> **Circulate the written agenda and any background material in advance.** Doing so gives everyone time to suggest changes to the agenda and to prepare for the meeting.

>> **Keep meetings to one hour or less.** You can force people to sit in a room for hours, but you can't force them to keep their minds on the activities and information at hand for that long. If necessary, schedule several meetings of one hour or less to discuss complex issues or multiple topics.

Conducting an efficient meeting

How you conduct the meeting can make or break it. The following tasks are essential for conducting a productive meeting:

>> **Start on time, even if people are absent.** After people see that you wait for latecomers, everyone will come late!

>> **Assign a timekeeper.** This person reminds the group when a topic has exceeded its allotted time for discussion.

>> **Assign a person to take written minutes of who attended, which items you discussed, and what decisions and assignments the group made.** This procedure allows people to review and clarify the information and serves as a reminder of actions to be taken after the meeting.

>> **Keep a list of action items that need further exploration, and assign one person to be responsible for each entry.** This step helps ensure that when you meet to discuss these issues again, you have the right information and people present to resolve them.

>> **If you don't have the right information or the right people to resolve an issue, stop your discussion and put it on the list of action items.** Discussing an issue without having the necessary information or the right people present is just wasting everyone's time.

>> **End on time.** Your meeting attendees may have other commitments that begin when your meeting is supposed to end. Not ending on time causes these people to be late for their next commitments or to leave your meeting before it's over.

Following up with the last details

Your meeting may be over, but your work isn't finished. Make sure you complete the following post-meeting tasks to get the greatest benefit from the session:

>> **Promptly distribute meeting minutes to all attendees.** These minutes allow people to reaffirm the information discussed at the meeting when it's still fresh in their minds, and minutes quickly remind people of their follow-up tasks. Try to distribute the minutes within 24 hours of the meeting, and ask recipients to let you know if they have any corrections or additions.

>> **Monitor the status of all action items performed after the meeting.** Because each action item is itself a miniproject, monitoring its progress increases the chances that people successfully complete it.

REMEMBER

Don't just talk about the suggestions outlined in the preceding sections for making your meetings more effective. Discussing them can't improve your meetings. Act on them!

Preparing a Written Project-Progress Report

The *project-progress report* is a project's most common written communication. The report reviews activities performed during a performance period, describes problems encountered and the corrective actions planned and taken, and previews plans for the next period.

This section helps you identify the audience for your project-progress report, provides pointers on what to include in your report, and suggests how to keep that content interesting so it doesn't put your team to sleep.

Making a list and checking it twice

A project-progress report is a convenient way to keep key audiences involved in your project and informed of their responsibilities. Decide who should get regularly scheduled project-progress reports by answering the following questions:

>> Who needs to know about your project?

>> Who wants to know about your project?

>> Whom do you want to know about your project?

REMEMBER

At a minimum, consider providing project-progress reports to your supervisor, upper management, the client or customer, project team members, and other people who are helping you on the project, as well as to people who are interested in or who will be affected by the project's results.

Knowing what's hot (and what's not) in your report

Preparing the project-progress report gives you an opportunity to step back and review all aspects of your project so you can recognize accomplishments and identify situations that may require your early intervention. Be sure to include some or all of the following information in your project-progress report for each performance period:

>> **Performance highlights:** Always begin your report with a summary of project highlights, such as "The planned upper-management review was successfully conducted on schedule" or "Our client Mary Fisher approved our training outline according to schedule." (Just remember to keep it to one page!)

>> **Performance details:** Describe the activities, outcomes, milestones, labor hours, and resource expenditures in detail. For consistency, identify each activity by its work breakdown structure (WBS) code (see Chapter 4 in this minibook for details).

>> **Problems and issues:** Highlight special issues or problems that you encountered during the period and propose any necessary corrective actions.

>> **Approved changes to the plan:** Report all approved changes to the existing project plan.

>> **Risk-management status:** Update your project risk assessment by reporting on changes in project assumptions, the likelihood of these updated assumptions occurring, and the effect of those updated assumptions on existing project plans.

>> **Plans for the next period:** Summarize major work and accomplishments that you have planned for the next performance period.

Figure 5-1 contains an example of a project-progress report format. Although you can expand each section of information, depending on the nature of your project, remember that the longer the report is, the less likely your intended audience is to read and understand it.

Earning a Pulitzer, or at least writing an interesting report

When you write your project-progress report, make sure it's interesting and tells the appropriate people what they need to know. After all, you don't want your report to end up as a birdcage liner. Use the following tips to improve the quality of each of your project-progress reports:

>> **Tailor your reports to the interests and needs of your audiences.** Provide only the information that your audience wants and needs. If necessary, prepare separate reports for different audiences. (See Chapter 2 of this minibook for more on defining your project's audiences.)

Monthly Progress Report					
Project Name		**Project Number**		**Project Manager** (First) (Last)	
Period Covered / / – / / (From) (To)		**Date Report Submitted** / /		**Report Prepared by** (First) (Last)	
Performance Highlights					
Major Accomplishments			Major Issues Encountered		
Detailed Performance					
Milestone/Activity		Start Date		End Date		Comments
WBS Code	Name	Planned	Actual	Planned	Actual	
Approved Changes to Plan Made during Period					
Risk-Management Status					
Plans for Next Period					

FIGURE 5-1: Example of a project-progress report.

» **If you're preparing different progress reports for different audiences, prepare the most detailed one first and extract information from that report to produce the others.** This approach ensures consistency among the reports and reduces the likelihood that you'll perform the same work more than once.

» **Produce a project-progress report at least once a month, no matter what your audience requests.** Monitoring and sharing information about project progress less often than once per month significantly increases the chances of major damage resulting from an unidentified problem.

» **Make sure that all product, schedule, and resource information in your report is for the same time period.** Accomplishing this may not be easy if you depend on different organization systems for your raw performance data.

If you track project schedule performance on a system that you maintain yourself, you may be able to produce a status report by the end of the first week after the performance period. However, your organization's financial system, which you use to track project expenditures, may not generate performance reports for the same period until a month later.

Address this issue in your project's start-up phase. Determine your sources for status data, the dates your updated data is available from each source, and the time periods that the data applies to. Then schedule your combined analysis and reporting so that all data describes the same time period.

» **Always compare actual performance with respect to the performance plan.** Presenting the information in this format highlights issues that you need to address.

» **Include no surprises.** If an element requires prompt action during the performance period (if, say, a key person unexpectedly leaves the project team), immediately tell all the people involved and work to address the problem. However, be sure to mention the occurrence and any corrective actions in the progress report to provide a written record.

» **Use your regularly scheduled team meetings to discuss issues and problems that you raise in the project-progress report.** Discuss any questions people have about the information in the project-progress report. (However, don't read verbatim to people from the written report they've already received — and, you hope, read!)

USING A PROJECT DASHBOARD

To make your written project-progress reports most effective, you want to include the greatest amount of information in the least amount of space. A *project dashboard* is an information display that depicts key indicators of project performance in a format that resembles an instrument panel on a dashboard. This format can convey the project's overall progress and highlight particular problems that require further attention.

When designing a dashboard for your project, take the following steps:

1. **Select the major categories of information.**

   Typical information categories that reflect important aspects of project performance include

   - **Results:** Desired products your team has produced to date

   - **Performance to schedule:** Dates that your team achieved milestones and started and completed activities compared to the schedule plan for milestones and activities

   - **Performance to resource budgets:** Labor hours, funds, and other resources your team has used to date compared to their budgeted amounts

   - **Risk management:** Current status of factors that may unexpectedly impede project performance

2. **Choose specific indicators for each information category.**

   Choose these indicators with the project's drivers and supporters. For example, a project that develops an operations manual for a piece of equipment may have the following indicators:

   - **Results:** The number of manual chapters written or the number of people who have approved the final manual

   - **Performance to schedule:** The number of milestone dates you've met and the number you've missed

   - **Performance to resource budgets:** The ratio of funds expended to those budgeted for all completed activities

   - **Risk management:** The number of original risks that may still occur or the number of new risks you've identified during the project

(continued)

(continued)

3. Select the format for each indicator.

You can display indicators in a table, bar graph, pie chart, or speedometer format. In addition, indicators often have a traffic light format:

- **Green light:** The element is proceeding according to plan.

- **Yellow light:** One or more minor problems exist.

- **Red light:** One or more serious situations require immediate attention.

Determine the specific criteria for green-, yellow-, and red-light status for each indicator in consultation with the project's drivers and supporters.

The following illustrations depict the types of displays in a project dashboard.

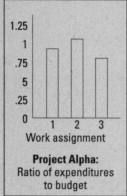

Project Alpha:
Ratio of expenditures
to budget

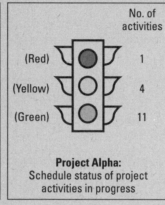

Project Alpha:
Schedule status of project
activities in progress

Project Alpha:
Percentage of
milestones
accomplished early
or on time to date

When creating a dashboard for your project, be sure to

- Work with the intended audiences of a report to select the categories, indicators, and their display formats.

- Always present *actual* indicator values alongside *planned* values.

- Keep the project dashboard report to one page or less.

Holding Key Project Meetings

Active, ongoing support from all major project audiences gives you the greatest chance for achieving project success. To gain that support, continually reinforce your project's vision and your progress toward it, and help your project's audiences understand when and how they can most effectively support your efforts. This section looks more closely at the three types of meetings you may hold during your project.

Regularly scheduled team meetings

Regularly scheduled team meetings give members an opportunity to share progress and issues and to sustain productive and trusting interpersonal relationships. These meetings also provide an opportunity to reaffirm the project's focus and to keep team members abreast of activities within and outside the project that affect their work and the project's ultimate success. Recognizing that most people work on several projects at the same time, these meetings can reinforce the team's identity and working relationships.

Consult with team members to develop a meeting schedule that's convenient for as many people as possible. If some people can't attend in person, try to have them participate in a conference call.

In addition to following the suggestions for productive meetings in the section "Move it along: Meetings that work," observe the following guidelines when planning and conducting regular team meetings:

>> Even though your team meetings are held regularly, before each meeting, prepare a specific agenda, distribute it beforehand, and solicit comments and suggestions.

>> Before the meeting, distribute the project-progress report for the most recent performance period (take a look at the previous section, "Preparing a Written Project-Progress Report," for details on this report).

>> Distribute any other background information related to topics on the agenda before the meeting.

>> Limit discussions that require more in-depth consideration; deal with them in other forums.

>> Start on time and end on time.

>> Prepare and distribute brief minutes of the meeting within 24 hours after its end.

Ad hoc team meetings

Hold ad hoc team meetings to address specific issues that arise during your project. An ad hoc meeting may involve some or all of your team's members, depending on the topic. Because issues often arise unexpectedly, do the following as you plan an ad hoc meeting:

>> Clarify the issue and what you hope to achieve at your meeting.

>> Identify and invite all people who may be interested in, affected by, or working on the issue.

>> Clearly explain the meeting's purpose to all meeting invitees.

>> Carefully document all action items that the attendees develop at the meeting, and assign responsibility for their completion.

>> Share the results of an ad hoc meeting with all team members who may be affected by the results, who have an interest in them, and/or whose support you need to implement them.

Upper-management progress reviews

An *upper-management progress review* is a meeting that a senior manager usually presides over, a project manager runs, and team members and representatives of all functional areas attend. This review gives you the chance to tell upper management about your project's status, its major accomplishments, and any issues that require their help. The review is also an opportunity for you to note ways to keep the project in line with major organization initiatives.

REMEMBER

Take every opportunity to help upper management remember why your project is important to them. They may have approved your project only months ago, but chances are your project is now just one of many activities in your busy organization.

TIP

Get the most out of your upper-management progress review by observing the following tips:

>> Identify the interests of your audience and explain how your project is meeting those interests.

>> Keep your presentation short; choose a few key messages and emphasize them.

>> Highlight key information but be prepared to go into more detail on issues if anyone asks you to do so.

>> Use both text and graphics to convey important information.

>> Allow time for questions.

>> Present updated information on project risks, and explain how you're addressing them.

>> Distribute a brief handout at the meeting that summarizes the key points of your presentation.

>> After the meeting, distribute notes that highlight issues raised and actions that you agreed on during the review.

Preparing a Project Communications Management Plan

With the diversity of audiences who will be looking for information about your project and the array of data you'll be collecting, it's essential that you prepare a project communications management plan to avoid duplication of effort and to ensure that nothing falls through the cracks.

A project *communications management plan* is a document that specifies all project communications generated throughout the project, their target audiences, their information content, and their frequency. Prepare an initial version of your project communications management plan in the starting the project stage of your project, and update it as needed in the carrying out the work stage. (Flip to Chapter 1 in this minibook for details on the distinct stages of a project.)

At a minimum, your plan should specify the following for all project communications:

>> **Target audience:** The people whose information needs are addressed through the project communication. (Check out Chapter 2 in this minibook for a discussion of how to identify and classify project audiences.)

>> **Information needs:** The information that the target audience wants and/or needs.

>> **Information-sharing activity:** The specific type of information-sharing activity to be used to transmit information to the target audience — written reports, presentations, and meetings, for example. (Check out the section "Choosing the Appropriate Medium for Project Communication" for more on when different types of information-sharing activities should be used.)

>> **Content:** The specific data to be shared in the project communication.

>> **Frequency:** When the information-sharing activity occurs (can be either regularly scheduled or ad hoc).

>> **Data collection:** How and when the data for the report is collected.

LinkedIn

Contents at a Glance

IN THIS CHAPTER

» **Getting to know your networking toolkit**

» **Understanding the different degrees of network connections**

» **Discovering LinkedIn features**

» **Comparing the different accounts**

» **Navigating the LinkedIn menu system**

Chapter **1**

Looking into LinkedIn

W hen we hear the terms "social networking" and "business networking," we always go back to one of our favorite phrases: "It's not *what* you know; it's *who* you know." Now imagine a website where both concepts are true, where you can demonstrate *what* you know and see the power of *who* you know. That's just one way to describe LinkedIn, one of the top websites today where you can do professional networking and so much more.

Social networking has garnered a lot of attention over the years, and while newer sites such as Pinterest, Instagram, and Snapchat are gaining in popularity, the two sites that most people think of first for social networking are Twitter and Facebook. Let us state right now, in the first chapter of this minibook, that LinkedIn is *not* one of those sites. You can find some elements of similarity, but LinkedIn isn't the place to tweet about what you had for lunch or show pictures of last Friday's beach bonfire.

LinkedIn is a place where relationships matter (the LinkedIn slogan). It was developed primarily for professional networking. When you look at its mission statement, LinkedIn's goal "is to help you be more effective in your daily work and open doors to opportunities using the professional relationships you already have." This is not a website that requires a lot of constant work to be effective. It's designed to work in the background and help you reach out to whomever you need while learning and growing yourself. The key is to set up your online identity, build your network, and steadily take advantage of the opportunities that most affect you or greatly interest you.

In this chapter, we introduce you to LinkedIn and the basic services it has to offer. You find answers to the questions "What is LinkedIn?" and, more importantly, "Why should I be using LinkedIn?" You discover how LinkedIn fits in with the rest of your professional activities, and then move on to the tangible benefits that LinkedIn can provide you, regardless of your profession or career situation. We discuss some of the premium account capabilities that you can pay to use, but rest assured that LinkedIn has a lot of free features. The last part of the chapter covers basic navigation of the LinkedIn site. You see the different menus and navigation bars, which you encounter throughout this minibook.

Understanding Your New Contact Management and Networking Toolkit

When thinking about how people can be connected with each other, it helps to picture a tangible network. For example, roads connect cities. The Internet connects computers. A quilt is a series of connected pieces of fabric. But what about the intangible networks? You can describe the relationship among family members by using a family tree metaphor. People now use the term *social network* to describe the intangible connections between them and other people, whether they're friends, co-workers, or acquaintances.

People used to rely on address books or contact organizers (PDAs) to keep track of their social networks. You could grow your social networks by attending networking events or by being introduced in person to new contacts, and then continuing to communicate with these new contacts. Eventually, the new contacts were considered part of your social network.

As people began to rely more and more on technology, though, new tools were created to help manage social networks. Salespeople started using contact management systems such as ACT! to keep track of communications. Phone calls replaced written letters, and cellular phones replaced landline phones. Then email replaced phone calls and letters, with text messaging increasingly handling short bursts of communication. Today, with the mass adoption of smartphones, laptops, and tablets, Internet browsing has dramatically increased. People manage their lives through web browsers, SMS (Short Message Service) communications, and apps on their smartphones.

Internet tools have advanced to the point where online communication within your network is much more automated and accessible. Sites such as LinkedIn have started to replace the older ways of accessing your social network. For example, instead of asking your friend Michael to call his friend Eric to see whether Eric's friend has a job available, you can use LinkedIn to see whether Eric's friend works for a company you want to contact, and you can then use LinkedIn to send a message through Michael to Eric (or in some cases, directly to Eric's friend) to accomplish the same task. (Of course, this assumes you, Michael, and Eric are all members of LinkedIn.)

In the past, you had no way of viewing other people's social networks (collections of friends and other contacts). Now, though, when folks put their social networks on LinkedIn, you can see your friends' networks as well as their friends' networks, and suddenly hidden opportunities start to become available to you.

Because of LinkedIn, you can spend more time researching potential opportunities (such as finding a job or a new employee for your business) as well as receiving information from the larger network and not just your immediate friends. The network is more useful because you can literally see the map that connects you with other people.

However, just because this information is more readily available, networking still involves work. You still have to manage your connections and use the network to gain more connections or knowledge. Remember, too, that nothing can replace the power of meeting people in person. But because LinkedIn works in the background guiding you in finding contacts and starting the networking process, you can spend your time more productively instead of making blind requests and relying solely on other people to make something happen.

Keeping track of your contacts

You made a connection with someone — say, your roommate from college. It's graduation day; you give him your contact information, he gives you his information, and you tell him to keep in touch. As both of you move to different places, start new jobs, and live your lives, you eventually lose track of each other, and all your contact information grows out of date. How do you find this person again?

One of the benefits of LinkedIn is that after you connect with someone you know who also has an account on LinkedIn, you always have a live link to that person. Even when that person changes email addresses, you'll be updated with his or her new email address. In this sense, LinkedIn always keeps you connected with people in your network, regardless of how their lives change. LinkedIn shows you a list of your connections, such as the list in Figure 1-1.

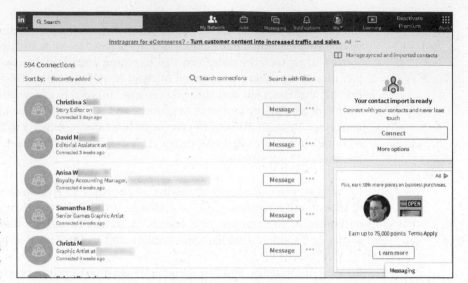

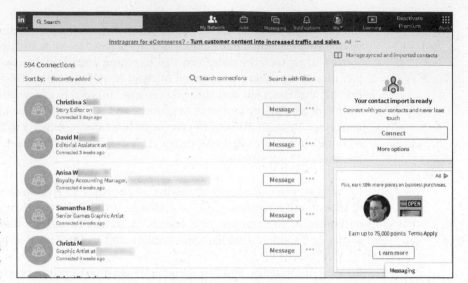 shows the LinkedIn Connections page with the following visible text elements:

594 Connections

Sort by: Recently added

Search connections   Search with filters

Manage synced and imported contacts

Christina S
Story Editor on
Connected 2 days ago
Message

David M
Editorial Assistant at
Connected 3 weeks ago
Message

Anisa W
Royalty Accounting Manager,
Connected 4 weeks ago
Message

Samantha B
Senior Games Graphic Artist
Connected 4 weeks ago
Message

Christa M
Graphic Artist at
Connected 4 weeks ago
Message

Your contact import is ready
Connect with your contacts and never lose touch
Connect
More options

 also shows an advertisement:
Plus, earn 50% more points on business purchases.
Earn up to 75,000 points. Terms Apply.
Learn more

FIGURE 1-1:
See all your connections in one centralized list.

Understanding the different degrees of network connections

In the LinkedIn universe, the word *connection* means a person who is connected to you through the site. The number of connections you have simply means the number of people who are directly connected to you in your professional network.

Here are the different levels of connectedness on LinkedIn:

>> **First-degree connections:** People you know personally; they have a direct relationship from their account to your account. These first-degree connections make up your immediate network and are usually your past colleagues, classmates, group members, friends, family, and close associates. Unlike Facebook, where everyone you connect to is a "friend," on LinkedIn, you can connect to friends who might not have a work, school, or group connection to you but whom you know personally outside those criteria. Similar to Facebook, though, you can see your list of first-degree connections' and they can see yours — provided your settings (and those of your connections) are configured so any connection can see other people's list of connections.

>> **Second-degree network members:** People who know at least one member of your first-degree connections: in other words, the friends of your friends. You can reach any second-degree network member by asking your first-degree connection to pass along your profile as an introduction from you to his friend.

>> **Third-degree network members:** People who know at least one of your second-degree network members: in other words, friends of your friends of your friends. You can reach any third-degree network member by asking your friend to pass along a request to be introduced to her friend, who then passes it to her friend, who is the third-degree network member.

The result is a large chain of connections and network members, with a core of trusted friends who help you reach out and tap your friends' networks and extended networks. Take the concept of Six Degrees of Separation (which says that, on average, a chain of six people can connect you to anyone else on Earth), put everyone's network online, and you have LinkedIn.

So, how powerful can these connections be? Figure 1-2 shows a snapshot of how someone's network on LinkedIn used to look.

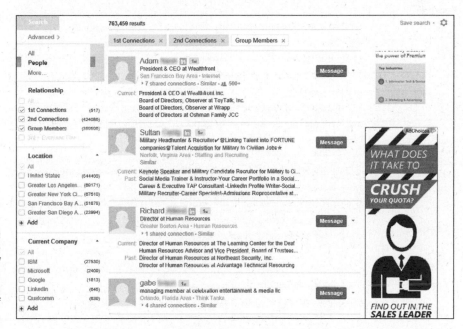

FIGURE 1-2:
Only three degrees of separation can give you a network of millions.

The account in Figure 1-2 has 517 first-degree connections. When you add all the network connections that each of these 517 people have, the user of this account could reach more than 424,000 different people on LinkedIn as second-degree network members. Add over 359,000 LinkedIn users who are members of groups that this account belongs to, plus millions of third-degree network members, and the user could have access to millions of LinkedIn users, part of a vast professional network that stretches across the world into companies and industries of all sizes. Such a network can help you advance your career or professional goals — and in turn, you can help advance others' careers or goals. As of this writing, the LinkedIn community has more than 500 million members, and LinkedIn focuses on your first-degree connections instead of your second- and third-degree network members, but the concept is still valid. Your network can be vast, thanks to the power of LinkedIn.

THE DIFFERENCE BETWEEN A USER AND A LION

Given all the power and potential to reach people around the world, some people — LinkedIn open networkers (LIONs) — want to network with anyone and everyone who's eager to connect with them. Their goal is to network with as many people as possible, regardless of past interactions or communications with that person.

One of your most prominently displayed LinkedIn statistics is the number of your first-degree connections. After you surpass 500 connections, LinkedIn displays not your current count of first-degree connections but just the message 500+. (It's kind of like how McDonald's stopped displaying the running total of hamburgers sold on its signs. Or are we the only ones who remembers that?) Part of the reason LinkedIn stops displaying updated counts past 500 is to discourage people from collecting connections. Many LIONs have thousands or even tens of thousands of first-degree connections, and the 500+ statistic is a badge of honor to them.

LIONs encourage open networking (that is, the ability to connect with someone you have never met or worked with in the past) by advertising their email address as part of their professional headline (for example, John Doe; Manager *firstname@lastname*.com), so anyone can request this person be added to her network. You can find more information at sites such as www.opennetworker.com.

LinkedIn offers a formal program — Open Profile — for people interested in networking with the larger community. You can sign up for this premium service any time after you establish a premium account. When you enable the Open Profile feature, you can send and receive messages with any other Open Profile member. We discuss this in the upcoming section, "Understanding LinkedIn Costs and Benefits."

We've been asked many times whether it's okay to be a LION and whether there is any meaning or benefit to having so many connections. Our answer is that we don't endorse being a LION *at all!* Although some people feel that they can find some quality hidden in the quantity, LinkedIn is designed to cultivate quality connections. Not only does LinkedIn heavily discourage users being a LION to the point of almost banning them, but also the random connections make it next to impossible to tap the real power and potential of LinkedIn.

Discovering What You Can Do with LinkedIn

Time to find out what kinds of things you can do on LinkedIn. The following sections introduce you to the topics you need to know to get your foot in the LinkedIn door and really make the site start working for you.

Building your brand and profile

On LinkedIn, you can build your own brand. Your name, your identity, is a brand — just like Ford or Facebook — in terms of what people think of when they think of you. It's your professional reputation. Companies spend billions to ensure that you have a certain opinion of their products, and that opinion, that perception, is their brand image. You have your own brand image in your professional life, and it's up to you to own, define, and push your brand.

Most people today have different online representations of their personal brand. Some people have their own websites, some create and write blogs, and some create profile pages on sites such as Facebook. LinkedIn allows you to define a profile and build your own brand based on your professional and educational background, as shown in Figure 1-3.

FIGURE 1-3:
Create a unified profile page to showcase your professional history.

Your LinkedIn profile can become a jumping-off point, where any visitor can get a rich and detailed idea of all the skills, experiences, and interests you bring to the table. Unlike a resume, where you have to worry about page length and formatting, you can provide substance and detail on your LinkedIn profile, including any part-time, contract, nonprofit, and consulting work in addition to traditional professional experience. You also have other options to consider; for example, you can

>> Write your own summary.

>> List any groups you belong to.

>> Describe any courses you have completed and test scores you have achieved.

>> Show any memberships or affiliations you have.

>> Cite honors and awards you have received.

>> Identify any patents or certifications you have earned.

>> Provide links to any publications you've written or published.

>> Give and receive endorsements of people's skills.

>> Give and receive recommendations from other people. (Recommendations are described in Chapter 4 of this minibook.)

>> Indicate your professional interests or supported causes.

>> Upload presentations, graphic design projects, or portfolio examples for others to view.

>> Upload videos that demonstrate a particular skill or past project.

>> Post website links to other parts of your professional identity, such as a blog, a website, or an e-commerce store you operate.

The best part is that *you* control and shape your professional identity. You decide what the content should be. You decide what to emphasize and what to omit. You decide how much information is visible to the world and how much is visible to your first-degree connections. (You find out more about the power of your profile in Chapter 2 of this minibook.)

Looking for a job now or later

At some point in your life, you'll probably have to look for a job. It might be today, it might be a year from now, or it may be ten years from now. The job search is, in itself, a full-time job, and studies show that as many as 85 percent of all jobs are found not through a job board such as Indeed or CareerBuilder, or a newspaper classified ad, but rather through a formal or informal network of contacts where the job isn't even posted yet. LinkedIn makes it easy to do some of the following tedious job search tasks:

>> **Finding the right person** at a target company, such as a hiring manager in a certain department, to discuss immediate and future job openings

>> **Getting a reference** from a past boss or co-worker to use for a future job application

>> **Finding information** about a company and position before the interview

>> **Enabling the right employers to find you** and validate your experience and job potential before an interview

>> **Searching posted job listings** on a job board such as the one on LinkedIn

The hidden power of LinkedIn is that it helps you find jobs you weren't looking for or applying to directly. This is when you're a *passive job seeker*, currently employed but interested in the right opportunity. As of this writing, hundreds of thousands of recruiters are members of LinkedIn, and they constantly use the search functions to go through the database and find skilled members who match their job search requirements. Instead of companies paying big money for resume books, they now have instant access to millions of qualified professionals, each of whom has a detailed profile with skills, experience, and recommendations already available.

This practice of finding passive job seekers is growing quickly on LinkedIn, mainly because of the following reasons:

>> **Companies can run detailed searches** to find the perfect candidate with all the right keywords and skills in his profile, and they then contact the person to see whether he is interested.

>> **LinkedIn users demonstrate their capabilities** by providing knowledge on the site, which gives companies insight into the passive job seeker's capabilities. Not only does LinkedIn give users the opportunity to share updates and knowledge, but it also hosts an extensive network of groups on the site. Each group runs its own discussion board of conversations, where LinkedIn users can pose a question or start a conversation and other LinkedIn members can provide insight or link to relevant articles and continue the discussion.

>> **Companies can review a person's profile** to find and check references ahead of time and interview only people they feel would be a great match with their corporate culture.

>> **Employed individuals can quietly run their own searches** at any time to see what's available, and they can follow up online without taking off a day for an in-person or phone interview.

LinkedIn research shows that "people with more than 20 connections are 34 times more likely to be approached with a job opportunity than people with fewer than 5 connections." Therefore, your connections definitely influence your active or passive job search.

Finding out all kinds of valuable information

Beyond getting information about your job search, you can use the immense LinkedIn database of professionals to find out what skills seem to be the most popular in a certain industry and job title. You can discover how many project managers live within 50 miles of you. You can even find current or past employees of a company and interview them about that job. LinkedIn now has millions of detailed Company pages that show not only company statistics but also recent hires, promotions, changes, and lists of employees closely connected with you.

Best of all, LinkedIn can help you find specific information on a variety of topics. You can do a search to find out the interests of your next sales prospect, the name of a former employee you can talk to about a company you like, or how you can join a start-up in your target industry by reaching out to the co-founder. You can sit back and skim the news, or you can dive in and hunt for the facts. It all depends on what method best fits your goals.

Expanding your network

You have your network today, but what about the future? Whether you want to move up in your industry, look for a new job, start your own company, or achieve some other goal, one way to do it is to expand your network. LinkedIn provides a fertile ground to reach like-minded and well-connected professionals who share a common interest, experience, or group membership. The site also provides several online mechanisms to reduce the friction of communication, so you can spend more time building your network instead of searching for the right person.

First and foremost, LinkedIn helps you identify and contact members of other people's professional networks, and best of all, you can contact them not via a cold call but with your friend's recommendation or introduction. (See Book 5, Chapter 4 for more information on recommendations.) In addition, you can find out more about your new contact before you send the first message, so you don't have to waste time figuring out whether this is someone who could be beneficial to have in your network.

You can also meet new people through various groups on LinkedIn, whether it's an alumni group from your old school, a group of past employees from the same company, or a group of people interested in improving their public speaking skills and contacts. LinkedIn groups help you connect with other like-minded members, search for specific group members, and share information about the group with other members.

Understanding LinkedIn Costs and Benefits

Signing up for LinkedIn is free, and many functions are open to all account holders, so you can take advantage of most of the opportunities that LinkedIn offers. You don't have to pay a setup or registration fee, but you can pay a monthly fee for a premium account to get additional functions or communication options. Finally, tailored solutions are available for corporations that want to use LinkedIn as a source for hiring quality candidates.

Weighing free versus paid accounts

There's not much difference between a free account and a paid account on LinkedIn. And the basic (free) account is anything but basic in usage.

Your free account with LinkedIn allows you to use most of LinkedIn's most popular features, including the following:

» Build a network of connections with no limits on size or numbers.

» Reconnect with any member of the LinkedIn network, provided that he or she knows you and agrees to connect with you.

» Create a professional and detailed LinkedIn profile.

» Give and receive an unlimited number of recommendations.

» Join or create up to 100 different LinkedIn groups.

» Perform an unlimited number of searches for LinkedIn members in your extended network of first- and second-degree members plus group members.

If you want to step up to a paid account, some of the main features include these:

» Send a message to anyone in the LinkedIn community — regardless of whether he or she is in your extended network — through an InMail messaging service. (*Note:* You get a limited number of InMail credits depending on your paid account level.)

» View more LinkedIn profile information of people not in your LinkedIn network when you conduct advanced searches.

» See more LinkedIn network profile information when you conduct advanced searches.

» See who has viewed your profile (if those viewers have not configured their settings to be anonymous when viewing profiles) and how they arrived at your profile.

» Obtain membership in the Open Profile program, which gives you unlimited Open Profile messages.

Comparing the paid accounts

LinkedIn offers a few levels of paid accounts, each with a specific level of benefits. For the most up-to-date packages that LinkedIn offers, check out the Free and Paid Accounts Help page at `http://www.linkedin.com/premium/products`, as shown in Figure 1-4. You can also click the Try Premium for Free link at the top right of your screen to see a comparison of the paid accounts.

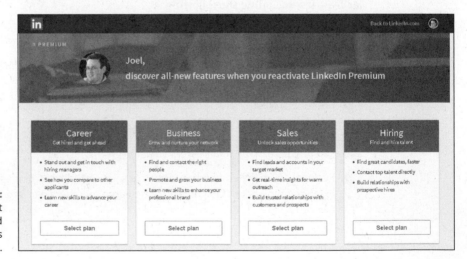

FIGURE 1-4: Learn about different paid account features on LinkedIn.

Every premium account comes with certain benefits regardless of the level you choose. These benefits include

>> Open Profile network membership

>> Unlimited Open Profile messages

>> Ability to see who viewed your profile

>> Access to premium content

>> One-business-day customer service for your LinkedIn questions

As of this writing, LinkedIn offers a variety of premium packages targeted at individual users: Premium Career, Premium Business, Premium Sales, and Premium Hiring. Each account level comes with specific benefits:

>> **Premium Career:** $29.99 per month, billed monthly, or $299.88 per year when you buy an annual subscription, at a 17 percent savings. This account includes the following:

- Three InMail credits per month, which allow you to contact any LinkedIn member regardless of whether he or she is in your network, as long as the other member agreed to receive InMail messages

- Ability to see who viewed your profile in the last 90 days and how they located you

WARNING

Even with this feature in a premium account, if the other person has her privacy settings configured to remove her visibility, you won't see her name when you look at who viewed your profile.

- Access to millions of online video courses taught by industry experts in the LinkedIn Learning library

- Salary insights that show you salary details when browsing job listings, without having to share your own personal data

- Applicant insights to see how you (and your skill set) compare to other candidates for a potential job

- Featured Applicant status when a recruiter searches for applicants, which means you are moved to the top section of a recruiter's search screen

>> **Premium Business:** $59.99 per month, billed monthly, or $575.88 per year when you buy an annual subscription, at a 20 percent savings. This account includes the following:

- Fifteen InMail credits per month

- Ability to view unlimited profiles when you perform a LinkedIn search, including any third-degree network members

- Ability to see who viewed your profile in the last 90 days and how they located you

- Business insights that give you the most up-to-date trends and information on how a company's growth rate and hiring trends are projecting, so you can research companies more effectively

- Many of the benefits of the Premium Career account, such as LinkedIn Learning, and applicant and salary insights

>> **Premium Sales (or Sales Navigator Professional):** $79.99 per month, billed monthly, or $779.88 per year when you buy an annual subscription, at a 19 percent savings. This account includes the following:

- Twenty InMails per month

- Help in finding recommended leads to reach out to, insight into how to reach out to them, and the ability to save those leads to your account

- Lead Builder and Recommendation tools to help you find the right people to close the deal in your sales life

>> **Premium Hiring (a.k.a. Recruiter Lite):** $119.95 per month, billed monthly, or $1,199.40 per year when you buy an annual subscription, at a 17 percent savings. This account includes these features:

- Thirty InMails per month.

- Advanced search engines geared for recruiting to help you find top talent even faster, and a guided search experience to navigate the LinkedIn network efficiently

- Smart Suggestions tools to help you find potential qualified candidates for your job listing that you may not initially considered

- Ability to create projects in LinkedIn, where you can track the progress of multiple applicants in a potential pool, categorize people in folders, attach notes to profiles, and set up automated reminders

Upgrading to a premium account

What's the value in getting a premium account? Besides the features listed in the previous section for each account level, premium accounts are designed to give you more attention in areas such as job searches. When an employer lists a job posting and collects applications through LinkedIn, premium account holders show up at the top of the applicant list (similar to the Sponsored result in a Google search) with a Featured Applicant status next to their name. LinkedIn provides special content in the form of emails, video tutorials, and articles that provide job search and professional development tips and advice from leaders in the industry. Finally, you get to see who has viewed your profile, which can be helpful when you're applying for jobs or trying to set up business deals. A premium account is not essential for everyone, so consider what you need from your LinkedIn experience and decide if upgrading is right for you.

TIP

As of this writing, LinkedIn gives you the option to try any premium plan for free during the first month, and it automatically charges your credit card each month afterward for the full amount, unless you bought a yearly plan, for which the charges renew every 12 months.

To upgrade to a premium account, we highly recommend starting by creating your free account and using the various functions on LinkedIn. If you find that after some usage, you need to reach the larger community and take advantage of some of the premium account features, you can always upgrade your account and keep all your profile and network information that you previously defined.

WARNING

If you're in charge of human resource functions at a small, medium, or large company and you are interested in using the Recruiter functions for your company, don't follow the steps in this section. Instead, visit `https://business.linkedin.com/talent-solutions` for more information on its Talent Solutions.

To subscribe to a premium account, just follow these steps (You must have created a LinkedIn account already; see Book 5, Chapter 2 for details.)

1. **Go to the LinkedIn home page at** `https://www.linkedin.com`.

2. **Click the Upgrade to Premium link at the top-right corner of the screen.**

3. **On the Premium Products page that appears, click the Select Plan button to bring up that premium account's specific options, as shown in Figure 1-5.**

   LinkedIn accepts Visa, MasterCard, American Express, or Discover to pay for your premium account. Make sure the billing address you provide matches the credit card billing address on file.

4. **Click the blue Start My Free Month button for the premium level to which you want to upgrade.**

5. **When asked to confirm if you want Monthly or Annual billing, click the type you want.**

   A green line appears under the box of your chosen type.

6. **Select the radio button beside the credit card or PayPal option to bring up the specific payment fields. Fill in the appropriate billing information, as shown in Figure 1-6, and then click the Review Order button.**

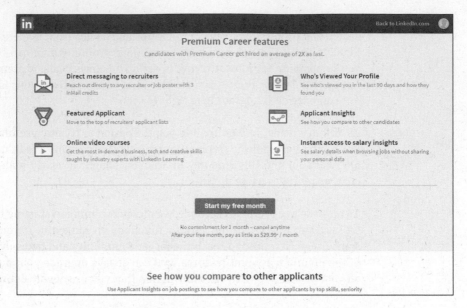

Premium Career features

Candidates with Premium Career get hired an average of 2X as fast.

Direct messaging to recruiters
Reach out directly to any recruiter or job poster with 3 InMail credits

Featured Applicant
Move to the top of recruiters' applicant lists

Online video courses
Get the most in-demand business, tech and creative skills taught by industry experts with LinkedIn Learning

Who's Viewed Your Profile
See who's viewed you in the last 90 days and how they found you

Applicant Insights
See how you compare to other candidates

Instant access to salary insights
See salary details when browsing jobs without sharing your personal data

Start my free month

No commitment for 1 month – cancel anytime
After your free month, pay as little as $29.99 / month

See how you compare to other applicants

Use Applicant Insights on job postings to see how you compare to other applicants by top skills, seniority

FIGURE 1-5:
Review the options for the premium account you are considering.

then $29.99 / month	then $24.99 / month ($299.88 annually)

Monthly after free trial	$29.99
Today's total	$0.00

Your free trial begins on **October 8, 2017** and will end on **November 8, 2017**. You can cancel anytime before **November 8, 2017** to avoid being charged and we'll send an email reminder **7 days before** the trial ends.

2 Select your payment method
Why do we need this for a free trial?

VISA · Discover · PayPal

First name *
Test

Last name *
User

Credit or debit card number *
Please enter a valid card number

Expiration date *
07 · 2021

Security code *
123

Country *
United States

Postal code *
67543

Review order

FIGURE 1-6:
Enter your billing information.

7. **Verify the information you've provided, and review the terms in the Review Your Order box.**

If you want, click the links to review LinkedIn's terms of service, refund policy, and how to cancel.

8. **Click the blue Start Your Free Trial button to complete the process.**

That's it! Expect to get emails from LinkedIn to help explain and demonstrate the new features that you can take advantage of on the website.

REMEMBER

If you decide to stop subscribing to a LinkedIn Premium account, you must go to your Settings & Privacy page, click Subscriptions on the left side of the screen, and then click the Downgrade or Cancel Your Premium Account link so you won't get billed anymore. (See "Looking at the Settings & Privacy page," later in this chapter, for information about how to reach and use this page.)

Navigating LinkedIn

When you're ready to get started, you can sign up for an account by checking out Book 5, Chapter 2. Before you do, however, take a look at the following sections, which walk you through the different parts of the LinkedIn website so you know how to find all the cool features we discuss in this minibook.

After you log in to your LinkedIn account, you see your personal LinkedIn home page, as shown in Figure 1-7. You'll use two important areas on your LinkedIn home page a lot, and we cover those areas in the following sections.

FIGURE 1-7:
Your LinkedIn
home page.

Touring the top navigation bar

Every page on LinkedIn contains links to the major parts of the site, and we call this top set of links the *top navigation bar* throughout this minibook. As of this writing, the major parts of the top navigation bar are as follows:

>> **Home:** Go to your personal LinkedIn home page.

>> **My Network:** View your connections on LinkedIn, add new connections, and import new connections.

>> **Jobs:** View the different job searches and postings you can do on LinkedIn.

>> **Messaging:** Go to your Messaging inbox to communicate with other LinkedIn members.

>> **Notifications:** Go to your Notifications page to see what your LinkedIn connections are doing, reading, and sharing, as well as daily rundowns on news items, the work anniversaries and birthdays of your connections, and suggestions for influencers or companies you can follow on LinkedIn.

>> **Me:** When you start your LinkedIn account, you'll see a generic icon in this spot. After you add a profile picture to your LinkedIn account, the icon changes to a thumbnail of your profile photo. When you click the drop-down arrow, you can choose to access your Settings & Privacy page, access the LinkedIn Help Center page, or manage your LinkedIn posts, job postings, or company pages.

You have to click each element in the top navigation bar to go to that direct page. For the Me icon, you need to click the drop-down arrow to see the various options for selection, as shown in Figure 1-8.

FIGURE 1-8:
Click the drop-down arrow to see options for this section.

Finally, other features may appear along the top right of the screen:

>> **Learning:** Back in 2015, LinkedIn acquired Lynda.com, one of the top sites for video tutorials on hundreds of business and technical subjects, put together by experts in their fields. LinkedIn turned this immense library into LinkedIn Learning, so its members can better educate themselves and improve or enhance their job skills. Clicking the Learning icon takes you to the Learning page.

>> **Post a Job:** This icon takes you directly to the LinkedIn Post a Job page.

>> **Work:** When you click the drop-down arrow, you can either access a number of LinkedIn services, such as LinkedIn groups, ads, ProFinder, and job postings, or go straight to one of LinkedIn's business services, such as Talent Solutions, Sales Solutions, or Learning Solutions.

TIP

At the bottom of this drop-down list is the Work option, where you can build a Company page.

Looking at the Settings & Privacy page

If you need to update any aspect of your LinkedIn account, click the Me icon, and then select the Settings & Privacy option. The page shown in Figure 1-9 appears.

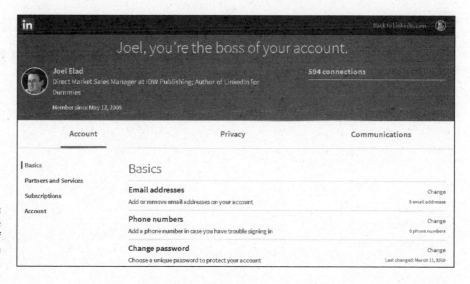

FIGURE 1-9:
You can change the details of your LinkedIn account.

Following are the settings you can access from this page:

>> **Account:** Update email addresses, your password, and language and security settings; upgrade, downgrade, or cancel your LinkedIn account; enable an RSS feed of your LinkedIn account, and more.

>> **Privacy:** Set how much of your profile is accessible by your contacts and how much information you want to make available to your network in terms of profile or status updates. Control your data and advertising preferences.

>> **Communications:** Set the frequency of the emails you receive from LinkedIn and which LinkedIn partners can reach you. Select how other LinkedIn members can communicate with you and who can send you invitations.

It's important to know where to find the Settings page in case you need to change something about your account.

Chapter **2**

Signing Up and Creating Your Account

When LinkedIn first launched, it grew primarily through invitations — you joined only if someone who was already a member invited you and encouraged you to join. However, membership is now open to anyone 14 years or older (as long as the user hasn't previously been suspended or removed from LinkedIn, of course). You can have only one active account, but you can attach multiple email addresses, past and present, to your account so that people can more easily find you.

You'll be presented with some configuration settings during the sign-up process that might confuse you until you're more familiar with the system. Fortunately, you can customize all those settings later, but for now, we suggest some initial settings. In addition, based on your initial settings, LinkedIn recommends people to invite to your network. This chapter touches on the initial recommendation process.

Joining LinkedIn

Many people join LinkedIn because a friend or colleague invited them. You can join just as easily without receiving an invitation, though. Everyone joins at the basic level, which is free. (You can opt for different levels of paid membership, as spelled out in Book 5, Chapter 1.) Being able to start at the basic level makes the sign-up process quite straightforward. Most importantly, the basic level still gives users the ability to take advantage of the most powerful tools that LinkedIn offers.

Joining with an invitation

When a friend or colleague invites you to join, you receive an email invitation. The email clearly identifies the sender and usually has *Invitation to connect on LinkedIn* as its subject line. (There's a chance, though, that the sender came up with a custom header.)

When you open the message, you see an invitation to join LinkedIn, such as the message shown in Figure 2-1. There might be some extra text if the person inviting you personalized the message. You also see a button or link that takes you back to LinkedIn to create your account, such as the Accept Joel's Invitation button shown in Figure 2-1.

FIGURE 2-1:
An invitation
to connect on
LinkedIn.

When you're ready to join LinkedIn with an invitation, you'll start with these two steps:

1. **Click the button or link from your invitation email.**

   A new window appears that goes to the LinkedIn website, as shown in Figure 2-2.

2. **Enter your correct first name and last name, and create a new password for your account.**

TIP

If you want to be known on LinkedIn by another version of your name (say a nickname, maiden name, middle initial, or proper name), or if you want to use a different email address from the one used for your invitation, you can change the details in those fields — First Name, Last Name, Email.

3. **Click the Join *Name's* Network button.**

You are taken to the next part of the sign-up process, where you provide basic information that LinkedIn will use to create your account. The remainder of the sign-up process is covered in "Completing the sign-up process," later in this chapter.

FIGURE 2-2:
Provide your name and create a password.

TIP

Try to choose a password that no one else can guess. You should use a combination of letters and numbers, and avoid commonly used passwords such as your name, the word *password*, a string of letters or numbers that are next to each other on the keyboard (for example, *qwerty*), or a password that you use on many other sites.

Joining without an invitation

If you haven't received an invitation to join LinkedIn, don't let that turn you into a wallflower. You can join LinkedIn directly, without an invitation from an existing user. Open your web browser and go to https://www.linkedin.com. You see the initial LinkedIn home page, as shown in Figure 2-3. When you're ready to join LinkedIn, simply provide your first name, last name, and email address, and enter a password in the boxes provided. Then click the Join Now button.

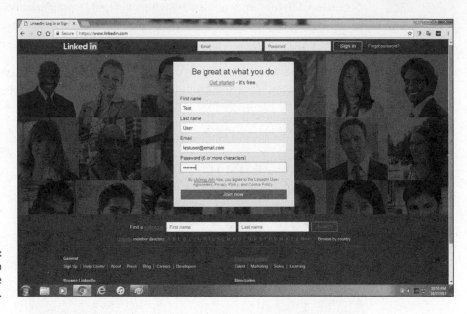

After you click the button, you advance to the next part of the sign-up process, where LinkedIn collects some basic information to create your account.

Completing the sign-up process

Whether you've been invited to join LinkedIn or created an account directly from its home page, LinkedIn requires some basic information beyond your name and email address to finish creating the basic account. When you're ready to complete the sign-up process, follow these steps:

1. **In the First, Let's Make Sure You're Recognizable window, select the country where you reside.**

   LinkedIn then asks for a zip code or a postal code, as shown in Figure 2-4.

2. **Provide your zip code or postal code, and then click the Next button.**

   You're taken to the next step, where LinkedIn starts to build your professional profile by asking about your current employment status and whether you are a student, as shown in Figure 2-5.

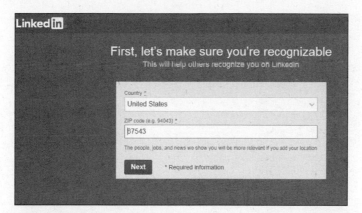

FIGURE 2-4:
Tell LinkedIn where you are located.

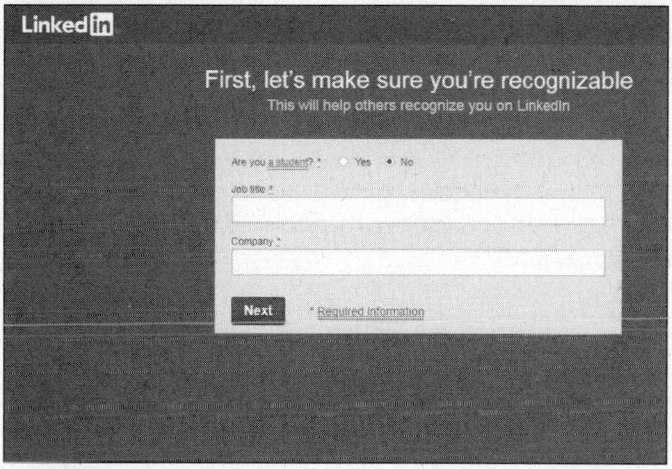

FIGURE 2-5:
Tell LinkedIn a little about yourself to create your account.

3. **Complete the fields regarding your student status and current employment.**

    Specifically, you need to provide the following information:

    - **Are You a Student?:** Select the appropriate radio button to indicate Yes or No.

    - **Job Title:** If you're not a student, indicate your current job title, whether you're employed, unemployed (a.k.a. "a job seeker"), or self-employed.

    - **Company:** LinkedIn asks for a company name and prompts you by showing existing companies in its database as you type in the name of your company, as shown in Figure 2-6. After you provide the company name, LinkedIn adds the Industry field. Use the drop-down list to identify which industry you feel you belong to, as shown in Figure 2-7.

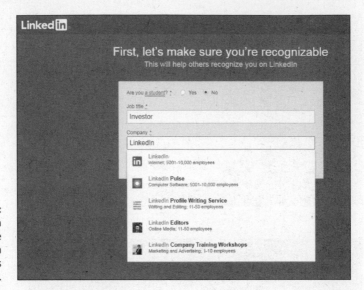

FIGURE 2-6:
LinkedIn can help associate you with known companies in its database.

TIP

If you find it difficult to choose an industry that best describes your primary expertise, just choose one that's closest. You can always change the selection later. If you're employed but looking for another job, you should still choose the industry of your current profession.

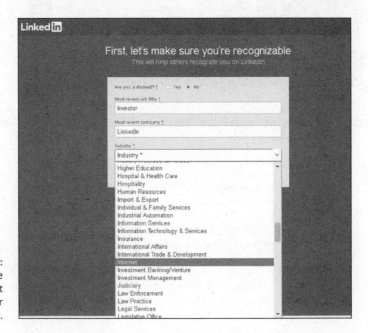

FIGURE 2-7:
Choose the industry that best matches your current job.

4. **Click the blue Next button to continue.**

   LinkedIn asks you what you're most interested in doing on the website, as shown in Figure 2-8.

5. **Click the option that best represents your goal for using LinkedIn.**

   LinkedIn tailors your remaining account creation prompts based on your choice here, but you'll still have access to fully customize your profile regardless of your choice. You can also skip this step by clicking the Not Sure Yet? I'm Open! option.

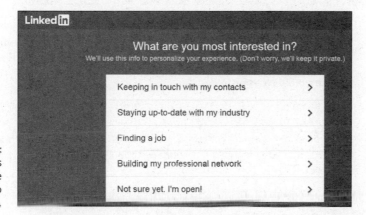

FIGURE 2-8:
LinkedIn helps you customize your account to your own needs.

REMEMBER

It might be tempting to start inviting friends and colleagues to connect with you right away, but you might want to work on creating your complete and up-to-date profile before flooding people's email inboxes with invitations. You can invite people to connect with you at any time.

6. **Confirm the email address for your account.**

   LinkedIn emails you a confirmation with a verification code to help verify the email account you're using, especially if you joined LinkedIn without an invitation.

   Open your email program and look for an email from LinkedIn Email Confirmation with the subject line *Please confirm your email address*. Open that email, and note the verification code. Go back to LinkedIn and enter the verification code in the box provided, as shown in Figure 2-9. Click the Verify button to proceed.

WARNING

If you skip the step of confirming your email with LinkedIn, you won't be able to invite any connections, apply for jobs on the LinkedIn job board, or take advantage of most other LinkedIn functions.

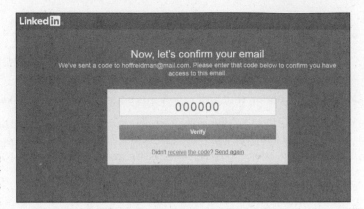

FIGURE 2-9:
Confirm your
email address
with LinkedIn.

7. **If you're asked to log in to your account, simply provide your email address and password when prompted and then provide the verification code.**

8. **Start building your network.**

   LinkedIn offers to import your contacts from your email program, as shown in Figure 2-10. You are walked through the steps of importing your address book and can also connect with existing members of LinkedIn. You can also do these tasks after you create your account by clicking Skip.

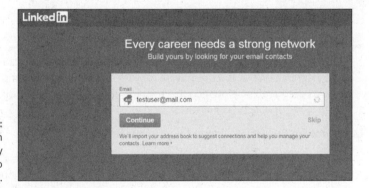

FIGURE 2-10:
LinkedIn can
help you identify
whom to add to
your network.

REMEMBER

As mentioned, it's best to create a complete profile before sending invitations. people's email inboxes with invitations. You can connect with people at any time.

9. **Start using the site based on your goals for using LinkedIn.**

   Suppose that you chose Finding a Job as the reason why you're setting up a LinkedIn account (in Step 5). You would be taken to the web page shown in Figure 2-11, where LinkedIn offers to set up a job alert so you're notified of jobs that might interest you. In this example, you can alter the title and location of the jobs you're searching for, and the frequency of the alert emails. After you make your choices, click the Create Alert button and LinkedIn will notify you that your job alert is saved. Or you can click Skip to go to the next step.

Based on the choice you made in Step 5, LinkedIn may prompt you for other features of its site, such as choosing companies or influencers to follow.

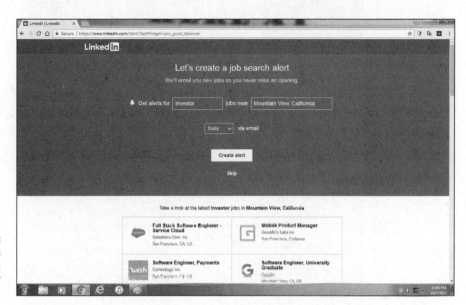

FIGURE 2-11: LinkedIn offers to help you reach your goals for using the site.

10. Upload a profile photo.

One of the most important elements of your LinkedIn profile is the profile photo you use to represent yourself. Your profile photo should indicate that you're a professional and responsible person. (In other words, this is not the social networking site to show off your party animal skills.) Locate a respectable photo of your face.

a. *Click the pencil icon, as shown in Figure 2-12, and follow the prompts to select a photo from your computer.*

b. *Rotate or crop your photo, if necessary, to capture your face (and the top of your shoulders if available), as shown in Figure 2-13.*

c. *Click Save to upload the photo.*

d. *Click Continue to assign it to your profile.*

LinkedIn prompts you to receive a link to download its mobile app.

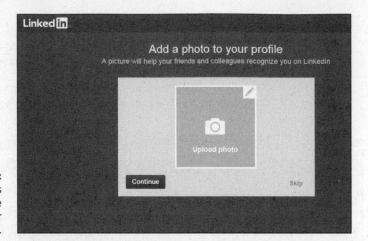

FIGURE 2-12:
LinkedIn offers
you the chance
to upload your
profile photo.

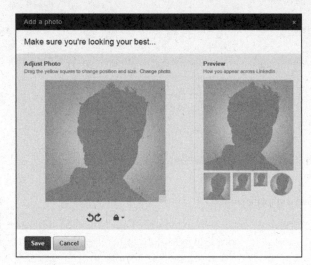

FIGURE 2-13:
Use LinkedIn's
tools to
customize
your photo.

11. **Provide your mobile number in the text box provided to receive the download link, and then click the Send an SMS button.**

Your LinkedIn home page appears.

You can also click the Apple Store or Google Play button to go directly to their app repositories, or click Next and install the app later.

12. Follow the prompts to guide you through the rest of the creation process.

You see pop-up messages offering you more information on aspects of LinkedIn, such as updating your background photo (see Figure 2-14) and sections you can add.

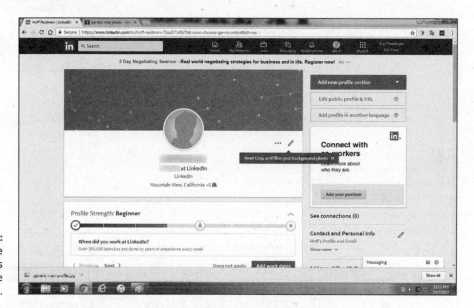

FIGURE 2-14:
Follow the LinkedIn prompts for more information.

13. Follow the long series of prompts to increase your profile strength.

The Profile Strength box appears below the main box that contains your name and profile photo. Scroll down to that section of your LinkedIn profile page (as shown in Figure 2-15) and click the blue button to provide the requested information to help complete your profile. You'll see prompts for areas such as work dates, your skills, educational background, past employers, and current job details.

Fill in information for each prompt and click the Save button to advance in the process. You can always click Skip to save a task for later.

After you complete the series of prompts, your profile page appears. From here, you can decide what to update next. For example, if you click the drop-down arrow next to the Add New Profile section, you'll see a list of sections you can update, as shown in Figure 2-16.

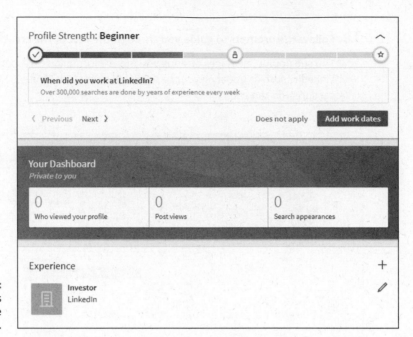

FIGURE 2-15:
LinkedIn prompts you to complete your profile.

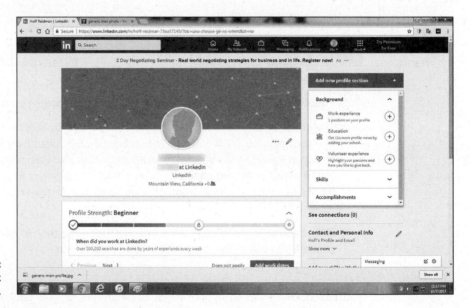

FIGURE 2-16:
Continue to work on your profile.

Starting to Build Your Network

You're ready to look at how to build your network, with tools and forms provided by LinkedIn. Your first step is to decide whom you want to invite to connect with you on LinkedIn.

Be sure to completely fill out your profile before you start inviting people to connect. Having a complete profile makes it easier to find former colleagues and classmates. After all, if you invite someone to connect whom you haven't spoken to recently, he'll probably take a quick look at your profile before responding. If he doesn't see a part of your professional history where he knows you, he will most likely ignore your invitation.

Your best bet now is to start using LinkedIn with some thought and planning. Here are some common pitfalls after signing up:

>> You feel compelled to start inviting friends and colleagues to connect with you right away, before working on your profile.

>> You get nervous and decide not to invite anybody beyond one or two close friends or family members.

>> You wonder about the value of LinkedIn (or get busy with your career and daily activities) and leave your account alone for a long period of time with no activity.

We've seen all three scenarios occur with various people who have joined LinkedIn, so don't feel bad if one of these is your natural reaction.

When you want to start using LinkedIn, begin by navigating to the home page and clicking Sign In. You're asked for your email address and LinkedIn password, which you provided when you joined the site. After you are logged in, you can access any of the functions from the top navigation bar.

Next, start thinking about whom you'd like to invite to join your network (see Figure 2-17). LinkedIn provides some neat tools to help you identify, in your existing networks, people you know and trust well enough to feel confident about inviting them and expecting that they will accept.

You can add connections by syncing your email account with LinkedIn. Start by clicking My Network at the top of any LinkedIn page, and then click the More Options link below the Connect button in the bottom-left section of the My Network page. This section incorporates some basic options to identify and grow your network:

>> Check the address book for your web-based email system, such as Yahoo! Mail, Gmail, Hotmail, and AOL.

>> Check your address book for contacts to invite by importing your desktop email contacts with the link provided.

>> Upload contact files from other applications.

>> Invite people to connect by their email address. (By specifying people's individual email addresses, you can decide whom you want to invite without sending a blind invitation to everyone in your address book.)

We cover these techniques in greater detail in Chapter 3 of this minibook. We recommend that you first spend a little time thinking about whom you want to invite. Then focus on setting up your profile, and then invite people to connect.

PRIVACY CONFIDENTIAL

When you give LinkedIn access to your existing contact lists (such as on Gmail or Yahoo! Mail), rest assured that LinkedIn respects your privacy. LinkedIn is a licensee of the TRUSTe Privacy Program. In its privacy policy, LinkedIn declares its adherence to the following key privacy principles:

- LinkedIn will never rent or sell your personally identifiable information to third parties for marketing purposes.

- LinkedIn will never share your contact information with another user without your consent.

- Any sensitive information that you provide will be secured with all industry standard protocols and technology.

IN THIS CHAPTER

» **Discovering the keys to a meaningful network**

» **Using the best strategies for expanding your network**

» **Sending connection requests**

» **Weeding out connections**

» **Dealing with invitations**

Chapter **3**

Growing Your Network

Maybe by now, you've signed on to LinkedIn, created your profile, searched through the network, and started inviting people to connect to you — and you're wondering, what's next? You certainly shouldn't be sitting around on your hands, waiting for responses to your invitations. LinkedIn is designed to open doors to opportunities using the professional relationships you already have (and, with luck, by creating new ones). The best use of it, therefore, is to capture as much of your professional network as possible in the form of first-degree connections to your LinkedIn network so that you can discover inside leads as well as friends of friends who can help you.

In this chapter, we discuss how you can grow your LinkedIn network and offer guidelines to keep in mind when growing your network. We also cover various search tools for you to use to stay on top of LinkedIn's growing membership and how others may relate to you.

To expand your network, you need to know how to send invitations as well as how to attract LinkedIn members and contacts who haven't yet taken the plunge into LinkedIn membership. All that is covered here, too. And finally, this chapter helps you deal with the etiquette of accepting or declining invitations that you receive, and shows you how to remove connections that you no longer want to keep in your network.

REMEMBER

An *invitation* is when you invite a colleague or a friend to join LinkedIn and stay connected to you as part of your network. An *introduction* is when you ask a first-degree connection to introduce you to one of his or her connections so you can get to know that person better.

Building a Meaningful Network

When you build a house, you start with a set of blueprints. When you start an organization, you usually have some sort of mission statement or guiding principles. Likewise, when you begin to build your LinkedIn network, you should keep in mind some of the keys to having and growing a professional network. These guiding principles help you decide whom to invite to your network, whom to search for and introduce yourself to, and how much time to spend on LinkedIn.

LinkedIn is different from the Facebook and Twitter sites because it focuses on business networking in a professional manner rather than encouraging users to post pictures of their latest beach party or tweet their latest status update. The best use of LinkedIn involves maintaining a professional network of connections, not sending someone an event invitation or a game request.

That said, you'll find variety in the types of networks that people maintain on LinkedIn. Much of that has to do with each person's definition of a meaningful network:

>> **Quality versus quantity:** As mentioned in Book 5, Chapter 1, some people use LinkedIn with the goal of gaining the highest number of connections possible, thereby emphasizing quantity over quality. Those people are typically referred to as LinkedIn open networkers (LIONs). At the other end of the spectrum are people who use LinkedIn only to keep together their closest, most tightly knit connections without striving to enlarge their network. Most people fall somewhere in between these two aims.

The question of whether you're after quality or quantity is something to keep in mind every time you think of inviting someone to join your network. LinkedIn strongly recommends connecting only with people you know, so its advice is to stick to quality connections. Here are some questions to ask yourself to help you figure out your purpose:

- Do you want to manage a network of only people you personally know?

- Do you want to manage a network of people you know or who might help you find new opportunities in a specific industry?

- Do you want to promote your business or expand your professional opportunities?

- Do you want to maximize your chances of being able to reach someone with a new opportunity or job offering, regardless of personal interaction?

>> **Depth versus breadth:** Some people want to focus on building a network of only the most relevant or new connections — people from their current job or industry who could play a role in their professional development in that industry. Other people like to include a diversity of connections that include anyone they have ever professionally interacted with, whether through work, education, or any kind of group or association, in hopes that anyone who knows them at all can potentially lead to future opportunities. For these LinkedIn users, it doesn't matter that most of the people in their network don't know 99 percent of their other connections. Most people fall somewhere in between these two poles but lean toward including more people in their network.

Here are some questions to keep in mind regarding whether you want to focus on depth or breadth in your network:

- Do you want to build or maintain a specific in-depth network of thought leaders regarding one topic, job, or industry?

- Do you want to build a broad network of connections who can help you with different aspects of your career or professional life?

- Do you want to add only people who may offer an immediate benefit to some aspect of your professional life?

- Do you want to add a professional contact now and figure out later how that person might fit with your long-term goals?

>> **Strong versus weak link:** We're not referring to the game show *The Weakest Link*, but rather to the strength of your connection with someone. Beyond the issue of quality versus quantity, you'll want to keep differing levels of quality in mind. Some people invite someone after meeting him once at a cocktail party, hoping to strengthen the link as time goes on. Others work to create strong links first and then invite those people to connect on LinkedIn afterward.

This issue comes down to how much you want LinkedIn itself to play a role in your business network's development. Do you see your LinkedIn network as a work in progress or as a virtual room in which to gather only your closest allies? Here are some questions to keep in mind:

- What level of interaction needs to have occurred for you to feel comfortable asking someone to connect with you on LinkedIn? A face-to-face meeting? Phone conversations only? A stream of emails?

- What length of time do you need to know someone before you feel that you can connect with that person? Or, does time matter less if you have had a high-quality interaction just once?

- Does membership in a specific group or association count as a good enough reference for you to add someone to your network? (For example, say you met someone briefly only once, but she is a school alum: Does that tie serve as a sufficient reference?)

>> **Specific versus general goals:** Some people like to maintain a strong network of people mainly to talk about work and job-related issues. Other people like to discuss all matters relating to their network, whether it's professional, personal, or social. Most people fall somewhere in between, and herein lies what we mean by the "purpose" of your network. Do you want to simply catalog your entire network, regardless of industry, because LinkedIn will act as your complete contact management system and because you can use LinkedIn to reach different parts of your network at varying times? Or do you want to focus your LinkedIn network on a specific goal, using your profile to attract and retain the right kind of contact that furthers that goal?

Here are some more questions to ask yourself:

- Do you have any requirements in mind for someone before you add him to your network? That is, are you looking to invite only people with certain qualities or experience?

- Does the way you know or met someone influence your decision to connect to that person on LinkedIn?

- What information do you need to know about someone before you want to add him to your network?

REMEMBER

By the way, this isn't a quiz — there is no one right answer to any of these questions. You decide what you want to accomplish through your network, and how you want to go from there. Also remember that although you might start LinkedIn with one goal in mind, your usage and experience might shift you to a different way of using the site. If that happens, just go with it, as long as it fits with your current goals.

After you establish why you want to link to other people, you can start looking for and reaching out to those people. In the next section, we point you to a number of linking strategies that can help you reach your goals for your network. When you start on LinkedIn, completing your profile helps you get your first round of connections, and you're prompted to enter whatever names you can remember to offer an invitation for them to connect with you. Now you're ready to generate your next round of connections, and to get into the habit of making this a continual process as you use the site.

Importing Contacts into LinkedIn

One of the most popular (and necessary) activities people use the Internet for is email. Your email account contains a record of the email addresses of everyone you regularly communicate with via email. And from your established base of communications, LinkedIn offers a way for you to ramp up your network by importing a list of contacts from your email program.

Importing your email contacts into LinkedIn eliminates the drudgery of going through your address book and copying addresses into LinkedIn.

Importing a contacts list from your email system

This section shows you how to use the LinkedIn function to import your email contacts into LinkedIn. To do so, follow these steps:

1. **Click the My Network icon on the top navigation bar to display your network page.**

2. **Click the More options link below the Your Contact Import Is Ready section on the left side of the screen.**

    The Sync Contacts screen appears, as shown in Figure 3-1. Your email address on file Is already entered in the email address text box in the middle of the screen.

    Below your email address is a row of buttons representing Gmail, Yahoo! Mail, Outlook, and AOL, an email message icon (for inputting a list of email addresses manually), and an upload icon (for uploading a file of email addresses).

3. **Click Continue to use the prefilled address, replace the email address by typing a new email address and then click Continue, or click one of the buttons to select an email system from which to import your contacts.**

    The Sign In window appears for your email account, as shown in Figure 3-2.

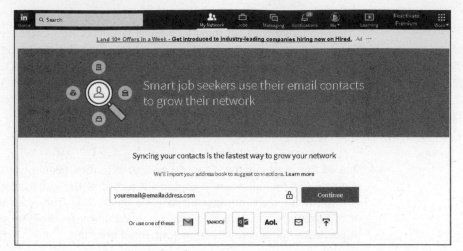

Smart job seekers use their email contacts to grow their network

Syncing your contacts is the fastest way to grow your network

We'll import your address book to suggest connections. Learn more

youremail@emailaddress.com   Continue

Or use one of these:

FIGURE 3-1:
Sync your email
contacts with
LinkedIn.

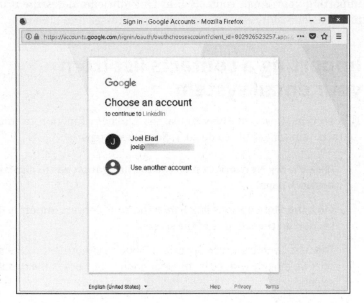

Sign in - Google Accounts - Mozilla Firefox

https://accounts.google.com/signin/oauth/oauthchooseaccount?client_id=802926523257.app...

Google

Choose an account

to continue to LinkedIn

J   Joel Elad
       joel@

⬤   Use another account

English (United States) ▼   Help   Privacy   Terms

FIGURE 3-2:
Select the email
address account
to sync.

4. **Follow the prompts to connect your email account with LinkedIn.**

   At the end of the prompts, you'll be asked to allow LinkedIn to access your
   email contacts, as shown in Figure 3-3.

5. **Click the Allow button.**

   LinkedIn spends some time accessing the account and checking to see whether
   any of your contacts are already on LinkedIn. Then the screen shown in
   Figure 3-4 appears, with a list of people from your email account who have
   LinkedIn accounts but are not currently connected to you.

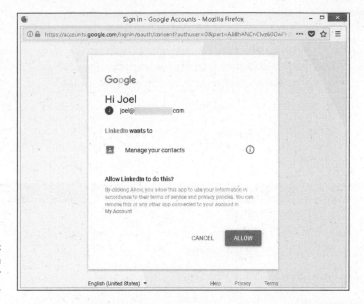

FIGURE 3-3:
Let LinkedIn
access your
email account.

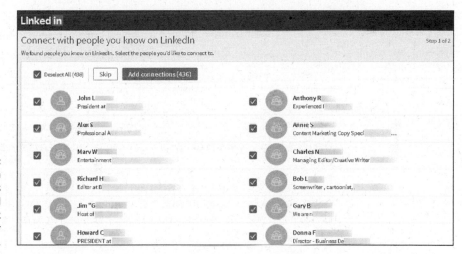

FIGURE 3-4:
Choose which
LinkedIn contacts
from your email
whom you want
to invite to your
network.

6. **Choose whom you want to invite to be your LinkedIn connections:**

   - *Add Connections:* Add everyone as a connection. Each of them will receive an automated invitation to connect with you. Because you can't tailor the messages to these people, this option isn't recommended. You must go to each person's profile page, and click Connect to send a customized invitation.

- *Deselect All:* Deselect every check box. You can then go through the list and selectively select the connections you want to add today. You can't add customized invitation text to these connection requests. Connect from each person's profile page to customize the invitation text.

- *Skip:* Skip this screen and move on with the process.

A new screen appears, as shown in Figure 3-5, with the names of people imported from your email account who don't have a LinkedIn account.

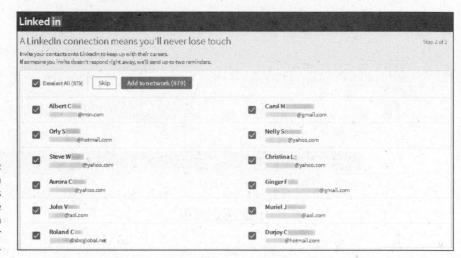

FIGURE 3-5:
Choose which email contacts you want to invite to use LinkedIn and join your network.

7. **Decide whom you want to invite to LinkedIn and add as a first-degree connection.**

   You see slightly different buttons than in Step 6. Click Add to network to add everyone, click Deselect All and manually choose people you want to invite to LinkedIn and add as a connection, or click the Skip button to move to the next step.

TIP

If you decide to skip Step 6 or 7, you'll be able to review LinkedIn's imported list of people at a later date by clicking the email system button, as you did in Step 3.

8. **To sync additional email accounts with LinkedIn, repeat Steps 2 to 7.**

   In this way, you can look for new contacts whom you can invite to your network. LinkedIn should be able to interface with any email account that can be accessed over the Internet from your computer. Some work email systems may be inaccessible depending on security levels set by your employer.

Checking for members

When you fill out your LinkedIn profile, you create an opportunity to check for colleagues and classmates as well as import potential contacts and invite them to connect with you and stay in touch using LinkedIn. However, that search happens only after you define your profile (and when you update or add to your profile). After that, it's up to you to routinely check the LinkedIn network to look for new members on the site who might want to connect with you or with whom you might want to connect. Fortunately, LinkedIn provides a few tools that help you quickly scan the system to see whether a recently joined member is a past colleague or a classmate. In addition, it never hurts to use your friends to check for new members, as we discuss in a little bit.

Finding classmates

Through LinkedIn, you can reconnect with former classmates and maintain that tie through your network, no matter where anyone moves. For you to find them to begin with, of course, your former classmates have to properly list their dates of education. And, just as with the search for former colleagues, it's important to do an occasional search to see which classmates joined LinkedIn.

To search for classmates — and add them to your network, if you want — follow these steps:

1. **While logged in to your LinkedIn account, go to** www.linkedin.com/alumni.

   If you've prefilled in at least one educational institution, the Alumni window for your most recent Education entry appears, as shown in Figure 3-6. If the screen is blank, you haven't yet added any education entries to your profile.

2. **Filter the results for a better list.**

   Click any of the classifications, such as Where They Live or Where They Work, to add filters and get a more precise list. You can also change the years of attendance in the boxes provided to see a different set of candidates, and to search by a specific graduation date.

3. **Look over the list of potential classmates and connect with anyone you recognize.**

   You can always click the name of the classmate to see his or her profile first, or just click the Connect link below the name to send an invitation to connect. If you have any shared connections, you can hover your cursor over the connection symbol and number next to the person's picture to see what connections you have in common.

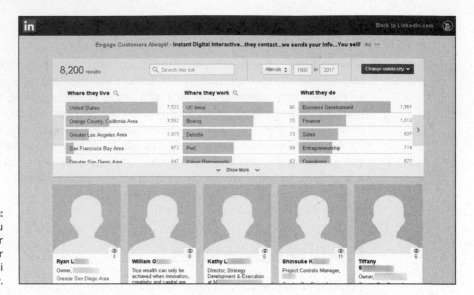

FIGURE 3-6:
The schools you identified in your profile appear in the Alumni window.

TIP

Before you invite people, click their name to read their profiles and see what they've been doing. Why ask them about their recent accomplishments or activities when you can read it for yourself? By doing your homework first, your invitation will sound more natural and be more likely to be accepted.

4. **Repeat the process for other schools by clicking the Change University button, as shown in Figure 3-7, and selecting another school from your educational history.**

When you select a new school, you see the same screen as shown in Figure 3-6 but for the newly selected school. You can filter those results and invite whomever you recognize.

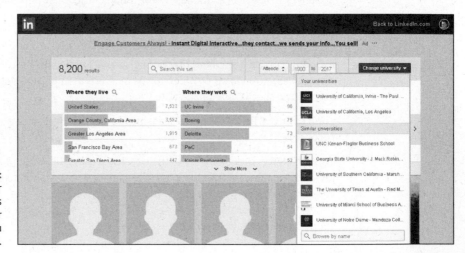

FIGURE 3-7:
Check for classmates from other schools you attended.

TIP

For more about sending invitations, see the "Sending Connection Requests" section, later in this chapter.

Using the People You May Know feature

One of the most common ways for you to increase your network is by using LinkedIn's suggestion system that it calls People You May Know. Given all the data that LinkedIn imports and the global network it maintains, it can use people's profile data, email imports, common experience, education, and LinkedIn activity or other commonalities to predict who may be in the same network with you.

You can access the People You May Know feature in several places. Occasionally, a section of your home page news feed as well as the middle section of your My Network page, as shown in Figure 3-8, are dedicated to this feature.

FIGURE 3-8: LinkedIn asks whether you know people to add to your network.

When you click Connect for someone, that spot is updated with a new potential connection for you to consider. As you scroll down, the page is updated with rows of people to whom you can send a connection request.

Here are some things to keep in mind as you review this section:

» **Study the connections you have in common.** A little symbol and a number at the bottom left corner of someone's picture indicates that you and this person have shared first-degree connections. You can hover your mouse over that number to see a pop-up window of those connections. LinkedIn will automatically sort people with more shared connections to the top of the page, assuming that if you have a lot of shared connections, perhaps that person belongs in your network.

>> **Some people have an Invite button.** If you see an email address and the Invite button instead of the Connect button, the person is a contact whom you imported to your LinkedIn account who isn't currently on LinkedIn. If you click the Invite button, LinkedIn will send that person an invitation to join LinkedIn, similar to the invitation you sent as an example in Book 5, Chapter 2.

>> **Don't spend a lot of time reviewing your connections.** Instead, visit this page every once in a while to see whom you may want to connect with.

REMEMBER

>> **Visit a person's profile first before clicking Connect.** We can't stress this enough. When you click Connect from the People You May Know page, LinkedIn sends that person a generic invitation. If you click the person's name instead and then click Connect, a screen appears where you can write a customized message. (This topic is covered in detail in "Sending Connection Requests," later in this chapter.)

Browsing your connections' networks

Although it's helpful for LinkedIn to help you search the network, sometimes nothing gives as good results as good old-fashioned investigation. From time to time, browse the network of a first-degree connection to see whether he or she has a contact that should be a part of your network. Don't spend a lot of your time this way, but doing spot check by choosing a few friends at random can yield nice results.

Why is this type of research effective? Lots of reasons, including these:

>> **You travel in the same circles.** If someone is a part of your network, you know that person from a past experience, whether you worked together, learned together, spoke at a conference together, or lived next door to each other. Whatever the experience, you and this contact spent time with other people, so chances are you have shared connections — or, better yet, you'll find people in that person's network whom you want to be a part of your network.

>> **You might find someone newly connected.** Say that you've already searched your undergraduate alumni contacts and added as many people as you could find. As time passes, someone new may connect to one of your friends.

TIP

One effective way to keep updated about the people whom your connections have recently added is to review your notifications. LinkedIn may create a section of the news feed to show you this information.

» **You might recognize someone whose name you didn't fully remember.** Many of us have a contact whom we feel we know well, have fun talking to, and consider more than just an acquaintance, but we can't remember that person's last name. Then, when you search a common contact's network and see the temporarily forgotten name and job title, you suddenly remember. Now you can invite that person to join your network. Another common experience is seeing the name and job title of a contact whose last name changed after marriage.

» **You might see someone you've wanted to get to know better.** Have you ever watched a friend talking to someone whom you wanted to add to your network? Maybe your friend already introduced you, so the other person knows your name, but you consider this person a casual acquaintance at best. When you see that person's name listed in your friend's network, you can take the opportunity to deepen that connection. Having a friend in common who can recommend you can help smooth the way.

WARNING

Looking through your friend's contacts list can be a cumbersome process if he or she has hundreds of contacts, so allow some time if you choose this technique.

To browse the network of one of your connections, follow these steps:

1. **Click the My Network icon in the top navigation bar to bring up your network page.**

2. **Under the Your Connections header, click the See All link.**

3. **Click the name of a first-degree connection.**

   Alternatively, search for the name by using the Search box on the home page. Then, select the name in the search results list.

   When perusing the person's profile, look for a See All *X* Connections link in the top-right corner, above the name and the Contact and Personal Info section. If you don't see this link, you can't proceed with this process because the person has chosen to make his or her connection list private. If that's the case, you need to select a different first-degree connection.

4. **Click the Connections link of the first-degree connection.**

   The connection's connection list appears (see Figure 3-9).

5. **Look through the list and find someone to whom you'd like to send an invitation. Click the person's name to display his or her profile, as shown in Figure 3-10.**

Find connections of your connections.

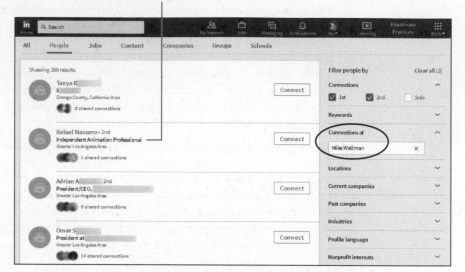

FIGURE 3-9:
You can look
through your
friend's network.

FIGURE 3-10:
Pull up the
person's profile
to add the person
to your network.

6. Click the blue Connect button.

LinkedIn prompts you with an option to customize the invitation, as shown in
Figure 3-11.

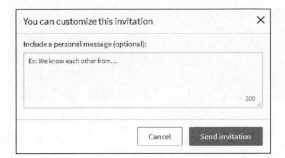

FIGURE 3-11:
Send a custom
invitation to your
new contact.

7. **To customize the invitation, click in the text box and write a message (up to 300 characters) to describe your connection to this person.**

    Remind the person you want to connect with exactly how you know him or her. Perhaps you simply have to indicate that you are a colleague, classmate, business partner, or friend, or have another association with this person.

8. **Click the blue Send Invitation button.**

    Presto! You're finished.

Sending Connection Requests

You can check out previous sections of this chapter to find out how to search the entire user network and find people you want to invite to join your network. In this section, we focus on sending out the invitation, including how to go about inviting people who haven't yet joined LinkedIn.

Sending requests to existing members

When you're on a LinkedIn page and spot the name of a member whom you want to invite to your network, follow these steps to send that person a connection request:

1. **Click the person's name to go to his or her profile page.**

    You might find people to invite by using one of the methods described in "Checking for members," earlier in this chapter. You might also find them while doing an advanced people search 4. Figure 3-12 shows a member's profile page.

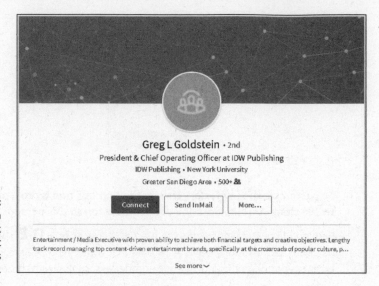

FIGURE 3-12:
Add a person
to your network
from that
person's
profile page.

2. Click the blue Connect button to start the connection request.

The Invitation page appears.

3. If requested, provide the person's email address to help prove that you know the person (see Figure 3-13).

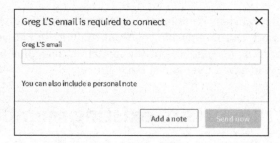

FIGURE 3-13:
For some
members, you
must know their
email address.

4. (Optional but recommended) Click the Add a Note button and enter your invitation text in the Add a Note field.

We highly recommend that you compose a custom invitation rather than use the standard "I'd like to add you to my professional network on LinkedIn" text. In the example in Figure 3-14, we remind the person how we recently met, acknowledge one of his achievements, and ask him to connect.

5. Click the blue Send Invitation button.

When the other party accepts your connection request, you're notified by email.

FIGURE 3-14:
Customize your
invitation text.

Greg L'S email is required to connect ✕

Greg L'S email

gregsemailaddress@emailaccount.com

Include a personal message (optional):

Hey, Greg, congratulations again on being promoted to Publisher of IDW! I can't wait to see what projects come out next! I thought we could stay connected via LinkedIn and talk about future ideas and the comic book industry.

Joel   69

Cancel   Send invitation

Understanding why you shouldn't use canned invitations

If you're having a rough or busy day, you might be tempted to send the canned invitation that LinkedIn displays when you go to the invitation request page. We all have things to do and goals to accomplish, so stopping to write a note for each invitation can grow tedious. However, it's important to replace that text with something that speaks to the recipient, for the following reasons:

» **The other person might not remember you.** Quite simply, your recipient can take one look at your name, see no additional information in the note that accompanied it, and think, "Who is this person?" A few might click your name to read your profile and try to figure it out, but most people are busy and won't take the time to investigate. They are likely to ignore your request. Not good.

» **The other person could report you as someone he doesn't know.** Having someone ignore your request isn't the worst possibility, though. Nope, the worst is being declined as unknown. Recipients of your invitation see an I Don't Know This Person button. If several people click this button from an invitation you sent, LinkedIn will eventually consider you a spammer and will suspend you — and possibly even remove your profile and account from the site!

» **You offer no motivation for a mutually beneficial relationship.** When people get an invitation request, they understand pretty clearly that you want something from them, whether it's access to them or to their network. If you've sent a canned invitation, they can't answer the question, "What's in it for me?" A canned invitation gives no motivation for or potential benefit of being connected to you. A custom note explaining that you'd like to swap resources or introduce that person to others is usually enough to encourage an acceptance.

» **A canned invitation implies that you don't care.** Some people will look at your canned invitation request and think, "This person doesn't have 30 to 60 seconds to write a quick note introducing herself? She must not think much of me." Worse, they may think, "This person just wants to increase her number of contacts to look more popular or to exploit my network." Either impression will quickly kill your chances of getting more connections.

Sending requests to nonmembers

Only members of LinkedIn can be part of anyone's network. Therefore, if you want to send a connection request to someone who hasn't yet joined LinkedIn, you must invite that person to create a LinkedIn account first. To do so, you can either send your invitee an email directly, asking him or her to join, or you can use a LinkedIn function that generates the email invitation that includes a link to join LinkedIn.

Either way, you need to have the nonmember's email address, and you'll probably have to provide your invitee with some incentive by offering reasons to take advantage of LinkedIn and create an account. (You get some tips for doing that in the next section.)

When you're ready to send your request using LinkedIn, follow these steps:

1. **Click the My Network icon in the top navigation bar, and then click the More Options link on the My Network page that appears.**

   The More Options link is below the Your Contact Import Is Ready section. The Add Connections window appears.

2. **Click the Email Message button along the bottom middle of the page.**

   The screen shown in Figure 3-15 appears.

3. **In the box provided, fill in the email addresses of the people you want to invite to LinkedIn.**

4. **To personalize the invitation request to nonmembers a bit, select from a list of preprogrammed phrases or reasons to join LinkedIn, which will be included in the invitation.**

   Simply select the radio button next to the phrase you want included. As an extra step, you may want to contact those people via email or phone first to let them know that this request is coming and encourage them to consider joining LinkedIn.

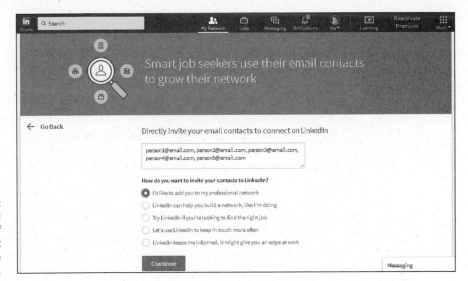

FIGURE 3-15:
Fill in the email
addresses of
anyone you want
to invite to join
LinkedIn.

5. **Click the blue Continue button.**

   A confirmation message pops up.

6. **To return to the Sync Contacts page, click the Go Back link in the top left.**

   You can repeat the process at any time to invite additional people to join LinkedIn and be added to your network.

Communicating the value of joining LinkedIn

So you want to add some people to your network, but they haven't yet signed on to LinkedIn. If you want them to accept your request by setting up their account, you might need to tout the value of LinkedIn. After all, utilizing your existing and growing network is one of the most powerful sales tools, which is why all types of businesses — from e-commerce stores and retail businesses to service directories and social networking websites — use LinkedIn. Offering to help them build their profile or use LinkedIn effectively wouldn't hurt either.

REMEMBER

As of this writing, LinkedIn does not allow you to personalize your invitation to nonmembers (beyond choosing a canned phrase as detailed in the previous section), so you'll need to make this pitch either via email or directly with the person you are recruiting.

So, how do you make your pitch? If you send a thesis on the merits of LinkedIn, it'll most likely be ignored. Sending a simple "C'mon! You know you wanna . . ."

Growing Your Network

request may or may not work. (You know your friends better than we.) You could buy them a copy of this book, but that could get expensive. (But we would be thrilled! C'mon! You know you wanna . . .) The simplest way is to mention some of the benefits they could enjoy from joining the site:

>> **LinkedIn members always stay in touch with their connections.** If people you know move, change their email addresses, or change jobs, you still have a live link to them via LinkedIn. You'll always be able to see their new email addresses if you're connected (assuming that they provide it, of course).

>> **LinkedIn members can tap into their friends' networks for jobs or opportunities, now or later.** Although someone might not need a job now, he or she may eventually need help, so why not access thousands or even millions of potential leads? LinkedIn has hundreds of millions of members in all sorts of industries, and people have obtained consulting leads, contract jobs, new careers, and even start-up venture capital or funding for a new film. After all, it's all about "who you know."

>> **LinkedIn can help you build your own brand.** LinkedIn members get a free profile page to build their online presence, and can link to up to three of their own websites, such as a blog, personal website, social media page, or e-commerce store. The search engines love LinkedIn pages, which have high page rankings — and this can only boost your online identity.

>> **LinkedIn can help you do all sorts of research.** You might need to know more about a company before an interview, or you're looking for a certain person to help your business, or you're curious what people's opinions would be regarding an idea you have. LinkedIn is a great resource in all these situations. You can use LinkedIn to get free advice and information, all from the comfort of your own computer.

>> **Employers are using LinkedIn every day.** Many employers now use LinkedIn to do due diligence on a job seeker by reviewing his or her LinkedIn profile before an interview. If you're not on LinkedIn, an employer may see this as a red flag and it could affect your chances of getting the job.

>> **A basic LinkedIn account is free, and joining LinkedIn is easy.** People have a lot of misconceptions about monthly fees or spending a lot of time updating their LinkedIn profiles. Simply remind people that joining is free, and that after they set up their profiles, LinkedIn is designed to take up little of their time keeping an active profile and benefitting from having an account.

Removing people from your network

The day might come when you feel you need to remove someone from your network. Perhaps you added the person in haste, or he repeatedly asks you for favors or introduction requests, or sends messages that you don't want to respond to. Not to worry — you're not doomed to suffer forever; simply remove the connection. When you do so, that person can no longer view your network or send you messages, unless he pays to send you an InMail message.

To remove a connection from your network, just follow these steps:

1. **While logged in to your LinkedIn account, click the My Network icon, on the top navigation bar.**

2. **Under the Your Connections header, click See All.**

   Your list of connections appears, as shown in Figure 3-16.

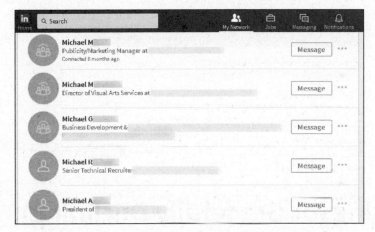

FIGURE 3-16:
Find the connection you want to remove.

3. **Scroll through the list to find the connection to remove.**

4. **To the far right of the person's name, click the three dots next to the Message button, and then select Remove Connection from the drop-down list that appears, as shown in Figure 3-17.**

   A pop-up box appears, warning you of what abilities you'll lose with this removal and asking you to confirm you want to remove the connection.

5. **To remove the person from your network, click the Remove button, as shown in Figure 3-18.**

   Your removed connection won't be notified of the removal.

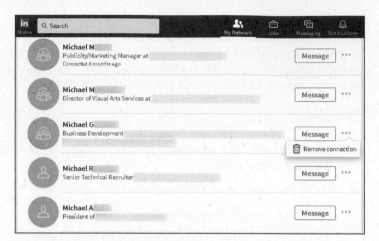

FIGURE 3-17:
Remove your
connection to
this person.

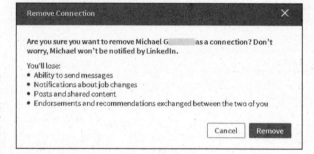

FIGURE 3-18:
Make sure you
understand what
you'll lose by
removing this
connection.

Accepting (or Gracefully Declining) Invitations

In this chapter, we talk a lot about how and why you might send invitations and add people to your network, and even cover what to do when you need to remove someone from your network. But what about the flip side of that coin — that is, being the invitee? In this section, we offer some guidance on what to do when you have to decide whether to happily accept or gracefully decline an invitation.

When you receive an invitation to join someone's network of connections and you're not sure whether to accept or decline the invitation, ask yourself these questions:

>> **How well do you know this person?** With any luck, the inviter has included a custom message clueing you in to who he or she is, in case you don't remember. You can, of course, click the name to read that person's profile, which

usually helps trigger your memory. If you don't know or remember this person, you probably don't want to add him to your network just yet. If you do know the person, you need to consider whether he or she is worth adding to your network.

>> **Does this person fit with the goals of your network?** As mentioned early in this chapter, it's easier to put together a network when you've established a sense of the purpose you want it to serve. When you're looking at this invitation, simply ask yourself, "Does accepting this invitation help further my goals?"

>> **Is this someone with whom you want to communicate and include in your network?** If you don't like someone or don't want to do business with him or her, you should certainly not feel obligated to accept the invitation. Keep in mind that these people will have access to your network and can hit you up with introduction messages and recommendation requests.

If you're thinking of declining an invitation, you can simply ignore the invitation message or click the X button on the screen to ignore the invitation. Optionally, you can respond to the person who sent you the invitation. Some people prefer to respond to be professional or polite, for example. If you decide to send a response message, instead of just ignoring the invite, here are some tips to help you do so gracefully:

>> **Respond quickly.** If you wait to respond to the invitation and then decide to go ahead and decline the invite, the other person might be even more offended and confused. Respond quickly so that this issue isn't hanging over anyone's head.

>> **If necessary, ask for more information.** If you feel uncomfortable because you don't know the person well but want to consider the invitation before you decline, respond with a request for more information, such as, "I appreciate your interest, but I am having trouble placing our previous meetings. What is your specific interest in connecting with me on LinkedIn? Please let me know how we know each other and what your goals are for LinkedIn. Thanks again."

>> **Respond politely but with a firm no.** You can simply write something along the lines of, "Thank you for your interest; I appreciate your eagerness. Unfortunately, because I'm not familiar with you, I'm not interested in connecting with you on LinkedIn just yet." Then, if you want, you can spell out the terms in which you might be interested in connecting, such as if the opportunity ever arises to get to know the person better or if he or she is referred to you by a friend.

IN THIS CHAPTER

» **Understanding recommendations**

» **Writing a good recommendation**

» **Requesting a recommendation**

» **Declining a recommendation or a request for one**

» **Managing your recommendations**

Chapter **4**

Exploring the Power of Recommendations

E ndorsements and testimonials have long been a mainstay of traditional marketing. But really, how much value is there in reading testimonials on someone's own website, like the following:

Maria is a great divorce attorney — I'd definitely use her again.

ELIZABETH T. LONDON

or

Jack is a fine lobbyist — a man of impeccable character.

EMANUEL R. SEATTLE

Without knowing who these people are, anyone reading the testimonials tends to be highly skeptical about them. At the very least, the reader wants to know that they're real people who have some degree of accountability for those endorsements.

The reader is looking for something called *social validation.* Basically, that's just a fancy-shmancy term meaning that people feel better about their decision to conduct business with someone if other people in their extended network are pleased with that person's work. The reader knows that people are putting their own reputations at stake, even if just to a small degree, by making a public recommendation of another person. You don't have to look much further than Yelp, HomeAdvisor, or Amazon reviews to understand this point.

As this chapter shows you, the LinkedIn recommendations feature offers you a powerful tool for finding out more about the people you're considering doing business with, as well as a means to publicly build your own reputation. We walk you through all the steps needed to create a recommendation for someone else, request a recommendation for your profile, and manage your existing recommendations.

Understanding Recommendations

The LinkedIn recommendation process starts in one of three ways:

>> **Unsolicited:** When viewing the profile of any first-degree connection, click the More button below the person's profile picture to display the menu shown in Figure 4-1. To give an unsolicited recommendation, select the Recommend option.

FIGURE 4-1:
You can start a recommendation with any first-degree connection.

- >> **Requested:** To request a recommendation from a first-degree connection, select Request a Recommendation in the drop-down menu shown in Figure 4-1. You might ask for a recommendation at the end of a successful project, for example, or before your transition to a new job.

- >> **Reciprocated:** Whenever you accept a recommendation from someone, you have the option of recommending that person in return. Some people do this as a thank you for receiving the recommendation, others reciprocate only because they mistakenly think they can't leave a recommendation until someone leaves them one, and still others don't feel comfortable reciprocating unless they truly believe the person deserves one. You should decide in each circumstance whether to reciprocate. (Sometimes the situation might be awkward, such as if you get a recommendation from a supervisor or boss.)

REMEMBER

After the recommendation is written, it's not posted immediately. Instead, it goes to the recipient for review, and he or she has the option to accept it, reject it, or request a revision. So even though the majority of recommendations you see on LinkedIn are genuine, they're also almost entirely positive because they have to be accepted by the recipient.

LinkedIn shows all recommendations you've received as well as links to the profiles of the people who recommended you, as shown in Figure 4-2. Allowing people to see who is endorsing you provides social validation.

FIGURE 4-2:
Recommendations on a profile page.

The quality and source of recommendations matter. A handful of specific recommendations from actual clients talking about how you helped them solve a problem are worth more than 50 general recommendations from business acquaintances saying, "I like Sally — she's cool," or "Hector is a great networker." And any recommendations that heartily endorse the number of cocktails you had at the last formal event probably need revision. Check out "Gracefully Declining a Recommendation (or a Request for One)," later in this chapter, if you're receiving those kinds of statements.

Writing Recommendations

We suggest that you practice making some recommendations before you start requesting them. Here's the method to our madness: When you know how to write a good recommendation yourself, you're in a better position to help others write good recommendations for you. And the easiest way to get recommendations is to give them. Every time you make a recommendation and the recipient accepts it, he or she is prompted to give you a recommendation. Thanks to the basic desire to be fair that most exhibit dealing with their network, many people will go ahead and endorse you in return.

Choose wisely, grasshopper: Deciding whom to recommend

Go through your contacts and make a list of the people you want to recommend. As you build your list, consider recommending the following types of contacts:

>> **People with whom you've worked:** We're not going to say that personal references are worthless, but they tend to ring hollow next to specific recommendations from colleagues and clients. Business recommendations are much stronger in the LinkedIn context. Your recommendation is rooted in actual side-by-side experiences with the other party, you can be specific regarding the behavior and accomplishments of the other party, and your examples will probably be appreciated by the professional LinkedIn community at large.

>> **People you know well:** You may choose to connect with casual acquaintances or even strangers, but reserve your personal recommendations for people with whom you have an established relationship (friends and family). Remember, you're putting your reputation on the line with recommendations. Are you comfortable risking your rep on them?

Recommend only those people whose performance you're happy with. We can't say it enough: Your reputation is on the line. Recommending a doofus just to get a recommendation in return isn't worth it! Here's a great question to ask yourself when deciding whether to recommend someone: Would you feel comfortable recommending this person to a best friend or a family member? If not, you have your answer.

When you complete your list, you're probably not going to write all the recommendations at once, so we suggest copying and pasting the names in a word processing document or a spreadsheet so that you can keep track as you complete them.

Look right here: Making your recommendation stand out

Keep the following in mind when trying to make your recommendation stand out from the rest of the crowd:

- >> **Be specific.** Don't just write that the person you're recommending is great. Instead, mention his specific strengths and skills. If you need help, ask him whether he can think of any helpful elements you could highlight in your recommendation.

- >> **Talk about results.** Adjectives and descriptions are fluff. Clichés are also useless. Tell what the person actually did and the effect it had on you and your business. It's one thing to say, "She has a great eye," and another to say, "The logo she designed for us has been instrumental in building our brand and received numerous positive comments from customers." Detailed results make a great impression, from the scope of difficulty of a project to the degree of challenge the person faced.

- >> **Tell how you know the person.** LinkedIn provides only two basic overall categories to represent your relationship to the person you're recommending: professional and education. If you've known this person for 10 years, say so. If she's your cousin, say so. If you've never met her in person, say so. Save it for the end, though. Open with the positive results this person provided, or the positive qualities the person exhibited in your interaction; then qualify the type of interaction.

- >> **Reinforce the requestor's major skills or goals.** Look at her profile. How is she trying to position herself now? What can you say in your recommendation that will support that? The recipient will appreciate this approach. For example, if you read her profile and see that she's focusing on her project management skills as opposed to her earlier software development skills, your recommendation should reinforce the message she's trying to convey in her profile.

> » **Don't gush.** By all means, if you think someone is fantastic, exceptional, extraordinary, or the best at what she does, say so. Just don't go on and on about it, and watch the clichéd adjectives.
>
> » **Be concise.** Although LinkedIn has a 3,000-character limit on the length of recommendations, you shouldn't reach that limit. Make your recommendation as long as it needs to be to say what you have to say, but no longer.

TIP

Don't be afraid to contact the requestor and ask for feedback on what you should highlight in your recommendation of that person. He knows his own brand better than anyone, so go right to the source!

Creating a recommendation

Now you're ready to write your first recommendation. To create a recommendation, first you need to pull up the person's profile:

1. **Click the My Network icon in the top navigation bar of any page.**

2. **When your network page appears, click the See All link under the Your Connections header.**

    Your list of connections appears.

3. **Select the person you're recommending.**

REMEMBER

Your recommendation goes directly to that person, not to prospective employers. Any prospective employer who wants a specific reference can request it by contacting that person directly on LinkedIn.

4. **Visit the profile of the person you want to recommend.**

Before you write up your recommendation, review the person's experience, summary, professional headline, and other elements of his profile. This helps you get a sense of what skills, attributes, or results should be reflected in your recommendation. After all, if the person you want to recommend is trying to build a career as a finance executive, your recommendation will serve him better if you focus on finance instead of his event planning or writing skills.

After you inform yourself a bit more about the person and have thought about what you are going to say, you can get your recommending groove on. Follow these steps:

1. **Click the More button below the person's profile picture, and then click Recommend in the drop-down list that appears.**

    The Write *X* a Recommendation page appears, as shown in Figure 4-3.

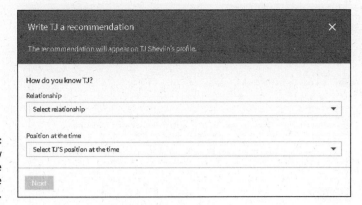

FIGURE 4-3:
Tell LinkedIn how you know the person you are recommending.

2. **Define your relationship:**

   a. *Under Relationship, define the basis of the recommendation. You have several options, including whether you were a colleague, client, or supervisor.*

   b. *Define the other person's position at the time.* Select at least one position that the other party held. You can enter only one recommendation per position, but you can recommend the other party for multiple positions.

   c. *Click Next.*

3. **In the text box shown in Figure 4-4, enter the text for your recommendation.**

   Throughout this chapter, we stress staying specific, concise, and professional while focusing on a person's results and skills.

REMEMBER

   The recommendations you write that are accepted by the other party appear also in your profile on the Recommendations tab. Believe it or not, people judge you by the comments you make about others, so read your recommendation before you post it and look for spelling or grammatical errors. (You may want to prepare your recommendation in a word processing program so you can use its spelling and grammar checks, and then cut and paste your newly pristine prose.)

4. **Click Send.**

   The recommendation is sent to the recipient.

   After you send your recommendation, the other person must accept it before it's posted. Don't take it personally if she doesn't post it, or at least not right away. After all, it's a gift, freely given. The primary value to *you* is in the gesture to the recipient, not the public visibility of your recommendation. And if she comes back with requested changes to the recommendation, by all means accommodate her as long as it's all true and you feel comfortable with it. It's a service to her, not you.

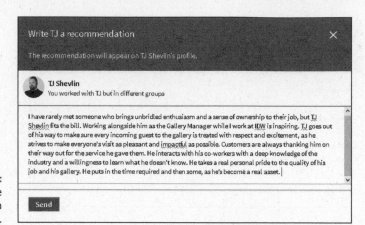

FIGURE 4-4:
Write the
recommendation
here.

Requesting Recommendations

In an ideal world, you'd never request a recommendation. Everyone who's had a positive experience working with you would just automatically post a raving recommendation on LinkedIn. But the reality is that most likely only your raving fans and very heavy LinkedIn users are going to make unsolicited recommendations. Your mildly happy customers, former bosses whose jokes you laughed at consistently, and co-workers you haven't seen in five years could all stand a little prompting.

Be prepared, though: Some people feel that recommendations should only be given freely, and they may be taken aback by receiving a recommendation request. So it's imperative that you frame your request with a personal message, not just a generic message from LinkedIn.

Don't be afraid to consider off-line methods of requesting a recommendation, such as a phone call or a face-to-face meeting, to make the request more personal and more likely for the person to say yes.

Choosing whom to ask

Request recommendations from the same people you might write them for: colleagues, business partners, and educational contacts. The only difference is that you're looking at it from his point of view.

Relationships aren't all symmetrical. For example, if someone hears us speak at a conference and buys this book, that person is our customer. Our customers know our skills and expertise fairly well — perhaps not on the same level as a consulting client, but still well enough to make a recommendation. We, on the other hand, might not know a customer at all. We're open to getting to know him, and are willing to connect, but we can't write a recommendation for him yet.

Creating a polite recommendation request

When you identify a person whom you want to write your recommendation, you're ready to create a recommendation request. To get started on authoring your request, follow these steps:

1. **Click the Me icon, on the top navigation bar, and then click View Profile.**

2. **Scroll down to the Recommendations header, and click the Ask to Be Recommended link (to the right of the header).**

   The Ask for Recommendations box appears.

3. **Enter the name of the first-degree connection:**

   a. *Below the Who Do You Want to Ask? header, start typing the name of the first-degree connection, as shown in Figure 4-5.*

   b. *When the name appears in the list, click it.*

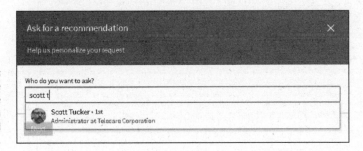

FIGURE 4-5:
Select the position to be associated with your requested recommendation.

4. **Define your relationship with the person in the drop-down boxes provided, as shown in Figure 4-6, and then click Next.**

   Similar to the process of writing a recommendation, LinkedIn asks you to define the basis of your relationship with this person (Professional or Educational) and your position during the time when the other person is basing her recommendation of you.

Exploring the Power of Recommendations

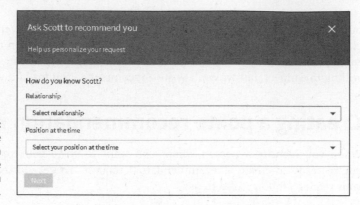

FIGURE 4-6:
Confirm the
person from
whom you're
requesting a
recommendation.

5. Type your message in the field provided.

The same etiquette is recommended here as in other requests: Don't just accept the boilerplate text that LinkedIn fills in, but rather customize it to create a personal note, as shown in Figure 4-7. You can customize only the body of your message.

TIP

Don't forget to thank the person for the time and the effort in leaving you a recommendation!

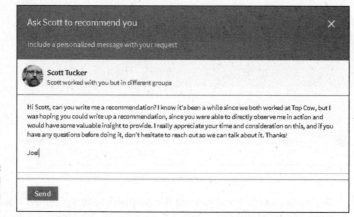

FIGURE 4-7:
A customized
recommendation
request.

6. Check your spelling and grammar.

You can write your message first using a program such as Microsoft Word, run the spelling and grammar check, and then cut and paste your message into the space provided, if you like.

7. Click Send.

The recommendation request is sent to the intended recipient.

REMEMBER

Giving people some context as to why you're making the request helps motivate them, especially if they're nervous about or don't know how to use LinkedIn. Let them know you're available for any technical or follow-up help. Also, even though you should be asking only people who would be comfortable recommending you (you are, aren't you?), you still want to give them a gracious way to decline. After all, you're asking a favor. The person you're contacting is in no way obligated. Don't expect anything, and you won't be disappointed.

TIP

There's no such thing as too many recommendations as long as the quality is good. However, if you start accepting mediocre recommendations (on the assumption that "something is better than nothing"), people will start to think that a lot of them are fluff. LinkedIn doesn't give you control over the display order, either, so you have all the more reason to make sure that the recommendations displayed are good quality.

Gracefully Declining a Recommendation (or a Request for One)

Unfortunately, not everyone writes good recommendations — and not all your LinkedIn connections have read this minibook — so eventually, someone will write a recommendation that you don't want in your profile.

No problem. Just politely request a replacement when you receive it. Thank him for thinking of you, and give him the context of what you're trying to accomplish:

> Wei:
>
> Thank you so much for your gracious recommendation. I'd like to ask a small favor, though. I'm trying to position myself more as a public speaker in the widget industry, rather than as a gadget trainer. Because you've heard me speak on the topic, if you could gear your recommendation more toward that, I'd greatly appreciate it.
>
> Thanks,
>
> Alexa

If he's sincerely trying to be of service to you, he should have no problem changing it. Just make sure you ask him for something based on your experience with him.

WARNING

You may receive a request for a recommendation from someone you don't feel comfortable recommending. If it's because she gave you poor service or was less than competent, you have to consider whether you should even be connected to her at all because, after all, LinkedIn is a business referral system.

Perhaps you don't have sufficient experience with her services to provide her a recommendation. If that's the case, just reply to her request with an explanation:

> Alexa:
>
> I received your request for a recommendation. Although I am happy to be connected to you on LinkedIn and look forward to getting to know you better or even work together in the future, at this time I just don't feel as though I have enough basis to give you a substantive recommendation.
>
> After we've worked together on something successfully, I'll be more than happy to provide a recommendation.
>
> Thanks,
>
> Wei

Managing Recommendations

Relationships change over time. Some get better, others get worse, and still others just change. As you get more recommendations, you might decide that you don't want to display them all or you would like some of them updated to support your current branding or initiatives.

Fortunately, neither the recommendation you give nor those you receive are etched in stone (or computer chips, as the case may be). You can edit or remove recommendations you've written at any time, and you can hide or request revisions to those you receive.

Editing or removing recommendations you've made

To edit or remove a recommendation you've made, follow these steps:

1. **Click the Me icon, on the top navigation bar, and then click View Profile from the drop-down list that appears.**

2. **Scroll down to the Recommendations header, and click the pencil icon (edit) to the far right of the header.**

   A Manage Recommendations window appears, containing all the recommendations you've received or given as well as pending requests.

3. Click the Given tab.

All the recommendations you've made are listed in reverse chronological order, as shown in Figure 4-8.

Manage recommendations ✕

Received (10) | Given (22)

Lynn Northrup
Freelance Editor
February 4, 2016, Joel worked with Lynn but at different companies

I worked with Lynn on several Dummies titles and I thought she was not only a solid and efficient Editor, but it was effortless and enjoyable to work with her. She was always able to provide guidance and shepherd a projection to completion with the confidence that helped everyone get their job done!

[Delete] [Revise]   ⊙ Visible to: Public

Brendan MacNeil, BA
Chief Executive Officer
August 31, 2014, Joel was a client of Brendan's

Brendan was an outstanding contributor to my event, and he can be a vital asset to any event requiring some planning. He was brought it to help set up and handle on-site logistics for the 2013 So Cal Comic Con in Oceanside. He was early, helpful throughout the entire day, easy to work with, and handled every task with ease. He is able to maneuver himself and arrange the necessary elements to an event through discipline, intuition and the right attitude.

Hidden recommendations (2)   [Save]

FIGURE 4-8:
Delete or change the visibility of a recommendation.

4. To change the visibility of a recommendation:

a. *Click its Visible To X link.* The screen updates and displays three options you can assign for the recommendation's visibility, as shown in Figure 4-9.

b. *Make your selection.* You can choose Only You, Your Connections, or Public. If you change to Only You or Your Connections, you'll be limiting who can view the recommendation.

5. To delete a recommendation, click the Delete button.

LinkedIn will display a message box asking you to click Yes to confirm the recommendation removal.

6. When you're finished, click the Save button to save your changes.

Handling new recommendations you've received

When you receive a recommendation from someone, you see it on your Recommendations page, under the Received tab, with the You Have X Pending Recommendations link. Click that link to read the full text, as shown in Figure 4-10.

Exploring the Power of Recommendations

CHAPTER 4 Exploring the Power of Recommendations   427

FIGURE 4-9:
Change the
visibility of your
recommendation.

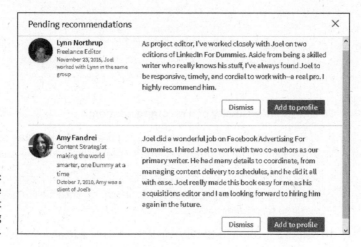

FIGURE 4-10:
Here is where
you can accept
an incoming
recommendation.

When you receive a recommendation, you have these options:

>> **Add it to your profile.** Click the Add to Profile button to add this recommen-
dation, as stated, to your profile.

>> **Get rid of it.** If you aren't happy with the person's recommendation or aren't
interested in having the recommendation in your profile, click the Dismiss
button. If you want, you can send the person a brief note explaining why
you're not adding the recommendation to your profile or requesting changes.

>> **Ignore it.** Until you take action, the recommendation is pending and will not appear in your profile. Perhaps you don't want the recommendation to become visible until a certain event happens, such as applying for a different job. You can return to this screen at any time to add the recommendation or ask for changes.

Removing or requesting to revise a recommendation

To remove a recommendation you've received or to request a revision, do the following:

1. **Click the Me icon, in the top navigation bar, and then click View Profile in the drop-down list that appears.**

2. **Scroll down to the Recommendations header, and click the pencil icon (edit) to the far right of the header.**

   The Recommendations page appears.

3. **If necessary, click the Received tab.**

   Doing so takes you to the Recommendations You've Received page.

4. **Scroll down the page to find the recommendation in question.**

5. **To remove a recommendation, change the slider (on the right of the recommendation) from Show to Hide, as in Figure 4-11.**

   Your recommendation will be hidden after you complete this process. At any time, you can come back to this window and change the slider from Hide to Show, to return the recommendation to your profile.

6. **When you want changes made to your recommendation:**

   a. *Click the Ask for Revision button (just below the recommendation you want to revise).* A message to the other party appears, as shown in Figure 4-12.

   b. *Write your message.* Detail what revisions you would like the person to make, such as adding specific details, including or removing a certain project, or highlighting previously unmentioned skills you now need to help make a career change.

   c. *Click the Send button to send the message.*

7. **To save your choice, click the Save button at the bottom of the box.**

Exploring the Power of Recommendations

FIGURE 4-11:
Remove a
recommendation
by changing its
visibility to Hide.

Manage recommendations ✕

Received (10)   Given (22)

You have 2 pending recommendations

to help market and promote his books. I hope to be able to work with Joel in the future on other book projects.

[Ask for revision]   Show ⬤

Michael Bellomo
Graduate Student, Master of Public Policy Program
July 15, 2008, Michael was a client of Joel's

Joel Elad is a superb freelance writer who is great to work with and a true expert on his subject matter.

[Ask for revision]   Show ⬤

Steven Hayes
Executive Editor for For Dummies series
July 15, 2008, Steven was a client of Joel's

Joel was an ideal choice when we needed an author to create content for a new, developing-on-the-fly series. His expertise in the worlds of tech, online business, and social networking have helped him create best selling content for Wiley. I look forward to working with him more in the future.

[Ask for revision]   Show ⬤

Hidden recommendations {2}   [Save]

FIGURE 4-12:
Ask your friend to
revise his or her
recommendation
of you.

Ask Michael for a revision ✕

Include a personalized message about what revisions you're asking for

Michael Bellomo
Michael was a client of yours

Hi Michael, can you please revise your recommendation for me? Specifically could you change...

[Send]

Negotiating the social graces concerning recommendations might feel awkward at first, but with practice you'll quickly become comfortable. By both giving and receiving good recommendations, you'll build your public reputation, increase your social capital with your connections, and have a good excuse for renewing relationships with people you haven't contacted recently.

Chapter **5**

Finding Employees

W hen you have a handle on the key elements of improving your LinkedIn profile and experience, it's time to look outward toward the LinkedIn network and talk about some of the benefits you can reap from a professional network of tens of millions of people.

Whether you're an entrepreneur looking for your first employee, a growing start-up needing to add a knowledgeable staffer, or a part of a Fortune 500 company filling a recent opening, LinkedIn can provide a rich and powerful pool of potential applicants and job candidates, including the perfectly skilled person who isn't even looking for a job!

When it comes to looking for an employee, one of the benefits of LinkedIn is that you aren't limited to an applicant's one- or two-page resume and cover letter. Instead, you get the full picture of the applicant's professional history, coupled with recommendations and his or her knowledge and willingness to share information. Even if you find your candidate outside LinkedIn, you can use the site to perform reference checks and get more information about the person. This information can augment what you learn from the candidate during the hiring process and from the references he or she provides. LinkedIn cannot replace your hiring process, but it can help you along the way.

In this chapter, we cover the basics of using LinkedIn to find an employee for your company or start-up. We begin with the basics of how you can post your job listing on LinkedIn and review applicants. We then move on to using LinkedIn to screen potential candidates, and finish the chapter with search strategies you should employ to find the right person.

Managing Your Job Listings

LinkedIn offers a Talent Solutions page for companies to manage their job listings. Click the Work icon on the top navigation bar on the home page, and select Talent Solutions from the drop-down list that appears. The Talent Solutions home page appears, as shown in Figure 5-1. This is where you can start the process of creating a job listing, reviewing the applicants you get, and paying LinkedIn to post the listing. You can also post a job without using Talent Solutions, but if you're managing a company account that will need more than the occasional job posting, you may want to investigate Talent Solutions further.

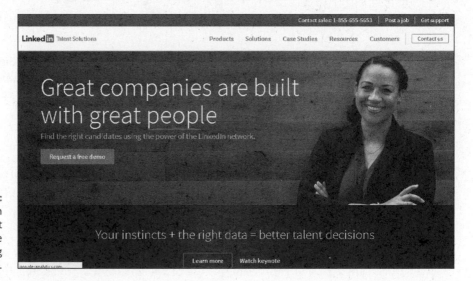

FIGURE 5-1:
LinkedIn offers a Talent Solutions page for managing your job listings.

You set the cost for each job listing with a daily budget, and are charged only when potential job candidates click your job listing. You can cancel the job listing at any time, so you don't have to run the listing for a long time if you get enough candidates quickly. You can pay for your job listing with PayPal or a major credit card such as Visa, MasterCard, American Express, or Discover.

TIP

If you know you're going to need multiple or ongoing job postings on LinkedIn, consider LinkedIn Recruiter to get discounts on job postings and InMail. You can get more information by completing a request for a demo at `https://business.linkedin.com/talent-solutions/recruiter`.

You can choose to renew your listing at the end of the 30-day window. Your *date posted* (the date you set up the job listing) is updated with the renewal date instead of the original posting date, so the listing appears at the top of search results. Renewing a job listing costs the same as the initial job posting.

WARNING

You can advertise only one open position per job listing. If you solicit applications for more than one position in a single job listing, LinkedIn will remove your listing.

Posting a job listing

To post your job opening, follow these steps:

1. Click the Work icon on the top navigation bar, and select Post a Job from the drop-down list that appears.

The screen shown in Figure 5-2 should appear, although some users will need to set the company, location, and job title first before tackling the other details.

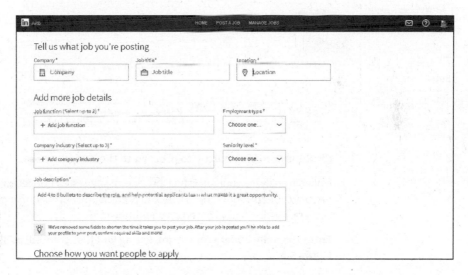

FIGURE 5-2: Start composing your job posting here.

2. Using the text boxes and lists provided, enter the required information about your company and the job you're offering.

LinkedIn asks for your company name, the job title, and the job location. As you fill in those fields, LinkedIn will try to fill in options for skills under the Job Function box and the industry your company represents. You should also add job function skills and industries that pertain to your job posting, as well as the employment type and seniority level.

Next, compose your job description in the text box provided (refer to Figure 5-2) or copy the description from another source and paste it into the box. If you paste the text, make sure the formatting (spacing, bullet points, font size, and so on) is correct.

3. **Scroll down and fill in the Choose How You Want People to Apply section, as shown in Figure 5-3.**

   You can receive applications at one of the email addresses you have listed in your profile or at another email address. Or supply a direct URL for applicants to use.

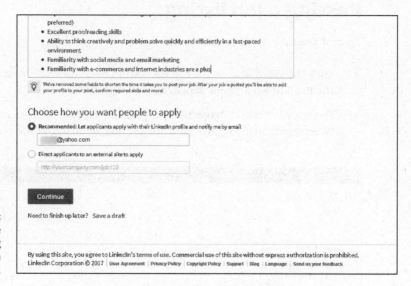

FIGURE 5-3:
Enter candidate routing information here.

4. **Click the Continue button to proceed to the budget phase.**

   LinkedIn analyzes your job listing, provides a suggested budget you can spend per day to keep your listing active, and predicts the number of applications you'll receive in 30 days based on your budget.

5. **Enter the daily budget for the job listing you just created, as shown in Figure 5-4.**

6. **Click the Continue button to proceed.**

   After LinkedIn has gathered your daily budget limit, it needs your billing information, as shown in Figure 5-5.

7. **Review your order, provide payment information, and click the blue Post Job button.**

   Look over the details of your order, and then scroll down and make sure you have a major credit card or a PayPal account on file to pay for the job listing.

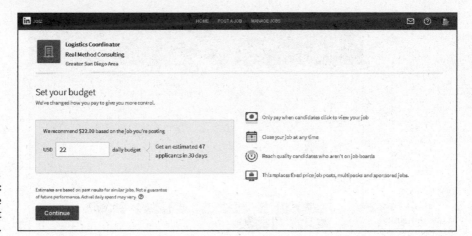

FIGURE 5-4:
Decide on the
daily PPC budget
you want to set.

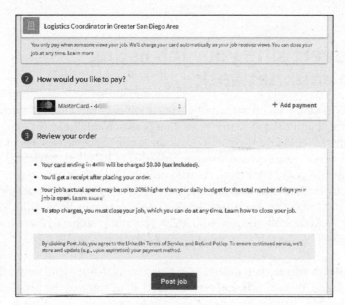

FIGURE 5-5:
Confirm the
details for your
job listing.

That's it! You have completed the all-important first step: posting your job list-ing. You receive a job posting confirmation, as shown in Figure 5-6. The listing is available by clicking the Jobs link (in the top navigation bar) and looking in the Your Jobs box along the right side of your Jobs home page.

You have two options for improving your job posting right after creating the post. You can decide whether you want your profile summary to appear with the job listing by leaving the appropriate check box selected (refer to Figure 5-6), and you can add required skills to the job listing by clicking the Add Skill link and adding the particular skills you want in your applicants. Click the blue Finish button to complete your choices.

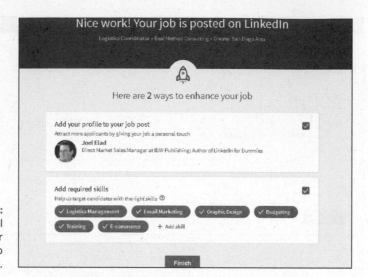

FIGURE 5-6:
Make some final
touches on your
LinkedIn job
listing.

Advertising your job listing to your network

Traditionally, when someone posted a job opening on the Internet using one of those ubiquitous job search sites, that person would hope the extensive pool of job seekers would find the posting and the appropriate parties would submit resumes and cover letters. When you use LinkedIn to fill a job, however, you still benefit from the pool of job seekers who search LinkedIn's Jobs page, but you have a distinct advantage: *your own network.* You're connected to people you know and trust, people you have worked with before so you know their capabilities, and most importantly, people who know you and (you hope) have a better idea than the average person as to what kind of person you would hire.

LinkedIn enables you to share your job listing using social networking sites Facebook and Twitter, and you can also send all or some of the people in your network a message, letting them know about your job opening and asking them if they, or anyone they know, might be interested in the job. When you're ready to advertise your job listing, follow these steps:

1. **Click the Me icon (your profile photo), on the top navigation bar, and select Job Postings (under the Manage header) from the drop-down list that appears.**

   After you've posted your job, the position is listed in the Jobs window, which automatically loads any active job postings.

2. **Click the three dots to the right of the job listing, and then click Share Job from the drop-down list that appears (see Figure 5-7).**

   Next, you'll select one or more networks in turn for sharing the job listing.

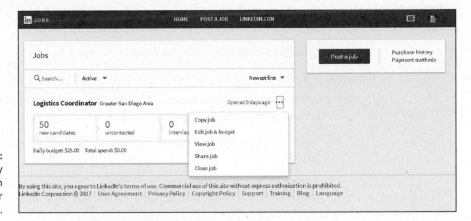

FIGURE 5-7:
See key
information
about your
new job listing.

3. **To share the job listing on LinkedIn:**

    a. *Click the LinkedIn icon.* A Share box appears that you can send to your LinkedIn network in a variety of ways (see Figure 5-8).

    b. *To generate an automatic network update, leave the Share an Update check box selected.*

    c. *To change the privacy settings for this update, select whom you want to share with by using the appropriate drop-down box to select an audience.*

FIGURE 5-8:
LinkedIn lets you
ask your network
for help.

4. **To send the listing to individual connections:**

   a. *Select the Send to Individuals check box.*

   b. *Start typing name of a first-degree connection in the To box.*

   c. *When the name you want appears in the list below the To box, click the name, which then moves to the To box.*

   d. *Continue to type additional names, up to a recommended maximum of ten people.*

   When you're sending the listing to individual connections, feel free to edit the text in the message box to make it sound as if it's coming from you, or leave the default message in place.

5. **Look over the text in the window again, making sure you have the right people selected, and then click the Share button (see Figure 5-9).**

   Your LinkedIn connections will receive a message in their LinkedIn inboxes and, depending on their notification settings, an email with this message as well. They can click a link from the message to see the job listing and either apply themselves or forward it to their contacts for consideration.

FIGURE 5-9: Proofread your message and then send it!

6. **To generate a message for Twitter or Facebook:**

   a. *Click the Twitter or Facebook icon.*

   b. *Enter your login information for the network.* A window appears that interfaces directly with Twitter or Facebook.

   c. *Draft an update or a tweet and click to send it directly to your network.*

Reviewing applicants

After you've posted your job listing on LinkedIn, you should expect to get some applicants for the position. Every time someone applies for that job, you receive an email from LinkedIn notifying you of the application. In addition, LinkedIn records the application in the Applicants number of the Active Jobs window. (Refer to Figure 5-7.)

When you're ready to review the applicants for your job, follow these steps:

1. **Click the Me icon, and then select Job Postings (under the Manage header) from the drop-down list that appears.**

   You should be taken to the Active Jobs screen, as shown in Figure 5-7 in the previous section. Click the job title of the job listing you want to review, which brings you to the Overview screen, as shown in Figure 5-10.

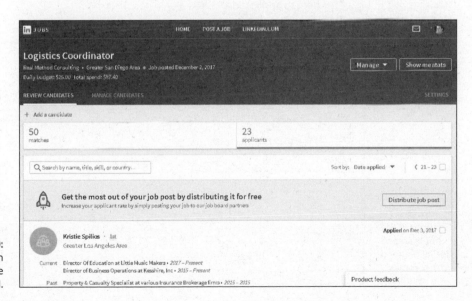

FIGURE 5-10: Review your open job listings to see who has applied.

2. **Click an applicant's name to see his LinkedIn profile and read up on his experience.**

REMEMBER

You should review all the potential applicants first, labeling them Good Fit or Not a Fit (see the next step), before moving onto the next phase, where you start contacting and interviewing potential matches.

3. **Click the check box to the right of an applicant's name, to display the options shown at the top of Figure 5-11, and then take one or more of the following actions:**

- *Not a Fit:* Label the person as Not a Fit. The applicant's name will be archived.

- *Good Fit:* Label the applicant as a Good Fit. The person's name will be moved from the Review Applicants screen to the Manage Candidates screen.

- *Contact:* Send the applicant a message.

- *Share Profile:* Share the person's application with other people, such as other members of a hiring committee.

- *Add Note:* Add your own notes about a particular applicant, which can be seen only by you.

- *More:* Display a menu to Save to PDF (the person's LinkedIn profile, that is) or Download Resume, if at least one person attached a resume to his or her job application.

FIGURE 5-11:
Go through the applicants to decide on good fits for your company.

4. **To automatically send a potential candidate a message that you're interested, click the Interested button.**

The candidate will be moved to the Manage Candidates screen.

Be careful about clicking the Interested button, because the message is sent to the potential candidate automatically and you can't customize the message.

WARNING

5. **To archive the person's name and remove that individual from active consideration, click the Not Interested button.**

This has the same effect of clicking the Not a Fit button for that person.

6. **After you've reviewed the potential applicants, scroll to the top of the screen and click the Manage Candidates header.**

The Manage Candidates screen appears, as shown in Figure 5-12, where you can keep track of which applicants you have contacted with messages, conducted phone screens, and conducted in-person interviews.

In addition, the following buttons appear (some of which are the same as the ones in the review applicants phase; refer to Step 3):

- *Move To*: Assign the candidate's name to the different phases in the applicant timeline, such as Contacted, Replied, Phone Screen, Interview, Offer, or Hire.

  You can access the Move To functions also by clicking the Move To button at the bottom right of the candidate's information.

TIP

- *Contact:* Send the candidate a message.

- *Share Profile:* Share the candidate's profile with other people.

- *Add a Note:* Include a note next to the candidate's name.

- *Archive:* Archive the applicant's information; it will no longer be visible on your Manage Candidates screen.

- *More:* Display a menu to Save to PDF (the person's LinkedIn profile, that is) or Download Resume, if at least one person attached a resume to his or her job application.

7. **Click the name of an applicant.**

The person's profile appears so you can review his or her qualifications further.

8. **If you think the applicant is worth pursuing, contact the person to set up the next part of your application process.**

You can contact the person by clicking the Message button on his or her profile page, or by clicking the Contact button or the Message button on the Manage Candidates page (refer to Step 6). The screen shown in Figure 5-13 appears, with a preprogrammed message that you can edit or replace.

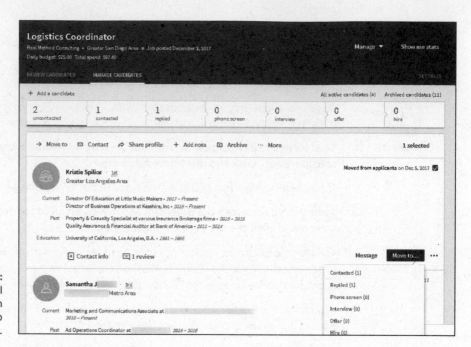

FIGURE 5-12:
Review potential applicants whom you want to interview.

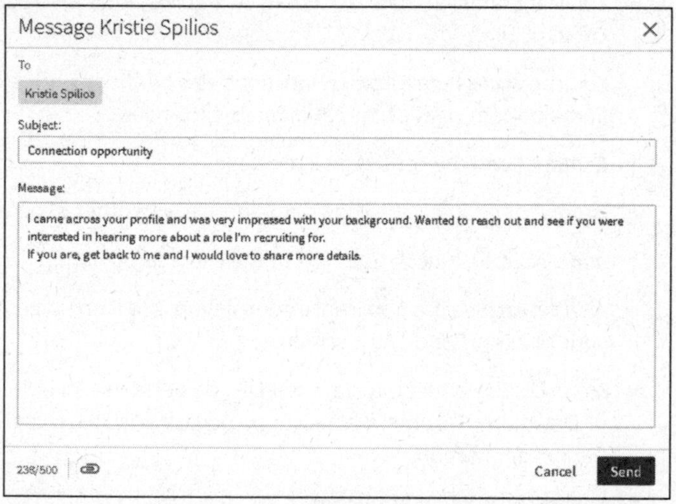

FIGURE 5-13:
Send a potential applicant a message.

Screening Candidates with LinkedIn

After you use LinkedIn to post a job request, you can continue to use LinkedIn to assist you in the screening part of your hiring process. In addition to asking for references from the applicant or possibly ordering a background check from an independent background check agency, you can use LinkedIn to verify information in your applicant's resume and application at any stage of the process, without paying a dime!

Here are some strategies to keep in mind:

>> **Start by thoroughly reviewing the applicant's profile.** When you review an applicant's profile, compare it with her resume, cover letter, and application. Is she consistent in how she presents her experience?

>> **Read through the applicant's recommendations and follow up.** If your candidate has received recommendations, go through them, noting the date the recommendation was written, and see whether any are applicable toward your open position. Pay particular attention to recommendations from former bosses or co-workers. If necessary, ask your candidate whether you can contact the recommender through InMail and use that person as a reference.

>> **See whether you're connected to your candidate.** When you pull up your candidate's profile, you see whether she is a second- or third-degree network member, which would mean one or two people connect you with the candidate. If so, contact that person (or ask for an introduction to reach the correct party) and ask for more information about the candidate. Chances are good that you'll get a more honest assessment from someone you know rather than the recommendations provided by the candidate. Understand, however, that although the two people may be connected, they may not know each other that well, or their connection may be outside the professional expertise you're looking to learn about from this job candidate.

>> **Evaluate the candidate's total picture.** If your candidate mentions any websites, blogs, or other online presence in her profile, look at the listed interests and group affiliations and see whether they add to (or detract from) your picture of the job candidate.

Because most LinkedIn users have already defined each position they've held, the companies where they've worked, and the years of employment, you can get a sense of their abilities, what they've handled in the past, and depending on the completeness of their profile, examples of their past accomplishments.

TIP

As helpful as LinkedIn can be when reviewing a candidate, don't be afraid to use other Internet websites and searches to gain a well-rounded view of the candidate in question.

Using Strategies to Find Active or Passive Job Seekers

One of the powers of LinkedIn is its ability to find not only the active job seeker but also the passive job seeker or someone who doesn't even realize he or she wants a new job! You can tap an extensive network of professionals who have already identified their past experiences, skill sets, interests, educational backgrounds, and group affiliations.

The best piece of advice for this type of search comes from Harvey Mackay and the book he wrote back in 1999, *Dig Your Well Before You're Thirsty* (Currency Books): You should be building a healthy network and keeping your eye on potential candidates before you have a job opening to fill. The earlier you start, and the more consistent you are with the time you spend weekly or monthly expanding your network, the easier it is to identify and then recruit a potential candidate to fill your opening.

You should take specific steps to make your strategy a reality. Whether you start this process in advance or just need to fill a position as soon as possible, here are some tactics to consider:

>> **Perform detailed advanced searches.** If you want the perfect candidate, search for that candidate. Put multiple keywords in the Advanced Search form, look for a big skill set, narrow your search to a specific industry, and maybe even limit your range to people who already live close to you. If you come up with zero results, remove the least necessary keyword and repeat the search. Keep doing that until you come up with potential candidates.

>> **Focus on your industry.** If you know that you're probably going to need software developers, start getting to know potential candidates on the LinkedIn site and stay in touch with them. Look for people to connect with, whether or not they share a group affiliation with you, and actively network with these people. Even if they say no to a future job opportunity, chances are good that someone in their networks will be more responsive than the average connection.

>> **Start some conversations in the Groups section.** After you've found some LinkedIn groups full of like-minded or interesting professionals, start exchanging information! Pose a question or start a group discussion that you would ask in an interview to potential candidates, and see who responds. Better yet, you'll see *how* the people respond and be able to decide from their answers whom to focus on for a follow-up. You can then review their public profiles and send them a message.

6

Business Writing

Contents at a Glance

Chapter **1**

Planning Your Message

Think for a minute about how you approached a recent writing task. If it was an email, how much time did you spend considering what to write? A few minutes? Seconds? Or did you just start typing?

Now bring a more complex document to mind: a challenging letter, proposal, report, or marketing piece. Did you put some time into shaping your message before you began writing — or did you just plunge in?

This chapter demonstrates the power of taking time before you write to consider *whom* you're writing to, *what* you truly hope to achieve, and *how* you can deploy your words to maximize success.

Adopting the Plan-Draft-Edit Principle

Prepare yourself for one of the most important pieces of advice in this minibook: Invest time in planning your messages. That means *every* message, because even an everyday communication such as an email can have a profound effect on your success. Everything you write shows people who you are.

How many times have you received an email asking for something, but the message was badly written and full of errors? Or a long, expensively produced document with an abrupt and sloppy email cover note? A poorly written email doesn't help the cause — whatever the cause is.

REMEMBER

No, you shouldn't lean back in your chair and let your mind wander into blue-sky mode before writing every email. The planning we recommend is a step-by-step process that leads to good decisions about what to say and how to say it. It's a process that will never fail you, no matter how big (or seemingly small) the writing challenge. And it's simple to adopt — in fact, you may experience surprising immediate results. You may also find that you enjoy writing much more.

This strategic approach has no relation to how you learned to write in school, unless you had an atypical teacher who was attuned to writing for results, so start by tossing any preconceived ideas about your inability to write over the side.

When you have a message or document to write, expect to spend your time this way:

>> Planning — one third

>> Drafting — one third

>> Editing — one third

In other words, give equal time, roughly speaking, to the jobs of deciding what to say (the content), preparing your first draft and finally, and fixing what you wrote.

See Chapter 2 in this minibook for no-fail writing strategies and Chapter 3 for editing tips and tricks.

Fine-Tuning Your Plan: Your Goals and Audience

A well-crafted message is based on two key aspects: your goal and your audience. The following section shows you how to get to know both intimately.

Defining your goal: Know what you want

Your first priority is to know exactly what you want to happen when the person you're writing to reads what you've written. Determining this is far less obvious than it sounds.

Consider a cover letter for your resume. Seen as a formal but unimportant necessity toward your ultimate goal — to get a job — a cover letter can just say:

Dear Mr. Blank, here is my resume — Jack Slade

Intuitively you know that isn't sufficient. But analyze what you want to accomplish and you can see clearly why it falls short. Your cover letter must yield the following results:

>> Connect you with the recipient so that you're a person instead of one more set of documents

>> Make you stand out — in a good way

>> Persuade the recipient that your resume is worth reading

>> Show that you understand the job and the company

>> Set up the person to review your qualifications with a favorable mind-set

You also need the cover letter to demonstrate your personal qualifications, especially the ability to communicate well.

If you see that your big goal depends on this set of more specific goals, it's obvious why a one-line perfunctory message can't succeed.

A cover letter for a formal business proposal has its own big goal — to help convince an individual or an institution to finance your new product. To do this, the letter's role is to connect with the prospective buyer, entice him to actually read at least part of the document, predispose him to like what he sees, present your company as better than the competition, and show off good communication skills.

How about the proposal itself? If you break down this goal into a more specific subset, you realize the proposal must demonstrate the following:

>> The financial viability of what you plan to produce

>> A minimal investment risk and high profit potential

>> Your own excellent qualifications and track record

>> Outstanding backup by an experienced team

>> Special expertise in the field

>> In-depth knowledge of the marketplace, competition, business environment, and so on

Spelling out your goals is extremely useful because the process keeps you aligned with the big picture while giving you instant guidelines for content that succeeds. Because of good planning on the front end, you're already moving toward *how* to accomplish what you want.

To reap the benefit of goal definition, you must take time to look past the surface. Write every message — no exceptions — with a clear set of goals. If you don't know your goals, don't write at all.

Invariably one of your goals is to present yourself in writing as professional, competent, knowledgeable, empathetic, and so on. Create a list of the personal and professional qualities you want other people to perceive in you. Then every time you write, remember to be that person. Ask yourself how that individual handles the tough stuff. Your answers may amaze you. This technique isn't mystical; it's just a way of accessing your own knowledge base and intuition. You may be able to channel this winning persona into your in-person experiences, too.

Defining your audience: Know your reader

You've no doubt noticed that people are genuinely different in countless ways — what they value, their motivations, how they like to spend their time, their attitude toward work and success, how they communicate, and much more. One ramification of these variables is that they read and react to your messages in different and sometimes unexpected ways.

As part of your planning, you need to anticipate people's responses to both your content and writing style. The key to successfully predicting your reader's response is to address everything you write to someone specific, rather than an anonymous, faceless anyone.

When you meet someone in person and want to persuade her to your viewpoint, you automatically adapt to her reactions as you go along. You respond to a host of clues. Beyond interruptions, comments, and questions, you also perceive facial expression, body language, tone of voice, nervous mannerisms, and many other indicators. (Check out *Body Language For Dummies,* 3rd Edition by Elizabeth Kuhnke to sharpen your ability to read people.)

Obviously a written message lacks all in-person clues. So for yours to succeed, you must play both roles — the reader's and your own. Doing this isn't as hard as it may sound.

GENERATION GAPS: UNDERSTANDING AND LEVERAGING THEM

In business today, understanding young people is important to older ones, and vice versa. If you're a member of Generation X or Generation Y, understanding Baby Boomers is especially useful because they still constitute more than 70 percent of business owners and probably a similar percentage of all top jobs.

You may quibble about the following descriptions — especially of your own cohort — but the generalizations are still illuminating. Supplement these ideas with your own observations and you discover ways to make higher-ups happy without necessarily compromising your own values:

- **Baby Boomers** (born 1946 to 1964) are highly competitive and define themselves by achievement. Many are workaholics. They respect authority, loyalty, position, and patience with the hierarchy and slow upward progress. They would like today's young people to advance the same way they did: earning rewards gradually over time. They are good with confrontation and prefer a lot of face-to-face time, so hold meetings often. They resent younger people's perceived lack of respect, low commitment level, expectations of fast progress, and arrogance about their own superior technology skills. And careless writing! Well-planned and proofed messages score high points with Boomers, and they are more likely to prefer long, detailed accounts. They like phone calls but resent telephone run-arounds and response delays.

- **Generation X'ers** (born 1965 to 1980) are literally caught in the middle. They are often middle managers and may constantly translate between those they report to and those who report to them. They are hard working, individualistic, committed to change, and technologically capable, but lack the full enthusiasm toward technological solutions of Gen Y. They value independence and resourcefulness (having been the first latchkey children) and like opportunities to develop new skills and receive feedback. Their preferred communication mode is generally email, the short efficient kind. They'd rather skip the meetings.

- **Generation Y members** (born after 1980) expect their technical skills and input to be recognized and rewarded quickly. They are highly social and collaborative, preferring to work in teams, and like staying in touch with what everyone is doing. They want to be given responsibility but also like structure and mentoring. They don't see the point of long-term commitment and expect to spend their careers job-hopping. Generation Y'ers prefer to interact through texting, instant messaging, and social media, and will use email as necessary, rather than in-person or telephone contact. A subgroup, the Millennials (born 1991 or later), are even more technocentric in their communication preferences.

Unless you're sending a trivial message, begin by creating a profile of the person you're writing to. If you know the person, begin with the usual suspects, the demographics. Start by determining the following:

>> How old? (Generational differences can be huge! See the sidebar "Generation gaps: Understanding and leveraging them.")

>> Male or female?

>> Engaged in what occupation?

>> Married, family, or some other arrangement?

>> Member of an ethnic or religious group?

>> Educated to what degree?

>> Social and economic position?

After demographics, you have *psychographic* considerations, the kind of factors marketing specialists spend a lot of time studying. Marketers are interested in creating customer profiles to understand and manipulate consumer buying. For your purposes, some psychographic factors that can matter follow:

>> Lifestyle

>> Values and beliefs

>> Opinions and attitudes

>> Interests

>> Leisure and volunteer activities

You also need to consider factors that reflect someone's positioning, personality, and in truth, entire life history and outlook on the world. Some factors that may directly affect how a person perceives your message include the following:

>> Professional background and experience

>> Position in the organization: What level? Moving up or down? Respected? How ambitious?

>> Degree of authority

>> Leadership style: Team-based? Dictatorial? Collaborative? Indiscernible?

>> Preferred communication style: In-person? Short or long written messages? Telephone? Texting? PowerPoint?

>> Approach to decision-making: Collaborative or top-down? Spontaneous or deliberative? Risk-taker or play-it-safer?

- » Information preferences: Broad vision? Detailed? Statistics and numbers? Charts and graphs?

- » Work priorities and pressures

- » Sensitivities and hot buttons

- » Interaction style and preferences: A people person or a systems and technology person?

- » Type of thinking: Logical or intuitive? Statistics-based or ideas-based? Big picture or micro oriented? Looking for long-range or immediate results?

- » Weaknesses, perceived by the person or not: Lack of technological savvy? People skills? Education?

- » Type of people the person likes — and dislikes

TIP

Do you know, or can you figure out, what your reader worries about? What keeps him up at night? What is his biggest problem? When you know a person's deepest concerns, you can effectively leverage this information to create messages that he finds highly compelling.

And of course, your precise relationship to the person matters — your relative positioning; the degree of mutual liking, respect and trust; the *simpatico* factor.

No doubt you're wondering how you can possibly take so much into consideration, or why you want to. The good news is, when your message is truly simple, you usually don't. More good news: Even when your goal is complex or important, only some factors matter. We're giving you a lengthy list to draw on because every situation brings different characteristics into play. Thinking through which ones count in your specific situation is crucial.

For example, say you want authorization to buy a new computer. Perhaps your boss is a technology freak who reacts best to equipment requests when they have detailed productivity data — in writing. Or you may report to someone who values relationships, good office vibes, and in-person negotiation. Whatever the specifics, you need to frame the same story differently. Don't manipulate the facts — both stories must be true and fair.

REMEMBER

You succeed when you take the time to look at things through the other person's eyes rather than solely your own. Doing so doesn't compromise your principles. It shows that you're sensible and sensitive to the differences between people and helps your relationships. It shows you how to frame what you're asking for. See the section "Framing messages with *you*, not *I*" later in this chapter for more on these techniques.

Brainstorming the best content for your purpose

Perhaps defining your goal and audience so thoroughly sounds like unnecessary busywork. But doing so helps immeasurably when you're approaching someone with an idea, a product, or a service that you need her to buy into.

Suppose your department is planning to launch a major project that you want to lead. You could write a memo explaining how important the opportunity is to you, how much you can use the extra money, or how much you'll appreciate being chosen for the new role. But unless your boss, Jane, is a totally selfless person without ambition or priorities of her own, why would she care about any of that?

You're much better off highlighting your relevant skills and accomplishments. Your competitors for the leadership position may equal or even better such a rundown, so you must make your best case. Think beyond yourself to what Jane herself most values.

A quick profile (see the preceding section) of Jane reveals a few characteristics to work with:

>> She likes to see good teamwork in people reporting to her.

>> She's a workaholic who is usually overcommitted.

>> She likes to launch projects and then basically forget about them until results are due.

>> She's ambitious and always angling for her next step up.

Considering what you know about Jane, the content of your message can correspond to these traits by including the following:

>> Your good record as both a team player and team leader

>> Your dedication to the new project and willingness to work over and beyond normal hours to do it right

>> Your ability to work independently and use good judgment with minimal supervision

>> Your enthusiasm for this particular project, which, if successful, will be highly valued by the department and company

Again, all your claims must be true, and you need to provide evidence that they are: a reminder of another project you successfully directed, for example, and handled independently.

Your reader profile can tell you still more. If you wonder how long your memo needs to be, for example, consider Jane's communication preferences. If she prefers brief memos followed by face-to-face decision-making, keep your memo brief but still cover all the points to ensure that you secure that all-important meeting. However, if she reacts best to written detail, give her more info up front.

REMEMBER

Reader profiling offers you the chance to create a blueprint for the content of all your messages and documents. After you've defined what you want and analyzed your audience in relation to the request, brainstorm the points that may help you win your case with that person. Your brainstorming gives you a list of possibilities to review. Winnowing out the most convincing points is easy — and organizing can involve simple prioritizing, as you see in Chapter 2 of this minibook.

TIP

Thinking through how to profile your reader works the same way if you're writing a major proposal, business plan, report, funding request, client letter, marketing piece, PowerPoint presentation, or networking message. Know your goal. Figure out what your audience cares about. Then think widely within that perspective.

Writing to groups and strangers

Profiling one person is easy enough, but you often write to groups rather than individuals as well as to people you haven't met and know nothing about. The same ideas discussed in the preceding section apply with groups and strangers, but they demand a little more imagination on your part.

TIP

Here's a good tactic for messages addressed to groups: Visualize a single individual — or a few key individuals — who epitomize that group. The financier Warren Buffet explained that when writing to stockholders he imagines he's writing to his two sisters: intelligent but not knowledgeable about finance. He consciously aims to be understood by them. The results are admirably clear financial messages that are well received and influential.

Like Buffet, you may be able to think of a particular person to represent a larger group. If you've invented a new item of ski equipment, for example, think about a skier you know who'd be interested in your product and profile that person. Or create a composite profile of several such people, drawing on what they have in common plus variations. If you're a business strategy consultant, think of your best clients and use what you know about them to profile your prospects.

Imagining your readers

Even when an audience is new to you, you can still make good generalizations about what these people are like — or, even better, their concerns. Suppose you're a dentist who's taking over a practice and you're writing to introduce yourself to your predecessor's patients. Your basic goal is to maintain that clientele. You needn't know the people to anticipate many of their probable concerns. You can assume, for example, that your news will be unwelcome because long-standing patients probably liked the old dentist and dislike change and inconvenience, just like you probably would yourself.

You can go further. Anticipate your readers' questions. Just put yourself in their shoes. You may wonder

>> Why should I trust you, an unknown entity?

>> Will I feel an interruption in my care? Will there be a learning curve?

>> Will I like you and find in you what I value in a medical practitioner — aspects such as kindness, respect for my time, attentiveness, and experience?

TIP

Plan your content to answer these intrinsic questions and you can't go wrong. Note that nearly all the questions are emotional rather than factual. Few patients are likely to ask about a new doctor's training and specific knowledge. They're more concerned with the kind of person he is and how they'll be treated. This somewhat counterintuitive truth applies to many situations. The questions are essentially the same for an accountant or any other service provider.

When writing, you may need to build a somewhat indirect response to some of the questions you anticipate from readers. Writing something like "I'm a really nice person" to prospective dental patients is unlikely to convince them, but you can comfortably include any or all of the following statements in your letter:

I will carefully review all your records so I am personally knowledgeable about your history.

My staff and I pledge to keep your waiting time to a minimum. We use all the latest techniques to make your visits comfortable and pain-free.

I look forward to meeting you in person and getting to know you.

I'm part of your community and participate in its good causes such as . . .

REMEMBER

Apply this strategy to job applications, business proposals, online media, and other important materials. Ask yourself, whom do I want to reach? Is the person a human resources executive? A CEO? A prospective customer for my product or service? Then jot down a profile covering what that person is probably like as well as her concerns and questions. Everyone has a problem to solve. What's your reader's problem? The HR person must fill open jobs in ways that satisfy other people. The CEO can be counted on to have one eye on the bottom line and the other on the big picture — that's her role. If you're pitching a product, you can base a prospective customer profile on the person for whom you're producing that product.

TIP

If you're an entrepreneur, building a detailed portrait of your ultimate buyers is especially important to your success. The more you know about your prospects, the better you can deliver what they need.

Making People Care

Sending your words out into today's message-dense world is not unlike tossing your message into the sea in a bottle. However, your message is now among a trillion bottles, all of which are trying to reach the same moving and dodging targets. So your competitive edge is in shaping a better bottle — or, rather, message.

Any message you send must be well crafted and well aimed, regardless of the medium or format. The challenge is to make people care enough to read your message and act on it in some way. The following sections explore the tools you need to ensure your bottle reaches its target and has the effect you desire.

Connecting instantly with your reader

Only in rare cases these days do you have the luxury of building up to a grand conclusion, one step at a time. Your audience simply won't stick around.

REMEMBER

The opening paragraph of anything you write must instantly hook your readers. The best way to do this is to link directly to their central interests and concerns, within the framework of your purpose.

Say you're informing the staff that the office will be closed on Tuesday to install new air-conditioning. You can write:

> *Subject: About next Tuesday*
>
> *Dear Staff:*
>
> *As you know, the company is always interested in your comfort and well being. As part of our company improvement plan this past year, we've installed improved lighting in the hallways, and in response to your request that we . . .*

Stop! No one is reading this! Instead, try this:

> *Subject: Office closed Tuesday*
>
> *We're installing new air-conditioning! Tuesday is the day, so we're giving you a holiday.*
>
> *I'm happy the company is able to respond to your number 1 request on the staff survey and hope you are too.*

One of the best ways to hook readers is also the simplest: Get to the point. The technique applies even to long documents. Start with the bottom line, such as the result you achieved, the strategy you recommend, or the action you want. In a report or proposal, the executive summary is often the way to do that, but note that even this micro version of your full message still needs to lead off with your most important point.

Note in the preceding example that the subject line of the email is part of the lead and is planned to hook readers as much as the first paragraph of the message. Chapter 5 in this minibook has more ideas of ways to optimize your emails.

Focusing on WIIFM

The marketing acronym *WIIFM* stands for *what's in it for me*. The air-conditioning email in the preceding section first captures readers by telling them that they have a day off and then follows up by saying that they're getting something they wanted. Figuring out what's going to engage *your* readers often takes a bit of thought.

To make people care, you must first be able to answer the question yourself. Why *should* they care? Then put your answer right in the lead or even the headline.

If you're selling a product or service, for example, zero in on the problem it solves. So rather than your press release headline saying

> *New Widget Model to Debut at Expo Magnus on Thursday*

Try

> *Widget 175F Day-to-Night Video Recorder Ends Pilfering Instantly*

If you're raising money for a non-profit, you may be tempted to write a letter to previous donors that begins like many you probably receive:

> *For 75 years, Little White Lights has been helping children with learning disabilities improve their capacities, live up to their potential, and feel more confident about their educational future.*

But don't you respond better to letters that open more like this?

> *For his first five years of school, Lenny hated every second. He couldn't follow the lessons, so he stopped trying and even stopped listening. But this September Lenny starts college — because the caring people and non-traditional teaching at Little White Lights showed him how to learn. He's one of 374 children whose lives we transformed since our not-for-profit organization was established, with your help, nine years ago.*

The second version works better not just because it's more concrete but also because it takes account of two factors that all recipients probably share: a concern for children, and a need to be reassured that their donations are well used.

Highlighting benefits, not features

People care about what a product or service can do for them, not what it is.

>> *Features* describe characteristics — a car having a 200 mph engine; an energy drink containing 500 units of caffeine; a hotel room furnished with priceless antiques.

>> *Benefits* are what features give us — the feeling that you can be the fastest animal on earth (given an open highway without radar traps); the ability to stay up for 56 hours to make up all the work you neglected; the experience of high luxury for the price of a hotel room, at least briefly.

Benefits have more to do with feelings and experiences than data. Marketers have known the power of benefits for a long time, but neuroscientists have recently confirmed the principle, noting that most buying decisions are made emotionally rather than logically. You choose a car that speaks to your personality instead of the one with the best technical specs, and then you try to justify your decision on rational grounds.

The lesson for business writing is clear: People care about messages that are based on what matters to them. Don't get lost in technical detail. Focus on the effect of an event, an idea, or a product. You can cover the specs but keep them contained in a separate section or as backup material. Approach information the way most newspapers have always done (and now do online as well). Put what's most interesting or compelling up front and then include the details in the back (or link to them) for readers who want more.

Finding the concrete and limiting the abstract

The Little White Lights example in a previous section demonstrates how to effectively focus on a single individual and simultaneously deliver a powerful, far-reaching message. One concrete example is almost always more effective than reams of high-flown prose and empty adjectives.

Make things real for your readers with these techniques:

» **Tell stories and anecdotes.** They must embody the idea you want to communicate, the nature of your organization, or your own value. An early television show about New York City used a slogan along the lines, "Eight million people, eight million stories." A good story is always there, lurking, even in what may seem everyday or ordinary. But finding it can take some thinking and active looking.

» **Use examples — and make them specific.** Tell customers how your product was used or how your service helped solve a problem. Give them strong case studies of implementations that worked. Inside a company, tell change-resistant staff members how another department saved three hours by using the new ordering process, or how a shift in benefits can cut their out-of-pocket health-care costs by 14 percent. And if you want people to use a new system, give them clear guidelines, perhaps a step-by-step process to follow.

» **Use visuals to explain and break up the words.** Readers who need to be captured and engaged generally shy away from uninterrupted type. Plenty of studies show that people remember visual lessons better, too. Look for ways to graphically present a trend, a change, a plan, a concept, or an example. In a way that suits your purpose and medium, incorporate photographs, illustrations, charts, graphs, and video. When you must deliver your message primarily in words, use graphic techniques such as headlines, subheads, bullets, typeface variations, and icons — like those in this minibook!

» **Give readers a vision.** Good leaders know that a vision is essential, whether they're running companies or running for public office. You're usually best off framing your message in big-picture terms that make people believe the future will be better in some way. Don't make empty promises; instead, look for the broadest implications of an important communication and use details to back up that central concept and make it more real. Focusing a complicated document this way also makes it more organized and more memorable — both big advantages.

» **Eliminate meaningless hyperbole.** What's the point of saying something like, "This is the most far-reaching, innovative, ground-breaking piece of industrial design ever conceived"? Yet business writing is jam-packed with empty, boring claims.

WARNING

Today's audiences come to everything you write already jaded, skeptical, and impatient. If you're a service provider and describe what you do in words that can belong to anyone, in any profession, you fail. If you depend on a website and it takes viewers 20 seconds to figure out what you're selling or how to make a pur-chase, you lose. If you're sending out a press release that buries what's interesting or important, you're invisible. The solution: Know your point and make it fast!

TIP

Go for the evidence! Tell your audience in real terms what your idea, plan, or product accomplishes in ways they care about. Show them how

>> The product improves people's lives.

>> The non-profit knows its money is helping people.

>> The service solves problems.

>> You personally helped your employer make more money or become more efficient.

Proof comes in many forms: statistics, data, images, testimonials, surveys, case histories, biographies, and video and audio clips. Figure out how to track your success and prove it. You end up with first-rate material to use in all your communication.

Choosing Your Written Voice: Tone

Presentation trainers often state that the meaning of a spoken message is communicated 55 percent by body language, 38 percent by tone of voice, and only 7 percent by the words. Actually, this formula has been thoroughly debunked and denied by its creator — the psychologist Albert Mehrabian — but it does imply some important points for writing.

WARNING

Written messages come without body language or tone of voice. One result is that humor — particularly sarcasm or irony — is risky. When readers can't see the wink in your eye or hear the playfulness in your voice, they take you literally. So refrain from subtle humor unless you're really secure with your reader's ability to get it. Better yet: Be cautious at all times because such assumptions are dangerous.

But even lacking facial expression and gesture, writing does carry its own tone, and this directly affects how readers receive and respond to messages. Written tone results from a combination of word choice, sentence structure, and other technical factors.

Also important are less tangible elements that are hard to pin down. You've probably received messages that led you to sense the writer was upset, angry, resistant, or amused — even if only a few words were involved. Sometimes even a close reading of the text doesn't explain what's carrying these emotions, but you just sense the writer's strong feelings.

REMEMBER

When you're the writer, be conscious of your message's tone. Consistently control tone so it supports your goals and avoids undermining your message. You've probably found that showing emotion in the workplace rarely gives you an advantage. Writing is similar. Tone conveys feelings, and if you're not in control of your emotions when you write, tone betrays you.

The following sections explore some ways to find and adopt the right tone.

Being appropriate to the occasion, relationship, and culture

Pause before writing and think about the moment you're writing in. Obviously if you're communicating bad news, you don't want to sound chipper and cheery.

Always think of your larger audience, too. If the company made more money last month because it eliminated a department, best not to treat the new profits as a triumph. Current staff members probably aren't happy about losing colleagues and are worried about their own jobs. On the other hand, if you're communicating about a staff holiday party, sounding gloomy and bored doesn't generate high hopes for a good time. The same is true if you're offering an opportunity or assigning a nuisance job: Make it as enticing as possible.

REMEMBER

Just as in face-to-face situations, the moods embedded in your writing are contagious. If you want an enthusiastic response, write with enthusiasm. If you want people to welcome a change you're announcing, sound positive and confident, not fearful or peevish and resentful — even if you don't personally agree with the change.

TIP

Make conscious decisions about how formal to sound. After you work in an organization for a while, you typically absorb its culture without noticing. (In fact, most organizations don't realize that they have a culture until they run into problems when introducing change or a high-level hire.) If you're new to the place, observe how things work so you can avoid booby-trapping yourself. Read through files of correspondence, emails, reports, as well as websites and online material. Analyze what your colleagues feel is appropriate in content and in writing style. How formal is the communication for the various media used? Adopt the guidelines you see enacted.

WARNING

Every passing year seems to decrease the formality of business communication. Just as in choosing what to wear to work, people are dressing down their writing. This less formal style can come across as friendlier, simpler, and more direct than in earlier years — and should. But business informal doesn't mean you should address an executive or board member casually, use texting or abbreviations your reader may not understand, or fail to edit and proofread every message. Those are gaffes much like wearing torn jeans to work or to a client meeting.

And you want to be especially careful if you're writing to someone in another country — even an English-speaking one. Most countries still prefer a formal form of communication.

Writing as your authentic self

Never try to impress anyone with how educated and literate you are. Studies show that people believe that those who write clearly and use simple words are smarter than those whose writing abounds in fancy phrases and complicated sentences.

TIP

Authentic means being a straightforward, unpretentious, honest, trustworthy person — and writer. It doesn't mean trying for a specific writing style. Clarity is always the goalpost. This aim holds true even for materials written to impress. A proposal, marketing brochure, or request for funding gains nothing by looking or sounding pompous and weighty.

Being relentlessly respectful

REMEMBER

Never underestimate or patronize your audience, regardless of educational level, position, or apparent accomplishment. People are sensitive to such attitudes and react adversely, often without knowing why or telling you. In *all* work and business situations, take the trouble to actively demonstrate respect for your reader. Specifically, do the following:

>> Address people courteously and use their names.

>> Close with courtesy and friendliness.

>> Write carefully and proofread thoroughly; many people find poorly written messages insulting.

>> Avoid acronyms, jargon, and abbreviations that may be unfamiliar to some readers.

>> Never be abrupt or rude or demanding.

>> Try to understand and respect cultural differences.

Apply these guidelines whether you're writing to a superior, a subordinate, or a peer. You don't need to be groveling to an executive higher up the chain than you are (in most cases), though often you should be more formal. Nor should you condescend to those lower down. Consider, for example, how best to assign a last-minute task to someone who reports to you. You could say the following:

> *Madge, I need you to read this book tonight and give me a complete rundown of the content first thing tomorrow. Thanks.*

Or:

> *Madge, I need your help — please read this book tonight. The author is coming in tomorrow to talk about engaging us. I'm reading another of his books myself and if we can compare notes first thing tomorrow, I'll feel much more prepped. Thanks!*

Either way, Madge may not be thrilled at how her evening looks, but treating her respectfully and explaining *why* you're giving her this intrusive assignment accomplishes a lot: She'll be more motivated, more enthusiastic, more interested in doing a good job, and happier to be part of your team. At the cost of writing a few more sentences, you improve her attitude and perhaps even her long-range performance.

Smiling when you say it

People whose job is answering the phone are told by customer service trainers to smile before picking up the call. Smiling physically affects your throat and vocal chords, and your tone of voice. You sound friendly and cheerful and may help the person on the other end of the phone feel that way.

The idea applies to writing as well. You need not smile before you write (though it's an interesting technique to try), but be aware of your own mood and how easily it transfers to your messages and documents.

REMEMBER

Your feelings of anger, impatience, or resentment might be well grounded, but displaying them rarely helps your cause. People dislike negative, whiny, nasty messages that put them on the defensive or make them feel under attack.

Suppose you've asked the purchasing department to buy a table for your office and were denied without explanation. You could write to both your boss and the head of purchasing a note such as the following:

> *Hal, Jeanne: I just can't believe how indifferent purchasing is to my work and what I need to do it. This ignorance is really offensive. I'm now an associate manager responsible for a three-person team and regular meetings are essential to my . . .*

Put yourself in the recipients' places to see how bad the effect of such a message can be — for you. At the least, you're creating unnecessary problems; at worst, perhaps permanent bad feelings. Why not write the following instead, and just to the purchasing officer:

Hi, Hal. Do you have a minute to talk about my request for a small conference table? I was surprised to find that it was denied and want to share why it's important to my work.

REMEMBER

The best way to control your tone is to let emotion-laden matters rest for whatever time you can manage. Even a ten-minute wait can make a difference. Overnight is better, if possible, in important situations. You're far more likely to accomplish what you want when you come across as logical, reasonable, and objective. Positive and cheerful is even better.

Sometimes the challenge isn't to control bad feelings, but to overcome a blah mood that leads your writing to sound dull and uninspired when you need it to sound persuasive and engaging. Knowing your own daily patterns is helpful, so you can focus on the task that requires the most energy when you're most naturally up.

TIP

If you don't have the luxury of waiting for a good mood to hit before writing, try the following method. Churn out the basic document regardless of your spirits. Later, when you're feeling bouncier, inject the energy and enthusiasm that you know the original message is missing. Typical changes involve switching out dull passive verbs and substituting livelier ones, picking up the tempo, editing out the dead wood, and adding plusses you overlooked when you felt gray. Chapter 2 in this minibook is chock-full of ideas to enliven your language.

People naturally prefer being around positive, dynamic, enthusiastic people, and they prefer receiving messages with the same qualities. Resolve not to complain, quibble, or criticize in writing. People are much more inclined to give you what you want when you're positive — and they see you as a problem-solver rather than a problem-generator.

Using Relationship-Building Techniques

REMEMBER

Just about everything you write is a chance to build relationships with people you report to and even other people above them in the chain, as well as peers, colleagues, customers, prospects, suppliers, and members of your industry. More and more, people succeed through good networking. In a world characterized by less face-to-face contact and more global possibilities, writing is a major tool for making connections and maintaining them.

As with tone, awareness that building relationships is always one of your goals puts you a giant step ahead. Ask yourself every time you write how you can improve the relationships with that individual. A range of techniques is available to help.

Personalizing what you write

In many countries, business emails and letters that get right down to business seem cold, abrupt, and unfeeling. Japanese writers and readers, for example, prefer to begin with the kind of polite comments you tend to make when meeting someone in person: "How have you been?" "Is your family well?" "Isn't it cold for October?" Such comments or questions may carry no real substance, but they serve an important purpose: They personalize the interaction to better set the stage for a business conversation.

TIP

Creating a sense of caring or at least interest in the other person gives you a much better context within which to transact business. If you've thought about your audience when planning what to write (see the previous section, "Defining your audience: Know your reader"), you can easily come up with simple but effective personalizing phrases to frame your message. You can always fall back on the old reliables — weather and general health inquiries. If communication continues, you can move the good feelings along by asking whether the vacation mentioned earlier worked out well, or if the weekend was good — whatever clues you can follow up on without becoming inappropriate or intrusive. The idea works with groups, too: You can, for example, begin, "I hope you all weathered the tornado okay."

Some techniques you can use to make your writing feel warm are useful but may not translate between different cultures. For example, salutations like *Hi, John* set a less formal tone than *Dear John*. Starting with just the name — *John,* — is informal to the point of assuming a relationship already exists. But both ways may not be appropriate if you're writing to someone in a more formal country than your own. A formal address — *Mr. Charles, Ms. Brown, Dr. Jones, General Frank* — may be called for. In many cultures, if you overlook this formality and other signs of respect, you can lose points before you even begin.

Similarly, it feels friendlier and less formal to use contractions: *isn't* instead of *is not, won't* instead of *will not*. But if your message is addressed to a non-native English speaker or will be translated, contractions may be confusing.

Framing messages with *you*, not *I*

Just accept it: People care more about themselves and what they want than they do about you. This simple-sounding concept has important implications for business writing.

Suppose you're a software developer and your company has come up with a dramatically better way for people to manage their online reputations. You may be tempted to announce the following on your website:

We've created a great new product for online reputation management that no one ever imagined possible.

Or you could say this:

Our great new Product X helps people manage their online reputation better than ever before.

The second example is better because it's less abstract and it makes the product's purpose clear. But see if you find this version more powerful:

You want a better way to solve your online reputation management challenges? We have what you need.

TIP

When you look for ways to use the word *you* more, and correspondingly decrease the use of *I* and *we*, you put yourself on the reader's wavelength. In the case of the new software, your readers care about how the product can help them, not that you're proud of achieving it.

The principle works for everyday email, letters, and online communication too. For example, when you receive a customer complaint, instead of writing the following:

We have received your complaint about . . .

You're better off writing this:

Your letter explaining your complaint has been received . . .

Or:

Thank you for writing to us about your recent problem with . . .

Coming up with a *you* frame is often challenging. Doing so may draw you into convoluted or passive-sounding language — for example, "Your unusual experience with our tree-pruning service has come to our attention." Ordinarily we recommend a direct statement (such as, "We hear you've had an unusual experience with . . ."), but in customer service situations and others where you want to relate to your reader instantly, figuring out a way to start with *you* can be worth the effort and a brief dip into the passive. (See Chapters 2, 3, and 4 in this minibook for ways to expand your resource of techniques for fine-tuning your tone through word choice, sentence structure, and customized content.)

REMEMBER

In every situation, genuinely consider your reader's viewpoint, sensitivities, and needs. Think about how the message you're communicating affects that person or group. Anticipate questions and build in the answers. Write within this framework and you will guide yourself to create successful messages and documents. When you care, it shows. And you succeed.

Chapter **2**

Making Your Writing Work

Your writing style probably took shape in school, where literary traditions and formal essays dominate. This experience may have led you to believe that subtle thoughts require complex sentences, sophisticated vocabulary, and dense presentation. Perhaps you learned to write that way — or maybe you didn't. Either way: The rules of academic writing don't apply to the business world.

Real-world business writing is more natural, reader-friendly, and easier to do than academic writing — especially after you know the basics covered in this chapter.

Stepping into a Twenty-First-Century Writing Style

REMEMBER

In business you succeed when you achieve your goals. You need to judge business writing the same way — by whether it accomplishes what you want. The following characteristics of business writing work:

>> **Clear and simple:** Except for technical material directed at specialists, no subject matter or idea is so complex that you cannot express it in clear, simple language.

You automatically move forward a step by accepting this basic premise and practicing it.

>> **Conversational:** Business writing is reader-friendly and accessible, far closer to spoken language than the more formal and traditional style. It may even come across as casual or spontaneous. This quality, however, doesn't give you a free pass on grammar, punctuation, and the other technicalities.

>> **Correct:** Noticeable mistakes interfere with your reader's ability to understand you. Further, in today's competitive world, careless writing deducts points you can't afford to lose. People judge you by every piece of writing you create, and you need to live up to your best self. However, good contemporary writing allows substantial leeway in observing grammatical niceties.

>> **Persuasive:** When you dig beneath the surface, most messages and documents ask something of the reader. This request may be minor ("Meet me at Restaurant X at 4") to major ("Please fund this proposal; a million will do."). Even when you're just asking for or providing information, frame your message to suit your reader's viewpoint. Writing for your audience is covered in depth in Chapter 1 of this minibook.

All these indicators of successful business communication come into play in everything you write. The following sections break down the various components of style into separate bits you can examine and adjust in your own writing.

Aiming for a clear, simple style

Clarity and simplicity go hand in hand: Your messages communicate what you intend with no room for misunderstanding or misinterpretation. This requires the following:

>> Words your reader already knows and whose meanings are agreed upon — no forcing readers to look up words, no trying to impress

>> Sentence structure that readers can easily follow the first time through

>> Well-organized, logical, on-point content without anything unnecessary or distracting

>> Clear connections between sentences, paragraphs, and ultimately ideas, to make a cohesive statement

>> Correct spelling and correct grammar

REMEMBER

Writing with the preceding characteristics is transparent: Nothing stands in the way of the reader absorbing your information, ideas, and recommendations. Good business writing for most purposes doesn't call attention to itself. It's like a good makeup job. A woman doesn't want to hear, "Great cosmetology!" She hopes for "You look beautiful." Similarly, you want your audience to admire your thinking, not the way you phrased it.

TIP

One result of following these criteria is that people can move through your material quickly. This is good! A fast read is your best shot at pulling people into your message and keeping them from straying off due to boredom. These days, people are so overwhelmed and impatient that they don't bother to invest time in deciphering a message's meaning. They just stop reading.

Creating an easy reading experience is hard on the writer. When you write well, you do all the readers' work for them. They don't need to figure out anything because you've already done it for them. Make the effort because that's how you win what you want.

Applying readability guidelines

Guidelines for business writing are not theoretical. They're practical and supported by research studies on how people respond to the written word. Fortunately, you don't have to read the research. Most word-processing software, including Microsoft Word, and several websites have digested all the data and offer easy-to-use tools to help you quickly gauge the readability of your writing.

Several readability indexes exist (see the sidebar "Readability research: What it tells us"). In this section, we focus on the Flesch Readability Index because it's the index that Microsoft Word uses. The Flesch Readability Index predicts the percentage of people likely to understand a piece of writing and assigns it a grade level of reading comprehension. The grade level scores are based on average reading ability of students in the US public school system. The algorithm for the Flesch Readability Index is primarily based on the length of words, sentences, and paragraphs.

TIP

Word's version of the Index also shows you the percentage of passive sentences in a selection, which is a good indicator of flabby verbs, indirect sentence structure, and cut-worthy phrases. See the section "Finding action verbs," later in this chapter, for more on activating sentences that contain passive verbs.

Matching reading level to audience

Whatever readability index you use, your target numbers depend on the audience you're writing to (one more reason to know your readers).

Highly educated readers can obviously comprehend difficult material, which may lead you to strive for text written at a high educational level for scientists or MBAs. But generally this isn't necessarily a good idea. For most business communication — email, letters, proposals, websites — most readers (yourself included) are lazy and prefer easy material.

At the same time, usually you don't want to gear your use of language to the least literate members of your audience. So take any calculations with many grains of salt and adapt them to your audience and purpose. (The average reader in the US is pegged at a 7th- to 9th-grade reading level, depending on which study you look at.)

When you want to reach a diverse group with a message, you can segment your audience, just like marketers, and craft different versions for each. If a company needs to inform employees of a benefits change, for example, it may need different communications for top managers, middle managers, clerical staff, factory workers, and so on. Beyond assuming varying reading comprehension levels, you may need to rethink the content for each as well.

Assessing readability level

If you're writing in Microsoft Word 2016, to find the Readability Index choose File ⇨ Options ⇨ Proofing. (In Office 365, go to Word ⇨ Preferences ⇨ Spelling & Grammar.) In the When Correcting Spelling and Grammar in Word section, select the Check Grammar with Spelling and Show Readability Statistics options. Thereafter, whenever you complete a spelling and grammar check, you see a box with readability scores.

Several readability tests are available free online, including www.readability-score.com. On most sites, you simply paste a chunk of your text into a box and have the site gauge readability.

Example *print media* targets for general audiences follow:

>> Flesch reading ease: 50 to 70 percent

>> Grade level: 10th to 12th grade

>> Percentage of passive sentences: 0 to 10 percent

>> Words per sentence: 14 to 18, average (some can consist of one word, while others a great many more)

>> Sentences per paragraph: Average three to five

READABILITY RESEARCH: WHAT IT TELLS US

Serious studies to figure out what produces easy reading began in the early twentieth century and continue to be done in many languages in addition to English. The most influential researchers have been Rudolph Flesch — for which the Flesch Readability Index is named — and Robert Gunning, who more picturesquely called his measurement system the Fog Index. Both worked with American journalists and newspaper publishers in the late 1940s to lower the reading grade level of newspapers. And sure enough, newspaper readership went up 45 percent.

Recent grade-level ratings of what we read are illuminating. Overall, the simpler and clearer the language, the higher the readership. A few examples of necessary grade levels follow:

- Most romance novels: 7
- Popular authors, including Stephen King, Tom Clancy, and John Grisham: 7
- The UK's *Sun* and *Daily Mirror:* 9
- *The Wall Street Journal:* 11
- *Sydney Sun-Herald:* 12
- *London Times:* 12
- *The Guardian:* 14
- *Times of India:* 15
- Academic papers: 15 to 20
- Typical government documents: Over 20

A recent British university study applied readability criteria to online newspapers and the results mirror print studies: *The Sun* was easiest to read and *The Guardian* the most difficult.

For online media, the targets are tighter. Reading from a screen — even a big one — is physically harder for people, so they are even less patient than with printed material. Sentences work best when they average 8 to 12 words. Paragraphs should contain one to three sentences.

Select a section or an entire document of something you wrote recently in Word or for a website. Review the Readability Statistics to find out if you need to simplify your writing. If the statistics say that at least a 12th-grade reading level is required (on many Word programs, the index doesn't show levels above 12) and less than 50 percent of readers will understand your document, consider rewriting. Or do the same if you used more than 10 percent passive sentences.

The next section provides lots of suggestions for rewriting, but for now consider any or all of the following:

>> Substitute short, one or two syllable words for any long ones.

>> Shorten long sentences by breaking them up or tightening your wording.

>> Break paragraphs into smaller chunks so that you have fewer sentences in each.

>> Look for words that are a form of the verbs *have* or *to be* (*is, are, will be,* and so on). These verbs are weak and often result in passive verb construction.

>> Review the rewrite to make sure that your message still means what you intended and hasn't become even harder to understand.

Then recheck the statistics. If the figures are still high, repeat the process. See if you can get the grade level down to 10, then 8. Try for less than 10 percent passive. Compare the different versions.

Finding the right rhythm

You may wonder whether basing your writing on short simple sentences produces choppy and boring material reminiscent of a grade school textbook. Aiming for clear and simple definitely should not mean dull reading.

Becoming aware of rhythm in what you read, and what you write, can improve your writing dramatically. Like all language, English was used to communicate orally long before writing was invented, so the sound and rhythm patterns are critical to how written forms as well as spoken ones are received.

Think of the worst public speakers you know. They probably speak in a series of long, complex sentences in an even tone that quickly numbs the ear. Good speakers, by contrast, vary the length of sentences and their intonation. As a writer, you want to do the same.

REMEMBER

In everything you write, aim to build in a natural cadence. Rhythm is one of the main tools for cajoling people to stay with you and find what you write more interesting. Just begin each sentence differently from the previous one and try alternating short, plain sentences with longer ones that have two or three clauses.

Good public speakers vary the lengths of their sentences to keep listeners' ears engaged. They avoid long, complex sentences, and they know that short punchy words and phrases need to be doled out carefully for maximum effect. As a writer, you want readers to have a similar experience.

Fixing the short and choppy

Even a short message benefits from attention to sentence rhythm. Consider this paragraph:

> *John: Our screw supply is low. It takes three weeks for orders to be filled. We should place the order now. Then we won't have an emergency situation later. Please sign this form to authorize this purchase. Thank you. — Ted*

And an alternate version:

> *John: Our screw supply is low. It takes three weeks for orders to be filled, so we should place the order now to avoid an emergency later. Please sign the attached form to authorize the purchase. Thanks. — Ted*

REMEMBER

For long documents, varying your sentence length and structure is critical. Few people will stay with multiple pages of stilted, mind-numbing prose.

Notice too that when you combine some short sentences to alternate the rhythm, easy ways emerge to improve the wording and edit out unneeded repetition. You may choose to go a step further and write a third version of the same message:

> *John: I notice that our screw supply is getting low. Since an order will take three weeks to reach us, let's take care of it now to avoid an emergency down the line. Just sign the attached authorization and we're all set. — Ted*

Leaving aside how this was edited, which is discussed in the next chapter, notice how much more connected the thoughts seem, and how much more authoritative the overall message feels. With little rewriting, the writer comes across as a more take-charge, efficient professional — someone who is reliable and cares about the entire operation, rather than just a cog going through the motions.

Fixing the long and complicated

Many people have a problem opposite to creating short, disconnected sentences. Maybe you tend to write lengthy complicated ones that end up with the same result: dead writing.

TIP

The solution to never-ending strings of words is the same — alternate sentence structures. But in this case, break up the long ones. Doing this produces punchier, more enticing copy.

A number of basically good writers don't succeed as well as they might because they fall into a pattern that repeats the same rhythm, over and over again. An example taken from an opinion piece written for a workshop:

> *I strongly support efforts to improve the global economy, and naturally may be biased toward the author's position. While this bias may be the reason I responded well to the piece in the first place, it is not the reason why I consider it an exceptional piece of writing. Not only is this article extremely well researched, its use of cost-benefit analysis is an effective way to think about the challenges.*

The monotonous pattern and unending sentences serve the ideas poorly. One way to rewrite the material:

> *I strongly support efforts to improve the global economy and this probably inclined me to a positive response. But it's not why I see it as an exceptional piece of writing. The article is extremely well researched. Further, its cost-benefit analysis is an effective way to think about the challenge.*

Again, simply varying the sentence length and structure quickly improves the overall wording and flow. Notice that you can take liberties with the recommended short-long-short sentence pattern and use two short sentences, then two more complex ones, for example.

Spend ten minutes with a recent piece of your writing that's at least half a page long. Scan it for rhythmic patterns. You may find a balanced flow with varying types of sentences. Or you may see sets of short, choppy sentences. Experiment with recombining some of them into longer ones. If you find too many long, convoluted sentences, break some of them up so short, terse ones are interspersed. Read the reworked text in its entirety and see whether it reads better.

REMEMBER

Everyone has particular ways of writing that leave room for improvement. Strive to recognize your own weaknesses and you'll be a giant step closer to better writing because you can apply fix-it techniques as part of your regular self-editing process. You can draw on a bunch of methods in Chapter 3 of this minibook.

Achieving a conversational tone

New business writers are often told to adopt a conversational tone, but what does that mean? Business correspondence written during the nineteenth century and even most of the twentieth seems slow, formal, and ponderous when you read it now. Today's faster pace of life results in a desire for faster communication, both in terms of how you deliver messages and how quickly you're able to read and deal with them.

REMEMBER

Conversational tone is something of an illusion. You don't really write the way you talk, and you shouldn't. But you can echo natural speech in various ways to more effectively engage your audience.

Rhythm, described in the preceding section, is a basic technique that gives your copy forward momentum and promotes a conversational feeling. Sentence variety engages readers while unrelieved choppy sentences or complicated ones kill interest.

Additional techniques for achieving conversational tone include the following:

>> **Infuse messages with warmth.** If you think of the person as an individual before you write, content that's appropriate to the relationship and subject will come to you, and the tone will be right.

>> **Choose short, simple words.** Rely on the versions you use to *talk* to someone, rather than the sophisticated ones you use to try and impress. See the later section "Choosing reader-friendly words" for examples.

>> **Use contractions as you do in speech.** For example, go with *can't* rather than *cannot,* and *I'm* rather than *I am.*

>> **Minimize the use of Inactive and passive forms.** Carefully evaluate every use of the *to be* verbs — *is, was, will be, are,* and so on — to determine if you can use active, interesting verbs instead.

>> **Take selective liberties with grammatical correctness.** Starting a sentence with *and* or *but* is okay, for example, but avoid mismatching your nouns and pronouns.

>> **Adopt an interactive spirit.** As online media teaches, one-way, top-down communication is so yesterday. Find ways in all your writing to invite active interest and input from your reader.

If you ignore the preceding guidelines — and want to look hopelessly outdated — you can write a long-winded and lifeless message like the following:

Dear Elaine:

I regret to communicate that the meeting for which we are scheduled on Tuesday at 2 p.m. must be canceled. Unfortunately the accounting information anticipated for receipt on Friday will not be able to meet the delivery deadline.

I am contemplating an appropriate rescheduling. Please inform my office of your potential availability at 3 p.m. on the 2nd. — Carrie

Yawn — and also a bit confusing. Or you can write a clear, quick, crisp version like this:

Elaine, I'm sorry to say we're postponing the Tuesday meeting. The accounting info we need won't be ready till Wednesday. Bummer, I know.

Is Thursday at 3:00 okay for you? — Carrie

TIP

Although the second example feels casual and conversational, these aren't the actual words Carrie would say to Elaine in a real phone conversation. This exchange is more likely:

Hi. How are you? Listen, we got a problem. The project numbers are running way late. I won't have them till Wednesday. Yeah. So no point meeting Tuesday. How's Thursday look?

Online copy often works best when it carries the conversational illusion to an extreme. Pay attention to the jazzy, spontaneous-style copy on websites you love. The words may read like they sprang ready-made out of some genie's lamp, but more than likely a team of copywriters agonized over every line for weeks. Spontaneous-reading copy doesn't come easy: It's hard work. Some people — frequent bloggers, for example — are better at writing conversationally because they practice this skill consciously.

The next time you encounter bloggers or online writers whose voices you like, copy some text and paste it into a blank word-processing document (to separate the words from all the online bells and whistles). Read through the words carefully and analyze what you like in terms of words, phrases, and sentences. See if you can identify how the writers pull off their appealing breezy style.

Enlivening Your Language

The most important guideline for selecting the best words for business writing may seem counterintuitive: Avoid long or subtle words that express nuance. These may serve as the staple for many fiction writers and academics, but you're not striving to sound evocative, ambiguous, impressive, or super-educated. In fact, you want just the opposite.

Relying on everyday words and phrasing

The short everyday words you use in ordinary speech are almost always best for business writing. They're clear, practical, and direct. They're also powerful enough to express your deepest and widest thoughts. They're the words that reach people emotionally, too, because they stand for the most basic and concrete things people care about and need to communicate about. For example, *home* is a whole different story than *residence,* and *quit* carries a lot more overtones than *resign.*

Make a list of basic one- and two-syllable words. Almost certainly, they come from the oldest part of the English language, Anglo-Saxon. Most words with three or more syllables were grafted onto this basic stock by historical invaders: the French-speaking Normans and the Latin-speaking Romans for the most part, both of whom aspired to higher levels of cultural refinement than the Britons.

If you were raised in an English-speaking home, you learned Anglo-Saxon words during earliest childhood and acquired the ones with Latin, French, and other influences later in your education. Scan these previous two paragraphs and you know immediately which words came from which culture set.

REMEMBER

For this reason and others, readers are programmed to respond best to simple, short, low-profile English words. They trigger feelings of trust (an Anglo-Saxon word) and credibility (from the French). Obviously, we don't choose to write entirely with one-syllable words. Variety is the key — just as with sentences. English's history gives you a remarkable array of words when you want to be precise or produce certain feelings. Even in business English, a sprinkling of longer words contributes to a good pace and can make what you say more specific and interesting. But don't forget your base word stock.

TIP

If you're writing to a non-native English speaking audience, you have even more reason to write with one- and two-syllable words. People master the same basic words first when learning a new language, no matter what their original tongue, so all new English-speakers understand them. This applies to less educated readers too. Given the diverse and multicultural audiences many of your messages must reach, simplicity of language should rule.

This principle holds for long documents such as reports and proposals as much as for emails. And it's very important for online writing such as websites and blogs. When you read on-screen, you have even less patience with multi-syllable sophisticated words. Reading (and writing) on smartphones and other small devices makes short words the *only* choice.

Choosing reader-friendly words

The typical business English you see all the time may lure you toward long, educated words. Resist!

Consciously develop your awareness of short-word options. Clearer writing gives you better results. Opt for the first and friendlier word in the following pairs:

Use	Rather than
help	assistance
often	frequently
try	endeavor
need	requirement
basic	fundamental
built	constructed
confirm	validate
rule	regulation
create	originate
use	utilize
prove	substantiate
show	demonstrate
study	analyze
fake	artificial
limits	parameters
skill	proficiency
need	necessitate

The longer words aren't bad — in fact, they may often be the better choice. But generally, make sure that you have a reason for going long.

Focusing on the real and concrete

Concrete nouns are words that denote something tangible: a person or any number of things, such as cat, apple, dirt, child, boat, balloon, computer, egg, tree, table, and Joseph.

Abstract nouns, on the other hand, typically represent ideas and concepts. They may denote a situation, a condition, a quality or an experience. For example: catastrophe, freedom, efficiency, knowledge, mystery, observation, analysis, research, love, and democracy.

Concrete nouns are objects that exist in real space. You can touch, see, hear, smell, or taste them. When you use concrete nouns in your writing, readers bring these physical associations to your words, and this lends reality to your thoughts. Moreover, you can expect most people to take the same meaning from them. This isn't true of abstract words. Two people are unlikely to argue about what an apricot is, but they may well disagree on what exactly *independence* means.

TIP

When your writing is built on a lot of abstract nouns, you are generalizing. Even when you're writing an opinion or philosophical piece, too much abstraction doesn't fire the imagination. A lot of business writing strikes readers as dull and uninspiring for this reason.

Suppose at a pivotal point of World War II, Winston Churchill had written in the manner of many modern business executives:

> *We're operationalizing this initiative to proceed as effectively, efficiently, and proactively as possible in alignment with our responsibilities to existing population centers and our intention to develop a transformative future for mankind. We'll employ cost-effective, cutting-edge technologies and exercise the highest level of commitment, whatever the obstacles that materialize in various geographic situations.*

Instead he wrote, and said:

> *We shall not flag or fail. We shall go on to the end. We shall fight in France, we shall fight on the seas and the oceans, we shall fight with growing confidence and growing strength in the air, we shall defend our island, whatever the cost may be. We shall fight on the beaches, we shall fight on the landing grounds, we shall fight in the fields and in the streets, we shall fight in the hills; we shall never surrender.*

Which statement engages the senses and therefore the heart, even three-quarters of a century after this particular cause was won? Which carries more conviction? Granted, Churchill was writing a speech, but the statement also works amazingly when read.

TIP

While you probably won't be called on to rouse your countrymen as Churchill was, writing in a concrete way pays off for you too. It brings your writing alive. Aim to get down to earth in what you say and how you say it.

Using short words goes a long way toward this goal. Note how many words of the mock business-writing piece contain three or more syllables. Churchill's piece uses only three. And running both passages through readability checks (see the previous section "Applying readability guidelines") predicts at least a 12th-grade reading level to understand the business-speak with only 2 percent of readers understanding it. By contrast, Churchill's lines require only a 4th-grade reading level and 91 percent of readers understand them.

Making Your Writing Work

You may often find yourself tempted to write convoluted, indirect, abstract prose — because it's common to your corporate culture, or your technical field or the request for proposal you're responding to. Don't do it. Remind yourself that nobody likes to read that kind of writing, even though he may write that way himself. Take the lead in delivering lean, lively messages and watch the positive response this brings.

Finding action verbs

Good strong verbs invigorate. Passive verbs, which involve a form of the verb *to be,* deaden language and thinking, too. Consider some dull sentences and their better alternatives:

All department heads were invited to the celebration by the CEO.

The CEO invited all department heads to the celebration.

A decision to extend working hours was reached by the talent management office.

The talent management office decided to extend working hours. Or: *The talent management office is extending work hours.*

The idea is an improvement on the original design.

The idea improves the original design.

The annual report numbers were contradicted by the auditors.

The auditors contradict the annual report numbers.

Try also to avoid sentences that rely on the phrases *there is* and *there are,* which often bury the meaning of a sentence. Compare the following pairs:

There is a company rule to consider in deciding which route to follow.

A company rule determines which route to follow.

There are guidelines you should use if you want to improve your writing.

Use the guidelines to improve your writing.

For most dull passive verbs, the solution is the same: *Find the action.* Be clear about *who* did *what* and then rework the sentence to say that.

You may need to go beyond changing the verb and rethink the entire sentence so it's simple, clear, and direct. In the process, take responsibility. Passive sentences often evade it. A classic example follows:

Mistakes were made, people were hurt, and opportunities were lost.

Who made the mistakes, hurt the people, and lost the opportunities? The writer? An unidentified CEO? Mystery government officials? This kind of structure is sometimes called the *divine passive*: Some unknown or unnamable force made it happen.

To help you remember why you generally need to avoid the passive, here's a favorite mistake. When a group of people were asked to write about their personal writing problems and how they planned to work on them, one person contributed the following:

> *Many passive verbs are used by me.*

REMEMBER

Take the time to identify the passive verbs and indirect constructions in all your writing. Doing so doesn't mean that you must always eliminate them. You may want to use the passive because no clearly definable active subject exists — or it doesn't matter:

> *The award was created to recognize outstanding sales achievement.*

Or you may have a surprise to disclose that leads you to use the passive for emphasis:

> *This year's award was won by the newest member of the department: Joe Mann.*

TIP

Using the passive unconsciously often undermines your writing success. Substitute active verbs. They can be short and punchy, such as *drive, end, gain, fail, win, probe, treat, taint, speed.* Or they can be longer words that offer more precise meaning, such as *underline, trigger, suspend, pioneer, model, fracture, crystallize, compress, accelerate.* Both word groups suggest action and movement, adding zing and urgency to your messages.

Crafting comparisons to help readers

Comparisons help your readers understand your message on deeper levels. You can use similes and metaphors, which are both analogies, to make abstract ideas more tangible and generally promote comprehension. These devices don't need to be elaborate, long, or pretentiously literary. Here are some simple comparisons:

> *Poets use metaphors like painters use brushes — to paint pictures that help people see under the surface.*
>
> *Winning this award is my Oscar.*
>
> *Life is like a box of chocolates.*
>
> *The new polymer strand is 10 nanometers in width — while the average human hair is 90,000 nanometers wide.*
>
> *From 15,000 feet up the world looks like a peaceful quilt of harmonious colors where no conflict could exist.*

MAKING UP FRESH COMPARISONS

Playing with comparisons is a classic schoolroom game, and you can experiment today as a means of finding new ways to express your ideas. Simply think about bringing together two different things so one is seen differently.

Take 15 minutes and assemble a short list of things, activities, or experiences on the left side of a page of blank paper or a screen. For example, you can list your new project, writing your resume, making your boss happy, the new product you're selling, or playing a computer game.

Think about what that item is like — how you can describe it visually or through the other senses. Think about how it makes you feel. Brainstorm about other things that have similar characteristics. Try to avoid clichés and instead come up with something you find interesting.

Write your idea for each item on your list on the right side. Come up with an idea for every item just to give yourself the practice, even if some of your comparisons aren't brilliant. Use your new skill when you're writing an important document, trying to explain something difficult, or making your best persuasive argument.

For example, you might brainstorm for a comparison by finishing statements such as the following:

Winning this contract is as good as . . .

This new service will change your thinking about life insurance, just like X changed Y.

Saving a few dollars by investing in Solution A instead of Solution B is like . . .

Whatever device you use, effective comparisons do the following:

>> **Create mental images.** You can give readers a different way to access — and *remember* — your ideas and information.

>> **Align things from different arenas.** Using the familiar to explain the unfamiliar can be especially helpful when you introduce new information or change.

>> **Heighten the effect of everyday practical writing.** Just as in well-written fiction, a great comparison in a business document engages the reader's imagination and boosts your message's memorability.

>> **Make intriguing headlines that grab attention.** If you saw a blog post titled, "How Learning to Ride a Bike Is Like Working at Home," you'd be likely to read it just to find out what the two things have in common.

Using Reader-Friendly Graphic Techniques

Good written messages and documents are well thought out, as covered in Chapter 1 in this minibook, and presented clearly and vividly, as shown in the previous sections of this chapter. But there's one more aspect to highlight. Your writing must not only meet audience needs and read well but also look good.

REMEMBER

Whether your material appears in print or online, every message and document you create is a visual experience. More than readability is at stake; readers judge your message's value and credibility by how it looks. Whether you want to write an effective resume, proposal, report — or just an email — design can make or break your writing.

The following sections show you how to use various graphic techniques to maximize your message's appeal. And rest assured, you don't need to purchase special software or other tools to easily implement these good design principles.

Building in white space

To coin a comparison (see the sidebar "Making up fresh comparisons"):

> *Add white space to your writing for the same reason bakers add yeast to their bread to leaven the denseness by letting in the light and air.*

TIP

Help your writing breathe by providing plenty of empty space. The eye demands rest when scanning or reading. Don't cram your words into a small, tight space by decreasing the point size or squeezing the space between characters, words or lines. Densely packed text is inaccessible. If you have too many words for the available space, cut them down. We show you many ways to do that in Chapter 3 in this minibook.

Always look for opportunities to add that valuable white space to your message. Check for white space in everything you deliver. Factors that affect white space include the size of the typeface, line spacing, margin size, and column width, and graphic devices such as subheads, sidebars, and integrated images.

Toying with type

Type has numerous graphic aspects and effects. Following are some of the most powerful, as well as easiest to adjust.

Fonts

Using an easy-to-read simple typeface (or font) is critical. For printed text, *serif fonts* — fonts with feet or squiggles at the end of each letter — are more reader-friendly because they smoothly guide the eye from letter to letter, word to word. However, *sans-serif fonts* (ones without the little feet) are favored by art directors because they look more modern and classy. The sans-serif face Verdana was specifically designed for screen work and often used for it.

TIP

You need to choose your font according to your purpose. For long print documents, serif remains the better choice for the same reason that books still use it — ease of reading. But you can to some extent mix your faces. Using sans-serif headlines and subheads can make a welcome contrast. (For example, Times New Roman and Helvetica work nicely together.) But generally, resist the temptation to combine more than two different typefaces.

WARNING

Avoid fancy or cute typefaces for any purpose. They're not only distracting but may not transfer well to someone else's computer system. They can end up garbled or altogether missing in action. Recruitment officers sometimes find a candidate's name entirely missing from a resume because their systems lack a corresponding typeface and end up omitting these important words.

And never type an entire message in capitals or bold face, which gives the impression that you're shouting. Avoid using italics on more than a word or two because such treatments are hard to read.

Point size

Like font choice, the best point size for text depends on the result that you're trying to achieve. Generally, somewhere between 10 and 12 points works best, but you need to adjust according to your audience and the experience you want to create. Small type may look great, but if you want readers 55 and older to read your annual report, 8-point type will kill it.

Online text suggests a similar 10- to 12-point range for body copy, but calculating the actual onscreen experience for a wide range of monitors and devices is complicated. Online text often looks different on different platforms. Err on the side of a generous point size.

Never resort to reducing the size of your typeface to fit more in. Someone once has to persuade his boss to cut back his "Message from the CEO" because it was longer than the allocated space. He resisted sacrificing more than a few words. Then he was shown what his message would look like in the 6-point type necessary to run the whole thing. He quickly slashed half his copy to create a better presentation.

Margins and columns

For both online and print media, avoid making columns of type so wide that the eye becomes discouraged in reading across. If breaking the copy into two columns isn't suitable, consider making one or both margins wider. Also avoid columns that are only three or four words wide, because they're hard to read and annoying visually.

Be selective in how you justify text. Left-justified text is almost always your best choice for body copy. Right-justified text is difficult to read because each new line starts in a different spot. Fully justified copy (on both left and right) often visibly distorts words and spacing to make your words fit consistently within a block of text (unless it is professionally typeset, like this book). Worse yet, full justification eliminates a good way to add white space through uneven lines.

Keeping colors simple

Using color to accent your document can work well, but keep it simple. One color, in addition to the black used for the text, is probably plenty. See whether an accent color sparks your message by using it consistently on headlines or subheads or both.

WARNING

Using a lot of different colors — even on a website — strikes people as messy and amateur these days. Designers prefer simple, clean palettes that combine a few colors at most. So should you. And do not place any type against a color background that makes it hard to read. Backgrounds should be no more than a light tint. *Dropped or reversed-out type* — for instance, white type on a black or dark background — can look terrific but only in small doses, such as a caption or short sidebar. An entire page of reversed-out type, whether in print or onscreen, makes a daunting read.

REMEMBER

If you're producing a substantial document or website in tandem with a graphic designer, never allow graphic effect to trump readability and editorial clarity. To most designers, words are just part of a visual pattern. If a designer tells you the document has too many words, certainly listen; it's probably true and you do want the piece to look good. But just say no if playing second fiddle to the visual undermines your copy. Graphics should strengthen, not weaken, your message's effect and absorbability.

Adding effective graphics

On the whole, if you have good images and they're appropriate, flaunt them. This doesn't really apply to an email or letter, but graphics certainly help long documents and anything read online.

Appropriateness of graphics depends on your purpose. A proposal can benefit from charts and graphs to make financials and other variables clear and more easily grasped. A report may include photographs of a project under way. A blog with a fun image related to the subject is more enticing. Additional possibilities for various media include images of successful projects to support credibility, illustrations of something yet to be built, change documentation, and visualizations of abstract ideas.

Your own resources and time may be limited. But when visual effect matters — to attract readers or when you're competing for a big contract, for example — take time to brainstorm possibilities. Wonderful online resources proliferate, and many are free. With some imagination and research, you can use your computer to produce a good chart or graph.

WARNING

Images must feel appropriate to your readers. If not, you create a negative reaction. Even with websites, research shows that people value the words most and are put off by images unrelated to the subject. And generally stay away from clip art that's packaged with your word-processing software or other design tools. Clip art must be totally appropriate to your medium and message or cleverly adapted to look original or else it instantly cheapens your message in the viewer's eye.

Breaking space up with sidebars, boxes, and lists

Print media in the past decade have increasingly used graphic techniques to draw readers in with as many ways as they can come up with. Today's readers are scanners first. Think of your own behavior when opening up a newspaper or magazine. You most likely scout for what interests you and then read the material, in whole or at least in part, if it appeals to you. When you get bored, you quickly stop reading and start scanning again.

Good headlines and subheads are critical to capture readers' attention and guide them through a document. But you must also pay major attention to writing:

>> Captions accompanying photos and other images

>> Sidebars and boxes offering additional background, sidelights, or information

>> Interesting quotes or tidbits used as pullouts in the margins or inside the text

>> Small tight summaries of the article, or introductions, at the beginning

>> Bulleted or numbered lists of examples or steps

>> Icons (such as the Tip and Remember icons in this book) that denote something of special interest

All these devices serve three important purposes.

>> **Along with images, they break up unrelieved blocks of type that discourage the eye.** In fact, on a printed page, some print editors use the dollar bill test: If you can lay down a bill on a page and it doesn't touch a single graphic device, add one in.

>> **They offer different ways to capture a reader's attention.** A summary, caption, or box may draw you in to read the entire piece, or at least some of it.

>> **Using graphic devices helps to convey ideas and information more clearly and effectively.** People absorb information in different ways. Taking lessons from the online world, today's editors offer readers choices of what they want to read, and where they want to start.

REMEMBER

All these graphic techniques should be part of your writing repertoire. Do you need them for every email you write? Of course not. But strategies and elements such as subheads and bullets can still help get your message across. For long documents and materials intended to be persuasive, draw on all the techniques that suit your goals and audience.

Chapter **3**

Improving Your Work

I f you expect to create a successful email, letter, or business document in just one shot, think again. Don't ask so much of yourself. Few professional writers can accomplish a finished piece — whether they write novels, plays, articles, websites, or press releases — with their first draft. This especially includes writers known for their simplicity and easy reading.

Editing is how writers write. For them, writing and editing are inseparable because they wouldn't dream of submitting work that is less than their best. Unfortunately, many people are intimidated by the notion of editing their work. But equipped with effective methods and techniques, you can edit with confidence. Mastering hundreds of grammar rules is not necessary to becoming a good editor. Know the clues that reveal where your writing needs work, and you can sharpen what you write so it accomplishes exactly what you want. This chapter gives you the groundwork.

Changing Hats: Going from Writer to Editor

The writer and editor roles reinforce each other:

» In writing, you plan your message or document based on what you want to accomplish and your analysis of the reader (covered in Chapter 1 in this minibook), brainstorm content possibilities, organize logically, and create a full draft. Always think of this piece as the *first draft* because every message, whatever its nature and length, deserves editing and will hugely benefit from it.

>> In editing, you review your first draft and find ways to liven word choice, simplify sentences, and ensure that ideas hang together. You also evaluate the macro side: whether the content and tone deliver the strongest message to your audience and help build relationships. (All this is covered in Chapter 1 in this minibook.) Furthermore, as you make a habit of regularly editing your writing, your first-draft writing improves as well.

>> In proofreading, you review your writing in nitty-gritty detail to find and correct errors — mistakes in spelling, grammar, punctuation, facts, references, citations, calculations, and more.

Don't expect to discard the editing process down the line as you further refine your writing abilities. Professional writers never stop relying on their editing skills, no matter how good they get at their craft.

Improving your editing abilities goes a long way toward improving the effect of everything you write. The following tools and tricks make you a more capable and confident self-editor.

Choosing a way to edit

You have three main ways to edit writing. Try each of the following and see which you prefer — but realize you can always switch your editing method to best suit a current writing task or timeline.

Option 1: Marking up printouts

Before computers, both writers and editors worked with hard copy because it was the only choice. For about a century before computers, people wrote on typewriters, revised the results by hand, and then retyped the entire document. If you were reviewing *printer's proofs* — preliminary versions of material to be printed — you used a shorthand set of symbols to tell the typesetter what to change.

These symbols offered uniformity; every editor and printer knew what they meant. Typing and printing processes have changed radically, but the marks are still used today and remain a helpful way for communicating text changes between people.

TIP

Many professional writers still edit their work on printouts because on-screen editing strains the eyes and makes you more error-prone. You may find that physically editing your copy with universal marks to be more satisfying; you have something to show for your editing efforts when you're finished. Editing on paper can help you switch over to the editor's side of the table. Of course, you must then transfer the changes to your computer.

Proof marks vary between the US and UK, and some organizations have special marks or special meanings.

Option 2: Editing on-screen

After you draft a document, you can simply read through it and make changes. Younger writers may never have considered any other system. With a few mouse clicks or keystrokes, you can substitute words and reorganize the material by cutting and pasting. The down side to this method of editing is that you're left with no record of the change process. (See the next section for a useful alternative.)

When maintaining a copy of your original text matters, save your new version as a separate document. Amend its name to avoid hassle later, in case a series of revised versions develops.

Keep your renaming simple yet specific. If the document is titled *Gidget*, title the edited version *Gidget 2*, for example, or date it *Gidget 11.13*. When you edit someone else's document, tack on your initials: *Gidget.nc*, for example. Be sure your titling allows for easy identification of the various versions to avoid time-wasting confusion later.

Option 3: Tracking your changes

Most word-processing software offers a handy feature to record every change you make to the text in a document. In Word 2016, choose Review, then choose Track Changes.

When you choose to track changes, all changes show up on the copy in a color other than black or in small text boxes off to the side (depending on your choice of screen view). Deletions appear as strikethrough text or off to the side.

The system takes some personal trial and error but provides a useful tool for your editing experiments.

When you're tracking changes on an extensively edited document, you can end up with something quite complicated. You can spare yourself the nitty-gritty of every deletion and insertion by selecting to view as Final with All Your Proposed

Improving Your Work

Changes Included. You don't lose your edits; they're just hidden from immediate view.

When you finish editing, save a version that shows the revisions, and then go back to the Review tab and choose Accept or Reject Changes. Accept all changes, or go through your document section by section or even sentence by sentence. You emerge with a clean copy; save this version separately from the original. Proof the new version carefully because new errors creep in when you edit.

TIP

The Track Changes tool can help you improve your writing process and offers a way to share refinement stages with others when needed. (Numerous online tools, such as Google Docs, help you share document development.) But when you ultimately send the message to your audience, be sure your final saved version does not reveal the change process: Turn Track Changes off.

Distancing yourself from what you write

REMEMBER

The first step for a self-editor is to consciously assume that role. Forget how hard some of the material was to draft, or how attached you are to some of the ideas or language. Aim to judge as objectively as you can whether your message succeeds and how to improve it.

Your best tool to achieve this distance is the one that cures all ills: time. Chapter 1 in this minibook suggests that for everything you write, allocate roughly one-third the available time to planning, one-third to drafting, and one-third to editing. But ideally, that last third isn't in the same continuous time frame as the first two stages.

TIP

Try to build in a pause between drafting and editing. Pausing overnight (or longer) is highly recommended for major business documents. If your document is long or important, try to edit and re-edit in a series of stages over days or even weeks. Some copy, such as a website home page or a marketing piece, may never be finished. It evolves over time.

For short or less consequential messages, an hour or two between drafting and editing helps. A top-of-your-head email or text message that doesn't seem important can still land you in a lot of trouble if you send it out without vetting. If an hour isn't possible, just a quick trip to the coffee maker to stretch your legs can clear your mind and refresh your eyes.

So put the message away and then revisit it after a planned delay. When you return, you see your words with fresh eyes — an editor's rather than the writer's.

Reviewing the Big and Small Pictures

Your job when self-editing is to review what you wrote on two levels:

>> **The macro level:** The thinking that underlies the message and the content decisions you made.

>> **The micro level:** How well you use language to express your viewpoint and ask for what you want. (This topic is discussed in Chapter 4 in this minibook.)

Assessing content success

Start your edit with a big-picture review, using the fresh eyes and mind you gain by putting the piece aside for a while.

Improving Your Work

Read through the entire document and ask yourself the following:

>> Is what I want very clear from reading the message?

>> Does the content support that goal?

>> Is anything missing from my argument, my sequence of thoughts, or my explanations? Do I include all necessary backup information?

>> Do I give the reader a reason to care?

>> Do I include any unnecessary ideas or statements that don't contribute to or that detract from my central goal?

>> Does the tone feel right for the person or group with whom I'm communicating?

>> Does the entire message present me in the best possible light?

>> How would I react if I were the recipient rather than the sender?

>> Could my reader misunderstand or misinterpret my words?

TIP

The initial editing challenge is to drill to the core of your message. If you followed the step-by-step process to create the document presented in Chapter 1 in this minibook, check now that you met your own criteria and that every element works to accomplish your goal.

Your objective answers to these nine questions may lead you to partially or substantially revamp your content. That's fine — there's no point working to improve the presentation until you have the right substance.

You may choose to do the big-picture revision right away, or plan for it and proceed to the second stage, which is the micro-level of editing, or crafting the words. It's much easier to make the language more effective when you know exactly what message you want to deliver.

Assessing the effectiveness of your language

You have two ways to get instant, objective feedback on how well you used language.

>> **Use a readability index.** Most word-processing software can give you a good overview of the difficulty of any written piece. As Chapter 2 in this minibook details, Word's Readability Statistics box provides helpful information on word, sentence, and paragraph length; the number of passive constructions; and the degree of ease with which people can read and understand your message. Use these statistics to pinpoint your word-choice problems.

» **Read it aloud.** Reading what they write aloud is a favored method for many writers. As you speak your writing quietly — even under your breath — you identify problems in flow, clarity, and word choice. Asking someone else to read your words aloud to you can put you even more fully in the listener role.

In addition to telling you whether you achieved a conversational tone, the read-aloud test alerts you to eight specific problems common to poor writing. Solutions to four of these problems are in Chapter 2 in this minibook:

» **Problem 1:** A sentence is so long it takes you more than one breath to get through it.

   Solution: Break up or shorten the sentence.

» **Problem 2:** You hear a monotonous pattern, with each sentence starting the same way.

   Solution: Change some of the sentence structures so you alternate between long and short, simple and complex.

» **Problem 3**: All or most sentences sound short and choppy, which creates an abrupt tone and dulls the content.

   Solution: Combine some sentences to make reading the text smoother.

» **Problem 4:** You stumble over words.

   Solution: Replace those words with simpler ones, preferably words that are one or two syllables long.

The read-aloud method can reveal four additional challenges. Each problem is dealt with in greater detail in following sections. For now, here's a quick overview:

» **Problem 5:** You hear yourself using an up-and-down inflection to get through a sentence.

   Solution: Make the sentence less complicated.

» **Problem 6:** You hear repeat sounds produced by words ending in *-ize, -ion, -ing, -ous,* or another suffix.

   Solution: Restructure the sentence.

» **Problem 7:** You notice numerous prepositional phrases strung together.

   Solution: Change your wording to make fewer prepositions necessary.

» **Problem 8:** You hear words repeated in the same paragraph.

   Solution: Find substitutes.

REMEMBER

If you read your copy aloud and practice the fix-it techniques prescribed in Chapter 2 in this minibook and the following sections, you give yourself a gift: the ability to bypass grammar lessons. After you know how to spot a problem, you can use shortcut tools to correct it. Even better, track your own patterns and prevent the problems from happening.

Everyone writes with his or her own patterns. The better handle you gain on your own patterns, the better your writing and the faster you achieve results.

Now for some detail on handling problems 5, 6, 7, and 8.

Avoiding telltale up-down-up inflection

Fancy words, excess phrases, and awkward constructions force sentences into an unnatural pattern when read aloud. The effect is rather like the typical up-down-up-down inflection of the tattletale: I know who **DID** it.

Read the following sentence aloud and see what pattern you force on your voice:

All of the writing that is published is a representation of our company, so spelling and grammatical errors can make us look unprofessional and interfere with the public perception of us as competent businesspeople.

Simply scanning the sentences tips you off to its wordiness. This single sentence contains two phrases using *of*, two statements with the passive verb *is*, and three words ending in *-ion*. They produce an awkward, wordy construction. Plus, the sentence contains 34 words — far more than the average 18 recommended — and more than 5 words have three or more syllables (see Chapter 2 of this minibook).

You don't need to be a linguistic rocket scientist to write a better sentence. Just go for simple and clear. Break up the long sentence. Get rid of the unnecessary words and phrases. Substitute shorter friendlier words. One way:

All our company's writing represents us. Spelling and grammar errors make us look unprofessional and incompetent.

After you simplify, you can often find a third, even better way to write the sentence. A third pass may read:

When we make spelling and grammar mistakes, we look unprofessional and incompetent.

Looking for repeat word endings

Big clues to wordy, ineffective sentences come with overused suffixes — words ending in *-ing, -ive, -ion, -ent, -ous,* and *-y.* Almost always, these words are three or more syllables and French or Latinate in origin. Several in a sentence make you sound pompous and stiff. They often force you into convoluted, passive constructions that weaken your writing and discourage readers. (See "Moving from Passive to Active," later in this chapter, for more on activating passive construction.)

TIP

Sprinkle these words throughout your written vocabulary but never let them dominate. Try for one per sentence, two at most. Avoid using a string of these words in a single sentence. Find these stuffy words either visually, by scanning what you write, or orally — read the material out loud and you'll definitely notice when they clutter up your sentences.

In the following sections, you see examples of overly suffixed wording and how to fix it. If you are unenthusiastic about grammar lessons, proceed happily: The goal is to help you develop a *feel* for well-put-together sentences and how to build them. After you notice problems, you can correct them without thinking about rules.

The *-ing* words

Consider this sentence:

> *An inspiring new idea is emerging from marshalling the evolving body of evidence.*

One short sentence with four words ending in *-ing!* Read it aloud and you find yourself falling into that up-down inflection. You can fix it by trimming down to one *-ing* word:

> *An inspiring new idea emerges from the evidence.*

Here's a sentence written for this chapter:

> *Besides, there's something more satisfying about physically editing your copy and using the universal markings.*

The five words ending in *-ing* weren't spotted until the third round of editing! After you see a problem like this, play with the words to eliminate it. Then check that it matches your original intent. The sentence was rewritten this way:

> *Besides, you may find it more satisfying to physically edit your copy with the universal marks.*

When you're both the writer and editor, you're doubly responsible for knowing what you want to say. Fuzzy, verbose writing often results from your own lack of clarity. So when you spot a technical problem, think first about whether a simple word fix will work. But realize that you may need to rethink your content more thoroughly. After you're clear, a better way to write the sentence emerges, like magic.

If you edit someone else's work, knowing the writer's intent is harder. You may not understand what the author is going for, and then it's all too easy to shift her meaning when you try to clarify. You may want to ask the author how to interpret what she wrote. Or make the changes and, as appropriate, check that they are okay with the writer. Don't be surprised if he or she objects. The writer/editor relationship is often a tense and complicated one.

The *-ion* words

The following is cluttered with -*ion* words and incredibly dull:

> *To attract the attention of the local population, with the intention of promoting new construction, we should mention recent inventions that reduce noise pollution.*

Reading aloud makes this sentence's unfriendliness instantly clear. Also note that piling up lots of -*ion* words leads to a very awkward passive sentence structure.

The problem with too many -*ion* words can be more subtle, as in this sentence from an otherwise careful writer:

> *Whether they are organizing large demonstrations, talking with pedestrians in the street, or gathering signatures for a petition, their involvement was motivated by the realization that as individuals within a larger group, they had the potential to influence and bring about change.*

In addition to two words with the -*ion* suffix, the sentence also contains three ending in -*ing*. The result is a rambling, hard to follow, and overly long sentence that feels abstract and distant. This sentence is challenging to fix. One way:

> *They organized large demonstrations, talked with pedestrians, and gathered signatures. Their motivation: knowing that as individuals, they could influence and bring about change.*

Does it say exactly the same thing as the original? Perhaps not, but it's close. And more likely to be read.

Notice that after the -*ion* and -*ing* words were cut down, some of the cluttery phrases become more obvious.

>> Of course, pedestrians are *in the street* — so why say it?

>> The phrases *for a petition* and *had the potential* are both overkill.

TIP

Always look for phrases that add nothing or offer unnecessary elaboration — and cut them. Your writing will improve noticeably.

The *-ize* words

Similarly to *-ion* and *-ing* words, more than one *-ize* per sentence works against you.

He intended to utilize the equipment to maximize the profit and minimize the workforce.

TIP

In fact, you rarely need these kind of Latinate words at all. In line with the principle of using short, simple words as much as possible, shift *utilize* to *use* and *maximize* to *raise*. And you can more honestly state *minimize* as *cut*.

Modern business language keeps inventing *-ize* words, essentially creating new verbs from nouns. *Incentivize* is a good example. Consider this quote from a government official that appeared in a newspaper article:

It would be a true homage to her memory if we are able to channelize these emotions into a constructive course of action.

Aside from the fact that *channel* is better than *channelize* for the purpose, note how made-up, long words are typically embedded in abstract, verbose thinking.

The *-ent, -ly,* and *-ous* words

Words with the *-ent, -ly,* or *-ous* suffixes are usually complicated versions of words available in simpler forms.

A silly example that combines all these forms shows how using long words forces you into that unnatural rhythm, passive structure, and wordy phrases full of unnecessary prepositional phrases.

Continuous investment in the pretentiously conceived strategic plan recently proved to be an impediment to the actualization and inadvertently triggered the anomaly.

WARNING

Unfortunately, much modern business writing is filled with convoluted language, clichés, and hyperbole at the expense of substance. When you try to edit some of it — such as the preceding silly example — you're left with nothing at all. Unfortunately, the fact that no one is impressed with empty writing and no one likes to read it doesn't stop people from producing it.

But research is under way to correlate good writing and communication with the bottom line. Towers Watson, a global management-consulting firm, conducts high-profile surveys on the financial impact of effective communication, and the American Management Association is interested in the ROI-writing connection. Meanwhile, the lesson is clear: Don't write in empty business-speak — it won't reward you.

Pruning prepositions

Another good way to reduce wordiness is to look for unnecessary prepositional phrases — that is, expressions that depend on words such as *of, to,* and *in.* Here are a few examples along with better alternatives:

> **Original:** *Our mission is to bring awareness of the importance of receiving annual checkups to the people of the community.*

> **Revised:** *Our mission is to build the community's awareness of how important annual checkups are.*

> **Original:** *But it is important not to forget that you have to still use the rules of traditional writing.*

> **Revised:** *But remember, you must still use traditional writing rules.*

> **Original:** *He invested 10 years in the development of a system to improve the performance of his organization.*

> **Revised:** *He spent 10 years developing a system to improve his organization's performance.*

Try any and all of the following to cut down wordy phrases:

>> **Use an apostrophe.** Why say the *trick of the magician,* when you can say *the magician's trick?* Why write *the favorite product of our customers,* when you can write *our customers' favorite product?*

>> **Use a hyphen.** Rework *the CEO's fixation on the bottom line* to *the CEO's bottom-line fixation.*

>> **Combine two words and remove an apostrophe:** The phrase *build the community's awareness* can also read well as *build community awareness.*

Cutting all non-contributing words

Extra words that don't support your meaning dilute writing strength. Aim for concise. Use the set of clues described in the previous sections and zero in on individual sentences for ways to tighten. Here's a case in point:

With the use of this new and unique idea, it will increase the profits for the magazine in that particular month.

Extra words hurt the sentence's readability and grammar. Even though the sentence is fairly short already, it manages to jam in two prepositions (*of* and *for*), an altogether useless phrase *(with the use of)*, and an unnecessary word repetition — *new* and *unique*. Of course, the sentence construction is confusing as a result. A better version:

This new idea will increase the magazine's profits in that particular month.

TEXTING AND INSTANT MESSAGING: WHEN AND WHERE TO USE THE STYLE

The terse style of texting and instant messaging follows time-honored traditions.

Probably since the first humans drew on cave walls, people have looked for faster and easier ways to communicate big ideas with written symbols. The Romans chipped their messages into stone tablets and monuments. This was such hard going that they jammed in strings of abbreviations and acronyms that still challenge historians. The ancient Egyptians also depended on word shortcuts to make their point on stone surfaces. They liked abbreviations and often skipped words that were obvious (to them, at least). In the nineteenth century, news was sent by telegraph and people found tapping out every letter of every word too slow. Again, words were abbreviated to their minimal intelligible form or omitted.

There's nothing inherently wrong with finding faster ways to type on tiny keyboards. In fact, many language gurus believe that texting improves writing because it teaches conciseness. But when you assume everyone understands those abbreviations and symbols, you may have a problem.

In general, many older people may not readily read text-style messages (see the information on generation gaps in Chapter 1 of this minibook), and even younger readers may not like it as a common language. Writing in a manner your readers are unlikely to understand simply doesn't make sense.

Further, many readers who are comfortable with texting shortcuts still expect a more formal style in other media, including email. So don't risk your credibility by transferring informal texting strategies to other business writing. Limit texting style to appropriate media and audiences that you're sure will respond in kind.

An objective look at your sentences may reveal words and phrases that obviously repeat the same idea. Here's a sentence written for this chapter, which talks about editing hard copy from a computer printout.

Of course, you must then transfer your changes to the original on your computer.

In context, the original document was clearly on the computer, so the unnecessary phrase was cut:

Of course, you must then transfer the changes to your computer.

Consider this explanation of how Track Changes works:

Now when you make a change, the alteration is indicated in a color and any deletion is shown on the right.

The rewrite:

Your changes then show up in color, and deletions appear outside the text on the far right.

The revision works better because it eliminates unnecessary words and with them, the passive construction of *alteration is indicated* and *deletion is shown*.

TIP

Take aim at common phrases that slow down reading. Substitute simple words. The words on the left are almost always non-contributors; choose those on the right.

Wordy	Better
at this time	now
for the purpose of	for, or to
in accordance with	under
in an effort to	to
in order to	to
in regard to	about
in the amount of	for
in the event of	if
in the near future	soon
is indicative of	indicates
is representative of	represents
on a daily basis	daily

Moving from Passive to Active

Most people write too passively. They use too many verbs that are forms of *to be*, which force sentences into convoluted shapes that are hard for readers to untangle. Worse, all those *to be* verbs make writing so dull that many readers don't even want to try. Chapter 2 in this minibook describes passive verbs in context of writing. This section covers the topic from the editing angle.

TIP

Active verbs say everything more directly, clearly, concisely, and colorfully. If you want to transform everything you write quickly, pay attention to verbs and build your sentences around active ones.

Thinking action

TIP

Active voice and action verbs are not the same thing grammatically, but this isn't a grammar guide. For practical purposes, don't worry about the distinction. Just remember to cut back on the following word choices:

>> **Is + an *-ed* ending:** As in, *Your attention is requested.*

>> **Are + an *-ed* ending:** As in, *The best toys are created by scientists.*

>> **Were + an *-ed* ending:** As in, *The company executives were worried about poor writers who were failing to build good customer relations.*

>> **Was + an *-ed* ending:** As in, *The ice cream was delivered by Jenny.*

>> **Will be + have + an *-ed* ending:** As in, *We will be happy to have finished studying grammar.*

>> **Would be + an -ed ending:** As in, *The CEO said a new marketing plan would be launched next year.*

The solution in every case is the same: Figure out *who* does *what*, and rephrase the idea accordingly:

>> *We request your attention.*

>> *Scientists create the best toys.*

>> *Company executives worry that bad writers fail to build good relationships.*

>> *Jenny delivered the ice cream.*

>> *We're happy to finish studying grammar.*

>> *The CEO plans to launch a new marketing plan next year.*

Verbs endings with -*en* raise the same red flag as those ending in -*ed*. For example, *I will be taken to Washington by an India Airways plane* is better expressed as *An India Airways plane will fly me to Washington.*

REMEMBER

When you rid a sentence of *to be* verbs, you win a chance to substitute active present tense verbs for boring, passive past tense ones. Many professionals work this tactic out on their own through years of trial and error. Writing in the present tense takes a bit more thought at first but quickly becomes a habit. Use present tense everywhere you can and see your writing leap forward in one giant step.

TIP

Look closely at all your sentences that contain *is, are,* and the other *to be* verbs. See whether an action verb can bring your sentences to life. Often, you can use the present tense of the same verb:

> **Original:** *He is still a pest to the whole office about correct grammar.*

> **Revised:** *He still pesters the whole office about correct grammar.*

At other times, think of a more interesting verb entirely:

> **Original:** *She is intending to develop a surprise party for the boss.*

> **Revised:** *She is hatching a surprise party for the boss.*

Trimming *there is* and *there are*

TIP

Big-time culprits in the passive sweepstakes are the combinations *there is* and *there are.* This problem is easy to fix — just commit never to start a sentence with either. Keep away from *there will be, there have been,* and all the variations. Don't bury them inside your sentences, either.

Check out the following examples and improvements:

> **Original:** *There were 23 references to public relations in the report.*

> **Revised:** *The report cited public relations 23 times.*

> **Original:** *There is a helpful section called "new entries" at the top of the page.*

> **Revised:** *A helpful section called "new entries" appears at the top of the page.*

> **Original:** *It's expected that in the future, there will be easier ways to communicate.*

> **Revised:** *We expect easier ways to communicate in the future.*

In every case, using an active verb does the trick, and almost all reworked sentences are in the present tense.

Cutting the *haves* and *have-nots*

Like the *to be* verbs, using the various forms of the verb *to have* signals lazy writing. Find substitute words as often as possible. A few examples and possible rewrites:

> **Original:** *He said he had intentions to utilize the equipment he had been given by the company.*
>
> **Revised:** *He said that he plans to use the equipment the company gave him.*
>
> **Original:** *We have to make use of the talents we have.*
>
> **Revised:** *We must use our own talents.*

Using the passive deliberately

Despite all the reasons for minimizing passive sentences, passive verbs are not bad. You need them on occasions when the actor is obvious, unknown, unimportant, or the punch line. For example:

> *The computer was developed in its modern form over a number of years.*
>
> *After long trial and error, the culprit was finally Identified as the Green Haybarn.*

You can also make a case for using the passive voice when you need to frame a message in terms of *you* rather than *we* or *I*. When writing to a customer, for example, you may be more effective to begin as follows:

> *Your satisfaction with the product is what we care about most.*

Rather than this:

> *We care most about your satisfaction with the product.*

The second statement gives the impression that it's all about us. Of course, don't write an *entire* letter like the first opening — just the first sentence.

The passive is also useful when you don't want to sound accusatory. *The bill has not been paid* is more neutral than *You failed to pay the bill.*

Sidestepping Jargon, Clichés, and Extra Modifiers

Relying on words that have little meaning wastes valuable message space and slows down reading. Overused expressions also dilute the effect, and insider language can confuse outside readers. Jargon, clichés, and unhelpful adjectives are hallmarks of unsuccessful business writing.

Reining in jargon

Almost every specialized profession has its *jargon:* terminology and symbols that shortcut communication and, in some cases, make group members feel more professional and inside. If a physicist is writing to other physicists, she doesn't need to spell out the formulas, symbols, and technical language. Her audience shares a common knowledge base.

Similarly, a lawyer can write to colleagues in the peculiar language he and his peers mastered through education and practice. A musician can exchange performance notes with other musicians in a way that means little to non-musicians.

WARNING

The risk arises when people talk or write to anyone other than fellow-specialists and use inside jargon. You forget that the general public does not share your professional language. If, for example, you're a scientist who needs to explain your work to a journalist, report on progress to company executives, order supplies, negotiate employment, or chat at a party, you're best avoiding scientific jargon.

REMEMBER

Outside of specialized fields, we are all generalists. We want to be addressed in clear, simple language that we can immediately understand. Judging by their messages to clients, many attorneys and accountants are among those who forget this basic principle — or perhaps no longer remember how to communicate in plain English.

But business writers face an additional challenge. A specialized, jargon-laden language flourishes full of buzzwords that mean little — even to those who use it. For example, a technology company states in a publication:

> *These visible IT capabilities along with IT participation in the project identification process can drive the infusion of IT leverage on revenue improvement in much the same way as IT has leveraged cost cutting and efficiency.*

What does it mean? Who knows? All too often, corporate writers string together a set of buzzwords and clichés that communicate little beyond a reluctance to think.

WARNING

Of course, sometimes a writer or organization deliberately chooses to bury a fact or a truth behind carefully selected words and phrases. Then you might argue that a message built on empty business jargon works well. But don't deliberately distort the truth, write without substance, or mask either situation with bad writing. Doing so just doesn't work, and it may boomerang. This widely circulated Citigroup press release made the bank look ridiculous:

> *Citigroup today announced a series of repositioning actions that will further reduce expenses and improve efficiency across the company while maintaining Citi's unique capabilities to serve clients, especially in the emerging markets. These actions will result in increased business efficiency, streamlined operations, and an optimized consumer footprint across geographies.*

Translation: *We're firing a lot of people to improve our numbers.*

To avoid producing empty business-speak, steer clear of words and phrases such as the following:

best practice

blue-sky thinking

boil the ocean

boots to the ground

core competency

drinking the Kool-Aid

from the helicopter view

full service

optimization

over the wall

peel the onion

robust

scalable

shift a paradigm

take it to the next level

think outside the box

360-degree view

value proposition

vertical

world class

If you're writing a press release, for a website, or other promotional copy, check it for buzz-wordiness by asking yourself: Could this copy be used by any company, in any industry, to describe any product or service? If I substitute down-to-earth words for the clichés, does the message have meaning? Will my 17-year-old nephew laugh when he reads it?

Cooling the clichés

Jargon can be seen as business-world clichés. English, like all languages, has an enormous trove of general clichés, expressions that are so overused they may lose their effect. A few random examples that can turn up in business communication: *All's well that ends well, barking up the wrong tree, beat around the bush, nice guys finish last, a stitch in time, read between the lines.*

Clichés are so numerous they often seem hard to avoid. Often they're idioms, a popular shorthand was of communicating ideas, found in every language. And they can be used well in context. But be on the lookout for any that don't carry your meaning or that trivialize it. Instead, say what you want more simply, or perhaps develop an original comparison, described in Chapter 2 in this minibook. And never forget that idioms and clichés are rarely understood by non-native English speakers, so try to avoid them when writing to these audiences.

Minimizing modifiers

The best advice on using descriptive words — adjectives and adverbs — came from the great nineteenth-century American novelist Mark Twain:

> *I notice that you use plain, simple language, short words and brief sentences. That is the way to write English — it is the modern way and the best way. Stick to it; don't let fluff and flowers and verbosity creep in.*

> *When you catch an adjective, kill it. No, I don't mean utterly, but kill most of them — then the rest will be valuable. They weaken when they are close together. They give strength when they are wide apart. An adjective habit, or a wordy, diffuse, flowery habit, once fastened upon a person, is as hard to get rid of as any other vice.*

Twain wrote this advice in 1880 to a 12-year-old boy who sent him a school essay, but he's right on target for today's business communicators.

If depending on buzzwords and clichés is Sin #1 of empty business-speak, overuse of adjectives is Sin #2. Consider, for example,

> *The newest, most innovative, cutting-edge solution to the ultimate twenty-first century challenges . . .*

UNCLEAR WRITING IS AGAINST THE LAW!

By long tradition, the worst examples of opaque, confusing, and hard to understand writing come from none other than government. However, plain language movements have gathered steam in a number of countries, including the US and Britain, since the 1970s. Advocates point out that clear writing is essential for people to access services, follow regulations, and understand the law.

In the US, sustained work by several non-profit groups led to passage of the Plain Writing Act of 2010, which requires federal agencies to write all new publications, forms, and publicly distributed documents in a "clear, concise, well-organized" manner that follows the best practices of plain language writing. Extending the law to government regulations is the next effort.

In England, the campaign against small-print, bureaucratic language is similarly vigorous, but a corresponding law has not been passed.

In both countries, efforts to clarify legal writing are underway as well. And an organization called PLAIN — the Plain Language Association International (www.plainlanguagenetwork.org) — serves as a central resource for the plain language movement globally.

A special point of interest: Some studies demonstrate that the guidelines for better writing are basically the same across different languages: short words, short simple sentences, fewer descriptive words, and good graphic techniques (see Chapter 2 in this minibook) work well for Swedish writing, just as for English.

Other interesting US sites include The Plain Writing Association (www.plain-writing-association.org) and the Center for Plain Language (www.centerforplainlanguage.org). These and related websites offer a wealth of useful information and good before-and-after writing examples from both the public and private sectors. Movement leaders hope that promoting clear language in government will have a much-needed effect on corporate writing.

What, another solution?

TIP

Adopt whenever possible the fiction writer's mantra: Show, don't tell. Adjectives generally communicate little. In fiction, and especially scriptwriting, writers must find ways to bring the audience into the experience so they draw their own conclusions about whether a character makes bad decisions, is unethical, feels ugly or pretty, is suffering pain, and so on.

In business writing, *show, don't tell* means giving your audience substance and detail: facts, ideas, statistics, examples — whatever it takes to prove they need your product or idea. Stating that something is innovative proves nothing. Adding an adverb, such as *very innovative*, just multiplies the emptiness.

Take a piece of marketing or website copy, either your own or someone else's, and highlight all the adjectives and adverbs. Then eliminate most or all of the words you identified. Examine what's left. Does it say anything meaningful? If not, can you replace the copy with something real?

Welcome opportunities to replace empty rhetoric with substance! There's no substitute for good content. Use good writing techniques (as presented throughout this book) to make that content clear, straightforward, and lively.

In Chapter 4 in this minibook, you move from sentence building to creating solid paragraphs, solving organization problems, using strong transitions, and fixing the technical problems that typically handicap many business writers.

Chapter **4**

Troubleshooting Your Writing

As you explore in Chapter 3 in this minibook, good self-editing requires you to look at your writing on two levels — macro and micro. Chapter 3 focuses on how you assess your content and present your material effectively. This chapter drills down to even more specific editing issues: techniques for organizing material and improving sentences and words.

REMEMBER

Each of us has our own writing demons, persistent problems that show up in everything we write. Happily, most of these issues fall into common categories that you can correct with common-sense approaches. Even better, you don't need to master hundreds of grammar rules. This chapter gives you a repertoire of practical fix-it techniques. After you absorb them and begin putting them into practice, they enable you to head off problems *before* they pull you off-message or undermine your success.

Organizing Your Document

Many people, including a number of experienced writers, say that organization is their biggest challenge. If you follow the process outlined in Chapter 1 in this minibook, which shows you how to plan each message within the framework of your goal and audience, you may be able to sidestep the organization challenge substantially.

But this may not altogether solve your problems, especially when documents are lengthy or complicated, written by more than one person, or simply strike you as confusing or illogical once drafted. You may need to review the organization at that point and reshuffle or recast material. The following techniques help. You can implement them at the writing stage or the editing stage.

Paragraphing for logic

You may remember being told in school to establish a thesis sentence and develop each paragraph from that. If you found this advice dumbfounding, you're not alone.

TIP

Here's a much easier way to look at paragraphs. Just accept the idea that each chunk should contain no more than three to five sentences. If you write your document that way, you easily achieve an inner logic and produce a series of self-contained units, or paragraphs.

If you routinely produce uninterrupted strings of sentences, don't despair: Make the fixes later, during the editing stage. Read over what you've written and look for logical places to make breaks.

Can't decide where to insert breaks? Use the following technique:

1. **Scan your text to find places where you introduce a new idea or fact — or where you change direction.**

   Break the flow into paragraphs at these points.

2. **If your paragraphs are still more than three to five sentences, go through the piece again and make decisions on an experimental basis. You'll check later to see if they work.**

   The three- to five-sentence guideline is a general one that applies to print material. But an occasional one-sentence paragraph is fine and adds variety. When you write for online reading, paragraphs should be shorter.

3. **Look carefully at the first sentence of each newly created paragraph.**

   See whether the new first sentence makes sense in connecting with what follows — or whether it connects better with the preceding paragraph. If the latter, move the sentence up a paragraph and break to a new paragraph where it now ends.

   If a sentence seems not to belong with either paragraph, it may need to stand as its own paragraph — or be rephrased.

4. **Look at your paragraphs again in order and check whether any wording needs adjustment.**

Pay particular attention to the first and last sentences of each paragraph. You want each paragraph to link to the next. Using transitions helps with this. (Read more about these in the later section "Working with transitions.")

If you don't like the sequence of paragraphs when you scan the entire message, fool around with shuffling them. Adjust the language as necessary so that your paragraphs still clearly relate to each other.

TIP

You might find repeated words or entire ideas during this step, so make the necessary cuts and smooth everything out.

REMEMBER

The point of paragraphing is clarity. You want to deliver information in absorbable or usable chunks that lead from one to the next, rather than a single, long, confusing word dump.

Sometimes the reason you have trouble organizing your material is because you don't yet understand it well enough to effectively present it to others. Ask yourself: What *is* my point? What are the components of my argument? Number or list them if you haven't yet done so. (Omit the numbers later if that's better for your purpose.) Also ask yourself whether you are missing critical pieces and need to research for them.

Building with subheads

TIP

Another strategy for organizing, useful on its own or to supplement the paragraphing strategy described in the preceding section, is to add a few simple subheads. Subheads as an excellent graphic technique, as you discover in Chapter 2 in this minibook. They are also useful guideposts for planning what you write and, during the editing process, can be added to help clarify your message.

Suppose you're composing an email telling your staff that new technology will be installed department-wide. The new system is technical, so you anticipate plenty of questions and some resistance. You want your memo to head off many of the possible challenges.

To organize your own thoughts and avoid writer's block, turn your brainstorming of content (see Chapter 1 in this minibook) into a series of subheads. You might write the following:

>> System X24A: Rollout starts March 6

>> Who is affected?

>> Advantages of the new system

>> Changes in how we'll work

>> Tech training plans

>> March 6: Department Q&A meeting

Arrange your subheads in a logical order and then fill in the information under each subhead. As you write under each heading, additional topics may emerge that you didn't think of initially — for example, how the new system affects your team's interface with payroll. Find a logical place in your sequence of subheads and add the new one.

In your final message, discard the subheads if you want or leave them in. Subheads usually work well to pull your readers through a message and keep them organized as well. The overall effect on readers, even those who only scan the message, is that they see you have the situation well in hand and have thoroughly thought everything out. This feeling alone inspires greater confidence in both you and the new system, making people more receptive to the change.

REMEMBER

Long, complex documents benefit from the subhead strategy too. For a report or proposal, for example, identify the necessary sections and write a headline, rather than a subhead, for each. Then write a set of subheads for each section.

Drafting headings and subheads is a great way to be sure that you cover all the right bases, identify missing pieces early, and build in good organization from the project's start. You also break up the writing process into doable bits so it's far less formidable.

Use a consistent style for all your headings. The Microsoft Word program offers built-in styles, so it just takes a click to apply one.

Working with transitions

Transitions, those low-key words and phrases, are like the connective tissue that holds your skeleton together and empowers you to move where you want. Transitions tell readers how all the ideas, facts, and information in a piece of writing connect to each other. They smooth your writing and pull people along in the direction you want to take them.

TIP

Good transitions signal good writing and good thinking. They help you organize your own ideas as a writer. And for the reader, they promote the feeling that your argument is sensible and even unassailable. Transitions are important tools for all writing — and essential for persuasive copy.

Transitions can consist of single words, phrases, or sentences. They can be put to work within a sentence, to link sentences, or to connect paragraphs. Think of them in several categories:

To continue a line of thought — or to shift a line of thought, use the following:

additionally	on the other hand
also	but
and	however
consequently	alternatively
for example	originally
furthermore	nevertheless
mainly	despite
so	in other words
sometimes	conversely

To establish a sequence or time frame, try these:

as soon as	ultimately
at the moment	finally
first . . . second . . . third	later
to begin with	next
to conclude	for now

To reinforce a desired focus or tone, choose one of the following:

disappointingly	it sounds good, but . . .
invariably	counterintuitively
luckily	of particular interest
unfortunately	at the same time

REMEMBER

Transitions give you a good way to begin paragraphs or sections, while putting that information in context of the full message. The following are examples of whole sentences that serve as transitions:

Based on this data, we've made the following decisions.

Here's why the problem arose.

We should pay special attention to the sales figures.

We now have four choices.

A number of questions were raised at the meeting. The most significant:

Notice how these introductory statements set up a super-simple way to organize subsequent material, including within long, complicated documents.

As with all writing principles, there can be too much of a good thing. When you give your writing the read-aloud test and it sounds stilted and clumsy, review your transitions — you may need to remove some. Do so and you still have a well-organized, convincing message.

Working in lists: Numbers and bulleting

Lists offer an excellent way to present information in a compact, to-the-point manner. They suit readers' Internet-trained text-skimming habits, and most people like them. They also automatically promote graphic variation, another plus for your document (see Chapter 2 in this minibook).

Numbered lists

Use numbered lists to present sequences of events, procedures, or processes. For example, a numbered list can guide readers on how to do something:

Follow these steps to activate the new software.

1. *Turn on your computer.*

2. *Choose Preferences in your graphics program.*

3. *Select Formatting, and then . . .*

Scout actively for opportunities to organize a sequence by dates or milestones:

1. *Jan. 7, Deadline 1: Submit preliminary budget estimates.*

2. *Feb. 10, Deadline 2: Submit adjusted numbers.*

3. *March 4, Deadline 3: Finalize department budget.*

These techniques may sound simple-minded, but they bestow a clarity that is so unambiguous, few people can misinterpret your meaning.

TIP

You can also use numbered lists in more sophisticated ways. Bloggers use them to present blog posts in a popular and reader-friendly style: a number-centered headline followed by each numbered point, spelled out. For example:

The 7 Tricks for Warp-Speed Writing That Professionals Don't Want You to Know

Many experienced bloggers think up a headline like that first, marshal their ideas around it, and then write the copy. In addition to its reader appeal, this format channels your knowledge in a different way and helps you uncover ideas you didn't know you knew.

Numbering is also a staple for speechwriters:

I'm going to give you five ways to boost your power to close the sale.

The technique works every time because audiences like knowing how much is ahead of them, and they love ticking off the speaker's progress (and their own). It helps people retain information a bit better, too.

You need to know when to stop, though. In a speech, listeners can usually handle no more than five numbered items. In print, as with bullets, limit yourself to seven. (However, something is magnetic about ten.)

Also as with bullets, make items on your lists parallel in structure — begin them with the same part of speech. And they should work visually by being approximately the same length.

Bulleted lists

Between on-screen writing habits and Microsoft PowerPoint everywhere, writing has become a bullet-heavy experience.

Like numbering, bullet lists convey information tightly and neatly. They're appropriate for summarizing, offering checklists, and providing information-at-a-glance. What's more, readers like them — but only up to a point. Used incorrectly, bullets can kill. Audience interest, that is.

TIP

To successfully use bulleting, take account of these guidelines:

>> **Don't use too many.** Research shows that people can't absorb more than about seven bullets. They tune out after that because each bullet typically makes a separate point and gives little logical connection to hold onto.

If you must present more than seven bullets, break them into more than one list and intersperse some narrative material.

» **Use the same sentence structure for every bullet.** Start each item similarly. Sentence structure must be parallel so as not to confuse readers.

You can begin bullet points with action verbs, such as when you present accomplishments in a resume:

- *Authorized . . .*
- *Generated . . .*
- *Streamlined . . .*
- *Overhauled . . .*
- *Mentored . . .*

» Or you can compose a bullet list that starts with nouns, such as:

When you weekend in Timbuktu, be sure to pack

- *Tropical microfiber clothing*
- *Sunglasses with a good UV coating*
- *Sunhat with extra-long visor*

WARNING

» Don't be lazy and create bulleted lists of unrelated mix-and-match thoughts, like this:

Here are goals to aim for in business writing:

- *You want a conversational but professional tone.*
- *When you quote numbers, check that your readers use those systems.*
- *Don't be emotional or make things up.*
- *Jane is trying to standardize a similar look on charts and graphs. Once she does so, use that standard.*

» You can refine this list by rearranging points two through four to start like the first one:

- *You want to check that all numbers quoted are in line with systems your readers use.*
- *You want to avoid emotion or making things up.*

» But that approach produces an annoying repetition of *you want*. The solution is to find an introductory sentence that covers the points you want to make. For example:

In business writing, try to use a

- *Conversational but professional style*
- *Non-emotional tone*

- *Number systems familiar to your readers*

- *Consistent style for charts and graphs*

>> **Punctuate and format bullets consistently.** In this book, the first phrase or sentence is often bold, followed by a colon (for a phrase) or a period (for a sentence). No one way of formatting is right for every organization and every situation. Figure out your style, or your organization's, and apply it consistently to all your lists.

WARNING

>> **Give bullet points meaning.** Don't depend on bullet points to convince people of something or expect readers to fill in the gaps between them. Bullets are only formatting.

Tell readers what your bullets mean with good narrative writing or a quick introduction that puts the bullets in context. In a bio or resume, for example, using all bullets to describe your assets defies readability. Begin with a well-written overall description of your current job followed by a list of your accomplishments, but put the information in context. For example, a job description can end with *Consistent performance beyond company goals for three years,* followed by your bullet evidence. Use no more than five to seven bullets, stated in parallel sentences.

Don't make formatting decisions, such as using bulleted and numbered lists, lightly. They may be easy to write, but you undermine your success if they don't present your message as clearly as possible. When you use such formatting devices, take a hard look during the editing stage to see if you might present your material better (and be more persuasive) in narrative form.

Catching Common Mistakes

Unlike the common cold, common writing problems can be treated and even prevented. The prescription is simple: Be aware of your own mistakes, which are nearly always consistent.

Improving your grammar is a personal thing, so if you want a solid grounding, scout what's out there in books and on the Internet. Choose a resource compatible with your learning style and dig in. Consider starting out with *English Grammar For Dummies* or *English Grammar Workbook For Dummies*, both by Geraldine Woods.

The grammar-related goals in this minibook are as follows:

>> Raise your consciousness so that you can recognize some of your own problems.

>> Give you practical tips for fixing those problems that require little grammar know-how.

>> Relieve you of some of your worries. What you're doing may be perfectly okay for today's less formal communication.

Infinitely more can — and has — been written about writing it right. See the sidebar "The journalist's grammar guidelines," later in this chapter, for what may be the most succinct rundown ever created.

The following sections tip you off to problems found in even solid writing — all are easily fixed and make the writing more effective. One general guideline to help you relax: When your own writing confronts you with a grammar problem that's hard to resolve or that you can't figure out, write the sentence differently to sidestep the challenge.

Using comma sense

Stop stressing about commas! If visual cues don't work for you, use oral ones. The reading-aloud trick recommended in Chapter 3 of this minibook is a surefire way to find out when you need a comma. Note the difference in the following:

> *Eat Grandpa!*

> *Eat, Grandpa!*

If you read the words aloud to say what you presumably intend — that Grandpa should eat — the first option sounds this way:

> *Eat* (pause and downward inflection) *Grandpa*

A pause signals the comma is needed. And most assuredly, this sentence needs the comma.

Too many commas can also be a problem:

> *The use of the Internet, is part of a new culture, that more and more of the younger generations are entering into.*

Read this sentence and you hear that it works better without pauses where the two commas are placed. They interfere with smooth reading and should be cut.

Badly placed commas in cases like this often signal a wording problem. A better version, once the too-obvious parts are cut:

Using the Internet is part of a new younger-generation culture.

TIP

Reading aloud can also cure runaway or run-on sentences that typically depend on misused commas. Here's one:

Grammar is something that everyone can always touch up on, the writers should use simple punctuation, properly place punctuation marks, things like too many commas and semicolons can confuse the reader.

The read-aloud test shows that a sustained pause calls for a new sentence after *touch up on*. The comma between the two middle thoughts doesn't work either because an *and* should connect them. Insert that conjunction and it's clear that you need a period after *marks* because to read meaningfully demands another sustained pause. The result follows:

Grammar is something that everyone can always touch up on. Writers should use simple punctuation and properly place punctuation marks. Things like too many commas and semicolons can confuse the reader.

Another way of fixing this paragraph is to connect the whole second part with a transition and cut some redundancy:

Writers should use simple punctuation and properly place punctuation marks, because too many commas and semicolons can confuse the reader.

Train your ear and with a little practice, you improve your punctuation quickly.

Using *however* correctly

As with commas, reading aloud gives you the clue about how to include *however* in your writing.

Many decent writers undercut themselves with sentences like these:

I'd like to go to the office, however, my car won't start.

Expense reports are due on Jan 15, however, exceptions can be made.

Reading these sentences aloud shows that long pauses are necessary before each *however*. You can break up both statements into two sentences with periods after *office* and *Jan. 15*. The second sentence in each case starts with *However*.

Alternatively, you can sidestep the "however" problem and also refine your wording by the following:

>> Replacing the *however* with *but*. If this substitution works, go with *but*. It's correct and less stuffy as well.

>> Using *however* only to begin sentences.

>> Moving a *however* that falls in the middle of the sentence to the beginning and see whether the meaning holds. For example:

> *He agreed with Jane, however, she was wrong.*

> *He wants to know, however, so he can plan his vacation.*

Moving *however* to the front makes nonsense of the first sentence. With the second sentence, moving it retains the basic sense.

Matching nouns and pronouns

Using the wrong pronoun is common, even in the work of professionals. *Pronouns* have a simple function — to stand in for nouns so you don't have to keep repeating them. One cause of confusion is when to use *me* instead of *I*, *he* rather than *him*, and so on. For example:

> *Just between you and I, Jean was correct.*

> *Mark, Harold, and me will go to the conference.*

Both sentences are wrong. One way to figure that out is to switch the wording so the correct pronoun becomes obvious. In the first sentence, if you substitute *us* for *you and I*, it works fine. But if you substitute *we*, the sentence sounds absurd and you're clearly wrong.

In the second sentence, you can choose to say *We will go to the conference*, and the singular for *we* is *I*, so that pronoun is correct. Or you can eliminate Mark and Harold from the scene, in which case you obviously must say *I*, not *me*.

As a general rule, go with what seems natural; but check yourself out. Try adding or subtracting words, as in the previous examples.

Another cause of confusion is when to use a plural possessive pronoun (like *their*) as opposed to a singular pronoun (*his, its*). In these situations, stay alert to the original noun:

A journalist must always be attuned to their readers' interests.

Everyone should use their discount when ordering online.

Both are wrong because both nouns (*journalist* and *everyone*) are singular, not plural. But the first sentence raises other issues. If I correct the first sentence as follows:

A journalist must always be attuned to his readers' interests.

Will I be accused of sexism? Perhaps, but the jury is still out on how to avoid this. You can do one of the following:

>> Say *his or her readers,* but that repetition gets tiresome.

>> Switch back and forth between the masculine and feminine. This approach works in longer documents.

>> Change the original noun to plural:

Journalists must always be attuned to their readers' interests.

>> Rework the sentence to avoid the problem entirely:

Journalists must always be attuned to reader interest.

You can alter the second sentence to: *Use your discount when ordering online.*

REMEMBER

Some pronoun issues reflect cultural differences. In the US, an organization is considered singular, so you say:

The company is widely criticized for its actions.

But in the UK, the plural is used:

The company is widely criticized for their actions.

Weighing *which* versus *that*

Almost always, choose *that* rather than *which*. The latter word refers to something specific. When you're not sure which to use, try using *that* and see whether the sentence has the same meaning. If it does, keep the *that.* For example:

The report that I wrote at home is on John's desk now.

But if you find that *that* doesn't reflect your meaning, you may mean *which.*

Note that you can write the sentence this way:

The report, which I wrote at home, is on John's desk now.

The second version calls attention to *where* you wrote it. And observe that you need two commas to set off the clause. *Which* always requires two commas unless the phrase appears at the end of the sentence. Another instance:

We provide afternoon breaks, which, we know, help reduce stress.

You're using *which* correctly if you can eliminate the phrase inside the commas *(we know)* without changing the sentence's basic meaning. If you remove the non-essential phrase, the sentence becomes:

We provide afternoon breaks that help reduce stress.

Does this sentence carry the same meaning as the original? Basically yes, but if the "we know" is important, it doesn't. For a sentence to carry your meaning, you must know what you want to communicate.

Pondering *who* versus *that*

Contemporary writing is chock-full of *that's* and very few *who's*. People have become depersonalized into objects. The following sentences are all incorrect:

The new office manager that started on Monday already called in sick.

My friend, that I've known for 20 years, is planning to visit.

The first person that said he was ready changed his mind.

REMEMBER

Always use *who* when referring to people. Inanimate objects and ideas are *that*. You may choose to refer to animals as *who*, but some prefer *that*.

Choosing *who* versus *whom*

Grammar enthusiasts insist that you differentiate between the word used as a subject *(who)* and as an object *(whom, as in to whom)*. But adhering to the rule can land you in some stuffy places.

To whom should I address the package?

With whom should I speak?

To whom it may concern . . .

The following version of the first two sentences work better for general business writing:

Who should I address this package to?

Who should I speak to?

THE JOURNALIST'S GRAMMAR GUIDELINES

Business writers can learn a lot from journalists, whose full-time work is figuring out how to present ideas and information in the clearest, most succinct, and most interesting way possible. Unfortunately, as the newspaper industry shrinks, it provides an ever-smaller training ground for writers.

This classic list of rules was originally taken from a bulletin board at Denver's *Rocky Mountain News* and has appeared, with different add-ons, in a number of journalism books. *The Rocky Mountain News* stopped publishing in 2009, but many a writer keeps this demonstration of grammar pitfalls on hand.

1. Don't use no double negatives.

2. Make each pronoun agree with their antecedent.

3. Join clauses good, like a conjunction should.

4. About them sentence fragments.

5. When dangling, watch your participles.

6. Verbs has to agree with their subjects.

7. Just between you and I, case is important too.

8. Don't write run-on sentences they are hard to read.

9. Don't use commas, which aren't necessary.

10. Try to not ever split infinitives.

11. It's important to use your apostrophe's correctly.

12. Proofread your writing to see if you any words out.

13. Correct speling is essential(!)

14. Avoid unnecessary redundancy.

15. Be more or less specific.

16. Avoid clichés like the plague.

In the case of the last example, simply don't use such an archaic phrase. Always find a specific person who may be concerned, and use her name. If that's impossible, use a title *(Dear Recruitment Chief)* or a generic address *(Dear Readers)*.

Beginning with *and* or *but*

Like other wording choices addressed in this section, grammatical standards have relaxed, and only the rare individual complains about sentences that begin with *and* or *but*. *The Wall Street Journal* does it, the *New York Times* does it. And so can you.

But don't do it so often that it loses its effect. Starting sentences with these conjunctions adds to your rhythmic variety and gives you a way to add a little verve, especially to online writing. It works best with short sentences.

Because can be used the same way, although I still hear people repeating the schoolroom mantra against starting sentences with that word. And *or* and *yet* can also start a sentence.

Ending with prepositions

An often-quoted piece of wit attributed to Winston Churchill underscores the silliness of strictly obeying some rules:

> *This is the sort of bloody nonsense up with which I will not put.*

Obviously it's more natural to say,

> *This is the sort of bloody nonsense I won't put up with.*

Similarly, sentences such as these that end with prepositions are fine:

> *Leave on the horse you rode in on.*
>
> *See if the answers add up.*
>
> *He's a man I can't get along with.*
>
> *We didn't know where he came from.*
>
> *Don't make fun of grammarians, just because some of their ideas don't go where you want to.*

TIP

Many stock phrases end with prepositions and there's no reason not to use them wherever they fall in a sentence. This especially applies if writing "correctly" requires an unnatural-sounding manipulation of language. The general guideline for business writing is: Use what feels comfortable in conversation.

Reviewing and Proofreading: The Final Check

Before sending your message or document into the world or to its target audience of one, review it at both the big-picture macro level (see Chapter 3 in this mini-book) and the close-in micro level (everything covered in this chapter).

REMEMBER

Editing is essential, but often the process unintentionally shifts meaning and introduces new mistakes. So plan to review any passages you reworked at least one extra time.

Checking the big picture

After you've edited your message or document and are satisfied with the writing, it's time to return to the big picture and assess your overall message in terms of content, effect, and tone. It's not sufficient to send a technically perfect message that isn't geared to accomplishing what you want!

Forgetting all the work and the decisions that went into what you've written and edited, look at your text as a self-contained piece and consider the following:

>> Is my *purpose* — what I want to accomplish — absolutely clear?

>> Does the piece support my sub-agenda? For example, does it promote the relationships I want to build, represent me in the best professional light, and contribute toward my larger goals?

>> Do I get to the point quickly and stay on message? Does every element of the message support the result I want?

WHEN HAVE I FINISHED EDITING?

Painters have the same question about knowing when they've finished a painting. With writing, stop editing before you begin to change the meaning of your message. And stop before you compress all the life out of it. Overly general, bland writing doesn't work well. Don't cut the examples, anecdotes, or details that engage readers and help them understand.

You're better off saying less but saying it fully. For example, plan a series of emails on a subject rather than jamming the information into one overly long one. Or focus an article on one aspect of a subject and keep the color.

>> Does the message move well and smoothly from section to section, paragraph to paragraph?

>> Is the level of detail right? Not too much, not too little, just enough to make my case?

Step even further back and read your document from your recipient's viewpoint:

>> Will the reader know what I want and exactly how to respond?

>> Is the message a good match in terms of tone, communication style, and audience characteristics? Does it focus on what's important to the reader?

>> If I were the recipient, would I care about this message enough to read it — and respond?

>> Did I provide appropriate evidence to support the case I'm making? What unanswered questions could the reader possibly have?

>> If I were the reader, would I give the writer what he or she wants?

>> Can anything in the message possibly be misinterpreted or misunderstood? Could it embarrass anyone?

>> How does it look? Is it accessible and easy to read? Does it have plenty of white space and good graphic devices? Does it need visuals?

>> And finally, will I feel perfectly fine if this document is forwarded to the CEO, tweeted to thousands of strangers, mailed to my grandmother, or printed in a daily newspaper?

Correct any problems using ideas and tips in this book, plus your own common sense. Chapter 1 in this minibook tells you how to understand your goals and your audience and build messages that draw the response you want. Choosing appropriate graphic options is covered in Chapter 2 in this minibook and in the previous sections of this chapter.

Proofreading your work

In professional communication circles, proofreading is seen as separate from writing and editing. But in these economically tight times, copywriters, journalists, and even book authors often wear all three hats. Many publications now outsource their proofing services or eliminate them. If you've noticed a growing number of mistakes in what you read, that's the reason.

SUREFIRE PROOFREADING TIPS

Here are some ways to do the best job proofing your own work or someone else's:

1. Use one of the systems explained at the beginning of Chapter 3 in this minibook so your proofreading is systematic and clear.

2. Be sure to keep an original, unedited version.

3. Try to proofread when your eyes and mind are fresh, and take frequent breaks.

4. Proofread more than once — ideally three times — allowing some time between sessions.

5. Carefully check sentences before and after every change you make, because editing often generates new errors.

6. Pay special attention to the places where you find an error, because errors often clump together (perhaps you were tired when you wrote that part).

7. Look for words that are often misspelled. Every grammar book has these lists, and you can easily find one online. (Keep a copy on your desk.)

8. Examine all the little words, including on, *in, at, the, for, to.* They may repeat or go missing without your noticing.

9. Look up all words you aren't sure about. Choose a dictionary you like (online or print), or just Google the word.

10. Triple-check names, titles, numbers, subheads, and headlines.

11. Rest your eyes regularly, especially if you're proofreading on-screen. Looking out a window into the distance helps. So does setting your computer screen to a comfortable brightness.

12. Try enlarging the on-screen type for easier viewing, but not so much that you don't see the entire sentence, paragraph, or section.

13. Read challenging portions of text backward. This approach is often useful with material that is highly technical or contains numbers.

14. Recheck all the places where a mistake would prove most embarrassing: headlines, lead sentences, and quotes.

TIP

On a daily basis, obviously proofreading is all up to you. But you can still reach out for help. Many writers use a buddy system to back them up on important material, and you can too. A colleague, friend, or partner may be happy to supply editing advice with you in exchange for the same help. As the saying goes, two sets of eyes are better than one.

Creating your very own writing improvement guide

Most writers are highly consistent in the errors they make, so creating a list of your writing shortfalls helps you sharpen — and ultimately speed up — your writing.

Treat yourself to an in-depth session to review either a major document or a batch of smaller messages. Or gather information and insights over time. Better yet, do both.

Start by thoroughly editing your selected work using the various criteria explained in this minibook. Look for patterns of errors and less-than-wonderful writing. You will benefit by addressing these particular problems.

Record the challenges — and the solutions — systematically. An example follows:

My Problems	Solutions
Too many words ending in *ing*	Find substitutes for most and rewrite as necessary
Too many sentences longer than 17 words	Break them up or tighten by cutting
Need to fix sentence rhythm often	Read them aloud and add or cut words so they move better
Too many sentences per paragraph	Break them up
Too many long words	Replace with short ones, mostly
Too much passive voice	Keep an eye on Word's Readability Index; find more interesting verbs that promote an action feel
General wordiness	Cut, tighten, rewrite
Too many qualifiers (*you might, you can, you should*) and extra phrases	Cut the hedge words and write in present tense!

This analysis produces a road map that the writer can use to review everything he or she writes, from an email to a home page to a proposal.

TIP

Get even more specific and add categories, such as words you often misspell or incorrect use of possessives. Scout for solutions in this book and other sources, and equip yourself with tools to lick the problem. Identifying your personal roadblocks goes a long way toward fixing them.

DOESN'T MY COMPUTER CATCH GRAMMAR GOOFS?

Microsoft Word and other word-processing software have grammar-checking features that identify possible mistakes and indicate potential fixes. While these tools can help, accepting the corrections unquestioningly is like trusting a smartphone's word-guessing function.

Pay attention to the corrections and changes your word-processing software wants to make, in both spelling and grammar, and evaluate them thoroughly.

To care about what you write is a different way of thinking. Do you really need to plan, draft, edit, cut, rewrite, add, subtract, edit, and proofread everything you write? You be the judge. But before you decide that most of the process isn't necessary, consider whether or not your reputation and effectiveness are on the line nearly every time you write. They probably are.

Try out the plan/draft/edit process in small ways, such as for everyday messages, and see whether you start getting what you want more often. When you practice the plan/draft/edit process on the small stuff, you're ready to use it for the big stuff: proposals, reports, articles, websites, blogs, and marketing materials.

Chapter **5**

Writing Emails That Get Results

L ove it or hate it, you can't leave it — email is the central nervous system of business life all over the world. Companies may declare e-free Fridays or add newer media such as instant messaging or social networks for basic communication, but you probably still find that your work life centers on managing your inbox and outbox.

The volume and omnipresence of email in your life gives you the opportunity to accomplish your immediate and long-range goals, or screw up both. This chapter shows you how to make the most of this powerful medium and sidestep the traps.

REMEMBER

Of course another communication channel may replace email soon, but it hasn't happened yet. In any case, the guidelines in this chapter apply to whatever comes next, maybe with minor adaptations to formatting and style. The essentials of good communication hold steady.

Fast-Forwarding Your Agenda In-House and Out-of-House

If you're wishing for a way to show off your skills, judgment, competence, and resourcefulness and have decision-makers pay attention, *shazam* — email is *the* opportunity.

Yes, everyone is overwhelmed with too much email and wants most of it to go away. The reasons are twofold: Most email is unrelated to your interests and needs, and most of it is badly thought out and poorly written. Take a look through your own inbox. You're likely to find that most of it falls into one of those two categories — or both.

Then take a look at your outbox. Ask yourself (and be honest) how many messages you carelessly tossed off without planning or editing. You may feel that this is the nature of the medium — here one minute, gone the next, so it's not worth investing time and energy. But email is the tool you depend on to get things done, day in and day out.

Moreover, email has become the delivery system for many forms of communication. In earlier times, you'd write a cover letter to accompany a resume, for example. Today you deliver it electronically. But a cover letter for a job application is still a cover letter — no matter how it's delivered. A short business proposal may also be sent by email, but it, like a cover letter, needs to be well written. Resist the temptation to write such material in an off-the-top-of-your-head fashion.

REMEMBER

Good emails bring you the results you want. Even more, writing good emails every time — no exceptions — brings you amazing opportunities to reach the people you want to reach with a message *about you*: how intelligent, resourceful, and reliable you are, for example, and how well you communicate. Even those humdrum in-house emails contribute incrementally to your positive image as an efficient professional and give you a long-range advantage way past accomplishing your immediate goal.

Send direct, well-written emails that have a clear purpose and respect people's time, and you get respect back. People notice and respond to well-written messages, though admittedly, most do so unconsciously.

The higher you go in an organization's hierarchy, the more people tend to recognize good writing and value it because they see so little of it these days. Executives are acutely aware of how badly written emails, even on mundane matters, can create the following:

>> Misunderstandings that generate mistakes

>> Needless dissent among employees and departments

>> Inefficiency, because countering unclear messages demands much more communication

>> A staggering waste of collective time and productivity

Smart leaders are even more aware of how poor email messaging can affect an organization's interface with the world at large, resulting in the following:

>> Weakened company image and reputation

>> Disaffected customers

>> Missed opportunities to connect with new customers

>> Long-term damage to relationships with the public, investors, suppliers, lenders, partners, media, regulators, and donors — all of which directly affect the company's bottom line

Take email seriously and it will give you many happy returns. Decision-makers in your workplace who value clear communication will value you all the more. In addition:

>> **Email offers huge opportunities to develop relationships in the course of doing business.** To build and sustain a network of trusted colleagues and contacts in-house and out can only benefit you over the long term.

>> **Email gives you access to the loftiest heights.** Fifteen years ago, the idea that you could directly write to your CEO or the hiring manager of your dream employer was unthinkable. Now you can, and she may read it and even respond — if you make your message good.

>> **Email is your ticket to reaching people all over the world.** Without it, international trade would depend on mail systems and faxes for making initial contact. Surely email is the unsung hero of globalization.

TIP

If you're an independent entrepreneur, a consultant, a freelancer, or an outside contractor, recognize that emails can make or break your enterprise. Written well, emails can help generate what you need: in-person meetings, opportunities to compete for business, new agreements, relationships of trust, and ways to promote what you do.

Getting Off to a Great Start

Your first imperative in drafting an email: Draw your reader to open it — and read it. Sound easy? Not at all, given the sheer volume of messages that motivate most people to press the Delete key. That's another reason why every email you send must be good: You don't want a reputation for sending pointless, hard-to-decipher messages that lead people to ignore the important ones that you craft carefully.

With email, the lead has two parts — the subject line and the opening sentence or paragraph. We explore each in detail in the following sections.

Writing subject lines that get your message read

Take another look at your inbox and scan the subject lines. Note which ones you opened and why. Most of them probably fall into one of these categories:

>> Must-read because of essential information:

- *Subject: New location, May 3rd meeting*

>> Must-read because of urgency:

- *Decision on Plan A needed today*

>> Must-read because of who the writer is (in which case, the *From* matters, too):

- *From: President White*

- *Subject: Department reorganization planned*

>> Want-to-read because you need the information or it may be valuable:

- *Subject: Free tools to recover deleted files*

>> Want-to-read because it looks like a good deal:

- *Subject: Lowest iPhone price ever*

>> Want-to-read because it's from a trusted source:

- *From: Kickstarter*
- *Subject: Projects we love: mobile murals*

>> Want-to-read because it sounds interesting or fun:

- *From: Bronx Zoo*
- *Subject: Come see our tiger cubs!*

REMEMBER

Few messages are required reading. Your challenge in writing email subject lines is to zero in on what's most likely to concern or interest your reader. But you must always be fair. Don't promise something in the package that isn't there after your reader opens it.

To create a good subject line that keeps fingers off that Delete key:

1. **Figure out what's most relevant to your reader in the message — why the person should care.**

2. **Think of the most concise way of saying it.**

3. **Put the key words as far to the left as possible so your recipient understands the meat of your message quickly and easily.**

Subject lines work best when they're as specific as possible. Here are two examples of emails you probably wouldn't open because the subject lines are too vague and general to capture your interest, along with suggestions for improving the message:

Poor: *Important question*

Better: *Where is tomorrow's workshop?*

Poor: *June newsletter*

Better: *New Twitter techniques in June issue*

Ensuring that the most important words appear in your recipient's inbox window and aren't cut off for lack of space — or because the person is reading on a smartphone or other handheld device — is worth the thought every time. Very few people pay attention to this simple principle, so build this habit to reap a big advantage.

Following are a few examples of truncated subject lines from emails:

The Coach's Corner: 9 ways to . . .

Did you ever wish that y . . .

Express yourself with a perso . . .

Suppose that the full subject line for the last one was *Express yourself with a personalized dish.* Had the line begun *Your personalized dish,* or *Your name on stoneware,* you might have opened the email.

Investing in good, accurate subject lines always rewards you. You may not be able to deliver the whole of your subject in the limited amount of characters your recipient's inbox allows, but try to get the gist across. Ordinarily, you needn't aim to be clever; but if the message is important, spend some time to make the first few words intriguing.

WARNING

If you can't come up with a tight subject line that communicates the core of your message, consider the possibility that your message may not have a core — or any meaning at all — to your reader. Review both the subject line and the entire message to see whether you're clear on why you're writing and what outcome you want.

Be sure to review your subject line after you write the message. You may shift tack in the course of writing. In fact, the writing process can lead you to think through your reason for creating the message and how to best make your case. Drafting the message first and then distilling the subject line is often easier.

TIP

Don't be lazy about changing the subject lines of long message threads. If you don't, people may overlook your new input. Later, both you and the recipient may be frustrated when looking for a specific message. Try for some continuity, however, so it doesn't look like a different topic. If the first email of a series is identified as *Ideas for Farber proposal,* for example, a new subject line might say *Farber proposal update November 3.* Keep the subject lines obviously relevant to everyone concerned.

Most people use email as their personal database to draw on as needed, so always label messages in ways that make them findable.

Using salutations that suit

The greeting you use is also part of the lead. Draw on a limited repertoire developed for letters:

> *Dear*
>
> *Hi*
>
> *Hello*

You can use *Greetings* or something else, but be sure it doesn't feel pretentious.

Follow with first name or last as appropriate, using the necessary title (Miss, Ms., Mrs., Mr.). For the plural, Mesdames and Messieurs are over the top for English speakers. For groups, you can sometimes come up with an aggregate title, such as *Dear Software X Users, Dear Subscribers,* or *Hi Team.* Don't be homey or quirky. Using *folks,* for example, can grate on people. Avoid generalizations such as *Dear Customer* if you're writing to an individual. These days, people expect to be addressed by name.

TIP

Often, people who know each other well or are transacting business in a series of emails dispense with the title, and simply start the message with the person's name — for example, *John.* That's fine if doing so feels comfortable. In general, don't omit a name and plunge right into your message because you'll miss an important chance to personalize. You can, however, build a name into the opening line, as in, *I haven't heard from you in a while, Jerry, so thought I'd check where things stand.*

Drafting a strong email lead

REMEMBER

The first sentence or two of your message should accomplish the same goal as the lead of a newspaper article: Attract your readers' attention, present the heart of what you want to say, and give them a reason to care. Plus, you need to tell readers what you want.

Because email leads usually include the same information that appears in the subject line, try not to repeat the same wording or the same information. Email copy occupies valuable real estate. Your best chance of enticing people to read the entire message is to make the lead and everything that follows tight.

Your email lead can consist of one sentence, two sentences, or a paragraph, as needed. When the subject line clearly suggests your focus, you can pick up the thread. For example:

> *Subject: Preparing for the August meeting*
>
> *Hi Jenn,*
>
> *Since we need the materials for the Willow conference in less than a week, I'd like to review their status with you ASAP.*

Often you need a context or clarifying sentence before you get to your request:

> *Subject: Timing on design hire*
>
> *Hilary, you mentioned that you'd like to bring in a graphic designer to work on the stockholder report ASAP. However, I won't be able to supply finished copy until April 3rd.*

Note how quickly both of these messages get to the point. Your everyday in-house messages should nearly always do so, whether addressed to peers, subordinates, or immediate supervisors. But never sacrifice courtesy. The right tone is essential to make your message work. That topic is described later in the sidebar "Finding the right tone for email."

In the case of messages to people outside your department or company, you often need to include more framing. Suppose you're responsible for fielding customer complaints and must write to an irate woman who claims your company sold her a defective appliance:

> *Dear Ms. Black,*
>
> *Your letter about your disappointment with the new Magnaline blender has been brought to my attention. I am happy to help resolve the problem.*

REMEMBER

A good subject line and lead rarely just happen: You achieve them by thoughtful planning. That doesn't mean you can't draft the complete email and then go back and strengthen or change the lead. In fact, you may prefer to figure out the main point through the writing process itself. Just be sure you leave time to edit when you proceed that way. See this minibook's Chapters 3 and 4 for more on editing and revising.

Building Messages That Achieve Your Goals

You build a successful email at the intersection of goal and audience. Intuition can take you far, but analyzing both factors in a methodical way improves all your results. Knowing your goal and your audience is especially critical when you're handling a difficult situation, trying to solve a problem, or writing an important message.

Clarifying your goals

Email often seems like a practical tool for getting things done. You write to arrange a meeting, receive or deliver information, change an appointment, request help, ask or answer a question, and so on. But even simple messages call for some delving into what you really want.

Consider Amy, a new junior member of the department, who hears that an important staff meeting was held and she wasn't invited. She could write the following:

> *Tom, I am so distressed to know I was excluded from the staff meeting last Thursday. Was it just an oversight, or should I take it as a sign that you think my contribution has no value?*

Bad move! Presenting herself as an easily offended childish whiner undermines what she really wants — to improve her positioning in the department. Instead of using the opportunity to vent, Amy can take a dispassionate look at the situation and build a message that serves her true goal:

> *Tom, I respectfully request that I be included in future department meetings. I am eager to learn everything I can about how we operate so I can do my work more efficiently and contribute more. I'd appreciate the opportunity to better understand department thinking and initiatives.*

With external communication, knowing your goal is just as important. For example, if you're responsible for answering customer complaints about defective appliances and believe your goal is to make an unhappy customer go away, you can write:

> *We regret your dissatisfaction, but yours is the only complaint we have ever received. We suggest you review the operating manual.*

If you assume your job is to mollify the customer on a just-enough level, you may say:

> *We're sorry it doesn't work. Use the enclosed label to ship it back to us, and we'll repair it within six months.*

But if your acknowledged goal is to retain this customer as a future buyer of company products while generating good word of mouth and maybe even positive rather than negative tweets, you're best off writing this:

We're so sorry to hear the product didn't work as you hoped. We're shipping you a new one today. I'm sure you'll be happy with it, but if not, please call me right away at my direct phone number . . .

For both Amy's and the customer service scenarios, keeping your true, higher goals in mind often leads you to create different messages. The thinking is big picture and future-oriented: In Amy's case, the higher purpose is to build a relationship of trust and value with a supervisor and gain opportunities. In the unhappy customer case, you want to reverse a negative situation and cultivate a loyal long-term customer.

TIP

Be the best person you can in every message you send. Every email is a building block for your reputation and future. And email is never private: Electronic magic means your message can go anywhere anyone wants to send it — and you can't erase it, ever.

Assessing what matters about your audience

After you're clear on what you want to accomplish with your email, think about your audience — the person or group to whom you're writing. One message, one style does not fit all occasions and individuals. As you discover in Chapter 1 in this minibook, when you ask someone to do something for you in person, you instinctively choose the best arguments to make your case. You adapt your arguments as you go along according to the other person's reactions — her words, body language, expression, tone of voice, inflection, and all the other tiny clues that tell you how the other person is receiving your message in the moment you're delivering it.

An email message, of course, provides no visual or oral feedback. Your words are on their own. So your job is to think through how your reader is most likely to respond and then base what you write on that.

Anticipating a reader's reaction can take a little imagination. You may find you're good at it. Try holding a two-way conversation in your head with the person. Observe what she says and how she says it. Note any areas of resistance and other clues.

You also have another surefire way to predict your reader's reaction: Systematically consider the most relevant factors about that person or group. Chapter 1 in this minibook gives you a comprehensive list of factors that may relate to what you want to accomplish.

Do you need to consider so many aspects when you're drafting every email? No, if your goal is really simple, such as a request to meet. But even then, you're better off knowing whether this particular recipient needs a clear reason to spend time with you, how much notice she prefers, if she already has set feelings about the subject you want to discuss, and so on. You can tilt the result in your favor — even for a seemingly minor request — by taking account of such things.

The more major your message is, the more factors you may need to consider. Or perhaps just one facet of the person's situation or personality may be overwhelmingly important. To shape the right message, check out the section on knowing your reader in Book 6, Chapter 1 for what's relevant to the person and the case at hand. Think about the factors that are most relevant in the context of what you're asking for.

REMEMBER

Audience analysis becomes instinctive with practice. And your better results soon reinforce its value.

Certain characteristics are always important. Considering your reader's age, for example, may seem rude or politically incorrect, but business writers beware — especially with emails. Different generations have genuinely different attitudes toward work, communications, rewards, authority, career development, and much more. If you're a Generation Y'er (born after 1980) or Generation X'er (born 1965 to 1980), you need to understand the Boomer's (born 1946 to 1964) need for respect, hierarchical thinking, correct grammar, courtesy, in-person communication, and more. This topic is described fully in Book 6, Chapter 1.

We often ask participants in writing workshops to create detailed profiles of their immediate supervisors. Pretend that you're an undercover agent and you're asked to file a report on the person you report to. Take 20 minutes and see what you can put together. First scan the demographic, psychographic, positioning, and personality traits outlined in Book 6, Chapter 1 and list those you think seem relevant to defining that person (for example, age, position, information preferences, hot buttons, and decision-making style). Then fill in what you know or intuit about the person under each category. You'll probably find that you understand far more about your boss than you think.

Read through the completed profile and you'll see major clues on how to communicate with that important person on a routine basis, as well as how to work with her successfully overall and make yourself more highly valued. You may uncover ways to strengthen your relationship or even turn it around.

Suppose you're inviting your immediate supervisor, Jane, to a staff meeting where you plan to present an idea for a new project. You hope to persuade her that your project is worth the resources to make it happen. First clarify your goal or set of goals. Perhaps, in no particular order, you aim to do the following:

>> Obtain Jane's buy-in and endorsement

>> Get input on project tweaks sooner rather than later

>> Gain the resources you need for the project

>> Demonstrate what a terrific asset you are (a constant)

You know Jane is heavily scheduled and the invite must convince her to reserve the time. What factors about her should you consider? Your analysis may suggest the following:

>> **Demographics:** Jane is young for her position, and the first woman to hold that job. Observation supports the idea that she feels pressured to prove herself. She drives herself hard and works 60-hour weeks.

>> **Psychographics:** She is famously pro-technology, a true believer, and an early adaptor.

>> **Positioning:** She has the authority to approve a pilot program but probably not more. She is most likely being groomed for higher positions and is closely monitored.

>> **Personality/communication style:** She likes statistics. She likes evidence. She's an impatient listener who makes decisions when she feels she has just enough information. Her hottest button is being able to show her own manager that she's boosted her department's numbers. How to do that probably keeps her up at night, along with how to impress her boss for her next promotion. She takes risks if she feels reasonably sheltered from bad consequences.

Presto! With these four points, you have a reader profile to help you write Jane a must-come email — and even more importantly, a guide that enables you to structure a meeting that accomplishes what you want.

Determining the best content for emails

After you know your goal and audience, you have the groundwork in place for good content decisions. You know how to judge what information is likely to lead the person or group to respond the way you want. (See Chapter 1 in this minibook for guidance on how to address groups and construct a reader who epitomizes that group.)

FINDING THE RIGHT TONE FOR EMAIL

In everyday emails, your tone contributes hugely to coming across as empathetic, so never overlook it. Chapter 1 in this minibook describes tone as it applies to all writing; here, you find out about tone in electronic communications.

Often you can identify the appropriate tone by briefly thinking about the person you're writing to. Imagine yourself in conversation with him and determine where the atmosphere falls along the spectrum of formal and professionally reserved to casual and friendly.

If you're writing to someone you don't know or to a group, edge toward the more formal but avoid sounding stilted or indifferent. Conveying a degree of warmth and caring is nearly always appropriate because people respond well to that.

Strive for positive energy in all your emails unless for some reason it feels inappropriate. Granted, you have limited ways to express enthusiasm and must balance word choice and content to achieve a positive tone. Punctuation offers the option of exclamation points. Many people use them more freely nowadays because electronic communication offers so few ways to sound excited. But don't scatter them everywhere and make yourself look childish. This recommendation also holds for emoticons, all those cute symbols popularized by texting. Unless you know your reader well, do not use them. Older people especially may regard you as lightweight. Remember, too, that some graphic emoticons don't translate between various technologies and may be auto-replaced with who knows what!

TIP

To figure out what you need to say, play a matching game: What information, facts, ideas, statistics, and so on will engage the person and dispose her to say yes?

Think about audience *benefits*. This important marketing concept applies to all persuasive pitches. Benefits speak to the underlying reasons you want something. A dress, for example, possesses features such as color, style, and craftsmanship, but the benefit is that it makes the wearer feel beautiful. When you're planning a message and want it to succeed, think about the audience and goal, and write down your first ideas about matching points and benefits.

For example, to draw Jane from the preceding section to that meeting, the list may include the following based on your analysis:

>> Evidence that the idea works well somewhere else

>> Information on how cutting-edge technology will be used

>> Potential for the idea to solve a major problem for the department

>> Suggestion that other parts of the company will also be interested and impressed

Many other ideas may be relevant — such as it's great for the environment, and it gives people more free time — but probably not to Jane.

Structuring Your Middle Ground

Think of your email message like a sandwich: The opening and closing hold your content together and the rest is the filling. Viewed in this way, most emails are easy to organize. Complicated messages full of subtle ideas and in-depth instructions or pronouncements are inappropriate to the medium anyway.

Email's typical orientation toward the practical means that how you set up and how you close count heavily — but the middle still matters. Typically the in-between content explains why — why a particular decision should be made, why you deserve an opportunity, or why the reader should respond positively. The middle portion can also explain in greater detail why a request is denied, or provide details and technical backup, or describe a series of steps to accomplish something.

Figure out middle section content by first brainstorming what points will accomplish your goal in terms of your target audience, as outlined in the previous sections. Then do the following:

1. **Write a simple list of the points to make.** One example is the list created to convince Jane to come to a meeting with a positive mind-set in the "Determining the best content for emails" section.

2. **Scan your list and frame your lead.**

   Your *lead* is the sentence or paragraph that clearly tells readers why you're writing and what you want in a way most likely to engage their interest. Starting with the bottom line is almost always your best approach for organizing a message. Remember the reporter's mantra: Don't bury the lead.

Skipping the subject line for now, a get-Jane-to-the-meeting message can begin like this:

Hi Jane,

I'm ready to show you how using new social media can help us increase market share for our entire XL line. After checking the online calendar for your availability, I scheduled the demo for March 5 at 2. Can you meet with me and my team then?

To structure the middle, consider the previously identified points that are most important to Jane:

>> Evidence that the idea works well somewhere else

>> Opportunity to use cutting-edge technology

>> Potential to solve a major problem

>> Potential for wide company interest

You then simply march through these points for the body of the message. For example:

My research shows that two companies in related industries have reaped 15 to 20 percent increases in market share in just a few months. For us, the new media I've identified can potentially move XL out of the sales doldrums of the past two quarters.

Further, we'll be positioning our department at the cutting edge of strategic social media marketing. If we succeed as I anticipate, I see the entire company taking notice of our creative leadership.

The thinking you did before you started to write now pays handsome dividends. With a little reshuffling of the four points, you have a persuasive memo that is organized and logical. You know your content and how it fits together.

This process may sound easy to do with an invented example, but working with real ideas and facts is even easier.

REMEMBER

Your biggest strength in building a successful message in any format is to know your story. Organizing a clear email is rarely a problem after you determine your content. You simply need to know such factors as the following:

>> How the person you want to meet with may benefit by seeing you

>> Why your recipient will find your report or proposal of interest

>> Why the employment manager should read *your* resume

Review the list you assemble, decide which points to include, and put them in a logical order. Your list may include more thoughts than you need for a convincing message, and you can be selective. That's fine. Just enough is better than too much.

This basic premise works with longer, more formal documents as well.

Closing Strong

After you write your lead and the middle, you need to close (and perhaps circle back to fill in or hone your subject line).

TIP

When you use the guidelines in the previous sections to begin messages and develop the middle, your close needs only to reinforce what you want. An email doesn't need to end dramatically. You just want to circle back to the beginning and add any more relevant information to the "ask." For example:

>> If you requested a decision, writing something like the following is sufficient: *I look forward to knowing your decision by October 21st.*

>> If you're delivering a report, your close might be this: *I appreciate your review. Please let me know if you have any questions or if you'd like additional information.*

>> In the case of the memo to Jane, the closing might be simply, *Please let me know if March 5th at 2 p.m. works for you. If not, I'm happy to reschedule.*

Sign off with courtesy and tailor the degree of formality to the occasion and relationship. If you're writing to a conservative person or a businessman in another culture, a formal closing such as *Sincerely* is often best. The same is true for a resume's cover letter, which is essentially a letter in email form and should look like a letter.

But in most situations, less formal end-signals are better, such as the following:

Thanks!

I look forward to your response.

Best regards

Avoid cute signoffs such as *Cheers.* Always end with your name — your first name if you know the person or are comfortable establishing informality. Even if your reader is someone who hears from you all the time, using your name personalizes the message and alerts her that the communication is truly finished.

Your finished message needs one more thing: the subject line. Consider at this point the total thrust of your content. Then decide what words and phrases work best to engage your audience's interest.

The *Jane* subject line, for example, needs to get across that your message is a meeting invitation, suggest what it's about, and emphasize that it is worth her time. Perhaps:

Need you there: May 3rd Demo, Social Media Project

Perfecting Your Writing for Email

Email deserves your best writing, editing, and proofreading skills. Often the message is *who you are* to your audience. You may be communicating with someone you'll never meet, in which case the virtual interaction determines the relationship and the success of the message. At other times, crafting good email messages wins you the opportunity to present your case in person or progress to the next stage of doing business.

WARNING

PRACTICING EMAIL SMARTS

Email is a great facilitator in many ways, but it definitely has limits. Email's easiness can lead you to inappropriate use. Don't use it to do the following:

- **Present complicated issues or subjects:** Of course you can attach a report, a proposal, or another long document to an email, but don't expect an email in itself to produce an investment, donation or other high-stakes buy-in.

- **Wax philosophical or poetic:** Readers look to email for practical communication and are annoyed by windy meanderings — even (or especially) if you're the boss.

- **Spam:** Send email only to people directly concerned with the subject and don't send unnecessary replies. Don't forward cute anecdotes or jokes unless you're sure the particular person welcomes that. And don't forward chain letters: They can upset recipients. Don't forward anything without reading it thoroughly and carefully.

- **Amuse:** Generally avoid sarcasm and irony (and most humor), because it can be misinterpreted against your interests.

Never respond to poorly considered and written emails with poor emails of your own. You don't know who else may see them, and even those who write poorly — perhaps through a feeling of executive privilege — may disrespect you for doing the same. Enjoy feeling superior (without expressing it, of course)! Your excellent emails reward you over the long run as almost nothing else can.

REMEMBER

People look for clues about you and draw conclusions from what you write and how you write it. Even if your ideas are good, incorrect grammar and spelling lose you more points than you may suspect, no matter how informal your relationship with the recipient seems.

The following sections run through some top tips for crafting text that perfectly suits email.

Monitoring length and breadth

Keep emails to fewer than 300 words and stick to one idea or question. Three hundred words can go a long way (the memo to draw Jane to the meeting in the previous section was less than 150 words).

Such limits are hard to consistently observe, but you're wise to remember how short people's attention spans are, especially for online reading. That's why you benefit from knowing your central point or request, and opening with it. Don't bury it as a grand conclusion. Nor should you bury any important secondary questions at the end.

TIP

Aim to make emails as brief and tight as you can. If your message starts to grow too much, reconsider whether email is the appropriate format. You may choose to use the message as a cover note and attach the full document. Or you may want to break the message into components to send separately over a reasonable space of time. But realize that you risk losing your audience if you send a series of messages.

Styling it right

Choose words and phrases that are conversational, friendly, businesslike, and unequivocally clear. Email is not the place for fanciful language and invention. Put your energy into the content and structure of your message.

Try to make your presentation transparent, eliminating all barriers to understanding. Your messages may end up less colorful than they could be, and that's okay. Clear, concise language is especially relevant to messages directed at overseas audiences.

Going short: Words, sentences, paragraphs

The business writing guidelines presented in Chapter 2 in this minibook apply even more intensely to email. You want your message to be readable and understood in the smallest possible amount of time.

Draw on the plain old Anglo-Saxon word stock, mostly one-syllable words. Use two-syllable words when they express ideas better, use three syllables when they're the best choice, but reserve more lengthy and complex words for when they serve a real purpose.

Short sentences work for the same reason. Aim for 10 to 15 words on average. Paragraphs should contain one to three sentences to support comprehension and build in helpful white space.

Using graphic techniques to promote clarity

The graphic techniques discussed here don't require special software or a degree in fine arts. They're simply ways to visually present information and make your writing more organized and accessible.

TIP

Do everything you can to incorporate generous *white space* (areas with no text or graphics) into your writing. Don't crowd your messages and leave them (and the reader) gasping for air. White space allows the eye to rest and focuses emphasis where you want it.

Add subheads

Subheads are great for longer emails. You can make the type bold and add a line of space above it. Subheads for email can be matter of fact:

Why decide now

Step 1 (followed by Step 2 and so on)

Final recommendation

Pros and cons

Background

This technique neatly guides the reader through the information and also enables you as a writer to organize your thinking and delivery with ease.

Drafting all your subheads *before* you write can be a terrific way to achieve good organization. Choose a message that you already wrote and found challenging. Think the subject through to come up with the major points or steps to cover, and then write a simple, suitable subhead for each. Put the subheads in order and add the relevant content under each. (Each section need not be more than a paragraph long.) Now check whether all the necessary information to make your point is there — if not, add it. Your message is sure to become clearer and more cohesive and persuasive.

Providing your own structure in this way may make writing easier, particularly if you feel organizationally challenged. It helps ensure that you don't leave out anything important, too.

Here's an extra trick. If you feel that you have too many subheads after drafting the message, cut some or all of them. You still have a solid, logically organized email. Just be sure to check that the connections between sections are clear without the subheads.

Bring in bulleted and numbered lists

Bullets offer another excellent option for presenting your information. They are

>> Readily absorbed

>> Fast to read

>> Easy to write

>> Useful for equipment lists, examples, considerations, and other groupings

However, observe a few cautions:

>> Don't use more than six or seven bullets in a list. A long stretch of bullets loses all effect; they become mind numbing and hard to absorb.

>> Don't use bullets to present ideas that need context or connection.

>> Don't mix and match. The items on your list must be *parallel,* so that they begin with the same kind of word — a verb, a noun, or in the case of the preceding bullet list, an adverb.

Never use bullet lists as a dumping ground for thoughts that you're too lazy to organize or connect. If you doubt this advice, think of all the bad Microsoft PowerPoint shows you've seen — screens rife with random-seeming bullets.

Numbered lists are also helpful, particularly if you're presenting a sequence or step-by-step process. Instructions work well in numbered form. Give numbered lists some air so that they don't look intimidating — skip a space between each number.

Consider boldface

Making your type bold gives you a good option for calling attention to key topics, ideas, or subsections of your message. You can use bold for lead-ins:

> **Holiday party coming up.** *Please see the task list and choose how you want to contribute . . .*

You may also use bold to highlight something in the body of the text:

> *Please see the task list and choose your way of contributing **by December 10.***

If you overload your message with boldface, you undermine its reason for being. Keep in mind that boldface doesn't always transfer across different email systems and software, so don't depend on it too much for making your point.

Underlining important words or phrases is another option.

Respect overall graphic impact

REMEMBER

Avoid undercutting your content through bad graphic presentation. Plain and simple is the way to go. Use plain text or the simplest HTML — no tricky, cute, or hard-to-read fonts. Don't write entire messages in capitals or italics, and don't use a rainbow of color — that's distracting rather than fun for readers. Avoid that crammed-in feeling. People simply do not read messages that look dense and difficult. Or they read as little of them as possible. Like everything else you write, an email must look inviting and accessible.

Using the signature block

Contact information these days can be complex. Typically you want people to find you by email or telephone. Plus there's your tagline. Your company name. Your website. Your blog. The book you wrote. The published article. Twitter. Facebook. LinkedIn. Professional affiliations and offices.

Decide on a few things you most want to call attention to and refrain from adding the rest. Better yet, create several signature blocks for different audiences. Then you can select the most appropriate one for the people to whom you're writing. Don't include your full signature block every time you respond to a message, especially if you incorporate a logo, which arrives as an attachment. Check your email program's settings so the automatic signature is minimal or absent.

7

Digital Marketing

Contents at a Glance

Chapter **1**

Understanding the Customer Journey

Think about the last important purchase you made. Perhaps you bought a car, hired a babysitter, or switched coffee suppliers at your office. Chances are, you consulted the Internet to read reviews, got recommendations from friends and family on social sites such as Facebook, and boned up on the features, options, and price of the product or service before you made your choice. Today, purchases and purchasing decisions are increasingly made online. Therefore, regardless of what you sell, an online presence is necessary to capitalize on this trend.

This new digital landscape is affecting organizations in more than just the lead and sales generation departments, though. Savvy companies use the Internet not only to drive awareness and interest in what they offer, but also to convert casual buyers into brand advocates who buy more and encourage members of their network to do the same.

In many ways, nothing in marketing has changed. Marketing is still about developing a mutually beneficial relationship with prospects, leads, and customers. We call the development of this relationship the *customer journey.* In this chapter, you create a customer journey for your organization and learn about the role digital marketing plays in that journey.

REMEMBER

The role of your digital marketing is to assist in moving a prospect, lead, or customer from one stage of the customer journey to the next.

Creating a Customer Avatar

Because the role of your marketing is to move people through a series of stages from cold prospects to rabid fans and promoters, you must first attain clarity on the characteristics of your ideal customers. You want to understand their goals, the challenges they face meeting those goals, and where they spend time consuming information and entertainment. Creating a customer avatar will give you this clarity. Other terms for *customer avatar* are *buyer persona*, *marketing persona*, and *target audience*, but *customer avatar (or just avatar)* is the term we use throughout this minibook.

A *customer avatar* is the fictional, generalized representation of your ideal customer. Realistically, unless your product or service fits in a narrow niche, you'll have multiple customer avatars for each campaign. People are so much more than their age, gender, ethnicity, religious background, profession, and so on. People don't fit neatly into boxes, which is why broad, generic marketing campaigns generally don't convert well; they don't resonate with your audience.

REMEMBER

It's crucial that you understand your customer avatar and make it as specific as possible so that you can craft personalized content, offers, and marketing campaigns that interest members of your audience or solve their problems.

The exercise of creating a customer avatar affects virtually every aspect of your marketing, including the following:

>> **Content marketing:** What blog posts, videos, podcasts, and so on should you create to attract and convert your avatar?

>> **Search marketing:** What solutions is your avatar searching for on search engines such as Google, YouTube (yes, YouTube is a search engine), and Bing?

>> **Social media marketing:** What social media sites is your avatar spending time on? What topics does your avatar like to discuss?

>> **Email marketing:** Which avatar should receive a specific email marketing campaign?

>> **Paid traffic:** Which ad platforms should you buy traffic from and how will you target your avatar?

>> **Product creation:** What problems is your avatar trying to solve?

>> **Copywriting:** How should you describe offers in your email marketing, ads, and sales letters in a way that compels your avatar to buy?

Any part of the marketing and sales process that touches the customer (which is pretty much everything) improves when you get clear on your customer avatar. After all, you're aiming toward a real person — one who buys your products and services. It pays to understand the characteristics of that person so that you can find and present him or her with a message that moves this person to action.

Components of your customer avatar

The customer avatar possesses five major components:

>> **Goals and values:** Determine what the avatar is trying to achieve. What values does he or she hold dear?

>> **Sources of information:** Figure out what books, magazines, blogs, news stations, and other resources the avatar references for information.

>> **Demographics:** Establish the age, gender, marital status, ethnicity, income, employment status, nationality, and political preference of the avatar.

>> **Challenges and pain points:** What is holding the avatar back from achieving his or her goals?

>> **Objections:** Why would the avatar choose not to buy your product or service?

In some cases, you need to conduct a survey or have conversations with existing customers to accurately flesh out your customer avatar. In other cases, you may already be intimately familiar with the characteristics of your ideal customer. In any case, move forward. Don't wait for surveys or interviews to be conducted to create your first draft of an avatar. Instead, go ahead and make assumptions despite having no data or feedback, and put completing your research on your short list of to-do's. In the meantime, you can begin benefiting from the avatar you've created.

TIP

Giving a customer avatar a name assists in bringing this fictional character to life. In addition, your team members have a way to refer to each avatar among themselves.

Using the five elements described in this section, we created a worksheet that we complete each time we create a new customer avatar. The worksheet helps you hone in on the ideal customer and pair him or her with the right message. In the following sections, we go into more detail about this worksheet so that you can use it in your own business.

Introducing Agency Eric: A customer avatar example

For this real-life example, we use the introduction of a new offer by DigitalMarketer. The company began selling a new type of digital marketing training product called certification classes. This training product, which includes exams, certificates, and badges, appeals to a new ideal customer. Of course, having a new ideal customer means that a new customer avatar must be built.

As a result, we defined four distinct buyer personas who would be interested in certifications and training from the company:

>> **The marketing freelancer:** Wants to distinguish herself from the other freelancers she is competing with in the marketplace

>> **The marketing agency owner:** Wants to add to the services he can offer his clients and to sharpen the marketing skills of his employees

>> **The employee:** Wants to distinguish himself at his place of employment or to secure a new job or promotion within his existing job

>> **The business owner:** Wants to sharpen her own marketing skills and the skills of her internal marketing team members

From the buyer personas, four new customer avatars were born. We call one of these new avatars, pictured in Figure 1-1, Agency Eric.

FIGURE 1-1: Agency Eric is a customer avatar who purchases the certification product from DigitalMarketer.

The next section describes the approach to filling out each section of the customer avatar worksheet so that you can define your customer avatars.

Getting clear on goals and values

The customer avatar creation process begins with identifying the goals and values of one of your ideal customers. Make note of the goals and values that are relevant to the products and services you offer.

Being aware of your customer avatar's goals and values drives decisions that you make about the following:

>> **Product creation:** What products or services can you develop to assist the avatar in meeting his or her goals?

>> **Advertising:** How can you describe these offers in your ads and sales copy?

>> **Content marketing:** What blog posts, podcasts, newsletters, and other content vehicles might your avatar respond to?

>> **Email marketing:** How can you tailor your email subject lines and body copy to be consistent with the avatar's goals?

At DigitalMarketer, the Agency Eric avatar owns a digital marketing agency and manages a team of marketers providing services to clients. One of Agency Eric's goals (shown in Figure 1-2) is to increase the capabilities of his team. Agency Eric knows that a more capable team will result in satisfied customers.

GOALS AND VALUES

Goals:
Eric wants to
- Increase agency business
- Increase the capabilities of his team
- Scale his business

Values:
Eric is committed to
- Professional development for himself and his employees
- Providing value for his clients
- Using "white hat" marketing principles

FIGURE 1-2: Understanding the goals and values of your avatar is important.

Because Agency Eric has this goal, he is likely to open and respond to an email that promotes the company's Content Marketing Certification with the following subject line:

Need Content Marketing training?

Finding sources of information and entertainment

This section of the customer avatar worksheet is critical to determining where your customer avatar is spending his time on and offline. What books does he read? What celebrities does he follow? What blogs does he read? This is vital information when considering where you will advertise and how you will target those advertisements.

TIP

The key to truly understanding where your customer is getting information and entertainment is in identifying niche sources. Identifying these niches is fairly simple using the But No One Else Would trick. To use this trick, you simply complete sentences such as the following:

>> My ideal customer would read [*book*], but no one else would.

>> My ideal customer would subscribe to [*magazine*], but no one else would.

>> My ideal customer would attend [*conference*], but no one else would.

The idea is to find the niche books, magazines, blogs, conferences, celebrities, and other interests that your ideal customer — but no one else — would be attracted to. For example, if you sell golf products, you wouldn't assign Tiger Woods as a celebrity. Tiger Woods is a celebrity your customer avatar would follow, but a large percentage of people interested in Tiger Woods are not golfers and aren't likely to buy your golf products.

Instead, choosing a more niche golfer such as Rory McIlroy allows you to hone in on your ideal customer and exclude people who wouldn't find value in your product. If you find these niches when buying traffic from ad platforms such as Facebook, you can often laser-target your audience by focusing on prospects who have these niche interests, while excluding less-than-ideal prospects.

Honing in on demographics

Applying demographic information brings your customer avatar to life. In this section, you add information to your avatar such as age, gender, marital status, and location.

TIP

Although the usual demographics are critical, the exercise of filling in the Quote field (shown in Figure 1-3) can be particularly helpful to get inside the head of your ideal customer. The Quote field is how this avatar might define himself or herself in one sentence, or is the motto the avatar lives by. For instance, the quote for Agency Eric is "I surround myself with people smarter than I." This sentence says a lot about this avatar's character and motivation to purchase the marketing training products. Brainstorm ideas for your avatar's quote with your team or someone who knows your business well.

Age: 40

Gender: Male

Marital Status: Married

#/Age of Children: 2 (Age 8 & 10)

Location: Orlando, Florida

Quote: "I surround myself with people smarter than I."

Occupation: Digital Marketing

Job Title: CEO/Founder

Annual Income: $150,000

Level of Education: College Graduate

Other: Spends time on LinkedIn looking for talent.

Demographic information for your customer avatar is also useful for choosing targeting options in ad platforms such as Facebook. Bring your avatar to life as much as possible, even by visualizing the person if you can. When you're writing content, email, or sales copy, it can be beneficial to write as though your avatar were sitting across the table from you. Demographic information such as age, gender, and location give your persona a look and feel.

Adding challenges and pain points

This section of the worksheet can help drive new product or service development. It can also help inspire the copy and ad creative you'll use to compel your ideal customer to action. *Copy* is any written word that makes up your ad, email, web page, social media post, or blog post. *Ad creative* is an object that communicates information in visual form, such as an image, a GIF (graphics interchange format), a video, an infographic, a meme, or another form of artwork that you use to convey your message. You use copy and ad creatives to call out to your audience, capture people's attention, and address how your product or service adds value to their lives by solving a pain point or a challenge they face.

When selling certifications to Agency Eric, for example, the company would do well to build solutions to his challenges and pain points and use language that addresses them in its marketing messages. For example, this avatar would respond to sales copy like the following:

> Are you tired of losing proposals simply because you don't offer content marketing services to your clients? Certify your team with DigitalMarketer's Content Marketing Mastery Course and Certification.

Copy like this receives a response from Agency Eric because it is specific to one of his pain points, which is the fear of losing business to competitors (see Figure 1-4).

FIGURE 1-4:
Understanding
the challenges
and pain points
of your customer
informs your
marketing efforts.

CHALLENGES AND PAIN POINTS

Challenges:
Eric is challenged with
- Scaling his agency business
- Finding, training, and retaining top marketing talent
- Keeping his marketing skills sharp while being CEO

Pain points:
Eric's pain points are
- Fear of losing business to competitors
- Fear of his agency falling behind the digital marketing scene

Preparing for objections

In the final section of the customer avatar worksheet, answer why your customer avatar might choose to decline the offer to buy your product or service. The reasons your avatar doesn't buy are called *objections,* and you must address them in your marketing. For example, if we know that Agency Eric is concerned with the amount of time his team members will be out of the office or unable to work while getting trained, we can send an email that overcomes that objection with a subject line like this:

> Get Content Marketing Certified (in one business day).

TIP

You can prepare your own customer avatar as we discuss with the help of a resource from DigitalMarketer. Find it at www.digitalmarketer.com/customer-avatar.

Getting Clear on the Value You Provide

An important part of planning for digital marketing success is understanding the value your organization brings to the marketplace. The value your company provides is far greater than the products or services it sells. People don't buy products or services — they buy outcomes.

Imagine a group of people who are discontent for one reason or another. This group of people are in what we call the Before state (see Figure 1-5). No matter what you're selling, you're trying to reach a group of prospective customers who are in this Before state. To gain some insight, write the adjectives that describe your prospective customer before she has experienced your product or service. Is she sad? Out of shape? Bored?

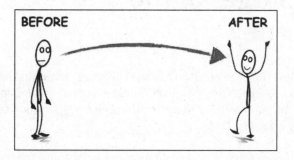

Now, leap forward into the future, to the point after your prospective customer has experienced your product or service. What is her After state? How has this person changed? In the same place where you took notes about her Before state, describe her After state. Is she happier? Healthier? More excited?

The shift from the Before state to the After state is what your customer is buying. This shift (or outcome) is the value that your business brings to the marketplace. Furthermore, the role of your marketing is to articulate this move from the Before state to the After state.

The understanding of this transition from Before to After is what allows you to craft what is called a statement of value. This statement is important because it sums up the value of your product or service. To craft your statement of value, simply fill in the blanks on the sentence shown in Figure 1-6.

STATEMENT OF VALUE

_____ enables
(Product Name)

_____ to experience
(Customer)

_____

_____

FIGURE 1-6:
Fill in the blanks on your statement of value.

The role of your marketing is to assist in moving a prospect, lead, or customer from one stage of the customer journey to the next. At the beginning of this journey, your customer is in the Before state. By the end, you will have taken your customer on a journey to that customer's ideal After state.

Knowing the Stages of the Customer Journey

If your business has acquired even a single customer, some kind of customer journey is in place. Perhaps this customer journey was not created intentionally, but it does exist. Or perhaps you call it something else in your organization, such as a marketing or sales pipeline.

Regardless of what you call it, becoming intentional about the movement of cold prospects, leads, and existing customers through the stages of this journey is the purpose of your marketing. When you've properly charted your ideal customer journey, you quickly find the bottlenecks that are restricting the flow of prospect to lead, lead to customer, and customer to raving fan.

We can't overstate the importance of sequence in marketing, and particularly in digital marketing. Moving cold prospects from one stage of the customer journey to the next must be done seamlessly and subtly. You're not likely to convert a complete stranger into a brand advocate overnight, but you can gradually move the prospect from one stage of the relationship to the next. To move people through the stages of the customer journey, go through the following eight steps. A worksheet that visualizes the steps of the customer journey is provided in the final section of this chapter.

Step 1: Generating awareness

Every repeat customer and raving fan of your business was, at one time, a stranger to your company. She had no idea what problems you solve, what products you sell, or what your brand stands for. The first step on her journey from cold prospect to raving fan is awareness. If awareness is your issue, you should employ the following digital marketing tactics:

>> **Advertising:** Advertising, both online and offline, is a reliable and effective method of raising awareness.

>> **Social media marketing:** Billions of people access social media sites such as Facebook, Twitter, and LinkedIn every day. Social media marketing is an inexpensive method of raising awareness.

>> **Search marketing:** Billions of web searches on sites such as Google and Bing are processed every day. Basic search marketing techniques direct some of that traffic to your website.

Figure 1-7 shows an awareness campaign from TransferWise, a company created by the same people who built Skype. TransferWise is a relatively new company in the money transfer business, and it uses the Facebook advertising platform to raise awareness of the service. Notice how the language used in this ad focuses on teaching what TransferWise is and how you benefit from using the service.

FIGURE 1-7:
A Facebook advertisement focused on the goal of awareness.

Step 2: Driving engagement

It's not enough to simply make a cold prospect aware of your business, products, and brand. You must engineer your marketing to capture the attention of your prospect and engage him. For a digital marketer, that engagement almost always takes the form of valuable content made freely available in the form of

>> Blog posts

>> Podcasts

>> Online videos

For example, the grocery store Whole Foods prides itself in selling fresh, organic foods from its hundreds of brick-and-mortar locations. The supermarket chain's online strategy includes its Whole Story blog, which engages its ideal customer with content relevant to the products the company sells. Blog articles with titles such as "9 Refreshing Summer Drinks You Need to Try Right Now" (see Figure 1-8) show existing and prospective customers how to use the products sold at Whole Foods.

9 Refreshing Summer Drinks You Need To Try Right Now

Like 0   Tweet

G+1   3

By Kate Rowe, July 12, 2016 | Meet the Blogger | More Posts by Kate

The summer heat is now upon us, but you can stay cool with refreshing, family-friendly drinks right now. We're all about using unexpected ingredients, making juice in the blender, and finding shortcuts to delicious summer sippers.

FIGURE 1-8:
An engaging blog post from the Whole Foods blog.

REMEMBER

A prospect, lead, or customer may spend anywhere from a few minutes to a few years at any one of the stages in this customer journey. For example, a prospect might become aware of your blog and engage with it for a year or more before moving to the next phase of the journey. Others will sprint through multiple stages of the journey in the space of a few minutes. A healthy business has groups of people at all stages of the journey at all times.

Step 3: Building subscribers

The next step in the customer journey is to graduate a prospect from the "merely aware and engaged" stage to the stage of being a subscriber or lead. A *subscriber* is anyone who has given you permission to have a conversation with him. Savvy digital marketers create lists of subscribers by building social media connections on sites such as Facebook and Twitter, attracting podcast subscribers on services such as iTunes and Stitcher, or generating subscribers from webinar registrations.

Offline companies might build subscription online by offering aware and engaged prospects the ability to receive physical mail or request a consultative sales call or product demo.

But the Holy Grail of lead generation in the digital marketing realm is email subscription. Email is, by far, the cheapest and highest-converting method of moving a prospect through the rest of the stages of this customer journey. We tell you more about email marketing in Chapter 5 of this minibook, but for now, take a look at an example of an effective email marketing campaign from one of the world's largest furniture retailers, IKEA.

IKEA builds social media subscribers on Facebook, Twitter, Pinterest, and more, but acquiring email subscribers is clearly the focal point of IKEA's digital marketing efforts. Upon visiting the IKEA website, you're asked in multiple locations to join IKEA's email list. Figure 1-9 shows an email opt-in form from the IKEA website.

FIGURE 1-9:
An email subscription offer from furniture retailer IKEA.

Step 4: Increasing conversions

At this stage, the goal is to elevate the commitment level of the prospect by asking him or her to give you a small amount of time or money. Low-dollar products or services, webinars, and product demos are all good offers to make during this stage.

Up to this point, the relationship with this prospect through the first three stages of the customer journey has been passive. The goal of stage 4 is not profitability, but rather an increased level of connection between the prospect and your business. One company that achieves this increased connection is GoDaddy, which allows you to, among other things, register a domain name for a website as well as host and design one for your business. GoDaddy uses a low-dollar domain registration offer with a two-year purchase (see Figure 1-10) to acquire customers and ramp up the commitment level.

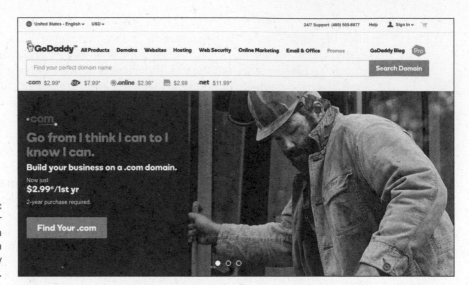

FIGURE 1-10:
A low-dollar offer
from domain
registration
company
GoDaddy.

Step 5: Building excitement

Your marketing should intentionally encourage your customer to use the offer that your lead or customer accepted in Step 4. The business term for getting your prospect to take advantage of an offer is *customer onboarding*. Regardless of whether the conversion in Step 4 was a commitment of time or money, the relationship with this customer or prospect has a much greater chance of success if she received value from the transaction.

DigitalMarketer has a community called DigitalMarketer Lab, made up of thousands of entrepreneurs, freelancers, and small business owners. Each new DigitalMarketer Lab member receives an onboarding packet (see Figure 1-11) from the company through post mail that teaches Lab members how to get the most out of their new purchase. This packet builds excitement by explaining all the benefits of being a member, and it shows members exactly how to get started receiving those benefits. By building excitement and teaching customers to be successful, we've seen dramatically lower cancellation rates.

REMEMBER

The value of the offers you make should far outweigh the price paid by your customer. Deliver great products and services and create marketing campaigns that encourage the use of those products and services. After all, your customers aren't likely to continue buying or promoting your brand to others if they aren't using the product or service themselves.

FIGURE 1-11:
This onboarding packet builds excitement and teaches the customer how to be successful with the product.

Step 6: Making the core offer sale and more

At this stage, prospects have developed a relationship with your brand. They may have invested a bit of time or money with you. People who develop this rapport with your company are much more likely to buy a more complex, expensive, or risky product or service from you. We call this jump from passive prospect to buyer *ascension*.

Unfortunately, this is where most businesses start and end their marketing. Some ask cold prospects to make risky investments of time and money with a company they know nothing about. This is the equivalent of proposing marriage to someone on a first date: The success rate is low. Other brands stop marketing to a customer after that particular customer has converted (made a purchase) instead of staying in touch with and converting that person into a repeat buyer.

In the ascension stage, customers or prospects purchase high-ticket products or services, sign up for subscriptions that bill them monthly, or become loyal, repeat buyers. Assuming that you have done the hard work in stages 1–5 of the customer journey, you should find that some of your leads and customers are ready to buy more, and buy repeatedly. That's because you've built a relationship with them and effectively communicated the value you can bring to their lives. When you market to your customers in this sequence, they're on the path to becoming brand advocates and promoters (see the upcoming sections about Steps 7 and 8). We discuss different strategies for selling more to your existing customers in Chapter 2 of this minibook when we cover profit maximizers.

Step 7: Developing brand advocates

Brand advocates give you testimonials about the fabulous experience they've had with your brand. They are fans of your company and defend your brand on social media channels and, if asked, leave great reviews for your products or services on sites such as Yelp or Amazon.

Your ability to create brand advocates depends on the relationship you have with these leads and buyers. When you've reached this step, your customer and your company are like close friends in the sense that developing the relationship to this level took time and effort, and maintaining that relationship — one that is mutually beneficial to both parties — will take time and effort also.

You build this relationship by adding value, delivering on the promise of your product (meaning that it actually does what you claim it will do), and with responsive customer service. By consistently delivering quality products and services, you can turn people into brand advocates and ultimately move them into the final step: brand promoter.

Step 8: Growing brand promoters

Brand promoters go beyond advocacy and do everything from tattooing your logo across their chest (think Harley-Davidson) to dedicating hours of their free time blogging and using social media to spread their love of your brand online. The difference between an advocate (Step 7) and a brand promoter is that the promoter actively spreads the word about your business, whereas the advocate is more passive.

For brand promoters, your company has become part of their life. They know that your brand is one that they can trust and depend on. Brand promoters believe in you because your brand and your products have delivered exceptional value again and again. They have committed not only their money but also their time to you.

Preparing Your Customer Journey Road Map

For successful businesses, the customer journey doesn't happen by accident. Smart digital marketers engineer marketing campaigns that intentionally move prospects, leads, and customers from one stage to the next. After you become aware of your ideal customer journey, the tactics that should be employed become clear.

For example, if you determine that you have an issue building subscribers (Step 3 of the customer journey), you want to deploy tactics that generate email leads (covered in Chapter 5 of this minibook) and social media connections to move customers through this part of the customer journey.

Creating a customer journey road map that clearly delineates the eight stages that we cover in the previous section of this chapter (see Figure 1-12 for just such a road map) is a fantastic way to plan and visualize the path that an ideal customer will take from cold prospect to brand promoter. Gather the stakeholders in your company and complete a customer journey road map for at least one of your major products or services. Brainstorm which campaigns and offers to use at each step of the customer journey to make people aware of your product and move them from awareness to their desired After state onto the path of a brand promoter.

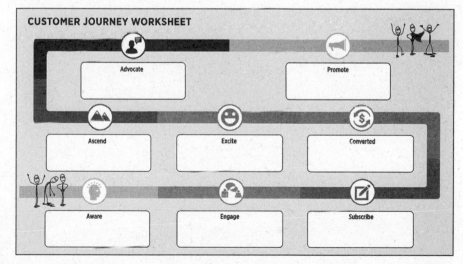

FIGURE 1-12: Create a customer journey road map for at least one of your core offers.

You can create your own customer journey road map with a resource from Digital-Marketer by going to www.digitalmarketer.com/customer-journey.

TIP

Chapter **2**

Crafting Winning Offers

Whether you're asking people to buy something, give you their contact information, or spend time reading your blog, you're making an offer. The way in which you make your offers — and perhaps more important, the sequence in which you make them — will make or break you online.

You should think of creating and nurturing relationships with your customers in the same way that you develop relationships with your friends and family. Your business might sell business to business (B2B) or business to consumer (B2C), but all businesses sell human to human (H2H). Real, individual people are buying your products and services.

Consider how perfect strangers become a married couple. The marriage proposal is an offer that is made after a sequence of other offers is made and deemed successful by both parties. Sure, the occasional marriage proposal on the first date occurs, but most relationships begin with a series of positive interactions over a period of time.

Although most people aren't likely to propose marriage on a first date, many businesses do the equivalent of that with their prospects. They ask cold prospects to buy high-ticket, complex, and otherwise risky products and services before the relationship is ready for that offer. On the other hand, a customer who has received tremendous value from your company over a period of time is much more likely to make a high-dollar, complex, or otherwise risky purchase.

In this chapter, we unpack the different types of offers you can make, the goals of those offers, and the order in which you should present them to prospective, new, and loyal customers. The offers explained in this chapter focus on Acquisition and Monetization campaigns.

Offering Value in Advance

Doing business online is different from doing business in person or even over the phone. In many cases, the prospective customer has no further information about your business than what is presented to her online. To acquire new leads and customers, you need to build trust and *lead with value* to build a relationship with your prospects or customers.

A successful relationship is a two-way street. Both sides of the relationship must benefit from the relationship, and because your company wants to begin this new relationship with a prospect, it makes sense for you to provide value first. Prospects won't become loyal customers if you don't first provide some value that builds trust in advance of asking them to buy. The good news is that you can provide this value with something as simple as an insightful, informative blog post or podcast that helps them solve a problem. You offer this value for free and with no strings attached to begin a healthy and mutually beneficial relationship.

We call acquisition offers that lead with value *entry point offers*, or EPOs. An EPO in a dating relationship equates to offering to buy someone a cup of coffee. This coffee offer, which has begun many healthy dating relationships, is a relatively risk-free proposition that provides value upfront. When your goal is to acquire a customer (and not a spouse), the EPO is a way of allowing large amounts of prospective customers to get to know, like, and trust your business without much risk.

There are three types of EPOs:

>> **Ungated:** You usually present this type of offer in the form of a blog post, video, or podcast, and it does not require contact information or a purchase to get value.

>> **Gated:** A gated offer requires contact information (name, email address, and so on) to get value.

>> **Deep discount:** This offer requires a purchase but at an extreme discount, usually 50 percent or greater.

It pays to provide tremendous value to your prospective customers when you're trying to gain their trust. This idea can seem counterintuitive to some people because they don't see the immediate return on this investment.

The goal of your marketing is to transform people from being completely unaware of your products or services to being raving fans who promote your products and services to anyone who will listen. The foundation of the relationships you build with your customers is built on offers that provide value in advance of the purchase.

Designing an Ungated Offer

Offers that require no risk on the part of prospective customers are the most powerful way to begin to cultivate strong relationships with customers. An *ungated offer* such as an informative article, video, or podcast gives value without asking for contact information or a purchase. That said, these are still offers. You are offering value to prospects in exchange for their time. And for many people, no other resource is more precious than time.

The value provided by the business is generally made available to prospects using content such as blog posts, social media updates, or videos. Successful digital marketers make free content available that provides one of the following values:

>> **Entertainment:** People pay a lot of money to be entertained, and content that makes a person laugh is content that is likely to be remembered. It's why commercials try to make you laugh (think the gecko from Geico or Flo from Progressive); they have only 30 to 60 seconds to cut through all the noise and get you to remember their product or service. Poo-Pourri's video advertisements on YouTube and Friskies' and Buzzfeed's Dear Kitten campaigns are prime examples of marketers providing entertaining content that gets their message across.

>> **Inspiration:** People are highly moved by content that makes them feel something. The sports and fitness industry taps into this sentiment with taglines like Just do it, by Nike, or Fitbit campaigns showing everyday people (as opposed to celebrities and professional athletes) achieving their goals using Fitbit. Weight-loss businesses also use inspirational content by using successful customer testimonials and before and after images.

>> **Education:** Ever go to YouTube to watch a how-to video? From DIY projects to how to rebuild a car engine, you can easily find educational content online. People want knowledge, and providing it helps build trust. Entire blogs, sites, YouTube channels, and businesses are built around educating people, to great success. That's why Wikipedia gets roughly 16 billion page views a month.

The first two value propositions (entertainment and inspiration) can be difficult to execute. But the third is within the grasp of every company.

REMEMBER

The production of content by brands is at an all-time high. An absolute glut of content is produced on blogs, YouTube channels, and social media sites every day. That said, an insatiable demand still exists for great ungated content. Don't make the mistake of thinking that because this content is free, it does not deserve the time and energy of your other offers. An ungated offer is, in many cases, the first transaction that a prospective customer will have with your company, and you should make it a successful one.

Designing a Gated Offer

To graduate someone from the stage of prospect to lead, you need a gated offer that requires prospects to submit their contact information to receive value. A *gated offer* provides a small chunk of value that solves a *specific* problem for a *specific* market and is offered in exchange for the prospects' contact information. That contact information is typically an email address, at a minimum. Returning to the dating relationship analogy earlier in the chapter, a gated offer is the equivalent of a first date. A gated offer might take the form of a white paper, a case study, or a webinar. For example, Figure 2-1 shows how OpenMarket makes valuable information available in the form of a white paper that requires contact information.

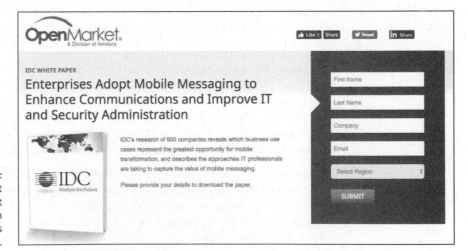

FIGURE 2-1:
OpenMarket asks for contact information in exchange for this white paper.

REMEMBER

A gated offer is an exchange in value. No money changes hands; instead, you provide your new lead something of value in exchange for the right to contact the lead in the future. Gated offers are free, and a common notion among digital marketers is that because they're giving the gated offer away for free, the product or service offered doesn't have to be of high quality. That's a mistake. Free does not mean low quality. When someone exchanges his contact information and gives you permission to follow up with him, he has given you value, and a transaction has taken place. This prospect has given you something that's typically private, as well as some of his time and attention. You need to return that value if you hope to build the relationship that is required for lifelong customers. The end goal of a gated offer is to gain leads so that you can nurture them into customers over time.

Revisit the definition of a gated offer (a gated offer provides a small chunk of value that solves a *specific* problem for a *specific* market and is offered in exchange for prospects' contact information) — and pay particular attention to the specific parts. Specificity is the key to a successful gated offer because it makes your offer more relevant to your audience. A lead form that simply states "Subscribe to our newsletter" is not a gated offer that will get you high conversions because it does not solve a specific problem. In the next section of this chapter, we discuss how to make your gated offer convert prospects by making it specific in terms of problem-solving, which will make your gated offer more relevant to your audience.

Zeroing in on what matters

In the previous section, we establish the idea that a specific and relevant gated offer works best for generating high opt-ins. But what does making the offer specific and relevant entail? High-converting gated offers include one, or a combination, of the following five aspects, in a specific form:

>> A promise

>> An example

>> A shortcut

>> A solution

>> A discount

Including at least one of these five items will help your conversion rates. The following sections take a look at each of these items.

Crafting Winning Offers

Making a specific promise

Making a specific promise is one of the simplest things you can do to increase the number of leads you receive from a gated offer. Look at the offer that you're delivering and think about how you can make the benefit of the offer more evident. Consider how you can speak to the specific desired end result of your prospect.

Craft a clear promise and then make sure that your promise is in the title of your gated offer. Generic or clever titles generally decrease the conversions on your gated offer. Many marketers are guilty of coming up with cutesy titles or using industry jargon in the title that their market may not understand. In your gated offer's title, talk less about your product and more about your target audience. Specifically communicate, in the gated offer's title, the benefit the gated offer will provide that target audience. Speak to the conversation that is going on inside the mind of your customer, not the one that you're having around the business table. Ask yourself, what are your target audience's concerns, fears, or desires? Think of the desired end result that your customer is seeking, and put that in the title. The gated offer shown in Figure 2-2 delivers a specific promise that resonates with its market.

FIGURE 2-2:
Copyblogger's gated offer clearly states what people can expect when they input their contact information.

Giving a specific example

In our experience, the best way to give a specific example in your gated offer is to deliver it in the form of a case study. If you have examples of real customers and prospects who have overcome problems with your product or service, these can work well as gated offers.

For instance, if your company sells surveillance cameras to universities, you might create a case study entitled "How State University Reduced Campus Crime by 73 Percent" that details how the university used surveillance camera technology to reduce acts of crime on the State campus. This headline clearly states the benefit and uses an example to add specificity to the gated offer.

Offering a specific shortcut

A gated offer that can save a person time is appealing and often converts well. For example, a gated offer that delivers a list of healthy snacks a person can eat throughout the day is a useful shortcut for someone looking to eat a more nutritious diet.

Answering a specific question

The fourth way you can make your gated offer more specific is by raising and answering a specific question. If the answer to the question is valuable, your prospects opt in to get the answer to that specific question, and after you've answered the question, you will have delivered on your promise and helped to establish yourself as an authority on the subject, which in turn helps build trust and moves the prospect closer to becoming a customer.

Delivering a specific discount

Price discounts can be a great way to spur sales, and many companies offer coupons that slash prices in the hope of creating a buying frenzy. But instead of handing out discounts, consider asking a prospect to opt in to receive the discount. For instance, your gated offer might say, "Join our Discount Club and receive 10% off any order." This wording is effective because it specifically tells the prospect how much she'll save.

Generating leads with educational content

In this section, we discuss five forms that your gated offer can take. These gated offers offer value by educating the lead on a particular topic related to your brand while also highlighting features of a solution, product, or service you provide.

TIP

Your gated offer does not have to be the length of a Tolstoy novel. Besides being ultraspecific, gated offers should be easy to consume — they should not be a 14-day course or a 300-page book. Rapid consumption of the gated offer is important because you want to provide value to your lead as quickly as possible. The faster your gated offer provides value, the quicker a lead can become a paying customer. Because most gated offers can be sent digitally, they can be delivered instantly, which allows the lead to receive the value of the gated offer quickly. Ideally, prospects receive value from your gated offer within minutes of giving you their contact information. Speedily delivering value helps to build a positive relationship with leads, as well as to quickly move them through the customer journey. (Turn to Chapter 1 in this minibook for more information on the customer journey.)

Free reports

Reports (also called guides) are among the most common types of gated offers and are usually mostly text and images. Reports usually offer facts, news, and best practices that are relevant to your industry and your target market. If you use a report as your gated offer, however, be careful. Reports can be lengthy and complex, thus they often take more time to be consumed, which means that the report will take longer to deliver on its value. Therefore, whenever possible, keep your reports as succinct and specific as possible so that they can quickly deliver their value and help to establish or reinforce a positive relationship with your lead or customer.

White papers

As is true of a report, a white paper is an authoritative guide that concisely informs readers about a complex issue and aims to help leads understand an issue, solve a problem, or make a decision. Although the white paper helps to educate your prospects, it also helps to promote your business's products or services. White papers can often be very effective at generating business-to-business (B2B) leads.

Primary research

Primary research is research that you or your business collects. It can include interviews and observations. When you take the time to create new research, you're providing a service and saving others from having to do their own primary research, which is why people opt in to a gated offer of this nature.

Webinar training

If you're an expert in your field, or can partner with one, you can host an online training via a webinar that teaches or demonstrates a topic that is relevant to both your brand and to your target audience. You create a gated offer that requires prospects to fill out a registration form for the webinar, thus capturing prospects' contact information and allowing you to follow up with them after the webinar takes place.

Sales material

In some cases, the most desired pieces of information for your market are pricing and descriptions of your products or services. This information helps people who are interested in buying your product or service make informed decisions. The sales material gated offer tends to be longer, in text and content examples such as images or customer testimonial videos, than the other examples in this chapter so far. However, this length is necessary because a person generally needs more information before making a purchase, especially if a big-ticket item is involved. However, this also means that anyone who opts in is more likely to be a qualified lead. A *qualified lead* is someone who is actively seeking more information about your products or services because he or she is interested in buying from you. (An unqualified lead may not have been nurtured enough to make a purchase yet, or isn't sure of what your company does or even what solution he or she seeks.)

IKEA provides a wonderful example of the sales material gated offer. The Scandinavian chain collects contact information in exchange for its catalog, which lists all its products. Figure 2-3 demonstrates IKEA's gated offer, and because IKEA can deliver its catalog digitally, it speeds up the delivery of value to the new lead.

FIGURE 2-3:
IKEA's sales catalog is an ideal example of a sales material gated offer.

Crafting Winning Offers

Generating leads with tools

Tools make powerful gated offers because they often deliver value *much faster* than the educational gated offers discussed in the previous section. Although white papers, reports, and case studies require someone to invest time in order to receive value, a tool is often immediately useful.

Handout or cheat sheet

Though similar to a free report, both handouts and cheat sheets provide a different value to prospects. A handout or cheat sheet is generally short (one page or so) and cuts straight to an ultraspecific point, making the information easily digestible. You can deliver handouts and cheat sheets as checklists, mind maps, or blueprints, to name a few examples. Figure 2-4 shows an example of a handout as a gated offer.

FIGURE 2-4:
A handout is a prime example of useful content that can be gated.

Resource list

If people are learning to do something that you're an expert in, chances are they'll want to know what tools you're using to get it done. This type of gated offer makes a list of tools or resources (be it of apps, physical products, hardware, or other items) available to the new lead or prospect. The toolkit or resource aggregates the list so that the lead doesn't have to keep searching for more information.

Template

A template is the perfect example of a proven, well-tested shortcut to better results and can make a tremendous gated offer. A template contains a proven pattern for success that requires less work on the part of the person using it. It might come in the form of a spreadsheet preconfigured to calculate business expenses. Or it can be a layout for designing a custom home. Templates make powerful gated offers because the prospect can put the tool to immediate use.

Software

Software can work well as a gated offer. You might, for example, offer full access to a free software tool that you developed or a free trial (that lasts for 14 days, perhaps) of your software in exchange for an email address. Software companies often offer a free trial of their software as a gated offer. A software gated offer can turn a lead who is on the fence about purchasing the product with a risk-free means of acquiring it, while also providing the company a way to follow up with that lead.

Discount and coupon clubs

Discount and coupon clubs offer exclusive savings and early access to sales. This is an effective type of offer that acquires contact information and allows you to continue the conversation by reminding members of specials and rewards available to them.

Quizzes and surveys

Quizzes and surveys are fun and engaging for people to take and can be a great way to generate new leads. For instance, a beauty company might offer a "What's Your Skin Type?" quiz. These types of content are intriguing to members of your market because they want to know the results of the quiz or survey. To obtain the results of the quiz or survey, the prospect must first opt in by entering an email address. If the quiz or survey results provide value to your market, this type of gated offer can be powerful.

Assessment

You can develop a gated offer that assesses or tests prospects on a particular subject. At the end of the assessment, offer prospects a grade and information on actions they can take to improve their grade, which would likely be a tool or service that you provide. For example, this assessment can serve as a rubric for grading a blog post. Figure 2-5 shows an assessment offer that has been generating leads for HubSpot, a company that sells marketing software, for years. Leads can use the assessment from HubSpot to grade their marketing and make it better.

Filling out the gated offer checklist

We've tested gated offers in a lot of different niches and developed an eight-point checklist of factors that can improve your overall level of success by making more effective gated offers. You don't have to be able to check off every one of the factors in the checklist, but if you find that your gated offer meets very few of these criteria, you have reason to be concerned.

We tell you about each of the factors on the checklist in the following sections.

FIGURE 2-5:
HubSpot
generates leads
with its gated
offer of its
Website Grader
assessment.

Point 1: Is your offer ultraspecific?

The more specific the promise of your gated offer is, the better it will perform after you provide that promise. By delivering on your promise, you have given value. This, of course, assumes that the promise you are making is compelling to the market you're approaching. Make sure that your gated offer isn't vague and that it offers an ultraspecific solution to an ultraspecific market.

Point 2: Are you offering too much?

Believe it or not, your gated offer will perform better if it delivers on one big thing rather than a number of things. We live in a multitasking world, so you want to be sure that your gated offer focuses on one topic or theme and provides one path for your lead to take. If you include too many paths or offers, your leads can get distracted and go off course as they try to follow all the ideas presented in your gated offer, thereby causing them to not opt in. If possible, offer a single solution to a single problem rather than numerous solutions to numerous problems.

Point 3: Does the offer speak to a desired end result?

The members of your market are searching for solutions. What does your market *really* want? If you can craft a gated offer that promises that solution, prospects will gladly give you their contact information (and their attention) in return.

Point 4: Does the offer deliver immediate gratification?

Your market wants a solution and wants it *now*. Establish and communicate how long it will take your leads to consume and derive value from your gated offer so that they know what to expect. If it takes days or weeks, your gated offer is not delivering immediate gratification — not by a long shot.

Point 5: Does the offer shift the relationship?

The best gated offers do more than inform; they actually change the state and mind-set of your prospects so that they're primed to engage in business with your company. After your leads have taken advantage of your offer, determine whether the value it provides will actually teach the leads how and why they should trust and buy from you. For example, if you sell gardening tools and supplies, a checklist entitled "15 Tools You Need to Create a Successful Container Garden" educates prospects on the tools they need while simultaneously moving them closer to purchasing the products you sell.

Point 6: Does the offer have a high perceived value?

Just because your gated offer is free doesn't mean that it should *look* free. Use good design through the use of professional graphics and imagery to create a gated offer of high perceived value in the mind of your lead.

Point 7: Does the offer have a high actual value?

The right information at the right time can be priceless. The gated offer that delivers something priceless will enjoy very high conversion rates, but if you're promising value, you *have* to deliver on it. A gated offer has high actual value when it lives up to its promise and delivers the goods.

Point 8: Does the offer allow for rapid consumption?

You don't want your gated offer to be a roadblock in the customer's journey toward becoming a customer. Before customers buy from you, they want to receive value from your gated offer. You want the gated offer to help move the lead to the next step, so ideally the gated offer should deliver value immediately. In other words, avoid long e-books or courses that take days or months to deliver their value.

TIP

Why do we keep insisting that your gated offer be quickly and easily consumable? Because after your gated offer has been consumed, you want to make the next offer whenever possible. There is (usually) no better time to make an offer than directly after someone has taken a prior offer. However, few will buy from you if they have not received the value from the last offer you made — your gated offer. So be sure that your gated offer quickly delivers value, allowing you to then make an offer to purchase something, which we discuss in the next section.

Designing Deep-Discount Offers

Acquiring leads is the goal of the gated offer discussed in the previous section, but how do you acquire buyers? Remember that the key to success online is the sequence of the offers you make to new leads and customers. The best way to acquire buyers is by making an offer at such a deep discount that it is difficult to refuse. A *deep-discount offer* is an irresistible, low-ticket offer made to convert leads and cold prospects into buyers.

REMEMBER

The goal of a deep-discount offer is not profit. In fact, selling deep-discount offers may come at a net loss to your company. Offering deep discounts may therefore seem counterintuitive, but the goal of this type of offer is to acquire buyers. Deep-discount offers change relationships; they turn a prospect into a customer, and that's a big deal. After a prospect makes a successful purchase with your company, she is far more likely to buy from you again. Deep-discount offers bring you one step closer to achieving your goal of converting a prospect to a repeat buyer and possibly even a raving fan.

In the following sections, we discuss the six different types of deep-discount offers you can employ.

Using physical premiums

As the name suggests, physical premiums are physical products. Offer something that your market desires and discount it deeply. DIY Ready, a company in the DIY and home décor space, offers a $19 bracelet kit for free. The new customer need only enter his or her credit card to pay for shipping and handling to receive the bracelet kit. This is a physical product that do-it-yourselfers find highly desirable. Figure 2-6 demonstrates what this physical premium offer from DIY Ready looks like.

FIGURE 2-6:
A Free + Shipping
offer is a typical
deep-discount
offer.

Employing a book

A physical book can make an excellent deep-discount offer. Books have an extremely high perceived and actual value. If you need to establish authority and trust with your market before making more complex or higher-ticket offers, the book is a great deep-discount offer to employ. Consider offering the book at a steep discount, or free plus shipping and handling. Although we don't recommend a physical or digital book for generating leads, it's a highly effective way to convert prospects and leads into customers. Remember, the objective of a deep-discount offer is to change the relationship with a lead or prospect and turn the person into a customer.

Leveraging the webinar

Webinars are one of the most versatile offers available to digital marketers. You can conduct free webinars to generate leads, plus you can offer a webinar as a product. Remember that when you're charging for anything and particularly a webinar, you should deliver value beyond what you've charged to attend.

TIP

When employing a webinar to serve as a deep-discount offer, you may not want to use the term *webinar* in your offer. People generally associate that term with something free. Consider calling your deep-discount-offer webinar a teleclass, online training, or boot camp instead, and it can be prerecorded or held live.

Selling software

Software and application plug-ins are effective deep-discount offers because software saves people time and energy, so these are highly sought-after commodities. When you use software as a deep-discount offer, the deep discount price is likely to cause a buying frenzy, resulting in a highly successful acquisition campaign.

Splintering a service

If your business has a high-dollar product or service, you can take a small piece of that product, also known as a *splinter*, and sell it *à la carte*. The key is to offer a piece of your service that can stand alone at an incredibly low price.

An example of a company that uses this approach is Fiverr, an online marketplace that offers tasks and services starting at $5. Figure 2-7 shows one of these Fiverr services, which include creating business logos. This is an excellent example of offering *part* of a highly sought-after service at a deep discount that will help turn a lead into a customer and can ultimately lead to more sales. After a person has bought from you, he's likely to buy from you again.

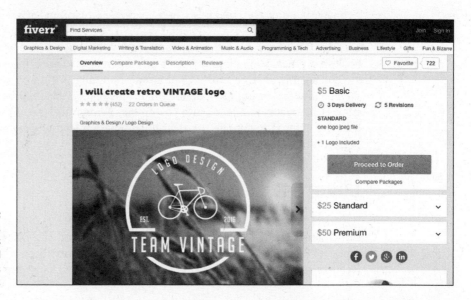

FIGURE 2-7: Through Fiverr, larger services can be splintered into smaller, single projects.

Because you're breaking out a part or splinter of your service, you don't have to create a new service. Instead, you're offering a portion of an existing product or service.

Brainstorming little victories to offer your leads

Because deep-discount offers are low priced, low risk, and highly desirable, they help your leads overcome doubt about your business or product. Less monetary risk is involved for the leads, so they're willing to take a chance and become customers. However, it can be harder for a marketer or a business owner to overcome the self-doubt that leads may have about themselves or their ability to reach the After state that your product or service promises to take them to. That's why the best deep-discount offers lead the customer to a little victory.

A little victory is something that helps inspire your leads and gives them confidence that they can accomplish whatever solution or goal you're offering, as well as the confidence that your product or service will help to get them there. A little victory gives your prospects hope and a taste of achieving the whole thing — of making it to the other side of the tunnel, so to speak. Keep in mind that little victories are usually quick to achieve and help deliver value to your customer.

For instance, if you're in the fitness world, you can offer your seven-day juice cleanse at a deep discount as a deep-discount offer. When describing the offer to potential buyers, you state that completing this juice cleanse is the hardest part of your program — because getting started is often the hardest part. If they can get through your seven-day cleanse, they'll know that the toughest part is behind them.

As you go through your products and services to determine which will make the best deep-discount offer, ask yourself what little victory this product or service can provide your customers. Brainstorm how it will give them hope, how it will help to get them over the hump of self-doubt. Helping your customers see that success is possible not only for the smiling customers in your testimonials but also for *them*, personally, will help make your offer more potent and enable you to build positive relationships with your newly acquired customers.

Filling out the deep-discount offer checklist

Previous sections talk about the various forms your deep-discount offers could take and the importance of little victories. Next, look over the five-point deep-discount offer checklist, presented in the following sections, so that you can ensure that your offer can convert leads and prospects into buyers.

Point 1: Does it lower the barrier to entry?

To start, your deep-discount offer should be low risk. The offer shouldn't be expensive, time consuming, or difficult to understand. The best offers at this stage are often impulse buys, like the pack of gum you grab while you wait in line at the supermarket. The price of your offer depends on your market. Leads shouldn't have to pause to consider whether they can afford your deep-discount offer; the price should remove that barrier. Again, the purpose of this offer is not profit. A good rule of thumb is to make these offers at $20 or below.

Point 2: Is the value clear?

Make your deep-discount offer easy to understand. You want to be able to quickly explain the value and entice the lead into buying. Therefore, your deep-discount offer should not be complex. Impulse buys are not complicated offers.

Point 3: Is it useful but incomplete?

WARNING

The keyword here is *useful*. Your deep-discount offer should not be a bait-and-switch offer. If the deep-discount offer doesn't deliver on its promise, you'll tarnish your relationship with that customer. You may have gained a quick sale with the deep-discount offer but lost a potential lifelong customer. This offer must be useful in its own right, but it is not the whole package.

Point 4: Does it have a high perceived value?

As with the gated offer before it, use good design to create a deep-discount offer with a high-quality look and feel. You don't want your new customers to feel ripped off; instead, you want them to feel as though the deep-discount offer they just bought from you was a steal.

REMEMBER

People don't buy products and services online, but rather buy pictures and descriptions of products and services online. If you want to sell online, you need to employ design and copywriting that communicate the value of the products and services you're offering.

Point 5: Does it have a high actual value?

Be sure that your deep-discount offer makes good on its promise and delivers value. This situation builds trust with your new customers, and when they're ready to buy again, they will remember the positive experience they had with you.

Discovering your deep-discount offer

The offer you use to acquire customers likely exists inside your *core offer*, which is a higher-priced or more complex product or service. Your core offer is often your flagship product or service. Look at your core offer and see what piece or pieces can stand on their own. What can you splinter off and still deliver value with that piece?

Here are some questions to ask to help you discover your deep-discount offer(s):

>> **What's the cool gadget that your market wants, but doesn't necessarily need?** What's your impulse buy? What's your stick of gum?

>> **What's the one thing everyone needs, but doesn't necessarily want?** This can be a product or service that people know they need but aren't exactly excited about. The product may not be sexy, but it's critical to a process that people engage in. For instance, if someone has a candle-making hobby, the wick may not be as fun or interesting as the colored waxes or scented oils, but it's an essential ingredient.

>> **What's a valuable service that you can perform quickly and inexpensively, one that will deliver results in advance and get your foot in the door?** This idea goes beyond giving someone a free quote or estimate; it gives customers a taste of how you can positively affect their lives. For example, a roofer could offer a deep discount on gutter cleaning as a deep-discount offer. After completing the job, the roofer could point out any necessary improvements that the roof or gutters need. That's a deep-discount offer that provides value first and then gets your foot in the door.

>> **What little victory or victories does your deep-discount offer provide?** How do you help the customer overcome self-doubt?

Maximizing Profit

As this chapter explains, you use ungated, gated, and deep-discount offers to acquire new customers and buyers. But when do you actually make a profit? The cost of acquiring new customers is often the most expensive one that businesses incur. After you have a buyer, asking that buyer to buy from you again makes sense. You want to turn that customer you spent so much time and money acquiring into a *repeat customer*.

The marketing campaigns you employ to sell more, or more often, to the leads and customers you've acquired are called Monetization campaigns, and these campaigns have a number of different types of offers to employ. In the following sections, we tell you how to implement and improve your monetization offers.

REMEMBER

Most companies are running Monetization campaigns (making high-dollar and complex offers) directed at ice-cold prospects and brand new leads. Although it would be fantastic to be profitable without needing to warm up a prospect with ungated, gated, and deep-discount offers, making that work is very difficult. The sequence of the offers you make to people is extremely critical to avoid being the business that is asking its prospects for too much, too soon.

Making an upsell or cross-sell offer

The first type of monetization offer we discuss is the immediate upsell, and it's one you're probably already familiar with even if you've never heard the term. An example of the immediate upsell is the famous "Do you want fries with that?" offer made at McDonald's. Upsells offer customers more of what they already bought. The purchase they are currently making and the upsell should lead the customer to the same desired end result. In the McDonald's example, adding fries to your order gets you a bigger meal. The cross-sell offer, on the other hand, makes an offer related to the first purchase. For example, a clothing retailer might offer dress shoes to a man who just purchased a suit.

Amazon.com (and virtually every other successful online retailer) uses upsell and cross-sell offers to increase the number of items people purchase. Amazon's Frequently Bought Together and Customers Who Bought This Item Also Bought sections contain immediate upsell and cross-sell offers to help ensure the sale and possibly increase the basket size. For example, after we select a book for $17.98, Amazon suggests other products that we may want to make with this purchase, as shown in Figure 2-8. If we accepted all the suggested upsells, the amount of our purchase would increase from $17.98 to $44.96.

FIGURE 2-8: Amazon expertly uses upsells and cross-sells to increase the basket size of its customer and get the sale.

In Figure 2-8, the item being searched for is *Harry Potter and the Cursed Child,* and Amazon offers some related Harry Potter books that would serve as an upsell and increase the basket size. But Amazon also offers cross-sells in the form of other fantasy books that may appeal to a fan of Harry Potter because they are of the same genre.

Because the cross-sell may not be as relevant to the first purchase, a cross-sell can feel like it's coming out of left field, which can be jarring to and unwanted by the customer. That's why you have to be careful with cross-sells, or you risk annoying your customers. Imagine buying a Mac computer and having Apple ask before you've even left the store whether you want to buy an iPhone or an iPad. That said, if the cross-sell truly complements the initial purchase, your customers will welcome the offer, and you'll welcome the additional revenue.

Building bundles and kits

Bundles and kits are other forms that your monetization offer can take. A bundle or a kit is taking one of your stand-alone products and combining it with other like items that you or one of your business partners sells. For example, if you sell men's razors, you might bundle the razor with a shaving kit that includes all the essential items a man needs to shave with, from the brush to the after-shave. This essential shaving kit will cost more than an individual razor, which increases your revenue per sale. Do you have products or services that you can combine to create a new value proposition?

Tacking on a slack adjuster

Slack adjusters can have a dramatic impact upon the bottom line. A *slack adjuster* is a product or service that you offer at a price point much higher than your typical offer. The price is generally 10 to 100 times higher than your usual offers. Although this product or service will appeal to only a very small portion of your market, those that do make this high-ticket purchase will have a dramatic impact on your revenue.

For example, Starbucks sells cups of tea and coffee, but the company also sells coffee makers. The coffee maker is far more expensive than the $6 cup of coffee. Most people stick to their usual beverage and ignore the coffee maker, but a few buy the coffee maker. When a product is that much more expensive than the core offer, only a small number of slack adjuster sales is needed to make an impact.

Recurring billing

Sometimes called a continuity offer in digital marketing circles, a recurring billing offer charges the customer periodically — usually each month or year. This may take the form of a club or some other type of membership, or a subscription such as a monthly gym membership. In the latter case, the gym charges a membership fee 12 times a year. You also find recurring billing in content and publishing with subscriptions to Netflix or *Cosmopolitan* magazine, and in e-commerce with products like Dollar Shave Club and Birchbox. Look to your products or services and consider how you can make a sale once and get paid over and over again.

Recurring billing can be a difficult sell because of the commitment that goes along with it. To overcome this issue, clearly communicate the advantage provided by the recurring billing offer and lower the perceived risk by clearly communicating the cancellation. For instance, the cooking delivery company Blue Apron often states in its offers that you can cancel anytime. In the dating analogy earlier in this chapter, a recurring billing offer is akin to a marriage proposal. Customers must decide whether they want to commit to you for an extended period.

Chapter **3**

Pursuing Content Marketing Perfection

C ontent is the heart and soul of any digital marketing campaign — the foundation on which your search, social, email, and paid traffic campaigns are built. Without content, Google has nothing to discover on your website, Facebook fans have nothing to share, newsletters have no news, and paid traffic campaigns become one-dimensional sales pitches.

Content goes beyond blogging; content includes YouTube videos, product and pricing pages on e-commerce sites, social media updates, and much more. Each piece of content acts as a stepping stone on the path from lead to customer, and from customer to engaged, frequent buyer.

This chapter begins the quest of using content to generate fans, followers, and customers by outlining the often-misunderstood strategy behind content marketing. We examine the many different forms that content marketing takes and its uses throughout a prospect's journey toward becoming a loyal customer.

Knowing the Dynamics of Content Marketing

At its core, the Internet is a place where people gather to discover, interact with, and share content. Whether that content is a funny cat video that gives you a much-needed laugh, an inspiring podcast about a single mom surviving cancer, or an article teaching you how to fix a leaky faucet, content is what people crave.

Engaging with valuable content is a natural, or native, experience on the Internet. People are drawn to content that teaches them something, inspires them, or makes them laugh or cry, and people share and talk about content that has provided them some form of value.

With the low-cost (or no cost) of publishing platforms such as WordPress, YouTube, and iTunes, even the smallest of brands can produce content for the web. This ease of publishing, however, is a double-edged sword because the constantly changing nature of the Internet requires the rapid production of content. Although your brand stands to reap the enormous rewards associated with content publishing, doing so without a plan can lead to frustration.

People have a nearly insatiable demand for content on the Internet. According to the most conservative estimates, every minute more than 1,000 blog posts are produced and 72 hours of new video are uploaded to YouTube. This glut of content underscores the importance of proceeding with content marketing only after you have made a plan, because you must create quality content to cut through the noise. And quality demands a plan. Without a plan, your content assets still have a chance to go viral, but that's more than likely to be the result of dumb luck. A plan helps to ensure the success of your digital marketing campaign.

TIP

Marketers often confuse the term *blogging* with *content marketing.* Although blogging is a powerful and versatile content marketing channel, it's only one part of a well-balanced content strategy. If you're among the many marketers who blog with no clear direction, you should commit a few hours to designing a content plan before writing another blog post. Well-executed content marketing includes planning what content you will produce, for what audience, and for what purpose. Many companies and personal brands that are frustrated with digital marketing can trace that frustration back to the time-consuming act of creating content with no clear audience or objective. You'll find the entire process much easier and much more lucrative when you have a good sense of your direction.

Finding Your Path to Perfect Content Marketing

Although "perfect" content marketing may sound like hype, it's actually obtainable. When you gain an understanding of the true principles of this critical discipline and content marketing's connection to all other facets of your digital marketing mix, you can quickly see the path to content marketing perfection.

Content marketing is about anticipating the needs of your customers and prospects, and building content assets that satisfy those needs. For example, the cloud-based software company FreshBooks anticipated a prospective customer's need for pricing information. The web page shown in Figure 3-1 represents perfect content marketing in this scenario: The content succinctly and clearly communicates the differences in its plans and the varying price levels, provides contact information for those who may have more questions and want to talk to a representative, and offers a free trial. The content on this page completely satisfies the need for pricing information.

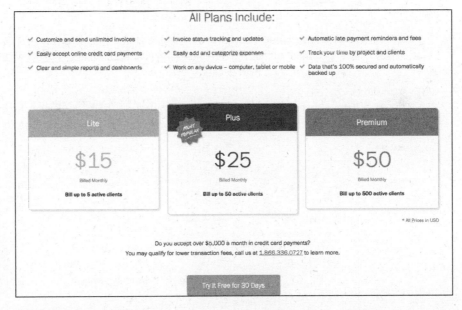

FIGURE 3-1: This content on FreshBooks is designed to meet a prospective customer's needs when looking for pricing.

For a prospective customer of FreshBooks to make an informed buying decision, the pricing page is necessary. Before they commit, people want to know what they're buying and how much it will cost. Failure to conveniently provide that information for the prospect will result in lost sales.

Understanding the marketing funnel

The path from stranger to buyer is often conveyed using the metaphor of a funnel. Ice-cold prospects enter the wide top of the funnel and some, you hope, exit through the much narrower bottom of the funnel as customers. Content can, and should, assist the prospect in graduating from one stage of the marketing funnel to the next.

A basic marketing funnel has three stages that take a prospect from stranger to buyer:

TIP

>> **Awareness:** The prospect must first become aware that he has a problem and that you or your organization can provide a solution.

Raising problem and solution awareness is where your blog will shine. Use your blog to educate, inspire, or entertain prospects and existing customers.

>> **Evaluation:** Those who move through the awareness stage must now evaluate the various choices available to them, including your competitor's solutions and, of course, taking no action to solve the problem at all. People can, after all, decide to live with the problem and not purchase the product or service that could solve that problem.

>> **Conversion:** Those who move through the evaluation stage are at the moment of truth — purchase. The goal at this stage is to convert leads into frequent and high-ticket buyers.

REMEMBER

These three stages of awareness, evaluation, and conversion form what is known as a *marketing funnel*. Figure 3-2 conceptualizes the marketing funnel.

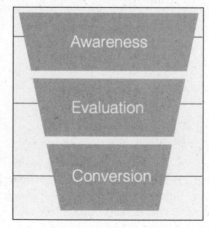

FIGURE 3-2:
The three-step marketing funnel.

Cold prospects cannot evaluate your solution until they are first aware of the problem *and* your solution. If prospects are unaware of the problem or the solution that you offer through your product or service, they obviously won't buy. Therefore, conversions are impossible until prospects have first evaluated the possible courses of action they can take, which include buying your product, buying a competitor's product rather than yours, or doing nothing and living with the problem. To move prospects through a marketing funnel, you need to provide content designed to satisfy their needs at each of the three stages:

>> Content at the top of the funnel (TOFU) that facilitates awareness

>> Content at the middle of the funnel (MOFU) that facilitates evaluation

>> Content at the bottom of the funnel (BOFU) that facilitates conversion

TIP

Blogs are fantastic facilitators of awareness (top of funnel) — but they do a poor job of facilitating evaluation (middle of funnel) and conversion (bottom of funnel). Also, at the risk of pointing out the obvious, evaluation and conversion are super critical to your business. To move prospects through the middle and bottom of the funnel, you need other content types, as shown in Figure 3-3 and explained in detail in the following sections.

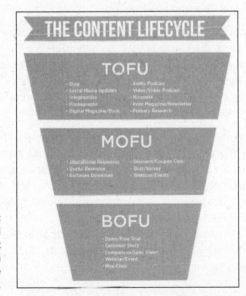

FIGURE 3-3:
You need different content types at each stage of the marketing funnel.

Top of funnel (TOFU) content marketing

The prospects entering the top of your funnel are unaware of your solution and often unaware that they even have a problem that needs to be solved. As a result, you need content that people can freely access, as opposed to content that requires prospects to give you their contact information or make a purchase. After all, you have yet to prove your value to them.

At the top of the funnel, make free ungated content (which we cover in greater detail in Book 7, Chapter 2) available that provides one of the following values:

» Entertains

» Educates

» Inspires

Choose two or three of the following content types to deliver TOFU content that will raise awareness about the solutions you provide through your products or services:

» **Blog posts:** Arguably the most recognized form of online content, blogs are an excellent way of raising awareness. For example, the fashion company J.Crew raises awareness of the products it sells by creating blog posts about fashion styles and tips for accessorizing. The J.Crew blog reader (and potential customer) gets some inspiration and solutions to the problem of what to wear and how to look fashionable; the post also alludes to the fact that J.Crew carries the clothing needed to pull off the look.

» **Social media updates:** As with blogs, social media platforms (such as Facebook) are fantastic at creating awareness. Whether it's a Pinterest board by Dreyer's Ice Cream that lists every flavor of ice cream the company sells, or a tweet by Airbnb about the ten perfect Paris food experiences, these social media updates give their followers free, valuable information while also bringing the solutions their company provides to the forefront.

» **Infographics:** Infographics are an interesting and engaging way to display content. Typically, infographics contain fun images with contrasting, eye-catching colors, and the way infographics break up text makes this form of content easily consumable by the viewer. Infographics are highly effective at delivering content that is both entertaining and educational, quickly. Whether it's an infographic by IMDb about the best of the year in movie entertainment, or an infographic by Casper Mattress providing tips on better sleeping habits, this type of content delivers value that a consumer wants, and it raises brand awareness effectively as well.

» **Photographs:** Pictures are powerful because they can explain a lot in a single image. Photographs also help to break up blocks of text in a piece of content, which keeps that content from becoming boring or intimidating to read. With a photograph, a kitchen design company can show completed projects that effectively demonstrate what the company does while raising awareness of what the company can do for another customer's kitchen.

>> **Digital magazines and books:** Digital magazines and books are popular, and are another way to distribute content and raise brand awareness. E-books and e-magazines are similar to the blog strategies discussed in Chapter 4 of this minibook. Therefore, you can look to your blog to inspire your content for your e-book or e-magazine.

>> **Audio and video podcasts:** Another form of content that you can use at the top of the funnel is a podcast. With a podcast, you package and distribute your content differently from textual content. A podcast delivers consumable content on the go. Subscribers can listen to the podcast on their commute to work or during their workout, or any other time they choose. They have a more flexible way to consume the content, in contrast to a blog post or a social media update that is less conducive to multitasking. Also, you can use podcasts to effectively promote your product or service while providing value to your prospects. If you sell outdoor equipment, for example, each episode of your podcast can give tips and tricks about hunting, fishing, camping, and other outdoor activities while also subtly reminding your listener of the outdoor equipment available at your store.

>> **Microsites:** A microsite is essentially an auxiliary blog about a specific topic that is put on a different site with its own links and address; a microsite is accessed mainly from a larger site. For instance, DadsDivorce.com is a separate domain of the men's family law firm Cordell & Cordell. DadsDivorce.com provides free content for divorcing fathers and is designed to raise awareness about the services and solutions Cordell & Cordell can provide.

>> **Print magazines and newsletters:** This type of content can require a bigger budget than digital content, but if going this route falls within your budget, print magazines and newsletters are still a great way to raise awareness. For example, the *Lego Club Magazine* contains plenty of entertaining comic-book-style content for LEGO's target customer. Magazines and newsletters help sales by inspiring shoppers based on what they see in print.

>> **Primary research:** This is research you go out and collect yourself, such as surveys, interviews, and observations. Although this data can be difficult and time consuming to gather, primary research is powerful because only a finite amount of primary research exists. Specifically, when you take the time to create research, you're providing a service and saving people from having to do their own primary research. For this reason, primary research can stir a good deal of awareness among your prospects.

TIP

Do you need all these content types at the top of the funnel? Heck, no. Most businesses focus on posting content to a blog and to social media channels such as Facebook, Twitter, LinkedIn, and Pinterest. After you've mastered blogging and social media updates, you might want to add more top-of-funnel content to the mix, such as a podcast or a print newsletter.

The big goal at the top of the funnel is to make prospects problem aware and solution aware. In Figure 3-4, notice how Whole Foods uses its Whole Story blog to raise awareness for the seafood the grocery store sells. In this way, Whole Foods is reminding its audience of the products it sells, making its audience solution aware while providing people with recipes they find valuable.

FIGURE 3-4:
Whole Foods raises awareness of products it sells while providing value to its blog audience.

Unfortunately, the top of the funnel is where most organizations begin and end their content marketing efforts. Smart content marketers know that, with a bit more effort, they can move prospects from awareness to evaluation at the middle of the funnel.

Middle of funnel (MOFU) content marketing

The big goal for content you use at the middle of the funnel is to convert problem aware and solution aware prospects into leads. You're looking to grow your email lists and gain more leads at this point of the funnel. DigitalMarketer uses free content to incentivize prospects to submit their contact information (such as their email address) and opt in to receive future marketing in exchange for valuable content. We call this type of content *gated offers,* which we discuss in Chapter 2 of this minibook.

A *gated offer* is a small chunk of value that solves a *specific* problem for a *specific* market and is offered in exchange for prospects' contact information.

Gated offers often take the form of content such as the following:

>> **Educational resources:** As discussed in Book 7, Chapter 2, educational resources for gated offers often exist in the form of free reports, white papers, primary research, webinar training, and sales material. These types of content resources educate the consumer on a particular topic related to your brand while highlighting features of a solution, product, or service you provide. An educational resource can include a case study packed with professional tips and a detailed breakdown of some of your strategies.

REMEMBER

Educational resources (and all forms of MOFU content, for that matter) must be of high quality or the consumer is likely to feel cheated. Also, if prospects feel that the content you gave them in exchange for their contact information is subpar, your brand awareness suffers. Keep in mind that the point of the MOFU is to help people evaluate your company and entice them to make a purchase. You entice with quality, not garbage.

>> **Useful resources:** Useful resources are tools such as

- Handouts or cheat sheets
- Resource lists
- Templates
- Software
- Surveys
- Assessments
- Discount and coupon clubs
- Quizzes and surveys

We explain these useful tools, which serve as powerful content for MOFU, in Book 7, Chapter 2. Instead of using a consumer's time (such as an e-book that may take an hour or more to read), useful resources promise that they will not only educate your prospects but also save them time. These resources save them time because the content is easy to consume and the resource is complete; it doesn't depend on another resource to deliver its value but can stand alone. For example, a company that sells vegetable gardening tools can create a resource called the "Seed Starting Cheat Sheet" that allows people with an interest in gardening to quickly determine the best time to plant popular vegetables in the garden.

Don't pin all your lead-generation hopes to a passive gated offer on your home page or the sidebar of your blog, because the gated offer can get lost among the many elements of your site. A missed gated offer won't capture leads. Be sure to also create a dedicated landing page for every gated offer (some call this a *squeeze page*) and drive traffic directly to that page using social media, email marketing, search engine optimization (SEO), and paid traffic. A dedicated landing page increases opt-ins. See Figure 3-5 for an example of a landing page.

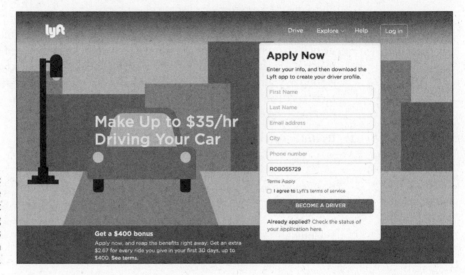

FIGURE 3-5: Rideshare company Lyft uses a landing page to start its driver application process.

The goal at the middle of the funnel is to convert prospects who were unaware of your product or service into people with whom you can now follow up. As they say, however, you can't deposit leads in the bank. To generate revenue, you need content that assists your prospects in making decisions at the point of sale.

Bottom of funnel (BOFU) content marketing

At the BOFU, you're looking to convert leads into customers and customers into higher-ticket customers. What types of content will your new lead need to make an informed purchase decision? Your leads may be reading your blog and downloading your gated offers (all of which helps to convert them), but to move them on through to the point of making a purchase, you also need to offer content that helps them decide whether to buy.

Here are examples of content types that work well at the bottom of the funnel:

» **Demos:** The downside of buying a product online is that customers can't hold the product in their hands — they have only an image (or two) and a description to base their purchasing decisions on, which can make people hesitate to buy. Offering a demo can help with this problem. A demo shows the product or service you offer in action, so that consumers can see how it works. It's as close to touching the product as they can get from their screen. So find a way to demonstrate your product or service through content such as video, screen shots, webinars, or schematic drawings.

» **Customer stories:** Customer stories are customer testimonials and reviews. Customer stories are fantastic at the bottom of the funnel because they allow a prospect to see how someone else experienced success with your product or service. You provide your prospects with peer reviews, which have a powerful effect on decision making. As shown in Figure 3-6, Salesforce.com supplies leads who are at the BOFU with plenty of customer success stories to prove that its product can take care of their needs.

» **Comparison and spec sheets:** When someone at the BOFU is debating over different products, comparisons and spec sheets are handy resources that people use to compare products side by side (whether the comparison is between similar products that you offer or between your product and your competitor's product). For example, the tax preparation software TurboTax might show a side-by-side comparison to the features and pricing of its competitor, TaxAct.

» **Webinars and events:** As previously stated in this chapter and in Book 7, Chapter 2, you can use webinars and events at the middle of the funnel to gather leads, but you can also use them at the bottom of the funnel to convert those leads. At the bottom of the funnel, a webinar can be used to gather prospective customers in one place to ask questions about a complex, risky, or high-ticket product or service.

» **Mini-classes:** A mini-class is a type of event that you set up to teach a relevant topic to your target audience. At the end of the short class, you make your pitch for your product or service. You need to provide quality educational resources with the mini-class, but in the end, the purpose of the class is to pitch a higher-dollar product related to the class you just held.

TIP

Is creating content that drives awareness at the top of the funnel important? Absolutely. That said, particularly for existing brands, the place to start building content is usually at the bottom of the funnel. Your prospects need information such as pricing or how you compare to a competitor, so build content that satisfies those basic questions before you start writing blog posts or uploading podcasts.

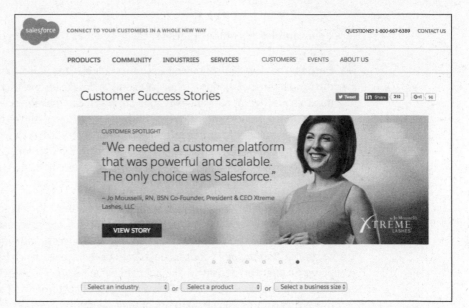

FIGURE 3-6:
Salesforce
creates content
that converts
at the BOFU by
telling customer
success stories.

Exploring the prospect's intent

The key to perfect content marketing is to understand your prospects' existing intent so that you can anticipate their future intent and predict which path or paths they will take. In foreseeing this, you can create the content assets needed to address that intent 24 hours a day, seven days a week.

Returning to the FreshBooks example, the software company that we refer to earlier in the chapter, a customer in the evaluation or conversion stage of the funnel might intend to compare FreshBooks to QuickBooks. The web page shown in Figure 3-7 satisfies that intent at both the middle and the bottom of the funnel. FreshBooks gives the prospect a comparison sheet that allows the customer to see the differences between FreshBooks and its competition, QuickBooks. The company knows that prospective customers want to see how it stacks up against QuickBooks. Satisfying that intent in the evaluation stage helps prospects move into the conversion stage.

TIP

If you're having difficulty brainstorming ideas for content that will satisfy your prospects' intent, gather a group of people in your organization who have contact with your customers and prospects. Salespeople, customer service representatives, trade-show workers, and others who hear the voice of the customer and prospect should be present. These members of your team can help you discover holes in your content that would satisfy a prospect's intent.

Accounting Purpose-Built for Small Business Owners

Frustrated by slow, bloated accounting software? FreshBooks is easy to use, backed by award-winning support and loved by millions.

	FreshBooks cloud accounting	QuickBooks
Invoices, expenses, and reports	✓	✓
Web and mobile access	✓	✓
Free online and phone support	✓	✓
Designed for service-based small business owners	✓	✗
Built-in time tracking features	✓	✗
Project tracking	✓	✗
Multi-currency billing	✓	✗
Late payment reminders	✓	✗
Award-winning customer support	✓	✗
Industry leading customer happiness score	✓	✗
Free trial period	30 Days	30 Days
Paid plans start at	$12.95/month	$12.95/month

* All prices in USD

FIGURE 3-7: FreshBooks uses a comparison sheet to move a prospect closer to conversion.

Brainstorm lists of intent at the top, middle, and bottom of the funnel. Then decide what content assets need to be built to satisfy that intent from awareness through conversion.

Providing a path to the next step

As a marketer, you need to provide a path from one piece of content to the next. People are busy and don't have the time or the patience to go digging through your site for the proper piece of content. They need to be able to find what they're looking for fast.

Failing to provide an easy-to-follow path to the next step isn't just bad marketing, it's a bad user experience, one that will cause people to hit the Back button on your site and leave it altogether. Smart content marketers anticipate the next logical intent and remove as much friction as possible to create a clear path to conversion.

The goal of every piece of content is to get the prospect to ascend to the next logical step in the customer journey. In the FreshBooks pricing page example shown in Figure 3-8, notice that FreshBooks has created a clear ascension path to a "Risk-Free Trial" of the software. Creating an ascension path is good marketing and results in a good user experience.

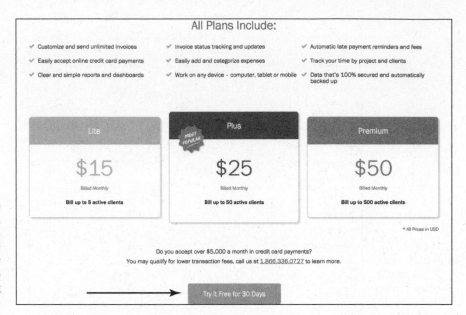

FIGURE 3-8:
FreshBooks
anticipates the
next logical
intent of a visitor
who needs to
obtain pricing
information.

TIP

How well an ascension offer performs depends on the relevance of the offer. Take time to anticipate the next logical step in the customer journey and create offers that are applicable to the piece of content they are currently consuming. For example, asking a visitor to listen to a podcast episode (a top-of-funnel content type) would be neither logical nor relevant from the FreshBooks pricing page in Figure 3-8. This person is visiting the pricing page because she is interested in buying, and the smart marketer anticipates that intent and makes the next logical offer — a free trial.

Segmenting your marketing with content

You won't truly understand your audience and what people really want until they have given you one of two things: their time or their money. They may answer survey questions and make comments that they are interested in this or that, but until they have committed a precious resource — time or money — you don't know for sure what interests them. This is good news for anyone creating content online, because when people spend time with content, they are showing interest.

For example, imagine that you own a company that sells healthy and nutritious meals to busy professionals, and you've been creating blog content about nourishing recipes. Your content falls into three main categories of recipes: vegan, vegetarian, and gluten free. What do you know about someone who visits a blog post about vegan recipes? Likewise for someone visiting a blog post about vegetarian recipes. It's pretty clear, right? These people have raised their hands and told you that they are (or are interested in becoming) vegan or vegetarian.

When people spend their valuable time consuming content, they are segmenting themselves. They are telling you what interests them. And thanks to the magic of ad retargeting, you can follow up with these prospects by using a relevant ascension offer without having to acquire their contact information.

Retargeting is the process of advertising to people based on their prior behavior. For example, you can configure retargeting ads so that they appear only to customers who bought a particular product or visited (showed interest) a particular product page or blog post. This approach allows you to show a very specific piece of content that is more likely to resonate with the segmented audience.

Appearing everywhere your customer expects

Marketers who want to create perfect content need to publish where their customers are. That means publishing content that meets prospects' intent in any channel, and at every stage of the funnel where groups of prospects are searching for and sharing content. These channels include but are certainly not limited to the following:

>> A website or blog

>> Facebook

>> Twitter

>> LinkedIn

>> Pinterest

>> Instagram

>> YouTube

You can publish a single content asset across numerous channels to maximize exposure. For instance, DigitalMarketer turned a presentation about how to launch a podcast into a webinar, and then into a podcast episode, and finally into a blog post. Because the audience responded so enthusiastically to this content, DigitalMarketer saw the value and the need to repurpose it and distribute it throughout its channels.

Consider what content from your company has resonated with your audience. For example, can that video demo of your product be republished on your YouTube channel? Can you repurpose an article from your blog into a webinar, or a podcast episode into an article for LinkedIn Pulse? The opportunities to repurpose content are virtually limitless.

Customizing your content

You produce perfect content marketing materials to satisfy the intent of your *customer avatars* (also known as target audience or customer persona). But not all avatars are the same; they, like their real-life counterparts, don't all want or need the same solution. That's why customizing and then segmenting your content is essential. A particular piece of content can satisfy the intent of multiple avatars, or you can use it to target a single avatar.

For example, we produced a blog article called "6 Trending Digital Marketing Skills to Put on a Resume" to raise awareness (top of the funnel) for our marketing certification programs. This post probably wouldn't interest small business owners, but that was fine — we weren't targeting them. This article was specifically targeted to our employee avatar whose intent is to acquire skills that will land her a better job. Included in the post are two calls to action, which, as mentioned in Book 7, Chapter 2, is an instruction to your audience designed to convey urgency and provoke an immediate response. In the case of the trending skills blog post, the calls to action are customized to appeal to the employee avatar.

Executing Perfect Content Marketing

As we say earlier in this chapter, to execute perfect content marketing, you need a plan. Each offer you make often requires the creation of different pieces of content. As a result, the ideal is to make a content plan for each of your major offers using a resource we call the content campaign plan. The content campaign plan aligns your content marketing with business objectives such as generating leads and sales. You can see the content campaign plan template in Figure 3-9 and can fill out your own by visiting www.digitalmarketer.com/content-campaign.

Following are the steps for creating your first content campaign plan:

1. Choose avatars.

2. Brainstorm content assets.

3. Choose the vehicle and channel.

4. Plan for ascension.

Read on to find out more about each of these steps.

OFFER	AVATAR 1	AVATAR 2	AVATAR 3	AVATAR 4	AVATAR 5		
AWARENESS							
EVALUATION							
CONVERSION							
ASSET	DESCRIPTION	AVATAR(S)	VEHICLE(S)	CHANNEL(S)	OWNER	ASCENSION	
ASSET A							
ASSET B							
ASSET C							
ASSET D							
ASSET E							
ASSET F							
ASSET G							

FIGURE 3-9: The content campaign plan organizes your content strategy for each individual product or service offer.

Step 1: Choosing avatars

Decide which avatars (also known as a *buyer persona*) this content targets. Because each avatar has different intents, motivations, and problems he responds to, each avatar requires different content to move him through the awareness, evaluation, and conversion stages. You therefore need to determine which existing content to use or what new content to create to move the avatar through the top, middle, and bottom of the funnel.

For example, a wealth management firm attempting to sell financial planning should approach a young professional much differently than a near retiree. Some content will appeal to both, but the most effective content will speak directly to a specific avatar.

Step 2: Brainstorming content assets

Use what you know about your customer avatar to create descriptions for content that you can create to reach that persona.

REMEMBER

Plan to create content at all three stages of the marketing funnel: awareness, evaluation, and conversion. In the wealth management firm example, what content could the firm produce at the top of the funnel to increase awareness for the young professional avatar? What could it produce to move the retiree avatar through the conversion stage?

Step 3: Choosing the vehicle and channel

The *vehicle* of the content refers to the form the content will take. Will it be text, an image, a video, or an audio asset? The *channel* refers to where the asset will be published — such as your blog, a Facebook page, or a YouTube channel.

The vehicle can sometimes determine the channel, and vice versa. For example, a video asset often gets published on YouTube, Facebook, and your blog, whereas an image asset is more likely to be on Pinterest.

Step 4: Planning for ascension

In the final step of the content campaign plan, you connect your content to your business goals. Build offers into each piece of content that allow prospects to get more value, either by consuming more content, giving you their contact information for follow-up, or buying a product or service.

TIP

Any call to action is better than none at all, but the highest-converting ascension offers are relevant to the content the prospect is consuming. For example, a blog post entitled "10 Ways to Grow More Nutritious Organic Tomatoes" would do well to make an offer such as "50% Off and Free Shipping on Organic Tomato Seeds" rather than an offer for carrot seeds.

If you want to create content that converts prospects at all stages of the funnel, create a content campaign plan and execute it. It works.

Distributing Content to Attract an Audience

Today, content plays an important role in all major forms of traffic generation. Convincing cold (and even warm) prospects to visit your website is difficult without first leading with valuable content.

The processes you develop to distribute content, and thus generate traffic to it, are as important as the processes surrounding the creation of that content. Entire books are devoted to the nuances of traffic generation using the methods of email marketing, search, social media, and paid traffic. However, it's worth mentioning how each of these major traffic generation methods interacts with the content you produce.

Marketing through email

Email is still the best method for making offers and sending more content, so growing and maintaining your email lists are critical tasks, which is why growing your email list is built into your content strategy. After you've produced a content asset, such as a blog post or a podcast episode, use your email list(s) to drive traffic to that piece.

To write the email for your new piece of content, first create the subject line of the email message. Often the subject is the same as the title of the content, but there are other strategies to naming your email subject line, such as scarcity headings such as "FINAL notice (Just hours left . . .)" or by piquing curiosity with subject lines such as "THIS is why I do what I do . . . ." We describe these strategies in more detail in Chapter 5 of this minibook.

Next, open your email with a short, punchy introduction that pulls people into the main body of your email, where you pique the email subscriber's interest and describe what he can expect from the content. Explain this email's relevance to the reader and what he has to gain from it (also known as the *benefit*). Also, be sure to include a call to action that instructs the subscriber to click the hyperlink to your content. Use two to three hyperlinked calls to action to make clicking them as convenient as possible.

Capturing leads through search marketing

Search engines, such as Google and Bing, are important content distribution channels to leverage. When prospects reach your site by querying a search engine (they might be searching for *dslr camera reviews* or *crepe recipes* in Google or Bing) but haven't selected an ad, they are using search marketing. The traffic driven to that content wasn't paid for but was found naturally by the users.

TIP

Today, search marketing is simple. The search engines, particularly Google, have become adept at sending traffic to the content that is most likely to satisfy the intent of the searcher. If you're committed to creating content assets that satisfy the intent of your various customer avatars, you'll get plenty of love from Google and other search engines.

Using social media to drive traffic to your site

After you have created a piece of content, use the social media platform(s) that your business participates in to drive traffic to that content. Driving traffic on social media may take several forms, such as a tweet on Twitter or an update on

Facebook or LinkedIn. This update announces the new content and provides a hyperlink to it.

When you write text for a social media update, your brand's personality should determine how you announce this new content. For instance, if your brand is a refined jewelry store, you may want to use a formal tone in your copy.

The length of the copy depends on restrictions (such as on Twitter) and the complexity of the offer. Simple offers don't require the same amount of description as complex offers do. Regardless of the length of the copy, be sure that the social media update piques the viewer's curiosity, describes the benefit of the content, and has a clear call to action, such as the home improvement store Lowe's Facebook post shown in Figure 3-10. This social media update meets all three of these requirements effectively.

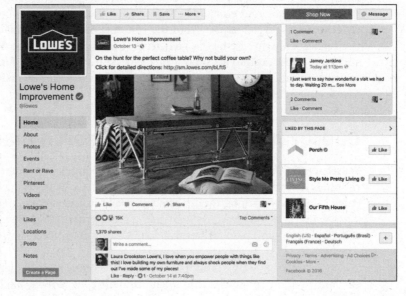

FIGURE 3-10:
On Facebook, Lowe's establishes the benefit of the content and gives a clear call to action for the viewer to click.

Paying for traffic

As the name suggests, paid traffic takes the form of ads that promote your content and helps your content gain reach, or exposure. You can display ads on many different platforms, including search engines and social media. Paid traffic can be highly effective at generating leads because it helps you to segment your visitors and make use of retargeting.

REMEMBER

When a prospect visits a piece of content, she places herself into a particular segment of your potential buyers. She's indicating an interest in the offer, topic, problem, or solution found on that page, and you can take advantage of ad retargeting networks such as Google and Facebook to show ads to this prospect based on the content she has visited.

Although many marketers may be reluctant to pay to send traffic to content, such as blog posts and podcasts, paid traffic has a major advantage: It's predictable. When you cut a check to Facebook, for example, to promote a piece of content, you will get traffic. This is why, at all times but especially when buying ads for your content, you must ensure the exceptional quality of your content. The last thing you want to do is spend money to send traffic to poor-quality content.

Use paid traffic to promote quality content that gives value to the consumer and aligns with your business goals. This will help you move people from one part of the funnel to the next, progressing from ice-cold prospect to a lead to customer to repeat customer and, ideally, to raving fan.

Chapter **4**

Blogging for Business

The topic of blogging deserves in-depth discussion. Blogging is one of the most powerful and versatile digital marketing tools at your disposal. You can think of your blog as a home for content of every type, including text, graphics, audio, and video. Functionally, though, a blog is just a tool that helps you manage certain pages of your website.

The power of a well-executed business blog lies in its capability to generate awareness for your company, brands, customer-facing employees, products, and services. When done right, the business blog becomes a critical part of your marketing mix. If done improperly, however, a business blog can become a frustrating, time-consuming chore that gives you zero return for your effort.

Although you should always keep the customer journey in mind, the main purpose of your business blog is to create aware and engaged prospects who eventually convert into leads and sales. Although in other content areas, building ungated, gated, and deep-discount offers (discussed in Chapter 2 of this minibook) into your content is critical, the goal of your blog is not the immediate conversion of a prospect into a lead or customer.

REMEMBER

Marketing is about the sequence of the offers you make to prospects, leads, and customers. Your blog content is one of the entry point offers (EPOs) that you make to cold prospects who know nothing about you or your company. But content is also something you can distribute via email, social media, and paid traffic to even your best customers to keep your business at the forefront of people's minds and provide additional value.

In this chapter, we give you strategies for successful business blogging. We point you toward effective tools to use for blogging ideas, tell you how to find and work with content creators to keep your blog diverse and interesting, and help you brainstorm effective headlines for your blog articles. The final part of this chapter provides a list of the elements by which you can audit your blog to make sure it's as effective as you can make it.

Establishing a Blog Publishing Process

To produce a blog that has an effect on the bottom line, you need a process. The unsuccessful business blog fails to plan. Putting together a blog-publishing process helps you do the following:

>> Fine-tune aspects of your blog, such as style, tone, topics, offers, mediums.

>> Plan your content and identify content gaps while considering what your audience *wants* you to write about.

>> Maximize your content's immediate effect as well as its long-term effect as a resource.

Your blog-publishing process should include a way to generate blog post ideas, utilize content segments for consistent planning, find and work with content creators, edit content, and broadcast new content. The following sections break down the details of each part of this process.

Brainstorming blog post ideas

In this section, you learn which tools are available to you while you're brainstorming post ideas or ways to frame your content.

Get inspiration from your customer avatar

The customer avatar process outlined in Chapter 1 of this minibook gives you an abundant source of information for brainstorming blog post ideas for your blog. What blog posts, videos, podcasts, and so on should you create to attract and convert your avatar?

Start by looking at the five components of your customer avatar:

>> **Goals and values:** What is the avatar trying to achieve? What values does he hold dear?

>> **Sources of information:** What books, magazines, blogs, and other publications does the avatar reference for information?

>> **Demographics:** What is the age, gender, and marital status of the avatar?

>> **Challenges and pain points:** What holds the avatar back from achieving her goals?

>> **Objections:** Why might the avatar choose not to buy your product or service?

Answer each of those questions about your avatar and use those answers to brainstorm ideas for content. Use the information you know about your target market to create content that solves your avatar's problem, enters the conversations she's having, speaks to her goals, and meets her objections head-on.

Do some research on BuzzSumo

BuzzSumo is an online tool that allows you to analyze what content is performing well on social media for a topic. The number of social media shares that a blog post receives is a good indication of content that the audience likes. The topics receiving the most attention from social media are the ones you should consider for your blog.

Start by searching keywords and phrases that your audience is likely to be searching for. With the BuzzSumo tool, you can also adjust the content type that you search for. You can choose from these categories: Articles, Infographics, Guest Posts, Giveaways, Interviews, and Videos. BuzzSumo allows you to adjust the date range for the content it searches, so if you're searching for content that's been making a *buzz* lately, or content that was published in the last year, your options are open.

Want to see how your competition's content is performing? Type in its domain to see all its content in order of social popularity. Figure 4-1 shows the BuzzSumo ranking of content on Typepad's blog by social popularity. Want to see what is performing well with people you admire in your industry? Search their names and BuzzSumo generates their most popular content.

Monitor your own data

The savvy blogger watches how the audience responds to content by monitoring data points. These data points help you determine what you should produce more of in the future.

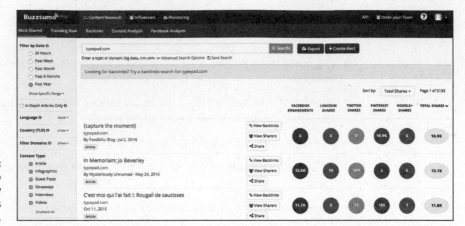

FIGURE 4-1:
Use BuzzSumo
to identify
content that is
working well.

Google Analytics is a free tool that allows you to view data about how your visitors are using your website. You can use Google Analytics to determine which blog posts on your website receive the most traffic, which posts people spend the most time on, and where the traffic comes from (for example, Twitter, Google, and email).

You should also keep an eye on the number of social shares on each blog post. If you use a content management system such as WordPress or Squarespace, you can install social sharing buttons that allow blog visitors to easily share your content with their network on sites such as Twitter, Facebook, or Pinterest. Figure 4-2 shows a blog post with high social engagement and shares. The data-driven blogger can find inspiration and create content that mimics posts with high social share count.

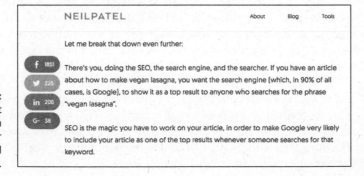

FIGURE 4-2:
A recent
post from
DigitalMarketer
with high social
engagement.

And finally, when distributing your content through an email newsletter, keep an eye on the open and click-through rates on each email. Content that interests your audience gets a relatively higher percentage of opens and clicks than content your audience finds less interesting.

Use information pulled from your internal data sources to shape your content calendar, prioritizing what the data tells you concerning your audience's interests.

Establishing content segments

Your blog should not be reinventing itself from week to week and month to month. You and your audience can derive more value from your blog if you create a predictable structure to the types of content you publish. To offer a predictable structure, you create content segments. A *content segment* is a blog post format that repeats on a set schedule and follows a similar style and template.

You're likely already familiar with content segments whether you're aware of it or not. The radio, television, and print mediums have used segments for decades. For example, the Letters to the Editor segment is a staple of the newspaper industry that appears day after day. Buzzfeed, an online social news and entertainment website, runs a daily post called "Here's What People Are Buying on Amazon Right Now." Figure 4-3 shows Moz, a company that creates SEO software and resources for digital marketers, featuring a weekly video blog post called Whiteboard Friday.

FIGURE 4-3: An excerpt of a segmented post from Moz.

Many post types are adaptable as segments. For example, you can run the link roundup post every week or month on your blog. Simply curate and compile a list of links that your audience would find interesting and publish it along with a description of what people can expect if they visit that link.

Segments are great pieces to have on your calendar for a variety of reasons. One is that you can offer outside writers consistent exposure on your blog. Another reason is that they're easily repeatable and quickly consumable because the format is always the same. Your audience will recognize them and grow to expect them as you continue to publish them, providing people with consistent value.

Working with content creators

To produce the content necessary to grow your blog, you're likely to need a team of writers. An outside writer is someone not associated with your brand who creates content assets for your blog. Those content assets are typically written articles, but the content can also take the form of audio, video, and images for your blog. Acquiring quality outside content creators gives your blog a broad range of perspectives and can help give authority and reach to your blog. This is especially true if the content creator is an *influencer* — that is, someone who has an above-average effect in his or her niche. Influencers often have a following of their own and are connected to key players in media outlets, consumer groups, or industry associations.

Finding content creators

One place to start when you're hunting for content creators is to search for blogs that are similar to yours in topic. Use a search engine, such as Google, and enter one of the following search queries:

- [your blog topic] blogs

- [your blog topic] blogger

- [your blog topic] author

- [your blog topic] speaker

For instance, if your blog is on the vegan lifestyle, you can search for *vegan blogs* and find links to top vegan blogs and authors who have contributed to those blogs.

TIP

Don't just search the first page of the search engine results page. Search deep into the results pages, many pages in — this is where you might stumble upon a good writer who may not be receiving very much traffic. These bloggers are very receptive to contributing content to other blogs to receive more exposure for their own blog.

You can also search for content creators on Twitter. Most content creators use Twitter to distribute links to their content. Use an app such as Followerwonk to search Twitter Bio's for terms such as the following:

[your blog topic] blogger

[your blog topic] writer

[your blog topic] author

[your blog topic] speaker

Another way you can find content creators is to visit blogs that are writing about topics that are the same as, or related to, your own and contact their guest bloggers. Often, these are freelance writers and bloggers who would be willing to write for your blog for money and exposure to your audience.

Next, you may be able to find content creators from your best commenters. These are people who leave the most in-depth and thoughtful comments on your articles. Not only are these commenters engaged with you, they know your style, and they may be writers and speakers looking for exposure.

Finally, you can create a Write for Us page on your site or blog so that interested writers can contact you. But be careful: You can get many low-quality content creators sending requests from your Write for Us page, which is why you want to include guidelines. Listing what you expect from content creators helps to detract the ones who aren't fit for your blog as well as draw the kind of authors you're looking for. Here are the elements to include on your Write for Us page to attract high-quality writers:

>> **Acceptance of bylined articles:** Most writers want to know that you will include a byline with a link to their website; let them know you do.

>> **Statement that you pay for articles:** If you pay for articles, you increase the response rate by letting writers know on the Write for Us page. You don't have to include how much you pay.

>> **Content categories:** Outline the topics you want guest writers to write about.

>> **Examples:** Link to sample articles that model the posts you want from guest writers.

>> **A form:** Include a form that the interested writer can fill out to contact you. Ask for the writer's name and email, at a minimum. To filter out low-quality submissions, ask interested writers to submit writing samples; we suggest ask for three writing samples.

MarketingProfs does an excellent job of creating a very detailed Write for Us page to help find quality content creators; see Figure 4-4 for an excerpt.

Write for MarketingProfs

Yes! We accept **bylined "how to" articles** and **opinion pieces** for our website and daily newsletter, MarketingProfs Today.

We also publish daily **summaries of research findings** based on polls, surveys, and research studies conducted by marketers, academia, PR firms, and other researchers.

1. Contribute bylined "how to" articles for MarketingProfs.com

Bylined articles of **800-1,000 words or so of body text**, written from an objective viewpoint and conveying valuable **how-to** content (**practical** advice, **actionable** tips, and **useful** know-how) in a fresh, approachable voice are more likely to meet MarketingProfs standards—and therefore more likely to be accepted for publication. See, as examples, the following three articles:

1. 13 'Old-School' Marketing Techniques That Take Your Facebook Fan Page From Wimpy to Wow

2. Run Your Website Like a Magazine

3. 10 Ways to Entice Your Whole Company (Not Just Marketing) to Blog

We will inform you if your article has been accepted for publication; expect to hear from us within a week or so of our having received your email. If we choose not to accept your article, you may or may not hear from us, depending on how crowded our inbox is.

Articles accepted for publication will be edited for clarity and brevity and to conform to the MarketingProfs house style. We will likely change your title, too, so you might want to suggest some alternatives.

So, if you are interested in joining the hundreds of MarketingProfs contributors of how-to marketing articles—on a one-time or a regular basis—here are some guidelines:

1. Articles should be original to the author and **unpublished elsewhere**.

2. Articles should offer readers **clear advice, takeaways, and practical how-to tips** about a specific marketing topic or approach to marketing. Bullet points are good. Meandering text is not—but keep in mind that **800-word minimum**.

3. At the beginning of your article, **list two or three bullet points summarizing its key takeaways**—the lessons learned and the how-tos contained in the article. They will be published along with the article.

4. Include a **brief bio** of 25 words, including LinkedIn and Twitter contact info, if available, and a recent **headshot** (make sure your entire head is in the picture).

FIGURE 4-4:
An excerpt from MarketingProfs' Write for Us page.

Acquiring content creators

After you find content contributors who interest you, it's time to reach out to them. Understand that outside content creators will produce content for your blog for one of two reasons: money or exposure (or both).

For writers doing it for the first reason, the process is simple: You cut them a check, and they create a piece of content for you. As a rule, the more specialized the knowledge your writer needs, the more the content will cost you. It's a supply and demand thing. If you're unsure how much the going rate for a writer is, you can visit sites such as Craigslist and ProBlogger Job Board to browse through the open jobs.

Aside from money, what you can offer writers is exposure to your audience. If your blog has impressive amounts of traffic, social shares, or comments from readers, share that information with the outside writers you are courting. You will find that the more exposure you have to offer writers, the less you will have to pay for their content. In fact, after your blog reaches a critical mass, you won't need to pay a dime for content — writers will come to you for the exposure.

TIP

Keep in mind that the reach the writer brings to the table will affect how much you have to pay him or her. The more influence and followers your guest writer has, the more money and exposure that author will require from you.

Ensuring success with content creators

The best way to ensure success from an outside writer is to be prepared with guidelines for your blog. These guidelines, like those on the Write for Us page, communicate what types of content perform best on your blog, what audience you gear your articles toward, and other standards for an outside writer's work to meet. For instance, if your blog doesn't accept certain kinds of images (stock or personal photography, for example), indicate those restrictions in your guidelines. If you require your images to be a certain size, with a certain resolution and with a specific border, list those requirements. Your guidelines are the information your writers need to shape the content you want them to provide you, and having guidelines will save you a mess of editing, formatting, and image polishing when you receive their final work. After connecting with outside writers who have indicated interest in writing for you, send them your guidelines so that they know what to expect. You can send the guidelines in a separate document or paste them directly into your correspondence.

Next, lead with examples by showing writers articles on your own blog that you want their article to model. Also, provide links to content that has done well in the past to help the writers get a sense of what direction to take the article.

After writers know what you expect based on your guidelines and the examples you've provided, ask the writers for information about the post they intend to write for you. Have them give you the following information:

>> **The working title:** The title of a blog post, also called a *headline,* is a promise to the reader. The working title isn't necessarily the headline that will be published on your blog, but it is a guiding statement for the writer as he produces the post.

>> **The outline:** You want to know how the post will lay out, details for each section, and what images the writer expects to use. The more detail you receive from the writer upfront, the greater the chance for the article's success.

When writers send back the working title and outline, approve or make suggestions and ask questions until you're satisfied that their efforts will generate a post that is publishable on your blog.

Last, discuss time frames and deadlines. Depending on the type of post, expect the writer to take between one and three weeks to develop the first draft. If you've never worked with someone before, ask her to write the first 25 percent and send it to you or your editor for review. This preview will allow you to make adjustments and work with the writer before she completes the post.

Be sure to respect the writers' time as they've respected yours and set expectations on turnaround time. How long will they have to wait until you send back edits or questions? How long before they know their post is approved? When will you communicate their publish date to them? With guidelines, timing, and expectations set, you ensure that your content creating process can go off without a hitch.

Editing the first draft

After a contributor has submitted a first draft (on time, you hope!), you approach the draft for a technical edit. This is the edit you perform to ensure that this piece of content is publishable in its current state, or can be brought up to standard without an overhaul of the content.

First, compare the final post to the headline and outline the writer submitted earlier in the process. Does it deliver on the promise in the working title? Does it stay true to the outline? Point out any areas of concern you have. Pay particular attention to areas that deviate from the stated promise in the working title or that the writer omitted from the expected outline.

Next, run down your guidelines to verify that the post meets your publishing criteria. Is the tone right for your blog? Does it deliver the types of content your audience expects from your blog? Do images meet the standard and specifications set by your guidelines? Does your writer have the necessary permissions secured to use images in the content?

After you established that the post does or does not meet your guidelines, go through the meat of the post to see what edits you need to make. What does the writer need to expand on? What should he remove? What can he clarify for the audience?

Decide whether the post needs to go back to the writer for further revisions and edits, or if you will publish as is or with minor edits from you or your editorial team. If you return the post to the writer, communicate a follow-up deadline in order to reach your publishing date. Your notes should clarify exactly what you're hoping for in the revisions, and what edits need to be made.

Copyediting the post

After you have a publishable post (one that fulfills the promise and meets your standards), you should perform a thorough copy edit. Edit the post to meet your language style (do you capitalize certain words by company standards? Hyphenate words that others don't?), or add clarifying sentences that you believe your audience needs to connect the dots.

Next, go through the post line by line, checking for misspellings and grammar errors, among other things. You should edit for formatting, flow, tone, and to ensure that links, images, and video work as expected. The goal of the copy edit is to ensure that the content is free of errors, including misspellings, grammar errors, and broken links.

Applying Blog Headline Formulas

Everything we discuss in this chapter is a moot point if you don't create blog post titles, also called headlines, that entice and engage your audience. The headline is the most important part of your post because it cuts through the noise to grab your readers' attention and convince them to give you their precious time by reading your article.

But how do you come up with these stellar blog headlines that increase clicks? You follow a formula. There are six different categories that great blog headlines fall into, and we detail each of them in the following sections.

Tapping into self-interest

The first headline formula is the self-interest headline. These are your bread-and-butter blog post titles and should be used frequently. Self-interest headlines are usually direct and speak to a specific benefit that your audience will gain by reading your blog post. These headlines start to answer the "What's in it for me?" question, as well as help prequalify readers by giving them a clue about what the article entails.

Here are some sample self-interest headlines:

Grow Your Website Traffic with the 3-Step Content Marketing Plan

How to Retire in Style Even if You Haven't Started Saving

Top 10 Organic Food Markets in Austin, Texas

Piquing curiosity

If self-interest headlines work because they communicate a direct benefit of reading a blog post, curiosity-based ones succeed for the exact opposite reason. These headlines pique the interest of readers without giving away too much information, which leads to a higher number of clicks. Curiosity headlines create an itch that needs to be scratched, and readers have a hard time resisting reading the blog post. Be careful, though, because curiosity-based headlines can fall flat if you miss the mark. Because curiosity headlines are more ambiguous, you might annoy your reader when the content fails to live up to the expectations set by the headline. So make sure that your curiosity headline doesn't mislead your reader.

Here are some examples of curiosity headlines:

25 Things You Didn't Know Your iPhone Could Do

Grill the Perfect Beef Filet with the "Butterfly Process"

This is Why You Should Never Drink Raw Milk

TIP

It's rarely a good idea to use pure curiosity in a blog post title. Instead, as with the example preceding headlines, combine curiosity with benefit to craft a powerful blog post headline. For example, you might be interested in reading a blog post about grilling the perfect beef filet, but the added curiosity created by the butterfly process makes the headline even more compelling.

Employing urgency and scarcity

The most powerful way to get someone to read your blog post is to impart urgency or scarcity with your headline. Headlines that communicate urgency and scarcity tell readers they must act *now*, or they'll miss something. Don't overuse this technique, or you'll likely aggravate your audience. Use urgency and scarcity headlines only when you truly have a deadline, limited quantity, or limited availability.

Here are some urgency and scarcity headlines:

Get Tickets Now! Woody Allen Speaking at Lincoln Center on October 15th

Free Photography Classes: Last Chance for Open Enrollment

New Book Reveals Ancient Weight Loss Secret; Supplies Are Limited

Issuing a warning

Often, people will be more motivated to take action to avoid pain than gain a benefit. Well-crafted warning headlines, such as the following, incorporate the promise that you can protect yourself from a threat if you take action:

The Big Lie Hiding in Your Apartment Rental Contract

Warning: Don't Buy Another Ounce of Dog Food Until You Read This

Is Your Child's Mattress Harmful to His or Her Health?

Borrowing authority

A fundamental characteristic of humans is that we look to the behavior of others when making decisions. You can leverage this trait in your headlines by mentioning a person's success story, citing familiar and influential names, or highlighting how many people are already using a product or service.

Smart marketers use this *social proof* — the propensity for people to make choices based on the choices other people have made — wherever they can. The more people making that choice and the more influential those people are, the more influential the social proof.

Consider these social proof headlines:

Why 1000s of Bostonians Will Gather in Boston Common on December 8th

What Dr. Oz Eats for a Midnight Snack

The New Justin Timberlake Video Everyone Is Talking About

Revealing the new

Keeping your audience informed about new developments in your field builds authority and keeps your audience tuned in. Blog posts that center on the cutting edge need a headline that stands out and conveys the newness or urgency of the latest information. These headlines often work well when combined with a curiosity element and are known as news headlines.

Take, for example, these news headlines:

Ancient Human Cancer Discovered in 1.7 Million-Year-Old Bone

Vibrant New Species Discovered Deep in the Caribbean

New Tool Changes Webinars Forever

Auditing a Blog Post

When you're reading or editing a blog post, putting your finger on the *specific* reasons a post is falling short of fabulous can be difficult. Communicating what needs to be improved to a writer or content team can be even more difficult — that is, these things are difficult if you don't have a process or don't know what to look for. To audit your blog post, you should examine ten elements. The following sections discuss each element to help you learn to evaluate and improve each one.

Present an exceptional headline

In the "Applying Blog Headline Formulas" section, earlier in this chapter, we list the six categories that headlines often fall into. No matter which headline formula, or combination of formulas, you're using, exceptional headlines have three aspects in common.

>> The headline contains a promise of what people will gain from reading the post.

>> Although the headline uses as many words as needed to convey the promise, it's concise and avoids fluff words, which are redundant, unnecessary words or phrases that add little to the headline and slow the reader down, such as *really, just, very,* and *rather.* Here's an example of a headline with fluff words:

Why It Is Very Important to Basically Avoid Fluff Words That Are Rather Empty and Sometimes a Little Distracting in Your Headlines and in Your Writing

Here's a better, more compelling headline:

How Fluff Words Drive Your Readers Away and How You Can Avoid Them in Your Writing

>> The headline is compelling without being misleading or full of hype.

Headlines that don't work well are often merely statements or incomplete phrases. For example, consider three blog headlines found on a fitness and nutrition website:

Chocolate for Breakfast

Benefits of Meditation

Win the War Against Childhood Obesity

Notice how all three headlines are simply statements of (presumably) fact. They can be dramatically improved, and often by a simple alteration such as

Chocolate for Breakfast?

7 Benefits of Meditation

How to Win the War Against Childhood Obesity

Although these modified headlines aren't perfect, they're considerably more effective than their originals. Adding a question mark to the first headline is a better way to pique a reader's interest. Putting a number in the middle headline eliminates vagueness and adds specificity. Finally, the addition of *How to* in the last headline turns a statement into a promise.

If you're struggling to come up with a headline for your piece, you can often find one hiding in the opening or closing of the article. Look for the promise statement that conveys the benefit of the article in your introduction or conclusion. You'll likely find the beginnings of a headline there.

Include a strong introduction

The weakest part of an article is often the introduction. Sometimes a blog post can go from being good to great if you just chop off the first five paragraphs to get the reader to the point quicker. Exceptional introductions contain the following elements:

>> Intro copy is extremely easy to consume and develops a rhythm for the post.

>> Intro copy draws readers in and compels them to read the entire article.

When writing your introduction, here's a trick you can use: Open the post with a punchy, curiosity-building sentence. Keep it short (rarely longer than eight words). The first sentence is intended to create a greased chute (a term coined by copywriter Joe Sugarman) that starts the reader sliding down the page.

Here are a few examples of this type of opening line:

You've finally found it.

Here's the big misconception . . .

Stop me if you've heard this before.

After you get readers started down the chute, keeping them moving is much easier; getting them started is the difficult part.

Offer easy-to-consume content

One of the goals of a blogger is for people to read the entire article, from start to finish, and not bounce to somewhere in between. Blog content isn't doing its job if it isn't easy to consume. To ensure that your content is easy to read, be sure that

>> The copy is formatted in a way that makes the article easy to consume.

>> The transitions between ideas and subheadlines are smooth.

Blog articles aren't like books. An exceptional blog should not consist of dense, long paragraphs with few to no images or video. Long, uninterrupted blocks of text are intimidating to a reader, not to mention visually unappealing. Help move the reader through the content by breaking up text with the following:

>> Bulleted lists

>> Numbered lists

>> Block quotes

>> Subheadings

>> Artwork and images (such as pictures, GIFs, infographics, and embedded videos)

>> Bold font

>> Italics

Next, look for changes between ideas and other areas where readers might slow down or stop reading. At the points that may block readers, make sure to include transitions. Transitions help to tie the article together, enhance reader comprehension, and help keep readers engaged and moving down the page to the final sentence. Figure 4-5 shows an excerpt of a blog post that uses figures, headings, bulleted lists, a bold font, and short paragraphs to break up text and make the content easy to read.

A final point: Break up paragraphs. Long paragraphs in blog posts are like speed bumps, slowing readers down and deterring them from fully consuming the article. When you're laying out your blog post, break up paragraphs that are longer than three lines to improve consumption.

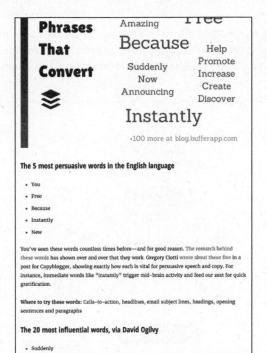

FIGURE 4-5: A blog post uses formatting in a way that makes the content easy to consume.

Inside the figure:

Phrases That Convert

Amazing   Free
Because   Help
Suddenly   Promote
Now   Increase
Announcing Create
           Discover

Instantly

+100 more at blog.bufferapp.com

The 5 most persuasive words in the English language

- You
- Free
- Because
- Instantly
- New

You've seen these words countless times before—and for good reason. The research behind these words has shown over and over that they work. Gregory Ciotti wrote about these five in a post for Copyblogger, showing exactly how each is vital for persuasive speech and copy. For instance, immediate words like "instantly" trigger mid-brain activity and feed our zest for quick gratification.

Where to try these words: Calls-to-action, headlines, email subject lines, headings, opening sentences and paragraphs

The 20 most influential words, via David Ogilvy

- Suddenly

Satisfy your goal

Although a blog has many goals, such as branding, providing your audience value, and establishing yourself as an authority, the main goal of a blog is to generate quality leads that ultimately lead to sales. The keys to higher conversion rates from blog content are as follows:

>> **Relevance:** The offer you make in the post needs to relate to that article's topic. The more congruent the offer, the more likely you'll secure a conversion.

>> **Consumption:** If the copy is difficult to get through, readers will leave your page in frustration.

To help meet the goal, be sure to include the following in each article that you publish:

>> A clear call to action (CTA) that is relevant to the subject matter of the article

>> Effective copy and design for the call to action so that it compels readers to take the desired action

>> A call to action that is located in one or more prominent positions within the post, giving it a better chance of being seen

Figure 4-6 shows a call to action from *The New York Times* that pops up over the blog post, catching visitors' attention before visitors leave the site. This CTA has a simple message and design that helps to grab attention and generate clicks.

FIGURE 4-6:
An article from the NYT with a strong CTA.

Include quality media

The images, videos, and audio files that you include in an article make up the media of your post. Quality media that loads quickly is extremely important to the success of an article. Media that takes longer than three seconds to load, or is of poor quality, causes readers to become frustrated and seek out blog content that doesn't make them wait or that looks fuzzy. Committing to the production of high-quality media is one way to stand out in an industry saturated with content. Therefore, be sure to include high-quality images, videos, and audio that are clean and crisp. Also, look for instances where media can further explain or enrich a point made in an article.

Hiring a full-time photographer or graphic designer may not be necessary, but try to avoid using stock images and video. Often, stock forms of media look too staged or forced, plus they don't always match well with the topic of your piece.

Provide a compelling close

Your article's closing paragraph can take your post from good to great. Effective conclusions tie the piece together. Therefore, by the close, any curiosity loops that your heading may have opened need to be answered, and you must have delivered on the promise of the article; otherwise, readers feel cheated and might form a negative impression of your brand. You can finish a post by using humor, wit, or insight, or otherwise incite emotions that compel readers to comment, share, or visit more pages on your blog.

REMEMBER

The conclusion is the make-or-break portion of your article that makes readers decide to share the post, comment, click your call to action, or dive deeper into your site. Your closing doesn't have to be epic, but be sure that the article doesn't end abruptly. The simplest way to close a piece is to restate the intro and ask the reader to comment and share.

Use search engine optimization

Done right, effective search engine optimization (SEO) helps your blog posts rank higher in search engines, such as Google, which will improve your chances of having your blog posts found by your audience. To optimize your blog post, choose a relevant keyword or keyword phrase that is unique to your post and include that keyword in the

>> Title tag

>> Body text

>> Image alt attribute

>> Universal resource locator (URL)

>> Meta description

Another important way to optimize your blog is to cross-link related and relevant sites to your blog article. You can link to other sites that aren't associated with your brand but are relevant to the topic of the article. You can also cross-link to other blog posts you've written that elaborate on or enrich a point that you make in your latest post.

Categorize your topics

As your blog expands, you may find yourself covering a larger base of topics. This is where categorizing and organizing your blogs posts comes into play. For instance, an economics blog may cover a wide variety of topics, such as tax tips, financial planning, budget and saving, and others. To help readers find what they are looking for, include categories, also called tags, on each post you publish.

Including categories helps to improve user experience, which in turn increases the value that you bring to your audience. Although it's often as simple as selecting a box by using your mouse, selecting the right category for your blog posts is an important checkpoint of any blog post audit.

Deliver on the promise

If the goal of the headline and introduction is to make a compelling promise, the job of the body of the blog post is to ensure that the article delivers completely on that promise. If the post doesn't fulfill the promise made, amend your headline or get back to work on the blog post. Nothing destroys the reputation of your blog quicker than writing a great headline and failing to deliver in the article.

That said, this element of the audit is about more than simply delivering on the promise. You're also making sure that every idea presented in the post is appropriately fleshed out and doesn't leave your audience confused or needing more information to understand the point. Look for areas in the post that you can strengthen by adding

>> Media (images, video, audio)

>> Examples

>> Data

>> Internal or external links to more information

Go the extra mile with each and every article, and you'll see results. Consider producing fewer posts that are exceptionally complete, as opposed to a high volume of content that leaves the audience wanting.

Keep professional consistency

What's the voice or personality of your brand? Is it professional? Snarky? Academic? Whatever it may be, produce content that reinforces your brand. For instance, a law firm blog probably shouldn't use curse words in its articles. But an edgy motorcycle blog has a better chance of getting away with using certain four-letter words because doing so might be more consistent with its brand. Therefore, whatever the topic of your article, be sure that it remains in line with your brand's personality.

Also, and perhaps more important for some organizations, ensure that the newest blog post doesn't contradict something else that you've published on the blog or anywhere else. For example, if you have a fashion blog with a post last year about the sins of wearing undershirts, but your newest blog post centers on the importance of undershirts and doesn't address what has changed since your past article on the topic, you're going to confuse and lose readers because of your inconsistency.

Chapter **5**

Following Up with Email Marketing

I magine that it's seven o'clock on a Tuesday morning. You wake up to the beeping of your alarm, roll out of bed, and stumble to the kitchen, where the coffee that you programmed to brew last night is just finishing its drip cycle. You grab a mug, add some cream and a tiny sprinkle of sugar, and sit down at the kitchen table. Then you check your email.

If you're anything like most adult Americans, this routine may be familiar. Email is not only part of our daily routines, but also one of our primary sources of information. It probably isn't a surprise to you that email has a higher return on investment than any other channel by far. In fact, email returns an average 4,300 percent return on investment for businesses in the United States.

Email plays an important role in digital marketing because it helps move customers from one stage of the customer journey (see Chapter 1 in this minibook for more on the customer journey) to the next in a way that yields high return on investment. Because email is both cost effective and time effective, not to mention one of the first channels that most customers turn to, this channel often yields the best results.

In this chapter, we show you how to create an email plan that gives your customers a reason to come to you again and again as you grow your business through dynamic, relationship-based marketing.

Understanding Marketing Emails

To start, it's important to understand the types of marketing emails that businesses send. The key to success in email marketing is employing the right type of email at the right time.

Figure 5-1 shows the goals of three types of emails — promotional, relational, and transactional — and how they're used in marketing strategy.

PRIMARY GOAL BY EMAIL TYPE	CUSTOMER SERVICE	BRAND AWARENESS	LEAD GENERATION	RETENTION & LOYALTY	ENGAGEMENT & NURTURING	SALES & UPSELLS
TRANSACTIONAL:	✔	✔	✔	✔	✔	✔
RELATIONAL:		✔	✔	✔	✔	✔
PROMOTIONAL:			✔	✔	✔	✔

FIGURE 5-1: The primary goals of each email type.

Promotional emails

Promotional emails present the leads and customers on your email list with an offer. The offers could be promotional content, a gated offer such as a white paper or webinar (see Chapter 2 in this minibook for more on gated offers), a brand announcement, product release, event announcements, or trial offers, just to name a few.

Promotional emails are the most common marketing emails. This isn't surprising. Because 66 percent of consumers have made a purchase as a direct result of an email marketing message, we know that promotional emails work.

REMEMBER

Promotional emails provide value and help tee up sales. They're great for lead generation, retention, loyalty, engagement, nurturing, sales, and upsells. They should be part of any email marketing strategy. The problem is that many companies use them as the only part of their email marketing strategy, so they miss out on opportunities to relate to customers in diverse ways that are often more effective.

Relational emails

Relational emails deliver value to your customers by providing free content and information such as subscriber welcomes, newsletters, blog articles, webinar guides, surveys, social updates, contest announcements, and more.

Relational emails may not sell a product or brand directly, but they build relationships with the customer by adding value upfront. For example, when your email subscriber receives a piece of high-quality content in an email newsletter, he or she is interacting with your brand in a deeper, more meaningful way.

Transactional emails

Transactional emails are sent in response to an action that a customer has taken with your brand. They include messages such as order confirmations, receipts, coupon codes, shipping notifications, account creation and product return confirmations, support tickets, password reminders, and unsubscribe confirmations.

These emails reengage customers who have engaged with your business in some way (see "Reengagement campaigns," later in this chapter) and give the customer an idea of the voice behind your brand.

Do you follow up quickly and deliver what you promised? Do you have systems in place that give the customer true value? Do you respect your customers' wishes? The leads and customers on your email list are observing how you conduct business, and your transactional email is a big part of that.

THE CHEMISTRY OF TRANSACTIONAL EMAILS

Think about the last time you purchased something you loved — a pair of boots you'd wanted for years, a new snowboard, a great bottle of wine, or dinner at your favorite restaurant. Now consider the way you felt when you made that purchase. You were excited, right?

As you purchase a product that you've been wanting, your brain is flooded with feel-good endorphins. You're happy about that product. Perhaps an hour later, you get a shipping confirmation with information about the key features of that snowboard or an email listing recipes for dishes that go with that wine. You've already made a feel-good purchase, and when the marketer reengages you when you're still on that high, you move farther along on your customer journey.

Transactional emails meet all the primary goals of marketing. They offer a customer service experience, tell customers about your brand, generate leads, increase customer retention and loyalty, engage customers, and even help with sales. Yet most businesses rarely use transactional emails properly, mistakenly assuming that promotional and relational emails are more effective.

Research shows, however, that transactional emails have the highest open rates of the three types and produce 2 percent to 5 percent more revenue than standard bulk email does. We've come to a fascinating conclusion: Transactional emails are chemically more likely to be successful (see the nearby sidebar "The chemistry of transactional emails").

Sending Broadcast and Triggered Emails

Email best practices say that you shouldn't just send every email to every subscriber on your list, and time management best practices say you can't spend every day manually sending emails to customers. For these reasons, your emails should be divided into two types: broadcast and triggered.

Broadcast emails

Broadcast emails are emails that you manually send to your entire list at a given time. They aren't responses to customer actions; you send them at a specific time and for a specific purpose. What we're going to say next may make you a bit upset, but we'll say it anyway: Overusing broadcast emails can hurt your customer relationships and cause customers to stop proceeding on the customer journey. Broadcast emails should be used for only three purposes:

>> **Newsletters:** You should send your regular daily, weekly, or monthly email newsletter to your entire list as promised when your subscribers subscribed.

>> **Promotions:** Not all promotions should be broadcasted to your entire audience. Only major promotions that you feel deliver value to your entire customer base should be sent to everyone. The rest should be sent to a segmented list.

>> **Segmentation:** Send a broadcast email to your entire list to determine the specific interests of certain customers and then segment your email lists.

Triggered emails

Most of the emails that you send should be *triggered emails,* which are fully automated. After you get the content honed and ready, you can let your email service provider do the work for you.

Triggered emails automatically go out after customers take a specific action. But there's a catch: Just because you can trigger something doesn't mean you should. In this day of detailed digital automation, you can probably get data to trigger an email every time your customer logs on to a computer or pours a cup of coffee. But that would just annoy your customers. Specific actions that trigger an automated email for each customer action might include

>> New subscriber welcome email

>> Gated offer email (see Book 7, Chapter 2 for more on gated offers)

>> Registration confirmations

>> Purchase receipts

>> Segmented promotion

>> Referral requests after customers leave a review

>> Abandonment of a shopping cart

>> Reengagement after a subscriber has ignored your brand emails for a specific period

Building a Promotional Calendar

The first question many business owners ask us is when to send email. This question is a good one because a great email campaign will engage customers as never before if it's sent at the right time. Conversely, if an email is sent at the wrong time, it won't be as effective as it could be.

The first thing you should do as a business owner or marketer after you decide to start an email marketing strategy is come up with a promotional calendar. That way, you'll know when to send the messaging your customers need when they want to receive it.

REMEMBER

Using a promotional calendar gives you the opportunity to elicit action. It mobilizes your subscribers to do something that you want them to do — buy something, ask for information, call you, or come to a store, for example. The right message delivered at the right time elicits action.

Cataloging your products and services

Before you can build an accurate, all-encompassing promotional calendar, you have to know exactly what you're promoting. Spend some time carefully cataloging every product and service that your business offers and taking some time to understand how to promote it best. DigitalMarketer uses a promotional asset sheet (see Figure 5-2) to keep a detailed record of our assets. Every time a new asset is released, an asset sheet is added to the list. And every time the promotional calendar is updated or an email campaign starts, those asset sheets are updated.

Be sure that whatever record you keep of your promotional assets contains the following information:

>> Name of the product or service

>> Price (both full price and sale price)

>> Where the transaction occurs

>> Whether you've sold this product or service via email before

>> Whether past marketing efforts worked (and why or why not)

>> When you last promoted this product or service

>> How many emails you sent about this product

>> Whether the product is currently available to promote (and if not, why not)

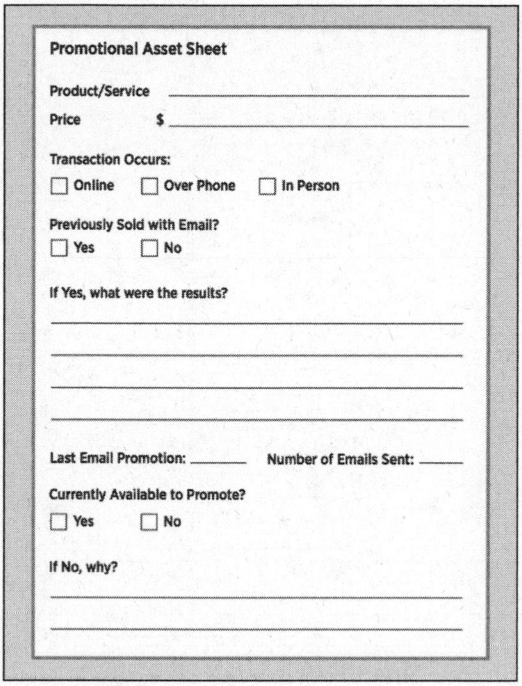
Promotional Asset Sheet

Product/Service ______

Price $ ______

Transaction Occurs:

☐ Online ☐ Over Phone ☐ In Person

Previously Sold with Email?

☐ Yes ☐ No

If Yes, what were the results?

______

Last Email Promotion: ______ Number of Emails Sent: ______

Currently Available to Promote?

☐ Yes ☐ No

If No, why?

______

FIGURE 5-2: A promotional asset sheet.

You may be wondering why you should spend so much time cataloging your marketing efforts. Wouldn't that time be better spent, perhaps, marketing those assets? The truth is that by carefully tracking the sales of your products, as well as the marketing campaigns that correspond with your sales, the job of marketing those assets becomes much easier. When you know what you have available to sell and the results of the promotions you've employed in the past, you can simply do more of what's working and less of what isn't.

The time you spend cataloging and analyzing these assets and the campaigns surrounding them is valuable marketing time. We believe that all marketers should gather the promotional assets from all the products and services they offered so that they know exactly what they can sell, how they can sell it, whom to sell it to, and (perhaps most important) when to sell it.

Creating an annual promotional plan

After you catalog your assets, create an annual promotional plan. This plan aligns your 12-month revenue goals with your annual promotions and marketing efforts to help you reach your goals. Figure 5-3 shows a sample worksheet.

MONTH	GOALS	SET PROMOS	REVENUE GOALS		POTENTIAL PROMOTIONS
1 JAN.			TARGET: $ ___ EXPECTED: $ ___ REMAINING: $ ___		
2 FEB.			TARGET: $ ___ EXPECTED: $ ___ REMAINING: $ ___		
3 MAR.			TARGET: $ ___ EXPECTED: $ ___ REMAINING: $ ___		
4 APR.			TARGET: $ ___ EXPECTED: $ ___ REMAINING: $ ___		
5 MAY			TARGET: $ ___ EXPECTED: $ ___ REMAINING: $ ___		
6 JUNE			TARGET: $ ___ EXPECTED: $ ___ REMAINING: $ ___		
7 JULY			TARGET: $ ___ EXPECTED: $ ___ REMAINING: $ ___		
8 AUG.			TARGET: $ ___ EXPECTED: $ ___ REMAINING: $ ___		
9 SEPT.			TARGET: $ ___ EXPECTED: $ ___ REMAINING: $ ___		
10 OCT.			TARGET: $ ___ EXPECTED: $ ___ REMAINING: $ ___		
11 NOV.			TARGET: $ ___ EXPECTED: $ ___ REMAINING: $ ___		
12 DEC.			TARGET: $ ___ EXPECTED: $ ___ REMAINING: $ ___		

FIGURE 5-3:
An annual promotional planning worksheet.

TIP

You can download your own 12-Month Promotional Planning Worksheet at http://www.digitalmarketer.com/email-planning.

Developing a marketing plan

Creating and developing an annual marketing plan takes some time, but after it's done, you have a solid framework for building your promotional calendar. Follow these steps:

1. **Write your 12-month revenue goals.**

Consider your target revenue goals, and figure out where you want to be each month to reach those goals.

2. **List your nonrevenue goals.**

This list could include nonrevenue growth opportunities such as the launch of a blog or podcast, the release of a book, or the opening of a new location.

3. **Slot holiday promotions into the appropriate months.**

For many retail businesses, November and December are key sales times and thus require strategic marketing. Other businesses may have peak promotion at varying times, such as before a major conference or during a certain season.

4. **Slot annual promotions into the appropriate months.**

These promotions may include major sales, product releases, or events.

5. **Denote seasonality.**

Every business has slow and busy months, so note those months in your plan so that you can build appropriate promotion during those times.

6. **Slot nonrevenue goals into the appropriate months.**

Are you planning to release a new book or launch a new blog in March? You need space on the promotional calendar for these nonrevenue initiatives.

7. **Break your revenue goals into monthly allotments.**

Keep seasonality in mind (see Step 5).

8. **Add your standard revenue projections.**

Include promotional efforts, major events, standard rebilling contracts, and subscriptions.

9. **Subtract your expected revenue from the target revenue.**

After doing this, consider how you can fill in the remaining revenue needed. This step is where your marketing efforts come into play.

10. **Brainstorm additional promotional ideas that could generate the revenue you need to reach your goals.**

Will you need to add new products or services to promote to reach your target revenue? Can you find new ways to offer the existing products and services you already have?

11. **Spot-check and adjust.**

Ask yourself whether your calendar helps you meet your goals in a way that will be both effective and practical.

12. **List additional items that you need to meet your target.**

You may need to launch a new product or service, or to create a sales presentation, for example.

Creating a 30-day calendar

The next step is to get down into the nitty-gritty of what you're going to do for the next 30 days.

A promotional campaign should have three goals:

>> **Monetization:** Making money or making a sale

>> **Activation:** Moving your customer forward on the customer journey

>> **Segmentation:** Becoming more aware of customers' needs and desires so you can segment your list and deliver value

For your first 30 days, we recommend that you set one of these promotional goals for each week and reserve the fourth week for a wildcard campaign. A wildcard campaign gives you the chance to try something new, get creative, test new ideas, or try to replicate your most successful campaigns.

You can use a monthly planning worksheet (see Figure 5-4) so that you can easily track which promotions you're running and how they do. You might also plan a backup promotion for each campaign in case the primary campaign falls, so that you still reach revenue goals regardless of how the campaigns perform.

FIGURE 5-4:
A 30-day promotional planning worksheet.

TIP

You can download your own monthly email planning worksheet at http://www. digitalmarketer.com/email-planning.

Creating a 90-day rolling calendar

When your 30-day promotional plan is up and rolling, you can plan a bit farther in advance with a 90-day rolling calendar. We call this calendar a *rolling calendar* because by repeating similar promotions every 90 days or so, you keep your customers informed and engaged without making the same offers with the same campaign goals over and over again.

TIP

Use a calendar application such as Google Calendar or hang a dry-erase board with a 90-day calendar template on it in your office so that you and your team can routinely map out a schedule that meets your revenue targets without repeating the same promotions too often. When viewing your 90-day calendar, you might find that you have three monetization campaigns in April, but none in May. Moving a monetization campaign or two to May will make it more likely that you hit your revenue targets in May and reduce the number of monetization offers you send to your email list in April.

Creating Email Campaigns

How do you create email campaigns that move your customers along the customer journey in a way that creates long-term brand engagement? And how do you do so without spamming or annoying your customers the way so many brands can do? This section walks you through five types of email campaigns so that you know how to build email campaigns that will work for your business.

A campaign structure page (like the one in Figure 5-5) will help you keep track of each campaign and the purpose of each email in the campaign.

SAMPLE CAMPAIGN STRUCTURE

EXAMPLE BUSINESS: Mattress Store (Physical or e-commerce)

DAY #	EMAIL TYPE	SUBJECT LINE
1	Welcome	Welcome to the Mattress Store (20% off coupon)!
2	Best of #1	Is Facebook stealing your sleep?
3	Best of #2	This made me think of you

FIGURE 5-5: A sample campaign storyboard.

Indoctrination campaigns

An *indoctrination campaign* is a triggered campaign sent immediately following an initial subscription. This campaign is designed to teach new subscribers about your brand and convince them that they've made a good decision by joining your email list and, by extension, becoming a part of your community. See Figure 5-6 for an example of an indoctrination email.

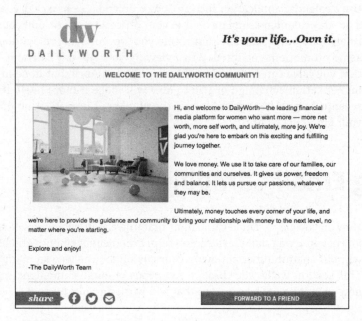

FIGURE 5-6: An example indoctrination email that welcomes a new subscriber.

Customers don't sign up for your email lists on a whim. Instead, they probably were introduced to your brand and then considered the value of your email list. Perhaps they were given the opportunity to get value in advance with a gated offer. (Discover more about gated offers in Book 7, Chapter 2.) Or perhaps they were signed up as they made a purchase or engaged with your website. In all cases, an indoctrination campaign reaffirms positive action and shows your customers that they made the right choice.

The fact that customers made a positive choice to join your email list, however, doesn't mean that they're fully engaged with your brand. They don't know you well enough to anticipate your every word. They may not recognize your name in their inbox and are still unsure about the value they can expect from you.

A carefully crafted indoctrination campaign can help move customers down the path of their customer journeys. (See Book 7, Chapter 1 for more on the customer journey.) In the aggregate, when you add an indoctrination campaign, you see a positive effect on the open and click-through rates of the email you send to these subscribers in the future because they know, like, and trust you better.

Indoctrination campaigns generally run one to three emails and introduce customers to the brand on a deeper level. These campaigns help you put your best foot forward with new subscribers, introducing them to who you are and what you stand for.

Your indoctrination campaign should do the following things:

>> Welcome and introduce new subscribers to your brand.

>> Restate the benefits of being a subscriber.

>> Tell subscribers what to expect.

>> Tell subscribers what to do next.

>> Introduce subscribers to your brand voice or personality.

Engagement campaigns

An *engagement campaign* is an interest-based, triggered campaign sent immediately following a subscriber action. It's designed to make a relevant offer and potentially a sale to subscribers. The role of an engagement campaign is to turn subscribers into converts by prescribing the next logical step based on what you know those people are interested in.

Before you craft an engagement campaign, ask yourself two questions:

>> **What next step do you want your customer to take?** You may want her to make a purchase, opt in to a gated offer, or engage with your brand on your website.

>> **Do you believe that the customer is ready to take that next step?** If the customer isn't ready, you only annoy and alienate her if you push her to take that step.

Sometimes it does hurt to ask — especially when you're asking too much too soon from a valuable customer.

WARNING

Your engagement campaign should do the following things:

>> Turn subscribers into converts. A conversion might be buying a product or service, scheduling an appointment, or registering for a webinar.

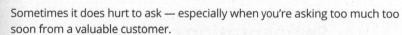

Following Up with Email Marketing

- >> Consider what the customer is interested in now and what will interest him next. Refer back to your customer journey and design your engagement campaigns to move the email subscriber to the next stage in that journey.

- >> Reference the previous positive action.

- >> Overcome or inoculate against known objections to converting.

- >> Prescribe the next logical step.

- >> Ask for an order or a next step.

Ascension campaigns

An *ascension campaign* is a triggered campaign sent immediately following a purchase to start the value loop designed to turn ordinary buyers into buyers who purchase from your brand again and again.

If a customer just bought a tent and four sleeping bags, for example, you could assume that she's looking to head out to the campground, and you could send her a coupon code for a camp stove. If a customer just bought a subscription to a social media training event, you could offer him follow-up training on email marketing.

An ascension campaign is a great way to move customers along the customer journey and build a long-term relationship with them. In an ascension campaign, you give customers what they want and then a bit more.

An ascension campaign should do the following things:

- >> Overcome or inoculate against known objections.

- >> Prescribe the next logical step.

- >> Increase the average value of customers by selling more to them, more often.

- >> Increase customer trust.

- >> Make customers ascend to fans.

Segmentation campaigns

A *segmentation campaign* is a manual campaign sent to your entire database as a promotion designed to segment your subscribers by interest.

Consider a small publishing company that sells high-interest nonfiction books to teachers and librarians. That company is releasing a series of science books on gardening and plant growth. The books have similar content, but some target early learners, others middle-school students, and still others high-school students. The marketing department, being wise and astute in the best practices of email marketing, decides to send out a segmentation campaign. The department staff craft an email listing the books that are available, with clear guidance on what age level each book is appropriate for. Then the staff sends the email as a broadcast campaign to the company's entire mailing list. This campaign makes the company's entire list aware of the new product, and possibly more important, the resulting click data allows the company to segment the list by which subscribers are interested in early-learning content, which are interested in middle-school content, and which are interested in high-school content. The marketing department can create audience segments and send additional emails that meet those customers' exact interests. Figure 5-7 shows a segmentation email from Home Depot. The email lists six categories in which subscribers can get savings. When a subscriber selects one of these categories, the marketing team knows that this person responded to this email and clicked a particular product category. That person would then be segmented, and Home Depot would likely send follow-up emails on the product the subscriber selected.

$ SAVINGS CENTRAL >
Find amazing items at new low prices.

UP TO 40% OFF Kitchen & Bath Essentials >	**UP TO 30% OFF** Storage Essentials >
UP TO 25% OFF with Appliance Special Buys >	**UP TO 30% OFF** LAST DAYS TO SAVE Select Custom Blinds & Shades >
UP TO 30% OFF Select Garage Storage >	**$100 OFF** All Weber Genesis® Grills >

FIGURE 5-7:
Example of a segmentation campaign email.

Reengagement campaigns

A *reengagement campaign* is a triggered campaign sent to any subscriber who has not opened or clicked an email in the past 30 to 60 days. This campaign is designed to reengage those subscribers with the brand. Perhaps subscribers got extremely busy and didn't check their email diligently. They may have gone through life changes and now have different interests. Or maybe they got frustrated with you and chose to disengage. A reengagement campaign can help those customers get back on the customer journey.

Figure 5-8 shows an effective reengagement email.

FIGURE 5-8:
An example reengagement campaign.

REMEMBER

Email deliverability is greatly affected by disengaged users. Best practices in email list management require that customers who aren't engaged be reengaged or removed from the list. If you run a reengagement campaign and still don't get a response from some customers, you can unsubscribe those customers and protect your email list from deliverability issues.

Writing and Designing Effective Emails

If you want people to read your emails, you have to write and design emails that they want to read. But with thousands of companies writing and sending emails every day, you have to make your emails stand out.

Although email writing and design are art and not formula, this section lists a few tips to hone your copywriting and email design skills so that your messages stand out.

Harvesting proven email copy

Go into your own email account and check the last ten messages that you opened. Look at the copy and the design. Then ask yourself the following questions:

>> Did the headline grab your attention?

>> What hooks and leads did the copywriter use?

>> What benefits of the product or service are mentioned?

>> What proof or stories grabbed your attention?

>> What was the call to action?

When you've read the emails that grabbed your attention, see whether you can use them as templates for emails that meet your own business goals. There's no need to reinvent the wheel if it's already been invented for you. (If you want to use the example emails that we include in this minibook and hone them to fit your marketing goals, feel free to do so.)

Answering four questions

To write great email copy, you have to figure out why a customer would engage with the promotion. Answer these four questions:

>> **Why now?** Consider whether the promotion you have should offer new or on-sale items. Also consider whether it's seasonal or timely; that is, whether it's something that customers want or need now more than at another time.

>> **Who cares?** Decide who in your target audience is most affected by having (or not having) what you're selling.

>> **Why should they care?** You need to let customers know how their lives will be different if they have your product or service.

>> **Can you prove it?** Provide case studies, testimonials, or news stories to prove that your customers' lives will be changed if they engage with your product or service.

Great email copy answers these questions in the body of the email in a way that clearly demonstrates to the customer the value of your promotion.

Knowing why people buy

People always buy things for a reason. By considering the reasons why people make purchases as you write email copy, you can hone in on what makes a customer click Buy. People generally buy things for four reasons:

>> **Personal gain:** A product or service will help them reach personal goals or desires.

>> **Logic and research:** Customers have done their research, and this product seems like a logical fit to meet a particular need.

>> **Social proof or third-party influence:** Customers' friends have told them that the product or service is great, and they want to be part of it, or they see a large number of people doing something and want to do it, too. Nothing attracts a crowd like a crowd.

>> **Fear of missing out:** People have a genuine fear of missing an opportunity or of being the only person not to have something important.

Consider which of these motivations you think will drive your customers and then address that reason in your email copy.

Writing effective email subject lines

Because most people spend only three to four seconds deciding whether to open an email, the subject line is the most important piece of email copy you can write. A good subject line piques interest and entices a customer to open the email. Then your email body copy can do the rest to drive engagement.

Subject lines can be tough nuts to crack. One company has its marketing team write 25 subject lines for each email and then choose a favorite to use in the email campaign. This operation may be time consuming, but the company continually receives higher-than-average open rates for its industry and higher-than-average email engagement. You may not have the resources to write 25 full subject lines for each email, but it's a good idea to consider several options for each send, especially triggered sends that you'll use over time.

You can use three types of subject lines to give people different reasons to open an email. We discuss these types in the following sections.

Curiosity subject lines

Curiosity subject lines pique the interest of subscribers and encourage them to click to find out more. For example, Kate Spade, a clothing retailer, sent an email to its subscriber list with the subject line, *Ready for your close up?* That email contained an offer for Kate Spade's jewelry products and used a curious subject line to increase the number of people opening the email.

Benefit subject lines

Benefit subject lines clearly state the reason why subscribers should open the email and the benefits they receive for doing so. For example, OfficeVibe, a Software as a Service (Saas) company that helps managers measure the engagement and satisfaction of their employees, sent an email to its subscribers with the subject line, *38 Employee Engagement Ideas,* which clearly states the benefit the subscriber will get by opening the email. The opposite of a benefit subject line is a warning subject line. For example, OfficeVibe also sent an email to its subscribers with the subject line, *11 Statistics That Will Scare Every Manager.* This subject line type should be used sparingly, but, when appropriate, it can be very effective.

Scarcity subject lines

Scarcity subject lines cause subscribers to feel that they may miss out on something important if they don't open the email and engage with it. For example, Home Depot sent an email to its subscribers with the subject line, *Hurry! Labor Day Savings End Tonight* to encourage subscribers to take advantage of its Labor Day sale before it was over.

Writing body copy

Copywriting isn't a formula, but an art. It's also true that through some formulaic chunking, you can create email copy quickly and effectively.

This chunking method is based on the answers to the questions that we list in "Answering four questions," earlier in this chapter. By breaking your copy into four major chunks and allowing each chunk to answer one of the questions, you can ensure that your copy addresses the major points you're trying to cover.

Each chunk of copy should have one link. That way, by the time customers read the entire email, they've had all their questions answered and have been given multiple opportunities to find out more by clicking a link.

Here's how we recommend that you chunk your email:

>> **Introduction:** In this section, answer the question "Who cares?" by showing customers that they should care about this promotion and why.

>> **Body:** Next, help your reader to answer the question "Why should they care?" by explaining the proven benefits or results of the product or service.

>> **Close:** The close of your email is a great time to answer the question "Why now?" Tell customers, if it applies, that they have a limited time to engage with the promotion.

>> **P.S.:** A postscript is a fantastic place to answer the question "Can you prove it?" by sharing social proof such as a testimonial, positive review, or story of a customer whose life has been changed by the product or service.

REMEMBER

Include a link to a relevant place on your website in each chunk of the email. It's okay if multiple links go to the same location. Just make sure that customers are given ample opportunity to engage further.

Cuing the Click

You've written a killer subject line. You've chunked up your copy beautifully, and each chunk contains a relevant link. You have a product or service that you believe in. You're 99.4 percent of the way to your goal. But you still have one more thing to do: You have to cue the click by asking people very clearly to perform the action of clicking.

Here are a few methods that may be effective for you:

>> **Pose a benefit-driven question.** Example: "Would you like to learn to grow tomatoes indoors? Click <link> to find out."

>> **Connect proof with product.** Example: "Our customers are able to grow 20% more winter tomatoes using our Indoor Tomato Trellis! See how it works here: <link>"

>> **Show the "after."** Example: "When you have the Indoor Tomato Trellis, you'll enjoy ripe tomatoes picked from the vine even in the coldest winter months. Get the Indoor Tomato Trellis here: <link>"

For more on the before and after of marketing, visit Book 7, Chapter 1.

>> **Present a takeaway.** Example: "This is your last chance to get the Indoor Tomato Trellis at 35% off: <link>"

Getting More Clicks and Opens

When you go through your inbox, you probably pay close attention to only a few emails — maybe 10 percent.

What went wrong with the 90 percent of emails that you didn't engage with? Maybe they didn't have great copy or design, or you didn't like the sender's products or services. Maybe you don't have a trusted relationship with the senders, and those emails just got lost in the sea of emails in your inbox.

As we say earlier in "Writing effective email subject lines," you have about three to four seconds to grab your reader's attention, so a great subject line, perfect copy and design, and an awesome promotion aren't always enough. That may seem a bit unfair.

To get you over this final hump, here are some tips to give your emails an extra boost:

>> **Get the timing right.** Send your emails at times when others aren't sending email. Then your emails will stand out in people's inboxes and get a higher open rate. We've found that the best times to send emails are from 8:30 to 10 a.m., 2:30 to 3:30 p.m., and 8 p.m. to midnight.

>> **Call people by name.** Our research shows that emails with a first name in the subject line garner a 23 percent higher open rate. That's an amazing boost, but don't use this trick too often. It loses its effectiveness if overused.

>> **Be positive in the morning and negative at night.** We all wake up bright-eyed and excited to face the new day (okay, after we've had our coffee). Take advantage of that fact by sending positive email messages during the morning hours. In the evenings, negative messages are better accepted.

TIP

If you're going to send a negative message — perhaps about a declining market or an urgent need — make sure that you offer a solution to the problem as part of your email. No one likes to be made to feel hopeless.

>> **Be controversial or relevant.** Stand out in the inbox by bringing up controversial topics (even if you worry that some of your subscribers won't agree with you) or relevant content.

>> **Use odd or specific numbers.** Everyone has ten tips for doing just about everything. Try using different numbers: "6 ways to change your business tonight," "14 simple ideas to teach your child math," or "The $234,423 idea that changed everything," for example.

TIP

Never round up your numbers up. Doing that makes you sound like a liar. If you have only nine amazing ideas for holiday décor, say you have nine amazing ideas. Saying that you have ten and then delivering only nine makes you look dishonest.

>> **Keep your subject line short.** The best subject lines have six to ten words, or 25 characters. Short subject lines are easy to read and view on a smartphone while still piquing customer interest.

» **Use a second subject line.** Most email providers have a second area of displayed content on every email. In many email systems, this area is referred to as the description, but if it's left blank, it defaults to the first line of copy. Instead of accepting the default, write a second, strong subject line and place it in the description section to tell your customers more about your email's content.

» **Include symbols in the subject line.** Using a symbol in the subject line can increase opens by as much as 15 percent. This symbol can be professional, such as a copywriting symbol, or playful, such as a snowman for a winter holiday promotion email.

TIP

We find loads of great symbols to use in subject lines at http://emailstuff. org/glyph. The site offers cool things such as a clock to symbolize a sale that's about to end. Tick-tock.

» **Press Play.** Instead of including a link, embed a still image of a video with a Play button superimposed on top. This technique can dramatically increase click-through rates in email campaigns.

» **Ask customers for their thoughts.** This strategy results in the highest click-through rate of all campaign types we run, so we replicate it and get high click-through rates on emails again and again. This strategy involves asking a question and listing four to five answers, each with a link (see Figure 5-9). All the links go to the same place, where customers can find answers to the questions.

» **Combine video and questions.** Video consistently yields high click-through rates and high customer engagement. Include a video and a "your thoughts" question in an email, and have subscribers watch the video to get the answer.

TIP

Many marketers worry that they don't have the charisma or budget to make highly professional video. Don't be afraid! Because email is about relationships, a simple conversational video can show your personality and voice to your subscribers, and allow you to connect with them in a new way.

» **Add a countdown.** Phrases such as "Four days until this sale is over forever!" and "You'll never get this deal again!" increase the urgency of the promotion. You can increase the urgency even more by adding a countdown clock or timer to show customers exactly how much time they have.

» **Use animated GIFs.** Pretty or funny moving images in an inbox catch people's attention. If you have access to a designer who can make custom animated GIFs, have that person create some for you. If not, sites such as Giphy (https://giphy.com) offer free GIFs that you can use to give your emails an extra edge.

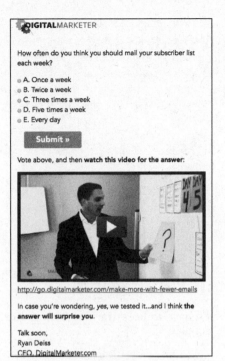

FIGURE 5-9:
An example of a "your thoughts" email that engages the audience.

Ensuring Email Deliverability

Everything we've talked about so far is moot if your emails aren't reaching your subscribers' inboxes. Did you know that 21 percent of emails worldwide never reach the desired recipients? A whole lot of work, effort, and brilliance are being wasted on emails that end up floating around in cyberspace.

How do you make sure that all your work isn't wasted? It comes down to one simple thing: You have to prove that you aren't a spammer and that you have no intention of being one.

Sadly, the Internet service providers responsible for determining whether you are sending spam consider bulk mailers to be guilty until proven innocent. They assume that emails are spam from the outset, and until you can show them that you don't act like a spammer, your email deliverability will be affected.

In the following sections, we provide some methods for improving deliverability. Most of these methods are very technical. If you're a tech wizard, go forth and set up your infrastructure to ensure deliverability. If you need help with technical stuff, find a local tech person or call your email service provider, and get some systems in place to ensure that your emails reach the people you want to reach.

Monitoring your reputation

To ensure deliverability, you have to keep track of how you're interacting with your list. Do the following things:

>> Monitor the complaint rates and the volume of complaints you're receiving. Your email service provider should provide reporting capabilities on the number and rate of complaints your emails are receiving.

>> Respond to complaints in a timely manner.

>> Make sure that you unsubscribe and stop sending email to anyone who unsubscribes. Your email service provider should provide a path to unsubscribe from every email and automatically remove those that unsubscribe from your email list.

>> Keep your message volume steady. Don't send a million emails one month and then none for six months.

>> Check your blacklist status on the major blacklist sites including Spamhaus (`https://www.spamhaus.org/`) and Spamcop (`https://www.spamcop.net/`). These major blacklist sites are referenced by mailbox providers such as Google's Gmail to help them determine whether your email should be delivered to the inbox. Each blacklist has its own process for removal from its blacklist; you can find this information on its website.

Proving subscriber engagement

The best way to assure the Internet service providers (ISPs) that you're not a spammer is to prove that you engage your subscribers with every single email you send. If people are opening your emails, reading what you have to say, and then clicking relevant links, you aren't a spammer.

Subscriber engagement rates are based on the following factors:

>> **Your open rate:** This rate isn't the number of emails that are opened, but the percentage.

>> **Your lateral scroll rate:** This rate is how far recipients scroll down on your emails.

>> **Your hard and soft bounce rate:** A bad email address is considered to be a hard bounce. A soft bounce can happen for many reasons, including a full inbox or accidental flagging as spam.

WARNING

If you continue to send emails to addresses that reject your mail, you look like a spammer.

TIP

Export your entire list, and send it to a company called BriteVerify (www.briteverify.com/). This company runs an analysis of your list and tells you which addresses are definitely good, which ones are questionable, and which are bad. If you expunge the questionable and bad emails from your list, you're practicing good list hygiene and increasing deliverability.

>> **Unsubscription and complaint rates:** If you receive high numbers of unsubscriptions or complaints, examine your campaigns to see whether you're doing something to upset subscribers.

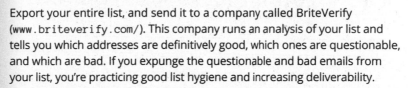

Following Up with Email Marketing

Index

C

call to action (CTA), 637–638

campaign plan (content marketing)
  ascension offers, 616
  brainstorming, 615
  channels, 616
  customer avatars, 614, 615
  overview, 614–615
  vehicle of content, 616

canned invitations (LinkedIn), 407–408

cap (capitalization), defined, 107

capacity plan (aggregate plans), 146

capital, defined, 74–76

capital accounts, 110

capital expenditures, 65, 91

capital intensive, 57

capital utilization test, 115

capitalization (cap), defined, 107

cash balances, 72

cash distributions from profit, 24

cash dividends, 74

cash flow, 21–22, 116. *See also* statement of cash flows

catch-all solutions (Six Sigma), 173

categorizing topics (blog posts), 639–640

categorizing work (WBS), 325–326

cause and effect, determining
  correlation, 167
  DOE methodology, 168–169
  fishbone (Ishikawa) diagram, 165–166
  FMEA, 166–167
  Pareto chart, 164–165

Center for Plain Language, 511

challenges and pain points component (customer avatar), 565–566

channels (content marketing), 616

character, displaying through decision-making, 231–235

cheat sheets (digital marketing), 586

checklist
  deep-discount offers, 593–594
  gated offers, 587–590

chief accounting officer (controller), 57

chunking (email), 659–660

Churchill, Winston, 481

clarity of writing
  overview, 470–471
  paragraphing, 514–515

classified balance sheet, 57, 61

classmates, finding on LinkedIn, 399–401

clean opinion (auditor's report), 119–120

clichés, minimizing use in writing, 510

clients/customers (project management), 265

closing processes (project management), 250, 257

clusters (run chart), 171

collaborators (project management), 265

color, readability and, 487

columns, readability and, 487

command-and-control management style, 238

commas, proper use of, 522–523

commitment (project management), 251

common stock, 108

communication
  communicating decisions, 212–213
  communications management plan, 353–354
  decoded messages, 337
  encoded messages, 337
  formal, 277, 340
  generational differences, 451
  informal, 277, 340
  listening, 338–339
  mediums, 337
  meetings, 342–345, 351–353
  messages, 337
  noise, 337
  one-way communication, 337
  overview, 335–336
  project dashboard, 349–350
  project management, 251
  project-progress report, 345–348
  receiver, 337
  senders, 337
  two-way communication, 338
  written reports, 340–342

type, 485–487

white space, 485

graphical view (WBS), 328

graphics interchange format (GIFs), 565, 664

green belts (Six Sigma), 160

gross margin (gross profit), 33, 37

gross margin ratio, 105–106

gross requirements (inventory record), 149

group meetings, 277

groups, planning messages for, 455

Groups section (LinkedIn), 444

groupthink, 237

guides (free reports), 584

Gunning, Robert, 473

H

H2H (human to human), 577

handouts, 586

hard bounce (email), 665

Hay Group, 238

headlines (blog)

curiosity, 632

news, 633

self-interest, 631

social proof, 633

urgency and scarcity, 632

warning, 633

hierarchic decision-makers, 180

hierarchical method. *See* top-down strategy

hierarchy diagram (WBS), 328

histogram, 171

Home option (LinkedIn top navigation bar), 374

home page (LinkedIn), 373

human to human (H2H), 577

hyperbole, using in business writing, 460

I

IASB (International Accounting Standards Board), 25

IKEA

email marketing, 571

gated offers, 585

implementing decisions

action plan, 214–215

adapting to changing realities, 217–218

metrics, 215–216

reflecting on results, 218

setting priorities, 217

implicit knowledge, 219

income smoothing, 29

income statement

active reader of, 38–40

assets, 45–47

deconstructing profit, 40–45

expenses, 11–12, 47–51

gross margin, 37

investment business, 35–36

liabilities, 45, 47–51

minus signs, 36

misconceptions, 53

misleading reports, 54

net income, 11, 36–37

operating costs, 37–38

overview, 10–11, 31–32

product-oriented business, 32–34

revenue, 45–47

sales revenue, 11, 13, 37

service-oriented business, 34–35

tips for, 12–13

unusual gains and losses, 51–53

income tax expense, 73–74

income tax payable account, 50–51, 73–74

indented-outline format (WBS), 328–329

indirect method of reporting (statement of cash flows), 83–84

indoctrination campaigns (email marketing), 652–653

inferences, checking, 339

inflation, 254

inflection, in business writing, 498

influencers, 626

infographics (TOFU content marketing), 604

informal communication, 277, 340

information resource, LinkedIn as, 366

information sources component (customer avatar), 564

information-sharing activity (communications management plan), 353

informed decision-making
    determining how much information is enough, 197–198
    emotional environment, 196–197
    objectivity, 194–195
    perspective, 195–196
    research, 194
    separating fact from speculation, 196

initiating processes (project management), 250–252

initiators, project, 286, 288–289

InMail messaging service (LinkedIn), 368

innovation
    building culture that values, 182–183
    early adopters, 182
    early majority, 182
    laggards, 182
    late majority, 182
    overview, 181–182

innovators, 181

inputs (MRP), 148–149

inspirational value (digital marketing), 579

instant messaging, 503

intangible assets, 71

integrative decision-makers, 180

interest expense, 73

internal balance sheet, 61

internal groups (audience list), 265

internal rate of return, 254

International Accounting Standards Board (IASB), 25

interpersonal issues, handling, 241–242

introductions
    blog posts, 635–636
    LinkedIn, 392

intuitive decision-making, 218–221

inventory
    assets, 9

cash flow and, 86–87
    cost of goods sold, 46–47
    cost of goods sold expense and, 69
    MRP, 149

investing activities, 17, 18, 65–67, 91, 99–101

Investing For Dummies (Tyson), 99

invitations (LinkedIn)
    canned invitations, 407–408
    defined, 392
    to existing members, 405–407
    to nonmembers, 408–409
    responding to, 412–413

involuntary bankruptcy, 61, 76

Ishikawa (fishbone) diagram, 165–166

J

jargon, minimizing use in writing, 508–510

J.Crew, 604

job listings (LinkedIn)
    advertising to network, 436–439
    overview, 432–433
    posting, 433–436
    reviewing applicants, 439–442

job search (LinkedIn), 364–366

Jobs option (LinkedIn top navigation bar), 374

Jobs page (LinkedIn), 436

justification (scope statement), 283

justifying project
    beneficiaries, 289–290
    confirming feasibility, 292–293
    identifying initiator, 286, 288–289
    identifying real users, 290–291
    identifying related projects, 293
    objectives, 297–302
    for organization, 294–295
    project champion, 290
    project requirements, 291–292
    project title, 286–287
    research, 295–296
    scope of work, 296–297

M

About the Authors

John A. Tracy (Boulder, Colorado) is Professor of Accounting, Emeritus, at the University of Colorado in Boulder. Before his 35-year tenure at Boulder, he was on the business faculty for 4 years at the University of California at Berkeley. Early in his career, he was a staff accountant with Ernst & Young. John is the author of several books on accounting and finance, including *The Fast Forward MBA in Finance* and *Accounting Workbook For Dummies*. His son, Tage C. Tracy, joined him as coauthor on *How to Read a Financial Report*, now in its 8th edition. John and Tage have also coauthored *Cash Flow For Dummies* and *Small Business Financial Management Kit For Dummies*. John received his BSC degree from Creighton University. He earned his MBA and PhD degrees at the University of Wisconsin in Madison. He is a CPA (inactive status) in Colorado.

Mary Ann Anderson is an operations consultant and an adjunct professor in operations management at the University of Texas McCombs School of Business. She has served as the faculty advisor for the Supply Chain Management and Engineering route to business majors and teaches numerous courses, ranging from manufacturing and service operations management to project management to supply chain strategy and logistics, as well as being an instructor in the Master of Science in Technology Commercialization program. She received a master's in engineering, concentrating in operations engineering, from the Massachusetts Institute of Technology. She received her bachelor's in electrical engineering from Kettering University (formerly the General Motors Institute), with a minor in business administration.

Ms. Anderson is also an active consultant. She specializes in operations management, business process analysis and improvement, supply chain management, and project management. She has developed integrated strategy-marketing-operations computer simulations using the system dynamics computer simulation methodology for multiple firms, and she has published articles in such journals as *The Systems Thinker*.

Ms. Anderson has served as a manufacturing strategist for a start-up firm, and her consulting clients include such firms as Ford Motor Company, Sony Entertainment, HP, and Shell, as well as the National Aeronautics and Space Administration (NASA) and the state of Texas. Prior to her teaching and consulting work, she held a variety of positions as an engineer for the General Motors Corporation.

Dr. Edward G. Anderson, Jr., is an associate professor of operations management at the University of Texas McCombs School of Business and an IC2 Institute Research Fellow. He is the faculty advisor for the BBA in the Science and Technology Management program and codirector for research for the McCombs Health Care Delivery Innovation Initiative. He received his doctorate from the Massachusetts Institute of Technology and his bachelor's degree, with majors in history and electrical engineering, from Stanford University.

Dr. Anderson's research interests include outsourced product development (distributed innovation) and project management, knowledge management, supply chain management, and computer simulation. He also has published research in national security, particularly counterinsurgency policy. He has published articles in *Management Science, Organization Science, Production and Operations Management, MIT Sloan Management Review,* and *System Dynamics Review.* He is also the coauthor of the book *The Innovation Butterfly: Managing Emergent Opportunities and Risks During Distributed Innovation,* which describes leadership metrics, planning, and organization in the complex adaptive system that is innovation management.

Dr. Anderson won the prestigious Wickham Skinner Early-Career Research Award from the Production and Operations Management Society. He has received research grants from the National Science Foundation (twice), SAP, and Hewlett-Packard. He is the department editor of *Production and Operations Management* for Industry Studies and Public Policy and was president-elect of the System Dynamics Society for 2013. Professor Anderson has consulted with Ford, Shell, Dell, and multiple other corporations and holds six U.S. and E.U. patents from his prior career as a product design engineer at the Ford Motor Company.

Dr. Geoffrey Parker is professor of management science at Tulane University in the A. B. Freeman School of Business and serves as director of the Tulane Energy Institute. He is also a faculty fellow at the MIT Sloan School's Center for Digital Business. Parker received a bachelor's in electrical engineering and computer science from Princeton University, a master's in electrical engineering (technology and policy program) from MIT, and a PhD in management science from MIT. He has spent much of his career studying coordination in supply chains, especially when firms outsource complex work. Dr. Parker has also contributed to the field of network economics and strategy as codeveloper of the theory of "two-sided" markets. Dr. Parker's work appears in journals such as *Harvard Business Review, MIT Sloan Management Review, Energy Economics, Journal of Economics and Management Strategy, Management Science, Production and Operations Management, Strategic Management Journal,* and *System Dynamics Review.*

Dr. Parker has worked on projects with multiple firms, including AT&T, Cellular South, Chrysler, ExxonMobil, Hewlett-Packard, IBM, International Postal Corporation, Microsoft, PJM, SAP, Thomson Reuters, and the United States Postal Service. Current research includes studies of distributed innovation, business platform strategy, and the design and performance of energy markets. His research is funded by grants from the National Science Foundation, the U.S. Department of Energy, and multiple corporations. He serves or has served as a National Science Foundation panelist and associate editor at multiple journals and as president-elect of the Industry Studies Association. Dr. Parker grew up in Oxford, Ohio, where he worked as an electronics technician and machinist in the

Instrumentation Laboratory at Miami University. Before graduate school, he held multiple positions in engineering and finance at General Electric in North Carolina and Wisconsin.

Dawna Jones believes business can be better for the people it serves and employs and for the planet that sustains us all. When not exploring the world or enjoying the great outdoors, she can be found on her website: www.FromInsight ToAction.com. Her business podcast, *Evolutionary Provocateur*, is on http://www. Management-Issues.com and on iTunes. She regularly hosts business innovation webinars, exchanging ideas worldwide toward healthier workplaces and restoring care for Nature.

Stan Portny, president of Stanley E. Portny and Associates, LLC, is an internationally recognized expert in project management and project leadership. During the past 35 years, he's provided training and consultation to more than 200 public and private organizations in consumer products, insurance, pharmaceuticals, finance, information technology, telecommunications, defense, and healthcare. He has developed and conducted training programs for more than 100,000 management and staff personnel in engineering, sales and marketing, research and development, information systems, manufacturing, operations, and support areas.

Stan provides on-site training in all aspects of project management, project team building, and project leadership. In addition, Stan can serve as the keynote speaker at your organization's or professional association's meetings. To understand how Stan can work with you to enhance your organization's project-management skills and practices, please contact him at Stanley E. Portny and Associates, LLC, 20 Helene Drive, Randolph, NJ 07869; phone 973-366-8500; e-mail Stan@StanPortny.com; website www.StanPortny.com.

Joel Elad, MBA, is the head of Real Method Consulting, a company dedicated to educating people through training seminars, DVDs, books, and other media. He holds a master's degree in Business from UC Irvine, and has a bachelor's degree in Computer Science and Engineering from UCLA. He also operates several online businesses and co-founded the So Cal Comic Con.

Joel has written seven books about various online topics, including *Facebook Advertising For Dummies, Starting an Online Business All-In-One For Dummies, Starting an iPhone Application Business For Dummies,* and *Wiley Pathways: E-business.* He has contributed to *Entrepreneur* magazine and Smartbiz.com, and has taught at institutions such as the University of California, Irvine, and the University of San Diego. He is an Educational Specialist trained by eBay and a former Internet instructor for the Learning Annex in New York City, Los Angeles, San Diego, and San Francisco.

Joel lives in San Diego, California. In his spare time, he hones his skills in creative writing, Texas Hold 'Em poker, and finance. He is an avid traveler who enjoys seeing the sights both near and far, whether it's the Las Vegas Strip or the ruins of Machu Picchu. He spends his weekends scouring eBay and local conventions for the best deals, catching the latest movies with friends or family, and enjoying a lazy Sunday.

Natalie Canavor is a nationally known expert on business writing whose mission is to help people communicate better so they can get what they want — whether that means a job, a promotion, or a successful business. Natalie creates practical writing workshops for businesspeople, writers, and professionals in every walk of life. Her unconventional approach meshes the best strategies from many writing venues: feature articles and columns, video scripts, websites, presentations, print and online marketing materials, and copywriting. She finds that given a planning structure and set of down-to-earth techniques, most people can dramatically improve their writing.

Natalie is the author of *Business Writing in the Digital Age* (Sage Publications), a textbook for advanced and graduate-level students of business and public relations. And with Claire Meirowitz, she coauthored *The Truth About the New Rules of Business Writing* (Financial Times Press), a quick guide to better writing. Natalie is happy to consult with organizations that see the value of raising the bar on writing, and travels to present custom workshops for businesses, associations, and other groups. Find her at Natalie@businesswritingnow.com.

Ryan Deiss (pronounced "Dice") is cofounder and CEO of DigitalMarketer.com, the leading provider of digital marketing training and certifications to small and mid-sized businesses. Ryan is also the founder and host of the Traffic & Conversion Summit, the largest digital marketing conversion conference in North America, and the creator of the "Customer Value Optimization" methodology.

Ryan's online business endeavors began at age 19, when he launched his first website from his freshman dorm room so that he could make some extra money to buy an engagement ring for his college sweetheart. It worked! Not only did the girl say "Yes," but his single little website ballooned into more than 500 sites, and a hobby had grown into a business.

Today, his digital media and e-commerce group, NativeCommerce.com, owns and operates hundreds of properties including DIYReady.com, MakeupTutorials.com, DIYProjects.com, SurvivalLife.com, and Sewing.com (just to name a few), and according to *Shark Tank* star Daymond John, "His companies practically own the Internet." He is also a bestselling author, and is considered one of the most dynamic speakers on modern digital marketing today.

Most important, Ryan is a proud dad of four wonderful kids, Jonathan, Joyce, Ruth, and Timothy, and husband to Emily . . . the girl who said "Yes" and inspired it all.

Russ Henneberry is the Editorial Director for DigitalMarketer. Prior to joining DigitalMarketer, Russ was on the content marketing team for Salesforce.com; he also helped to launch a blog for a well-known marketing SaaS, growing it from 0 to 120,000 unique visitors per month in less than a year.

Russ got his start in search engine optimization and pay-per-click marketing, managing 20 developers and over 600 digital marketing projects for small to mid-sized businesses. It was at Salesforce that Russ began to master the art of content marketing at all stages of the sales and marketing funnel to create value for a company.

In his time at DigitalMarketer, front-end traffic to DigitalMarketer content has increased by 1,125 percent. The content marketing team, under Russ's management, generates thousands of leads and front-end sales per month by developing and executing a truly "full funnel" content marketing strategy. Connect with Russ on Twitter: @RussHenneberry.

Russ lives in St. Louis, Missouri, with his wonderful wife Sarah, his two amazing children, Thomas and Mary Grace, and an extremely enthusiastic dog named Buck.

Publisher's Acknowledgments

Acquisitions Editor: Amy Fandrei

Project and Copy Editor: Susan Pink

Proofreader: Debbye Butler

Production Editor: Siddique Shaik

Cover Image: © BUTENKOV ALEKSEI/ Shutterstock